THE CHURCH'S BIBLE

General Editor
Robert Louis Wilken

• •

The Song of Songs
Richard A. Norris Jr.

Isaiah
Robert Louis Wilken

1 Corinthians
Judith L. Kovacs

ISAIAH

*Interpreted by Early Christian
and Medieval Commentators*

Translated and Edited by

Robert Louis Wilken

with
Angela Russell Christman
and
Michael J. Hollerich

WILLIAM B. EERDMANS PUBLISHING COMPANY
GRAND RAPIDS, MICHIGAN

Wm. B. Eerdmans Publishing Co.
4035 Park East Court SE, Grand Rapids, Michigan 49546
www.eerdmans.com

© 2007 Robert Louis Wilken
All rights reserved

Hardcover edition 2007
Paperback edition 2021

ISBN 978-0-8028-7981-3

Library of Congress Cataloging-in-Publication Data

Isaiah: interpreted by early Christian and medieval commentators /translated and edited by
    Robert Louis Wilken with Angela Christman and Michael Hollerich.
p. cm. — (The church's Bible)
Includes bibliographical references and indexes
ISBN 978-0-8028-7981-3 (pbk.: alk. paper)
1. Bible. O.T. Isaiah — Commentaries.
    I. Wilken, Robert Louis, 1936- .
    II. Christman, Angela Russell. III. Hollerich, Michael J.
BS1515.53.I83 2007
224'.10609 — dc22
                2007010831

Scripture quotations for the translation of Isaiah are from *A New English Translation Of The Septuagint*, translated by Albert Pietersma, © 2006 by International Organization for Septuagint and Cognate Studies. Used by permission of Oxford University Press, Inc.

To the Sisters of
Our Lady of the Angels Monastery
Crozet, Virginia

Contents

Series Preface	x
Acknowledgments	xii
Interpreting the Old Testament	xiii
Introduction to the Christian Interpretation of Isaiah	xx
Preface to Isaiah	**1**
Isaiah 1	**14**
Isaiah 2	**30**
Isaiah 4	**43**
Isaiah 5	**50**
Isaiah 6	**61**
Isaiah 7	**90**
Isaiah 8	**108**
Isaiah 9	**118**
Isaiah 11	**132**
Isaiah 12	**154**
Isaiah 13	**158**
Isaiah 14	**168**
Isaiah 15–16	**182**
Isaiah 19	**192**
Isaiah 20	**199**
Isaiah 24	**202**

Isaiah 25	208
Isaiah 26	217
Isaiah 28	232
Isaiah 29	241
Isaiah 35	253
Isaiah 40	263
Isaiah 41	281
Isaiah 42	291
Isaiah 43	303
Isaiah 44	316
Isaiah 45	329
Isaiah 46	347
Isaiah 48	356
Isaiah 49	363
Isaiah 50	380
Isaiah 51	390
Isaiah 52:1-12	400
Isaiah 52:13–53:12	412
Isaiah 54	431
Isaiah 55	440
Isaiah 56	450
Isaiah 60	459
Isaiah 61	470
Isaiah 62	482
Isaiah 63	488
Isaiah 64	499
Isaiah 65	508
Isaiah 66	522
APPENDIX 1: *Authors of Works Excerpted*	537

Contents

APPENDIX 2: *Sources of Texts Translated* — 545
Index of Names — 567
Index of Subjects — 569
Index of Scripture References — 574

Series Preface

The volumes in The Church's Bible are designed to present the Holy Scriptures as understood and interpreted during the first millennium of Christian history. The Christian Church has a long tradition of commentary on the Bible. In the early Church all discussion of theological topics, of moral issues, and of Christian practice took the biblical text as the starting point. The recitation of the Psalms and meditation on books of the Bible, particularly in the context of the liturgy or of private prayer, nurtured the spiritual life. For most of the Church's history theology and scriptural interpretation were one. Theology was called *sacra pagina* (the sacred page), and the task of interpreting the Bible was a spiritual enterprise.

During the first two centuries interpretation of the Bible took the form of exposition of select passages on particular issues. For example, Irenaeus, bishop of Lyons, discussed many passages from the Old and New Testaments in his defense of the apostolic faith against the Gnostics. By the beginning of the third century Christian bishops and scholars had begun to preach regular series of sermons that followed the biblical books verse by verse. Some wrote more scholarly commentaries that examined in greater detail grammatical, literary, and historical questions as well as theological ideas and spiritual teachings found in the texts. From Origen of Alexandria, the first great biblical commentator in the Church's history, we have, among others, a large verse-by-verse commentary on the Gospel of John, a series of homilies on Genesis and Exodus, and a large part of his *Commentary on the Epistle to the Romans*. In the course of the first eight hundred years of Christian history Christian teachers produced a library of biblical commentaries and homilies on the Bible.

Today this ancient tradition of biblical interpretation is known only in bits and pieces, and even where it still shapes our understanding of the Bible, for example, in the selection of readings for Christian worship (e.g., Isaiah 7 and Isaiah 9 read at Christmas), or the interpretation of the Psalms in daily prayer, the spiritual world that gave it birth remains shadowy and indistinct. It is the purpose of this series to make available the richness of the Church's classical tradition of interpretation for clergy, Sunday school and Bible class teachers, men and women living in religious communities, and serious readers of the Bible.

Anyone who reads the ancient commentaries realizes at once that they are deeply spiritual, insightful, edifying, and, shall we say, "biblical." Early Christian thinkers moved in the world of the Bible, understood its idiom, loved its teaching, and were filled with awe before its mysteries. They believed in the maxim, "Scripture interprets Scripture." They knew something that has largely been forgotten by biblical scholars, and their commentaries are an untapped resource for understanding the Bible as a book about Christ.

The distinctive mark of The Church's Bible is that it draws extensively on the ancient commentaries, not only on random comments drawn from theological treatises, sermons, or devotional works. Its volumes will, in the main, offer fairly lengthy excerpts from the ancient commentaries and from series of sermons on specific books. For example, in this volume there are long passages from commentaries on the prophet Isaiah by Eusebius of Caesarea, Jerome, and Cyril of Alexandria. Some passages will be as brief as a paragraph, but many will be several pages in length, and some longer. We believe that it is only through a deeper immersion in the ancient sources that contemporary readers can enter into the inexhaustible spiritual and theological world of the early Church and hence of the Bible

It is also hoped that longer passages will be suitable for private devotional reading and for spiritual reading in religious communities, in Bible study groups, and in prayer circles.

ROBERT LOUIS WILKEN
GENERAL EDITOR

Acknowledgments

Angela Christman and Michael Hollerich have been with this project from the beginning. They have read the ancient commentaries and other works, chosen passages for inclusion, translated them into English, and written editorial introductions to chapters. They have also offered wise counsel in dealing with the many problems that emerged as the commentary took shape. Without their contribution this volume would have not been possible.

I am grateful to Bryan Stewart, who did some translations, edited the final version of the manuscript, and made many valuable suggestions. I also wish to thank Brian Marinas, Charles Schultz, and Richard Bishop for early drafts of translations of select passages, and Eric Miller for suggestions of early medieval texts. Fr. Stephen Ryan, O.P., helped in the preparation of some Syriac texts. Gary Anderson was generous in providing answers to questions of interpretation and finding obscure Old Testament references.

I am also grateful to Moisés Silva, the translator of Isaiah in the *New English Translation of the Septuagint*. Early on he made his translation available to me, and it is that translation of the Septuagint that is used in the Commentary. I am grateful to Oxford University Press for permission to use *A New English Translation of the Septuagint* for the book of Isaiah. I wish also to thank the editors of the Works of St. Augustine for the Twenty-First Century and New City Press for permission to use recent translations of writings of Augustine.

Finally, Bill Eerdmans' unfailing support over the years has been a source of encouragement and inspiration. I thank him for his friendship, love of jazz, and budding devotion to the Washington Nationals.

Robert Louis Wilken

Interpreting the Old Testament

For most of the Church's history (the early Church, the Church during medieval times, and the Reformation era) the Old Testament was a book about Christ and the Church. As the historical study of the Bible gained ascendency in the twentieth century, however, the Old Testament came to be understood chiefly within the framework of ancient Near Eastern history, culture, and literature. The books of the Old Testament were of course written before the coming of Christ; one task of interpretation, therefore, will always be to set them within the context in which they were first composed. The first Christians, however, recognized that these books were not simply documents from the past but living testimonies to the marvelous things that happened in their own time and continue to happen. St. Jerome said, "Isaiah is an evangelist and apostle, not only a prophet. . . . This book of the Bible contains all the mysteries of the Lord and proclaims him as Emmanuel born of a virgin, as a worker of glorious deeds and signs, as having died and been buried and rising from hell, and, indeed, as the Savior of all the nations."[1]

In calling Isaiah an evangelist and apostle Jerome reflects the practice of the New Testament. After Christ's ascension Philip met an Ethiopian who was returning home from Jerusalem. The Ethiopian was reading the Bible and came to the passage in Isaiah that read: "As a sheep led to the slaughter or a lamb before its shearer is dumb, so he opens not his mouth. In his humiliation justice was denied him. Who can describe his generation? For his life is taken up from the earth" (Isa 53:7-8 as quoted in Acts 8:32-33). When the Ethiopian read this passage, he asked Philip, "To whom do these words refer, to the prophet himself or to someone else?" Philip said they referred to Christ, and beginning with this scripture "he told him the good news of Jesus" (Acts 8:34-35). The book of Isaiah spoke with uncommon clarity about Christ.

It was not only Isaiah, however, that spoke of Christ; the books of Moses, Ezekiel and Jeremiah, the Minor Prophets, the Psalms, and the Wisdom Books also spoke clearly of Christ. According to Luke, when Jesus met two of his disciples on the road to Emmaus he instructed them in the Scriptures "beginning with Moses and all the prophets" and "interpreted to them in all the scriptures the things concerning himself" (Luke 24:27). The Epistle to the Hebrews begins with seven quotations from the Psalms and other

---

1. Prologue to the *Commentary on Isaiah* (CCSL 73:1).

books of the Old Testament and applies them directly to Christ. "To what angel," he writes, "did God ever say, 'Thou art my Son, today I have begotten thee'? [Ps 2:7]. To whom did he say, 'I will be to him a father, and he shall be to me a son'? [2 Sam 7:14]. Of the angels he said, 'Who makes his angels winds, and his servants flames of fire' [Ps 104:4], but his Son he says, 'Thy throne, O God, is forever and ever' [Ps 45:6] . . ." (Heb 1:5-14). Both the Gospel of Matthew and the Gospel of John interpret the words of Zechariah, "Lo, your king comes to you, humble and mounted on an ass, and on a colt, the foal of an ass" (Zech 9:9), as a depiction of Christ's entry into Jerusalem (Matt 21:5; John 12:15).

But the Old Testament is a very large book, and it is not obvious how everything that is found in it (e.g., the ritual of the Day of Atonement in Leviticus 16 or the love poetry of the Song of Songs) derives its meaning from Christ. It may be useful, in introducing these commentaries, to say a few things about how the church fathers went about the business of interpreting the Old Testament. The simple answer is that they followed the example of the writers of the New Testament. Origen of Alexandria, the first major interpreter of the Bible in the Church's history, said that "the apostle Paul, 'teacher of the Gentiles in faith and truth,' taught the Church . . . how it ought to interpret the books of the Law."[2] In 1 Corinthians Paul had written that the Israelites in the desert "drank from the supernatural Rock which followed them, and the Rock was Christ" (1 Cor 10:4), to which he added that these things were "written down for us as types" (1 Cor 10:11). Paul knew of course that the events recorded in the book of Exodus had taken place centuries earlier. God had delivered the Israelites from the oppression of the Egyptians and led them safely through the Red Sea into the Sinai desert. While they made their way back to the land of Israel, God sustained them with manna from heaven and water drawn from rocks. Nevertheless, St. Paul says that what happened in the desert centuries ago is not simply past history. These ancient events are dramatic rehearsals of the deeds of Christ, the Son of God.

Accordingly, Origen believed that Paul, by his example, had provided a "rule of interpretation" for understanding the Old Testament. "Take note," he writes, "how much Paul's teaching differs from the plain meaning. . . . What the Jews thought was a crossing of the sea, Paul calls baptism; what they supposed was a cloud, Paul says is the Holy Spirit." And what Exodus calls a "rock," Paul says was "Christ." Christian interpreters, says Origen, "should apply this rule in a similar way to other passages." In other words, Paul has given the Church a model of how the Old Testament is to be interpreted, and it is the task of later expositors to discern how other passages are to be understood in light of Christ's coming. Augustine made precisely the same point on the basis of the passage from 1 Corinthians. How Paul understands things in this passage, says Augustine, "is a key as to how the rest [of the Old Testament] is to be interpreted."[3]

Following St. Paul, the church fathers argued that a surface reading of the Old Testament, what Origen calls the "plain" meaning, missed what was most important in the Bible, Jesus Christ. The subject of the Scriptures, writes Cyril of Alexandria, is "the mystery of Christ signified to us through a myriad of different kinds of things. Someone

2. *Homily on Exodus* 5.1.
3. *Against Faustus* 12.29.

might liken it to a glittering and magnificent city, having not one image of the king but many, and publicly displayed in every corner of the city.... Its purpose is not to provide us an account of the lives of the saints of old. Far from that. Its purpose is to give us knowledge of the mystery [of Christ] through things that make the word about him clear and true."[4]

To drive home the point the church fathers also cited the passage in Ephesians where St. Paul interprets the famous words about the institution of marriage in Genesis as referring to Christ and the Church. The text in Genesis reads: "For this reason a man shall leave his father and mother and be joined to his wife, and the two shall become one flesh" (Gen 2:24). Paul comments, "This mystery is a profound one, and I am saying that it refers to Christ and the church" (Eph 5:31-32). In Paul's interpretation the words from Genesis do not simply signify Christ but are speaking *about* Christ; that is to say, marriage takes its meaning from the mystery of Christ. At the beginning of his *Literal Commentary on Genesis* Augustine cites this passage from Ephesians and the text from 1 Corinthians 10 to show that the Old Testament cannot be understood in a strictly literal or historical way. "No Christian will dare say that the narrative must not be taken in a figurative sense. For St. Paul says, 'Now all these things that happened to them were symbolic' (1 Cor 10:11). And he explains the statement in Genesis, 'And they shall be two in one flesh' (Eph 5:31), as a great mystery in reference to Christ and to the Church."[5]

The customary term for this kind of exegesis is "allegory," a word first introduced into Christian speech by St. Paul in the Epistle to the Galatians: "It is written that Abraham had two sons, one by a slave and one by a free woman. But the son of the slave was born according to the flesh, the son of the free woman through promise. Now this is an allegory; these women are two covenants" (Gal 4:22-24). The root meaning of allegory is that there is "another" sense, another meaning, besides the plain sense. Sarah and Hagar are not simply names of the wives of Abraham; they also signify two covenants, one associated with Sinai and the other with the Jerusalem above. The rock in the desert that Moses struck and from which water flowed is not simply a rock; it is also Christ.

Allegory is not distinctive to Christian exegesis of the Old Testament. It was used by Greek literary scholars in the ancient world to interpret the *Iliad* and *Odyssey* of Homer, and it was employed by Jewish thinkers — for example, Philo of Alexandria — to interpret the Pentateuch. Christian allegory has similarities to this kind of allegory, but what sets it apart is that it is centered on Christ. Allegory in Christian usage means interpreting the Old Testament as a book about Christ. St. Ambrose wrote: "The Lord Jesus came and what was old was made new."[6] Everything in the Scriptures is to be related to him. As a medieval commentator put it, "All of Divine Scripture is one book, and that one book is Christ, because all of Divine Scripture speaks of Christ, and all of Divine Scripture is fulfilled in Christ."[7] Allegory, or, if one prefers, "spiritual exegesis," is interpreta-

---

4. PG 69:308c.
5. Augustine, *Literal Commentary on Genesis* 1.1.1.
6. *Interpretation of Job and David* 1.4.12 (PL 14:802a).
7. Hugh of St. Victor, *De arca Noe morali* 2.7 (PL 176:642c-d).

tion of the Old Testament in light of the new reality of Christ. In the words of Henri de Lubac, the distinguished theologian and historian of early Christian exegesis: "The conversion of the Old Testament to the New or of the letter of Scripture to its spirit can only be explained and justified, in its radicality, by the all-powerful and unprecedented intervention of Him who is himself at once the Alpha and the Omega, the First and the Last.... Therefore Jesus Christ brings about the unity of Scripture, because he is the endpoint and fulness of Scripture. Everything in it is related to him. In the end he is its sole object. Consequently, he is, so to speak, its whole exegesis."[8]

With these considerations in mind consider a few examples. Isaiah 63:1-3: "Who is this that comes from Edom, in crimsoned garments from Bozrah, he that is glorious in his apparel, marching in the greatness of his strength? 'It is I, announcing vindication, mighty to save.' Why is thy apparel red, and thy garments like his that treads in the winepress? 'I have trodden the winepress alone, and from the peoples no one was with me.'" In the early Church this passage was understood to refer to Christ's ascension. The words "who is this that comes from Edom?" were spoken by the angels who received Christ in heaven after his ascension, and "crimsoned garments" was thought to refer to his garments stained by the blood of his passion. In answer to the questions of the heavenly host Christ says, "I have trodden the winepress alone...." In his commentary on Isaiah 63 Cyril of Alexandria writes: "His appearance was altogether strange and foreign to the powers above. They were astonished at seeing him come up, and said: Who is this that comes from Edom? (63:1). Edom can be translated either 'of wheat' or 'of earth,' Bozrah as either 'of flesh' or 'fleshly.' So they are asking, 'Who is this one from the earth, this earthling?' And the crimsoned garments from Bozrah mean that his clothes were reddened from flesh, or, rather, from blood. He is glorious in his apparel. The heavenly powers, strong and wise and filled with heavenly glory, were looking upon Christ, even in the flesh, as a mighty one, thoroughly invincible, who manifests his divinity as well as his humanity to them."[9] Although this interpretation of Isaiah 63 may be foreign to current readers, it was almost universal in the early Church. Just as the "suffering servant" in Isaiah 53 was interpreted in reference to Christ's passion, so Isaiah 63 was an oracle about Christ's ascension.

A different kind of example can be found in an ancient paschal homily preached in the second century by Melito, bishop of Sardis in Asia Minor. Melito was a gifted orator who used his rhetorical skills to open the Scriptures to his congregation: "If you wish to see the mystery of the Lord, look

at Abel who is similarily murdered (Gen 4:1-8),
at Isaac who is similarly bound (Gen 22:1-9),
at Joseph who is similarly sold (Gen 37:28),
at Moses who is similarly exposed (Exod 2:3),
at David who is similarly persecuted (1 Samuel 23–26),
at the prophets who similarly suffer for the sake of Christ (Matt 5:12).

---

8. *Medieval Exegesis* (Grand Rapids: Eerdmans, 1998), 1:235-37.
9. PG 70:1381b-d.

Interpreting the Old Testament

Look also at the sheep which is slain in the land of Egypt, which struck Egypt and saved Israel by its blood."[10] Here specific moments in Christ's suffering and death are seen foreshadowed in the lives of great figures in the Old Testament.

Some books, for example, Proverbs, do not yield readily to allegory. The passage, "If one gives answer before he hears, it is his folly and shame" (Prov 18:13), stands quite comfortably on its own. Likewise there is much in the historical books of the Bible that is spiritually and morally applicable in its own right, such as the story of Joseph in Genesis or of David in 2 Samuel. On the other hand, the book of Leviticus and the Song of Songs cry out for a spiritual interpretation if they are to be read profitably by Christians. Taken only in its literal sense Leviticus, as Origen once observed, is more of an obstacle to faith than a means of exhortation or edification.[11] It is surely significant that books such as Leviticus and the Song of Songs are seldom read in Christian worship today. Without allegory, that is, a spiritual interpretation related to Christ, they languish.

The early Church read the Old Testament as the Word of God, a book about the triune God, Father, Son, and Holy Spirit, the God who "was and is and is to come." What the text of the Bible meant when it was written, as far as that can be determined, is part of interpretation, but it can never be the last word, nor even the most important word. A historical interpretation can only be preparatory. A Christian understanding of the Scriptures is oriented toward the living Christ revealed through the words of the Bible, toward what the text means today in the lives of the faithful and what it promises for the future. God spoke once, said St. Bernard, but he speaks to us continually and without interruption.[12]

In reading the commentaries on the Old Testament in The Church's Bible, the reader might note the ways in which interpretation turns on specific words or images. For example, the Song of Songs uses the phrase "well of living water" (4:15), an image that also occurs in Jer 2:13, "they have forsaken me, the fount of living water," in Zech 14:8, and in Jesus' discourse with the Samaritan woman (John 4:7-15). In its original literary setting it is crowded in with a number of other images and seems rather innocuous. In his homilies on the Song of Songs, however, Gregory of Nyssa takes "living water" to be an image of the divine life, which is "life-giving." He writes: "We are familiar with these descriptions of the divine essence as a source of life from the Holy Scriptures. Thus the prophet, speaking in the person of God, says: 'They have forsaken me, the fountain of living water' (Jer 2:13). And again the Lord says to the Samaritan woman, 'If you knew the gift of God, and who it is that is saying to you, "Give me a drink," you would have asked him, and he would have given you living water' (John 4:10). And again the Lord says, 'If anyone thirst, let him come to me and drink. He who believes in me, as the Scripture has said, "Out of his heart shall flow rivers of living water"' (John 7:38-39)." By relating what is written in the Song of Songs to other passages from the Old Testament and especially to the words of Jesus in the Gospel of John, Gregory is able to interpret the phrase "living water" in the Song of Songs as "life" flowing from the divine Word of God like water to refresh the soul.

Once a deeper significance of a word or phrase or image is discerned, texts from

---

10. Melito of Sardis, *Paschal Homily* 59-60.
11. Homily 5.1 on Leviticus.
12. *Sermones de diversis* 5.1 (PL 183:554).

the Old Testament resonate with the fullness of the revelation in Christ. The Bible becomes a vast field of interrelated words, all speaking about the same reality, the one God revealed in Christ whose work was confirmed by the Holy Spirit in the life of the Church. The task of the interpreter (and of this series) is to help the faithful look beyond the surface, to highlight a word here, an image there, to find Christ in surprising and unexpected places, to drink at the bountiful spring whose water is ever fresh. Though early Christian exegesis may on first reading appear idiosyncratic and arbitrary, it must be remembered that it arose within the life of the Church and was practiced within a tradition of shared beliefs and practices, guided by the Church's faith as expressed in the creed. Exegesis was not about novelty but about finding the triune God in new and unexpected places within the Scriptures.

The Text of the Old Testament

Most modern English versions of the Old Testament are based on the original Hebrew (and Aramaic) version as it has come down to us in the text established by Jewish scholars (the "Masoretes") in Palestine from the 6th to the 9th centuries. The Masoretic Text is the only complete version of the Hebrew Old Testament, and for centuries it has been used by Christians as well as by Jews. In recent years this text has been amended as new evidence, for example, from the Dead Sea Scrolls, has become available. But modern editions still depend chiefly on the Masoretic Text.

The early Christians, however, did not use the Hebrew version of the Bible. Few spoke or read Hebrew, and the version of the Old Testament read in the churches and used as the basis for biblical commentaries and preaching was a Greek translation of the Hebrew made by Jews before the time of Christ. This translation is usually called the Septuagint (because there were said to be seventy translators). The term may originally have referred only to the books of the Torah, the Pentateuch, that is, the first five books of the Bible. Today, however, the Septuagint (LXX) designates the Greek translation of all the books of the Hebrew Bible, including the Prophets, the Historical Books, and the Wisdom Books, as well as a significant body of other books that go by the name Old Testament Apocrypha, for example, the Wisdom of Solomon, Sirach, the books of the Maccabees, Judith, and Tobit. These latter books are available in English translation in the Revised Standard Version and in the New Revised Standard Version. This Greek Jewish Bible (or translations based on it) was the Bible of the early Church. In the early 5th century, however, St. Jerome translated the Old Testament from Hebrew into Latin, and this version, known as the Vulgate, eventually came to be used by medieval Christian commentators writing in Latin.

Besides the Septuagint, early Christian commentators had access to several other translations made in the first and second centuries A.D. These are identified by the name of the translator: Aquila, Symmachus, and Theodotion. All three were proselytes to Judaism, and Aquila's translation, which was particularly literal, came to be preferred to the Septuagint by Greek-speaking Jews.

Because the ancient commentators were basing their interpretations on the Greek version of the Old Testament (or translations based on it), the actual wording of the text sometimes differs from that of the Hebrew, and hence of modern English versions. Sometimes the differences are minor, but they can also diverge significantly. For example, at Isa 2:2 the Hebrew reads: "It shall come to pass in the latter days that the mountain of the house of the LORD shall be *established* as the highest of the mountains...." In the Septuagint the verse reads: "For in the last days the mountain of the Lord shall be *manifest*...." This is of course a minor variation, yet the term "manifest" lent itself to an interpretation that highlighted that the Church that began in Jerusalem came to be known throughout the world.

A more significant variant occurs in Ps 22:1 (LXX 21:1). In the Hebrew the verse reads: "My God, my God, why hast thou forsaken me? Why art thou so far from helping me, from the words of my groaning?" In the Septuagint the second part of the verse reads: "The words of my transgressions are far from your salvation." This reading posed a serious challenge for the interpreter because the psalm was understood to be spoken by Christ. The first words, "My God, my God, why hast thou forsaken me?" are of course the words of Christ on the cross, and other phrases in the psalm were understood to refer to Christ. Yet, if Christ is speaking, how can he say that God's salvation is far from his "transgressions," that is, from his "sins"?

The Greek and Latin versions of the Song of Songs diverge significantly from the Hebrew, and the variants often suggest interpretations that would not be supported by the Masoretic Text. At the very beginning, for example, at 1:2, the Hebrew reads "For your love is better than wine," but the Greek (and the Latin following the Greek) read "For your breasts are better than wine," offering a more erotic version of the text that commentators exploited.

Because the church fathers were commenting on the Septuagint (or a version based on the Septuagint, e.g., the Latin), the commentaries in this series provide translations of the text on which their expositions are based.

In general we have tried to provide fairly lengthy selections from the commentaries so that the reader can see how the interpretation derives from the text and how the text under discussion is related to other passages in the Bible. In addition to passages from commentaries and homilies on the book under consideration, we have made a selection of occasional comments on particular verses drawn from theological writings, spiritual treatises, sermons, and other works from the early Church.

We had hoped to be able to provide material on every verse or pericope in each chapter, but that proved unrealistic for the longer books, for example, Genesis, Isaiah, and the Psalms. The ancient commentaries are lengthy and repetitious. We have tried to choose selections that are spiritually, exegetically, or theologically interesting and significant. Readers who wish to check particular passages for which we have not provided excerpts can consult the many translations of ancient commentaries that are now becoming available.

In the excerpts the specific text under discussion is printed in bold. When a passage is cited from elsewhere in the Scriptures, it is printed in italics. LXX refers to the Septuagint and Vg. to the Vulgate, the medieval Latin translation.

The authors and works from which the selections are taken are given in the appendixes.

ROBERT LOUIS WILKEN

Introduction to the Christian Interpretation of Isaiah

Among the ancient Jewish prophets Isaiah was the most beloved, the most esteemed, and the most quoted by early Christians. His book contained all the mysteries of the Lord, his birth from a virgin, his miracles, his suffering, death, and resurrection, as well as prophecies of the Church's mission to the nations. Augustine said that Isaiah contains more prophecies of Christ and of the Church than all the other prophets. Over time Isaiah's soaring language and unforgettable imagery were woven into the tapestry of Christian worship, life, and thinking.

Already in the New Testament the story of Christ was punctuated with citations from the prophet Isaiah: "In those days came John the Baptist in the wilderness of Judea, proclaiming, 'Repent, for the kingdom of heaven is at hand.' For this is he who was spoken of by the prophet Isaiah when he said, 'The voice of one crying out in the wilderness: Prepare the way of the Lord, make his paths straight'" (40:3; Matt 3:1-3). Jesus' birth is announced with the memorable words: "Behold, a virgin shall conceive and bear a son, and they shall name him Emmanuel" (7:14; Matt 1:23). When Jesus read from the prophets in his home synagogue in Nazareth, the text for that Sabbath day was from Isaiah 61, "The Spirit of the Lord God is upon me, because he has anointed me to bring good news to the poor...." After the reading he began his discourse with the words: "Today this scripture has been fulfilled in your hearing" (Luke 4:21). In answer to the question of the disciples of John the Baptizer, "Are you he who is to come, or shall we look for another?" Jesus responded by citing verses from Isaiah 29, 35, and 61 (Matt 11:2-6); and to explain why Jesus instructed those whom he healed to keep silent about him, Matthew quotes a passage from Isaiah 42 (Matt 12:15-21).

In the Epistle to the Galatians St. Paul cites a passage from Isaiah 54 to depict the Jerusalem above "who is our mother": "Rejoice, you childless one, you who bear no children, burst into song and shout, you who endure no birth pangs; for the children of the desolate woman are more numerous than the children of the one who is married" (Gal 4:27). In the Acts of the Apostles Philip explains to the Ethiopian eunuch that the phrase "like a sheep he was led to slaughter" (Isa 53:7) refers to Jesus (Acts 8:26-40). And in 1 Peter the apostle uses words from Isaiah to urge his readers to follow the example of Jesus, who patiently bore suffering: "He committed no sin, and no deceit was found in his

Introduction to the Christian Interpretation of Isaiah

mouth. When he was abused, he did not return abuse; when he suffered, he did not threaten.... By his wounds you have been healed" (1 Pet 2:22-24; Isa 53:5-7).

Because of the prominence of Isaiah within the New Testament, a tradition of interpretation took root early in the Church's history. For certain passages — 7:14 (virgin birth), 28:16 (a precious cornerstone), 40:3 (a voice crying in the wilderness), 52:13–53:12 (the suffering servant), 54:1 (the heavenly Jerusalem) — the New Testament gave the words of the prophet very specific meanings. But Isaiah is a very large book, sixty-six chapters in all, and it was not immediately evident how to interpret many of its oracles. It was one thing to highlight key texts cited in the New Testament or used in the Church's worship, quite another to begin with chapter 1 and work through the book verse by verse with the aim of interpreting each passage in light of the coming of Christ and the mission of the Church. For example, the New Testament seldom cites from the oracles against the nations (chs. 13–23),[1] and only rarely alludes to passages from chapters 30–39.[2] In truth Isaiah offered a formidable challenge to the Christian interpreter.

Only by looking at the gradual reception of Isaiah in the early Church can one see how much of what seems familiar (and self-evident) to later Christian readers was discerned over time.[3] To mention a few examples: The famous passage in chapter 2 about beating "swords into plowshares" is not mentioned in the New Testament, nor chapter 9, "Unto us a child is born, unto us a son is given," nor chapter 40, "Comfort ye, comfort ye my people," so familiar from Handel's *Messiah*. Likewise, "A shoot from the stump of Jesse" (11:1) and "Arise, shine, for thy light is come" (60:1) do not appear. The New Testament makes no reference to the "ox" and the "ass" (1:2) that became associated with the crèche of the Christmas season, nor does it allude to the seven gifts of the Spirit in 11:2 (in the Septuagint version).

Although the Christian interpretation of Isaiah began with the New Testament, it was only as Christians lived with the book, heard it read in public worship, sang its "canticles" (e.g., 12:1-6), pondered its words and images, and debated difficult passages, that its fuller meaning was uncovered. The actual text of Isaiah is the beginning of what Isaiah means for Christians, not the ending.

Several examples can illustrate the point. Isaiah 60, an oracle on the restoration of Jerusalem, is not cited in the New Testament. It begins with the words: "Arise, shine; for your light has come, and the glory of the LORD has risen upon you." In the version read by the church fathers, the first part of the verse reads, "Shine, shine, O Jerusalem; for your light has come." Early Christian interpreters understood the phrase "glory of the LORD" to refer to Christ, who had shined first on the Israelites, that is, on Jerusalem, and then on the nations. The prophet, writes Cyril of Alexandria, calls the one who appeared "'the glory of the Lord,' for Christ has risen like a kind of sun shining all around with a divine and spiritual light to bring the radiance of true knowledge of God to those who are eager to believe. He is the glory of God the Father, for in him and through him and with him

---

1. An exception is "Let us eat and drink, for tomorrow we die" (22:13), cited in 1 Cor 15:32.
2. Exceptions are 34:4 in Matt 24:29 and 35:5-6 in Matt 11:5-6.
3. For a fascinating survey of the appropriation of Isaiah over the centuries see John F. A. Sawyer, *The Fifth Gospel: Isaiah in the History of Christianity* (New York: Cambridge University Press, 1996); also Brevard S. Childs, *The Struggle to Understand Isaiah as Christian Scripture* (Grand Rapids: Eerdmans, 2004).

God is glorified." Because the text goes on to speak of the "darkness" that covered the nations, this section of Isaiah came to be associated with bringing the gospel to all peoples. In time it became associated with the Feast of Epiphany, which celebrates the manifestation of God's glory in all the world, symbolized by the coming of the three wise men from the East to worship the infant Christ. To this day Isaiah 60:1-3 is read in most Christian churches on the Feast of Epiphany.

The chant of the seraphim in Isaiah 6, "Holy, holy, holy," appears in the New Testament in the hymn of praise sung by the four living creatures around the throne of God in the book of Revelation: "And the four living creatures, each of them with six wings, are full of eyes all round and within, and day and night they never cease to sing, '**Holy, holy, holy, is the Lord God Almighty** (6:3), who was and is, and is to come!'" (Rev 4:8). From there it passed over into the Eucharistic Liturgy in the hymn known in the Christian East as the Trisagion and in the Christian West as the Sanctus: "Holy, holy, holy, Lord of Power and Might. Heaven and earth are full of your glory. Hosanna in the highest. Blessed is He who comes in the name of the Lord. Hosanna in the Highest."

But another part of chapter 6 not referred to in the New Testament also became part of the Eucharistic Liturgy among Syriac-speaking Christians. When Isaiah has the vision of the Lord seated on a throne surrounded by the seraphim, he says: "Woe is me! For I am lost; for I am a man of unclean lips." Then one of the seraphim lifts "a burning coal which he had taken with tongs from the altar" (6:6) and touches the prophet's lips. The seraph says: "Behold, this has touched your lips; your guilt is taken away, and your sin forgiven (6:7)." Several commentators took the "burning coal" to signify the consecrated bread of the Eucharist that brings forgiveness of sins when it touches the lips of the communicant. This interpretation passed over into the Liturgy, where it is mentioned in the words recited before giving communion to the faithful: "The propitiatory **live coal** of the body and blood of Christ our God is given to the true believer for the pardon of offenses and the forgiveness of sins forever." The same passage from Isaiah is also the source of the priest's prayer before he reads the gospel in the Liturgy: "Cleanse my heart and my lips, that I may worthily proclaim your gospel," an apt association given the early Christian practice of calling Isaiah an evangelist.

The book of Isaiah offered Christians a cornucopia of words and images to speak about familiar things: for Christ's passion the garments stained red (63:1ff.), for Christ who wounds with his love (Song 2:5) the "chosen arrow" (49:2), for the Eucharist the "feast of wine" (25:6), for the Church the tent that is enlarged (54:2). By meditating on these figures and not only on the explicit statements in the gospels or the epistles, Christians were able to enter more deeply into the mystery of Christ and the Church. For the first Christian readers of Isaiah, the interpretation of his book became an ongoing adventure of discovery and discernment. Isaiah's rich and versatile vocabulary proved to be more redolent of the things of God than that of any of the other ancient prophets. Over time the oracles of his book shimmered with meanings that were seen only dimly in the first generations.

Christ was the key to the interpretation of the Old Testament. Origen of Alexandria, the greatest and most influential biblical commentator in the early Church, said that one had to have the mind of Christ to interpret the law and the prophets. "We are not able to understand the law rightly," he wrote, "if Jesus does not read it to us, for when he reads it to us we grasp his mind and meaning. For did he not understand its meaning who said, 'We have the mind of Christ that we might understand the gifts bestowed on us by God, and we impart this in words' (1 Cor 2:12-13)? And those who met Jesus on the road to Emmaus also understood, for they said: 'Did not our hearts burn within us while he opened to us the scriptures on the road?' For 'beginning with the law of Moses and going on to the prophets he read to them from the scriptures and revealed to them everything that was written there concerning himself' (Luke 24:32, 27)."[4]

In many cases the meaning of a passage seemed to lie on the surface of the text. An example is the opening of Isaiah 43: "But now thus says the LORD, he who created you, O Jacob, he who formed you, O Israel: 'Fear not, for I have redeemed you; I have called you by name, you are mine.'" In his commentary on Isaiah Eusebius of Caesarea explains this passage as follows: "The text says, **For I redeemed you** (43:1). The manner of the redemption is made plain by the all-wise Paul, in speaking about Christ, the savior of us all, when he says that the God and Father was pleased to recapitulate all things in him, 'things in heaven and things on earth' (Eph 1:10). In him there is universal redemption, in him absolution and forgiveness of the deeds of the past, and through spiritual kinship with him and sanctification we reach maturity and are lifted up to communion with our God and Father. Therefore he says, **I have called you by name** (43:1). Which name? The name by which we are called is **you are mine**, for we are Christ's. His is the fair name by which we have been called."

In other cases the sense had to be teased out of the text. The technique for doing this was often word association. A word or an image in a passage from Isaiah seemed to echo a word or image in the New Testament, and that in turn suggested how the text from Isaiah was to be understood. The church fathers viewed Scripture as a single book spoken by the Holy Spirit. Cyril of Alexandria saw in the phrase "a plan formed of old" (25:1) a reference to Eph 1:9-10: "For he has made known to us in all wisdom and insight the mystery of his will, according to his purpose which he set forth in Christ as a *plan* for the fullness of time, to unite all things in him, things in heaven and things on earth." Accordingly, Cyril took Isaiah 25 to refer to the Incarnation and the expression "feast of wine" (in 25:6) to signify the Eucharist.

Of course, there are many passages to which the church fathers give a fairly straightforward historical exposition. They discuss the circumstances of an oracle, for example, the reign of an Israelite king, and sometimes make a moral or spiritual application of the text. On occasion they will refer to other sources, such as the *Antiquities* of Josephus or Greek historical works, like Xenophon's *History*. In the main, however, the historical information used to interpret Isaiah is drawn from the Bible itself, from books such as 1 and 2 Samuel and 1 and 2 Kings. These historical passages in the commentaries show that the ancient commentators took seriously the history that was narrated in the Old Testament; it was not simply a springboard to reach other things. It had its own integrity and meaning. Yet it must be acknowledged that modern commentaries are superior for understanding the historical and literary setting of the oracles of Isaiah. We have,

---

4. *Homilies on Joshua* 9.8.

however, included some examples of historical interpretation that illustrate how Christians saw themselves in continuity with the history of biblical Israel.

Christian Critique of Judaism

Christian commentators saw discontinuity as well, and the text of Isaiah offered abundant opportunity to mount a critique of Israel, and, perforce, of the Jews of their own day. Isaiah's vocation as a prophet in ancient Israel was to speak on behalf of God to the people of Israel. At times his language is highly charged and he denounces the Israelites as a willful and rebellious people who worship false gods. In the first chapter he calls them a "sinful nation, a people laden with iniquity" (1:4). Several such passages are cited in the New Testament with reference to Jews who do not believe in Christ. For example, in the Gospel of John we read: "He has blinded their eyes and hardened their heart, lest they should see with their eyes and perceive with their heart and turn for me to heal them" (6:9-10 at John 12:40; also see Jesus' invocation of this passage in Mark 4:12). The song of the vineyard from chapter 5 lies behind Jesus' parable of the vineyard in Matt 21:33-46. In Isaiah the vineyard brings forth "wild grapes," and in Matthew the "kingdom" will be taken away from the Jews and "given to a nation producing the fruits of it" (Matt 21:43).

Christianity began as a movement among the Jews, and from the beginning Christian writers drew on the prophets to support and defend their belief in Christ. Christians claimed the Jewish Scriptures, the Christian Old Testament, as their own, but the Jews used the same sacred book. They also possessed the Hebrew versions of the Scriptures, and interpreted the prophets quite differently from Christians. Jews took the prophecies to refer to the rebuilding of Jerusalem and the reestablishment of a Jewish kingdom in the land of Israel. Christians believed that the prophecies referred to the coming of Christ and interpreted the oracles about Jerusalem and Zion in relation to the Church. In other words, Christian commentators had to contend with an alternate tradition of interpretation. This conflict is most evident in Jerome's *Commentary on Isaiah*.

Furthermore, the Jews belonged to well-established communities many of which had been established in the cities of the Mediterranean world centuries before the rise of Christianity, and they enjoyed certain legal rights and privileges. Christians were members of a new movement that claimed to be the inheritor of the Jewish tradition, but they did not observe the laws that were clearly set down in the Old Testament (e.g., keeping the Sabbath). That is, the Christian way of reading the Old Testament seemed to be refuted by the words of the Bible itself. Even pagan critics who observed the practices of both communities realized that they could use the Jewish Scriptures (the Christian Old Testament) to mount arguments against Christianity.

Such was the historical and social setting in which Christians read the book of Isaiah. In ancient Israel the aim of the prophet was to bring the people to repentance, and his words of reproach were accompanied by words of pardon, comfort, and hope. Christians, however, took the prophets' denunciations of the idolatry of the ancient Israelites as a judgment on the Jews of their day for not accepting Christ, and asserted that the Jews did not understand their own books. As skilled polemicists formed in the highly developed rhetorical culture of the ancient world, Christian thinkers were delighted to find in Isaiah a stockpile of invectives to deploy in their polemics against the Jews. Not surprisingly, these passages in the ancient commentaries — along with critiques directed at early Christian heretical groups (e.g., the Gnostics or Arians or Pelagians) — do not make for edifying reading today.

These polemical passages, particularly those directed at the Jews, posed a dilemma during the preparation of this commentary. In the context of the ancient world in which Christianity was seeking to establish and define itself against well-established Jewish communities a vigorous polemic is understandable. These passages, however, carried different meanings when they were read by Christians in medieval Christian societies where Jews were discriminated against and even in modern times when Jews were considered an alien presence in Christian societies. Read today, they only help to perpetuate stereotypes of the Jews that have shaped negative Christian attitudes in the past. If, on the other hand, they were ignored, this commentary would misrepresent an aspect of the early Christian interpretation of Isaiah that is nearly ubiquitous. So we have included a number of representative passages that reflect this tradition of interpretation. They can be found particularly in chapters 5, 6, 8, and 28. But since the purpose of this series is to provide excerpts for spiritual reading and resources for the theological appropriation of the Bible, and not simply to offer a representative cross section of early Christian biblical interpretation, it seemed advisable not to include many of the sharply polemical passages.

Commentaries and Homilies on Isaiah

We have drawn chiefly on the four complete commentaries on Isaiah from the early Church written by Eusebius of Caesarea, Jerome, Cyril of Alexandria, and Theodoret of Cyrus. A fifth commentary by John Chrysostom is preserved in an Armenian translation, but it did not yield much of value for this series. Origen's huge commentary on the first thirty chapters of Isaiah is lost, but there are extant nine homilies dealing with select verses from Isaiah. From John Chrysostom there is a commentary on chapters 1–8 drawn from his homilies as well as a collection of five homilies dealing with Isaiah 6. Chapters 1–16 are treated in a Greek commentary that goes under the name of Pseudo-Basil.

The book of Isaiah was also cited often in sermons and homilies on other biblical books, in theological and polemical writings, and in spiritual and devotional works. Since comments on passages from these books, though occasional, are often illuminating, in the excerpts we draw freely on a wide range of authors who did not write commentaries on Isaiah, for example, Irenaeus of Lyons, Tertullian, Gregory of Nyssa, Gregory of Nazianzus, Basil of Caesarea, Ephrem the Syrian, Ambrose, Augustine, Gregory the Great, Symeon the New Theologian, Bernard of Clairvaux, and Aelred of Rievaulx.

Using This Commentary

The writers excerpted in this collection were variously commenting on the Septuagint (LXX), the Greek version of the Old Testament, an early Latin version based on the Greek (Old Latin), a Syriac version, or a Latin version based on the Hebrew (Vulgate). That is to say, they were expounding a different version of Isaiah than the Hebrew that is the basis for modern English versions. Jerome had a knowledge of Hebrew and will sometimes give a Latin translation of the Hebrew as well as of the Septuagint, and several commentators had at their disposal Greek versions prepared by Jews after the rise of Christianity. These go by the names of their translators, Symmachus, Aquila, and Theodotion, and are sometimes cited in selections in this commentary. But most of the fathers were reading only the Greek, Latin, or Syriac versions, which sometimes differ significantly from the Hebrew. If readers look up some of the biblical passages discussed here in a modern English translation, they may find what appears to be a different text altogether.

A good example is Isa 11:2. In the Hebrew version there are six gifts of the Spirit: "the spirit of wisdom and understanding, the spirit of counsel and might, the spirit of knowledge and the fear of the LORD." However, because of the way the Septuagint rendered the Hebrew, the sixth gift becomes "godliness" and the next line becomes a seventh gift, "the spirit of the fear of God." The Christian interpretation of the text takes its cue from the Septuagint version.

In the commentary each chapter is prefaced with a modern English translation of the Septuagint version of Isaiah. This was prepared by Moisés Silva for *A New English Translation of the Septuagint* (*NETS*). For biblical names the *NETS* uses an English translation of the Greek form, for example, Iudaia instead of Judea, Iakob for Jacob, Libanos for Lebanon, but in our translation we have used more familiar spellings. Notes on textual variations have not been included.

For citations from Isaiah in the excerpts we have generally used the *NETS* version, though changing the names to more familiar English spelling. However, since some commentators were citing a Latin version or a Syriac version or a different Greek version or from memory, the text of Isaiah sometimes differs from what is printed at the head of the chapter in the Septuagint. We have translated the text as it is cited. For other books of the Bible we have used, where possible, the RSV, but here too citations are often from memory and will differ in small ways from the received text. In some cases we have called attention to changes, but because they are so frequent, more often they pass unmentioned. The reader should keep in mind that the biblical text is very fluid and will often differ from modern English versions. Far from dismissing this as a failing, early Christian interpreters took the fluidity of the biblical text as an opportunity to discover more than one meaning in a text.

In contrast to the approach taken by modern commentators, the approach of the church fathers to the biblical text is often piecemeal. In the line-by-line commentaries, interpreters will sometimes discuss the literary or historical context of a passage, but more often they lift out a word or words or an image, and relate that to other passages in Scripture, to the Church's faith as confessed in the creeds, or to the Eucharist or Baptism.

Introduction to the Christian Interpretation of Isaiah

In other words, the framework of interpretation is shaped not by the literary form of the book or its historical origin but by the Church's faith, practice, and teaching. For example, chapter 66 begins: "Heaven is my throne and the earth is the footstool of my feet.... All these things my hand has made." Gregory of Nyssa (and other commentators), following the prologue to the Gospel of John and St. Paul, took this to mean that the world came into being by the agency of the divine Logos: "The prophet 'speaking in the person of the Father' asserts: **"My hand made all these things"** (66:2). **Hand** in his enigmatic language signifies the power of the Only-Begotten. And the apostle says that all things are *from* the Father and *through* the Son (1 Cor 8:6)."

It is understandable, then, that the church fathers were drawn to certain passages and were less interested in others. That is one reason why we have not provided a running commentary on every verse of Isaiah. Not all the material in the ancient commentaries on Isaiah will be of interest to modern readers. There is also much repetition. Judicious selection seemed the way of prudence. Consequently only certain verses receive commentary, and some chapters are ignored completely. We have tried to provide comment on the most important passages (and many of lesser importance), but this commentary is a selection, and like any selection it may seem partial and incomplete where it should be full. The list of chapters treated is given in the table of contents.

The arrangement of the material within each chapter is as follows. After the modern English translation of the Septuagint version there is an editorial comment that briefly discusses the central themes of the chapter and highlights particular features of the interpretation. Then follows a passage, sometimes quite lengthy, from one of the four complete commentaries on Isaiah. This may be followed by shorter excerpts from one of the other commentaries. Here the order is dependent on how the excerpts treat the text. Then follow shorter excerpts chosen at random from other writings (sermons, theological treatises, devotional works, and liturgical texts) as well as from the commentaries. These are arranged according to the verses in the chapter, which are printed in bold at the beginning of each section. When there is more than one excerpt, they are given in chronological order.

The passage from Isaiah being commented on is printed in bold; citations from other biblical books and from elsewhere in Isaiah are in italics. References to passages in Isaiah give only chapter and verse (e.g., 64:12, not Isa 64:12), except where such citations might lead to confusion with other biblical books.

One final comment about the terminology of the church fathers. The term "type" means a model, a representation, a figure that anticipates something that is to come. A clay statue is a "type" of a bronze or marble statue. Hence the type points to the end product, the thing itself, the "truth." A type could be a person or an event or a thing. The "sacrifice" of Isaac is a type of the sacrifice of Christ, the exodus through the Red Sea a type of Baptism, the bronze serpent on the pole a type of the crucifixion, and the sacrifices of animals in the Old Testament types of the perfect sacrifice of Christ.

The term "economy" refers to God's ordered plan of redemption realized in the history of Israel and the coming of Christ. It is often used to refer specifically to Christ's sojourn on earth and hence to the Incarnation.

Sources for the Interpretation of Isaiah

Biographical information on the authors whose writings are excerpted in this volume is provided in an appendix. In another appendix the sources from which the individual excerpts are taken are listed in the order in which they appear.

ROBERT LOUIS WILKEN

Preface to Isaiah

This opening section gathers together excerpts from introductions to ancient commentaries on Isaiah, several passages from the New Testament, as well as occasional references to Isaiah in other early Christian writings. In Jewish tradition Isaiah was thought to have been martyred by King Manasseh because he claimed to have "seen" God (6:1). The account of his martyrdom is found in the apocryphal book The Martyrdom and Ascension of Isaiah, *and is alluded to in the Epistle to the Hebrews (Heb 11:37). In the eyes of the church fathers Isaiah was not only a prophet but also an evangelist, a point that Jerome accents in the preface to his commentary on Isaiah. "This book of the Bible," he writes, "contains all the mysteries of the Lord." So extensive were the passages that prefigured events in Christ's life that it seemed possible to recount the entire narrative of the gospel using the words of the prophet. In fact, an early medieval writer, Isidore of Seville, did just that, and the final excerpt includes some sections from his work,* Isaiah's Testimony, concerning Christ the Lord.*

The excerpt from Origen underscores a conviction that was at the heart of the interpretation of the Old Testament in the early Church: only those who have "met Jesus on the road to Emmaus" (Luke 24:27ff.) are able to understand the law and the prophets. We are able to grasp their meaning, says Origen, "when Jesus reads it to us." Chrysostom discusses Isaiah's compassion and his identification with the sufferings of those to whom he preached. "Nothing," he writes, "suits one for spiritual leadership more than being able to suffer with others." Eusebius reminds the readers of his commentary that much of the language of the book of Isaiah is metaphorical, and Cyril of Alexandria introduces his readers to the kings who ruled in Isaiah's time.

As a young man Augustine found the book impenetrable, gave up reading it after the first chapter, and never attempted to write a commentary on Isaiah. An indication of how important the Scriptures were in forming Christian thinking can be found in another passage from Augustine. In his Reconsiderations, *a work in which the elderly Augustine reviewed his writings, he observed that had he known 59:2, "your iniquities have made a separation between you and your God," he would not have written what he did in his early work* On the Immortality of the Soul. *In the* City of God *Augustine mentions the central principle guiding the interpretation of Isaiah in the early Church, that Isaiah has more prophecies about Christ and the Church than any other prophet, and cites at length Isaiah 53 on Christ and Isaiah 54 on the Church to make his point.*

ISAIAH

(1) The Letter to the Hebrews

And what more shall I say? For time would fail me to tell of Gideon, Barak, Samson, Jephthah, of David and Samuel and the prophets. . . . Some were tortured, refusing to accept release, that they might rise again to a better life. Others suffered mocking and scourging, and even chains and imprisonment. They were stoned, they were sawn in two. . . .[1] And all these, though well attested by their faith, did not receive what was promised, since God had foreseen something better for us, that apart from us they should not be made perfect.

(2) The Gospel according to Luke

And [Jesus] came to Nazareth, where he had been brought up; and he went to the synagogue, as his custom was, on the sabbath day. And he stood up to read; and there was given to him the book of the prophet Isaiah. He opened the book and found the place where it was written: **The Spirit of the Lord is upon me, because he has anointed me to preach good news to the poor. He has sent me to proclaim release to the captives and recovering of sight to the blind, to set at liberty those who are oppressed, to proclaim the acceptable year of the Lord** (61:1-2). And he closed the book, and gave it back to the attendant, and sat down; and the eyes of all in the synagogue were fixed on him. And he began to say to them, "Today this scripture has been fulfilled in your hearing."

(3) The Gospel according to John

When Jesus had said this, he departed and hid himself from them. Though he had done so many signs before them, yet they did not believe in him; it was that the word spoken by the prophet Isaiah might be fulfilled: **Lord, who has believed our report, and to whom has the arm of the Lord been revealed?** (53:1). Therefore, they could not believe. For Isaiah again said: **He has blinded their eyes and hardened their heart, lest they should see with their eyes and perceive with their heart, and turn for me to heal them** (6:10). Isaiah said this because he saw his glory and spoke of him.

(4) The Acts of the Apostles

But an angel of the Lord said to Philip, "Rise and go toward the south to the road that goes down from Jerusalem to Gaza." This is a desert road. And he rose and went. And behold, an Ethiopian, a eunuch, a minister of Candace, queen of the Ethiopians, in charge of all her treasure, had come to Jerusalem to worship and was returning; seated in his

---

1. This is a reference to the legend of Isaiah's martyrdom. See passage no. 5 from the *Martyrdom and Ascension of Isaiah*.

chariot, he was reading the prophet Isaiah. And the Spirit said to Philip, "Go up and join this chariot." So Philip ran to him, and heard him reading Isaiah the prophet, and asked, "Do you understand what you are reading?" And he said, "How can I, unless some one guides me?" And he invited Philip to come up and sit with him. Now the passage of the scripture which he was reading was this: **As a sheep led to the slaughter or a lamb before its shearer is dumb, so he opens not his mouth. In his humiliation justice was denied him. Who can describe his generation? For his life is taken up from the earth** (53:7-8). And the eunuch said to Philip, "About whom, pray, does the prophet say this, about himself or about some one else?" Then Philip opened his mouth, and beginning with this scripture he told him the good news of Jesus. And as they went along the road they came to some water, and the eunuch said, "See, here is water! What is to prevent my being baptized?" And he commanded the chariot to stop, and they both went down into the water, Philip and the eunuch, and he baptized him.

(5) Martyrdom and Ascension of Isaiah

And Belkira[2] accused Isaiah and the prophets who were with him, saying: "Isaiah and the prophets who were with him prophesy against Israel and Judah. . . . And Isaiah himself said: 'I see more than Moses the prophet.' Moses, however, said that *no man can see God and live* (Exod 33:20). But Isaiah insisted: 'I have seen God (6:1), and behold I am alive.' Know therefore, O king, that they are false prophets."

Because of these visions, therefore, Beliar[3] was angry with Isaiah, and he dwelt in the heart of Manasseh, and Manasseh sawed Isaiah in half with a wood saw. And while Isaiah was being sawed, his accuser, Belkira, stood by, and all the false prophets stood by, laughing and maliciously rejoicing because of Isaiah. And Belkira, through Mekembekus, stood before Isaiah, laughing and deriding. And Belkira told Isaiah: "Say, 'I have lied in everything I have spoken; the ways of Manasseh are good and right, and also the ways of Belkira and those who are with him are good.'" And he said this to him when he began to be sawed in half. And Isaiah was absorbed in a vision of the Lord, and though his eyes were open, he did not see them.

(6) Origen of Alexandria

Jesus reads the law to us when he reveals the mysteries of the law. For we who belong to the catholic Church do not reject the law of Moses, we embrace it, on the condition that Jesus read it to us. For we are not able to understand the law rightly if Jesus does not read it to us, for when he reads it to us we grasp his mind and meaning. For did he not understand its meaning who said, *We have the mind of Christ, that we might understand the gifts bestowed on us by God and we impart this in words* (1 Cor 2:12)? And those who met Jesus

---

2. An agent of the devil.
3. The devil.

on the road to Emmaus also understood, for they said: *Did not our hearts burn within us while he opened to us the scriptures on the road? For beginning with the law of Moses and going on to the prophets he read to them from the Scriptures and revealed to them everything that was written there concerning himself* (Luke 24:32, 27).

(7) Eusebius of Caesarea

At times the Spirit disclosed his revelations to the prophet Isaiah clearly, and his words have no need of an allegorical interpretation. The plain meaning alone suffices. On other occasions, however, the Spirit spoke through symbols that pointed to other realities, hinted at by expressive words and names — as in the case of dreams. A good example is the way Joseph's brothers are represented as eleven stars that appear to offer homage to him (Gen 37:9-10; cf. 37:5-8); another example is when he dreamed his brothers were collecting ears of corn, a sign that there would be famine (cf. Gen 37:6-7; 41:1-36). It is not dissimilar with Isaiah. Many of the things he prophesied were seen through symbols, and others were presented in elaborate fashion, words intended literally woven together in the same passage with others meant metaphorically. This same combining of disparate elements is also found in the teachings of our Savior, for example, when he is described as having instructed: *Do you not say that there are four months and harvest is coming? Lift up your eyes and see the fields, that they are white for the harvest* (John 4:35). Some of these words are to be taken literally but others metaphorically. So also with the prophet I am presently expounding. He will sometimes use words whose meaning is self-evident, such as, **What is your abundance of sacrifices to me? says the Lord; I have had enough of your burnt offerings**, (1:11). However, the following passage requires a metaphorical or spiritual interpretation: **My beloved had a vineyard on a hill in a very fertile place**, and so on (5:1).

(8) John Chrysostom

The remarkable quality of the prophet Isaiah is certainly evident in his book, but the apostle Paul, who knew Isaiah's virtues better than anyone else, shows Isaiah's greatness in his own inspired writings. In a single sentence he points to the elegance of Isaiah's style, his independence of spirit, his lofty ideas, and the exceptional clarity of his prophecy concerning Christ. Here is what he says: *Isaiah is so bold as to say,* **I have been found by those who did not seek me; I have shown myself to those who did not ask for me** (Rom 10:20; Isa 65:1).

Isaiah was also very compassionate. Not only did he struggle against the folly of the people, but he also proclaimed in his own distinctive language and with profound understanding the misfortunes that were about to overtake them. When their actions brought trouble upon them, he suffered no less than they. He was no less troubled and cried out more bitterly than his fellows.

This is the way of prophets and saints. They have more tender feelings for those in their care than parents, feelings that are almost unnatural. For no one, even those devoted to their children, ever burned with such love for their offspring as those saints who died on behalf of those to whom they spoke. They mourned and lamented for them, pleaded with God on their behalf when they knew hardship, were deported with them, and shared in their terrors. They underwent these things so that people might be spared God's anger and delivered from suffering. Nothing suits one for spiritual leadership more than being able to suffer with others.

This is why God raised the great Moses to a position of authority. By his actions he showed that he was devoted to his people. At one point he said to God: *If you will, forgive their sin, forgive them. And if not, blot me out of the book which you have written* (Exod 32:32). And Isaiah, when he saw the people perishing, said: **Leave me alone, for I am weeping bitter tears; do not labor to comfort me for the destruction of the daughter of my people** (22:4). Jeremiah also composed long lamentations when the city was laid waste. Ezekiel was taken into exile with the others, thinking that a foreign land would be easier to bear than staying in his own land. For he believed that in this calamity the greatest comfort he could give was to be present with those who suffered and to do what he could to help their situation. Daniel fasted for more than twenty days to help bring about the return from exile, and he fervently pleaded with God to free the Israelites from their bitter servitude (Dan 10:2-3). It appears that each of the saints displayed this same virtue.

In the same way, when David saw that God was going to chastise his people, he called down a plague on himself, saying: *I the shepherd[4] have sinned, and I the shepherd have done wickedness; but these sheep, what have they done? Let your hand, I pray you, be against me and against my father's house* (2 Sam 24:17). The patriarch Abraham stood far apart from evil and had nothing to do with the troubles that were to be visited on Sodom; nevertheless he prayed and beseeched God as if he himself were in danger. If God had not dismissed him and sent him away, he would have continued to speak and bend his efforts to stop the terrible conflagration (Gen 18:22-33).

The saints in the New Covenant displayed even greater virtue, for they were the beneficiaries of even more abundant grace and called to even greater trials. So Peter, when he heard Christ say that it is very difficult for the rich to enter heaven, was filled with anxiety and trembling, and asked this question: *Then who can be saved?* (Luke 18:26). He was, however, confident about himself. This kind of person does not think of himself but is concerned for the whole world. Paul's character, too, is displayed throughout his epistles. He did not want to see Christ before others were saved. It would be *far better,* he writes, *to depart and be with Christ. But to remain in the flesh is more necessary on your account* (Phil 1:23-24). The prophet Isaiah displays the same strength of character when he boldly proclaims God's oracles, rebukes sinners, and does not cease praying for those who oppose him.

---

4. Chrysostom adds the word **shepherd** as an exegetical elaboration of the passage.

(9) Jerome

Isaiah is an evangelist and an apostle as well as a prophet. For about himself and the other evangelists he announced: **How beautiful upon the mountains are the feet of him who brings good tidings, who publishes peace** (52:7). And God speaks to him as to an apostle: **Whom shall I send, and who will go to this people?** And he responds, **Here am I! Send me** (6:8).... This book of the Bible contains all the mysteries of the Lord and proclaims him as Emmanuel born of a virgin, as a worker of glorious deeds and signs, as having died and been buried and as rising from hell, and, indeed, as the Savior of all the nations.

(10) Augustine of Hippo

Ambrose told me to read the prophet Isaiah,[5] I think, because more clearly than others he foretold the gospel and the calling of the Gentiles. But I did not understand the first passage of the book, and thought the whole would be equally obscure. So I set it aside to be resumed when I had more practice in the Lord's style of language.

(11) Augustine of Hippo

The prophet Isaiah is not in the book of the Twelve Prophets. They are called "minor" prophets because their discourses are brief in comparison with those called "major" because they are longer. Among the latter is Isaiah, whom I connect with the two I have just discussed [Hosea and Amos], who prophesied during the same time. Isaiah reproached the people for their wrongdoing, taught them righteousness, and predicted the misfortunes that would befall them. But he also made many more prophecies than the other prophets about Christ and the Church, that is, about the king and the City which he founded, so much so that he was called an evangelist rather than a prophet by some commentators.[6] [Augustine then cites in its entirety 52:13–53:12.]

So much was said about Christ. And now let us listen to what follows, which concerns the Church. [He then cites 54:1-5.]

(12) Augustine of Hippo

What I wrote [in *Immortality of the Soul*[7]] — "the soul cannot be separated from eternal reason because they are not joined spatially" — I would not have said had I been more familiar with the Sacred Scriptures. For I would have been reminded of what is written:

---

5. In answer to Augustine's question about which books of the Bible he should read.
6. See the excerpt from Jerome.
7. *Immortality of the Soul* 1.6.11 (PL 32:1026).

Your sins separate you from God (59:2). There it is given to understand that we can speak of separation even of those things that are not joined spatially but spiritually.

(13) Cyril of Alexandria

Because the words of the holy prophets are filled with hidden meanings and predictions of divine mysteries, their language makes great demands on the reader. For *Christ is the end of the law and the prophets*[8] (Rom 10:4). I believe that if one wishes to understand clearly the subtlety and breadth of Isaiah's visions, one must examine very carefully with the eyes of the mind both the historical account and the spiritual meaning found in the text. Approached in this way, the text has much to offer the reader and its meaning will shine through clearly.

Isaiah prophesied during the reigns of Uzziah, Jotham, Ahaz, and Hezekiah. Let us begin by reviewing the history of each of these kings and speak briefly of their conduct. As we look at these things, we will see that the prophet's message was most pertinent and apropos the historical situation in which he spoke.

Uzziah, who was also known as Azariah,[9] was a pious man. As time passed, he grew more famous and more powerful. Under his leadership Judah conquered the neighboring nations, subjugated their leaders, and exacted tribute from them. Uzziah founded several cities, annexed others, and fortified the boundaries of the whole land of Judah. At this point in his life, however, a temptation common to all humans overtook him. After having won all these victories and enjoying the great luxury and widespread fame that resulted from them, he became preoccupied with his accomplishments. His arrogance grew like a sickness, so overpowering him that he grievously transgressed God's law. When it might have been appropriate for the priests to honor him for his accomplishments, he took matters into his own hands, entering the temple on his own and personally offering a sacrifice to God (2 Chr 26:16ff.). He thus displaced the proper ritual with this illegal and arrogant act. As a result, he immediately became a leper. This punishment publicly deprived him of every vestige of honor, since lepers were considered to be unclean.

At this point Uzziah's son Jotham succeeded him. Jotham was a devout man, but, according to the Scripture, he did not remove the so-called "high places." So the people of Israel continued to offer sacrifices to idols they themselves had made. According to Hosea, they went into the hills and the mountains to sacrifice under oaks, poplars, and other shady trees, since these places provided good shelter (Hos 4:13).

When Jotham's reign came to an end, Ahaz, a hideous and loathsome individual, took the scepter of leadership. During his reign the land was overflowing with despicable enmity toward God. Ahaz closed up the temple and refused to allow the people to honor the one God with the legally prescribed sacrifices. He stopped the celebration of the customary Jewish festivals, and after erecting pagan altars in every part of the city of Jerusa-

---

8. Cyril adds the words: **and the prophets**.
9. Cf. 2 Kgs 14:21–22; 15:1–34.

lem, he ordered the people to worship idols and to bow down to the hosts of heaven (cf. Zeph 1:5).[10] He even forced his own children to "pass through the fire,"[11] which means that he offered them as a burnt offering to unclean spirits. In short, there was no impious act he did not practice diligently.

After the reign of Ahaz, Hezekiah became king. He was a pious and devout man, a just ruler who zealously sought all that was good and a person who acted in accordance with God's will. Hezekiah did away with all the unlawful practices that had flourished during the time of Ahaz. He reopened the temple and ordered that the proper sacrifices and oblations to God be reinstituted. He issued a decree that the legally appointed priests should be honored and that the long-forgotten laws relating to the Passover be renewed. He destroyed the sacred precincts, idols, and altars of false gods, and commanded the scores of diviners, false prophets, and enchanters to be silent. In the eyes of God he was a good man.

Surely, therefore, during the reigns of those of whom we have just spoken, the God of all was provoked to condemn Israel when she was worshiping idols. On the other hand, when her leader was virtuous and the affections of the Israelites were turned toward true devotion, God was appeased and the day of judgment was put off. For this reason, the prophecy contains a somewhat ambivalent message. At some points, when Israel was acting impiously, Isaiah makes very grave threats. At other places, however, Isaiah speaks words brimming with promise for those who are good. All the while, his prophecy proclaims that the future redemption is to come through Christ and says that in later times Israel will be cut off from the household of God and that the full complement of the nations, being justified through faith in Christ, will be invited into the household of God.

It seems to me that the prophet Isaiah is crowned with the greatest of honor, not only in the eloquence of his own words but also because he is mentioned often by the apostles (e.g., Matt 3:3; John 12:38; Rom 10:20). Their references to him inextricably link his words with the sparkling joy of the message of the gospel.

(14) Isidore of Seville

Blessed Isaiah, the son of Amos, whose name is translated "Savior of the Lord," born from the tribe of Judah, noble in birth, honored and distinguished among all the prophets, prophesied under four kings of Judah who succeeded and were descended one from the other, Uzziah, Jotham, Ahaz, and in the end Hezekiah. He prophesied about Judah and Jerusalem and Israel and about Babylon and Philistia, Moab and Damascus, also Egypt and the Desert of the Sea, Idumea and Arabia, the Valley of Death and Tyre, and the land of the Negev. He met his end, however, under Manasseh, king of Judah, son of Hezekiah. Because Isaiah regularly censured Manasseh for his abominations before the Lord in Jerusalem, he was slain by being cut in half with a saw by Manasseh from his head down

---

10. False gods.
11. The wording of 4 Kgdms 16:3 in the LXX.

through his middle (Heb 11:37). Isaiah earned a double honor, the office of prophet and martyr. He was buried under the oak Rogel next to the waterfall that Hezekiah, king of Judah, had set up, when a dam was constructed with earth and dust.

Among the prophets Isaiah is certainly most revered because he narrated all the deeds of Christ in order and most fully, and he published in his own book very many clear testimonies of what was revealed to him by the Lord in the spirit of prophecy.

That Christ Was Born from the Stock of David

Isaiah foretold that Christ would be born according to the flesh from the seed of David, saying: **A branch *(virga)* will come forth from the root of Jesse.** Mary the Virgin *(virgo)* was born from the stock of David; **and a flower will arise from his root** (11:1). This refers to our Lord Jesus Christ, who was brought forth from the flesh from Mary. **And the Spirit of the Lord will rest upon him, the Spirit of wisdom and understanding, the Spirit of counsel and might, the Spirit of knowledge and piety, and the Spirit will fill him with the fear of the Lord** (11:2). Why are such great gifts of the Spirit proclaimed by God concerning him? Because the Holy Spirit does not dwell to the same measure in him as in us, but entirely, that is, in the fullness of divinity and grace. He is the one who **judges not according to the vision of the eyes and hearing of the ears, for justice is the girdle of his limbs, and faith the girdle of his affections** (11:3-5).

That Christ Was Born of a Virgin

The holy Isaiah in ancient times foretold his birth from the Virgin in this way: **And the Lord added that he speak to Ahaz, saying: Seek for yourself a sign from the Lord your God in the depth of the underworld or in the height above.** And he said: **Hear, therefore, O house of David,** that is, nation of David. His words were quite rightly addressed to the house of David from whose stock, that is, from Mary and from the Holy Spirit, Christ would be born. And he added: **On account of this the Lord himself will give you a sign: Behold, a virgin will conceive in her womb and bear a son, and you will call his name Emmanuel** . . . (7:10-14). Emmanuel is Hebrew for the Latin *Deus nobiscum,* that is, "God with us." The one whom the Virgin bore is named "God with us."

That Christ Was Born from a Virgin without Intercourse with a Man

The same prophet Isaiah says elsewhere that Christ was not born by male seed, but of a virgin: **Let the heavens drop down from above, and let the clouds rain justice; let the earth be opened and let it sprout forth a savior, and let justice arise at the same time; I the Lord created him** (45:8). The heavens, that is, the clouds, are the prophets, through whom Christ's coming was prophesied. Mary is the earth who bore him, not, however, by intercourse because the Lord alone brought him into being without the mingling of the seed of a man. Speaking in the person of the Father, Isaiah said: **Lo, I send among the foundations of Zion a Stone, approved, a precious, choice cornerstone, and he who will have believed on him will not be confounded** . . . (28:16).

ISAIAH

That God Was Made Flesh and Became a Man

The prophet Isaiah proclaims that the Lord would be born in the flesh: **A child**, he says, **has been born to us, a Son has been given to us. And the government is upon his shoulders; and his name will be called Marvelous, Counselor, God, Mighty, Father of the World to Come, the Prince of Peace. His empire will be increased, and there will be no end to his peace** (9:6-7). The **child** surely is Christ, because he was born a man for us. . . . Moreover, **A son has been given to us**: Whose son is this except the son of God? His **government upon his shoulders**, that is, because he himself first carried the cross on his shoulders. Pilate wrote the inscription of "king" on the cross over his shoulders and head: *Iesus Nazarenus Rex Iudeorum*: "Jesus of Nazareth, King of the Jews." His first name is **Marvelous**; second **Counselor**; third **God**; fourth **Mighty**; fifth **Prince of Peace**; sixth **Father of the World to Come**. Behold, God was born a child.

That Christ the Lord Did Wonders and Marvelous Deeds

The healings and marvelous deeds that Christ worked in the world were written down in advance long ago through the prophet Isaiah when he declared: **Behold, our God, he himself will come and save us. Then shall the eyes of the blind be opened, and the ears of the deaf will hear. Then shall the lame man leap like a deer, and the tongue of the dumb will be clear** (35:5-6). Likewise, concerning the same thing Isaiah says: **The Spirit of the Lord is upon me, because he anointed me; he sent me to the meek in order that I might heal the contrite in heart, announcing that he proclaims redemption to the captive and restores light to the blind** (61:1). And again Isaiah says: **For in the strength of his virtue he stirred up the dead with his voice**.[12] To be sure, many saints and prophets did wonders; yet none of them brought the dead back to life except by the word of the Lord. . . .

That Christ Suffered and That He Was Hanged on the Wood of the Cross

Isaiah declared that the Son of God would come to suffer when he said: **Who is that man who comes from Edom, with dyed garments from Bozrah? He is beautiful in his robe, walking in the multitude of his strength. I am he who speaks justice, and I am a defender in order to save. Why then are your clothing and vestments red just like the clothing of those who tread in a winepress? I treaded the winepress alone, and of the peoples there was none with me** (63:1-3). Truly the prophetic Spirit, contemplating God clothed in the flesh and coming to his passion, mentions that he was covered with blood, likening his bloodstained clothing to the clothing of those who tread a winepress. For men climb down from the vat stained blood-red from the redness of wine. This was also prefigured in Genesis in the person of Judah, from whose tribe Christ descended: *He will wash*, he says, *his own robe in wine and his own mantle with the blood red juice of a grape* (Gen 49:11), pointing to his flesh as "robe" and "mantle" and to his blood as "wine." The wine is a figure of the mystery of his blood, the blood of his cup.

---

12. Source of this citation unknown.

Preface to Isaiah

Likewise in Isaiah it is also written about him: **And his government will be upon his shoulders** (9:6), that is, he carried the wood of his own cross on his shoulders. He did not say that he had a crown on his head or a scepter in his hand or wore some peculiar clothing, but only the new King, the King of the Ages, Jesus Christ, bore on his shoulder his power and majesty. Isaiah also asserts: **Behold, my servant understands and will be exalted and lifted up and will be very lofty** (52:13), that is, through the victory of the cross, his royal power will exalt the form of a servant, that is, the flesh, which he had put on.

That He Died Not for His Own Sins but for Ours

The prophet Isaiah says: **For the iniquities of his people he was led to death.** And also: **All we like sheep have gone astray; each and every one has turned to his own way; and the Lord placed on him the iniquities of us all** (53:6).

That He Died

The prophet Isaiah also speaks about the death of the Lord: **Just as a sheep is led to death, and even as a lamb in the presence of the one shearing it is without a voice, so he did not open his own mouth. By the iniquities of his own people was he led to death** (53:7-8).

That Christ Rose from the Dead and Ascended into Heaven

Through the prophet Isaiah Christ announces: **Now I shall rise up, says the Lord, now I shall be exalted, and now I shall be lifted up** (33:10). A testimony to the resurrection and ascension of Christ is proclaimed as if to say: Now I shall rise up from the dead, now I shall be exalted in the sky, now I shall be lifted up in my kingdom. In another place Isaiah says: **Behold, my servant understands and will be exalted and will be elevated and will be very lofty** (52:13), which certainly pertains to the ascension to heaven and the glory of his kingdom.

That, After the Ascension of Christ the Lord into the Heavens, the Gift of the Holy Spirit Will Be Poured Forth upon the Apostles and the Faithful

The prophet Isaiah promises. **I shall pour forth my Spirit, says the Lord, and my blessing upon your seed, Jacob; and they will sprout forth among the grasses as willows beside flowing waters** (44:3-4). Likewise Isaiah says: **Let the Spirit be poured forth from on high** (32:15). Again he says: **When the Spirit of the Lord will have come like a violent river, and will have come to Zion** (59:19-20). And again: **The Spirit of the Lord, even as a flooding torrent, will come** (30:28), that is, the Spirit comes like the great sound of rushing waters.

That Christ Would Send the Apostles to Bear Witness to the Gentiles of the Glory of His Resurrection

The prophet Isaiah speaks out, saying: **I come to gather together all nations and tongues. And they will come and see my glory, and I shall place on them a sign** — certainly the sign of the cross — **and out of those who will have been saved I shall send men to the nations on the sea and into Africa and into Libya, bearing an arrow** — that is, the proclamation of the gospel — **into Italy, into Greece, and to islands far off and to those who have not heard about me and have not seen my glory; and they will announce my goodness among the nations** (66:18-19 Vg.). Here he speaks about the apostles, that they would proclaim the gospel through the whole world. The prophets were not silent about this, and in the Psalms it was foretold: *Into all the earth their sound is gone out, and into the ends of the world their words. There are no languages or dialects in which their voices should not be heard* (Ps 19:3-4).

That the Lord Would Give the Gospel to the Faithful as a New Law

Thus the prophet Isaiah declares: **He first says to Zion: Behold, I am present and I shall give good news to Jerusalem** (41:27), because surely the Lord came first to Zion and proclaimed the gospel to Jerusalem. And again Isaiah says: **the law will go out from Zion**, that is, the gospel of the New Covenant; **and the word from Jerusalem**, that is, the proclamation of the faith; and **He will judge the nations and will reprove many peoples** from far away (2:3-4), that is, the teaching of the gospel reproves nations believing in Christ for doing unlawful deeds.

That God Presents to the Faithful the Gift of the Grace of Baptism for Indulgence and Remission of Past Misdeeds

The prophet Isaiah promises: **You will draw water joyfully from the springs of the Savior; and you will say on that day: We confess to the Lord and invoke his name** (12:3-4). Who is that Savior, from whose springs the prophet says you draw water, except Jesus Christ, Savior of the world, who taught that you are cleansed by the water of holy baptism? Again Isaiah urges: **All who thirst, come to the waters, and you who do not have silver, hasten, buy, and eat. Come and buy wine and milk without silver or any exchange** (55:1).

That the Gentiles Are Converted to Belief in Christ

The prophet Isaiah already had made a prediction about this, saying: **The nations will come, and many peoples will come and will say: Come, and let us ascend to the mountain of the Lord, and to the house of the God of Jacob; and he will teach us about his good paths, and we shall walk on his footpaths** (2:2-3). Likewise Isaiah says: **They sought me, who previously did not ask about me; they found me, who did not seek me. And I said: Behold, I have come to the nation which did not call on my name**

(65:1). Again Isaiah says: **Everyone from all nations will bring a gift to the Lord on horses and on chariots and on litters and on mules and on carriages to my sacred mountain into Jerusalem into the house of the Lord; and I shall take some of them for priests and Levites, says the Lord** (66:20-21), that is, the faithful will make pilgrimage to the Lord's tomb.

Isaiah 1

₁A vision, which Esaias son of Amos saw — which he saw against Judea and against Ierousalem in the reign of Ozias and Ioatham and Achaz and Hezekias, who reigned over Judea.

2 Hear, O heaven, and give ear, O earth;
    for the Lord has spoken:
  I begat sons and raised them up,
    but they rejected me.
3 The ox knows its owner,
    and the donkey its master's crib;
  but Israel has not known me,
    and the people have not understood me.

4 Ah, sinful nation,
    people full of sins,
  evil offspring,
    lawless sons,
  you have forsaken the Lord
    and provoked to anger the Holy One of Israel!

5 Why should you be beaten anymore
    as you continue in lawlessness?
  Every head has become troubled,
    and every heart has become sad.
6 From the feet to the head
    — whether a sore or a bruise or a festering wound —
  there is no emollient to put on,
    nor oil nor bandages.

7 Your country lies desolate,
    your cities are burned with fire;

    in your very presence
        foreigners devour your land;
        and it has been made desolate, overthrown by foreign peoples.
8 Daughter Sion will be forsaken
    like a booth in a vineyard,
  and like a hut in a cucumber field,
    like a besieged city.

9 And if the Lord Sabaoth
    had not left us offspring,
  we would have become like Sodoma,
    and been made similar to Gomorra.

10 Hear the word of the Lord,
    you rulers of Sodoma!
  Pay attention to the law of God,
    you people of Gomorra!
11 What to me is the multitude of your sacrifices?
    says the Lord;
  I am full of burnt offerings of rams,
    and I do not want the fat of lambs
    nor the blood of bulls and goats —
12 not even if you come to appear before me.
    For who asked these things from your hands?
    You shall trample my court no more!
13 If you should offer fine flour, that would be futile;
    incense is an abomination to me.
  Your new moons and sabbaths and great day
    I cannot endure. Fasting and holidays,
14 as well as your new moons and your festivals,
    my soul hates.
  You have made me full;
    I will no longer forgive your sins.
15 When you stretch out your hands to me,
    I will turn away my eyes from you;
  even if you make many petitions,
    I will not listen to you;
    for your hands are full of blood.
16 Wash yourselves; become clean;
    remove the evil deeds from your souls
    before my eyes;
  cease from your evil deeds;
17   learn to do good;
  seek judgment,

>   rescue the one who is wronged,
> defend the orphan,
>   and do justice to the widow.

18 So come and let us argue it out,
        says the Lord:
    even though your sins are like crimson,
        I will make them white like snow;
    and though they are like scarlet,
        I will make them white like wool.
19 And if you are willing and listen to me,
        you shall eat the good things of the land;
20 but if you are not willing nor listen to me,
        the sword will devour you;
    for the mouth of the Lord has spoken these things.

21 How the faithful city Sion
        has become a whore!
    She that was full of justice,
        wherein righteousness lodged —
        but now murderers!
22 Your silver has no value,
        your taverners mix the wine with water.
23 Your rulers are disobedient:
        they are companions of thieves,
    loving gifts,
        running after a reward,
    not defending orphans,
        and not paying attention to the widows' cause.

24 Therefore, this is what the Sovereign, the Lord Sabaoth, says:
    Ah, mighty ones of Israel!
        For my wrath on my adversaries will not abate,
        and I will exact judgment from my foes!
25 And I will turn my hand against you,
        and will burn you to bring about purity.
    But the disobedient I will destroy,
        and I will remove from you all the transgressors,
        and humble all who are arrogant.
26 And I will set up your judges as at the former time,
        and your counselors as at the beginning.
    And after these things you shall be called the city of righteousness,
        the faithful mother city, Sion.

27 **For her captivity shall be saved**
   with judgment and with mercy.
28 **But the transgressors and the sinners shall be crushed together,**
   and those who forsake the Lord shall be brought to an end.
29 **For they shall be ashamed because of their idols,**
   which they themselves wanted;
   and they were embarrassed because of their gardens,
   which they desired.
30 **For they shall be like a terebinth**
   that has shed its leaves,
   and like an orchard that has no water.
31 **And their strength shall be like a stalk of flax,**
   and their works like sparks of fire;
   and the transgressors and the sinners shall be burned together,
   and there shall be no one to quench them.

*One of the first topics to be discussed in the commentaries on Isaiah was the nature of prophetic visions. How, the interpreters ask, does the **vision of Isaiah** (1:1) differ from other visions and dreams? Chrysostom also comments on the character of a prophet. Because Isaiah's visions took place under specific Israelite kings, for example, Uzziah, Jothan, Ahaz, and Hezekiah, the commentaries discuss the historical circumstances of the prophecies. But the church fathers find many other things in the opening chapter. Origen takes **vision** (1:1) to refer to the knowledge of God acquired by meditating on the Scriptures. Because the ox and ass in the traditional Nativity scene derive from 1:2, **the ox knows its owner, and the donkey [or ass] knows its master's crib** (1:2), we have included a passage from an oration by Gregory the Theologian (Gregory of Nazianzus) delivered at the celebration of Christmas [called Theophany or Birthday of Christ] that mentions the ox and the ass. There is also a charming allegory from Augustine on **the donkey knows its master's crib**. He interprets the donkey as the Christian who carries on his back Christ, a load that is not burdensome but uplifting. Tertullian uses the words **What to me is the multitude of your sacrifices?** (1:11) as an occasion to discuss spiritual prayer. Several commentators relate **Wash yourselves; become clean** (1:16) to the cleansing waters of Baptism.*

(1) John Chrysostom

The prophets did not hear things as others hear them, as Isaiah says: *God granted to me an ear to hear* (50:4). By calling what he has seen a vision Isaiah assures us that his words are trustworthy, but he also captures the attention of his hearers and directs them toward the One who revealed these things. It is the custom of all those who proclaim God's words to establish at the outset that they have said nothing on their own initiative, that their words are divine oracles and their writings have come down from heaven. Hence David says, *My tongue is like the pen of a ready scribe* (Ps 45:1). One should recognize, then, that the words come from the hand of God who holds the pen, not from David. It is not David's tongue that speaks but the grace that moves him. Another prophet says something similar: *I am a herdsman, and a dresser of mulberry trees* (Amos 7:14), so that no one would suppose that his words came from human wisdom. And if this is not enough, in another place it is said: *But as for me, I am filled with power, in the Spirit of the LORD, and with justice and might* (Mic 3:8).

God's grace made the prophets strong as well as wise, not only in body but also in character. Since they had to deal with a headstrong and impudent people who thirsted for the blood of the prophets and were well versed in murdering the saints, they surely needed great strength to overcome the assaults of their foes. Hence God says to Jeremiah, *I have made you like an iron pillar and a bronze wall* (Jer 1:18). And he commands Ezekiel: *Be not afraid, though you dwell among scorpions, nor be dismayed at their looks* (Ezek 2:6). And when Moses was sent, it appears that he was not only afraid of standing up before Pharaoh, but also particularly fearful of the Israelites themselves. When he spoke to God after he had left the barbarians [i.e., the Egyptians], he was very anxious about what he would say to those who did not believe that he came from God (Exod 3:11–4:17). So he worked signs to convince them, and rightly so. For if one man put such terror in him, even when he had helped him, what was he likely to experience dealing with such a recalcitrant people?[1]

That is why the prophet Micah received a Spirit not only of wisdom but also of power, as he proclaimed: *I am filled with power, in the Spirit of the LORD, and with justice and might* (Mic 3:8). Of Jeremiah it is said, *The word of God came to Jeremiah, the son of Hilkiah* (Jer 1:1-2). . . . And of Nahum it is said, *The commission received concerning Nineveh. The book of the vision of Nahum of Elkosh* (Nah 1:1). In the case of Nahum, he says the same thing as to the others but uses a peculiar expression in calling the possession by the Holy Spirit a *commission,* literally a "burden." He gave this name to the working of grace because the prophets uttered their oracles after the Spirit had laid hold of them. Paul always begins his letters with the title *apostle.*[2] As the prophets call their writings a "vision," an "oracle," a "burden" or a "commission," a "word," so he uses the term "apostle." Just as one who presents a vision or speaks the word of God does not proclaim his own opinions, so also by calling himself an apostle Paul does not teach his own ideas but what he has received from the one who sent him. The authority of an apostle derives from someone other than himself. Christ said, *Do not call anyone on earth your teacher, for you have one teacher, who is in heaven*[3] (Matt 23:10). All our teachings have their origin in the Lord who is in heaven, even if the ministers of his words are human beings.

Which Isaiah saw (1:1). It is not for us to say the precise manner in which the prophets saw the things they saw. For it is not possible to explain with words the manner of the vision. Only one who has experienced such a vision is able to know what it is like. If it is often impossible to describe the activities and movements in the natural world, how much more difficult it is to speak of the activity of the Spirit! One must be satisfied with indistinct images that allow one to see only dimly. The souls of the prophets, however, were pu-

---

1. Chrysostom is referring to the incident in which Moses had killed an Egyptian who was beating a Hebrew, and then the following day is accused by a Hebrew. Chrysostom is assuming that the person Moses had rescued on the first day is the same one who accused him the next. The text says, "Moses was afraid" (Exod 2:11-15).
2. For example, Rom 1:1; 1 Cor 1:1. "Apostle" means "one who is sent."
3. Chrysostom here paraphrases and conflates Matt 23:8-10.

rified by virtue. As clear water is illuminated when it receives the rays of the sun, so the souls of the prophets when illuminated by the gift of the Spirit had access to the future.

In the days of Uzziah, Jotham, Ahaz, and Hezekiah, kings of Judah (1:1). The prophet gives, of course, chronological data, so that the diligent reader will know the history of that time. If one understands the situation and the remedies that the prophets applied to the trials of the Israelites, the prophecy will be clearer and more understandable.

Sons have I begotten (1:2). This passage does not speak of God's goodness to all men, which he gives by bringing them into being, but of a special act of grace, by which they become God's children. God always begins by conferring benefits on human beings. When he made man he honored him even before he was born, saying, *Let us make man in our image, and according to our likeness* (Gen 1:26). In the New Covenant the honor is even greater. For he honors with the bath of regeneration not only those who have done nothing to merit it, but even those who have done many evil things. He honors with adoption not only those who have done nothing good, but even those who have committed great sins. Yet although his grace precedes human works, that does not mean that he takes no note of our works. Indeed, the virtuous person receives even greater honors.

(2) Cyril of Alexandria

One can discuss the prophets in two ways: first, insofar as they had knowledge of what was going to happen in the future, since these things had been revealed to them by the Holy Spirit; second, insofar as they were informed about the things that were happening in their own time of which they were spectators. Isaiah, it seems, was able to see with the eye of the mind what was going to happen to Judah at a later time. He saw enemies in full battle array ravaging the land, cities laid to waste, houses burned, and other things that accompany war. It is to these things that the beginning of the prophecy refers.

The vision of Isaiah the son of Amoz, which he saw concerning Judah and Jerusalem (1:1). The text helpfully mentioned the kings who lived at that time, so that what God reveals in the prophecy might be suited to the kind of life that each one followed.

The Israelites had not observed the law and had neglected the teachings that give life. They abandoned the God who is by nature one and gave themselves over to the service of unclean spirits in the mountains and the hills. In the forested ravines they worshiped and offered sacrifices to the works of their own hands. Their behavior was an offense to the God of all, and rightly so, as another of the holy prophets declared: *Arise, plead your case before the mountains, and the hills will listen to your voice. Hear, O Hills, the Lord's indictment, and listen, O Ravines, foundations of the earth, for the Lord is bringing a charge against his people, and the case against them will be opened* (Mic 6:1-2 LXX). The Lord's indictment which the prophet delivered was not directed against the mountains and the hills; it was aimed at the impiety of the people of Israel and the unclean spirits on the mountains and hills and in the wooded valleys. . . .

The words **I have begotten and raised up children** (1:2) mean that Israel was received by grace and made worthy to be treated as children begotten by God. Through faith in Christ, however, we have experienced the true spiritual rebirth, begotten by water and the Spirit. Even though Israel was the firstborn and was called a people, its relation to God was that of a servant. But to us God gave a name through adoption by the Spirit. *Because you are sons,* he says, *God has sent the Spirit of his Son into your hearts, crying, "Abba! Father!"* (Gal 4:6).

Note that the text says not only that he **begot these children**, but also that he **raised them up** (1:2), that is, he cared for them. At least this is the understanding of many interpreters. For after Israel had been liberated from slavery in Egypt, it was not abandoned by God or deprived of God's loving nurture. For Israel was **raised** by an extremely affectionate father who truly loved his child. As the psalmist relates, *He gave them bread from heaven. Humans ate of the bread of the angels* (Ps 78:24-25). This can be understood to refer to spiritual nurture, that the wisdom of the law and the teachings of the prophets was a food that led to the knowledge of the truth, that is, of Christ. As Paul says, *The law was our pedagogue leading to Christ* (Gal 3:24).

1:1
The vision of Isaiah

(3) Origen of Alexandria

The Lord blessed Isaac, the Scripture says, *and Isaac dwelled at the well of vision*[4] (Gen 25:11). The entire blessing the Lord gave Isaac was that he could dwell *at the well of vision.* How great a blessing for those who perceive it! Would that the Lord might grant me this blessing, that I would be worthy to dwell at the well of vision.

Who can know and comprehend **the vision that Isaiah son of Amoz saw** (1:1)? Indeed, who can know the vision of Nahum (Nah 1:1)? Or who can comprehend the content of the vision that Jacob had in Bethel as he was departing for Mesopotamia, when he asserted: *This is the house of God and the gate of heaven* (Gen 28:17)? For if someone could know and comprehend all the visions found in the law or the prophets, he would dwell *at the well of vision.*

Consider very attentively, then, that the great blessing Isaac was worthy of receiving was to dwell *at the well of vision.* As for us, will we ever be worthy even of passing alongside *the well of vision*? Isaac was worthy of staying at the [well of] **vision** and dwelling there; but we, who have been but a little enlightened by the mercy of God, can scarcely know or catch a glimpse of a single vision.

Yet, if I can have only one glimpse of the vision of God, I will have spent one day *at the well of vision.* And if I am able to grasp something not only according to the letter but also according to the Spirit, I will have spent two days *at the well of vision.* And if I am also able to grasp how the vision forms my life, I will have spent three days there.

In any case, even if I have not been able to understand everything, yet diligently study the Scriptures and *meditate day and night on the law of God* (Ps 1:1), and at no time

---

4. English versions transliterate the Hebrew name for the place, "Beer-lahai-roi"; the LXX translates it as "the well of vision."

cease studying, discussing, inquiring, and, most of all, praying to God and asking for understanding from him who *teaches men knowledge* (Ps 94:10), then it will seem that I dwell *at the well of vision*.

But if I am neglectful and do not study the Word of God at home nor come frequently to church to hear the Word — and I have noticed that some of you come to church only on festivals — well, people of this sort do not dwell *at the well of vision*. For I fear that those who neglect the Word of God, even when they come to church, will neither drink from the well of water nor be refreshed by it. For they are so absorbed with the cares and thoughts they brought with them that, even after drinking from the wells of the Scriptures, they go away thirsty.

Hurry then to apply yourselves so that the blessing of the Lord will come upon you, and you may be able to dwell *at the well of vision,* and the Lord will open your eyes to see *the well of vision.* Then you will receive from it *living water* (John 4:10-11) that can become in you *a spring of water welling up to eternal life* (John 4:14). But if someone comes to church only infrequently and draws only occasionally from the springs of the Scriptures, dismissing at once what he hears, or is preoccupied with other things, such a person will not dwell *at the well of vision*.

Do you want me to show you the one who never leaves *the well of vision*? It is the apostle Paul, who wrote: *And we all, with unveiled face, behold the glory of the Lord* (2 Cor 3:18).

(4) Didymus the Blind

It is fitting that when God reveals himself he converses with those who have an inner disposition to hear. In the Psalms the hymnist says, *then you spoke in a vision to your sons* (Ps 89:19), because to those who possess the spirit of adoption God the Word does not speak to the ear with his voice (cf. Rom 8:15). Because he is the true light, the Word illumines the mind of those whom he wishes to receive his divine utterances. He speaks by *vision* rather than to the ears. Indeed, when God spoke to Isaiah in this way — **The vision which Isaiah saw** (1:1) — it is not visible things, but inner words that followed. For how can the verse, **Hear, O heaven, and incline your ear, O earth, because the Lord has spoken: I have begotten and raised up sons, but they have abandoned me** (1:2), refer to something visible?

1:3
The ox knows its owner, and the donkey its master's crib; but Israel does not know me, and the people have not understood me.

(5) Augustine of Hippo

The birth of Christ from the Father was without a mother; the birth of Christ from his mother was without a father. Each birth was marvelous. The first was eternal; the second took place in time. When was he born from the Father? What is this business about "when"? You ask about "when," but there is no time here. Don't try to find out "when" in this matter. We can ask about "when" if we're talking about his birth from his mother. Then it's the right question. But it's not a good question when we're talking about his father. He was born of the Father, but that birth had nothing to do with time. He was born eternal from the eternal, co-eternal. Why are you astonished? He is God. Keep in mind that we are talking about divinity, and you will no longer be astonished.

When we say that he is born of a virgin, that is a great thing and you should be astonished. But he is God, so don't be astonished. Let astonishment give way to adoration. Let faith be present; believe what happened. Even if you don't believe, it still happened while you remain in your unbelief. He deigned to become a man; what more do you want? Is it a little thing that God humbled himself for you? The one who was God has become man. The inn was cramped, he was wrapped in diapers and placed in a manger. Who would not be astonished on hearing that? The one who fills the universe could find no room in an inn. He who was placed in a manger has become our food.

Let the two animals that approach the manger signify the two peoples.[5] **The ox knows its owner, and the donkey its master's manger** (1:3). Turn your attention to the manger. Don't be ashamed of being the Lord's donkey. If you carry Christ you won't go astray. You walk along the way, and the Way is sitting on you. Do you remember the little donkey brought to the Lord? You should not be ashamed that we are the Lord's donkey. Let the Lord sit on us and take us wherever he wants. We are his mount and are heading to Jerusalem. With him seated on us we are not weighed down, but raised up; with him showing the way we won't go astray. We are going to him, we are going by him, we will not lose our way.

(6) Gregory the Theologian

Make Christ's conception your own and leap before him, if not like John in the womb (Luke 1:41), then like David when the ark came to rest (2 Sam 6:14). Honor the *enrollment* (Luke 2:1), thanks to which you were enrolled in the heavens. Celebrate the Nativity by which you were loosed from the bonds of your birth,[6] and give honor to little Bethlehem, which has brought you back to paradise. And worship the crib through which you, who lacked reason *(logos)*, were fed by Reason *(Logos)* itself. Know your master — as Isaiah bids you — as the **ox knows its master, and the ass its master's crib** (1:3), that is, if you are pure according to the law and chew the cud of the Word and are fit for sacrifice. If, however, you are among those who are as yet unclean and unpalatable and unfit for sacrifice, and belong to the portion of the Gentiles, run with the star and bear your gifts with the Magi, gold and frankincense and myrrh, as to a King, and to God, and to one who is dead[7] for your sake. Glorify him with shepherds, sing a hymn with the angels, dance with the archangels. Let there be a common festival of the powers in heaven and the powers on earth. For I am persuaded that the heavenly host celebrates and keeps the festival with us today, since they love human beings even as they love God. . . .

---

5. Jews and Gentiles.
6. Because of being conceived in sin (Ps 51:7).
7. And anointed with myrrh, as was customary with the dead.

1:11
What to me is the multitude of your sacrifices?

(7) Tertullian

Prayer is the spiritual offering that abolished the earlier sacrifices. **What to me is the multitude of your sacrifices? says the Lord; I have had enough of burnt offerings and of the the fat of lambs, and I do not want the blood of bulls and goats** (1:11). What God asks of us the Gospel teaches: *The hour is coming when the true worshipers will worship the Father in spirit and in truth. For God is a spirit,* and so requires his worshipers to be such (John 4:23-24). We are the true worshipers and true priests, who, praying in spirit, offer a spiritual sacrifice, an offering fitting and acceptable to God. He asked that we offer this sacrifice, and he foresaw that we would do so. This sacrifice is offered with the whole heart, fed on faith, looked after by truth, perfect in innocence, pure in chastity, and garlanded with love. Moreover, we ought to escort this sacrifice with the pomp of good works, with psalms and hymns to God's altar that God may answer all our prayers.

For what has God, who requires that we pray, ever denied to prayer that comes from *spirit and truth?* How many testimonies of its effectiveness do we read and hear and believe! In ancient times prayer freed from fire and from beasts and from famine even though it was not prayer in the name of Christ. How much more effective is Christian prayer! It does not station the angel with a moist wind in the midst of fire (*Song of the Three Young Men* 27), nor muzzle lions (Dan 6:22), nor give bread to the hungry (2 Kgs 4:42-44); it does not escape suffering by transferring it elsewhere. Rather, Christian prayer supplies the suffering, the feeling, and the grieving; it expands grace by virtue, that faith may know what she receives from the Lord, when she understands what she suffers for the sake of God's name.

In days gone by prayer used to call down plagues, scatter the armies of foes, and hold back life-giving showers. Now, however, the prayer offered in righteousness averts God's anger, keeps watch over one's enemies, and makes supplication on behalf of persecutors. Is it any wonder that it knows how to commandeer the rains from heaven — prayer which was once able to procure fire from heaven?

Prayer alone conquers God. Christ, however, willed that it not be used to bring about evil. He gave it power only in the cause of good. And so prayer knows nothing except how to call back the souls of the departed from the way of death, to transform the weak, to restore the sick, to purge the possessed, to open prison bars, and to loose the bonds of the innocent. Likewise it washes away faults, repels temptations, extinguishes persecutions, consoles the faint-spirited, cheers the high-spirited, escorts travelers, appeases waves, makes robbers stand aghast, nourishes the poor, directs the rich, raises up the fallen, stops those who are falling, and supports those who are standing.

Prayer is the wall of faith; it is the arms and weapons against the foe who watches us continually. By day we are on guard; by night we keep vigil. Under the arms of prayer we hold up our general's standard while we await in prayer the angel's trumpet.

The angels also pray. Every creature prays. Cattle and wild beasts pray and bend their knees; and when they go forth from their haunts and lairs, they look heavenward with no idle mouth, making their breath vibrate each in their own way. The birds too, rising out of the nest, raise themselves up toward heaven, and in place of hands stretch their wings like a cross as though praying. What more, then, shall I say about the work of prayer? Even the Lord himself prayed, to whom be honor and power for ages unending.

(8) Augustine of Hippo

My powers, brothers, are very puny, but infinitely great are those of God's word. Give it free rein in your hearts. Then you can hear strongly what I say rather feebly, if you carry it out. The Lord has thundered at us through the prophet Isaiah as from his storm cloud. If you have any sense, you are terrified. He spoke plainly enough, after all, and the passage doesn't require explanation, but action. **What to me is the multitude of your sacrifices? Who asked these things from your hands?** (1:11-12). God seeks us, not what belongs to us. The Christian's sacrifice is giving of alms and kindness to the poor. That's what makes God lenient toward sins. Unless God were somehow made lenient toward sins, who would not be guilty? From those failings and sins without which this life is not lived, people are cleansed by giving of alms or kindness.

These are of two sorts of kindness: giving and forgiving, giving the good you have and forgiving the evil you suffer. These two sorts of kindness were described with a few words by the Lord, the good teacher, who shortened his words on the earth that they might be fruitful and not painful. Listen to what he commands: *Forgive, and you will be forgiven; give, and it will be given to you* (Luke 6:37-38). *Forgive, and you will be forgiven* refers to pardoning; *give, and it will given to you* refers to being generous. The kindness by which you forgive people costs you nothing. They ask your pardon straightaway, you grant it, and you lose nothing. You return home richer in charity. The other sort of kindness though, where we are told to spend money on the needy, seems difficult, because you'll no longer have what you give.

1:16
Wash yourselves; become clean; remove from your souls the evil deeds before my eyes.

(9) Clement of Rome

The ministers of God's grace spoke about repentance through the Holy Spirit, and the Master of the universe himself spoke of repentance with an oath: *"For as I live,"* says the Lord GOD, *"I do not desire the death of the sinner, but his repentance"* (Ezek 33:11). He added this good counsel as well: *Repent, O house of Israel, of your iniquity. Say to the sons of my people, Should your sins reach from earth to heaven, and be redder than scarlet and blacker than sackcloth, and should you turn to me with your whole heart and say, "Father!" I will heed you as though you were a holy people* (Ezek 33:11-20).[8] And in another place he writes: **Wash yourselves and make yourselves clean; rid yourself of the wickedness of**

---

8. Clement paraphrases the passage from Ezekiel.

Isaiah 1

your souls from before my eyes. **Cease to do evil; learn to do good, seek justice, correct oppression, defend the fatherless, and grant the widow justice. Come, now, let us reason together, says the Lord: though your sins are like scarlet, I will make them white as snow; and if they are red like crimson, I will make them white as wool. If you are willing and obedient, you shall eat the good things of the earth. But if you refuse and rebel, you shall be devoured by the sword. For the mouth of the Lord has spoken** (1:16-20). Therefore since he wanted all those he loved to have an opportunity to repent, he confirmed this by his almighty will. So, then, let us obey his great and glorious will, and let us prostrate ourselves before him and plead for his mercy and kindness.

(10) Origen of Alexandria

Moses, according to the command of the Lord, took *Aaron and his sons* (Lev 8:1). First he washed them, and then he clothed them. For you cannot be clothed unless first you were washed. Therefore **wash yourselves; make yourselves clean; remove the evil of your doings from your souls** (1:16). Unless you were washed in this way, you cannot put on the Lord Jesus Christ, as the apostle says, *Put on the Lord Jesus Christ, and make no provision for the flesh, to gratify its desires* (Rom 13:14). Therefore, let Moses wash you; let him wash you, and let him clothe you.

(11) Aphrahat

The [people] inquire of [the prophet]: "What can we do?" And he orders, **Wash and be clean; remove the evils of your works from my sight; cease from evil and learn how to do good. Seek out judgment and do good to the afflicted. Judge the case of the orphans and widows** (1:16-17). Again they ask the prophet: "When we have done this, what will happen to us?" He responds: **Thus says the Lord: When you have done these things, come and we will speak with each other** (1:18). And how do men speak with God, except in prayer which is without blemish? For prayer that is impure cannot converse with God. As it is written, God said in reply: **Even though you make many prayers, I will not listen; for your hands are full of blood** (1:15).

(12) Cyril of Jerusalem

Disciples of the New Testament and partakers of the mysteries of Christ, as yet by calling only, but before long by grace also,[9] *make yourselves a new heart and a new spirit!* (Ezek 18:31), that there may be gladness among the inhabitants of heaven. For if there is joy over one sinner who repents (Luke 15:7), according to the Gospel, how much more shall the salvation of so many souls move the inhabitants of heaven to gladness. As you have entered upon a good and most glorious path, run with reverence the race of godliness. For

---

9. Cyril was addressing catechumens who were in the last stages of preparing for Baptism.

the only-begotten Son of God is present here ready to redeem you, saying, *Come to me, all who labor and are heavy laden, and I will give you rest* (Matt 11:28). You who are clothed with the rough garment of your offenses, who are held *with the cords of your own sins* (Prov 5:22), hear the voice of the prophet commanding: **Wash yourselves; make yourselves clean; remove your iniquities from before my eyes** (1:16). And the choir of angels may chant over you: *Blessed are those whose iniquities are forgiven, whose sins are covered* (Ps 32:1). You who have just lighted the torches of faith, guard them carefully in your hands unquenched, that he, who once on this all-holy Golgotha opened paradise to the robber on account of his faith, may grant to you to sing the bridal song.

(13) Gregory of Nyssa

For only the Jordan among the rivers received in itself the first fruits of sanctification and benediction and conveyed from its unique source the grace of Baptism to the whole world. . . . Let us now consider some of the prophecies of this in words and speech. Isaiah cried out, saying, **Wash yourselves; make yourselves clean; remove the evil from your souls** (1:16). David says, *Draw near to him and be enlightened,*[10] *and your faces shall not be ashamed* (Ps 34:5). Ezekiel, who wrote more clearly and plainly than both, promises, *I will sprinkle clean water upon you, and you shall be cleansed; from all your uncleannesses and from all your idols I will cleanse you. A new heart I will give you, and a new spirit I will put within you; and I will take out of your flesh the heart of stone and give you a heart of flesh. And I will put my spirit within you* (Ezek 36:25-27). And Zechariah clearly prophesies about Joshua, that is, Jesus, that he was clothed with a dirty garment (namely, the flesh of a servant, which is our flesh), but then he was stripped of his stained clothes and adorned with clean and fair clothing. By this comparison he teaches us that in the baptism of Jesus we all cast off our sins like a tattered garment fit for a beggar and are clothed in the holy and beautiful raiment of regeneration.

(14) Didymus the Blind

Note how precisely the Scripture speaks. It refers here to **wicked deeds** that belong to **souls** (1:16), and are not seen by anyone but God. God says: do not pretend before me to **remove wicked deeds** from your **souls**. For I will see them even if I don't stand facing you. This can be likened to what is said by the Savior, that one ought to give alms in secret so that *the Father who sees into what is secret will repay* (Matt 6:4).

(15) Didymus the Blind

To those who are entangled with sins and as a result ignorant of the exercise of praiseworthy deeds, Isaiah says: **Cease from your wicked deeds; learn to do good** (1:16-17).

---

10. "Enlightenment" was a word for Baptism in the early Church.

Isaiah 1

For they have a free and unfettered choice to cease from being evildoers and to learn to do good. To such as these, the Lord speaks through Isaiah: **Remove from your souls the wicked deeds before my eyes** (1:16) — for I see your hidden actions. Therefore, not in word or in appearance only, but in truth earnestly strive for the **removal of wicked deeds** from the hidden part of your **souls**.

(16) Augustine of Hippo

So present yourselves to Christ the head as a body worthy of him, to the bridegroom as a worthy bride. The head can only have a body worthy of his, and so great a husband can only marry a wife worthy of him. *That he might,* it says, *present the glorious church to himself, without stain or wrinkle or any such thing* (Eph 5:27). This is the bride of Christ, who does not have a stain or wrinkle. You don't want to have any stain? Do what is written: **Wash yourselves; make yourselves clean; remove the wicked schemes from your hearts** (1:16). You don't want to have any wrinkle? Stretch yourself on the cross. You see, you don't only need to be washed but also to be stretched, in order to be without stain or wrinkle, because by the washing sins are removed, while by the stretching a desire is created for the future life, which is what Christ was crucified for.

Listen to Paul himself. Once he was washed he said: *He has saved us not because of the works of justice which we have done, but according to his own mercy, by the washing of rebirth* (Titus 3:5). Listen to him as he is stretched: *Forgetting,* he says, *what lies behind, stretched out to what lies ahead, I intentionally press on to the prize of the upward call of God in Christ Jesus* (Phil 3:13-14).

(17) Martyrius

At the beginning of our converse with God, as we stand before him, we should use those humble words of the blessed patriarch Abraham: *See, I have begun to speak in the LORD's presence, I who am but dust and ashes* (Gen 18:27). Let us also ponder this: how we, who are mortal beings continually bespattered with the mud of sins, have been held worthy to stand before *the King of kings and Lord of lords,* who *dwells in* the resplendent *light that none can approach* (1 Tim 6:15-16), to whose honor *thousands upon thousands* and *myriads of myriads* of angels and archangels *minister* (Dan 7:10) as they stand before him in fear and trembling. *Before him even the heavens are not pure* (Job 15:15), and though he strikes wonder in his angels (Job 15:15), yet he condescends to speak with weak and wretched human beings who have made themselves unclean by sins. For through the prophet he commanded the sinful people of Israel who were befouled by ugly deeds: **Wash, and be cleansed; remove your foul deeds from my sight. Then come, let us speak with one another, says the Lord** (1:16, 18).

1:18
Though your sins are like scarlet, they shall be as white as snow; though they are red like crimson, they shall become like wool.

(18) Basil of Caesarea

Jesus Christ came into the world to save sinners. *O come, let us worship and fall down, let us weep*[11] *before him* (Ps 95:6). The Word who invited us to repentance calls aloud, *Come to me, all who labor and are heavy laden, and I will give you rest* (Matt. 11:28). There is, then, a way of salvation, if we bend our wills to it. *Death in his might he has swallowed up, but the Lord GOD has wiped away tears from all faces* (Isa 25:7-8) of them that repent. *The LORD is faithful in all his words* (Ps 145:13), and spoke truly when he promised: **Though your sins be like scarlet, they shall be as white as snow; though they be red like crimson, they shall be like wool** (1:18). The great physician of souls, who is ready to deliver not you alone but all who are enslaved by sin, can heal your sickness. From him come the words; it was his sweet and saving lips that said, *Those who are well have no need of a physician, but those who are sick; I have not come to call the righteous, but sinners to repentance* (Luke 5:31-32).

(19) Augustine of Hippo

The Lord Jesus himself shone as brilliantly as the sun; his garments became as white as snow, and Moses and Elijah were talking to him (Matt 17:1-8). There was Jesus himself, brilliant as the sun, signifying that he is the *light which enlightens every man coming into this world* (John 1:9). What this sun is to the eyes of the body, he is to the eyes of the heart; what it is to bodies, he is to hearts.

As for garments, they are his Church. You see, unless garments are held in place by the person they clothe, they fall down. Of these garments one of the least and last hems, so to speak, was Paul. He says himself, you see, *For I am the least of the apostles*, and elsewhere, I am *the last* of the apostles (1 Cor 15:8-9). And in a garment the hem is the last and least part. Accordingly, just as that woman who was suffering from an issue of blood touched the Lord's hem and was healed,[12] so too the Church which comes from the Gentiles was healed and saved by the preaching of Paul.

What is surprising about white garments symbolizing the Church, when you hear the prophet Isaiah saying, **Though your sins are like scarlet, I will make them as white as snow** (1:18)? As for Moses and Elijah, that is to say, the law and the prophets, what do they avail unless they are conversing with the Lord? Unless they bore witness to the Lord, who would read the law, who the prophets? Notice how neatly the apostle puts it: *Through the law comes knowledge of sin. But now the justice of God has been manifested without the law* — that is, the sun — *attested by the law and the prophets* (Rom 3:20-21) — that is, the brilliance.

---

11. Instead of the word *kneel*, the LXX reads *weep*.
12. Mark 5:25-34; Luke 8:43-48.

Isaiah 1

1:19-20
If you are willing and obedient, you shall eat the good of the land.

(20) Augustine of Hippo

In Isaiah we read: **If you are willing and listen to me, you shall eat the good of the land; but if you are not willing and do not listen to me, you shall be devoured by the sword; for the mouth of the Lord has spoken** (1:19-20). Now with all their efforts of disguise the Pelagians here betray their purpose; for they plainly attempt to controvert the grace and mercy of God,[13] which we desire to obtain whenever we offer the prayer, *Your will be done, on earth as it is in heaven* (Matt 6:10), or again, *Lead us not into temptation, but deliver us from evil* (Matt 6:13). For indeed, why do we present such petitions in earnest supplication, if the result comes from him that wills and him that runs but not from God who shows mercy (Rom 9:16)? Now the wholesomeness of faith is this, that it makes us *seek, that we may find; ask, that we may receive, and knock, that it may be opened to us* (Matt 7:7).

*   *   *

Pelagius thought he had discovered great support for his cause in the prophet Isaiah; because by him God said, **If you are willing and listen to me, you shall eat the good of the land; but if you are not willing and do not listen to me, you shall be devoured by the sword; for the mouth of the Lord has spoken** (1:19-20). As if the entire law were not full of conditions of this sort; or as if its commandments had been given to proud men for any other reason than that *the law was added because of transgressions, till the seed should come to whom the promise had been made* (Gal 3:19). *Law came in, to increase the offense; but where sin increased, grace abounded all the more* (Rom 5:20). In other words, the conditions of the law were given that man might receive commandments, trusting as he did in his own resources, and that, failing in these and becoming a transgressor, he might ask for a deliverer and a savior; and that the fear of the law might humble him and bring him, as a schoolmaster, to faith and grace.

---

13. Pelagius had cited this passage, as well as other texts from Scripture (Deut 30:15; Rom 9:16; 1 Cor 7:36), to show that grace was dependent on the will, on human choice. Isa 1:19-20 seemed to support his position because it made the good that God gives conditional on what we do.

Isaiah 2

1 The word that came from the Lord to Esaias son of Amos concerning Judea and concerning Ierousalem.

2 For in the last days
>   the mountain of the Lord shall be manifest,
> and the house of God shall be on the tops of the mountains
>   and shall be raised above the hills;
> and all the nations shall come to it.
3   And many nations shall go and say,
> "Come, let us go up to the mountain of the Lord
>   and to the house of the God of Iakob;
> and he will declare to us his way,
>   and we will walk in it."
> For out of Sion shall go forth a law,
>   and a word of the Lord from Ierousalem.
4 And he shall judge between the nations,
>   and shall convict many people;
> and they shall beat their swords into plows,
>   and their spears into pruning hooks;
> and no more shall nation take up sword against nation,
>   neither shall they learn to wage war any more.

5 And now, O house of Iakob,
>   come, let us walk
>   by the light of the Lord!
6 For he has abandoned his people,
>   the house of Israel.
> Because their country, like that of the foreigners,
>   was filled with divinations as it had been at the beginning,
>   and many foreign children were born to them.
7 For their country was filled with silver and gold,

Isaiah 2

and there was no number to their treasures;
and the land was filled with horses,
and there was no number to their chariots.
8 And the land was filled with abominations,
the works of their hands,
and they worshiped the things their own fingers had made.
9 And so a person bowed down
and a man was humbled —
and I will not forgive them!
10 And now enter into the rocks,
and hide in the earth
from before the fear of the Lord,
and from the glory of his strength,
when he rises to crush the earth.
11 For the eyes of the Lord are lofty, but man is lowly,
and the loftiness of men shall be brought low,
and the Lord alone will be exalted
in that day.
12 For the day of the Lord Sabaoth will be
against everyone who is insolent and haughty,
and against everyone who is lofty and high,
and they shall be humbled;
13 both against every cedar of Lebanon,
of them that are lofty and high;
and against every acorn tree of Basan;
14 both against every mountain,
and against every lofty hill;
15 both every lofty tower,
and against every lofty wall;
16 both every ship of the sea,
and against every spectacle of beautiful ships.
17 And every person shall be humbled,
and the loftiness of men shall fall;
and the Lord alone will be exalted on that day.
18 They will hide all the works of their hands —
19 carrying them into the caves
and into the clefts of the rocks
and into the holes of the earth —
from before the fear of the Lord,
and from the glory of his strength,
when he rises to crush the earth.
20 On that day a man will throw away
to the vain ones and to the bats
his silver and gold abominations,

> which they made to worship,
> 21 to enter the holes of the solid rock
> and the clefts of the rocks,
> from before the fear of the Lord,
> and from the glory of his strength,
> when he rises to crush the earth.

According to most early Christian commentators, chapter 1 of Isaiah referred to events that had taken place in ancient Israel. Chapter 2, however, begins with a new oracle: **the word that came to Isaiah concerning Judea and Jerusalem** *(2:1). This suggested that the prophet was introducing a new topic. According to the Septuagint, the oracle in 1:1 was* **against** *Judea and Jerusalem, that is, directed against Israel's idolatry, whereas 2:1 read* **concerning** *Judea and Jerusalem, that is, what is going to happen in Judah and Jerusalem. Hence the oracle refers to the coming of Christ in Judea and the Church's mission that went out from Jerusalem to all the world. There is, however, one strong dissenter. Theodore of Mopsuestia argues that the accent on place in the text, that is, on Jerusalem, is not in keeping with Jesus' teaching that "God is spirit, and those who worship him must worship in spirit and truth" (John 4:24), and he is sharply critical of commentators who take the oracle as a type of events that took place at the time of Christ.*

Theodoret notes that the phrase **in the latter days** *(2:2) occurs at key places in the New Testament, for example, "in these last days" (Heb 1:2) and "in the last days" (Acts 2:17). This led commentators to interpret the opening verses of chapter 2 in reference to the time of Christ's coming, the gathering of the Church, the new spiritual Jerusalem, and the spread of the gospel from Jerusalem into all the world. Significantly, the phrase* **in the last days** *appears in the decree on Christ from the Council of Chalcedon, A.D. 451, to designate the time when the divine Son appeared as a human being and was born of the Virgin Mary. The image of the* **mountain** *(2:2) intrigued commentators, and Gregory the Great explains that it is an appropriate metaphor for the Virgin Mary, who surpasses all of God's elect.*

Origen has a lovely comment on the relation between the term "Word" in John 1, "the Word was with God," and **the Word came to Isaiah** *in 2:1, and in a sermon at the great Vigil of Easter Augustine meditates on the meaning of the term* **mountain** *in the Scriptures. The memorable passage (at least to our ears),* **They will beat their swords into ploughshares . . . and nation will not take up sword against nation** *(2:4), did not make as deep an impression on early Christians as it has on modern readers of the Bible. But several authors, for example, Tertullian and Athanasius, interpret it as referring to the end of warfare. Eusebius, displaying his characteristic interest in the historical and political fulfillment of prophecy, applies the passage to the peace brought by the Roman Empire. His coordination of the Pax Romana with the birth of Christ and the spread of the gospel was a well-known motif among early Christian apologists, with roots in the New Testament itself (cf. Luke 2:1ff.). But Eusebius hints at a more overtly political and contemporary application when he speaks of universal "peace and concord," words that were favorite themes in the age of Constantine.*

Isaiah 2

(1) The Letter to the Hebrews

In many and various ways God spoke of old to our fathers by the prophets; but in **these last days** he has spoken to us by a Son, whom he appointed the heir of all things, through whom also he created the world.

(2) Cyril of Alexandria

The present passage has certain features in common with the previous chapter, and one is inclined to interpret it along similar lines. It must be remembered that these oracles of God about Judea and Jerusalem were written down by the inspired prophet long ago, and the meaning of what is said about Judea and about Jerusalem seems opaque and not wholly clear. Let me, however, as far as I am able, attempt to explain the meaning of the vision briefly.

Although the prophet seems to be speaking of the destruction of the historical Judea and Jerusalem, in truth he is referring to the spiritual meaning of the events realized when Christ appeared and was manifested in the world. For this reason the prophet says a vision **concerning Judea and concerning Jerusalem** (2:1) instead of "*for the sake of* Judea and *against* Jerusalem" (1:1).[1]

When I speak of the historical Judea and Jerusalem, I am referring to the geographical region of Israel and to the religious practices of the Jews. When, however, I speak of the spiritual Jerusalem and Judea, I have in mind spiritual circumcision and the Church, those whose minds and hearts have been circumcised by Christ, not by a human hand. It was in reference to this circumcision that Jeremiah, one of the holy prophets, addressed the Jews, *Circumcise yourselves to the* LORD, *remove the foreskin of your hearts, O men of Judah and inhabitants of Jerusalem* (Jer 4:4). Saint Paul also recognized the kind of Jew who was circumcised spiritually rather than physically when he wrote: *For he is not a real Jew who is one outwardly, nor is true circumcision something external and physical. He is a Jew who is one inwardly, and real circumcision is a matter of the heart, spiritual and not literal* (Rom 2:28-29). One must, therefore, ask whether the prophet is speaking about the actual city of Jerusalem and Judea or whether he is referring to those things that happened spiritually at the coming of Christ. . . .

Isaiah's vision regarding the historical Jerusalem and Judea comes to an end at the beginning of the second chapter. What he had spoken of in the first chapter had already taken place. . . . In this second vision, he designates the time when the power of the devil will be overcome not in one part of the earth, not in one country or one city, but everywhere. The worship of idols and the practice of unholy rites will be completely destroyed, and the evil spirits that tyrannize mankind will be stamped out all over the world. This oracle was fulfilled **in the latter days** (2:1), that is, in the last times, the present age when the only-begotten son of God, the divine Word, born of a woman, shone forth in the world. At that time he presented the spiritual Judea, Jerusalem, the Church, to himself as

---

1. Inexplicably Cyril uses the preposition "for the sake of" here, even though his text reads "against Judea."

a holy virgin *without stain or wrinkle* (Eph 5:27), in the words of the Scriptures, *holy and blameless* (Eph 1:4). Isaiah, then, is speaking about the Church when he says, **In the latter days the mountain of the Lord shall be manifest, and the house of God shall be on the tops of the mountains, and shall be raised above the hills** (2:2).

The text says that Zion, the city in Judah that sits on a mountain, will be rebuilt. It is referring not to the actual city but to a spiritual building, the Church which is likened to a mountain. For the Church is indeed lifted up and conspicuous and known by all peoples throughout the world.

(3) Eusebius of Caesarea

The prophet gives the clearest sign as to the time when this prophecy (2:1-4) will come to pass. The sign he proclaims will be a time of universal peace among the nations, so that separate governments and multiple national authorities will no longer exist; it will be a time when the nations are no longer divided and rising up against one another, and the cities in each nation are not fighting and waging war against one another. Instead, peace and concord will reign everywhere, so that no longer will the tillers of the earth think to turn their tools into instruments of war, as they did in the past because of constant attacks from neighboring countries. This is precisely what happened after the coming of our Savior Jesus Christ. In ages prior to his time, one would not have found the same secure and peaceful state of affairs such as we have seen with our own eyes under the Roman Empire since the Savior's coming. Everywhere peaceful exchange prevailed among the nations, in both cities and countryside, so that the new law and the gospel word went forth unhindered from the land of the Jews and from the same Zion to fill the world and all the nations....

Since the prophetic text reads, according to Symmachus, **concerning Judea and Jerusalem** (2:1), one might reasonably say that the literal sense of this passage refers to Judea and Jerusalem. For the good news of grace and salvation had its beginning in Judea and Jerusalem. Christ, the Son of God, walked around Judea and Galilee and lived in Jerusalem for some time preaching the kingdom of God (Luke 8:1).... One might also identify the spiritual Judea with what the psalmist says, *God is known in Judea* (Ps 76:1). If *God is known in Judea,* the soul which has received the knowledge of God would truly be **Judea**. For this reason he calls the knowledge of God among the nations **Judea**. Thus the house of God which exists in Judea would be the Church of the nations which is called **house of God** and *is founded upon that* saving and unbreakable *rock* (Matt 7:25). The **mountain** (2:2) is the Word of God.

(4) John Chrysostom

It is clear from this passage that the prophets did not utter all their prophecies at the same time. Instead they were inspired in different circumstances, and what they announced in brief speeches was later compiled into one book.... The letters of Paul and the gospels were composed at one time, but the works of the prophets were composed under different circumstances. This is why Isaiah begins his discourse with a preface. The subject matter the prophet is about to discuss is different from what he had set forth in the previous chapter. Its theme is more elevated, because it deals with the calling of the nations, the splendor of the gospel, the extension of the knowledge of God throughout all the world, and peace over all the earth. . . .

It shall come to pass in the latter days that the mountain of the Lord will be manifest (2:2). Take note how precisely the prophet speaks. He indicates not only what is to happen but also when it would happen. Paul did the same when he wrote: *when the fullness of time had come* (Gal 4:4), and elsewhere, *as a plan for the fullness of time* (Eph. 1:10). So the prophet says: **in the latter days** (2:2). **Mountain** refers to the invincible strength of the Church's teachings. For even if one attacks a mountain with innumerable armies, throws spears or aims javelins, and brings up siege engines, nothing does it harm. The enemy is forced to retreat exhausted. So it is with those who attack the Church. Their assaults are in vain, and as they turn back they are ashamed to have expended all their strength. Exhausted by their flailing and weakened from hurling missiles, they are easily overcome by their enemies.

This kind of victory is paradoxical and can only be the work of God, not of men. It is marvelous not only that the Church was victorious, but in what way it conquered. It was hunted out, persecuted, and cut down in countless way, yet not only did it not falter, but it grew in strength and by its suffering overcame its adversaries.

(5) Theodoret of Cyrus

In this passage the prophet predicts that the worship of the true God will be known throughout the world, that idolatry will cease, and the **house of God** will be treated with the respect it is due. For by **mountains** and **hills** he signifies not only the arrogance but also the error which prevailed in former times. Temples were constructed to idols, groves planted, and sacrifices offered on high places and on the crest of hills. But after the appearance of our Savior the worship of idols was shown to be false, the beauty of truth was revealed, and the words of the prophets fulfilled. Moreover, by the phrase **last days** (2:2) he is referring to what happened after the manifestation of the Lord. So also the prophet Joel said: *In the last days I will pour out my spirit on all flesh* (Joel 2:28), a text that was fulfilled on the day of Pentecost (Acts 2:17). Further, the holy apostle declared: *In many and various ways God spoke of old to our fathers by the prophets; but in **these last days** he has spoken to us by a Son* (Heb 1:1).

2:1

The word that came from the Lord to Isaiah

(6) Origen of Alexandria

It is helpful to relate the phrase in the Gospel of John, *the Word was with God* (John 1:1), to the statement elsewhere in the Bible that the *Word came* to certain men. For example,

The word of the LORD *which came to Hosea the son of Beeri* (Hos 1:1), and **The word which came to Isaiah the son of Amoz concerning Judea and Jerusalem** (2:1), and *The word which came to Jeremiah concerning the drought* (Jer 14:1).

We must consider, then, how *the word of the* LORD *came to Hosea*, and how this is the **word which came to Isaiah the son of Amoz**, and again how the *word came to Jeremiah concerning the drought* so that we can discover how *the Word was with God* (John 1:1), since they are closely related to one another.

Most people will understand what is said of the prophets in a straightforward way, as though the Word of the Lord or the Word came to them. Just as we say that someone comes to someone, so the Son, who is confessed as divine, came to Hosea as the Word sent to him by the Father. According to the literal sense, he was sent to the son of Beeri, the prophet Hosea, but according to the mystical meaning, he was sent to the one who is saved — for Hosea means saved. The son of Beeri means son of wells, for each of the saved becomes a son of the spring which gushes forth from the depth of the wisdom of God.

It is not strange for the saint to be the son of wells, for a son frequently receives his name from virtuous deeds. One may be called a son of light because his works *shine before men* (Matt 5:16), another son of *peace* because he has the *peace of God which surpasses all understanding* (Phil 4:7), and, further, one may be called a *child of wisdom* because of the benefit that comes from wisdom, for Scripture says, *Wisdom is justified by her children* (Luke 7:35).

Therefore, the person who *searches all things, by the divine Spirit, even the depths of God,* so that he can exclaim, *O the depth of the riches and wisdom and knowledge of God!* (Rom 11:33), can be a *son of wells* to whom the Word of the Lord comes.

In the same way the **Word** also **came to Isaiah,** teaching him the things that will come upon **Judah and Jerusalem in the last days**.

2:2
And it shall come to pass in the last days that the mountain of the Lord shall be manifest. . . .

(7) Theodore of Mopsuestia[2]

After the terrible experiences the people had undergone, first being taken into captivity by the Assyrians and later being made subject to the Babylonians, the prophet predicts that there will be so great a transformation at this place [Jerusalem] that the mountain on which God was said to dwell would become manifest to all. It will far surpass every mountain and be exalted over all mountains and hills because it will be covered with God's glory. Many people from all parts of the world will assemble there, hastening to come to the mountain in which God is thought to dwell. There they would be instructed and learn how to conduct their lives. Foreigners would live in accord with the law ob-

---

2. Theodore is commenting on Mic 4:1-3, which duplicates Isa 2:2-4.

served there, and all would apparently hear the divine voice that obliges them to live according to the laws of Jerusalem. They would have good reason to do so because they had seen God's power bring justice to many who were ill-disposed toward us, censuring those who imagined themselves mighty, even if they seem distant from us. They will be judged for the wrongs they have committed against us, and punished in a way that is appropriate to their offenses.

I am, however, astounded by those who assert that the things the prophet said would happen to the Israelites when they return from Babylon are also to be taken as a type of what would happen at the time of Christ the Lord. I applaud them for saying that these words refer to the people's return from Babylon, but I am at a loss to know how one can say that this is a type of things that would take place at the time of Christ the Lord. For it is obvious that every type must have a representation of that of which it is said to be a type. There is, however, a significant difference between the verse, **For out of Zion shall go forth a law, and a word of the Lord from Jerusalem** (2:3), and what the Lord clearly said to the Samaritan woman, *Woman, believe me, the hour is coming when neither on this mountain nor in Jerusalem will you worship the Father* (John 4:21). And the reason he gives is this: *God is spirit, and those who worship him must worship in spirit and truth* (John 4:24). It seems evident that he has ruled out any honoring of places and also indicated that there is no reason to worship in Jerusalem rather than in another place. For all who have learned that God is incorporeal will understand that it does not matter where one worships him.

This verse, then, **out of Zion shall go forth a law, and a word of the Lord from Jerusalem** (2:3), is rightly applied to the return from Babylon. For then the Israelites returned to the place of Zion to carry out the prescribed form of worship there according to the provisions of the law. They could not worship God properly elsewhere. This is evident from another passage: *How shall we sing the Lord's song in a foreign land?* (Ps 137:4). How can this passage be a type of the things that happened at the time of Christ the Lord? For he laid down that the worship of God could be offered everywhere and that one should distinguish good or bad worshipers by the manner of their worship, not where it is practiced.

(8) Augustine of Hippo

The Gentiles will come from east and west; not to the temple of Jerusalem, not to arrive at the center of the earth, not to climb some mountain. Nevertheless, they are coming to the temple of Jerusalem, and to a certain center and to a certain mountain. For the temple of Jerusalem is now the body of Christ, about which he said, *Pull down this temple, and in three days I shall raise it up* (John 2:19). The central place they are coming to is Christ himself; he is at the center, because he is equally related to all; anything placed in the center is common to all. They are coming to the mountain, of which Isaiah declared: **In the last times the mountain of the Lord shall be manifest, prepared on the summit of the mountains, and it shall be lifted up above all the hills, and all the nations shall come to it** (2:2). This mountain was a small stone that grew till it filled the world, as Daniel said (Dan 2:34).

Approach the mountain, climb up the mountain, and when you climb it, don't go down. There you will be safe, there you will be protected; Christ is your mountain of refuge. And where is Christ? At the right hand of the Father, since he has ascended into heaven. "That's a long way; who can climb there, who can reach there?" If it is a long way from you, how can I say with truth "The Lord be with you"? Not only is he seated at the right hand of the Father, but he will also never withdraw from your hearts.

(9) Augustine of Hippo

We are celebrating in this solemn festival[3] the humility of the Lord, who *humbled himself, becoming obedient to the death, death even on the cross* (Phil 2:8). That is why we too are humbling our souls on this holy night by fasting, by watching, and by praying; nor is this glowing fervor of yours at odds with such humility. What else, after all, is a grain of mustard seed but the fervor of humility? It is by this grain that *mountains were carried into the heart of the sea* (Ps 46:2); that is, the great preachers of the gospels, the holy apostles, were carried from Judea to the nations, and the very heart of the world, that is, the secular thoughts of this age were captured by the mountains of which it is said, *Your justice like the mountains of God* (Ps 36:6); by the mountains of which it is said, *Shedding wonderful light are you from the everlasting mountains* (Ps 76:4).

Those very mountains, you see, had light shed on them, so that their summits glowed with fervor, and thus they brought the light which sheds light on every person, the mountain of mountains so to say, the king of kings and the holy of holy ones, both this one and themselves they brought into the heart of the sea, meaning for the faith of the nations; thus fulfilling what the prophet had foretold: **There will be manifest in the last times the mountain of the Lord, prepared on the summit of the mountains** (2:2); and also what he had said himself: *If you have faith like a grain of mustard seed, you will say to this mountain, Pick yourself up and throw yourself into the sea, and it will happen* (Matt 17:20).

It is these mountains that consecrated for us this night, on which the Lord rose again after being buried, the grain of mustard seed humbling itself by being covered up so as not to be seen, and then sprouting and growing and spreading its branches in all directions, so as to tower over everything else and invite the proud-hearted to take refuge and find rest in them like birds building their nests. May this mountain also dwell in your hearts; it will not, as you see, be cramped for space wherever love provides it with the broadest, most ample space.

(10) Council of Chalcedon

Following therefore the holy fathers, we confess one and the same our Lord Jesus Christ, and we all teach harmoniously that he is the same perfect in Godhead, the same perfect in manhood, truly God and truly man, the same of a reasonable soul and body;

---

3. This sermon was preached at the Easter Vigil.

consubstantial with the Father in godhead, and the same consubstantial with us in humanity, like us in all things except sin; begotten before ages of the Father in godhead, the same **in the last days** (2:2) for us; and for our salvation born of Mary the Virgin *theotokos* in manhood, one and the same Christ, Son, Lord, unique; acknowledged in two natures without confusion, without change, without division, without separation — the difference of the natures being by no means taken away because of the union, but rather the distinctive character of each nature being preserved, and each combining in one person and hypostasis — not divided or separated into two persons, but one and the same Son and only-begotten God, Word, Lord Jesus Christ; the prophets of old and the Lord Jesus Christ himself taught us about him, and the creed the fathers have handed down to us.

(11) Gregory the Great

The most blessed and ever Virgin Mary, Mother of God, can be called by the name **mountain** (2:2). Indeed, she was a mountain who by the dignity of her election completely surpassed the height of every elect creature.

Is it not proper, then, to call her a lofty mountain? For through her God brought about the conception of the eternal Word, raising her merits above the choir of angels up to the threshold of the Godhead.

Isaiah, prophesying in such admirable honor, said: **In the last days the mountain of the Lord's house will be made the highest mountain** (2:2). This **mountain** was made the highest because Mary shone above all the saints. And as a mountain implies height, so **house** signifies a dwelling place. Therefore, she is called **mountain** and **house**, because she, illuminated by incomparable merits, prepared a holy womb for God's only-begotten Son to dwell in. In sum, she became a mountain surpassing all other peaks because giving birth to God raised her above the angels; and she became the Lord's house because the divine Word dwelled in her womb when he assumed human nature.

She is rightly called a mountain that brings forth luscious fruit because she brought forth the best fruit of all, a new kind of human being. For this reason when the prophet contemplated her beauty, adorned in the glory of her fruit, he cries out: *There shall come forth a shoot from the stump of Jesse, and a branch shall grow from his roots* (11:1).

David, exulting in the fruits of this mountain, lifts his voice in prayer to God: *Let the peoples praise thee, O God; let all the peoples praise thee! The earth has yielded its fruit* (Ps 67:5-6). How did the earth yield its fruit? The Virgin did not conceive her Son by man's doing but by the Holy Spirit who overshadowed her (Luke 1:35). Therefore, the Lord promises David, king and prophet: *I will place the fruit of your womb upon your throne* (Ps 132:11).

So says Isaiah: *And the fruit of the earth shall be exalted* (4:2). For the one born of the Virgin was not only a holy man but also the mighty God. Elizabeth refers to this fruit when she greets the Virgin: *Blessed are you among women, and blessed is the fruit of your womb* (Luke 1:42).

Mary is rightly also called the mountain of Ephrem.[4] When she is raised up to ineffable dignity by giving birth to God, the dry branches of the human condition flower again in the fruit of her womb.

2:3-4
Out of Zion shall go forth the law, and the word of the Lord from Jerusalem.

(12) Justin Martyr

When the prophetic Spirit prophesied what was to come, he said: **For the law shall go forth from Zion, and the Word of the Lord from Jerusalem; and he shall judge between the nations, and shall convict many people; and they shall beat their swords into plowshares, and their spears into pruning hooks; and nation will not lift up sword against nation, neither shall they learn to wage war any more** (2:3-4). You can see that this has happened. For a company of twelve men **went forth from Jerusalem** into the world, and they were ordinary men, unskilled in speaking. But by the power of God they proclaimed to every race of humankind that they had been sent by Christ to teach the Word of God to everyone. And we who once killed each other not only do not wage war on our enemies, but in order not to lie or deceive our inquisitors we gladly die for the confession of Christ.

(13) Irenaeus of Lyons

Since the time of the coming of the Lord, the New Covenant that brings peace and the life-giving law went out into the whole world, as the prophets predicted: **Out of Zion shall go forth the law, and the word of the Lord from Jerusalem. And he shall rebuke many people. And they shall beat their swords into plowshares, and their spears into pruning hooks; neither shall they learn war any more** (2:3-4). If another law and word had gone forth from Jerusalem to bring about such great peace among the nations that received the Word, and were able to convince many other peoples of their folly, then it would seem that the prophets were speaking of someone other than Christ.

But if the law of liberty, that is, the word preached by the apostles, who **went forth from Jerusalem** through all the earth, brought about such a change in the world that nations did form their swords and spears into plows and into scythes for cutting grain, tools for peaceful ends, and have forgotten how to wage war, and, when struck, turn the other cheek, then the prophets have spoken these things of no one other than he who brought them about. This person is our Lord, and in him this oracle is fulfilled. For it was he himself who made the plough, and introduced the scythe, that is, the first sowing of the seed that led to the creation of Adam, and the gathering in of the produce **in the last times** (2:2) by the Word. For this reason, he joined the beginning to the end, and is the Lord of both. He has finally displayed the plough in which the wood is joined to the iron and has

---

4. The "hill country" near Shechem. See Josh 20:7.

cleared his land. For the Word, being firmly united to the flesh, and nailed to the cross, has reclaimed the savage earth.

(14) Cassiodorus

Out of Zion the loveliness of his beauty (Ps 50:2). Here Jerusalem is meant. It is within this city that the mountain gleams like gold metal on pure hearts. The apostles, on leaving the city, announced through the whole world Christ's lovely beauty. As Isaiah declares: **Out of Zion shall go forth the law, and the word of the Lord from Jerusalem** (2:3). Jerusalem is a revered city, a holy hilltop; we can rightly call that notable dwelling of our King the earth's citadel. Observe how fittingly we are instructed. In the previous verse the synagogue had said that Christ the Lord was summoning all nations; now she also points to the place from where his teaching flowed over the bounds of the whole world as from a clear and abundant stream. The words of the gospel are in harmony with the verse of the psalm (Ps 50:20), which traverses all nations beginning from Jerusalem, for Christ began to be proclaimed from there. His lovely beauty is known, as another psalm attests: *You are the fairest of the sons of men* (Ps 45:2).

2:4
They shall beat their swords into plows, and their spears into pruning hooks; and no more shall nation take up sword against nation, neither shall they learn to wage war any more.

(15) Tertullian

This passage means that the majesty of God will be revealed. **The temple of God above the top of the mountains** means Christ, the worldwide temple of God in which God is worshiped, that is established above all the principalities and powers. . . . **And nation shall not take up sword against nation,** that is, the sword of discord; **neither shall they learn war any more,** that is, bring about enmity, so that you may learn that the Christ who was promised was not one powerful in war, but a bringer of peace.

(16) Athanasius of Alexandria

Who is it who has joined in peace those who hated each other except the beloved Son of the Father, the Savior common to all, Jesus Christ, who in his love endured everything for our salvation? It had long been prophesied concerning the peace he brought, as the Scripture says: **They shall beat their swords into ploughshares, and their spears into pruning hooks; and nation will not take up the sword against nation, nor will they learn any more to wage war** (2:4). This is not beyond belief because the barbarians, who are by nature wild, still sacrifice to idols and rage against each other, and cannot bear to remain a single moment without a sword. But when they hear the teaching of Christ, they immediately turn from war to farming, and instead of arming their hands with swords they stretch them out in prayer; and in a word, instead of waging war with themselves, henceforth they arm themselves against the devil and the demons, subduing them with the weapons of sobriety and spiritual virtue. This is the indication of the Savior's divinity: what men were unable to learn from idols they have learned from him. This is no small refutation of the weakness and nothingness of the demons and idols.

2:8-9
They bow down to the work of their hands.

(17) Cyril of Alexandria

The God of all honored man by creating him by hand. He did not create man as he did all other creatures by means of a word, as when he said, *Let there be a firmament* (Gen 1:6), and it was so. Instead, as Moses says, he took dust from the earth and fashioned man from it (Gen 2:7). Man was made in the *image and likeness* of God (Gen 1:26-27), and he was appointed the ruler of everything on the earth (Gen 1:28). Man was further honored with the presence of the Spirit of Life, for *he breathed into his nostrils the breath of life* (Gen 2:7). But, as it says in the Scripture, *Man in his arrogance does not understand* (Ps 48:12 LXX). He began to worship graven images, as the prophet put it: **They bow down to the work of their hands, to what their own fingers have made. So man is humbled, and men are brought low** (2:8-9). Such arrogance dishonors God and demeans human nature. For one is certainly able to perceive the Creator by analogy from the beauty of the things he has created. *His invisible nature, namely, his eternal power and deity, has been clearly perceived in the things that have been made* (Rom 1:20).

2:12-13
For the day of the Lord Sabaoth will be against everyone who is insolent and haughty, against everyone who is lofty and high, and they shall be humbled.

(18) Didymus the Blind

The day of the Lord Sabaoth against every insolent and arrogant and lofty and exalted person (2:12), and a little later, **and against every cedar of Lebanon upon the heights, and against every acorn-bearing tree of Bashan** (2:13). All these savage trees, which have been planted upon idolatry and contempt, are trampled down and consumed by fire together with those who make specious arguments on their behalf, as Isaiah says elsewhere: *Lebanon will fall together with the high places* (10:34). For idolatry falls together with the demons and with humans who take their side, just as contemptuous people fall together with the boastful when God opposes the arrogant, according to the text in the divine Proverbs, *God opposes the arrogant* (Prov 3:34).

Isaiah 4

1 Seven women shall take hold of one man, saying,
 "We will eat our own bread
  and wear our own clothes;
 just let your name be called upon us;
  take away our reproach."

2But on that day God will gloriously shine on the earth with counsel, to uplift and glorify what remains of Israel. 3And what is left behind in Sion and remains in Ierousalem will be called holy, all who have been recorded for life in Ierousalem; 4because the Lord will wash away the filth of the sons and daughters of Sion and will cleanse the blood from their midst by a spirit of judgment and a spirit of burning. 5Then he will come; and as for every site of Mount Sion and all that surrounds it, a cloud will overshadow it by day and will be like smoke and like a light of fire burning by night. With all glory will it be covered. 6And it will serve as a shade from the heat, and as a shelter and a hideout from harshness and rain.

*John Chrysostom gives a fairly straightforward homiletical application of this chapter. Uncharacteristically he allegorizes the terms **cloud** and **heat** (4:5, 6). Eusebius of Caesarea provides a brief literal interpretation of 4:1 and then mentions an allegorical reading that applies the text to Christ and the Holy Spirit — very likely a reference to the christological interpretation that we find in a homily of Origen on Isaiah excerpted here (and in chapter 11 #15). Cyril of Alexandria takes the phrase **on that day** (4:2) to refer to the Incarnation, and the **cloud** (4:5) to signify Christ (cf. 1 Cor 10:1-5). Origen and Didymus understand **filth** and **blood** in 4:4 to refer to different kinds of sin. Gregory of Nyssa links the word **judgment** (4:4) with the passage in the Gospel of John, "The Father judges no one, but has given all judgment to the Son" (John 5:22), and uses the words of Isaiah as an occasion to discuss the unity of the three persons in the actions of the Holy Trinity.*

(1) John Chrysostom

The prophet presents the absence of men as the result of war and also as evidence of the extreme desolation of the Jewish people. The women of the city can no longer rely on their husbands to look after them, and they no longer expect protection. Their only desire is that they be freed of the reproach of being called "widows," a name that in ancient times was considered dishonorable.

Once the prophet has shaken their spirit by the threat of calamities, dramatized their woes, and exposed at length the horrors to come, he turns to words of comfort. The best kind of cure is not simply to cut and cauterize, but to apply a soothing remedy to the pain. The prophets use a similar technique. Not everything, he insists, will end in sadness. Troubles will give way to a better future. There will not only be an end to suffering, but there will be great splendor and a brilliant light. This is what is meant by the **glorious shining of God** (4:2) that dispels the darkness of discouragement, makes the day bright, and gives light to all. By the phrase **his counsel** (4:2) he indicates that God will do all things with understanding and wisdom.

It is not by chance that those who escaped evil were saved. They were the beneficiaries of a heavenly decree. Though surrounded by danger, they were delivered. Hence the prophet says: **all who have been recorded for life in Jerusalem will be called holy** (4:3). That is, those who have been set apart, found worthy, and marked with a seal will suffer no harm. It is fitting to call them **holy**, for not only have they been set apart for salvation, and this is God's will, but also they are holy because before as well as after their suffering they lived virtuous lives. Though they had been virtuous, through suffering they became more so. As gold when put to the fire is freed of impurities, so through trials those who are zealous in pursuit of the good are purged of indolence to become stronger and more virtuous. . . .

What does he mean by the words **with a spirit of judgment and a spirit of burning** (4:4)? He continues the metaphor of smelting of metals. In a foundry the blast of air fans the flame, and the coals turn hotter and burn up the dross. In the same way God's wrath, delivered by an army invading the city, was like a fire for them, not one that destroys but one that burns, refines, chastises, and corrects. The **spirit of judgment,** then, means a spirit of punishment, chastisement, and retribution. . . .

The **cloud** signifies comfort in misfortunes, and **heat** (4:5, 6) the radiance that accompanies consolation. A cloud in fierce heat is like a torch that shines brightly in darkness or at night. One protects from scorching heat, the other drives away gloom. Hence the prophet compared radiance to the blaze of the furnace and comfort to the shadow of the cloud.

(2) Cyril of Alexandria

Does the phrase **he shall come** (4:5) refer to the time when these things will take place, or to the one who emptied himself (cf. Phil 2:7) and came down from heaven to save the human race? The text can be understood to refer to either, to the time of his sojourn, or to

Christ himself. For when he came in grace he made the sons and daughters of the spiritual Zion, the Jerusalem that is free, blessed. In ancient times, when the *cloud* (cf. Exod 14:19-20) overshadowed the Israelites in the desert, God was their protector. This is why it says, **he will come, and there will be over the whole site of Mount Zion and over her assemblies a cloud by day** (4:5). To enable those who dwell on the spiritual Zion, namely, the Church, to endure the burning heat of this present life and to run the gauntlet of the fires of temptation that test them, the prophet says that Christ will be like a **cloud** (4:5) that surrounds and protects them. He dispels the darkness of ignorance and shines in their minds like a light in the dark or the blaze of a fire. As it was written about Israel: *the LORD went before them by day in a pillar of cloud to lead them along the way, and by night in a pillar of fire to give them light* (Exod 13:21). These things, however, should be seen as types or images of spiritual things. The truth, the thing itself, came through Christ, for he is the *truth* (John 14:6). For those who have been favored by God, says the prophet, it will be as though there is **a shade by day from the heat** and **a refuge and a shelter from the storm and rain** (4:6). He uses the terms **storm** and **rain** to signify the intensity of the trials and the force of the powers that assault them. Christ promises: *Every one then who hears these words of mine and does them will be like a wise man who built his house upon the rock; and the rain fell, and the floods came, and the winds blew and beat upon that house, but it did not fall, because it had been founded on the rock* (Matt 7:24-25). When the prophet adds, **with all glory it will be covered** (4:5), he means not only that the grace of Christ will cover believers but that his mercy will be freely dispensed to the whole world. They will be under the covering and tent of the one who is able to protect them and keep them out of harm's way.

**4:1
Seven women shall take hold of one man, saying, "We will eat our own bread and wear our own clothes; just let us be called by your name; take away our reproach."**

(3) Origen of Alexandria

Seven women suffer reproach and wander around asking someone to take them in and remove their **reproach** (cf. Isa 4:1). These seven women promise to eat their own bread and wear their own clothes — they seek not a man's bread but his name, to remove their reproach. They do not need the man's clothes. They have better clothes than he can provide. They have food that is more sumptuous than human nature can give. It is worth considering, therefore, whose women these are and what their reproach is.

The seven women are in fact one, the Spirit of God. The Spirit is one, but also sevenfold: *the spirit of wisdom and understanding, the spirit of counsel and strength, the spirit of knowledge and piety, the spirit of the fear of the Lord* (11:2-3). As Wisdom it suffers reproach from the many wisdoms that rise up against it. As the true Understanding it suffers reproach from false understandings. As Great Counsel it suffers reproach from counsel that is not good. As Strength it is abused by strength that is not strength but claims it is. As

Knowledge it is reproached by knowledge so called. As Piety it is accused by what passes for piety but promotes impiety. As the Fear of the Lord it suffers reproach from that which is thought to be fear. For many promise a genuine fear of God but do so without knowledge.[1]

(4) Eusebius of Caesarea

After he has described the ultimate desolation of the place with the preceding words (3:25-26), he then adds that, because so few men escaped being cut down *by the sword* (3:25), **Seven women shall take hold of one man** (4:1) and beg him for this one thing that they lacked (since they needed nothing else), namely, to be called by his **name** and to have him become a husband, so that they might not be abandoned and left with the shame of widowhood. Therefore, as though finding a rare survivor among all those who had perished, they say to him, **Just let us be called by your name; take away our reproach** (4:1).

That at any rate would be the literal meaning of the text. But other people have held that the "first man" is the Savior and that the **seven women** are the seven powers of the Holy Spirit, who embraced the "first man" because they found no one else who was able to receive them — they being *the spirit of wisdom and understanding, of counsel and strength, of knowledge and piety, and,* finally, *the spirit of the fear of God* (11:2-3).

4:4
The Lord will wash away the filth of the sons and daughters of Sion and will cleanse the blood from their midst by a spirit of judgment and a spirit of burning.

(5) Irenaeus of Lyons

In the *last days* (cf. Heb 1:1), *when the fullness of the time of liberty had arrived* (Gal 4:4), the Word himself in his own person **washed away the filth of the daughters of Zion** (4:4) by washing the disciples' feet with his own hands (John 13:5). This is the end to which the human race was destined, namely, to become inheritors of God. As in the beginning we were all brought into bondage by the actions of our first parents and made subject to death, so in these last days through the person of the last man all who were his disciples from the beginning, being cleansed and washed from those things that pertain to death, come to share the life of God. For the one who washed the feet of his disciples sanctified and made pure the entire body.

(6) Origen of Alexandria

Let us consider the words [of Jeremiah]. *"Even if you wash in lye and use much soap, still you are stained in your iniquities before me,"* says the Lord GOD (Jer 2:22). Does a sinful soul

---

1. Continuation of this passage is found in #15 of chapter 11.

which has washed itself in bodily lye suppose that it will put an end to its filth and its sin? Does anyone think that when he uses earthly soap to wash and cleanse himself, the soul is purified? Listen to what the Word says to the vine that has turned to bitterness and become alien: *"Even if you wash in lye and use much soap, still you are stained in your iniquities before me," says the Lord* GOD (Jer 2:22). Of course, lye and soap do not make one pure! Yet one must recognize that the Word has all power, including the ability to empower every word of Scripture. He has the power to heal all things; indeed, he has more healing power than the most powerful cleanser. *For the Word of God is living and active, sharper than any two-edged sword* (Heb 4:12). Hence whatever you need is in the power of the Word.

There is then a Word which is *lye* and a Word which is *soap*, and when this word is spoken it purifies filth of the sort alluded to in the text. However, the Word which is lye and the Word which is soap do not cleanse one of every kind of sin. There are sins which neither *lye* nor *soap* can cleanse, and the words of the text are addressed to those who think their sins can be washed away by lye and soap. *"Even if you wash in lye and use much soap, still you are stained in your iniquities before me," says the Lord* GOD (Jer 2:22). Certain wounds are healed by ointments, others by oil, and others need a bandage. Yet there are others about which it is said: *It is not possible to apply ointments or oil or bandages; your country is a desert, your cities are consumed by fire* (Isa 1:6-7). So it is with sins. Some foul the soul, and one needs the lye of the Word and the soap of the Word to purify one of these kind of sins. Yet there are other sins that cannot be cleansed in this way, for their filth is of a different order.

Note that the Lord speaks of different kinds of sins in Isaiah: **The Lord will wash away the filth of the sons and daughters of Sion and will cleanse the blood from their midst by a spirit of judgment and a spirit of burning** (4:4). The key terms are **filth** and **blood: filth** by a **spirit of judgment** and **blood** by a **spirit of burning**. Even if you have not committed a sin which leads to death (1 John 5:16-17), still you have sinned and become filthy. Therefore **the Lord will wash away the filth of the sons and daughters of Sion and will cleanse the blood from their midst by a spirit of judgment and a spirit of burning.** A **spirit of judgment** refers to the **filth**, a **spirit of burning** to the **blood.** Many of us when we sin grievously need neither lye nor soap, but the **spirit of burning.**

Now I understand why Jesus baptizes *in the Holy Spirit and in fire* (Luke 3:16). He does not baptize the same person *in the Holy Spirit and in fire*. He baptizes a holy person *in the Holy Spirit*, but someone who, after coming to faith and being found worthy of the Holy Spirit, still sinned, Jesus baptizes in fire. So the one baptized by Jesus in the Holy Spirit and the one in fire are not the same.

Happy, then, is the one who is baptized in the Holy Spirit and does not need the baptism of fire. And three times more unhappy is the one who has to be baptized in fire. Jesus, however, cares for each. For *a shoot shall come forth from the root of Jesse, and a branch will grow out of its root* (11:1), a *shoot* for those who are punished,[2] a *branch* for the righteous. So God is a *consuming fire* (Heb 12:29), and God is a *light* (1 John 1:5), a consuming fire to sinners, a light to the just and holy ones.

---

2. The term for "shoot" can also mean "rod" used for punishment. See 10:5.

(7) Didymus the Blind

Job says: *Even if I am pure with respect to actions, nevertheless I am filthy* (Job 9:30-31; Jer 2:22). For the earthly place is filthy in comparison to the pure life, not, however, in and of itself. As it is said, *as the rag of a bleeding woman is all our righteousness before you, O Lord* (64:6). This the Lord washes away according to what is written in Isaiah: **The Lord will wash away the filth of the sons and daughters of Zion, and he will purify the blood from their midst** (4:4). **Filth** would be involuntary transgressions, while **blood** signifies the things done intentionally. It will be washed away **by the spirit of judgment and the spirit of burning** (4:4). The **spirit of judgment** refers to discernment, and the **spirit of burning** to punishment. Together they bring about correction.

(8) Gregory of Nyssa

We learn from Scripture that the God of the universe judges all the earth (Rom 3:6), and we say that he is the judge of all things through the Son. When we hear that the *Father judges no one* (John 5:22), we do not think that Scripture contradicts itself. For the one who judges all the earth does this through *the Son, to whom he has given all judgment* (John 5:22). Everything done by the Only-Begotten has reference to the Father, so that he is judge of all and yet judges no one. For, as I have observed, he has given all judgment to the Son; and all the judgment of the Son is not alien to the Father's will. Hence it is not proper to say that there are two judges or that one is excluded from the authority and power of judgment.

So it is also with respect to the godhead. Christ is the *power of God and the wisdom of God* (1 Cor 1:24). And the Father exercises his power of overseeing or seeing (what we call godhead) through the Only-Begotten, who by the Holy Spirit brings all power to perfection and who judges, as Isaiah says, **by the spirit of judgment and the spirit of fire** (4:4). In this way he acts in accord with the saying in the Gospel spoken to the Jews. For he says: *If I by the Spirit of God cast out demons* (Matt 12:28). The whole is here understood by the part, that is, he includes every form of doing good in a statement that only mentions driving out demons. However, the action of doing good is one, and the term used for the work of doing good cannot be divided into many when the result of several operations is one.

As I have already mentioned, the principle underlying the power of overseeing and seeing is a unity in the Father, Son, and Holy Spirit. It comes forth from the Father as from a spring. It is made effective by the Son; and its grace is brought to perfection by the power of the Holy Spirit. There is no distinction of activity among the persons, as though an action were brought to completion individually by each of them or separately without jointly being overseen. Rather, all providence, care, and oversight of all things, whether in the visible creation or in the heavenly realm, whether preserving what is, correcting what is awry, or instructing those who are virtuous — all these actions are the work of one, not three, and are brought about by the Holy Trinity. This work is not divided into three parts according to the number of the persons contemplated by the faith, so that each of the acts viewed by itself would be the work of the Father alone, or the Only-Begotten individually, or by the Holy Spirit separately. While one Spirit, as the apostle says (1 Cor 12:11), distributes his good things to each person individually, this beneficent movement of the Spirit is not without beginning. We find that the power we conceive as preceding it, namely, the only-begotten God, makes all things. Without him nothing comes into being (John 1:3), but again I emphasize that the ultimate source of goodness issues from the Father's will.

Every good thing and every good name depend on the power and purpose which is without beginning. It is brought to completion by the power of the Holy Spirit through the only-begotten God without reference to time or extension. There is no delay or even a conception of delay in the movement of the divine will from the Father through the Son and to the Holy Spirit. Now the "godhead" is one of these good names and concepts; hence the word cannot be used properly in the plural, since the unity of operation rules out the plural number.

Isaiah 5

1 I will now sing for the beloved
    a song of the loved one concerning my vineyard:
The beloved had a vineyard
    on a hill, on a fertile place.
2 And I put a hedge around it and fenced it in,
    and planted a Sorech vine;
and I built a tower in the midst of it,
    and dug out a wine vat in it;
and I waited for it to produce a cluster of grapes,
    but it produced thorns.

3 And now, man of Ioudas
    and those who dwell in Ierousalem,
judge between me
    and my vineyard.
4 What more might I do for my vineyard
    and I have not done for it?
Because I waited for it to produce a cluster of grapes,
    but it produced thorns.

5 But now I will declare to you
    what I will do to my vineyard.
I will remove its hedge,
    and it shall be plundered;
and I will tear down its wall,
    and it shall be trampled down.
6 And I will abandon my vineyard;
    and it shall not be pruned or dug,
    and a thorn shall come up into it as into a wasteland;

and I will also command the clouds
   that they send no rain to it.

7 For the vineyard of the Lord Sabaoth
   is the house of Israel,
and the man of Ioudas
   is a beloved young plant;
I waited for him to produce justice,
   but he produced lawlessness —
nor did he produce righteousness,
   but a cry!

8 Ah, those who join house to house
   and bring field next to field,
so that they may take something from their neighbor!
   Will you dwell alone on the earth?
9 For these things were heard in the ears of the Lord Sabaoth.
   For if houses become many, large and beautiful ones shall be desolate,
   and there shall be no inhabitants.
10 For where ten yoke of oxen shall work,
   that land shall produce one jarful,
and he who sows six bushels
   shall produce three measures.
11 Ah, those who rise early
   and pursue strong drink,
who linger till evening,
   for wine will inflame them!
12 For with lyre and harp
   and drums and flutes do they drink the wine,
but do not regard the works of the Lord,
   or consider the works of his hands!
13 Therefore my people have become captive,
   because they do not know the Lord;
they have become a multitude of corpses
   because of famine and thirst for water.

14 And Hades has enlarged its appetite
   and opened its mouth without ceasing;
and her glorious ones and her great,
   and her rich and her pestilent shall go down.
15 A person shall be brought low, and a man shall be dishonored,
   and the eyes that are high shall be brought low.
16 But the Lord Sabaoth shall be exalted in judgment,
   and the Holy God shall be glorified in righteousness.

17 Then those who have been plundered shall graze like bulls,
    and lambs shall feed on the wastelands
    of those who have been displaced.

18 Ah, those who draw sins as with a long rope,
    and who draw transgressions as with a strap from a heifer's yoke,
19 who say, "Let him quickly bring near
    the things he will do,
    that we may see them;
and let the plan of the Holy One of Israel come,
    that we may know it"!
20 Ah, those who call evil good
    and good evil,
who make darkness light
    and light darkness,
who make bitter sweet
    and sweet bitter!
21 Ah, those who are wise in themselves,
    and knowledgeable in their own sight!
22 Ah, your strong ones who drink wine
    and the powerful ones who mix strong drink,
23 who acquit the ungodly one for the sake of bribes,
    and take away the right of the righteous one!
24 Therefore, as stubble will be burned by a coal of fire
    and burned up by a weakened flame,
so their root will be like fine dust,
    and their blossom go up like dust;
for they did not want the law of the Lord Sabaoth,
    but have provoked the oracle of the Holy One of Israel.

25 And the Lord Sabaoth was enraged with anger against his people,
    and he laid his hand on them and struck them;
    the mountains were provoked,
and their carcasses became like dung
    in the middle of the road.
In all these things his wrath has not turned away,
    but his hand is still high.
26 Therefore, he will raise a signal among the nations that are far away,
    and whistle for them from the end of the earth.
And behold they are coming, quickly, swiftly!
27 They will not hunger, nor grow weary,
    nor slumber, nor sleep,
nor will they loosen their girdles from their waist,
    nor will the thongs of their sandals be broken;

28 their arrows are sharp,
    and their bows bent,
their horses' hoofs were reckoned as solid rock,
    the wheels of their chariots as a tempest.
29 They rush like lions
    but stand by like a lion's whelp;
and he will seize and roar like a beast,
    and he will cast them out, and there will be no one who can rescue.
30 And he will roar because of them on that day,
    like the sound of a surging sea.
And they will look to the land,
    and behold, harsh darkness in their dismay.

Of particular interest is John Chrysostom's exposition of v. 7, **For the vineyard of the Lord of hosts is the house of Israel.** *In his view, not shared by all early Christian commentators, a text should be given an allegorical interpretation only when the scriptural writer indicates that his words have an allegorical meaning. In this chapter the prophet says that* **vineyard** *signifies the* **house of the Israel**, *hence an allegorical interpretation is appropriate. The song of the vineyard (5:1-2) lies behind the parable of the vineyard in the gospels (Matt 21:33-46 and parallels). The church fathers drew on this parable to interpret Isaiah 5 with reference to the Jewish rejection of Jesus, as can be seen in the selection from Theodoret of Cyrus. This theme is also developed on the basis of other texts from Isaiah, for example, 6:9-10.*

The words, **He looked for it to yield grapes, but it brought forth thorns** *(5:2), and* **those who draw iniquity with cords of falsehood, who draw sin as with cart ropes** *(5:18), lent themselves readily to homiletic application, as the selection from Augustine indicates. The references to* **the beloved** *(1:1) also left their mark on christological exegesis, both in the gospels (the Baptism of Jesus and his Transfiguration) and in the church fathers, as seen in Eusebius's trinitarian interpretation, in the excerpt from Theodoret, and in the unknown author of the* **Fourth Oration against the Arians,** *attributed to Athanasius.*

(1) The Gospel of Matthew

And when Jesus was baptized, he went up immediately from the water, and behold, the heavens were opened and he saw the Spirit of God descending like a dove, and alighting on him; and lo, a voice from heaven, saying, "This is **my beloved** (5:1; 42:1) Son, with whom I am well pleased."

*   *   *   **

He was still speaking, when lo, a bright cloud overshadowed them, and a voice from the cloud said, "This is **my beloved** (5:1; 42:1) Son, with whom I am well pleased."

* * *

"Hear another parable. There was a householder who **planted a vineyard, and set a hedge around it, and dug a winepress in it, and built a tower** (5:1-2), and let it out to tenants, and went into another country." . . . Jesus said to them, "Have you never read in the scriptures: *The very stone which the builders rejected has become the head of the corner; this was the* LORD's *doing, and it is marvelous in our eyes* (Ps 118:22-23)? Therefore, I tell you, the kingdom of God will be taken away from you and given to a nation producing the fruits of it." When the chief priests and the Pharisees heard his parables, they perceived that he was speaking about them. . . .

(2) John Chrysostom

Let me sing for my beloved a love song concerning his vineyard (5:1). After Isaiah has terrified the people with threats and offered them solace with kind words of hope, he applies a different kind of healing as he begins a new section similar to the first part of the prophecy. There he announced God's kindness to the people with these words: *Sons have I reared and brought up* (1:2). Then he proceeded to lay out their transgressions, saying, *they have rebelled against me* (1:2) and *Israel does not know me, my people does not understand* (1:3). Though here he uses different words, his approach is quite similar. If, however, his aim is to censure the people, why does he call his reproach a song?

When Moses was about to celebrate his victory, he sang a song with his sister Miriam. It was quite natural for him to begin with the words, *I will sing to the* LORD, *for he has triumphed gloriously; the horse and his rider he has thrown into the sea* (Exod 15:1). Likewise, after her marvelous and astonishing triumph Deborah also had a good reason to raise a victory song to praise and glorify God (Judg 5:1ff.). But it is surprising that Isaiah, who is about to reproach the people with stern words and an iron will, would announce to us that he is going to sing and calls his accusations a song. Isaiah, however, was not alone in this approach. Even the great Moses, who once sang a song of victory, later accused the Israelites in the words of a long song (cf. Deut 31:30–32:44) in which he asked, *Do you thus requite the* LORD, *you foolish and senseless people?* (Deut 32:6). After putting together a list of accusations against the people, he enjoined them to recite these charges in song (Deut 32:46), and even to this day we continue to sing the words of his song.

Why do Isaiah and Moses make their accusations in a song? In their spiritual wisdom they wanted to implant a very great thing in their listeners' souls. Nothing is more useful than to recall one's sins regularly, and nothing fixes something permanently in one's memory more than a melody. There are two further reasons why Isaiah uses a song. By couching his accusations in the form of a song, he hides the shame associated with the constant mention of their sins and consoles them in the despondency that weighs heavy on them. He does not want them to shrink from the gravity of the charges and, overcome with guilt, avoid dealing with their sins. He also uses the form of a song because people seem to be under some sort of compulsion to sing the words of a catchy tune again and again. As they repeat the words of this song, they will constantly be reminded of their sins, thus making it easier to teach them virtue.

You know, of course, that today many people do not even know the names of many books of the Bible, though most have the words of the Psalms on the tips of their tongues because the Psalms are sung. This is a good example of the power of melody. For this reason Isaiah announces: **I will sing for the beloved a song of the loved one concerning my vineyard** (5:1). **A song for the beloved,** he says, **concerning his vineyard.** I will sing about the beloved himself. I will sing for him, he says, and the song will be about his person and what belongs to him. Do not be surprised that Isaiah calls him **loved** and **beloved** even though he is about to bring accusations against him.

Is not this the most serious charge to bring against someone: to have been loved and to have enjoyed God's goodness, yet not to have become a better person? Another prophet, hinting at this same thing, said, *Like grapes in the wilderness, I found Israel. Like the first fruit of the fig tree, in its first season, I saw your fathers* (Hos 9:10). By referring to fruit, he indicates that the people are both lovely and desirable. They were, however, lovely and desirable not because of their own inherent virtue, but because of God's goodness. He states that God loved them *like grapes in the wilderness* and like *the first fruit of the fig tree*. If these examples seem unbefitting God, they certainly are appropriate to the excesses of the people, for the prophet continues, *But they came to Baal-peor and consecrated themselves to Baal, and they became detestable* (Hos 9:10).

God calls the people **beloved** and **loved.** These terms indicate that God initiated the loving relationship; it was not the people's own doing. Subsequently, the people demonstrated that they were in no way worthy of God's benevolence; in fact, their actions showed just the opposite. . . .

He built a watchtower in the midst of it, and hewed out a wine vat in it (5:2). Some interpreters suggest that the watchtower is the temple and that the wine vat is the altar. As grapes are gathered and brought to the wine vat, so the people offered their virtuous lives as sacrifices and offerings. As I have said before and will now say again, one must consider the point of the metaphor. What Isaiah is trying to get across throughout this section is that everything depends on God, who has blessed the people fully and has taken care of them in every possible way. . . .

I will make it a waste; it shall not be pruned nor dug (5:6). Again it is my view that Isaiah is speaking metaphorically. Anyone wishing to examine this passage more closely will see that he is speaking about the care God provided for the people by his teachings and commandments. Now, however, the people will no longer have the benefit of the things they had previously; instead they will be bereft of teachers, rulers, and prophets to correct them and to care for them. Just as vinedressers hoe and prune the vineyard under their care, those who care for souls threaten, frighten, instruct, and rebuke. But now they will be deprived of these and will be taken into exile in a strange land. . . .

And thorns shall grow up in it as in a wasteland; I will also command the clouds that they send no rain on it (5:6). Here he is talking about either the desolation of the city or the desolation of the people and the desolation of the soul of each person. Certain interpreters suggest that the **clouds** in this verse refer to the prophets since they receive their words from above and then pass them on to the people like rain. In this interpretation, this passage means that the prophets will no longer perform their customary role. Even though one or two of the prophets went into exile with the people, most of the prophets were silent. . . .

For the vineyard of the Lord of hosts is the house of Israel (5:7). Since the prophet uses many metaphors in the section, for example, vineyard, tower, wine vat, wall, and tilling, he indicates what they signify so that an unsophisticated reader would not think, for example, that he is talking about an actual vineyard. Hence he writes, **the vineyard of the Lord of hosts is the house of Israel**. My message, says the prophet, does not have to do with plants or inanimate life or stones and walls, but rather with our people. For this reason he adds: **And the men of Judea are his pleasant planting** (5:7). Judah was privileged among the ten tribes in that the temple was located there and God was worshiped there. And Judah, a powerful royal tribe, was more prosperous than the others. By calling them **beloved**, he subtly reproaches them and reminds them of the intensity of their love in earlier times.

We learn something else of great importance from this passage. And what might this be? It helps us know when one should interpret Scripture allegorically. As readers we cannot dictate the rules of interpretation, but must strive to be faithful to the sense of Scripture and use allegory only when it is appropriate. Here is what I mean. In the passage under discussion, Scripture speaks of a vineyard, a wall, and a wine vat. These things cannot be applied to any events or people one wishes, for the text itself explains what it means when it says, **For the vineyard of the Lord of hosts is the house of Israel** (5:7).

To take another example: Ezekiel describes *a great eagle with great wings that came to Lebanon and took the top of the cedar* (Ezek 17:3-6). The reader is not free to interpret this allegory any way he wishes. For Ezekiel himself tells us what the eagle and cedar signify. To take another example from later in the book of Isaiah: *The Lord is bringing up against them the waters of the River* (Isa 8:7). By providing the name of the king whom he has called a *river* Isaiah lets the reader know that he cannot apply what he says to whomever he wishes.

This rule of interpretation applies to the entire Bible. Whenever Scripture wishes to allegorize, it also offers an interpretation of the allegory. This has a double consequence. First, it shows that the passage should not be taken literally. Second, it prohibits unbridled allegorists from going astray and being led off in every possible direction. Why are you surprised that the prophets follow this procedure? The author of Proverbs does the same. For he warned: *Let your lovely hind and graceful filly accompany you, and let your spring of water be for you alone* (Prov 5:19, 17). Then he explains that he is speaking of one's lawful wife who is free, and warns against having anything to do with a prostitute or foreign woman. In the same way the passage before us in Isaiah tells us what the **vineyard** signifies.

* * *

Woe to those who are wise in themselves, and knowledgeable in their own sight! (5:21). To think oneself wise and to rely completely on one's own reasoning is no small fault. That is exactly what happened to the people being discussed in this passage. They said that evil

Isaiah 5

was good and good evil. The apostle Paul accused the pagan philosophers of this very thing when he said, *Claiming they were wise, they became fools* (Rom 1:22). Indeed, they were fools! Proverbs expresses the same idea when it inquires, *Do you see a man who is wise in his own eyes? There is more hope for a fool than for him* (Prov 26:12). Paul makes a similar accusation when he comments, *Never be conceited* (Rom 12:16), and *If any one among you thinks that he is wise in this age, let him become a fool that he may become wise* (1 Cor 3:18). He asserts that people should not delight in their native wisdom or ability to reason; instead they should set these things aside and surrender themselves to the guidance of the Holy Spirit.

(3) Eusebius of Caesarea

This passage is spoken in the person of the Holy Spirit, who announces, **I will now sing for the beloved a song of the loved one concerning my vineyard** (5:1). Instead of the Septuagint's **concerning *my* vineyard**, the Hebrew original and the other Greek translators read **concerning *his* vineyard**. For the speaker says, **I will sing for the beloved a song** that is neither mine nor composed by me, but by that same person, **the loved one**, who **sings concerning *his* vineyard a song** filled with lamentation and mourning. . . . This same person[1] composed it **concerning his vineyard** or **for his vineyard**, as a song of lamentation. He was both **the beloved** and **the loved one, beloved** by his God and Father,[2] and **the loved one** of the Holy Spirit. That is what is meant when the prophetic Spirit says, **I will sing for the beloved a song of the loved one concerning my vineyard**.

Through the song he recounts his favors toward his vineyard and rebukes its wickedness, prophesying what will happen to it in the future. So it was that God's **loved one** possessed the first people, the circumcised, as his share and portion, and utters a lament over its destruction because of his great love for it.

(4) Theodoret of Cyrus

Let me sing for my beloved a love song concerning my vineyard (5:1). There are many kinds of songs: festival songs, bridal songs, dirges, and songs of mourning. People sing, you see, not only at weddings but also at funerals. Thus blessed Moses, though he is speaking to the people of terrible things to come, calls his warning a *song* (Deut 31:30).

Symmachus translated this passage as follows: **I will sing to my beloved the song that my love addresses to its vineyard**. The term **beloved** signifies the only Son of God, the Word. *For God so loved the world that he gave his only Son, that whoever believes in*

---

1. That is, the Son or the Logos, whom Eusebius believed was the providential overseer of Israel's history even before the Incarnation.
2. See Mark 1:11, the Baptism of Jesus, and Mark 9:7, his Transfiguration.

him should not perish but have eternal life (John 3:16). Moreover, the Father himself testified to him from the heavens when he said: *This is my beloved Son, with whom I am well pleased* (Matt 3:17). This is the one who from the beginning planted the **vineyard** of Israel.

The beloved had a vineyard on a mountaintop, on a fertile place. I put a hedge around it and fenced it in, and planted it with a choice vine. I built a tower in the midst of it, and dug out a wine vat in it. And I waited for it to produce a cluster of grapes, but it produced thorns (5:1-2). He calls the people a vineyard, as blessed David did in the psalm: *Thou didst bring a vine out of Egypt; thou didst drive out the nations and plant it* (Ps 80:8). Similarly, God also spoke through the prophet Jeremiah: *Yet I planted a choice vine wholly of pure seed* (Jer 2:21). In the gospels, the Lord himself said, *There was a householder who planted a vineyard, let it out to tenants, and went into another country* (Matt 21:33). By **tower** he means a **booth** for someone watching the vineyard, using the same term he had used earlier (1:8), and by **wine vat** he means the altar of sacrifice. The term does not mean the sort of vat in which grapes are pressed for wine, but the vat in which grapes are stored prior to being pressed. These things are types that refer to the truth that was to come in Christ. For now we have the holy altars on which is pressed the sacramental wine of the true vine and over which we sing the songs of the true vintage festival. . . .

In the holy gospels the Lord himself did something similar: after setting forth the parable of the vineyard to the Jews, he interprets them as owners of the vineyard and hence responsible for it, asking: *What will the owner of the vineyard do to those tenants?* (Matt 21:40). Not only is there a resemblance between the two questions [of God in Isaiah and Jesus in Matthew], but both have the same sense. For in Isaiah he inquires: **What more might I do for my vineyard that I have not done for it?** (5:4); and in the gospels: *How often would I have gathered your children together as a hen gathers her brood under her wings, and you would not! Behold, your house is forsaken and desolate* (Matt 23:37-38).

(5) Pseudo-Athanasius of Alexandria

Many things are said about the Son in the Old Testament. In Psalm 2: *You are my son, today I have begotten you* (Ps 2:7). In the superscription to Psalm 9: *To the end concerning the hidden things of the son, a psalm of David* (Ps 9:1 LXX). In the superscription to Psalm 44: *To the end concerning the things that shall be changed . . . a song about the beloved* (Ps 44:1 LXX). And in Isaiah: **I will sing for my beloved a love song concerning his vineyard. My beloved had a vineyard** (5:1). Who is this **beloved** but the *only-begotten Son?* Also in Psalm 109: *From the womb I begot you before the morning star* (Ps 109:3 LXX). And in the book of Proverbs: *Before the hills he begot me* (Prov 8:25).

Isaiah 5

5:2
He looked for it to produce grapes, but it yielded wild grapes.

(6) Augustine of Hippo

Let me warn you, holy seedlings,[3] let me warn you, fresh plants in the field of the Lord, not to have it said of you what was said of the vineyard of the house of Israel: **I looked for it to produce grapes, but it produced thorns** (5:2). Let him find good bunches of grapes on you, seeing that he was himself a bunch of grapes trodden in the winepress for you (63:1-3). Produce grapes, live good lives. *For the fruit of the Spirit*, as the apostle says, *is charity, joy, peace, tolerance, kindness, goodness, gentleness, faith, self-control, chastity*[4] (Gal 5:22-23). We know how to plant and water outwardly, but as the apostle says, *Neither the one who plants is anything, nor the one who waters; but God who produces growth* (1 Cor 3:7). Our farmer, whose laborers we are, however, produces growth from within, and he now sees how you listen, he observes how you are in awe of him, or at least beginning to be in awe of him. So when that farmer comes, may he find in you what the apostle said: *My joy and my crown, all of you that are standing firm in the Lord* (Phil 4:1).

5:18
Ah, those who draw sins as with a long rope, who draw transgressions as with a strap from a heifer's yoke.

(7) Augustine of Hippo

Every man braids a rope for himself in his sins. The prophet warns: **Woe to those who drag their sins as with a long rope** (5:18). Who makes the rope long? Who adds sin to sin? How are sins added to sins? When sins that have been committed are combined with other sins! Someone committed a theft. To ensure that no one may find out he committed it, he seeks out an astrologer. It would be enough to have committed the theft; why do you want to join a second sin to the first? Then you have two sins. When you are forbidden to go to an astrologer, you rebuke the bishop. Now there are three sins. When you hear it said of you, "Cast him out of the Church," you reply, "I will go to the party of Donatus."[5] Now you have added a fourth sin. The rope is growing. Beware of the rope!

---

3. Augustine is preaching to the newly baptized.
4. Some ancient manuscripts, including Augustine's Latin version, include "chastity" after "self-control."
5. Donatus was the head of an early Christian schismatic group that held that the Church was composed of holy people and that the sacraments administered by priests who were impure were invalid.

5:21
Woe to those who are wise in their own eyes!

(8) Gregory the Great

Consider how holy men have a remarkable ability to keep before their inner eyes what they do not know in order to safeguard the virtue of humility. On the one hand they consider their weakness, and on the other they do not allow their hearts to be puffed up just because they have done something good. Knowledge is a virtue, but humility is its guardian.

One's mind, then, should be modest about everything it knows, lest the winds of pride blow away what the virtue of knowledge has gathered in. When you do something good, always call to mind the evils you have done. If you keep your faults in mind, your heart will never be heedlessly happy because of its good works. . . . Let everyone strive to be great in the practice of virtue, but nevertheless let each one know that to a certain extent he is in fact nothing. If not, one will attribute greatness to oneself and lose whatever good one has done. This is why the prophet warned: **Woe to you who are wise in your own eyes, and prudent in your own sight!** (5:21). And Paul: *Do not be prudent in your own sight* (Rom 12:16). And because of his pride it was said against Saul: *When you were little in your own eyes, I made you head of the tribes of Israel* (1 Sam 15:17). It is as if he had been told, "When you considered yourself little, I made you greater than the rest; but when you thought of yourself as great, I considered you little."

(9) Symeon the New Theologian

I beseech you who bear the name of children of God and who consider yourselves Christians, you priests and monks who teach others with vain words and act like masters — but falsely! — take these things to heart. Inquire of your elders and priests, gather yourselves together in the love of God; to begin with, first seek to learn these things by doing them and experiencing them yourselves. Then bend your will to behold the vision of God and become godlike through experience. Do not put on a performance as if you were on stage, putting on the clothes of an actor as if you had the dignity of an apostle. For if you rush to rule over others before you have knowledge of the mysteries of God, these words will apply to you: **Woe to those who are wise in their own eyes, and shrewd in their own sight!** (5:21). **Woe to those who make darkness light and light darkness!** (5:20). So I encourage all of you, brothers in Christ, first to lay a firm foundation of humility and on that build the edifice of virtue.

Isaiah 6

₁And it happened in the year that King Ozias died that I saw the Lord sitting on a throne, lofty and raised up; and the house was full of his glory. ₂And seraphim stood around him; the one had six wings and the one had six wings, and with two they covered their face, and with two they covered their feet, and with two they flew. ₃And they cried out one to another and said:

"Holy, holy, holy is the Lord Sabaoth;
 the whole earth is full of his glory."

₄And the lintel was raised at the voice with which they cried out, and the house was filled with smoke. ₅And I said: "O wretched man that I am! I am stunned, for being a man and having unclean lips, I live among a people having unclean lips; and I have seen the King, the Lord Sabaoth, with my eyes!"

₆Then one of the seraphim was sent to me, and he had in his hand a live coal that he had taken from the altar with the tongs. ₇And he touched my mouth and said: "Behold, this has touched your lips; and it will take away your transgressions and purify your sins." ₈Then I heard the voice of the Lord saying, "Whom should I send, and who will go to this people?" And I said, "Here am I; send me!"

9 And he said, "Go and say to this people:
   'You will listen by listening, but you will not understand;
   and looking you will look, but you will not perceive.'
10 For this people's heart has grown fat,
   and with their ears they have heard heavily,
   and they have shut their eyes,
 so that they might not see with their eyes,
   and hear with their ears,
 and understand with their heart,
   and turn — and I would heal them."
11 Then I said, "How long,

O Lord?" And he said:
"Until cities become desolate
   because they are not inhabited,
and houses, because there are no people,
   and the land will be left desolate.
12 And after these things, God will send people far away,
   and those who have been left will be multiplied on the land.
13 And still a tenth part is on it,
   and it will be plundered again,
like a terebinth or an acorn tree
   when it falls from its station."

The interpretation of Isaiah 6 is rich, varied, and provocative. Origen interprets the two seraphim as the divine Word, the eternal Son of God, and the Holy Spirit. This view was rejected by later interpreters because it seemed to subordinate the Son and the Holy Spirit to the Father, and Jerome refutes his exegesis point by point in his Commentary on Isaiah, *excerpted here, and also in a longer discussion in Letter 18. The church fathers discuss which person of the Holy Trinity was "seen" by Isaiah. Jerome, following John 12:41, thinks that it is the Son. But he also notes that, according to the Acts of the Apostles (18:26-27), it is the Holy Spirit who speaks in 6:9-10. But the central question was how Isaiah could have said that he* **saw** *God when the Gospel of John says, "No one has ever seen God" (John 1:18), and God said to Moses, "For man shall not see me and live" (Exod 33:20). In a long letter on the "vision of God" St. Augustine discusses at length the relevant biblical texts and the theological issues raised by the apparently contradictory statements in the Scriptures about "seeing God." Origen notes that it was only after the death of the wicked king Uzziah (who had defiled the Holy of Holies) that Isaiah was able to have a vision, suggesting that only when we purge our souls of evil will we be able to see God. Some took the* **burning coal** *(6:6) to signify Christ, who burns out our sin, and hence the Eucharist, which is taken from the altar and distributed to the faithful. In the Syrian tradition this interpretation is taken over in the Eucharistic Liturgy.*

Isaiah 6:9-10 raises the issue of predestination. Does God merely foreknow what choices people will make, or does he in some sense also determine them? These verses also appear at several places in the New Testament to explain Jewish rejection of the preaching of the gospel. Accordingly, they were invoked by the church fathers to criticize Jews for misunderstanding the prophecies about Christ. As the selection from Jerome shows, the Septuagint's translation appears to deflect the predestinarian implications of the original Hebrew text, which makes God the agent of the people's unbelief since he commands the prophet, **Make the heart of this people fat**. *By contrast, the Septuagint renders these verses as indicatives (***This people's heart has grown fat***). In his* Tractates on John *Augustine struggles with the implications of the passage as cited in John 12:39-40, namely, that Jewish unbelief seems to be attributed to God, and in the end he concludes that the judgments of God are beyond our ken, quoting St. Paul: "How unsearchable are his judgments, and how inscrutable his ways!" (Rom 11:33). The Greek fathers were uncomfortable with any understanding of God's sovereignty that seemed to threaten human free will and responsibility for moral acts. The selection from John Chrysostom is representative of this eastern Christian approach. The classic discussion of the biblical theme of "hard-*

ening" is found in Origen's work On First Principles *(3.1)*. However, since it focuses on the hardening of Pharaoh's heart in the book of Exodus rather than Isa 6:9-10, it is not included here.

(1) The Gospel of Matthew

Then the disciples came and said to him, "Why do you speak to them in parables?" And he answered them, "To you it has been given to know the secrets of the kingdom of heaven, but to them it has not been given. For to him who has will more be given, and he will have abundance; but from him who has not, even what he has will be taken away. This is why I speak to them in parables, because seeing they do not see, and hearing they do not hear, nor do they understand. With them indeed is fulfilled the prophecy of Isaiah which says: **You shall indeed hear but never understand, and you shall indeed see but never perceive. For this people's heart has grown dull, and their ears are heavy of hearing, and their eyes they have closed, lest they should perceive with their eyes, and hear with their ears, and understand with their heart, and turn for me to heal them** (6:9-10). But blessed are your eyes, for they see, and your ears, for they hear. Truly, I say to you, many prophets and righteous men longed to see what you see, and did not see it, and to hear what you hear, and did not hear it."

(2) The Gospel of John

When Jesus had said this, he departed and hid himself from them. Though he had done so many signs before them, yet they did not believe in him; it was that the word spoken by the prophet Isaiah might be fulfilled: *Who has believed our report, and to whom has the arm of the LORD been revealed?* (53:1). Therefore they could not believe. For Isaiah again said, **He has blinded their eyes and hardened their heart, lest they should see with their eyes and perceive with their heart, and turn for me to heal them** (6:10). Isaiah said this because he **saw** (6:1) his glory and spoke of him.

(3) The Acts of the Apostles

When they had appointed a day for [Paul], they came to him at his lodging in great numbers. And he expounded the matter to them from morning till evening, testifying to the kingdom of God and trying to convince them about Jesus both from the law of Moses and from the prophets. And some were convinced by what he said, while others disbelieved. So, as they disagreed among themselves, they departed, after Paul had made one statement: "The Holy Spirit was right in saying to your fathers through Isaiah the prophet: **Go to this people and say, "You shall indeed hear but never understand, and you shall indeed see but never perceive." For this people's heart has grown dull, and their ears are heavy of hearing, and their eyes they have closed; lest they should per-**

ceive with their eyes, and hear with their ears, and understand with their heart, and turn for me to heal them** (6:9-10). Let it be known to you, then, that this salvation of God has been sent to the Gentiles; they will listen."

(4) The Revelation to John

And round the throne, on each side of the throne, are four living creatures, full of eyes in front and behind; the first living creature like a lion, the second living creature like an ox, the third living creature with the face of a man, and the fourth living creature like a flying eagle. And the four living creatures, each of them with six wings, are full of eyes all round and within, and day and night they never cease to sing, "**Holy, holy, holy, is the Lord God Almighty** (6:3), who was and is and is to come!" And whenever the living creatures give glory and honor and thanks to him who is seated on the throne, who lives forever and ever, the twenty-four elders fall down before him who is seated on the throne and worship him who lives forever; they cast their crowns before the throne, singing, "Worthy art thou, our Lord and God, to receive glory and honor and power, for thou didst create all things, and by thy will they existed and were created."

(5) Origen of Alexandria

When King Uzziah was alive, the prophet Isaiah was unable to have visions. Uzziah had sinned and done what was evil in the sight of the Lord by deliberately breaking the divine law. He entered the Holy of Holies, and for this his face broke out with leprosy. Hence he was forced to go outside of the city and live among the unclean. One way of reading the text, then, is that it teaches that we will be able to see God only when we put to death the evil that rules our souls. This is the reason why the Scripture says: **In the year that King Uzziah died I saw the Lord** (6:1). . . .

As long as Uzziah is alive, we will not be able to see the glory of God. When he dies, however, we will be able to see the glory of God if the Word of God rules us who said: *I have set my king on Zion, my holy hill* (Ps 2:6), and anger no longer has any power over us. For the Word is lord over sin, as the apostle Paul ordered: *Let not sin therefore reign in our mortal bodies* (Rom 6:12). Those over whom sin reigns are miserable, for by giving themselves over to the rule of sin they are driven by their desires and despise the rule of God. Whoever loves his desires more than God is not a lover of God, as the apostle Paul wrote to Timothy: *They are lovers of pleasure rather than lovers of God* (2 Tim 3:4). This passage is not talking about strangers to the faith but those who are within the Church yet are *lovers of pleasure rather than God, holding the form of religion but denying the power of it* (2 Tim 3:4-5). So it was that immediately after the death of King Uzziah the prophet had a vision.

I saw the Lord sitting upon a throne, high and lifted up (6:1). What did Isaiah see? Not everyone who sees God sees him sitting upon a throne, high and lifted up. I know of another prophet who saw God sitting on a throne, but neither high nor lifted up. In Daniel it is written: *Thrones were placed* (Dan 7:9), but it was not high and lifted up.

Further, Joel says: *Let the nations bestir themselves to come up to the valley of Jehoshaphat; for there will I sit to judge all the nations round about* (Joel 3:12). It is plain here that God is depicted as sitting in a valley judging those who have been condemned. It is, however, quite another thing to see God sitting on a throne high and lifted up. In Micah, God is said to be *coming forth* and *coming down* (Mic 1:3). And, according to Genesis, when God saw Sodom, he came down: *I will go down to see whether they have done altogether according to the outcry which has come to me* (Gen 18:21). Thus God is sometimes seen on high and sometimes lower down depending on what is appropriate to the situation.

Isaiah announced: **I saw the Lord sitting on a throne, high and lifted up** (6:1). If I see God ruling over those on earth, I do not see him high and lifted up. If I see him ruling the celestial powers, I see him **sitting upon a throne, high and lifted up**. Who are these celestial powers? They are *thrones, dominions, principalities, and powers* (Col 1:16). And if I see God through the Word ruling over them, then **I saw the Lord sitting on a throne, high and lifted up; and his glory filled the house.** Just as his throne was elevated, so his dwelling place was filled with his **glory**. I do not think that a dwelling place **filled with his glory** exists on earth. The psalmist says, *The earth is the* Lord's *and the fullness thereof* (Ps 24:1). But you will not find the fullness of God's **glory** in the present age. But if someone builds a temple for God, the glory of God will be seen and the word of the prophet will be confirmed that said, **God's glory filled the house.** . . .

Above him stood the seraphim; each had six wings (6:2). The wings of the seraphim were arranged in this way: with two they covered the face — not their own faces but the face of God; with two they covered the feet — not their own feet but God's feet; and with two they flew. The text seems to contradict itself because, if they are standing, they are presumably not flying. Yet it is written: **Above him stood the seraphim; each had six wings; with two he covered his face, and with two he covered his feet, and with two he flew. And one called to another** (6:2). In fact, when these seraphim who are around God and know him intimately shout, **Holy, holy, holy** (6:3), they affirm the mystery of the Trinity, for they themselves are holy. Among things that exist nothing is more holy than the seraphim. And when they cry out, **Holy, holy, holy,** they do not speak quietly one to the other but shout their life-giving confession aloud for all to hear.

Who are these two seraphim? They are my Lord Jesus and the Holy Spirit. Do not, however, think that the nature of the Trinity is divided. Each name designates specific functions.

The seraphim hide the face of God because God's beginning is unknown. But they also cover God's feet, for we also do not comprehend the ultimate things about our God. It is possible to see only those things that take place between the beginning and the end. What happened before I do not know, for I know God only from the things which are. Likewise, what will come later I do not know, because it is still to come. *Who can tell a person what will come after him?* asks the book of Ecclesiastes (Eccl 10:14). If you tell me what is the beginning and what is the end, I will say with Isaiah, *You are gods.* For the prophets say: *Tell us the former things, what they are, that we may consider them, that we may know their outcome; or declare to us the things to come. Tell us what is to come hereafter, and I will say that you are gods* (41:22-23). If someone is able to say what is past or to predict the final things, he is God.

When the seraphim say, **The whole earth is full of his glory** (6:3), they are announcing the advent of my Lord Jesus Christ, for now the whole world is indeed filled with his glory. Or if it is not yet completely filled with his glory, in the future it will be filled with his glory. This is clear from the prayer that Jesus commanded us to pray to the Father. He said, *Pray then like this: "Our Father who art in heaven, Hallowed be thy name. Thy kingdom come, Thy will be done, On earth as it is in heaven"* (Matt 6:9-10). Clearly God's will is done in heaven, but it is not done fully on earth.

When Jesus took on human flesh, he claimed: *All authority in heaven and on earth has been given to me* (Matt 28:18). But does he who has power in heaven have no power on earth? Did he receive something from the world when he *came to his own* (John 1:11)? He came that God might be believed on earth as he is believed in heaven. So Christ as man received power that he did not have previously. But even to this day he does not yet possess all power on earth. For example, he does not yet rule over those who are sinners. When all power is given to him, his power will be complete and all things will be subject to him. There are, of course, some who do not wish to be subject to him; indeed, they are still subject to his enemy. Let us, however, ask, *Shall my soul not be subjected to God?* (Ps 61:2 LXX). For *from him comes my salvation* (Ps 61:2 LXX). . . .

And I said: "Woe is me, for I am lost . . ." (6:5). It is difficult to know why Isaiah would think so little of himself. But Scripture quite clearly testifies that his lips were cleansed by the seraph that was sent to take away his sin. This seraph was my Lord Jesus Christ, who is sent by the Father to take away our sins. It is he who says, *I have taken away your iniquity* (Zech 3:4) and cleansed your sins. Do not think that it is an affront to our nature if the Son has been sent to you from the Father. He came that you might know the unity of the divine Trinity. In this passage only Christ is sent to dispel Isaiah's sins. Yet it is absolutely clear that his sins were dispelled by the Trinity. Whoever believes in one person of the Trinity believes in all three persons.

Bring down from the heavenly altar, O Lord, tongs carrying a burning coal to touch my lips, for if the tongs of the Lord touch my lips, they will be cleansed! And if the Lord cleanses my lips and burns out my faults, as we have just said, the Word of God will be in my mouth and no unclean word will escape my lips. . . .

My eyes have seen the King, the Lord of hosts (6:5). Scripture asserts that no one shall see God's face and live (Exod 33:20), yet Isaiah says clearly that he saw the Lord of hosts. Some Jewish interpreters contend that Moses did not see God, and yet Isaiah claims to see him. For this reason he was persecuted and accused of blasphemy.[1] They have, however, not considered that the seraphim covered God's face with two wings. Although Isaiah says that he **saw the Lord,** he did not see God's face, just as Moses did not see his face. As Scripture says, Moses only saw his *back* (Exod 33:23). It is correct, then, to say that he saw the Lord even if he did not see his face. Thus, those who condemn Isaiah do so wrongly. . . .

In order to have the vision that Isaiah had, let us call upon Jesus, who gives eyes to those who cannot see. He is able to come and do this that we might perceive with unimpeded vision what is read in this passage. Let us, in return, promise never to make the

---

1. For this tradition see the passage from the *Martyrdom and Ascension of Isaiah* in the Preface.

body of Christ into the body of a prostitute (cf. 1 Cor 6:15-16) nor to do any of those things that would cause him grief. Let each of us speak in our hearts to God and beseech him to come now. For if Christ does not come to us, we will not be able to see what Isaiah saw.

I pray that the seraph will be sent to me and, by taking the burning coal in his forceps, purge my lips. Why does the text say **lips** (6:5)? Isaiah was holy, and had sinned only with the lips. That is why only his lips were cleansed. However, I am not as pure as Isaiah, for I cannot say that only my lips are unclean. I fear that I have an unclean heart, unclean eyes, unclean ears, and an unclean mouth. As long as I sin in all these parts of my body, I am totally unclean. If I see a woman and lust after her, I am an adulterer in my heart (cf. Matt 5:28), and I have unclean eyes. If evil thoughts arise in my breast, thoughts of adultery, of fornication, or of bearing false witness, then I have an unclean heart. *How beautiful upon the mountains are the feet of him who brings good tidings* (Isa 52:7). I fear that in chasing after evil things I also have unclean feet. I stretch out my hands to God, yet he turns from me and says: *When you spread forth your hands, I will hide my eyes from you* (Isa 1:15).

Who will cleanse me? Who will wash my feet? Come, Jesus, I have filthy feet. For my sake you became a servant; pour water into your basin. Come, wash my feet. I know I speak rashly, but I am afraid because you have said, *If I do not wash you, you will have no part in me* (John 13:8). Please wash my feet that I may have a part in you! But why do I say, "Wash my feet"? Peter was able to say this to Jesus because he had need only that his feet be washed. Otherwise he was wholly cleansed. But I, since I was once cleansed,[2] have need of the baptism about which the Lord said: *I have a baptism to be baptized with* (Luke 12:50). Why have I said these things? I am preparing myself and those who are listening to me for greater mysteries. If the Word of God descends to us, I am afraid that he may leave me or refuse to bless me. The Word of God left the people on account of one sinner, Achan — I repeat because of one sinner, Achan, son of Carmi, son of Zabdi, son of Zerah, of the tribe of Judah (Josh 7:1). Achan disobeyed God and was, therefore, condemned by God. And now there is a great crowd in Church because of the Paschal Feast, and also on the Lord's Day, which is a memorial of the passion of Christ (for the resurrection of the Lord is not celebrated only once a year, nor only once a week).[3] Pray to the Lord that his word will come to us. Even though you are sinners, pray to the Lord. For God hears the prayers of sinners. If you are afraid to call out to the Lord because of what someone said in the Gospel, *We know that God does not listen to sinners* (John 9:31), do not be afraid, and don't believe what he says. Remember that it was a blind man who said this. Believe rather in the one who does not lie and who promised, *Even if your sins are like crimson, they shall become as white as wool. If you are willing and obedient, you shall eat the good of the land* (Isa 1.18-19). If you want to hear God now, let us together call out to the Lord that the Word might come to us and we might be able to listen to the words of the prophets.

---

2. In Baptism.
3. "Passion" here means the death and resurrection of Christ, the "paschal mystery." In the early Church the Eucharist was often celebrated on Wednesday, Friday, and Saturday as well as on Sunday.

(6) Eusebius of Caesarea

When the prophet saw the **Lord of hosts** (6:5) he saw something other than the unbegotten, invisible, and incomprehensible deity. Whom did the prophet see if not *the only Son, who is in the bosom of the Father* (John 1:18), who, descending from his own majesty, limited himself and made himself visible and comprehensible to human beings? This was also the case when the Lord *appeared to Abram and said, "To your descendants I will give this land"* (Gen 12:7). Scripture continues, *So he built there an altar to the* LORD, *who had appeared to him* (Gen 12:7); a little later it adds, *When Abram was ninety-nine years old the* LORD *appeared to Abram* (Gen 17:1); and further on it says, *And the* LORD *appeared to him by the oaks of Mamre* (Gen 18:1). Concerning Isaac Scripture says, *From there he went up to Beer-sheba. And the* LORD *appeared to him the same night* (Gen 26:23-24). Elsewhere it speaks about Jacob's encounters with God this way, *I am the God who appeared to you in this holy place* (Gen 31:13 LXX), and *And Jacob came to Luz (that is, Bethel) . . . he and all the people who were with him, and there he built an altar, and called the place El-bethel, because there God had revealed himself to him* (Gen 35:6-7). Then it adds, *God appeared to Jacob again* (Gen 35:9).

In an earlier passage it is written that God appeared in human form and said to Jacob, *Your name shall no more be called Jacob, but Israel, for you have striven with God and men and have prevailed* (Gen 32:28); and Jacob *called the name of the place Peniel, saying, "I have seen God face to face, and yet my life is preserved"* (Gen 32:30). . . . From all of this we learn that the visions of God which came to the various persons mentioned in the Scriptures were not the same; they were all different. Yet God told Moses, *You cannot see my face; for man shall not see me and live* (Exod 33:20). He meant that the face of the Word of God, namely, the divine nature of the Only-Begotten Son of God, could not be comprehended by mortal nature. It was the glory of the Word which Ezekiel saw as through a glass darkly. He was seen by Abraham, having been fashioned in human form, and was under a tree and had his feet washed and shared in a meal. . . . In the text before us, Isaiah testifies that he saw his glory, that is to say, he saw the glory of our Savior Jesus Christ. . . .

Although the vision of the prophet Isaiah was different from that of Moses and Ezekiel, he too saw the glory of our Savior, though not with his physical eyes. His understanding was enlightened by the Holy Spirit. For just as one's physical eyes when furnished with the external light of the sun are enabled to see perceptible things, in the same manner, the eyes of the pure soul having been enlightened with intellectual light are able to see divine things. It is for this reason that our Savior taught with these words, *Blessed are the pure in heart, for they shall see God* (Matt 5:8). . . .

One cried out loudly to another, saying, "Holy, holy, holy is the Lord of Hosts; the whole earth is full of his glory" (6:3). The seraphim do not sound forth with one voice, nor do they all lift their voices in common, but one seraph proclaims to the other his awe and wonder before the One they behold. The descent of the glory of the Word from higher things to lower especially amazed them. Indeed, this was the greatest wonder — not only was heaven full of his glory but now he came to earth so that the whole earth is filled with his glory.

(7) Jerome

Sacred Scripture records that Uzziah, who illicitly assumed the role of a priest, was struck down with leprosy. When he died, the Lord again appeared in the temple, which had been polluted by the presence of Uzziah. From this we learn that if the leprosy of sin rules us, it is impossible for us either to see the Lord reigning in majesty or to know the mysteries of the Holy Trinity. For this reason, after the death of Pharaoh, who forced the Israelites to make bricks out of mud and straw, as recorded in the book of Exodus, the people cried out to God (Exod 2:23). When Pharaoh was still alive, they were unable to cry out to God.

The Hebrew states quite beautifully that it is not the Lord himself who **fills the temple** (6:1). His throne is in heaven, and the earth is his footstool. As we read in the Psalms, *The Lord is in his holy temple, the Lord's throne is in heaven* (Ps 11:4). It was **his train** that **filled the temple** (6:1). From the Gospel of John and the book of Acts we learn that it was the Lord who was seen in this vision. About these things John said: *Isaiah said this because he saw his glory and spoke of him* (John 12:41). There can be no doubt that he is referring to Christ. Moreover, in the Acts of the Apostles, when speaking to the Jews in Rome, Paul says: *The Holy Spirit was right in saying to your fathers through Isaiah the prophet:* **"Go to this people and say, 'You shall indeed hear but never understand, and you shall indeed see but never perceive.' For this people's heart has grown dull, and their ears are heavy of hearing, and their eyes they have closed; lest they should perceive with their eyes, and hear with their ears, and understand with their heart, and turn for me to heal them"** (Acts 28:24-27; 6:9-10). Here the Son is seen as reigning, but the Holy Spirit also speaks because the Spirit shares in the divine majesty and the unity of the Holy Trinity.

Someone might also ask how the prophet can say he saw the Lord, and not simply the Lord, but the **Lord of hosts**, when Christ himself later testifies according to the Evangelist John: *No one has ever seen God* (John 1:18). God also told Moses, *You cannot see my face; for man shall not see me and live* (Exod 33:20). To which we reply that the eyes of the flesh are unable to see the divinity of the Father, nor that of the Son, nor of the Holy Spirit, because in the Trinity there is one nature. The Trinity can be seen only with the eyes of the mind. It was to this that the Savior was referring when he said, *Blessed are the pure in heart, for they shall see God* (Matt 5:8). We read that Abraham saw God in a human form (cf. Gen 17:1; 18:1) and that Jacob wrestled with someone who seemed to be a man but was, in fact, God (Gen 32:24-30). Jacob named the place where he had wrestled with God Peniel, which means the face of God, for he declares, *I have seen God face to face, and yet my life has been preserved* (Gen 32:30). Ezekiel also saw God in *the form that had the appearance of a man* sitting above the cherubim and *below what appeared to be his loins it was fire, and above his loins it was like the appearance of brightness, like gleaming bronze* (Ezek 8:2). The nature of God cannot be perceived, but God reveals himself to human beings insofar as he wishes to be seen.

Above him stood the seraphim; each had six wings: with two he covered his face, and with two he covered his feet, and with two he flew. And one called to another and said: "Holy, holy, holy is the Lord of hosts; the whole earth is full of his glory" (6:2-3). In Hebrew there is some ambiguity whether the pronoun **his** refers to God or to each seraph. For this reason, it is difficult to determine whether the seraphim were covering their own faces and feet or whether they were covering the face and feet of God.

In Psalm 80 we read: *Thou who art enthroned upon the cherubim, shine forth* (Ps 80:1). *Cherubim* in our language signifies fullness of wisdom. Hence the Lord is clearly depicted as sitting upon the cherubim like a charioteer. I know of no other place in Scripture besides this one, however, where the **seraphim** stand above the temple or round about God. The psalm reads, *Thou who art enthroned upon the cherubim,* not *Thou who art enthroned upon the cherubim* and **seraphim**. Those who recite it this way when they are praying the psalms are in error. Scripture does not teach this. In Greek the seraphim are rendered as *empreestai*, which means "those who are burning" or "those who are on fire," as we read elsewhere in Scripture: *who makest the winds thy messengers, fire and flame thy ministers* (Ps 104:4). Hence in the Epistle to the Hebrews the apostle Paul[4] writes: *Are not all ministering spirits sent forth to serve, for the sake of those who are to obtain salvation?* (Heb 1:14). When Daniel describes the Lord in majesty, he adds: *a thousand thousands served him, and ten thousand times ten thousand stood before him* (Dan 7:10). The Lord then is made known among the cherubim, but among the seraphim he is partly made known, partly veiled. For the Lord's **face** and **feet** were concealed. This veiling indicates that we cannot know what happened in the past before the creation of the world and what will happen in the future after the end of the world. Don't be surprised that some things are veiled to the seraphim, for the apostles revealed the Savior to those who believed, but hid him from unbelievers. Furthermore, there was a veil before the ark of the covenant.

This passage indicates that it was not the Jewish temple that is filled with God's **glory**, as in former times, but **the whole earth is full of his glory** (6:3). God's glory filled the earth when God took on human form for our salvation and came to earth. When the people worshiped the golden calf, Moses prayed that God might forgive the sins of the people, and God responded, *I will be gracious to them, for as I live and my name lives, all the earth will be filled with the glory of the LORD* (Num 14:20-21). In Psalm 72 the psalmist sings, *May his glory fill the whole earth* (Ps 72:19). Later, in the gospels, the angels proclaim to the shepherds, *"Glory to God in the highest, and on earth peace among men with whom he is pleased!"* (Luke 2:14).

*   *   *

Some have interpreted this passage before me, Greeks as well as Romans, to mean that the Lord sitting upon a throne is God the Father, and the two seraphim that are said to be standing one at each side are our Lord Jesus Christ and the Holy Spirit.

*   *   *

But those who claim that the two seraphim are the Son and the Holy Spirit are impious.[5] For, as we have seen, according to John the Evangelist and Paul the Apostle it was the Son of God who was seen reigning in majesty and the Holy Spirit who spoke. . . .
And I said: "Woe is me! For I am lost; for I am a man of unclean lips, and I dwell

---

4. In the early Church St. Paul was often considered the author of the Epistle to the Hebrews.
5. Jerome has in mind Origen.

Isaiah 6

in the midst of a people of unclean lips; for my eyes have seen the King, the Lord of hosts (6:5). In the Hebrew we read, **Woe is me, for I am silent.** The prophet bemoans that he is not worthy to join the seraphim (whom we understand to be mighty angelic beings) in praising the Lord. Because he had unclean lips he thought he was unworthy to praise the Lord. And why did he have unclean lips? Because he lived among a sinful people. Hence the text is to be understood as follows: I was silent because I did not have the courage to reproach the impious King Uzziah. Therefore my lips are unclean, and I dare not join the angels in singing praises to the Lord. It is as though the words of the psalm were being spoken to me, *What right have you to recite my statutes or take my covenant on your lips?* (Ps 50:16). For indeed, *a hymn of praise is not fitting on the lips of a sinner* (Sir 15:9). . . .

Note also what was said to Jeremiah: *Before I formed you in the womb I knew you, and before you were born I consecrated you* (Jer 1:5). Jeremiah did not have unclean lips; instead he asserted, *I do not know how to speak, for I am only a youth* (Jer 1:6). In response, the Lord extended his hand, touched his mouth, and said, *Behold, I have put my words in your mouth* (Jer 1:9). In the case of Isaiah, who confessed, **I am a man of unclean lips, and I dwell in the midst of a people of unclean lips** (6:5), the Lord did not stretch out his hand; rather, one of the seraphim was sent by God, or flew to Isaiah of his own accord since he was charged with this task. And in his hand the seraph held a live coal. . . . When he touched Isaiah's mouth with it, Isaiah was cleansed of his former sins. A hand of God and of the seraphim was extended to the prophet so that the prophet, seeing a human hand, would not be terrified by being touched by something strange. . . .

And I heard the voice of the Lord saying, "Whom shall I send and who will go for us?" Then I said, "Here I am! Send me!" (6:8). The Lord does not say unequivocally whom he is sending. He leaves the matter vague so that the prophet might respond to the call voluntarily. When Isaiah responds, he does not do so out of rashness or overconfidence but out of trust. For his iniquity has been removed, and he has been cleansed of his sins. Think how Moses responded when the Lord said to him, *Come, I will send you to Pharaoh, the king of Egypt* (Exod 3:10). He begged, *Oh, my Lord, send, I pray, some other person, for I am not worthy* (Exod 4:13). . . . When he pleaded, *Send someone else*, Moses was not being recalcitrant but humble. Even though he had been instructed in all the wisdom of the Egyptians, he had heard nothing about his lips being cleansed. Isaiah did not volunteer to serve the Lord on the basis of his own merit but because he had been cleansed by the grace of God. . . . We say, then, that when Isaiah offered himself to be sent he was not rash but obedient.

(8) John Chrysostom

Christ said, *No one has ever seen God; the only Son, who is in the bosom of the Father, has made him known* (John 1:18). And elsewhere: *Not that any one has seen the Father except him who is sent from God; he has seen the Father* (John 6:46). And God said to Moses, *Man shall not see me and live* (Exod 33:20). How then can Isaiah say here that he saw the Lord (for the text says, **I saw the Lord** [6:1])? His words do not contradict Christ's sayings, but are in harmony with them. Christ was speaking about perceiving God fully, and no one has ever seen God in that way. Only the Only-Begotten has seen the divine nature in all its splendor and beheld the essence of God. The prophet saw what he was capable of seeing. He did not see the essence of God, he saw the form that God had assumed when he lowered himself to the level human weakness could reach.

That Isaiah did not see the fullness of God, nor indeed did anyone else, is clear from the words spoken by Isaiah. **I saw**, he says, **the Lord sitting** (6:1). It is obvious that God does not sit, for God has no bodily form. Note further that Isaiah not only says that God was sitting, but that he was sitting **upon a throne** (6:1). But God is neither limited nor circumscribed. How could God sit on a throne when God is everywhere and fills everything? *In his hands are the depths of the earth,* writes the psalmist (Ps 95:4). It is obvious, then, that Isaiah's vision was possible because of God's condescension to human capabilities. Another prophet hints at this same thing when he says, speaking in the name of God: *It was I who multiplied visions* (Hos 12:10). In other words, "I have been seen in many different ways." If God's essence had been totally unveiled, there would have been no need for him to be seen in different ways. But when God condescends to reveal himself to us, he appears in one way in one prophet and in another way in another prophet, taking different forms depending on the particular place and time. That is why God says: *I have multiplied visions and taken form in the hands of the prophets* (Hos 12:10).

I did not appear, God tell us, as I am in myself. I take on a form that can be seen by those who behold me. That is why at various different places in Scripture you see God sitting (cf. Isa 6:1), in full armor (34:6 and 63:1), having white hair (Dan 7:9), in a wind (1 Kgs 19:11), in fire (Exod 3:2; 1 Kgs 19:12). Sometimes you read of God's back (Exod 33:23), sometimes he is enthroned on the cherubim (Ps 80:1), and sometimes he takes the form of a shining, yet diaphanous, metallic substance (Ezek 1:4). . . .

Why, then, does God appear to Isaiah in the form of one sitting on a throne with seraphim next to him? He is imitating human behavior because he is speaking to human beings. God is about to pronounce a sentence concerning important matters for everyone, including of course the inhabitants of Jerusalem. He is handing down a two-sided verdict. On the one hand, it will bring punishment on the city and the whole nation; on the other hand, it will bring benefit to the whole world and offer the magnificent hope of immortality. It is customary for judges not to render judgment in secret but from an elevated bench before which everyone stands. In the same way God sits on a high throne with the seraphim standing around him and pronounces his verdict from there. . . .

Why did he say, **I saw the Lord sitting** (6:1)? Sitting upon a throne is always a symbol of judgment; as David said, *Thou hast sat upon the throne giving righteous judgment* (Ps 9:4). Daniel adds, *Thrones were placed and the one that was ancient of days took his seat* (Dan 7:9). The prophet is indicating that the act of sitting is symbolic of something else. And what might that be? It is symbolic of being firm, stable, established, immoveable, eternal, and immortal. Therefore the Scriptures say: *Thou art enthroned forever, and we are perishing forever* (Bar 3:3). "You," he says, "remain, you exist, and you live always the same." . . .

And around him stood the seraphim (6:2). Who exactly are these seraphim? They are incorporeal powers, heavenly beings whose virtue and blessedness is evident in the

Isaiah 6

name. In Hebrew, *seraphim* means "mouths of fire." What can we learn from this? That it is their nature to be pure, vigilant, alert, spirited, energetic, undefiled. That is why when the prophet David wanted to describe the devoted service, swiftness in carrying out tasks, and sheer energy of the heavenly beings, he said: *He makes his angels winds, and his ministers flames of fire* (Ps 104:4). By pointing to aspects of the natural world he is able to describe their speed, agility, and energy. These heavenly beings celebrate the Lord with pure voices, carrying out their tasks without interruption, and offering their service of praise continually. They are honored by being able to stand close to God's throne. Among the kings of the earth those who are most honored stand next to the throne. In the same way, because of their great virtue, these heavenly beings encircle the heavenly throne and continually enjoy a happiness beyond words as they delight in this blessed service.

Each had six wings: with two he covered his face, and with two he covered his feet, and with two he flew. And one called to another and said: "Holy, holy, holy is the Lord of hosts; the whole earth is full of his glory" (6:2-3). What does Isaiah want to convey to us with the term **wings**? Incorporeal powers, after all, cannot have wings. Once again the prophet is attempting to describe something that is ineffable by means of images from the world of the senses. As he adapted himself to his hearers then, he now adapts to us that we might grasp things that are beyond our understanding. What, then, do the wings signify? They signify the lofty and exalted nature of these powers. That is why the angel Gabriel appears flying down from heaven on wings (Dan 9:21), so that you might recognize his speed and agility. And why should one be surprised if Scripture uses such expressions to speak of the ministering powers and employs the same language to speak about the accommodation of the God of the universe to human capabilities? When David wanted to depict God's incorporeal nature and how swiftly he is present everywhere, he said: *He walks on the wings of the wind* (Ps 18:10). Of course the wind does not have wings, and God does not walk on wings. How could he, since he is present everywhere? As I have mentioned, he condescended to the limitations of his hearers and, by using things that were familiar, made it possible for them to understand higher things. David uses similar language when he wishes to depict divine aid and the assurance it brings: *Hide me under the shadow of thy wings* (Ps 17:8).

In this passage Isaiah not only uses the image of wings to convey to us that the seraphim were exalted and agile, but he intends to convey something more awesome. He shows that even if the vision was made possible by an act of condescension on God's part, as it most certainly was, the heavenly beings were unable even to reach this level. By hiding their feet and their faces and their backs they show that they were awestruck and trembled in fear, unable to bear the force of the lightning that shoots out from the throne. For this reason they covered their faces by extending their wings like a shield. For heavenly powers experience the same feelings in God's presence that we do when we cower in a corner at the rolling of thunder and the flashing of lightning. If the seraphim, these magnificent and awesome powers, cannot look at God seated upon his throne without fear, but must hide their faces and their feet, what words could I use to describe the folly of those who say they have seen God fully and known his very being?[6]

---

6. John is referring to Eunomius and his followers.

(9) Gregory the Theologian

No one has ever discovered nor can discover what God is by nature and in essence. . . . In our present life all that reaches us is but a little effluence, as it were a small beam from a great light. . . . Abraham, great patriarch though he was, was justified by faith, and the sacrifice that he offered was unique in that it foreshadowed the great one to come. Yet he did not see God directly. Indeed, he gave him food as a man (Gen 18:1-8). Yet he was commended because he worshiped God as he was able. . . . And Jacob wrestled with God in human form (Gen 32:22-32) . . . yet neither he nor anyone after him to this day from the twelve tribes . . . could boast that he had had a complete unobstructed vision of God.

For Elijah it was neither the strong wind, nor the fire, nor the earthquake, as Scripture tells us, but a light breeze that made known the presence of God (1 Kgs 19:11-13), not, however, God's nature. . . .

What will you say of Isaiah or Ezekiel, who were eyewitnesses of very great mysteries, and of the other prophets? For Isaiah **saw the Lord of hosts sitting on the throne of glory** (6:1), encircled by the six-winged seraphim, and was himself purged by the live **coal** (6:6) and equipped for his prophetic office. And Ezekiel describes the cherubic chariots of God, and the throne upon them, and the firmament over it, and the one that showed himself in the firmament, and in certain sounds, movements, and actions as well (cf. Ezek 1:4-28). Whether this was an appearance by day, visible only to the saints, or an unerring vision of the night, or an impression on the mind of the future as if it were the present, or some other ineffable form of prophecy, I cannot say. The God of the prophets knows, and those who are genuinely inspired know. But neither of these two prophets, nor any of their fellows, was ever privy to the very nature of God, or "stood" before the essence of God, as Scripture has it.[7] None saw, and none told of God's nature.

(10) Gregory of Nyssa

Someone may see a relation between Isaiah's vision and the words in the Song of Songs, *they beat me, they wounded me, they took away my veil, those watchmen of the walls* (Song 5:7). Isaiah saw someone sitting in **glory** upon a lofty, exalted **throne** (6:1), but he could not see his form and his extent. Had Isaiah been able, he would have spoken of this, for he described other things he saw, the number of the wings of the **seraphim** (6:2), their location and movement. But he mentions only the voice he heard, that the **lintels were raised** because of the singing of the seraphim, and that **the house was filled with smoke** (6:4). One of the seraphim touched his mouth with a **burning coal** (6:6); not only were his **lips purified** (6:7), but his ears were made capable of receiving God's word. Similarly, the bride says that she was struck and wounded by the watchmen of the city and her veil was removed; instead of a veil, the **lintel** was removed so that Isaiah's vision would not be hindered. In place of watchmen **seraphim** are mentioned; instead of a rod a **coal**; and burn-

---

7. Gregory has in mind Jer 23:18: "For who among them has *stood* in the council of the LORD to perceive and to hear his word. . . ."

ing heat in place of a blow. Both the bride and Isaiah have a common goal: purification. As the prophet was not harmed by the burning coal but was able to behold God's glory, the bride does not complain of the pain received from the watchman's blow, but is filled with pride that her veil has been removed

(11) Didymus the Blind

Scripture does not say "Abram saw God," but *God appeared to Abram* (Gen 12:7). As long as we are in the weakness of created nature, it is not possible to see God, but insofar as God is compassionate, it becomes possible, as, for example, when out of goodness he gave himself to be known by Abram. If, however, a text reads "he saw" instead of "he appeared," as in Isaiah's **I saw the Lord seated** (6:1) and what follows, we are to understand this from what happened to Abram, namely that this refers to God's giving of himself. One can see that the verb "to see" is sometimes used in the sense of "to understand" by looking at the words of Paul to the Romans, *his invisible things are perceived* [i.e., seen] *intelligibly from the creation of the world by the things he made* (Rom 1:20). And Moses, judging that God, whom he thought to be invisible, said, *Make yourself manifest to me, that I might see you* [i.e., clearly] (Exod 33:13 LXX). And again, *He is manifest to those who do not disbelieve him* (Wis 1:2). For if what is seen is of a visible nature, it would be possible for it also to appear to unbelievers. Here, however, it says, *He is manifest to those who do not disbelieve him,* that is, who have a mind illumined by divine light.

The matter is reversed in seeing sensible objects. First we see them, then, when an impression is formed in the mind from the perception, we conceive them. But intelligible things must give themselves to be known. The mind does not take the lead, except to prepare itself to know, and follows what allows itself to be seen.

(12) Augustine of Hippo

We know that God can be seen because Scripture says, *Blessed are the pure of heart, because they shall see God* (Matt 5:8). Or should I have said, not "we know," but "we believe"? For we have not seen God with the body, as we have seen this sunlight, nor with the mind, as we have seen in ourselves the very faith by which we believe that, but we have no doubt that it is true, only because it is recorded in that Scripture which we believe.

The apostle John, nonetheless, said something of the sort: *We know,* he declared, *that when he shall appear, we shall be like him, because we shall see him as he is* (1 John 3:2). See, he said he knew something that had not yet come about not by seeing but by believing. And so we were correct to say, "We know that God can be seen," though we have not seen him but we have believed in the authority which depends on the holy books.

Why, then, does that same authority say, *No one has ever seen God* (John 1:18)? Is the answer perhaps that the former testimonies are concerned with seeing God in the future, not that God has been seen? For it is said that they *shall see God,* and not that we have seen, but *we shall see him as he is.* Hence, *no one has ever seen God* is not opposed to these statements. For those who with a pure heart have wanted to be children of God will see him whom they have not seen.

What, then, does it mean, *I saw God face to face, and my soul was saved* (Gen 32:30)? Is not this also opposed to what was said, *No one has ever seen God?* And there are those words that were written concerning Moses, namely, that he was speaking with God *face to face, as one speaks to his friend* (Exod 33:11). And there is what the prophet Isaiah said in speaking of himself: **I saw the Lord of hosts sitting upon a throne** (6:1), and any other similar testimonies that can be produced from the same authority. How can they not be opposed to that statement that says, *No one has ever seen God?* And yet, the Gospel itself can also be thought to be in opposition to itself, for how is the statement in it, *He who sees me sees the Father* (John 14:9), true if *no one has ever seen God?* How is it true that *their angels always see the face of my Father* (Matt 18:10) if *no one has ever seen God?*

By what rule of interpretation shall we prove that these statements that seem opposed and in conflict are not opposed and in conflict? For it is in no way possible that this authority of the Scriptures is not truthful. . . .

By nature God is invisible, not only the Father but also the Trinity itself, one God. Because he is not only invisible but also immutable, he appears as he wills in what form he wills so that his invisible and immutable nature remains whole within him. But the desire of truly pious persons by which they long and avidly desire to see God does not, I believe, burn to gaze upon that form in which he appears when he wills, which is not himself, but to gaze upon that substance by which he is what he is.

The saintly Moses, his faithful servant, revealed the flame of this desire of his when he said to God, with whom he was speaking face to face like a friend, *If I have found favor before you, show yourself to me* (Exod 33:13 LXX). What, then, does this mean? Was that not God? If it was not God, Moses would not say to him, *Show me yourself,* but "Show me God," and yet, if he looked upon his nature and substance, he would have much less reason to say, *Show me yourself.* God was, therefore, in that form in which he had willed to appear, but he did not appear in his own nature, which Moses longed to see. That vision is, of course, promised to the saints in the next life. Hence the reply given to Moses is true, that *no one can see the face of God and live* (Exod 33:20), that is, no one can, while living in this life, see him as he is.

For many have seen him but have seen what was chosen by his will, not what was fashioned from his nature. And if one correctly understands it, this is what John said: *Beloved, we are now the children of God, and it has not yet appeared what we shall be. We know that when he appears, we shall be like him because we shall see him as he is* (1 John 3:2), not as human beings saw him when God willed and in the form in which he willed, not in the nature in which he was in himself hidden, even when he was seen, but *as he is.* This is what Moses asked of him when he said to him, *Show me yourself;* he asked this of him with whom he was speaking *face to face.* For no one has ever grasped the fullness of God, not by the eyes of the body, not even by the mind itself. For it is one thing to see; it is another to grasp the whole by seeing. . . . To say, then, that *no one has ever seen God . . .* means that no one has seen the fullness of his divinity.

6:3
Holy, holy, holy is the Lord God of hosts.

(13) The Liturgy of St. James

Priest: It is truly meet and right, fitting, and our bounden duty to praise You, to laud You, to bless You, to worship You, to glorify You, to give thanks to You, Maker of all things visible and invisible, the treasury of all good things, the source of life and immortality, the God and Lord of all, whom the heavens and the heaven of heavens and all the powers thereof do praise, the sun and moon and all the choir of the stars, earth, sea, and all that is in them, the assembly of the heavenly Jerusalem, the Church of the firstborn whose names are written in the heavens, the spirits of the righteous and prophets, the souls of the martyrs and apostles, angels, archangels, thrones, dominions, principalities, authorities, dread powers, cherubim with many eyes, and **the six-winged seraphim who with two wings cover their faces and with two their feet and with two they fly and cry one to the other** (6:2) with ceaseless voices in endless praise singing the hymn of victory of Your excellent glory, with clear voice singing and shouting, glorifying and crying and saying:

People: **Holy, holy, holy, Lord of hosts. Heaven and earth are full of your glory** (6:3). Hosanna in the highest! Blessed is he who comes in the name of the Lord! Hosanna in the highest! (cf. Matt 21:9).

(14) Ambrose of Milan

What is the meaning of the threefold utterance of the word **Holy**? If it is repeated three times, why is it one act of praise? Is not **Holy** repeated three times because the Father and the Son and the Holy Spirit are one in holiness? The seraphim spoke the name, not once, lest the Son should be excluded, not twice, lest the Spirit should be overlooked, not four times lest something created should be included. Furthermore, to show that the Trinity is one God, after the threefold **Holy** is spoken they add the singular, **the Lord God of hosts** (6:3). Therefore the Father is holy, the Son is holy, and also the Spirit of God is holy; the Trinity is adored, but does not adore, it is praised, but it does not praise. As for me, I believe as the seraphim believed, and adore God as did all the principalities and powers of heaven.

(15) Basil of Caesarea

The revelation of mysteries is the proper work of the Spirit, as it is written: *God has revealed to us through the Spirit* (1 Cor 2:10). How could thrones and dominions and principalities and powers live their blessed life if they did not behold *the face of the Father who is in heaven* (Matt 18:10)? For one cannot have a vision of God without the Spirit, in the same way that when the lights in the house go out at night, the eyes become blind and are useless, unable to tell, for example, whether one is stepping on gold or on iron. It is the same in the religious life. It is impossible to have a deep spiritual life according to God's law without the Spirit. That is as unlikely as an army maintaining its discipline in the absence of its commander or a chorus without its director.

How could the seraphim cry, **Holy, holy, holy** (6:3), if they had not been taught by the Spirit that true devotion requires them to lift their voices in praise of God's glory? If all his angels and all his hosts praise God, it is through the cooperation of the Spirit. Do not a thousand times a thousand angels and ten thousand times ten thousand ministering spirits stand before him (cf. Dan 7:10)? By the power of the Holy Spirit they are carrying out their distinctive work unfailingly. All the majestic and ineffable harmony of the highest heavens, whether in the worship of God or in the mutual concord of the celestial powers, is preserved only under the direction of the Spirit.

(16) Prudentius

> Now that we have nourished bodies,[8]
>   let us likewise feed our souls
> and set these mouths that chew and swallow
>   to other, more important goals —
> the framing of our songs of praise to
>   God the Father on his **throne** (6:1)
> among the cherubs and the **seraphs** (6:2).
>   He is supreme, the Lord alone,
>
> with neither ending nor beginning,
>   He is the *fons et origo*
> of everything that is, instilling
>   faith and virtue here below.
> Life he gives and then salvation,
>   through which comes immortality
> in heaven's precincts where his Spirit
>   reigns in light and purity.

(17) Cyril of Alexandria

The seraphim begin their doxology with a threefold repetition of **Holy,** and they conclude with the words **Lord of hosts** (6:3), thereby affirming that the one divine nature is a Holy Trinity. For when we confess the creed we say that there are three persons, the Father, the Son, and the Holy Spirit. There is no reason to divide these three into different natures simply because each bears a different name. The one divine Godhead is to be un-

---

8. Prudentius's poem is a prayer for after meals.

derstood in three persons. The holy seraphim bear witness that the **whole earth is full of his glory** because they are pointing to what is going to happen in the future, foretelling the mystery of Christ's coming in the flesh. For until the time when the Word became flesh, the devil, the transgressor, that dragon and apostate, was ruler of all things under heaven and created things were worshiped rather than the Creator and Maker (Rom 1:25). But, when the only Son of God, the Word, became flesh, the **whole earth** was **filled with his glory** (6:3). Every knee and every people and every tongue will bow before him and will serve him, as it is written (Phil 2:10-11). Inspired by the Spirit, David anticipated this day when he said: *All the nations thou hast made shall come and bow down before thee, O Lord* (Ps 86:9). This has indeed come to pass, for many nations have been called to his service and all worship him who on our behalf became like us and who alone remains above all things.

(18) Gregory the Great

David, Isaiah, and Paul lived at different times in the history of the world. But they did not differ in their thinking. Though they did not know one another face to face, they had a similar knowledge of God. David, in order to show forth that the triune God is the creator of all things, said: *Let God bless us, our God, let God bless us* (Ps 67:6-7). Lest he should be thought to have spoken of three Gods, because he mentioned God three times, to assert the unity of the Trinity he at once adds: *let all the ends of the earth fear him* (Ps 67:7). For by saying *him* instead of "them" he intimates that the three he named are one. When Isaiah was also praising the unity of the Trinity, he says that the voices of the seraphim cried out: **Holy, holy, holy**. However, lest he should appear to sever the unity of the divine nature, he added, **Lord God of hosts** (6:3). He did not say "Lords" or "Gods" but **Lord God**. In that way he indicated that the one who was three times called **Holy** was one God. And St. Paul, to show forth the work of the Holy Trinity, declares: *From him and through him and in him are all things* (Rom 11:36). And to indicate the unity of the Trinity he immediately adds: *To him be glory forever.* By not saying "to them," but *to him*, he makes clear that there is one God in three persons. The three phrases are spoken of the one God.

(19) Pseudo-Dionysius the Areopagite

The first rank of heavenly beings circles in immediate proximity to God (6:2).[9] Simply and ceaselessly this rank dances around an eternal knowledge of him. It is forever and totally thus, as befits angelic beings. In a pure vision it can not only look upon a host of blessed contemplations but it can also be enlightened in simple and direct beams. It is filled with divine nourishment that is abundant, because it comes from the original yet single stream, because the nourishing gifts of God bring oneness in a unity without diversity.

This first group is particularly worthy of communing with God and of sharing in

---

9. Dionysius is thinking of the seraphim in Isaiah 6.

his work. It imitates, as far as possible, the beauty of God's condition and activity. Knowing many divine things in so superior a fashion, it can have a proper share of the divine knowledge and understanding. The mystical knowledge of God has transmitted to the men of earth those hymns sung by the first ranks of the angels whose gloriously transcendent enlightenment is revealed in them. Some of these hymns, if one may use sensible images, are like the *sound of many waters* (Ezek 1:24; Rev 14:2) as they proclaim: *Blessed be the glory of the Lord from his place* (Ezek 3:12 LXX). Others thunder out that famous and venerable song acclaiming God: **Holy, holy, holy is the Lord of hosts. The whole earth is full of his glory.**

(20) Martyrius

The creation is full of the splendor of God's glory. The **seraphs** of fire **stand** (6:2) there to honor him, the ranks of many-eyed *cherubim* (Ezek 10:12) escort his majestic Being, the hands of spiritual powers dash around ministering to him, the thrones of angels fly hither and thither with their wings, and all the orders of spiritual beings serve his Being in awe, crying **Holy** in trembling and love, **as they cover their faces** (6:2) with their wings at the splendor of his great and fearful radiance, ceaselessly crying out to one another the threefold sanctification of his exalted glory, saying **Holy, holy, holy, Lord Almighty**, with whose glories both heaven and **earth are full** (6:3).

Let us therefore tremble at the magnitude of the sight of the Ineffable One, and at the sound which ceaselessly utters the praise of the Hidden Being. And let us be filled with awe and trembling, falling on our faces in fear before him. Let us recognize our earth-born nature, let us be aware of the base character of the dust we are made from, let us join the prophet in saying, with feeling and with a penitent heart, **Woe is our state of confusion** (6:5); let us lay bare the foulness of our sins quite openly, accusing ourselves forcefully — just as it is said: *The just man condemns himself at the very beginning of his words* (Prov 18:17 LXX).

This is what we should do at the commencement of our prayer, stating before God that we are not worthy to stand in his presence in our wretched state; and that, because our blind hearts have lost their sight through concentrating on what is below, dwelling in the darkness of the earth, we are unable to gaze on the great sight of him whose glory blinds the vision of the angels of light. Again, how are we able to speak with **unclean lips** (6:5) in the presence of his great holiness?

6:5
Woe is me . . . for I am a man of unclean lips.

(21) Maximus the Confessor

When through love the mind is ravished by the knowledge of God and stretches itself beyond things that have been made, it glimpses the transcendence and otherness of God.

Isaiah 6

Then, according to the divine Isaiah, it is astonished as it senses its own lowliness and utters with conviction the words of the prophet: **Woe is me, for I am stricken in heart. For I am a man with unclean lips, and I dwell in the midst of a people of unclean lips, and I have seen with my eyes the King, the Lord of hosts** (6:5).

(22) John Cassian

All those who are holy are struck with compunction because of the weakness of their constitution, and with daily sighs they scrutinize their different thoughts and the hidden and secret places of their conscience, humbly crying out, *Enter not into judgment with your servant, for no man living is righteous before thee* (Ps 143:2). And also: *Who will boast of having a chaste heart? Or who will have confidence that he is pure from sin?* (Prov 20:9). And again: *There is no one who is righteous upon the earth, who does what is good and does not sin* (cf. Pss 14:3; 53:3; Jer 5:1; Rom 3:10). And also: *Who understands his sins?* (Ps 19:12).

Those who are holy consider the righteousness of human beings as weak and imperfect and constantly in need of God's mercy. Indeed, one of God's prophets, whose iniquities and sins God cleansed with the fiery coal of his word that came from the altar, said, after contemplating God in wondrous fashion, and after seeing the lofty seraphim and a revelation of the heavenly mysteries: **Woe is me, for I am a man of unclean lips, and I dwell in the midst of a people with unclean lips.** In my estimation he would not have felt the uncleanness of his lips if he had not deserved to know the true and integral purity of perfection, thanks to his having contemplated God. Upon seeing God he immediately recognized an uncleanness in himself that was hidden to him previously. For when he says, **Woe is me, for I am a man of unclean lips,** he shows by what follows, **and I dwell in the midst of a people with unclean lips,** that he was speaking of his own lips and not of the people's uncleanness.

(23) Anaphora of the East Syrian Liturgy

Celebrant: Worthy of praise from every mouth, of confession from every tongue, and of worship and exaltation from every creature is the adorable and glorious name of the blessed Trinity, Father, Son, and the Holy Spirit, You who created the world by your grace and its inhabitants by your mercy, and bestowed great grace on mortal men. O my Lord, thousands of those on high bow down and worship your majesty. Myriads upon myriads of holy angels, a host of spiritual ministers of fire and spirit glorify your name; and with the holy cherubim and the spiritual seraphim they offer worship to your Sovereignty.

The celebrant kisses the altar, then, lifting up his hands, says in a loud voice:

Crying out and praising without ceasing, and proclaiming to one another and saying:

Response: Holy, holy, holy, Lord God Almighty. Heaven and earth are full of his praises (6:3). Hosanna in the highest! Hosanna to the son of David! Blessed is he who came and is to come in the name of the Lord! Hosanna in the highest! (Matt 21:9).

Meanwhile, the celebrant says the following prayer in a low voice, kissing the altar.

Celebrant: Holy are you, God; you alone are the Father of truth from whom is all fatherhood in heaven and on earth. Holy are you, Eternal Son, through whom all things were made. Holy are you, Holy Spirit, the Being by whom all things are sanctified.

Celebrant (in low voice): Woe to me, for I am dismayed because **I am a man of unclean lips and dwell in the midst of a people of unclean lips** (6:5), and my eyes **have seen the King, the Lord of hosts!** (6:5). How dreadful is this place, for this day I have seen the Lord face to face and this is none other than the house of God, and now, O Lord, let your grace be upon us, and purify our uncleanness and sanctify our lips and mingle, O my Lord, the voices of our feebleness with the hallowing of the seraphim and of archangels. Glory be to your mercies, you who have associated the earthly with spiritual beings.

6:6
A burning coal which he had taken with tongs from the altar

(24) Theodore of Mopsuestia

There were **live coals** on the **altar** (6:6): a figure of the Sacrament that was to be given to us. A piece of coal is at first black and cold, but when it is brought to the fire it becomes luminous and hot. The food of the holy Sacrament was going to be similar to this: at first it is laid upon the altar as common bread and wine mixed with water. But by the coming of the Holy Spirit it is transformed into body and blood, and thus it is changed into the power of a spiritual and immortal nourishment. . . . As the seraph drew nigh, purified, and forgave all the sins of the prophet, so also we ought to believe that by participation in the holy Sacrament our trespasses will be completely blotted out if we repent and are grieved and afflicted in our mind for our sins.

(25) Cyril of Alexandria

One of the seraphim is sent to Isaiah with **a burning coal** which he took from the **altar with tongs** (6:6). This is clearly a symbol of Christ, who, on our behalf, offered himself up to God the Father as a pure and unblemished spiritual sacrifice with a most pleasing fragrance. In the same way Christ is received from the altar.[10] We must, however, explain why Christ is like a **burning coal**. It is customary in Holy Scripture for the divine nature to be likened to fire. God appeared in this way to the people of Israel as they *stood before the Lord at Horeb,* which is Mount Sinai (Deut 4:10-12). Similarly, when Moses was watching his sheep in the wilderness, God appeared to him in the form of a fire in a bramble bush and spoke with him (Exod 3:1-6).

Although coal is wood by nature, when it is filled through and through with fire it contains fire's power and energy. I am convinced that one must view our Lord Jesus

---

10. In the Eucharist.

Isaiah 6

Christ in the same way, for *the Word became flesh and dwelt among us* (John 1:14). Although at the time of his sojourn he appeared on earth as a human being like us, the entire *fullness of the Godhead dwelt in him* (Col 1:19) because of the union. In this way, his human flesh was seen to have powers suited only to God. Thus, he could touch the bier and raise up the dead son of the widow (Luke 7:14). Likewise, after spitting in the clay, he put the mixture in the eyes of a blind man and restored his sight (John 9:6). One then might well liken the **burning coal** to Emmanuel, who, if he were placed on our lips, would wholly remove all our sins and *cleanse us from all unrighteousness* (1 John 1:9).

Yet how could Christ be placed on our lips? This happens whenever we confess our faith in him. This is why Paul wrote: *The word is near you, on your lips and in your heart (that is, the word of faith that we preach); because, if you confess with your lips that Jesus is Lord and believe in your heart that God raised him from the dead, you will be saved. For man believes with his heart and so is justified, and he confesses with his lips and so is saved* (Rom 10:8-10). Let God then be on our lips like a **glowing coal** that burns away the rubbish of our sins, purges the filth of our unrighteousness, and sets us on fire with the Spirit. You will grasp the meaning of this passage quite nicely if you see picking up the **burning coal with tongs** as faith and knowledge of him. Moreover, we bring Christ to ourselves with **tongs** when we receive the testimonies of the law and the oracles of the prophets. For by appealing to the testimonies of the law and the prophets, the apostles persuade those who hear them, and bring, as it were, a **burning coal** to their lips so that they might confess faith in Christ.

(26) Divine Liturgy of the Syro-Malakar Rite

[*While communicating the priest says*]: The propitiatory **live coal** (6:6) of the body and blood of Christ our God is given to me, a weak and sinful servant, for the pardon of offenses and the forgiveness of sins in both worlds forever. Amen.

[*When he communicates the people he says*]: The propitiatory **live coal** of the body and blood of Christ our God is given to the true believer for the pardon of offenses and the forgiveness of sins forever.

(27) Ephrem the Syrian

> The prophetess Anna embraced him
> And put her mouth to his lips.
> The Spirit rested on her lips, as on Isaiah's;
> His mouth was silent, but the **coal of fire** (6:6)
> Opened up his mouth by touching his lips.
> Anna's mouth too became fervent with the Spirit
> From his mouth,
> And she sang to him: "O royal Son, O lowly Son,
> You listen in stillness, You see, but are hidden,

You know but are unknown;
O God and Man, praise to Your name."

*   *   *

The seraph could not touch the **coal of fire** with his fingers, and the **coal** merely touched Isaiah's mouth; the seraph did not hold it, Isaiah did not consume it, but our Lord has allowed us to do both.[11]

6:9-10
And he said, "Go and say to this people: 'You will listen by listening, but you will not understand; and looking you will look, but you will not perceive.' For this people's heart has grown fat, and with their ears they have heard heavily, and they have shut their eyes, so that they might not see with their eyes, and hear with their ears, and understand with their heart, and turn — and I would heal them."

(28) Jerome

When Luke quotes this passage in the Acts of the Apostles, he uses the Septuagint version: *So, as they disagreed among themselves, they* — referring here to the Jews — *departed after Paul had made one statement: "The Holy Spirit was right in saying to your fathers through Isaiah the prophet:*

'Go to this people, and say,
"You shall indeed hear but never understand,
and you shall indeed see but never perceive."
For this people's heart has grown dull,
and their ears are heavy of hearing,
and their eyes they have closed;
lest they should perceive with their eyes,
and hear with their ears,
and understand with their heart,
and turn for me to heal them.'" (Acts 28:25-27, citing Isa 6:9-10)

The apostle Paul himself says in the next verse at what time this prophecy would be fulfilled: *Let it be known to you then that this salvation of God has been sent to the Gentiles; they will listen* (Acts 28:28). Therefore, we also read in Acts that when the Jews refused to believe, Paul and Barnabas said: *It was necessary that the word of God be spoken first to*

---

11. Ephrem is referring to the consecrated bread and wine in the Eucharist.

Isaiah 6

you. Since you thrust it from you, and judge yourselves unworthy of eternal life, behold, we turn to the Gentiles. For so the Lord has commanded us, saying, "I have set you to be a light to the Gentiles, that you may bring salvation to the uttermost ends of the earth" (Acts 13:46-47, citing Isa 49:6).

Therefore the interpretation of the Septuagint's reading is clear: at God's command the prophet Isaiah simply predicted what the people would do. The Hebrew, however, poses a difficult problem in the way that God directly commands the people **to hear with their hearing, and not understand, and seeing, to see, but not perceive**. And after the prophet is induced to speak and to beseech the Lord, God also instructs,

> **"Make the heart of this people blind,**[12]
> **and their ears heavy,**
> **and shut their eyes,**
> **lest they see with their eyes,**
> **and hear with their ears,**
> **and understand with their hearts,**
> **and turn and be healed."** (6:10)

We cannot appeal to the Septuagint version to avoid the apparent blasphemy in the Hebrew (**Hear and hear, but do not understand; see and see, but do not perceive** [6:9]), because we will discover testimonies of this type even in the Septuagint, for instance, that which is said in the book of Exodus to Pharaoh: *For this reason I have stirred you up, so that I might show my power in you* (Exod 9:16); but if he himself stirred Pharaoh up, he also hardened his heart so that he would not believe. This is spoken of others as well: *God gave them a spirit of stupefaction, eyes that they might not see, and ears that they might not hear* (Isa 29:10, as quoted in Rom 11:8); and in the Psalms, *Let their table become a snare and a trap, a pitfall and a retribution for them; let their eyes be darkened so that they cannot see, and bend their backs forever* (Ps 68:23-24 LXX, as quoted in Rom 11:9-10). The point is that the difficulty seems to lie not with those who do not see but with the one who gave them eyes so *that* they could not see.

Therefore, quite apart from this prophecy which we are now trying to interpret, the same problem exists in other passages; either they will be solved along with this one, or all alike will remain unsolved. The blessed apostle Paul expounds this problem more fully in his letter to the Romans. Because he pursues it through almost the whole letter, it is hubris to think that one can understand it in a brief discussion. Near the end he says, *God has consigned all men to disobedience, that he may have mercy upon all* (Rom 11:32). Marveling at the Lord's mysteries, he exclaims, *O the depth of the riches and wisdom and knowledge of God! How unsearchable are his judgments and how inscrutable his ways!* (Rom 11:33). And again, considering the unbelief of the Jews, he says, *Have they stumbled so as to fall? By no means! But through their trespass salvation has come to the Gentiles, so as to make Israel*

---

12. Jerome renders the verb meaning "to make fat" or "to make dull" as "make blind," influenced perhaps by the occurrence of "blinded" in the version of Isa 6:10 quoted in John 12:40: "He has blinded their hearts."

jealous (Rom 11:11). And a little later: *For if their rejection means the reconciliation of the world, what will their acceptance mean but life from the dead?* (Rom 11:15). And again: *Lest you be wise in your own conceits, I want you to understand this mystery, brethren: a hardening has come upon part of Israel, until the full number of the Gentiles come in, and so all Israel will be saved* (Rom 11:25-26). And just after that: *As regards the gospel they are enemies for your sake; but as regards election they are beloved for the sake of their forefathers. For the gifts and the call of God are irrevocable. Just as you were once disobedient to God but now have received mercy because of their disobedience, so they have now been disobedient in order that by the mercy shown to you they also may receive mercy. For God has consigned all men to disobedience, that he may have mercy upon all* (Rom 11:28-32).

Therefore, it is not the cruelty of God but his mercy, that one people should perish so that all might be saved — for part of the Jews not to see, so that the whole world might perceive. In the Gospel the Lord himself gives a symbolic interpretation to the miracle of the man born blind who had recovered his sight: *For judgment I came into this world, that those who do not see may see, and that those who see may become blind* (John 9:39). And in another text Simeon predicts, *Behold, this child is set for the fall and rising of many* (Luke 2:34). And so when they do not see, we see; when they fall, we rise. The prophet, who realized this, was saying something like this: "O Lord, you command me to speak to the Jewish people, so that they may hear and not understand the Savior, and they may see him and not perceive. If you want your command to be fulfilled and the whole world saved, which I too desire to happen, harden the heart of this people and cover their ears and close their eyes, lest they understand, lest they hear, lest they see. For if they shall see and be converted, and understand and be healed, the whole world will not receive healing." From this we conclude that if anyone repents he can be saved, no matter how grievous the sin. This too must be explained. For the greatness of the crime they have been judged unworthy of repentance, as the Lord himself cried over Jerusalem: *How often would I have gathered your children together as a hen gathers her brood under wings, and you would not!* (Matt 23:37).

(29) John Chrysostom

This is why I speak to them in parables, says Jesus, *because* **seeing they do not see** (Matt 13:13).

It was necessary, he says, to open their eyes because they did not see. Now if the disability was of a physical order, it was necessary to open their eyes. But since the disability was voluntary and self-initiated, he did not just say, "They do not see" but **seeing they do not see**, so that the disability is their own wicked doing. For they saw the demons being cast out and said, *It is by Beelzebul, the prince of demons, that he casts out demons* (Matt 12:24). They heard him as he led them toward God and demonstrated that he was in complete harmony with God, yet they argue, "He is not from God." Since they declared the opposite of what they saw and heard, therefore, he says, "I will deprive them of their hearing." For now it profits them nothing, but only makes the verdict worse. They didn't simply disbelieve; they actually framed an accusation against him and set traps. For his part, he does not speak in this way, because he does not want to make a mean-spirited accusation. So initially he did not speak with them in parables but with complete transparency; but after they became corrupted, he spoke from that time on in parables. Then, to keep them from thinking his words a bald accusation and saying, "Because he is our enemy, he lays this charge against us and accuses us," Jesus invokes the prophet, who holds the same opinion as his: *With them is indeed fulfilled the prophecy of Isaiah which says,* **You shall indeed hear but never understand, and you shall indeed see but never perceive**" (Matt 13:14). Do you see how precisely the prophet expresses his reproach? For he too does not say, "You do not see," but **You will see and you will not understand**; nor does he say, "You will not hear," but that **You will hear and not perceive**. Consequently, they first deprive themselves of sight and hearing, by plugging their ears, shutting their eyes, and hardening their hearts. For they didn't just "not hear," but **they heard heavily**; they did this, God says, **lest they should turn and I should heal them**, expressing their impassioned evil and enthusiastic perversity.

God speaks thus to attract and provoke them, by showing that if they converted he would heal them, much as if one were to say, "He did not want to see me, for which I am grateful; for if I had been found worthy of this response, I would have immediately given in to him." This shows how he might have been reconciled — hence the present statement, **lest they should turn, and I should heal them**. It demonstrates that they were *capable* of turning and, after repenting, of being saved. Finally, it shows that he did everything for the sake of their salvation, not for his own glory. If he hadn't wanted any of them to be saved, all he had to do was to remain silent rather than to speak in parables, by which means he now rouses them in foreshadowing the future. *For God does not desire the death of the sinner, but that he should turn and live* (Ezek 18:23).

In short: sin is not a result of nature nor is it by necessity nor by coercion. Listen to what he says to the apostles: *But blessed are your eyes, for they see, and your ears, for they hear* (Matt 13:16), by which he means not literal sight or hearing, but that which comes from the understanding. For his followers too were Jews and had been raised in the same circumstances; nevertheless, they did not ignore the prophecy, because their will and their judgment were well rooted in what was good.

(30) Augustine of Hippo

St. Paul says, *So neither he who plants nor he who waters is anything, but only God who gives the growth* (1 Cor 3:7). Some people, therefore, mutter among themselves, and when they have an opportunity say so out loud, wondering what the Jews did or how it was their fault, that it should become necessary *that the word spoken by the prophet Isaiah might be fulfilled, "Oh Lord, who has believed our report, and to whom has the arm of the Lord been revealed?"* (John 12:38, citing Isa 53:1).

To such people we reply as follows: The Lord, knowing the future, foretold the unbelief of the Jews through the word of the prophet — he *predicted* it, he did not *do* it. God does not force anyone to sin, even though he already knows men's future sins. The sins he foreknows are theirs, not his — no one else's but theirs. . . .

But the words that follow in the Gospel go further and pose a deeper question. For the Gospel of John goes on, *Therefore they could not believe. For Isaiah again said,* **He has blinded their eyes and hardened their heart, lest they should see with their eyes and perceive with their heart, and turn for me to heal them** (John 12:39-40, citing Isa 6:10). So we hear this sort of objection: "If they were unable to believe, what sin is it for a man not to do what he can't do? But if they did commit sin by not believing, therefore they were able to believe and did not. If, then, they were able, why does the Gospel say, *Therefore they could not believe. For Isaiah again said,* **He has blinded their eyes and hardened their heart**, so that, what is more serious, the cause of their unbelief is passed back to God, seeing that **He has blinded their eyes and hardened their heart**? This is said, mind you, not of the devil but of *God,* as the prophetic writing itself bears witness. For if we were to think that this had been said of the devil, that **He has blinded their eyes and hardened their heart**, we would have to explain how to show that the culpability of not believing lay with those of whom it is said, *they could not believe.* In that case, what will we answer regarding another testimony of the same prophet that the apostle Paul quotes, saying, *Israel failed to obtain what it sought. The elect obtained it, but the rest were blinded, as it is written,* **God gave them a spirit of stupor, eyes that they should not see and ears that they should not hear, down to this very day** (Rom 11:7).

So that is how the objection might run. You have heard it, brothers, and surely you see how serious it is. I will answer to the best of my ability. The Evangelist says, *They could not believe* (John 12:39) because this the prophet Isaiah did foretell; but the prophet foretold it because God foreknew that it would happen. If I am asked *why* they were not able, I answer briefly that they didn't want to: God foresaw their ill will, and he from whom the future cannot be hidden foretold it through the prophet.

But, you say, the prophet speaks of another cause, not of their willing. What cause does the prophet say? That **God gave them a spirit of stupor, eyes that should not see and ears that should not hear, and he has blinded their eyes and hardened their heart.**[13] I answer that their will deserved this. The way that God blinds and hardens is by withdrawing and by not assisting. And he can do this by a hidden judgment, but not by one that is unjust. The piety of believers has to keep this principle firm and uncompromised, just as the apostle Paul managed to do when facing exactly the same problem: *What then shall we say? Is there injustice on God's part? By no means* (Rom 9:14). If it is unthinkable that there be injustice on God's part, two things follow: when he gives his assistance, he acts mercifully; but when he does not give his assistance, he acts justly. For he always acts with considered judgment and not with rashness. Furthermore, if the judgments of the saints are just, how much more the judgments of the God who makes the saints holy and who justifies them? His judgments, therefore, are just but hidden.

And so when questions arise as to why one person is treated one way and another person a different way; why one person shall be blinded when God withdraws, and another shall be enlightened when God grants his assistance; let us not usurp the judgment of so great a Judge, but with the apostle cry out in fear and trembling, *O the depths of the*

---

13. Here Augustine runs together the form in which Isa 6:10 is quoted by Paul in Rom 11:7, and the form in which it is quoted in John 12:40.

riches and wisdom and knowledge of God! How unsearchable are his judgments and how inscrutable his ways! (Rom 11:33). As it is said by the psalmist, *Thy judgments are like the great deep* (Ps 36:6).

(31) Theodoret of Cyrus

The prophet predicts that the Jews will reject the Lord when he appears. Though they had **heard** the sacred oracles, they had not **listened** to them. And even though they **saw** many miracles, they did not want to **understand**. That is why in the holy gospels the Lord predicts: *For judgment I came into this world, that those who do not see may see, and that those who see may become blind* (John 9:39). In fact those who were physically blind saw him with the eyes of the soul, but those whose physical eyes were healthy were spiritually blind. Not only were their eyes shut, but also their ears were plugged up. For this reason the Lord urged: *He who has ears to hear, let him hear* (Matt 11:15).

Moreover, the prophet — or rather the God of the prophet — teaches in the passage that follows that they had deliberately allowed themselves to become afflicted with such maladies. Note what he says next: **For this people's heart has grown fat, and their ears have become hard of hearing, and they have shut their eyes, so that they might not see with their eyes, and hear with their ears, and understand with their heart, and turn — and I would heal them** (6:10).

These maladies are not the work of nature but of deliberate choice. They were not blind by nature, but they themselves shut their eyes. Offended by the divine oracles, they fought, as it were, against themselves and spurned the salvation that comes from sight and hearing and their offspring, repentance.

Isaiah 7

1And it happened in the days of Achaz son of Ioatham the son of Ozias, king of Ioudas, that King Raasson of Aram and King Phakee son of Romelias of Israel went up against Ierousalem to wage war against it, but could not besiege it. 2And it was reported to the house of Dauid, saying, "Aram has made an agreement with Ephraim." And his soul and the soul of his people were agitated as when a tree in the forest is shaken by the wind.

3Then the Lord said to Esaias, Go out to meet Achaz, you and the one who is left, your son Iasoub, at the pool on the upper road to the Fuller's Field. 4And you will say to him, Take care to be quiet and do not fear, nor let your soul be feeble because of these two logs of smoking firebrands, for when my fierce anger comes, I will heal again. 5And as for the son of Aram and the son of Romelias: Because they have plotted an evil counsel concerning you, saying, 6We will go up to Judea and, after talking with them, let us turn them toward us; and we will make the son of Tabeel king over it; 7this is what the Lord Sabaoth says:

> This counsel shall not remain,
>   nor shall it come to pass.
> 8 But the head of Aram is Damascus,
>   and the head of Damascus is Raasson,
> but yet within sixty-five years
>   the kingdom of Ephraim will cease from being a people.
> 9 And the head of Ephraim is Somoron,
>   and the head of Somoron is the son of Romelias.
> And if you do not believe,
>   neither shall you understand.

10And the Lord spoke further to Achaz, saying, 11Ask for yourself a sign of the Lord your God, in depth or in height. 12But Achaz said, I will not ask, nor will I put the Lord to the test. 13Then he said: "Hear now, O house of Dauid! Is it a small thing for you to provoke a fight with mortals? How then do you provoke a fight with the Lord?

14Therefore the Lord himself will give you a sign. Look, the virgin shall be with child and bear a son, and you shall name him Emmanouel. 15He shall eat butter and honey; before he knows or prefers evil things, he shall choose what is good. 16For before the child knows good or bad, he defies evil to choose what is good, and the land that you fear from before the two kings will be abandoned. 17But God will bring on you and on your people and on your ancestral house such days as have not yet come since the day that he took Ephraim away from Ioudas — the king of the Assyrians."

18And it shall be on that day that the Lord will whistle for the flies that rule part of the river of Egypt, and for the bee that is in the country of the Assyrians. 19And they will all come and rest in the ravines of the country, and in the clefts of the rocks, and into the caves, and into every crevice, and on every tree.

20On that day the Lord will shave with the great and drunken razor — which is beyond the river of the king of the Assyrians — the head and the hair of the feet, and he will cut off the beard.

21And it shall be on that day that a person will nourish a young cow of the cattle and two sheep, 22and it shall be because of the abundance of milk that they give, everyone that is left on the land will eat butter and honey.

23And it shall be on that day that every place where there used to be a thousand vines, worth a thousand shekels, will become barren ground and thorn. 24With dart and arrow they will enter there, for all the land will be barren ground and thorn; 25and every hill being plowed will be plowed, and fear will not come there; for it will be turned from the barren ground and thorn to a place where a sheep can feed and an ox can tread.

Chapter 7 is largely historical and deals with the Syro-Ephraimite War (734-733 B.C.). Accordingly the ancient commentators treat the historical circumstances that are the background for the chapter, drawing in the main on material from the historical books, for example, 2 Kgs 16:1-20. They also discuss the abominations of King Ahaz, one of the most reprehensible of Judah's kings. Apparently some commentators had tried to find an allegorical meaning in the historical events, but Cyril observes that if one considers the literal sense "trivial," one will not be able to understand what is written in passages such as this. The "spiritual sense," he writes, is beautiful, but when Holy Scripture presents historical material it is appropriate for the interpreter to consider its use and significance.

This chapter also has the verse, **If you do not believe, you will not understand** *(7:9), that has been so important in Western theological thought. On the basis of the Hebrew it is usually translated,* **If you do not stand firm in faith, you shall not stand at all.** *But the Septuagint version, and the Latin based on it, read the verse as* **If you do not believe, you will not understand**, *and in this form it passed into Christian tradition. The passage is cited often by Augustine, beginning as early as 387,[1] and was taken to mean that the understanding of the mysteries*

---

1. In his treatise *On Free Will* 1.2 and 2.2.

of God begins with faith. From this came the phrase fides quaerens intellectum, *faith seeking understanding.*

But this chapter is especially precious because it includes the famous passage on the virgin birth of Christ: **Look, a virgin shall conceive and bear a son, and you shall name him Emmanuel** (7:14). *Following the Gospel of Matthew, where this verse is cited (Matt 1:23), the church fathers break off the historical discussion to discuss the virgin birth, the Incarnation, and the person of Christ.*

In antiquity, as in modern times, the translation of the Hebrew term ʿalmah *was disputed. The Septuagint translated it "virgin," but Jewish translators, for example, Aquila, Symmachus, and Theodotion, translated it "young woman." Christian interpreters defended the translation "virgin" but also argued that the term "young woman" had the same sense. Ambrose makes the charming comment that Mary had read the passage in Isaiah and hence was ready to believe the angel Gabriel's announcement that a virgin would give birth to a son.*

(1) Gospel of Matthew

Now the birth of Jesus Christ took place in this way. When his mother Mary had been betrothed to Joseph, before they came together she was found to be with child of the Holy Spirit; and her husband Joseph, being a just man and unwilling to put her to shame, resolved to divorce her quietly. But as he considered this, behold an angel of the Lord appeared to him in a dream, saying, "Joseph, son of David, do not fear to take Mary your wife, for that which is conceived in her is of the Holy Spirit; she will bear a son, and you shall call his name Jesus, for he will save his people from their sins." All this took place to fulfill what the Lord had spoken by the prophet: **Behold, a virgin shall conceive and bear a son, and his name shall be called Emmanuel** (7:14) (which means, God with us). When Joseph woke from sleep, he did as the angel of the Lord commanded him; he took his wife, but knew her not until she had borne a son; and he called his name Jesus.

(2) John Chrysostom

As I have said on many occasions and now say again, the ancient prophecies were given not only that the Jews could learn about what was to come, but also, being instructed, to profit from this knowledge: through fear of imminent dangers they became wiser and through promises of good things to come they became more zealous in pursuit of the virtuous life. In each case they learned of God's power and his solicitude for them. . . .

If we are to understand what the passage before us says, we must pay close attention to the historical details. **In the days of Ahaz son of Jotham son of Uzziah, king of Judah, King Rezin of Aram [Syria] and King Pekah son of Remaliah of Israel went up against Jerusalem to wage war against it, but could not besiege it. It was reported to the house of David, saying, "Aram [Syria] has made an agreement with Ephraim"** (7:1-2).

These words are a historical account of what took place. But if one examines the text carefully and thoughtfully, there is much to learn from it about the wisdom of God and his care for the Jewish people. Neither does God stop the war at the beginning, nor does he allow the enemy to subdue the city. He allows the enemy to threaten with words, but he delays their attack. That is, he wishes to arouse the Jews and awaken them from their torpor and at the same time demonstrate his power. Even when danger is at hand, God is able to keep them safe, as though they were free of their difficulties. There are many examples of this in the Scriptures: the furnace in Babylon (Daniel 3), the den of lions (Daniel 6), and others. In this case the enemy was ready to attack the city, but after approaching the walls and alarming the inhabitants, was unable to take advantage of the situation. . . .

Again the Lord spoke to Ahaz, saying, "Ask for yourself a sign of the Lord your God, in the depth or in the height." But Ahaz said, "I will not ask, nor will I put the Lord to the test." Then Isaiah said: "Hear now, O house of David! Is it a small thing for you to provoke a fight with mortals? How then do you provoke a fight with the Lord? Therefore the Lord himself will give you a sign. Look, the virgin shall be with child and bear a son, and you shall name him Emmanuel" (Isa 7:10-14). Great is the Lord's condescension and great the king's folly. The king should have heeded the prophet and not doubted what he said. . . .

When Isaiah says, **Ask for yourself a sign**, the king, pretending to be a devout believer, responds, **I will not ask, I will not tempt the Lord**. However, Isaiah abruptly cuts him off. Faced with such hypocrisy, he sharpens his reproach. Considering the king unworthy of a reply, he turns instead to the people: **Hear now, O house of David! Is it a small thing for you to provoke a fight with mortals?** This statement is unclear and needs to be examined carefully. It seems to mean: "Do you think these are only my words? Do you think it is only I who say this? It is wrong to doubt human beings without cause; how much more to disbelieve God!" Disputing with God is a form of unbelief, a grave offense. . . .

Although Isaiah was unable to convince the king to ask for a sign, he did not give up. After he had corrected the king and shown that he was not taken in by his deceitful ways, he discloses a mysterious prophecy concerning the salvation of the world and the restoration of all things. The sign, he holds, was not given to Ahaz but to the Jewish people as a whole. At first it was offered to him, but when Ahaz proved himself unworthy, he addressed it to all the people. Therefore he says that he will give the sign **to you** in the plural, not **to you** in the singular. In other words, he is speaking to the house of David. There the sign will break forth. What, then, is the sign?

Look, the virgin shall be with child and bear a son, and you shall name him Emmanuel (7:14). As I have said, note that the sign was not given to Ahaz. This is not a matter of conjecture, for the prophet had reproached and accused him, saying: **Is it a small thing for you to provoke a fight with mortals? Therefore the Lord himself will give you** [plural] **a sign. Look, the virgin will be with child**. Now if she were not a virgin, it would hardly be a sign. A sign must be different from, indeed transcend, the ordinary workings of nature. It must be so strange and remarkable that those who see and hear it recognize its unique character. **Sign** means that it is significant. If it occurs in the ordinary course of things it could not be a sign. If he had said that a woman was to bear a child in the normal way, something that happens every day, why would he call that a sign? This is why he did not say, **Look, a virgin**, but **Look, the virgin**. By using the definite article he indicates to us that this is something noteworthy and unique....

In speaking of the birth he also tells us the name of the one who is to be born — not the name to be given to him, but a name appropriate to the things that would happen. In the same way the prophet calls Jerusalem the *city of righteousness* (Isa 1:26) although it was never actually named the city of righteousness. It was given this name because of what happened there.... In the same way the name **Emmanuel** is given to Christ because of what he would do. When he sojourned among us and became known on earth, God was most definitely among us and zealous for our welfare. Christ was neither an angel nor an archangel; it was the Lord himself who came among us to transform our lives. He spoke with prostitutes, ate with tax collectors, visited the homes of sinners, gave thieves boldness to speak up, attracted wise men, and went about everywhere doing good and uniting human nature to himself.

Isaiah predicts all these things when he announces the birth of Christ and the unspeakable and boundless good that will come from his nativity. When God is with his people, fear and trembling give way to confidence. And that is what has happened. The ancient and intractable evils were destroyed, the sentence on the whole race was removed, the tendons of sin were severed, the devil's tyranny was broken, paradise once closed to all was opened to a murderer and thief (Luke 23:42-43), the vault of heaven was thrown open, human beings had fellowship with angels, our nature was lifted up to the royal throne, the prison of Hades was emptied, and death, deprived of its power, became death in name only. Choirs of martyrs and women blunted the stings of Hades. Foreseeing all this, Isaiah leaped and danced, and with one word **Emmanuel**, God with us, he anticipated what was to come....

He shall eat butter and honey; before he knows or prefers evil things, he shall choose what is good. For before the child knows good or bad, he will reject evil to choose what is good (7:15-16). The eating of butter and honey has to do with Christ's humanity, not his divinity. God did not simply fashion a man to dwell in; he was conceived as a human being and went through the nine-month term, was born and kept in diapers and nursed by his mother — all this should shut the mouths of those who deny that he was a human being. For this reason the prophet who sees all this not only speaks of his birth and his remarkable infancy, but also says that as an infant he took the same kind of food as other children. There was nothing exceptional about it.

In some ways he was like us, in others not. To be born of a woman is commonplace, to be born of a virgin extraordinary. To take nourishment according to the law of nature like everyone else is usual, but to become a temple in which evil cannot dwell and to do no wrong is uncommon and unique and pertained to no one else. For this reason the prophet emphasizes both aspects of his person. Unlike us, Christ did not become good after doing evil; he was wholly virtuous from the beginning. As he himself said: *Which of you convicts me of sin?* (John 8:46) and *the ruler of the world is coming, and he has no power over me* (John 14:30).

Isaiah himself speaks of these things later in the book: *He committed no sin, and there was no deceit in his mouth* (53:9). Here he says something similar, namely, that before Christ knows or chooses evil — that is, from infancy, the age of innocence — he will

Isaiah 7

live virtuously and shun evil. **For before the child knows good or bad, he will reject evil to choose what is good** (7:16). These are matters of great moment, and he confirms what he says by repeating it. First he says, **before he knows or prefers evil, he shall choose what is good**, and then he adds, **Before the child knows good or bad, he will reject evil to choose what is good**.

Such an extraordinary thing could only be said of Christ. Paul often speaks of him in this way, and when John saw Christ he exclaimed, *Behold, the Lamb of God, who takes away the sin of the world!* (John 1:29). How much more should the one who takes away others' sins be himself without sin. Paul, as I have indicated, never wearies of proclaiming this. Christ had to die so that no unbeliever would think he could atone for his own sin. Paul mentions Christ's sinlessness in order to show that his death atones for our sins. This is why he said: *Christ being raised from the dead will never die again.... The death he died he died to sin* (Rom 6:9-10). Christ died not because of his own sin, but because of the transgression common to all. If it was not because he was subject to death that he died, as has been shown, it is certain that he will not die again.

7:9
If you do not believe, you shall not understand.

(3) Augustine of Hippo

The sacred and hidden mysteries of the kingdom of God require people first to believe so they become people who understand. Faith, you see, is a step toward understanding; understanding is the well-deserved reward of faith. The prophet says this plainly enough to all those who impatiently put the cart before the horse by looking for understanding and ignoring the need for faith. He states, **Unless you believe, you shall not understand**. Faith too, of course, has a kind of light of its own in the Scriptures: in the readings from the prophets, from the gospel, from the apostle. I mean, all those texts that are chanted to us at the appropriate time are lights in a dark place, to keep us going until the day. The apostle Peter says, *We have the prophetic word, to which you do well to pay attention, as to a light in a dark place, until the day dawns and the morning star rises in your hearts* (2 Pet 1:19).

(4) Augustine of Hippo

Catholic teaching holds that the Christian mind must first be nourished in simple faith that it might become capable of understanding sublime and eternal things. Thus the prophet asserts, **Unless you believe, you shall not understand**. It is precisely through such simple faith that we believe, before we can attain to the height of the knowledge of the love of Christ, so as to be filled with all the fullness of God.

(5) Augustine of Hippo

In your letter in which you ask that I discuss the question of the Trinity, you say that you had determined for yourself that "the truth about things divine must be attained more by faith than by reason. For," you continue, "if the faith of the holy Church were grasped by reasoned argumentation and not by pious belief, no one except philosophers and professors would possess happiness. But because it pleased God, who chose the weak things of this world in order to confound the strong (1 Cor 1:27), to save through the foolishness of preaching those who believe (1 Cor 1:21), we should not so much require reasoning concerning God as we should follow the authority of the saints."

See, then, whether in accord with your words you ought not rather, especially on this topic, on which above all our faith consists, to follow only the authority of the saints and not ask of me a rational account in order to understand it. For, when I begin to introduce you to some extent to an understanding of this mystery — and if God does not help interiorly I shall be utterly unable to do so — I shall do nothing else in my explanation than give a rational account to the extent I am able. And if you do not unreasonably demand of me or of any teacher that you may understand what you believe, correct your conviction, not so that you reject faith, but so that what you already hold with the firmness of faith you may also see with the light of reason.

Heaven forbid, after all, that God should hate in us that by which he made us more excellent than the other animals. Heaven forbid, I say, that we should believe in such a way that we do not accept or seek a rational account, since you could never believe if we did not have rational souls. In certain matters, therefore, pertaining to the teaching of salvation, which we cannot yet grasp by reason, but which we will be able to at some point, faith precedes reason so that the heart may be purified in order that it may receive and sustain the light of the great reason, which is, of course, a demand of reason! And so, the prophet stated quite reasonably, **Unless you believe, you will not understand**. There he undoubtedly distinguished these two and gave the counsel that we should believe first in order that we may be able to understand what we believe. Hence it was reasonably commanded that faith should precede reason. For if this command is not reasonable, it is, therefore, unreasonable. Heaven forbid! If that cannot yet be grasped, however slight the reason is that persuades us to this, it undoubtedly also comes before faith.

Hence the apostle Peter warns that we should be ready to respond to everyone who asks us for an account of our faith and hope (1 Pet 3:15). If an unbeliever asks me for an account of my faith and hope and I see that, before he believes, he cannot grasp it, I give him this very argument by which he may, if possible, see how preposterous it is to demand before faith an account of those things that he cannot grasp. But if a believer asks for an account in order that he may understand what he believes, we must look at his ability in order that, when an account has been given in accord with it, he may derive as great an understanding of his faith as is possible; a greater understanding if he grasps more, a smaller understanding if he grasps less. Yet until he comes to the fullness and perfection of knowledge, let him not depart from the journey of faith. This is the reason why the apostle declares, *And even if you have some other ideas, God will also reveal it to you; let us nonetheless continue to walk in the path to which we have come* (Phil 3:15-16). If, then, we are already believers, we have come to the way of faith, and if we do not give it up, we shall undoubtedly come not only to as great an understanding of incorporeal and immutable things as can be grasped in this life (though not by all), but also to the peak of contemplation, which the apostle calls *face to face* (1 Cor 13:12). For certain people, even the simplest who, nonetheless, walk with great perseverance in the path of faith, come to that most blessed contemplation. But there are those who somehow already know what the invisible, immutable, incorporeal nature is and refuse to hold onto the way that leads to so great an abode of happiness, because it seems foolish to them. That way is Christ crucified. And hence they cannot arrive at the temple of that rest by the light of which their mind is now touched as it sheds its ray from afar. . . .

I wanted to relate these things in order to encourage your faith toward a love for the understanding to which true reasoning leads and for which faith prepares the minds.

(6) Augustine of Hippo

For God himself whom we are seeking will, as I hope, grant us his help, so that our labor may not be fruitless and we may understand what is commanded in the holy psalm: *Let the heart of those who seek the Lord rejoice; seek his face always* (Ps 104:3-4 LXX). Now it would seem that what is always being sought, is never found; but how will the heart of those who seek the Lord rejoice and not grow sad, if they are unable to find what they are seeking? For the psalmist does not say, "Let the heart of those who find rejoice" but "let the heart of those who seek the Lord rejoice."

Yet the prophet Isaiah testifies that the Lord God can be found when he is sought: *Seek the* Lord, *and as soon as you find him call upon him, and when he draws near to you, let the godless man forsake his ways and the wrongdoer his thoughts* (55:6).

If, then, he can be found when he is sought, why is it said: *Seek his face always*? Is he perhaps to be sought even when he is found? Indeed, that is how one is to search out things beyond our comprehension, lest one think he has found nothing when he discovers just how incomprehensible what he is looking for is. Why, then, keep looking when one has comprehended the incomprehensibility of what one is looking for, unless because one knows he must not give up the search as long as he is making progress in seeking out incomprehensible things? One becomes better and better by seeking so great a good which is sought in order to be found, and found in order to be sought. For it is sought in order that it may be found all the sweeter, and is found in order that it may be sought more eagerly.

For what is said in the book of Sirach can be understood in this sense. For there Wisdom says, *Those who eat me shall still hunger, and those who drink me shall still be thirsty* (Sir 24:29). They eat and drink because they find; and because they are hungry and thirsty, they still go on seeking. Faith seeks; understanding finds. That is why the prophet asserts: **Unless you believe, you shall not understand**. Understanding, then, still goes on seeking the one it has found, for *God looked down upon the children of men, to see if there be one who understands and is seeking God* (Ps 14:2). For this reason, even when one has understanding, one continues to seek God.

(7) Cyril of Alexandria

Faith provides the root to nurture understanding because it is the beginning of genuine devotion and brings life to those who receive it. Thus the prophet Isaiah said, **If you do not believe, neither shall you understand** (7:9).

(8) Anselm of Canterbury

I acknowledge, O Lord, with gratitude, that you created this your image in me, so that, being mindful of you, I might think of you and love you. But this image, being worn away by my faults, has become effaced, and so covered by the smoke of my sins, that it cannot do what it was made to do unless you renew it and form it again. I do not try, O Lord, to plumb your depths; for that my understanding fails. Yet I long in some measure to understand your truth. I do not seek to understand and so believe, but rather to believe and so understand. This I believe: **Unless I have believed, I shall not understand** (7:9).

7:14
**Look, the virgin shall be with child and bear a son,
and you shall name him Emmanuel.**

(9) Tertullian

We must ask whether Christ received his flesh from the virgin. For only if he received its substance from his mother's womb is it certain that his flesh was human. If he received his being from his mother's womb, we can give clear proof of the human character of his flesh. By its name, its nature, its capacity for sensation, and its experience of suffering, it is clear that his flesh is human.

But we need to show why the Son of God had to be born of a virgin. It is to be expected that the one who was going to inaugurate a new birth had to be born in a new way, and Isaiah had foretold that the Lord would give a sign of this. What is that sign? **Look, a virgin shall conceive in her womb and bear a son.** Accordingly, a virgin did conceive and bore **Emmanuel,** God with us.

This is the new nativity, that man is born in God and in this man God is born, taking on the flesh of the ancient race, without, however, having its inception in the ancient seed. For he molded the flesh anew through a new seed, a spiritual seed, and purified it by the removal of its ancient stains. But, as is in other cases, this whole new manner of birth, being born of a virgin, was prefigured in ancient times.

When man was created by God the earth was still a virgin, not yet weighed down by human toil, no seed being cast into the ground. We know that from this virgin earth God created man as a living soul. If it is recorded that the first Adam came to be in this way, there is all the more reason that the *second Adam,* as the apostle declared (cf. 1 Cor 15:45,

47), would come forth from a virgin earth as a living spirit by God's action, that is, from a body not violated by human generation.

I should not let the opportunity pass to say something about the name Adam. Did the apostle not call Christ *Adam* (1 Cor 15:45) because as man he had an earthly origin? Here even reason comes to our aid: by reversing things God recovered his image and likeness that had been stolen by Satan.

For just as the devil's beguiling word that brought about death had penetrated the ear of Eve, who was still a virgin, in the same way God's life-giving Word had to enter into a virgin so that the one who had fallen into perdition because of a woman might be led back to salvation by means of the same sex. Eve believed the serpent, Mary believed Gabriel. The fault Eve introduced by believing, Mary by believing erased.

(10) Origen of Alexandria

Celsus[2] did not quote the prophecy in Isaiah that says Emmanuel shall be born of a virgin, because either he did not know it, though he professes to know everything, or if he had read it, he willfully said nothing of it to avoid appearing, against his intention, to support the doctrine which is contrary to his purpose. The passage reads as follows: **And the Lord spoke again to Ahaz, saying: "Ask a sign of the Lord your God, either in the depth or in the height." And Ahaz said, "I will not ask, neither will I put the Lord to the test." And he said, "Hear then, O house of David! Is it a small thing to you to strive with men? How also do you strive with the Lord? Therefore the Lord will give you a sign. Behold, a virgin shall conceive in her womb and bring forth a son, and you shall call his name Emmanuel"** (7:10-14), which is interpreted God with us (Matt 1:23). It is evident to me that Celsus ignored the prophecy out of wickedness. For though he quoted several things from the Gospel according to Matthew, such as the star that arose at the birth of Jesus and other miracles, he makes no mention of this whatsoever.

If a Jew should ingeniously explain it away by saying that it is not written, **Behold, a virgin**, but **behold, a young woman**, we should reply to him that the word 'almah, which the Septuagint translated by *parthenos* (virgin) and other translators by *neanis* (young woman), also occurs, so they say, in Deuteronomy applied to a virgin.[3] The passage reads as follows: *If a girl that is a virgin is betrothed to a man, and a man find her in a city and he lie with her, you shall bring both out to the gate of the city and stone them to death with stones, the young woman because she did not cry out in the city, and the man because he disgraced his neighbor's wife.* And after this: *If in the open country a man meets a girl that is betrothed and the man seizes her and lies with her, then only the man that lay with her shall die. But to the young woman you shall do nothing; in the young woman there is no sin punishable by death* (Deut 22:23-26).

---

2. Celsus was the author of a book against Christianity entitled *True Doctrine*. In it he had said that Mary had been convicted of adultery and had a child by a soldier named Panthera. Though the name Panthera was common, it was similar to the Greek word for virgin, *parthenos,* hence the offense to Christians.

3. The Hebrew term 'almah does not occur in the passage from Deuteronomy.

However, lest we appear to depend on a Hebrew word to gain the assent of those who do not understand whether or not to accept that the prophet said that this man would be born of a virgin (concerning whose birth it was said, *God with us*), let us explain what is said from the passage itself. The Lord, according to the scripture, told Ahaz, **"Ask a sign of the Lord your God, either in the depth or in the height"** (7:11). The sign that is given is this: **Behold, a virgin shall conceive and bear a son** (7:14). What sort of sign would it be if a young woman who was not a virgin bore a son? And which would be more appropriate as the mother of Emmanuel, that is, *God with us*, a woman who had intercourse with a man and conceived by female passion, or a woman who was still chaste and pure and a virgin? It is surely fitting that the latter should give birth to a child at whose birth it is said, *God with us*.

If, however, he explains this away by saying that it was Ahaz who was addressed in the words, **"Ask a sign of the Lord your God,"** we will argue: Who was born in Ahaz's time whose birth is referred to in the words **Emmanuel**, *which is God with us*? For if no one is to be found, obviously the words to Ahaz were addressed to the house of David, because according to Scripture our Savior was *of the seed of David according to the flesh* (Rom 1:3). Furthermore, this sign is said to be **in the depth or in the height** (7:11), since *this is he who descended and who ascended far above all heavens that he might fill all things* (Eph 4:10). I say these things as if speaking to a Jew who believes the prophecy. But perhaps Celsus or any who agree with him will explain to us how the prophet perceived the future, whether in this instance or in the others recorded in the prophecies. Has he foreknowledge of the future or not? If he has, then the prophets possessed divine inspiration. If he has not, let Celsus account for the mind of a man who ventures to speak about the future and is admired for his prophecy among the Jews.

(11) Ambrose of Milan

When Mary asked the angel, *How shall this be?* (Luke 1:34), she was not doubting what the angel said; she wanted to know how it would come about. How much more measured is her response than the words of the priest Zechariah. She asked, *How shall this be?* He replied, *How shall I know this?* (Luke 1:18). She responds to what is to happen; he remains doubtful of the news. He shows that he does not believe by saying that he does not know, and seeks to find someone else as warrant; she declares that she is ready to do what she is called for and does not doubt that it will take place. She asks only how it will happen when she says: *How shall this be since I have no husband?* Such a marvelous and unheard-of birth needed to be announced so that she could believe it. For a virgin to give birth is a sign of a divine mystery, not a human affair. Further, Mary had read the words, **Receive a sign: Behold, a virgin shall conceive and bear a son**. Therefore she believed that the prophecy would come true, but how it would happen she would not have read, for how it would be fulfilled had not been revealed even to so great a prophet.

Isaiah 7

(12) Pseudo-Basil of Caesarea

A virgin given in marriage to a man was found worthy to serve God's purpose in the Incarnation. In that way virginity was honored and marriage not despised. For virginity was chosen as being suited to sanctification, but because she was betrothed, marriage was honored.... An ancient author[4] explained why Mary married Joseph. The marriage with Joseph was planned so that Mary's virginity might remain hidden from the prince of this world. For the conventions of engagement were followed by the Virgin, almost as if to distract the evil one (who always preys on virgins). Hence the prophet announces: **Look, the virgin shall conceive and bear a son** (7:14). The tempter of virginity was deceived by their marriage. He knew that the coming of the Lord in the flesh would entail the destruction of his dominion....

(13) Gregory of Nyssa

Listen to Isaiah as he cries out: *For to us a child is born, to us a son is given* (9:6). Learn from the same prophet how the child is born, how the son is given. According to the law of nature? No, says the prophet. The Lord of nature is not a slave of the laws of nature. How then is the child born? Tell me. **Behold**, the prophet predicts, **the virgin shall be with child and bear a son, and they shall call him Emmanuel** (7:14), which translated means, *God with us*.

How marvelous! The virgin becomes a mother and remains a virgin. Observe this new thing in nature. With all other women, as long as one is a virgin one is not a mother. When a woman becomes a mother, she is no longer a virgin. Here, however, both names apply to one person. The same one is both mother and virgin. Her virginity was not an obstacle to giving birth, nor did giving birth destroy her virginity. It was fitting that he who came into human life to bring incorruptibility to all should himself have his beginning from a birth that preserved his incorruptibility.

It seems to me that Moses already knew about this mystery by means of the light by which God appeared to him when he saw the bush burning without being consumed (Exod 3:2). For Moses said, *I wish to go up closer and observe this great vision* (Exod 3:3). I believe that the term *go up closer* does not mean motion in space but drawing near in time. What was prefigured at that time in the flame of the bush was openly manifested in the mystery of the Virgin, once a period of time had passed.

Just as on the mountain the bush burned but was not consumed, so the Virgin gave birth to the light and was not corrupted. Nor should you consider comparing the Virgin to a bush to be inappropriate, for the bush prefigures the God-bearing body of the Virgin.

(14) Jerome

Isaiah speaks of the mystery of our faith and hope. **Look, a virgin shall conceive and bear a son, and shall call his name Emmanuel** (7:14). I know that the Jews are accustomed to

---

4. Ignatius of Antioch, *Ephesians* 19.1.

object that in Hebrew the word *'almah* does not mean a virgin but a young woman. That is true; the proper word for virgin is *bethulah*. However, a young woman or girl is not *'almah*, but *na'arah*. What then is the meaning of *'almah*? It refers to a hidden virgin, that is, one who is emphatically a virgin. For not every virgin is hidden and shut away from the occasional sight of men. So Rebecca, because of her extreme purity, and because she was a type of the Church as represented by her virginity, is said in Genesis to be an *'almah*, not *bethulah*, as may be shown from the words of Abraham's servant, spoken by him in Mesopotamia: *O Lord, the God of my master Abraham, if now you will prosper my way which I go, behold, I am standing by the spring of water; let the young woman who comes out to draw, to whom I will say, "Pray give me a little water from your jar to drink." And she will say to me, "Drink, and I will draw for your camels also," let her be the woman whom the Lord has appointed for my master's son* (Gen 24:42-44). Here where the text speaks of a virgin who comes forth to draw water, the Hebrew word is *'almah*, that is, a virgin who is secluded and carefully guarded by her parents. If this is not the case, let them show me where the word is applied to married women and I will admit that I am misinformed.

(15) Pacian of Barcelona

What is grace? It is the forgiveness of sin, that is, a gift. For grace is, literally, a gift. When Christ came and took on human nature, he presented to God this same human nature now freed from the power of sin, pure and innocent. **Behold**, Isaiah announces, **a virgin shall conceive and bear a son, and you shall call his name Emmanuel. He shall eat butter and honey by the time he knows how to refuse evil and choose the good** (7:14-15). And again it is written about him: *He committed no sin, nor was deceit found in his mouth* (53:9; 1 Pet 2:22). Shielded by his innocence, Christ went to the defense of man in the flesh of sin itself.

(16) Augustine of Hippo

You must appreciate, brothers and sisters, what a tremendous desire possessed the saints of old to see the Christ. They knew he was going to come, and all those living devout and blameless lives would exclaim, "Oh, if only that birth may find me still here! Oh, if only I may see with my own eyes what I believe from God's Scriptures!" And to prove to you how great was the desire of the saints who knew from the Holy Scriptures that a virgin was going to give birth, as you heard when Isaiah was read: **Behold, a virgin shall conceive in the womb, and shall bear a son, and his name shall be called Emmanuel.** The Gospel declares to us the meaning of the name **Emmanuel**, saying, *which is interpreted, God with us* (Matt 1:23). So don't let it surprise you, unbelieving soul, whoever you are, don't let it strike you as impossible that a virgin should give birth, and in giving birth remain a virgin. Realize that it was God who was born, and you won't be surprised at a virgin giving birth. So then, to prove to you how the saints and the just men and women of old longed to see what was granted to the old man Simeon, our Lord Jesus Christ said, when speaking to his disciples, *Many just men and prophets have wished to see what you see, and have not seen it; and to hear what you hear, and have not heard it* (Matt 13:17).

(17) Cyril of Alexandria

Some translators of the Holy Scriptures render this verse as follows: **A young woman shall conceive and bear a son**. The Jews think that the term **young woman** signifies the mother of the Lord, and that she should not be called a virgin. They believe that they will deprive the mystery of its power if she is called **young woman** rather than **virgin**. But this logic is faulty for many reasons, as anyone can see. First, even if it is said that the **virgin** is a **young woman**, that does not mean she is not a **virgin**.

Further, they contend that the prophet was speaking about the wife of Ahaz when he wrote, **Look, a young woman shall conceive and bear a son**, and the one who was born was Hezekiah, the son of Ahaz. But they have not examined the prophet's words carefully and have bent the text to their own views, basing their interpretation on this one point. But my good fellow, someone might object, who ever called Hezekiah Emmanuel? And who could demonstrate that **before he knew good or evil, he refused evil to choose the good** (7:16)? Let us then bid farewell to such sophistry and accept what is true and correct, namely, our conviction that the prophet with God's aid was referring to the holy Virgin. This then is truly an extraordinary sign contrary to expectation, at once **in the depth and in the height** (7:11) according to the divine promise.

For the only Son, begotten from above and from the Father by nature, emptied himself and came forth from the virgin's womb, born not from human seed but from the power and working of the Holy Spirit. Thus the holy Virgin promised through the voice of blessed Gabriel: *The Holy Spirit will come upon you, and the power of the Most High will overshadow you* (Luke 1:35). In the words of the text, **She will bear a son** (7:14). As for you, O house of David, the prophet says that you refused to put your trust in God but asked of him a sign to confirm what had been promised because you venerated idols. However, **you will call him Emmanuel**, that is, you will confess that God has appeared in human form. For when the only-begotten Word of God appeared among us, then *God was with us*. The one who is beyond all created things became one of us. Consider then what is said of him as God and as man, for then we can see that he is truly God and truly man.

To demonstrate that Christ was fully human the prophet says that he was nourished with food appropriate to infants, **butter and honey** (7:15). At the same time, when he became flesh he did not sin because he was God. **Before the child knows good or bad, he defies evil to choose what is good** (7:16). Before reaching puberty or the maturity that is endowed with judgment, one is incapable of distinguishing evil from good, nor acting on the basis of free choice. With God, however, whose nature is unlike ours, evil has no place whatsoever. God is not moved or tempted by evil thoughts, for in his very nature he is wholly opposed to evil. In the same way one would not say that light refuses to be darkness. It is of its very nature that light is not darkness. If it is darkness, it would no longer be light. Hence the prophet indicates that the divine nature always cleaves to the good when he says: **He defies evil to choose what is good** (7:16). This then is true about

Christ. He became flesh through the holy Virgin, being God by nature and begotten of God, at the same time from his mother and before her, indeed before all the ages as God. When he became man he did not relinquish his prerogatives as God, nor when he was man did he shun anything that belonged to human beings. For this reason one can believe that he truly came among us and by his birth sanctified our birth.

And the land that you fear will be abandoned before the two kings (7:16). It is as though one would say: When the Virgin who was pregnant gave birth, you, O house of David, would say: **You will name him Emmanuel** (7:14). Then all who laid waste the holy land departed. No longer will those willing to pillage the land see their way clear. This passage is to be understood spiritually. For when Emmanuel was born, the truly holy land and city, that is, the Church, became a beacon of hope. It struck down the spiritual foes, for when its enemies recognized that it was invincible, they fled, leaving it under God's gracious protection. *I will be to her, says the* LORD, *a wall of fire round about, and I will be the glory within her* (Zech 2:5).

(18) Theodoret of Cyrus

I am astonished at the effrontery of Jews who do not accept the prophecy concerning the Virgin. Aquila and Theodotion and Symmachus translate the term not as "virgin" but as "young woman." They should realize that the testimony of the Seventy[5] is more reliable than the witness of three, especially when this translation was unanimously accepted by all the translators. Moreover, the chronological facts give further support. The Seventy translated the Holy Scripture into Greek before the Incarnation of our Savior. They had no reason to falsify the passage. Furthermore, by God's grace they came to unanimous agreement. On the other hand, Theodotion, Aquila, and Symmachus translated Holy Scripture after the Lord's appearance. They were Jews and of course ill-disposed to accept the prophecies concerning the Lord. Nevertheless, the truth cannot be hidden. Furthermore, Moses the Lawgiver used the term "young woman" to refer to a "virgin": *If in the open country a man meets a young woman and sleeps with her* (Deut 22:25), then such and such will be done. Even if one grants that Moses the Lawgiver does not make the point explicitly, the use of the term **sign** (7:11) in the text gives sufficient proof of the meaning of the verse. This birth is called a sign, indeed a very great sign. If the birth was not that of a virgin, but of a married woman, why does one use the term "sign" for something that happens according to the ordinary processes of nature?

(19) Ephrem the Syrian

> When Aram and Ephrem dared to attack,
> Zion was afraid lest she be left bereft
> of the House of David (7:2). When Ahaz took flight

---

5. The seventy translators of the Septuagint. Theodoret refers to the legend that the seventy translators, although working independently, miraculously produced the same translation.

and abandoned her, Isaiah
gave her the good news of **Emmanuel**.
Behold, a virgin shall conceive and give birth (7:14)
without intercourse. Am I having a dream
or a vision that, behold, upon my lap[6]
is **Emmanuel**? I shall cease all else
and give thanks to the Lord of the universe each day.
"Whereas they despised virginity in Zion,
they honored Your mother, O Child of a Virgin who
clothed yourself in the virginity of your Mother.
To me You are Child,
Bridegroom and Son, even God."

(20) Leo the Great

Certainly, the things that pertain to the mystery of today's solemnity[7] are well known to you, dearly beloved, and you have heard about them often. Just as this visible light brings pleasure to healthy eyes, so our Savior's birth gives eternal joy to hearts that are well. We must never keep silent about it, even though we cannot explain it as it deserves. We believe that the question, *Who will recount his generation?* (Isa 53:8), pertains not only to the mystery by which the Son of God is coeternal with the Father, but also to this beginning by which *the Word was made flesh* (John 1:14).

And so, God the Son of God, equal to and of the same nature as the Father (from the Father and with the Father), Creator and Lord of the universe, wholly present everywhere and wholly surpassing all things, himself chose this day in the passage of time (which moves according to his own arrangement) to be born for the salvation of the world from blessed Mary, while at the same time preserving her honor. Her virginity was violated neither in conception nor in giving birth. As the Evangelist said: [All this took place] *to fulfill what the Lord had spoken by the prophet:* **Behold, a virgin will conceive in her womb and will give birth to a son, and his name will be called Emmanuel,** *which means, God with us* (Matt 1:22-23 and Isa 7:14).

By giving birth in this wonderful way the holy Virgin brought forth in a single offspring both a truly human nature and a truly divine one, because neither substance held its properties in such a way that there was a distinction of persons. Nor was the creature taken up into an association with its Creator as though one was the dweller and the other a dwelling; rather, each nature was intimately connected with the other.

Although there is one nature which is received and another which receives, yet the distinction between them is joined into so great a unity that there is one and the same Son — who says that he is inferior to the Father insofar as he is true man (John 14:28), and declares that he is equal to the Father insofar as he is true God (John 10:30).

6. Ephrem's hymn takes the form of a prayer of Mary to Christ.
7. This selection is taken from a sermon preached on Christmas Day.

(21) Venantius Fortunatus

> The prophets' tongue has sung the **Virgin's giving birth** (7:14):
> The angel takes the tidings to earth beneath the sky.
> The voice of men agrees, remembers what this girl has done,
> How she, a **virgin**, bore a man without man's seed.
> Concordant with this gospel, Isaiah tells
> What God inspires, he sounds the trumpet call,
> With eloquence abounding, and truly tells the mystery,
> And sings the **Virgin's** gift of our **Emmanuel**,
> Predicting from of old, that through the mother of the Lord
> Would Jesse's root produce a flower from his shoot.
> The **Virgin** is that shoot,[8] from which the Flower, Christ, has sprung,
> Whose living fragrance causes buried limbs to rise,
> As Lazarus, undone by death four days before,
> Received anew his breath from Christ, the fragrant Flower.
> Made holy in the womb (cf. Jer 1:5), the prophet Jeremiah
> Likewise foretold her in his vatic speech: *Behold,*
> *The days will come: from David will I cause a shoot*
> *To sprout, a king will reign, and wisely will he rule* (cf. Jer 33:14).
> The **Virgin** is this shoot, the king her infant son,
> The arbiter of justice, heir to world rule.
> The psalmist hymned the **Virgin** on his plectrum,
> When strings and voices sang their melody:
> *Of Mother Zion will they say: "One man here, one born there*
> *In her"* (Ps 87:5a), which means: He founded her, became a man in her.
> And then it says, *Most High is he who founded her* (Ps 87:5b):
> For she, the **Virgin** Mother, she is Mother Zion.

(22) Cassiodorus

Behold, a virgin will conceive and bring forth a son, and his name shall be called Emmanuel (7:14). And elsewhere: *All flesh shall see the salvation of God* (52:10). These words, shrouded in the darkness of long ago, were made clear by the brightness of the Lord's coming. The coming of the Lord revealed what was long hidden in obscurity. For what was hidden in the words of the Scriptures was now made clear in the things he did. Then the Word was made flesh and the **Virgin** gave birth. Then the dumb spoke, the deaf heard, the lame walked without limping, and other miracles bore witness to the Lord's character. By his coming, human nature, which had languished in darkness, was flooded with light through his mighty power.

---

8. Playing on Latin *virgo* ("virgin") and *virga* ("shoot," "branch," "staff"), a pun popular with Latin Christian writers.

(23) Bernard of Clairvaux

Let us see whether what Isaiah says about Aaron's blossoms (Num 17:8), which I have already mentioned,[9] sheds any light on this novel thing Jeremiah spoke about [when he said, *The Lord has created a new thing on earth; a woman shall enclose a man* (Jer 31:22)]. Isaiah says: **Behold, a virgin shall conceive and bear a son** (7:14). So you have a young woman, the Virgin. Do you also want to hear who the man is? He announces: **And he will be called Emmanuel**, *that is, God with us* (Matt 2:23). The woman enclosing the man is the Virgin conceiving God. Do you see how beautifully and harmoniously the marvelous deeds and mystical words of the saints agree? Don't you see what an astonishing and singular miracle took place through the Virgin and in the Virgin? Although the prophets used different kinds of signs at different times, they were animated by one Spirit and saw and foretold the same event. What was shown to Moses in the bush and the fire (Exod 3:2), to Aaron in the rod and the blossom, to Gideon in the fleece and the dew (Judg 6:37-40), this Solomon perceived clearly in the valiant woman and her price (Prov 31:10). Jeremiah prophesied this even more clearly when he spoke of the woman and the man. But it was Isaiah who stated it precisely by mentioning the **Virgin** and God, and Gabriel made it known to the Virgin herself when he greeted her. For it is she of whom the Evangelist wrote: *The angel Gabriel was sent by God to a virgin betrothed to Joseph* (Luke 1:26-27).

---

9. See excerpt #13 in chapter 11.

Isaiah 8

₁Then the Lord said to me, Take for yourself a scroll of a new large one and write on it with a man's pen, "In order to take plunder from the spoils quickly, for it is near," ₂and make reliable men my witnesses, Ourias and Zacharias son of Barachias. ₃And I went to the prophetess, and she conceived and bore a son. Then the Lord said to me, Name him "Swiftly Spoil, Quickly Plunder"; ₄for before the child knows how to call father or mother, it will receive the power of Damascus and the spoils of Samaria before the king of the Assyrians.

₅The Lord spoke to me yet further: ₆Because this people do not want the water of Siloam that flows gently, but want to have Raasson and the son of Romelias as king over you; ₇therefore, behold, the Lord is bringing up against you the mighty and abundant water of the River, the king of the Assyrians and his glory; and he will go up on your every valley and walk on your every wall; ₈and he will take away from Judea any man who can lift his head or who is capable to accomplish anything; his camp will be such as to fill the breadth of your country. God is with us.

9 Learn, you nations, and be defeated;
   listen as far as the end of the earth;
   be strong and be defeated;
   for if you become strong again, again you shall be defeated!
10 And whatever counsel you take, the Lord will scatter it;
   and whatever word you speak, it will not remain for you,
   because the Lord God is with us.

₁₁Thus says the Lord, With a strong hand do they reject the course of the way of this people, saying: ₁₂Never say "Hard," for whatever this people says is hard; but do not fear what it fears, neither be troubled. ₁₃Sanctify the Lord himself; and he himself will be your fear. ₁₄If you trust in him, he will become your sanctuary, and you will not encounter him as a stumbling caused by a stone, nor as a fall caused by a rock; but the house of Iakob is in a trap, and those who sit in Ierousalem are in a pit. ₁₅Therefore, many among them shall become powerless; and they shall fall and be crushed; and people who are in safety shall draw near and be taken.

16Then shall become manifest those who seal up the law so that they might not learn. 17And one shall say, "I will wait for God, who has turned away his face from the house of Iakob, and I will trust in him. 18Here am I, and the children whom God has given me, and they shall become signs and portents in Israel from the Lord Sabaoth, who dwells on Mount Sion." 19And if people say to you, "Seek those who utter sounds from the earth and the ventriloquists, the babblers who utter sounds out of their bellies," should not a nation be with its God? Why do they seek out the dead concerning the living? 20For he has given a law as a help, so that they may not speak a word such as this one, concerning which there are no gifts to give. 21And a harsh famine will come upon you; and it shall be that when you become hungry, you will be distressed, and you will vilify your ruler and your patachra [idol]. And they will look up to heaven above, 22and they will observe the earth below, but look: affliction and distress and darkness — dire straits and darkness so that they cannot see; (23)and the one who is in distress will not be perplexed for a time.

*Chapter 8 posed several problems for early Christian expositors. They realized that it was speaking about the Assyrian invasion of Syria and Samaria; consequently, they discussed the historical background of the text. But the mention of the **prophetess** who **conceived and bore a son** turned their attention back to chapter 7 and the prophecy of Christ's birth. Introducing Christ into the interpretation of the text in turn led some to allegorize Syria and Samaria as spiritual foes and the king of Assyria as the devil. An excerpt from Eusebius has been chosen to show how the argument from the fulfillment of prophecy could be used in both literal and figurative ways, with the literal interpretation applied to the Roman capture of Jerusalem during the First Jewish Revolt of A.D. 66-70. A short selection from a homily by Origen on Isa 8 is included because of its mordant criticism of ecclesiastical careerism. Jerome, following the citation of Isa 8:18 in Hebrews 2, gives the passage a christological interpretation and understands the **children whom God has given me** (8:18) to refer to preachers of the gospel. The phrases **stumbling caused by a stone** and **fall caused by a rock** (8:14) are cited twice in the New Testament, in Paul's discussion of Israel's unbelief in Romans 9 and also in 1 Peter, and this led Christian commentators to discuss Jewish rejection of Christ. As representative of this tradition of interpretation we have chosen a passage from Origen's* Commentary on Romans 9 *with its exposition of the two phrases (in his rendering),* **stone of stumbling** *and* **rock of offense**. *As the selection from John Cassian illustrates, the verse* **he has given a law to help them** *(8:20) was understood by some to refer to the natural law implanted in human beings at creation.*

(1) The Letter to the Romans

They have stumbled over the stumbling stone, as it is written, **Behold, I am laying in Zion a stone that will make men stumble, a rock that will make them fall; and he who believes in him will not be put to shame** (8:14-15; cf. 28:16).

(2) The Letter to the Hebrews

For he who sanctifies and those who are sanctified have all one origin. That is why he is not ashamed to call them brethren, saying, *I will proclaim thy name to my brethren; in the midst of the congregation I will praise thee* (Ps 22:22). And again, **I will put my trust in him**. And again, **Here am I, and the children God has given me** (8:17-18). Since therefore the children share in flesh and blood, he himself likewise partook of the same nature, that through death he might destroy him who has the power of death, that is, the devil, and deliver all those who through fear of death were subject to lifelong bondage.

(3) The First Letter of Peter

Come to him, to that living stone, rejected by men but in God's sight chosen and precious; and like living stones be yourselves built into a spiritual house, to be a holy priesthood, to offer spiritual sacrifices acceptable to God through Jesus Christ. For it stands in scripture: *Behold, I am laying in Zion a stone, a cornerstone chosen and precious, and he who believes in him will not be put to shame* (28:16). To you therefore who believe, he is precious, but for those who do not believe, *The very stone which the builders rejected has become the head of the corner* (Ps 118:22) and **A stone that will make men stumble, a rock that will make them fall** (8:14); for they stumble because they disobey the word, as they were destined to do.

(4) Jerome

For **large book** (8:1) the Septuagint translates **large and new book**, and for **I got reliable witnesses** (8:2), it reads **it is near and make reliable men my witnesses**. For **Uriah the priest**, it has only **Uriah**, and there are other minor alterations. First the prophet was sent to Ahaz (7:3-11), and Scripture records what was said to him. However, Ahaz refused to listen. Then the Lord himself spoke to Ahaz and told him to ask of the Lord a sign in the depth or in the height. To which the king responded: *I will not ask, and I will not put the LORD to the test* (7:12). The prophet then turned away from the impious king and addressed the words of God to the house of David, and gave it the promise that a virgin would bear a son whose name would be Emmanuel, that is, God with us. If God is called upon often in prayer, Samaria and Syria would be destroyed. The conqueror, however, would be the king of the Assyrians, who would later capture Judah. The result would be that the entire land of Judah would be laid waste.

Then, using another figure of speech, he portrays a virgin birth. And the Lord said to the prophet that he had never proclaimed the mystery of a new birth to the people, but he wrote that in this large book which we now read. How marvelous that the things human beings use for writing, human words and a pen, are able to capture the mysteries of God. What is written with a human pen? That a child born with the name **swiftly spoil, quickly plunder** (8:3) announces the end of the devil's reign. To save his creatures God did not send angels or prophets, but came down himself.

The prophet did what he was commanded and found two **reliable witnesses** (8:2), Uriah, a priest who is also a teacher of the law, as it is said in Malachi, *For the lips of a priest should guard knowledge, and men should seek instruction from his mouth, for he is the messenger of the LORD of hosts* (Mal 2:7), and Zechariah, son of Jeberechiah, who undoubtedly is a prophet. We read that during the reign of Ahaz when Zechariah[1] was a priest in the temple of the Lord, Ahaz ordered him to build an altar similar to the altar in Damascus (2 Kgs 16:10ff.). In the Book of the Days [the books of Chronicles] it is recorded that Hezekiah, the son of Ahaz, sought the Lord in the days of Zechariah, a prophet filled with the fear of God (cf. 2 Chr 29:1-2). Isaiah, fully worthy of the prophetic spirit, put himself at the service of the prophetess, that is, the Holy Spirit (in the Hebrew language the term is feminine, *ruach*): *Draw near to the Lord and be enlightened* (Ps 33:6 LXX). So the Lord was conceived by the Holy Spirit. And even though a human word is unable to explain the mystery of his nativity, Gabriel nevertheless used words to tell the Virgin herself that she would conceive: *The Holy Spirit will come upon you, and the power of the Most High will overshadow you; therefore the child to be born will be called holy, the Son of God* (Luke 1:35).

Some take the prophetess to be the holy Virgin Mary, for she was surely a prophetess. In the Gospel she exulted: *For behold all generations shall call me blessed; for he who is mighty has done great things for me* (Lk 1:48-49).

Isaiah was told that the child who had been named Emmanuel would now be called **"Swiftly Spoil, Quickly Plunder"** (8:3). *For he ascended on high, and led captivity captive, and received gifts among men* (Ps 68:18; Eph 4:8). Before he took on a human body and called God his Father and Mary his mother, the king of Assyria removed the strength of Damascus and took away the spoils of Samaria. Even before he was born, he saved his people Israel when they called upon God.

(5) Eusebius of Caesarea

This prophecy (8:1-4) is connected with the previous one (ch. 7). For she who was called a *virgin* in 7:14, and was said to bear *God with us,* is here called a **prophetess** (8:3). And if one should ask how she could conceive without being married, the prophecy now explains: **And I went to the prophetess, and she conceived and bore a son** (8:3). These things must be understood to be about the Holy Spirit under whose influence the prophet spoke. This same Holy Spirit then himself confesses that he went into the prophetess, and this reached its fulfillment in the birth of our savior Jesus Christ. . . .

In the preceding prophecy, at the time when Emmanuel was born, *before the child knows good or evil* (7:16), it is said that the land was forsaken by the two kings who attacked it, one the king of Samaria and the other of Damascus. This prophecy predicts that **before the child knows how to call "Father" or "Mother," he shall take the power of Damascus and the spoils of Samaria** (8:4), whose kings, according to his earlier prophecy (7:8), would be destroyed at the birth of Emmanuel.

---

1. Jerome means Uriah; see 2 Kgs 16:11.

I have already pointed out that, according to the same prophet Isaiah, in the time of Ahaz king of Judah, two kings made a covenant and attacked those ruled by David's successors; one king was ruler of the idolatrous Gentiles of Damascus, and the other, ruler of the Jewish people in the city of Palestine called Samaria, which we call Sebaste. Through the prophet God encouraged Ahaz with regard to these two kings: *Do not fear, and do not let your heart be faint because of these two smoldering stumps of firebrands* (7:4). And he foretells that the destruction of these men will be immediate, and proceeds to prophesy that at the birth of *God with us,* both their kingdoms will be utterly extinguished and destroyed. And we know from history that until the coming of our Savior Jesus Christ the kingdoms of Judea and Damascus continued, but that after he appeared to all, they came to an end in accord with the prophecy, for the Roman Empire absorbed them at the time of the preaching of our Savior....

8:5-7
The Lord spoke to me yet again: Because this people do not want the water of Siloam that flows gently, but want to have Raasson and the son of Romelias as king over you; therefore, the Lord is bringing up against you the mighty and abundant water of the River, the king of the Assyrians and his glory....

(6) Eusebius of Caesarea

It is clear that the only way to make this text intelligible is to explain it figuratively. Thus **the water of Siloam that flows gently** (8:5) signifies the gospel teaching of the word of salvation. The term **Siloam** means "sent." It is referring to God the Word sent by the Father, of whom Moses also says, *A ruler shall not fail from Judah, nor a prince from his loins, until he comes for whom it is stored up, and he is the expectation of nations* (Gen 49:10 LXX). For instead of *for whom it is stored up,* the Hebrew has "Siloam," the very word also used here in this prophecy, which means "the one that is sent."

And Raasson again was king of the idolatrous gentiles in Damascus, as was also the son of Romelias king of the Jews in Samaria, who abandoned the worship of their ancestors. And so God threatens that on those who will not accept **Siloam** — that is to say, Emmanuel, who is sent to them, and the son born of the prophetess, and his pleasant and fruitful word — but rather reject it, though it **flows softly** and **gently**, and choose for themselves the prince of idolatrous gentiles or the leaders of the apostasy of God's people, on them will he bring the strong and full flood of the **River**. The prophecy interprets the word **River** for us: it is the **king of the Assyrians** — meaning here again either figuratively the Prince of this world, or the power of Rome actually dominant, to which they were delivered, they who rejected **the water of Siloam that went softly** and embraced beliefs utterly hostile to good teaching. And at once surely and without delay the Roman army, under God's direction, came upon those who rejected the gospel of our Savior and refused **the water of Siloam that went softly**. They came through all their valleys, trod down their walls, took away from Judea every man who could raise his head or was able

Isaiah 8

to do anything at all, and so great was their camp that it filled the whole breadth of Judea. So was the prophecy fulfilled literally against them.

8:14
If you trust in him, he will become your sanctuary, and you will not encounter him as a stumbling caused by a stone, nor as a fall caused by a rock.

(7) Origen of Alexandria

Israel, who pursued the righteousness which is based on law, did not succeed in fulfilling the law (Rom 9:31). This passage, as we have already said, uses the term *law* in two different senses in the same verse. Certainly Israel pursued the righteousness which is based on law according to the letter, yet it has not succeeded in fulfilling the law. Which law did it not fulfill? No doubt the law of the Spirit. Otherwise the apostle would not have said that Israel did not succeed in fulfilling the law it pursued, to which it held fast, and which it possessed. So he explains why Israel was not able to fulfill the law: *Because they did not pursue it through faith, but as if it were based on works* (Rom 9:32).

At the beginning of my comments on the letter to the Romans, I discussed faith in Christ and works of the law at great length. To avoid repeating myself, I shall expound the present passage by citing a few statements of the apostle himself. For example, he says: *For being ignorant of the righteousness that comes from God, and seeking to establish their own, they did not submit to God's righteousness. For Christ is the end of the law, and every one who has faith may be justified* (Rom 10:3-4). Therefore, since they were pursuing a law not according to the works of God's righteousness but according to the works of their own righteousness, *they stumbled over the stumbling stone, as it is written: "Behold, I am laying in Zion a* **stone that will make men stumble, a rock of offense**, *and whoever believes in him will not be ashamed"* (28:16). It should be noted that in the prophet this testimony is written as follows: *Behold, I am sending for the foundation of Zion a select and beautiful cornerstone for its foundations, and whoever believes in him will not be ashamed* (28:16). But the apostle has inserted into this testimony, **stone that makes one stumble, a rock of offense** from another place in the prophet Isaiah where it is written: **You will not encounter him as a stone of offense or a stone that makes one stumble** (18:14). The apostle has taken from each place what suited his argument and adapted it accordingly.

It may seem surprising that the Lord Jesus, who is addressed with many good and life-giving names, should in this passage (which the apostle took from the prophet Isaiah) be called **a stone of stumbling and a rock of offense**. Surely only those names that designate something good and life-giving ought to be used of the good Lord and the Son of the good Father, names such as peace (Eph 2:14), righteousness (1 Cor 1:30), truth (John 14:6), door which opens to the Father (John 10:7), lion of the tribe of Judah (Rev 5:5), a lion's whelp who rises from sleep (Gen 49:9), sanctification, redemption (1 Cor 1:30), and whatever is appropriate to his majesty. But let us see if we are able to show to what extent **stone of stumbling and rock of offense** can rightly be applied to him.

The terms **stumbling** (Latin *offensio*) and **offense** (Latin *scandalum*) mean pretty much the same thing.[2] *Scandalum* is used to designate "hindrance," that is, when some kind of barrier is found on the path that blocks the steps of someone who is walking or climbing *(scandentis)* — hence the derivation of the word "hindrance" *(scandalum)*. The point is that because those who were in Zion were not traveling on good roads, they were running swiftly down the path of destruction, supporting one another in their evil deeds, as the prophet says: *The sinner is praised for the evil desires of his soul, and the evildoer is blessed* (Ps 9:24 LXX). When our Lord and Savior came, he reproached their ways, saying: *Woe to you, scribes and Pharisees* (Matt 23:13), and again, *Woe to you that are rich* (Luke 6:24), and again, *Woe to you, Jerusalem, who kills the prophets and stones those sent to you* (Matt 23:37). By saying many things of this sort and reproaching them he began to block the roads of their destruction, and by not allowing them to travel the wide road that leads to death he became for them a **stone of stumbling** and a **rock of offense**. One can also find this written in the prophet Hosea about those who are traveling on the road of sin: *Therefore I will hedge up her way with thorns; and I will obstruct her roads, and she will not find her path* (Hos 2:6).

If it seems appropriate, let us again put forth Paul as an example. He had received letters from the priests and was heading to Damascus to lead all the men and women who believed in Christ to Jerusalem as prisoners. When he was on that erring journey, the Lord Jesus met him on the road and struck him with blindness for a time. One could say then that with respect to Paul's goal on his erring journey, Christ had become for him a **stone of stumbling** and a **rock of offense**. Once he was converted, he believed in him who prevented him by blocking the road with the *thorns* (Hos 2:6) of his threat, and by believing in him he would not be *ashamed* (28:16).

(8) Augustine of Hippo

Take a look at the text: *Climb the mountain and die* (Deut 32:49-50). The bodily death of Moses stood for the death of his doubting, but his death took place on the mountain. What marvelous mysteries! When this has been definitely explained and understood, how much sweeter it is to the taste than manna! Doubting was born at the rock, but died on the mountain. When Christ was humbled in his passion, he was like a rock lying on the ground before their eyes. It was natural to have doubts about him; that humility was not holding out hopes for anything very great. His very humiliation naturally made him into a **stone of offense**. But once glorified by his resurrection, he was seen to be great; he is now a mountain. So now let doubt, which was born at the rock, die on the mountain. Let the disciples recognize where their salvation lies, let them summon up their hope again. Notice how that doubting dies, notice how Moses dies

---

2. Though Origen wrote in Greek, only a Latin version of this passage is extant, and the Latin translator has adapted the terminology to his readers.

on the mountain. Let him not enter the promised land; we don't want any doubting there; let it die.

8:18
Here am I, and the children whom God has given me, and they shall become signs and portents in Israel from the Lord Sabaoth, who dwells on Mount Sion.

(9) Jerome

The Lord commands that I **bind up the testimony for the Jews and hand on the law and seal for his disciples** (8:16), because he has hidden his face from the house of Jacob. Therefore, I look for and await my Lord, not only I but also the **children whom the Lord has given to me** (8:18), some who are prophets and others sons of prophets, *who were born not of the will of the flesh and blood, but of God* (John 1:13). These the apostle had in mind when he said: *My little children, with whom I am again in travail until Christ be formed in you* (Gal 4:19). These children, that is, prophets, have been given as **signs and portents in Israel**, according to what we read in Ezekiel: *And Ezekiel will be a sign to you* (Ezek 24:24). Moreover, in Zechariah the holy men and disciples of the prophets are *diviners* (Zech 3:8), that is, they are called observers of **portents and signs**, in that prophets are able to discern the signs of what is to come. So much for the literal sense.

But the blessed apostle in the letter written to the Hebrews, although it is not reckoned among the canonical Scriptures in the Latin-speaking churches, teaches that this passage ought to be understood with respect to the Lord and Savior. *That is why he is not ashamed to call them brethren, saying: "I will proclaim thy name to my brethren, in the midst of the congregation I will praise thee"* (Heb 2:11-12). And again, *I will put my trust in him* (Heb 12:13). And again: **Here am I, and the children God has given me.** *Since therefore the children share in flesh and blood, he himself also shared in their sufferings* (Heb 2:13-14). How these children became a **sign and portent** of the wisdom of the world and the pride of the Jews, that same apostle teaches, who said *that the Lord and Savior chose what is foolish in the world and what is weak that he might shame the wise and strong* (1 Cor 1:27). And the Savior said to the apostles: *Unless you turn and become like a child, you will not enter into the kingdom of heaven* (Matt 18:3).

Moreover, a child is made into a preacher of the new gospel, one who puts off the old man who was corrupted by uncontrollable desires, and is clothed with the new man who *is being renewed in knowledge after the image of its creator* (Col 3:10). The same apostle writes that **The Lord of hosts dwells on Mount Zion**: *You have come to Mount Zion and to the city of the living God* (Heb 12:22).

8:19
Now if people say to you, "Seek those who utter sounds from the earth and the ventriloquists, the babblers who utter sounds out of their bellies. . . ."[3]

(10) Origen of Alexandria

Now I want to explain why the text takes up the subject of the powerful wizardry of the "ventriloquists" when it says, **Now if people say to you, "Seek out the ventriloquists . . ."** (8:19). You will discover that all of those who promise to deliver the truth but who do not possess it are the slaves of their bellies,[4] and everything they do, to use a figure of speech, is for the sake of their bellies' pleasure and appetite. This includes not just pagans but those too who, while promising devotion to Christ, are actually heretics. And not only heretics; even among us, among those who are ministers of the church, you will discover people who strive to their uttermost to fill their bellies, that is, to gain honor and to put their hands on the Church's offerings. Such a person speaks from his belly, and the source of his words is in his belly; they do not flow from a good heart, or good thoughts, or the Holy Spirit. Therefore, when someone promises to teach, observe carefully whether his words have their origin in his belly or not.

8:20
For he has given a law as a help . . . .

(11) John Cassian

When God created each human being, he placed in him, as something natural, a knowledge of the law. If this law had been observed by every individual according to the Lord's plan, as was the case in the beginning, it would certainly not have been necessary for that other law to be given which he promulgated later in writing. For it was superfluous to offer an external means of health when the one that had been placed within continued to be effective. But since, as we have said, this latter one had already been utterly corrupted by the freedom to sin and by the practice of sinning, the severe stringency of the Mosaic law was imposed as its administrator and avenger and, to use the very words of Scriptures, as its **helper** (8:20). Thereby, through fear of punishment in the present life, human beings could not completely extinguish the good of natural knowledge. As the prophet says: **He gave the law as a help**. It is also described by the apostles as having been given as

---

3. The biblical text here refers to mediums or necromancers who claim to communicate with the dead. The word "ventriloquist" means literally "someone who speaks from their belly," because the voice is represented as coming from a source below. Origen gives the word an allegorical interpretation based on the etymology.

4. Probably an allusion to Phil 3:19: "Their god is the belly."

an "instructor" to little children (Gal 3:24), teaching them and protecting them, lest by a kind of forgetfulness they slip away from that discipline in which they had been instructed by nature.

That a complete knowledge of the law has been poured into every human being since the beginning of creation is clearly proved by this: before the law, and even before the Flood, we know that all the holy ones observed the commandments of the law without having read them in writing.

Isaiah 9

9.1(8.23) Do this first, do it quickly, O country of Zaboulon, the land of Nephthalim, and the rest who inhabit the seashore and the land beyond the Jordan, Galilee of the nations, the parts of Judea.

2(1) O you people who walk in darkness,
    see a great light!
O you who live in the country and in the shadow of death,
    light will shine on you!

3(2) Most of the people,
    whom you have brought back in your joy,
will also rejoice before you
    like those who rejoice at the harvest,
    and in the same way as those who divide plunder.

4(3) Because the yoke placed on them will be taken away,
    and the rod that is on their neck;
    for the Lord has scattered the rod of the exactors
    as on the day that was upon Madiam.

5(4) Because with reconciliation they shall repay
    every garment and cloak acquired by deceit;
and they will be willing to do so
    even if they have been burned by fire.

6(5) Because a child was born for us,
    a son also given to us,
whose sovereignty was upon his shoulder;
    and he is named Messenger of Great Counsel,
for I will bring peace upon the rulers,
    peace and health to him.

7(6) His sovereignty is great,
    and his peace has no boundary
upon the throne of Dauid and his kingdom,
    to make it prosper and to uphold it

Isaiah 9

with righteousness and with judgment
    from this time onward and forevermore.
The zeal of the Lord Sabaoth will do these things.

8(7) The Lord sent death against Iakob,
    and it came on Israel;
9(8) and all the people of Ephraim will know it,
    and those who sit in Samaria
    with pride and uplifted heart saying:
10(9) "The bricks have fallen,
    but come, let us hew stones
    and cut down sycamores and cedars
    and build ourselves a tower."
11(10) And God will strike those who rise up against them on Mount Sion,
    and he will scatter their enemies,
12(11) Syria from the rising of the sun
    and the Greeks from the setting of the sun —
    those who devour Israel with open mouth.
For all this his anger has not turned away;
    but his hand is still uplifted.

13(12) And the people did not turn back until they were smitten,
    and they did not seek the Lord.
14(13) So the Lord took away from Israel head and tail,
    great and small in one day —

(14) the elder and those who admire persons: this is the first part;
15   and the prophet who teaches transgressions: this one is the tail.
16(15) And those who congratulate this people will lead them astray,
    and they lead them astray in order to devour them.
17(16) Therefore God will not rejoice over their young people,
    nor will he have compassion on their orphans and widows;
    for they are all lawless and evil,
    and every mouth speaks injustices.
For all this his anger has not turned away,
    but his hand is still uplifted.

18(17) And the transgression will burn like a fire,
    and like dry grass will it be consumed by fire;
    and it will burn in the thickets of the forest
    and devour everything around the hills.
19(18) Because of the fierce anger of the Lord
    the whole land has been burned up,
    and the people will be completely burned as by fire.

A man will not have compassion on his brother,
20(19) but will turn aside to the right because he will be hungry,
and he will eat on the left;
but a man will not be satisfied
even if he eats the flesh of his arm.
21(20) For Manasse will eat Ephraim's, and Ephraim Manasse's,
because together they will besiege Ioudas.
For all this his anger has not turned away;
but his hand is still uplifted.

In the early Church chapter 9 was read in close conjunction with chapters 7 and 8, and some writers speak of three prophecies that complement one another. The phrase **a child was born for us** *(9:6) was taken to refer to Christ and* **sovereignty upon his shoulder** *(9:6) to his universal rule. The Septuagint does not translate the list of names that are so familiar from Handel's Messiah:* **Wonderful Counselor, Mighty God, Everlasting Father, Prince of Peace** *(9:6). For that reason Jerome, who had the Hebrew text before him, is one of the few ancient commentators to discuss these names. He suggests that the Septuagint did not render them in Greek because the translators thought them inappropriate for a* **child** *(9:6). But the Septuagint does include one name,* **Messenger of Great Counsel,** *and several interpretations of the phrase are provided. The phrase became a matter of dispute because the Greek term translated* **messenger** *also meant* **angel***. Taken in that way, the passage seemed to suggest that Christ was not God but a lesser being, and therefore commentators emphasize that he is divine. Some interpreters, such as Leo the Great, following the Evangelist Matthew, understood* **the people who sat in darkness** *and* **those who sat in the region and shadow of death** *to be the Gentiles, while others, such as John of Damascus, took this group to be those in Hades to whom Jesus brought the gospel when he descended to the dead (cf. 1 Pet 3:19). The Greek term for* **sovereignty** *(9:7) is* **archē***; it is also the term that is translated "rule" in Eph 1:19-20: "what is the immeasurable greatness of his power in us who believe, according to the working of his great might which he accomplished in Christ when he raised him from the dead and made him sit at his right hand in the heavenly places, far above all* **rule** *and authority and power and dominion." Accordingly some commentators took the phrase* **his sovereignty (archē) is great** *(9:7) to refer to Christ's universal rule.*

(1) The Gospel according to Matthew

Now when he heard that John had been arrested, he withdrew into Galilee; and leaving Nazareth he went and dwelt in Capernaum by the sea, in the territory of Zebulun and Naphtali, that what was spoken by the prophet Isaiah might be fulfilled:

**The land of Zebulun and the land of Naphtali;
toward the sea, across the Jordan,
Galilee of the Gentiles —
the people who sat in darkness have seen a great light,**

Isaiah 9

**and for those who sat in the region and shadow of death
light has dawned.** (9:1-2)

From that time Jesus began to preach, saying, "Repent, for the kingdom of heaven is at hand."

(2) Cyril of Alexandria

The prophet began his discussion by showing who were the first to believe, who became the first fruits of those called to knowledge of Emmanuel, when he said: *Here am I, and the children whom God has given me, and they shall become signs and portents in the house of Israel from the* LORD *Sabaoth, who dwells on Mount Sion* (8:18). Now he speaks of the region of **Zebulun and Naphtali** (9:1) which is next to the Sea of Tiberias, at the edge of the land of the Jews, bordering on Galilee of the Gentiles, but is different from the land of the Phoenicians. From that land most of the holy apostles would come. And blessed Matthew, giving us an account of their calling, narrates when Jesus first went into the region of **Zebulun and Naphtali,** There Jesus chose his holy apostles, and the Evangelist continues: *He left Nazareth and made his home in Capernaum by the lake in the territory of Zebulun and Naphtali, so that what had been spoken through the prophet Isaiah might be fulfilled*: **Land of Zebulun and land of Naphtali, on the road by the sea, across the Jordan, Galilee of the Gentiles — the people who sat in darkness have seen a great light, and for those who sat in the region and shadow of death, light has dawned** (Matt 4:13-16; 9:1-2). Then Matthew adds: *As he walked by the Sea of Galilee, he saw two brothers, Simon, who is called Peter, and Andrew his brother, casting a net into the lake — for they were fishermen. And he said to them, "Follow me, and I will make you fishers of men." Immediately they left their nets and followed him. As he went from there, he saw two other brothers, James son of Zebedee and his brother John, in the boat with their father Zebedee, mending their nets, and he called them. Immediately they left the boat and their father, and followed him* (Matt 4:18-22).

One should recognize that the Sea of Galilee, also called the Sea of Tiberias, is considered holy by the Scriptures. For there the holy disciples went about their work as fishermen. The God of all speaks through the voice of the prophet in the present, directing his words to the lands or the cities of the tribe of Zebulun and Naphtali which are located close to the Sea of Tiberias. He says that he will give them the cup of salvation and wine which rejoices the heart of man, the gospel of Christ: **Drink this first, do it quickly, O country of Zebulon and Naphtali** (9:1). Receive the saving gospel, but do it quickly, without any delay! The disciples responded swiftly and were prepared to go forth without delay believing in Christ. They followed immediately, leaving their nets and their father. There was no need for elaborate instruction. They heard: *Follow me, and I will make you fishers of men. Immediately they followed him* (Matt 4:19-20).

In the same way other holy apostles were called and became Christ's disciples. John writes about Christ the Savior of all. *The next day Jesus decided to go to Galilee. He found Philip and said to him, "Follow me." Now Philip was from Bethsaida, the city of Andrew and*

Peter. Philip found Nathanael and said to him, "We have found him of whom Moses in the law and also the prophets wrote, Jesus of Nazareth, the son of Joseph" (John 1:43-45). When he came to Jesus, he heard him saying, *I saw you under the fig tree before Philip called you.* He believed at once and cried out, *Rabbi, you are the Son of God! You are the King of Israel!* (John 1:47-49). Bethsaida, where Philip and Nathanael came from, was near the Sea of Tiberias. Blessed David mentions the commissioning of the disciples and says, *There is Benjamin entranced, the princes of Judah, their rulers, the princes of Zebulun, the princes of Naphtali* (Ps 68:27). To show that not only the holy disciples would be called at that time, but also the many Gentiles, the text says: **the rest who inhabit the seashore and the land beyond the Jordan, Galilee of the Gentiles. O you people who walk in darkness, see a great light! O you who live in the country and in the shadow of death, light will shine on you!** (9:1-2). The Gentiles lived in the night and in darkness because their minds were not enlightened with the true knowledge of God.

*   *   *

The prophet asserts that **a son is given to us** (9:6). The only-begotten Word of God became man for us not for his own sake but that he might renew human nature to what it was at the beginning. He became a ransom for the life of all, offering his own body as a fragrant offering to God the Father. The prophet says that **sovereignty will be upon his shoulder** (9:6). It seems to some that these words should be understood as follows: when our Lord Jesus Christ came to his saving passion, bearing the cross, he was lifted up, and through it ruled over everything under heaven, that is, he took the **sovereignty upon his shoulder**.

This saying of the prophet is persuasive and worthy of praise: With the term **shoulder** the prophetic word signifies strength, for all our strength is in the arms and the shoulders. Therefore, the Son is called the right hand and arm of God the Father. *Who has believed what we have heard? And to whom has the arm of the LORD been revealed?* (53:1). Christ ruled everything under heaven through his own power. He is the power of his God and Father.

He is called **Messenger of Great Counsel** (9:6), that is, messenger of God the Father. And wise John will testify of him, saying: *He who receives his testimony sets his seal to this, that God is true. For he whom God has sent utters the words of God* (John 3:33-34). And elsewhere he says to the holy apostles: *You are my friends if you do what I command you. No longer do I call you servants, for the servant does not know what his master is doing; but I have called you friends, for all that I have heard from my Father I have made known to you* (John 15:14-15). For this reason he calls Emmanuel **Messenger of Great Counsel**.

When he became man he attributed to his God and Father the power to carry out everything he did. This God the Father himself makes clear in the words: **I will bring peace upon the rulers, peace and health to them** (9:6). True peace Christ gave to his holy apostles as to his own. For all things which belong to the Father are his. For he said: *Peace I leave with you; my peace I give to you* (John 14:27). If it is said that Emmanuel himself receives **peace and health** (9:6), consider again the marvel of the incarnation in the flesh. He received **peace** from the world, namely, that everything was handed over to him by the Father, persuading the world to deal peaceably with him, by worshiping him and taking on the yoke of his kingdom. *No one*, he says, *can come to me unless the Father who sent me draws him* (John 6:44). And Isaiah somewhere announces: *Let us make peace with him, let those who come make peace with him* (27:5). Therefore he received peace from the Father in this way, as I have mentioned. We heard him speaking to his Father and God in heaven: "Those whom you gave me from the world, they are yours and you have given them to me" (cf. John 17:9-10).

He received **health** (9:6), that is, resurrection from the dead. Since he was said to be weakened for a short time, because he allowed his own flesh by the grace of God to taste death for all, he received **health**, that is, resurrection, and this he himself accomplished. He raised his own temple, for he exists as the power of the Father. If he is the resurrection and the life, what does life need to be made alive? And if he is seen to have raised the bodies of others by his own power, could he not raise up his own body before raising others? Moreover, he said to the Jews: *Destroy this temple, and in three days I will raise it up* (John 2:19). That the kingdom of Christ is unshakeable and firm he teaches when he said: **His sovereignty is great, and of his peace there will be no limit** (9:7). He no longer rules only Judea, but everything under heaven. And there will be no end of the **peace** which we offer to him. For we make **peace** with him, we worship him, as I have said, and through him and in him we worship the God and Father. And we are zealous to be rid of the sin which is a friend to war.

(3) Eusebius of Caesarea

A child was born for us, a son also given to us, whose sovereignty was upon his shoulder; and he shall be named Messenger of Great Counsel (9:6). The one who is called Emmanuel is here called **son** and **child**. **Son** and **child** occur in the third of three prophecies. The first is, *Behold, a virgin shall conceive and bear a son, and you will call his name Emmanuel*, to which is added, *before the child knows good and evil* (7:14-15). The second is, *And I went to the prophetess, and she conceived and bore a son*, to which is added, *before the child knows how to call on mother or father* (8:3-4). And the third is the text before us, **A child was born for us**. This child is the son given as a gift by God to those who believe in him. He has many names, as can be seen in the present text.

He is called **angel of great counsel**. This is an appropriate name, for he is superior not only to every mortal nature but also to angelic nature: he is said to be not merely an angel, but **angel of great counsel**. Who else would be the **great counsel** than the great God, and what else would it be than the plan (cf. Eph 1:10)[1] of the calling and salvation of all the nations? The angel is our Savior, who carried out the plan of his compassionate Father. According to the book of Hebrews, he was honored with a name greater than that of an angel (Heb 1:4), for he is said to have the **sovereignty upon his shoulder**. This is the sovereignty of the child that was promised, a sovereignty of glory and honor and king-

---

1. In Greek the terms for "counsel" and "plan" are the same.

ship. Universal sovereignty is on his shoulder, understood as the right arm of his divinity. Because he is God he is called **angel of great counsel**, for he alone comprehends the ineffable things of the fatherly counsel and became a messenger to those who are dear to God. . . .

His sovereignty will be great, and of his peace there will be no end (9:7). The phrase **his sovereignty will be great** can be understood to refer to the church that is spread throughout the whole world. Consider also the testimonies of the holy apostle concerning him when he says, *according to the working of his great might, which he accomplished in Christ when he raised him from the dead and made him sit at his right hand in the heavenly places, far above every rule and authority and power and dominion and above every name that is named* (Eph 1:19-21). So the sovereignty of our Savior will be great. Further, **of his peace there will be no end**. For it will be without termination, it will not grow old nor will it be circumscribed, as it is written: *In his days may righteousness and fullness of peace flourish* (Ps 72:7).

9:2
The people who sat in darkness have seen a great light, and for those who sat in the region and shadow of death light has dawned.

(4) Gregory the Theologian

Christ is born, glorify him. Christ comes from the heavens, greet him. Christ is on earth, be lifted up. *Sing to the* LORD, *all the earth* (Ps 96:1). And to join both together: *Let the heavens be glad, and let the earth rejoice* (Ps 96:11), for he is *heavenly,* then *earthly* (1 Cor 15:47). Christ is in the flesh, *rejoice with trembling* (Ps 2:11) and with joy. With trembling because of sin, with joy because of hope. Christ is born of a virgin; women, live as virgins that you may become mothers of Christ. Who does not worship the one who is *from the beginning* (John 1:1); who does not glorify the one who is *the last* (Rev 1:17)?

Again darkness is destroyed, again light comes into being (Gen 1:3-4). Again Egypt is punished with darkness; again Israel is enlightened by a pillar (Exod 10:21-23). **The people who were sitting in the darkness** of ignorance, let them **see a great light** (9:2). *The old has passed away; all things have become new* (2 Cor 5:17). The letter gives way, the Spirit triumphs (2 Cor 3:6); the shadows flee, and truth makes its entrance (cf. Rom 13:12). Melchisedech finds his fulfillment. The one without a mother is born without a father. In the first place he is without a mother, in the second without a father. The laws of nature are suspended; the world above is to be filled. Christ commands it; let us not stand against him. *Clap your hands, all peoples* (Ps 47:1), because *a child was born for us, and a son given to us, and sovereignty will be on his shoulder* (for with the cross it is raised up), and *his name will be called Messenger of Great Counsel* (9:6) of the Father.

Let John cry out: *Prepare ye the way of the Lord* (Matt 3:3). I too will cry out the power of this day. The one who is without flesh became flesh; the Word takes on the density of matter; the one who is invisible is seen; the one who cannot be touched is palpable; the one outside of time enters into time; the son of God becomes the son of man, *Jesus*

Christ, the same yesterday, today, and forever (Heb 13:8). Let the Jews be offended, let the Greeks make fun, let the heretics itch to talk. They will believe when they see him ascending to heaven, and if not then, when they see him coming from heaven and taking his seat as judge.

But that is for later. Now it is the Feast of Theophaneia[2] or the *Nativity*, for it is called both, two names for one thing. Through this birth, God appeared among human beings. On the one hand, the one who is and always is from what always is, beyond every cause and every reason — for there was nothing prior to the Word; on the other hand, later he was born for our sake, that the one who gave us existence might also give us well-being, or rather, because we had fallen from our well-being as a result of evil, he might restore us to himself by his Incarnation. The name "Theophany" is because of his appearing, the name "Nativity" because of his birth.

This festival we celebrate today, the coming of God to man, that we might make our way to God, or rather that we might return to God — for that is the proper expression, that we might cast off the old man and put on the new. *As in Adam we died, so in Christ we are made alive* (1 Cor 15:22), being born with Christ, crucified with him, buried with him, and raised with him. It is necessary that I undergo that lovely reversal, and as sorrowful things gave way to pleasant things, so more pleasant things followed the sorrowful. *Where sin increased, grace abounded all the more* (Rom 5:20), for if a taste [of the fruit in the Garden of Eden] brought condemnation, how much more does Christ's passion make us righteous. Therefore let us keep the feast, not as a secular holiday but in a godly way, not in the way of the world but in a way that transcends the world, not as our own but as the feast of the one who is ours, as that of our Lord, not as weakness but of healing, not as creation but as re-creation.

(5) Augustine of Hippo

So we should be aware of each kind of resurrection, both the spiritual and the bodily kind. The spiritual kind is referred to by the text, *Arise, you that are asleep, and rise up from the dead* (Eph 5:14); and by the other one, **Upon those who were sitting in the shadow of death light has risen** (9:2), and by the one I just mentioned, *If you have risen together with Christ, seek the things that are above* (Col 3:1).

(6) Proclus of Constantinople

Today the sun of justice sprang from the virginal cloud: **The people that sat in darkness have seen a great light** (9:2). Today the unsown seed grew up out of the uncultivated plain, and the hungry world rejoices for it. Today, without conjugal relations, a birth sprang from an uncorrupt womb, and all creation brings gifts to the child who has no father. The earth offers a manger; the rocks offer jars of water; the mountains, a cave; the

---

2. That is, the appearing of God.

cities, Bethlehem; the winds, obedience; the sea, submission; the waves, calm; the depths of the ocean, fish; the fish, a coin (Matt 17:27); the rivers, the Jordan; the wells, the Samaritan woman; the desert, John; the beasts, a foal; the birds, a dove; the Magi, their gifts.

The women offer Martha; the widows, Anna; the barren, Elizabeth; the virgins, Mary, Mother of God; the shepherds, a hymn of praise; the priests, Simeon; the children, palms; the persecutors, Paul; the sinners, the publican; the Gentiles, the Canaanite woman; the woman with a hemorrhage, her faith; the sinful woman, ointment; the trees, Zacchaeus; wood, the cross; the cross, the thief; the east, a star; the air, a cloud; Gabriel, his greeting: *Rejoice, full of grace, the Lord is with you* (Luke 1:28), and the Lord is from you, and the Lord is before you.

He came unto you according to his good pleasure; he came from you as he willed; he came before you, before every thought of mind, having been generated by God the Father ineffably, immutably, wondrously, impassibly, without corruption, without witnesses, without mediators, without supervisors, unspeakably and divinely. In heaven without a mother, on earth without a father. *Glory to God in the highest, and on earth peace among men with whom he is pleased* (Luke 2:14), now and forever.

(7) Leo the Great

Isaiah announces: **The people who were sitting in darkness have seen a great light. A light has arisen for those who were living in the realm of death's shadow** (9:1-2). Elsewhere Isaiah declares, *Nations that have not known you will call upon you, and people who do not recognize you will take refuge in you* (55:5). Therefore, let us rejoice in the day of salvation, dearly beloved. We have been taken up through the New Covenant to participate in him who was told by the Father through a prophet, *You are my Son, this day have I begotten you. Ask it of me, and I will give the ends of the earth for your possession* (Ps 2:7-8). Let us glory, therefore, in the mercy of the one adopting us. As the apostle says, *You did not receive a spirit of slavery again in fear, but you have received the spirit of adoption as children, in which we cry out, "Abba! Father!"* (Rom 8:15). It would be fitting and appropriate that the will of a father's testament be carried out by adopted sons. As the apostle adds, *If we suffer with him, we shall also be glorified with him* (Rom 8:17). Let those who are going to be co-heirs with Christ in glory participate in his lowliness as well.

(8) John of Damascus

Christ's soul, when it was deified, descended into Hades, in order that, just as *the Sun of Righteousness* (Mal 4:2) rose for those on the earth, so likewise he might bring light to those who were sitting under the earth **in darkness and death's shadow** (9:2). Just as he proclaimed peace to those on the earth, release to prisoners, and recovery of sight to the blind (cf. Isa 61:1), and became to those who believed the author of everlasting salvation and to those who did not believe a reproach of their unbelief, so he might do the same for those in Hades (cf. 1 Pet 3:19) *so that every knee should bow, in heaven and on earth and* *under the earth* (Phil 2:10). And thus after he had freed those who had been bound for ages, he rose from the dead, preparing for us the way of the resurrection.

(9) Symeon the New Theologian

You must learn and be convinced that **those who sit in darkness** will see **the great light shine** (9:2) if only they look toward it. Also, though it shone in the past, one should not think that people today cannot see it while they are still in the body. If it were impossible to see it, why did it shine then, and why does it still shine even when it is not seen? In fact, the light always existed (John 1:1) and always shone and still shines in those who have been cleansed. It shone in the darkness, and the darkness did not overcome it (John 1:5), and it shines now, and the darkness does not overcome it. It does not even touch it. But to state that now it has risen for the **people that sits in darkness** means that even now it reveals itself to those to whom it appears. Others, however, who are in darkness do not receive it. For he who is invisible has appeared, both by means of the body through physical eyes to all who beheld him, both believers and unbelievers, and he was also made known and the light of his godhead was revealed, yet only to those who showed their faith by deeds. It was those who would say to him: *Lo, we have left everything and followed you* (Matt 19:27).

9:6
A child was born for us, a son also given to us, whose sovereignty was upon his shoulder; and he shall be named Messenger of Great Counsel.

(10) Irenaeus of Lyons

In no other way could we have attained to incorruptibility and immortality than by being united to incorruptibility and immortality. But how could we be joined to incorruptibility and immortality, unless, first, incorruptibility and immortality had become what we are, so that the incorruptible might be swallowed up by incorruptibility, and the mortal by immortality, that we might receive the adoption of sons (Gal 4:5)?

For this reason Isaiah asks, *Who shall declare his generation?* (Isa 53:8). Since *he is a man, and who shall recognize him?* (Jer 17:9). But he to whom the Father in heaven has revealed him, knows him. He understood that the one *born not from the will of the flesh nor of the will of man* (John 1:13) is the Son of man, that is, Christ, the Son of the living God. . . . But that he is himself unlike all men who ever lived and in his own right God, and Lord, eternal King and the Incarnate Word, proclaimed by all the prophets, the apostles, and by the Spirit himself, may be seen by all who have attained to even a small portion of the truth. Now, the Scriptures would not have testified these things of him if, like others, he had been a mere man. But the Holy Scriptures testify to him in a double fashion: that he, unlike anyone else, was begotten in a remarkable way from the most high Father and also was born in a remarkable way from the Virgin. Further, that he was a man without comeliness, able to suffer, that he sat upon the foal of a donkey, that he was given vinegar and gall to drink, that he was despised among the people and humbled himself even to death, and that he is the holy Lord, **the wonderful counselor, the beautiful in appearance, and the mighty God** (9:6), coming on the clouds as the judge of men (Dan 7:13) — all these things the Scriptures prophesied of him.

(11) Tertullian

Come now, if you have read in the Psalms, *The L*ORD *reigned from the tree* (Ps 96:10).[3] I wonder what you understand by it, unless perhaps you think the reference is to some woodman as king of the Jews and not to Christ, who ever since his suffering on the tree has been king through his conquest of death. For although death reigned from Adam until Christ (cf. Rom 5:12-14), why should not Christ be said to have reigned from the tree, ever since he drove out the kingdom of death by dying on the tree of the cross?

In the same sense also Isaiah says, **Because to us a child is born** (9:6). What is new in this, unless he is speaking about the Son of God? And, **Unto us one is given whose government is placed upon his shoulder**. Which king ever displayed the sign of his dominion upon his shoulder, and not in a crown upon his head or a scepter in his hand, or some mark of appropriate apparel? No, only the new king of the new ages, Christ Jesus, the king of new glory, has lifted up upon his shoulder his own dominion and majesty, which is the cross, so that from henceforth, as the previous prophecy stated, he reigned as Lord from the tree.

(12) Pseudo-Ephrem the Syrian

> She carries an infant in her bosom,
> yet her virginity's seal is preserved.
> If anyone looks upon her,
> what can he say except
> "Here is the **Wonderful One**,"
> just as Isaiah spoke of old.
>
> The glorious Isaiah called Him "**God, the Valiant**";
> he called Him "the **wonderful**" too,
> because of His astonishing birth.
> For this reason let no one call Him
> anything apart from "**the Wonderful**."
>
> He entered by the ear[4]
> and resided in the womb in hidden fashion;

---

3. The phrase "from the tree" is not found in the Hebrew or the LXX, but Justin Martyr knew such a text (1 *Apology* 41).

4. By the word of the angel Gabriel to Mary.

He then left the womb without undoing her virginity's seal.
Likewise too when He left the tomb
He did so without undoing its seal.

Mary carried Him in honor
for nine months in her womb,
and when He sucked her milk
He too gave the drops of rain.
He is the prodigious **wonder**:
let the stance of all who deny Him be shattered!

(13) Ambrose of Milan

Your faith has saved you. Go in peace (Luke 7:50).[5] How simple this reading from the gospels, how deep its counsel! That is to be expected because the words are those of the **Great Counselor** (9:6). Let us consider their depth. Our Lord Jesus Christ realized that human beings could more readily be provoked to do what is right by kindness than by fear and that love is more effective in correcting someone than threats.

(14) Jerome

After the Lord has been called by two names (Emmanuel and Swiftly Spoil, Quickly Plunder), he is now given six others: **Wonderful, Counselor, God, Might, Everlasting Father, Prince of Peace**. These names are not to be joined together in groups of two — as some think — and read, Wonderful Counselor, Mighty God. Rather, they are to be read separately. . . . **Everlasting Father** signifies the Father of the future age and of the resurrection which will take place on the day we are judged. **Prince of Peace** has reference to what was said to the apostles: *Peace I leave with you; my peace I give to you* (John 14:27). One should not doubt that our peace, according to the apostle Paul, is the Savior (Eph 2:14-15). As to why the Septuagint does not translate these names, I think the reason may be that the translators were terrified to use names of such majesty to refer to a child and openly to call him God. Hence for these six names they have instead **messenger of great counsel, for I will bring peace upon the rulers, peace and health to him**.

(15) Maximus of Turin

To the apostles, who are already older in years, the Lord warns: *Unless you change and become like this child, you will not enter the kingdom of heaven* (Matt 18:3). He calls them back to that from which they came, and he insists that they return to their infancy, so that

---

5. Jesus said this to the woman who had anointed him with oil from an alabaster flask.

those who had grown old in their frail body might be born anew in good habits of innocence, as the Savior urges: *Unless one is reborn of water and the Holy Spirit, he will not enter the kingdom of God* (John 3:5). For this reason the apostles are told: *unless you change and become like this child.* He does not say "like these children," but *like this child.* He chooses one, he proposes one. Let us see, then, who he might be, who is proposed to the disciples to be imitated. I do not think that he is from the people, nor from the ordinary crowd, nor from the vast multitude — this one who was given, through the apostles, as an example of holiness to the entire world. I do not think, I say, that he is from the ordinary crowd but from heaven. For he is the child from heaven about whom the prophet Isaiah says: **A child is born to us, a son is given to us** (9:6). Clearly he is the child who, like an innocent, did not curse when he was cursed, did not strike back when he was struck (1 Pet 2:23). But rather in his suffering, he prayed for his enemies saying: *Father, forgive them, for they know not what they do* (Luke 23:34). So simplicity, which nature has given to infants, the Lord augmented with the virtue of mercy. This is the child, then, who is proposed to little ones to be imitated, and followed, for he himself commands: *Take up your cross and follow me* (Matt 16:24).

(16) Fulgentius of Ruspe

We know that Christ the Son of God is truthfully called by the words of the prophet **Mighty God**, when Isaiah says, **For a child is born to us, a son given to us, sovereignty rests on his shoulders, and he is named Wonderful Counselor, Mighty God, Everlasting Father, Prince of Peace** (9:6). Does not the apostle in one text point out the eternal power and divinity of this mighty God? Moreover, the true faith does not proclaim the eternal power and divinity of the Father in such a way that it does not believe in the eternal power and divinity of the Son or the Holy Spirit, since by nature the eternal power and divinity of the Father and the Son and the Holy Spirit are one. Therefore, Christ, the mighty God, is also truly God, just as divinity is truly mighty because it is power. Therefore, it is the true faith which truly believes and proclaims that Christ is the mighty God and knows that Christ crucified is the *power of God* and the *wisdom of God* as preached by the apostle (cf. 1 Cor 1:24); just as, in faith, he knows and acknowledges that, according to the flesh, the power is crucified, so he does not hesitate to confess that, according to the flesh, the divinity is crucified; for Christ the mighty God is God in such a way that he is his divinity; while he is mighty in such a way that he is his power.

9:7
His sovereignty is great, and his peace has no boundary.

(17) Eusebius of Caesarea

The expression **his sovereignty is great** (9:7) should be understood to refer to the Church spread throughout all the world, especially when one considers the testimonies

Isaiah 9

of the holy apostle concerning him. For example, it is said: *according to the working of his great might which he accomplished in Christ when he raised him from the dead and made him sit at his right hand in the heavenly places, far above every rule[6] and authority and power and dominion, and above every name that is named* (Eph 1:19-21). This, then, is what is meant by **his sovereignty is great**.

Further, the text reads: **to his peace there is no boundary** (9:7), because it is without end, ageless and unbounded. For this reason it is written: *In his days righteousness shall flourish, and peace abound* (Ps 72:7). After saying such things about the child who is born, he also adds this about him: **upon the throne of David and his kingdom, to establish it** (9:7). Observe carefully that he does not say "he will be set upon the throne of David," but simply, **upon the throne of David and his kingdom, to establish it**. What this means is that he will come in order to establish the throne of David and *the booth that is fallen* (Amos 9:11). From the time the people were taken in captivity to Babylon the kingdom of David was overthrown and destroyed. There were, however, prophecies that foretold that the throne of David would shine like the light of the sun through the whole inhabited world. He has come to fulfill this promise, being born *of the seed of David according to the flesh* (Rom 1:3), enlightening the souls of men, and strengthening his kingdom among the nations all over the world. In these he has **established the throne of David**, not with swords and spears but **with judgment and righteousness** (9:7). This he did **from this time onward and forever** (9:7). **From this time onward** signifies a **rule** with limits, that is, the time of his sojourn among men; **forever** indicates that his kingdom would be lasting and without limits.

---

6. See n. 2.

Isaiah 11

1 And a staff shall come out of the root of Iessai,
    and a blossom shall come up out of his root.
2 And the spirit of God shall rest on him,
    the spirit of wisdom and understanding,
    the spirit of counsel and might,
    the spirit of knowledge and godliness.
3 The spirit of the fear of God will fill him.
He shall not judge on the basis of repute,
    or convict on the basis of report;
4 but he shall administer justice to a humble one,
    and convict the humble ones of the earth;
and he shall strike the earth with the word of his mouth,
    and with breath through his lips he shall do away with the ungodly.
5 He shall be girded with righteousness around the waist,
    and bound with truth around the sides.

6 And the wolf shall graze with the lamb,
    and the leopard shall rest with the kid,
and the calf and the bull and the lion shall graze together,
    and a little child shall lead them.
7 And the ox and the bear shall graze together,
    and their young shall be together;
    and together shall the lion and the ox eat husks.
8 And the young child shall put its hand over the hole of asps,
    and on the lair of the offspring of asps.
9 And they will not hurt or be able to destroy
    anyone on my holy mountain;
because the whole earth has been filled to know the Lord
    like much water to cover seas.

10And there shall be on that day the root of Iessai, even the one who stands up to rule nations; nations shall hope in him, and his rest shall be honor.

11And it shall be on that day that the Lord will further display his hand to show zeal for the remnant that is left of the people, whatever is left from the Assyrians, and from Egypt and Babylonia and Ethiopia, and from the Ailamites, and from where the sun rises, and out of Arabia.

12 And he will raise a signal for the nations,
    and will gather the lost ones of Israel,
  and gather the dispersed of Ioudas
    from the four points of the earth.
13 And the jealousy of Ephraim shall be taken away,
    and the enemies of Ioudas shall perish;
  Ephraim shall not be jealous of Ioudas,
    and Ioudas shall not afflict Ephraim.
14 But they shall fly away in foreigners' ships,
    together they shall plunder the sea
    and those from the rising of the sun and Idumea.
  And they shall first lay their hands on Moab,
    but the sons of Ammon shall obey first.
15 And the Lord will make
    the sea of Egypt desolate;
  and will lay his hand upon the River
    with a violent wind;
  and will strike seven channels,
    so that he may cross in sandals.
16 And there shall be a passage
    for what is left of my people in Egypt,
  and it shall be to Israel
    as the day when he came out of the land of Egypt.

The first two verses of chapter 11 receive extensive commentary in the early Church. The church fathers took the first verse to refer to the Incarnation, when human nature "blossomed" to new life. Others, as the excerpt from Chrysostom indicates, thought the passage also showed that Christ was of the house and lineage of Jesse, that is, a descendant of King David. Jerome, the most learned of the ancient commentators, discusses several philological issues, including the view of some writers that the Hebrew word for **blossom** *(netser) in this passage is the source of the term "Nazarene" in Matt 2:23. He observes that "Nazarene" is written with the Hebrew letter "zayin," not "tsade" (as in "netser"), though the distinction between them cannot be expressed in Latin. The Greek term translated* **staff** *in v. 1 can be rendered "shoot" or "branch" or "rod" or "scepter," and in each selection we have rendered it according to the use the interpreter makes of it.*

    The second verse is the biblical basis for the seven gifts of the Holy Spirit, as in the hymn, "Veni, Creator Spiritus," that mentions the "seven-formed gift of the Spirit," Tu septiformis munere. *The gifts are wisdom and understanding, counsel and strength, knowledge and godliness, and fear of God. In the Hebrew text, however, there are only six gifts: wisdom, understanding, counsel, might, knowledge, and fear of the Lord. In the Septuagint version and others based on it, for example, the Latin,* **fear of the Lord** *is rendered* **the spirit of godliness (or piety)**, *and the final phrase,* **his delight shall be in the fear of the Lord** *(11:3), is translated* **the spirit of the fear of God**, *resulting in seven gifts. Gregory of Nazianzus takes the mention of the gifts of the Spirit as an occasion to discuss the nature of the Holy Spirit, and Augustine draws a parallel between the seven gifts and the seven beatitudes.*

The Virgin Mary also figures in the reading of this prophecy. Of particular interest are two kontakia, *liturgical poems or hymns, on Mary the Theotokos, Mother of God, by Romanos the Melodist, that draw on words and phrases from Isaiah 11. The peace of the messianic age spoken of in 11:6-9 was seen as a prediction of the civilizing effects of the gospel. Cyril of Alexandria says that Christ brought an end to savagery and introduced a gentle and a holy life, and Irenaeus sees in this text a promise of the restoration of a harmonious natural order.*

In Rom 15:12 St. Paul cites 11:10, **the root of Jesse shall come . . . in him shall the Gentiles hope**, *along with several other passages from the Psalms and Deuteronomy, to show that the Gentiles will share in the promises made to Israel. Following Paul, Cyril interprets 11:10 to refer to the calling of the Gentiles, but instead of citing Rom 15:12, he quotes another passage, Eph 2:11-13, where Paul says that those who were "strangers to the covenant of promise" and "once were far off have been brought near in the blood of Christ."*

(1) The Letter of Paul to the Romans

For I tell you that Christ became a servant to the circumcised to show God's truthfulness, in order to confirm the promises given to the patriarchs, and in order that the Gentiles might glorify God for his mercy. As it is written, *Therefore I will praise thee among the Gentiles, and sing to thy name* (Ps 18:49); and again it is said, *Rejoice, O Gentiles, with his people* (Deut 32:43); and again, *Praise the Lord, all Gentiles, and let all the peoples praise him* (Ps 117:1); and further Isaiah says, **The root of Jesse shall come, he who rises to rule the Gentiles; in him shall the Gentiles hope** (11:10).

(2) The Revelation to John

Then one of the elders said to me, "Weep not; lo, the Lion of the tribe of Judah, **the Root** of David (11:1, 10), has conquered, so that he can open the scroll and its seven seals."

*   *   *

"I Jesus have sent my angel to you with this testimony for the churches. I am **the root** (11:1, 10) and the offspring of David, the bright morning star."

(3) Cyril of Alexandria

The narrative now returns to the principal matter, the Incarnation of the only Son and the future dispensation of his birth from a woman according to the flesh. The prophet uses the term **staff** to refer to Christ **from the root of Jesse** according to the flesh. In addition, he is called a **blossom** (11:1). By **staff** [or scepter] it seems he is obliquely referring to his royal authority. For the staff is a sign of rule. Holy David said about the same Son, *Your throne, O God, endures forever and ever. Your royal scepter is a scepter of equity* (Ps. 45:6).

Staff can also signify that he possesses all things and holds all things together. He gives strength to the weak, for human nature is blown about and inebriated with unruly passions. For this reason blessed David, attributing to himself what is common to all human beings, sings: *Your rod and your staff, they comfort me* (Ps 23:4). He also *upholds the righteous* (Ps 37:17), as it is written. And he is called *glorious staff* and *magnificent rod* by the prophet (Jer 48:17). **Staff** can also have another significance, since the good shepherd lays down his life for his sheep (John 10:11). It was said of him through one of the holy prophets: *Shepherd thy people with thy staff, thy tribe, the flock of thy inheritance* (Mic 7:14). It also seems to some that, since he is judge and rewards each according to his works, it is fitting to call him **rod**. For it was said to him, when Israel behaved toward him like a drunken person and rashly became disobedient, *You shall shepherd them with a rod of iron, and dash them in pieces like a potter's vessel* (Ps 2:9). . . .

When the prophet says that the **staff from the root of Jesse** will appear to us, he sheds light on the mystery of Christ through figurative language. With the mind's eye he sees the only-begotten Word of God, through whom are all things, and in whom are all things, incarnate in the flesh, willingly emptying himself (Phil 2:7), undergoing human birth for us from a woman according to the divine plan (cf. Gal 4:4). As the prophet says: LORD, *I heard the report of you, and was filled with awe; I considered your works and was astounded* (Hab 3:2). These, then, are some of the reasons why he is called **staff**.

He is also called **blossom**. For human nature blossoms into life and immortality in him, and into the newness of the evangelical way of life. **Blossom** can be understood in another way, as spiritual fragrance. *I am a blossom of the plain, a lily of the valley* (Song 2:1 LXX). For he became for us the fragrance of the knowledge of our God and Father. Therefore, St. Paul exults: *Thanks be to God, who always leads us in Christ and through us spreads the fragrance of the knowledge of him everywhere. For we are the aroma of Christ to God among those who are being saved and among those who are perishing, to one a fragrance from death to death, to the other a fragrance from life to life* (2 Cor 2:14-16). On this **staff** or this **blossom from the root of Jesse** the Holy Spirit rested at the opportune time and brought about many works. The prophet mentions **the spirit of counsel and understanding, of knowledge and wisdom, of piety and the fear of God** (11:2).[1]

---

1. For some reason Cyril mentions only six gifts and omits **spirit of strength**. At the end of the section, however, he does refer to the **spirit of strength**.

In a skillful way the prophet does not present to us a Jesus who is a mere man who became a bearer of the Spirit by receiving the gifts that God bestows on human beings, but rather he declares him to be the divine Word incarnate, full of every good gift that pertains to his nature. At the same time he makes his own what belongs to human nature. For human beings receive God's grace as a gift from above. For the question is asked, *What have you that you did not receive?* (1 Cor 4:7). We have been enriched from without, from what is given to us, for what we have received from God is beyond our abilities.

When the only-begotten Word of God emptied himself, he did not shun the lowliness of the human condition. For the sake of mankind he became fully human and received the Spirit, not for himself but for us who are in need of every good thing that comes from God. If then it is said that he who is the giver of the Spirit received the Spirit and distributes the Spirit to the saints, not measuring out what he received but giving out of his own fullness, understand that he received the Spirit as a mark of his emptying (Phil 2:7). If you think of things in that way, you will have come to the truth.

Next in the text come the words: **And the Spirit of the Lord will rest upon him** (11:2). The Spirit had been given to the first fruits of human nature, that is, to Adam, but he became indifferent toward keeping the law that had been given to him. He disregarded the commandments, and sank into sin. Consequently the Spirit could find no resting place among human beings. *All have turned aside, together they have gone wrong; no one does good, not even one* (Rom 3:12, citing Ps 14:3). So when the only-begotten Word of God became man, he did not cease to be God. He became one of us, though without sin, and the Holy Spirit rested again on human nature, as in the first man, now as a kind of second first fruits of the human race, so that he might rest again on human nature and remain permanently in it by dwelling in believers' minds. Hence St. John said that he beheld the Spirit *descending from heaven* on Christ (John 1:32).

As we became co-heirs of the evil that came upon the one first formed, so we will share in the things that came to be through God's plan in the second first fruits of our race, that is, in Christ. Grace was not given to him partially as it is when it is said that the Spirit rested on the saints. The fullness of the godhead dwelled in his own flesh (cf. Col 1:19; 2:9), as in his own temple, with a human soul. He was animated by an intelligent soul, as the prophet makes clear: **The Spirit of the fear of God will fill him** (11:3).

The one Spirit works many different things. There is not one **Spirit for wisdom and another for understanding, another for counsel, another for strength**, and so on. The Word of God the Father is one, but his activity is manifold. For he is life and light and power. So also one should understand the Holy Spirit. Though he is one, his works are many. Therefore, all-wise Paul, enumerating the different kinds of gifts bestowed on us, said: *All these are inspired by one and the same Spirit, who apportions to each one individually as he wills* (1 Cor 12:11).

(4) Jerome

Up to the beginning of the vision of the fall of Babylon,[2] which Isaiah son of Amos saw, this whole prophecy is about Christ. We intend to explain it in portions, so that the arguments and expositions will not overwhelm the reader's memory.

The Jews interpret the **branch and the blossom from the root of Jesse** (11:1) as the Lord[3] himself, on the grounds that his royal power is symbolized in the **branch**[4] and his beauty in the **blossom**. We, however, understand the **branch from the root of Jesse** as holy Mary, the Virgin, who had no bush clinging to her,[5] and about whom we read above: *A virgin[6] shall conceive and bear a son* (Isa 7:14). **Blossom** refers to the Lord and Savior who said in the Song of Songs: *I am a blossom of the field and a lily of the valleys* (Song 2:1 LXX). For **root**, a translation found only in the Septuagint, *geza* is written in the Hebrew original, and Aquila, Symmachus, and Theodotion have all translated it into Greek as *kormos*, meaning "trunk." And **blossom**, which in Hebrew is called *netser*, they have translated as "shoot," in order to show that long after the Babylonian Captivity, when no one from the line of David possessed the glory of the ancient kingdom, Christ was born of Mary, as it were from Mary as "trunk."

All the orthodox writers have looked in vain [in the Old Testament] for the source of the line in Matthew's Gospel, *He shall be called a Nazarene* (Matt 2:23). Learned men from the Hebrews think it originated in this passage in Isaiah. But we must realize that the word *netser* [*nezer*] is written with the Hebrew letter *tsade*, whose character and sound, between a "z" and an "s," cannot be expressed in the Latin language. It is a kind of hissing sound that can be produced with difficulty by the pressure of the tongue when the teeth are pressed together. The city of "Sion" is written with the same letter. Furthermore, "Nazarenes," which the Septuagint translates as "holy ones" and Symmachus as "separated ones," is always written with the Hebrew letter *zayin*.

The Spirit of the Lord will come to rest on this **blossom** which springs suddenly from the trunk and **from the root of Jesse** (11:2) through the Virgin Mary. For *in him the whole fullness of divinity dwells bodily* (Col 2:9). The Spirit does not dwell in him partially as in the other saints, but according to the gospel written in the Hebrew language read by the Nazarenes, *The whole font of the Holy Spirit descended on him*.[7] *The Lord is the Spirit, and where the Spirit of the Lord is, there is freedom* (2 Cor 3:17). In the book of Matthew we read what is written later in Isaiah: *Behold, my servant whom I have chosen, my beloved with whom my soul is well pleased. I will put my Spirit upon him, and he shall proclaim justice to the Gentiles* (Matt 12:17-18, citing Isa 42:1-4). This is to be understood as referring to the Savior in whom the Spirit of the Lord rested. That is, the Spirit found in him a per-

---

2. Chapter 13.
3. That is, the Messiah.
4. Scepter.
5. Jerome has used a Latin word for a shrub or a bush, playing on the plant imagery of the prophetic text, but his language also carries sexual connotations to emphasize Mary's virginity.
6. In Latin "virgin" is *virgo*, while *virga* means "branch" or "rod."
7. This passage and the one cited a few lines later come from the lost *Gospel of the Nazarenes*, a Jewish-Christian gospel.

manent dwelling place. He would not fly away and later descend on him again. According to the testimony of John the Baptizer, he would remain in him continually: *I saw the Spirit descend as a dove from heaven, and it remained on him. I myself did not know him; but he who sent me to baptize with water said to me, "He on whom you see the Spirit descend and remain, this is he who baptizes with the Holy Spirit"* (John 1:32-33).

Further, in the Gospel mentioned above, we find these words: *And it came to pass when the Lord came up out of the water, the whole font of the Holy Spirit descended on him and rested on him and said to him, "My Son, in all the prophets I was waiting for you to come that I might rest on you. For you are my rest, you are my firstborn, you reign forever."*[8] He is called the Spirit of the Lord and the Spirit of Wisdom, for *all things were made through him, and without him was not anything made that was made* (John 1:3). And in the psalm is sung: *How magnificent are your works, O Lord! In wisdom you have made them all* (Ps 104:24). And the apostle writes: *Christ the power of God and the wisdom of God* (1 Cor 1:24). And in the book of Proverbs it is written: *The Lord by wisdom founded the earth; with prudence he established the heavens* (Prov 3:19).

As this same Word of God is called light and life and resurrection, so he is called the **spirit of wisdom and understanding, of counsel and strength, of knowledge and piety** and **the fear of the Lord**. That there are different names should not be taken to mean that there are different spirits. There is one and the same font and origin for all the virtues. Therefore, without Christ no one can be wise, or intelligent, or a giver of good advice, or strong, or knowledgeable, or pious, or full of the fear of God. It must be noted that the spirit of the Lord, of **wisdom and understanding, counsel and strength, knowledge and piety and the fear of the Lord** — that is, a seven fold number, who are called *seven eyes on a single stone* in Zechariah (Zech 3:9 LXX) — will come to rest on the **branch** and the **blossom** which has sprung up from Jesse, and thereby from the line of David.

11:1
A shoot shall come out of the root of Jesse,
and a blossom shall come out of his root.

(5) Justin Martyr

The first power after God the Father and Master of all is his Son the Word. How he was made flesh and became man we will say in what follows. As the blood of the grape was not made by man but by God, so it was announced that his blood should not come from human seed but from divine power. . . . Isaiah promised: **A star shall rise out of Jacob, and a blossom will come forth from the root of Jesse, and in his arm the nations will hope** (11:1; cf. 51:5; Num 24:17). The luminous star rose and the flower has blossomed from the root of Jesse — this one is Christ. He was conceived by the power of God from a virgin of the seed of Jacob, who was the father of Judah, the father of the Jews, as was made clear; Jesse was his ancestor according to the oracle, and he was the son of Jacob and Judah by lineal succession.

---

8. From the *Gospel of the Nazarenes*.

(6) Tertullian

Isaiah made the announcement, **There shall come forth a shoot out of the root of Jesse, and a blossom shall come up from the root, and the Spirit of the Lord shall rest upon him.** Then he goes on to recount its forms: **The Spirit of wisdom and understanding, the Spirit of counsel and might, the Spirit of knowledge and godliness; the Spirit of the fear of God shall fill him** (11:1-3). Thus in the figure of a flower he pointed to Christ, who was to rise up out of the shoot which had come forth from the root of Jesse — that is, the virgin of the offspring of David the son of Jesse; and in that Christ the entire substance of the Spirit was to come to rest. Not that it was to come as a later addition to him who even before his Incarnation has always been the Spirit of God — so that you may not use this as an argument that this prophecy refers to the Christ who as a mere man, solely of descent from David, will in the future [you say] acquire the spirit of his own God — but because from the moment that the flower bloomed in the flesh assumed from the stock of David, the entire operation of spiritual grace was to come to rest in him and, as far as the Jews were concerned, to come to an end. And the facts themselves bear witness to this, since from then onward the Spirit of the Creator no longer breathes among them. . . . So now there is that promise of the Spirit made in general terms by Joel: *In the last days I will pour out my Spirit upon all flesh, and their sons and their daughters shall prophesy, and upon my servants and my handmaids I will pour forth of my Spirit* (Joel 2:28). And in fact, if it was for the last days that the Creator promised the grace of the Spirit, while in the last days Christ has appeared as dispenser of spiritual things — for the apostle says, *But when the time was fulfilled, God sent his Son* (Gal. 4:4), and again, *Because the time is now short* (1 Cor 7:29) — it is clear also from that foretelling of the last times that this grace of the Spirit appertains to the Christ of him who foretold it. Place side by side the apostle's details and those of Isaiah: *To one*, he says, *is given by the Spirit the word of wisdom* (see 1 Cor 12:8-10), so at once Isaiah has set down, **The Spirit of wisdom**; *to another the word of knowledge*, and this must be the word of **understanding and counsel**; *to another faith, by the same Spirit*, which must mean **the Spirit of godliness and the fear of God**; *to another the gift of healings, to another miracles*, and this will be **Spirit of might**; *to another prophecy, to another discerning of spirits, to another diverse kinds of tongues, to another the interpretation of tongues*, which will be the **Spirit of knowledge**. See how both when he sets out the apportionments of the one Spirit and when he expounds their particular bearing, the apostle is in full agreement with the prophet.

(7) Hippolytus

The prophet [Jacob] calls the one who is descended from Judah and David according to the flesh *a lion's cub* (Gen 49:9), although he does not originate from David's seed but is conceived by the Holy Spirit and **comes forth** *from a holy shoot* (Gen 49:9 LXX) from the earth. Thus Isaiah predicts, **A shoot shall come forth from the root of Jesse, and a blossom shall flower from it** (11:1). What Isaiah calls a **blossom** is what Jacob calls a *shoot,* because he first sprouted forth and then blossomed in the world. The text that says, *He lay back and went to sleep, like a lion and a lion's cub* (Gen 49:9 LXX), refers to Christ's three-day sleep, as Isaiah also exclaims: *How has faithful Zion become a prostitute, she that was full of justice! Righteousness used to sleep in her, but now murderers* (Isa 1:21). And David likewise says: *I went to sleep and slumbered; I awoke, because the* LORD *shall be my help* (Ps 3:5), in order to show that his going to sleep and his resurrection had occurred. Jacob says, *Who will wake him?* (Gen 49:9 LXX), referring to the one of whom David had spoken, just as Paul says, *And of God the Father, who raised him from the dead* (Gal 1:1).

(8) Didymus the Blind

Revealing his servant, the Father says, *Behold, a man; his name is "the East"* (Zech 6:12 LXX; cf. also Zech 3:8 LXX). He calls him a *man* because of the Incarnation, but *the East* because he is the Sun of Righteousness which has arisen. For it is written of him in the last book of the Minor Prophets, in the mouth of the Father who has sent him, *The Sun of Righteousness will rise upon you who fear my name, and there will be healing in his wings* (Mal 4:2).

Having explained the reason for the sending of his servant *the East,* he says, *Because the stone before* the one whose light has shone *contains seven eyes . . .* (Zech 3:9). What is this stone but the Savior who has dwelt among us, who possesses a capacity for a sevenfold power of vision? This is what Isaiah says of him: **A staff shall come out of the root of Jesse, and a blossom shall come out of his root, and the Spirit of God shall rest upon him, the spirit of wisdom and understanding, the spirit of counsel and strength, the spirit of knowledge and piety, and the spirit of the fear of God shall fill him** (11:1-3).

Now consider the seven eyes of the Lord upon the stone, among which are the **spirit of wisdom** and that of **understanding**. What eye could be so bright as to take in all that is good and great, save the **spirit of wisdom**, and similarly the **spirit of understanding**?

What spiritual stone could be so endowed with eyes, being **counsel** and **strength** itself, as to contemplate everything with prudence and power, with knowledge and piety, filled with the Spirit of God, especially when it has assumed *the form of a servant* (Phil 2:6)? Nor did he receive just momentarily or externally the spirit that came to **rest upon him, the spirit of wisdom and understanding, of counsel and strength, of knowledge and piety**, for it is said to **come to rest upon him**. Each of the things that are named is peculiarly fit for him, although only the **spirit of fear** is said to come in such as way as to **fill** him.

This **spirit of fear** is known by another name as "reverence," as befits the human being born from Mary. The apostle writes about him using this very word: *In the days of his flesh, Jesus offered up prayers and supplications, with loud cries and tears, to him who was able to save him from death, and he was heard for his godly fear* (Heb 5:7).

(9) John Chrysostom

Though he used figures and metaphorical language, the prophet Isaiah predicted long ago not only that Christ would be a man and be born of a virgin, but also that he would be of the house of David. **A rod shall come out of the root of Jesse, and a blossom shall arise from his root . . .** (11:1-2). This Jesse was David's father, and it is clear from this that David came from the tribe of Jesse. The prophet predicted that the one who was to come would come not only from the tribe but even from the house of Jesse when he said: **A rod will come forth from Jesse's root**. For the prophet was not simply speaking of the **rod** but of [Christ] and his kingdom. He makes clear that he is not speaking about the **rod** because after he says **a rod shall come forth**, he adds: **And the spirit of wisdom and understanding shall rest on him**.

No one would be so senseless as to say that the grace of the Spirit came down on a piece of wood. It is clear that the Spirit came down on that spotless temple of the Spirit. This is why Isaiah did not say *it will come* but *it will come to rest*, because after coming he remained. The Evangelist John made this clear when he said: *I saw the Spirit descend as a dove, and it remained on him* (John 1:32).

(10) Leo the Great

In many and diverse ways (Heb 1:1), beloved, the divine goodness has always cared for the human race and mercifully imparted an abundance of gifts through his providence to all past generations. But *at the end of the times* (1 Pet 1:20) he has exceeded the customary measure of his goodness when, in Christ, mercy itself has come down to sinners, truth itself to those in error, and life itself to the dead. In assuming our lowly nature, the Word — coeternal with and equal to the Creator — brought it into union with his divinity. As God was born from God, the same one might be born man from man. This was promised from *the foundation of the world* (Eph 1:4) and had long been prophesied by many ways, by deeds and by words. Yet how many people would those figures and dark mysteries have saved, had not Christ fulfilled the ancient and hidden promises by his coming? What was to happen profited only a few believers; now its fulfillment has helped countless of the faithful.

So now we are led to believe not by signs and images, but we are confirmed by the evangelical history. We believe what has actually happened; we adore aided by the instruction of the prophets. There is no uncertainty because we know that these things were predicted by such venerable oracles. Here is what the Lord promised Abraham: *In your seed all the nations will be blessed* (Gen 22:18). And this is God's promise sung by David speaking with the spirit of prophecy: *The LORD swore to David and will not disappoint him: "One of the sons of your body I will set on my throne"* (Ps 132:11). And this same Lord predicted through Isaiah: *Behold, a virgin will conceive and bear a son, and they will call his name Emmanuel* (7:14), which means "God is with us." And again: **There shall come forth a shoot from the root of Jesse, and from this root a blossom will rise up** (11:1). It is certain that this **shoot** signifies the Blessed Virgin Mary,[9] who sprang from the stock of Jesse and David and was made fruitful by the Holy Spirit, bringing forth a new flower of human flesh, from a mother's womb to be sure, but through a virgin birth.

---

9. The same wordplay used by Jerome; see n. 5.

(11) Romanos the Melodist

Prelude

Today the Virgin gives birth to him who is above all being,
And the earth offers a cave to him whom no one can approach.
Angels with shepherds give glory,
And Magi journey with a star,
For to us there has been born
    A little Child, God before the ages (cf. 9:5).
Bethlehem has opened Eden, come, let us see;
We have found delight in secret, come, let us receive
The joys of paradise within the cave.
There the unwatered **root** whose **blossom** (11:1) is forgiveness has appeared.
There has been found the undug well
From which David once longed to drink.
There a virgin has borne a babe
And has quenched at once Adam's and David's thirst.
For this, let us hasten to this place where there has been born
    A little Child, God before the ages.
The mother's Father has willingly become her Son,
The infants' Savior is laid as an infant in a manger.
As she who bore him contemplates him, she says,
"Tell me, my Child, how were you sown, or how were you planted in me?
I see you, my flesh and blood, and I am amazed,
Because I gave suck and yet I am not married.
And though I see you in swaddling clothes,
I know that the **flower** of my virginity is sealed,
For you preserved it when, in your good pleasure, you were born.
    A little Child, God before the ages.

* * *

When you conceived without seed, O Mother of God,
Joseph was struck with wonder as he contemplated what was beyond nature,
And he brought to mind the rain on the fleece (Ps 71:6 LXX; Judg 6:36-38),
The bush unburned by fire (cf. Exod 3:2-4),
Aaron's rod which blossomed (Num 17:8).
And your betrothed and guardian bore witness and cried to the priests,[10]
    "A Virgin gives birth, and after childbirth remains still a virgin."

---

10. In this *kontakion* Joseph is speaking in direct discourse.

"What I see I cannot understand, for it surpasses the human mind,
How is it that the grass carries fire and is not burned?
A lamb carries a lion, a swallow an eagle, and the servant her Master (cf. 11:6-8)
In a mortal womb, in a manner uncircumscribed,
Mary carries my Savior as he wills,
So that everyone will say,
   'A Virgin gives birth, and after childbirth remains still a virgin.'
"Now I see Aaron's rod that blossomed without watering (Num 17:8),
Of which Isaiah son of Amos wrote for me.
See, he says, **a shoot will come out of Jesse, and the flower from its root**.
The rod of Aaron and Jesse — Mary,
Who flowered without cultivation. . . ."
   A Virgin gives birth, and after childbirth remains still a virgin.

(12) Maximus the Confessor

The holy prophet Isaiah says in his prophecy that seven spirits rested on the Savior who rose up **from the root of Jesse** (11:1). He knows that these were not seven spirits of God. What he has in mind is this: there are seven activities of the one Holy Spirit, and these he calls **spirits** (11:1) because the Holy Spirit brings about each individual activity perfectly and proportionately.

The divine apostle, on the other hand, speaks about the different activities of the one Holy Spirit as *varieties of gifts* (1 Cor 12:4) brought about by one and the same Spirit. If then the manifestation of the Spirit is granted to each person according to the measure of his faith, then each believer who shares in such a gift does so in proportion to his faith and to the interior disposition of his soul. He receives the appropriate action of the Spirit granted to him to the degree that he is able to perform this or that commandment.

One person receives, as it were, the word of **wisdom**, another the word of **knowledge**, another the word of **faith**, and still another something other of the gifts of the Spirit enumerated by the great apostle (1 Cor 12:8ff.). In this way one receives through the Spirit, according to the measure of one's faith, a gift of perfect, direct, and wholly spiritual love for God, while another receives from the same Spirit a gift of perfect love for the neighbor. As I said, the gift that is proper to each one is brought about by the same Spirit. If, like holy Isaiah, one calls these *gifts* **spirits,** he has not gone wrong. For as the Holy Spirit is the perfect agent of every gift, so he is found proportionately in every gift to a greater or lesser degree.

(13) Bernard of Clairvaux

What was the bush that Moses saw ablaze yet not burning up if not Mary giving birth yet not experiencing the pain of birth? What, I ask, did Aaron's rod that blossomed without being watered (Num 17:8) point to if not Mary conceiving although she had not known a man? Isaiah instructed us about the greater mystery of this wondrous miracle when he promised: **A shoot will come out of the root of Jesse, and a blossom shall come out of its root** (11:1), the shoot signifying the Virgin and the blossom the virgin birth.

11:2-3
And the Spirit of the Lord shall rest upon him, the spirit of wisdom and understanding, the spirit of counsel and might, the spirit of knowledge and godliness. The spirit of the fear of God will fill him.

(14) Irenaeus of Lyons

[At his baptism] the Spirit of God descended on Christ as a dove. This was the Spirit of whom it was said by Isaiah: **The Spirit of God shall rest upon him** (11:2). And again: *The Spirit of the Lord GOD is upon me, because he has anointed me* (61:1). This is the Spirit about whom the Lord says: *It is not you who speak, but the Spirit of your Father who speaks through you* (Matt 10:20). And again when he gave his disciples power to bring about a rebirth in God, he commanded them: *Go and make disciples of all nations, baptizing them in the name of the Father and of the Son and of the Holy Spirit* (Matt 28:19). God had promised that in the last times he would pour out this Spirit upon his servants and handmaids, that they might prophesy (cf. Joel 2:28-29; Acts 2:17-18). For this reason he also descended on the Son of God who had become the Son of man. By dwelling in him he grew accustomed to dwell in the human race, to find rest in human beings, and to dwell in God's handiwork. He carried out the Father's will, transforming their old habits into the newness of Christ.

David asked that the Spirit be sent to the human race when he prayed: *Uphold me with your guiding Spirit* (Ps 50:12 LXX). This same Spirit, as Luke says, descended upon the disciples on the Day of Pentecost after the Lord's Ascension, giving them power to bring life to the nations and to lay open a new covenant. Moreover, they praised God in all languages with one accord, and the Spirit brought the disparate tribes together, offering them to the Father as the first fruits of all nations (cf. Acts 2:1-11).

That is why the Lord promised to send the Comforter to unite us with God. For as dry flour cannot be made into a lump of dough or a loaf of bread without liquid, so we could not be made one in Christ Jesus without the water from heaven. In the same way, just as the dry earth cannot bring forth fruit without moisture, so we, who were once a dry tree, could not have brought forth a life that bears fruit without the gracious rain (cf. Ps 68:9).... The Lord, then, who received the Spirit as a gift from his Father, confers it upon those who are in fellowship with him, sending the Holy Spirit to all the earth.

Isaiah wrote that the dew, the Spirit of God, would descend on the Lord and be diffused throughout all the earth: **the spirit of wisdom and understanding, the spirit of counsel and strength, the spirit of knowledge and piety, the spirit of the fear of God** (11:2-3). He conferred this Spirit on the Church, sending the Comforter from heaven throughout the whole world.... We have need of the dew of God so that we are not consumed by fire, nor become sterile, and that we may have an advocate when we have been accused (1 John 2:1). The Lord entrusted the human race, which belonged to him, to the Holy Spirit after humanity had fallen among thieves (cf. Luke 10:30). *He had compassion* on humanity *and bound up his wounds* (Luke 10:33-34), giving *two denarii* (Luke 10:35), so that we, having received the image and inscription of the Father and of the Son through the Spirit, might make the gift fruitful and return it many times over to the Lord.

(15) Origen of Alexandria

Seven women suffer reproach and wander around asking someone to take them in and remove their reproach (4:1). These seven women promise to eat their own bread and wear their own clothes — they seek not a man's bread but his name, to remove their reproach. They do not need the man's clothes. They have better clothes than he can provide. They have food that is more sumptuous than human nature can give. It is worth considering, therefore, whose women these are and what is their reproach.

The seven women are in fact one, the Spirit of God. The Spirit is one, but also sevenfold: **the spirit of wisdom and understanding, the spirit of counsel and strength, the spirit of knowledge and piety, the spirit of the fear of the Lord** (11:2-3). As **Wisdom** it suffers reproach from the many wisdoms that rise up against it. As the true **Understanding** it suffers reproach from false understandings. As **Great Counsel** it suffers reproach from counsel that is not good. As **Strength** [or virtue] it is abused by strength that is not strength but claims it is. As **Knowledge** it is reproached by counterfeit knowledge. As **Piety** it is accused by what passes for piety but promotes impiety. As the **Fear of the Lord** it suffers reproach from that which is thought to be fear. For many promise a genuine fear of God but do so without knowledge.

Let us now consider how these seven suffer reproach. Look at the wisdom of this age, look at the wisdom of the rulers of this world, how they reproach the wisdom of my Christ, and how they reproach the wisdom of the true Judaism, according to which we are circumcised spiritually, not by being cut physically. And so understand how the wisdom of this age and of the rulers of this world curse Wisdom, and why a man is sought who can be with these seven **spirits** or seven women and remove their reproach. Who is that man? Jesus, who came forth according to the flesh **from the root of Jesse**, *was born from the seed of David according to the flesh and designated Son of God in power according to the Spirit of holiness* (Rom 1:3-4). **A branch came out of the root of Jesse**. The **branch** is not the Firstborn of every creature, not the one who was in the beginning with God as God the Word, but the **branch from the root of Jesse, who was born according to the flesh. And a flower came out of his root.**

Who is this **flower** and what is the **root**? Both inhere in the very same thing; their difference consists in what they do. For if you are a sinner, he is not a **flower** so far as you are concerned, nor will you see the **flower from the root of Jesse**. Rather, for you he will come as a **branch** [in the sense of a rod], as the apostle speaks of *rod*[11] and **flowers**. Of

---

11. The word for "rod" in 1 Cor 4:21 is the same as that for "branch" in Isa 11:1.

the rod he asks, *What do you wish? Shall I come to you with a rod?* And of the **flower** he inquires, *or with love in a spirit of gentleness?* (1 Cor 4:21). Therefore, **from the root of Jesse** has come forth a branch or rod of wisdom for him who is beaten as punishment, a rod for him who needs reproof, a rod for him who needs rebuke; but it has come forth as a flower for him who already has knowledge, does not need harsh correction, and certainly does not need punishment, but has already begun to flower in good health and to advance toward perfect fruit. First the flower appears, then after the flower a branch grows and produces fruit.

A shoot came out of the root of Jesse, and a flower will arise from his root, and there **will rest on him** seven women, the spirits of the Lord, **the spirit of wisdom and understanding will rest on him**. But the spirit of wisdom did not rest on Moses, the spirit of wisdom did not rest on Joshua the son of Nave, the spirit of wisdom did not rest on the individual prophets, not on Isaiah nor on Jeremiah.

Don't stone me as if I were a blasphemer because I want to glorify my Lord Jesus Christ. But be patient and consider what I am saying, and you will see that the Spirit did not come to rest on any of them — not that it did not *come* to them, only that it did not *rest* on them.... For everyone sins: *there is not a single just man on earth who only does good and does not sin* (Eccl 7:20), and *No one is pure from his birth, not even if his life be only one day; his months are numbered* (Job 14:4-5 LXX). Therefore, the spirit rests on no one. We can also prove this from the Gospel, because the Spirit came upon many but did not remain with them. A little before the Lord said, *My spirit shall not abide in man forever* (Gen 6:1-3). He does not say that it will not come, but that it *will not abide*. John saw only one on whom it remained, and this was the sign: *He on whom you see the Spirit descend and remain, he . . . is the Son of God* (John 1:33-34).

(16) Origen of Alexandria

The Holy Spirit rested on all those who prophesied, but he did not rest on anyone in the way he rested on the Savior. That is why it is written of him: **A shoot shall come out of the root of Jesse, and a flower shall come out of his root, and the spirit of God will rest on him, the spirit of wisdom and understanding** . . . (11:1-2). But perhaps someone will object: You have showed nothing more about Christ than what is written about other men. For just as it is said of others that it rested on them, so it is said of the Savior, **the spirit of God rested on him**. Note, however, that nowhere is it written that the Spirit of God rested on another person with seven powers; however, from this prophecy we learn that the essence of the divine Spirit, which because it cannot be expressed in one title requires many, rested on the **shoot which came out of the root of Jesse**.

I have another witness that allows me to teach that the Spirit rested on my Lord and Savior in an extraordinary way and quite differently than on other persons. That is John the Baptizer, who said of him: *He who sent me to baptize with water said to me, "He on whom you see the Spirit descend and remain, that is he"* (John 1:33). If God had said, *You will see the Spirit descend* without adding *and remain on him*, he would seem to have possessed nothing more extraordinary than others. But he added, *and remain on him*. This sign shows that the Savior possessed what no other person possessed. For about no one else was it written that the Holy Spirit remained on him.

(17) Aphrahat

[*For behold, upon the stone which I have set before Joshua, upon a single stone with seven facets, I will engrave its inscription, says the* LORD *of hosts . . .* (Zech 3:9).] And of this stone he said: *Lo, on this stone I will open seven eyes* (Zech. 3:9). And what are the seven eyes opened on the stone? Clearly it is the Spirit of God that rested on Christ with several works, as Isaiah the prophet said: **The Spirit of God shall rest and dwell on him, a spirit of wisdom and understanding, of counsel and of courage, of knowledge and of the fear of the Lord** (11:1-2). These were the seven eyes that were opened upon the Stone, and *these are the seven eyes of the* LORD, *which look on all the earth* (Zech 4:10).

(18) Gregory the Theologian

The Holy Spirit has always existed, exists now, and always will exist. He has no beginning and no end but is always joined with the Father and the Son and numbered with them. It is impossible for the Father ever to exist without the Son, or the Son without the Spirit: it would be acutely embarrassing for the godhead to advance, as it were, toward full perfection out of regret for a previous lack.

The Holy Spirit therefore is participated *in,* though the Spirit itself never participates (see 1 Cor 6:11); it perfects but is not perfected; *fills* (Wis 1:7) but is not itself filled; *makes holy* (1 Cor 6:11) but is not made holy; divinizes (cf. 1 Cor 3:16-17) but is not itself divinized; forever retains its identity with itself and the Persons with whom it is numbered; is unseen, timeless, unbounded, unchanging; with neither quality nor quantity, with neither form nor tangibility; perpetually self-moving, self-ruling, autonomous, and *almighty* (Wis 7:23) — even though, just as everything that belongs to the Son is referred to the First Cause [the Father], so too is everything that belongs to the Spirit — Life and life-giver; Light and source of light; Goodness itself and the source of goodness; the Spirit is *right* (Ps 51:10), *willing* (Ps 51:12), *Lord* (2 Cor 3:17), the one who *sends* (Acts 13:4) and *sets apart* (Acts 13:2), who builds a *temple* for himself (1 Cor 3:16) and who *leads the way* (Ps 143:10), who *works* and *apportions* his gifts *as he wills* (1 Cor 12:11): the Spirit of *adoption* (Rom 8:15), of *truth* (John 14:17), **of wisdom, of understanding, of knowledge, of godliness, of counsel, of strength, of fear** (11:2-3), as these have been counted [in Isaiah], by which Spirit the Father is known and the Son is glorified, and to whom alone he is known: one harmonious order, one adoration, worship, power, perfection, holiness.

(19) Ambrose of Milan

Remember that you received the seal of the Spirit: **the spirit of wisdom and understanding, the spirit of counsel and strength, the spirit of knowledge and piety, and the**

spirit of holy fear, and have preserved what you received. God the Father sealed you, Christ the Lord strengthened you and gave the guarantee of the Spirit in your heart, as you have learned in the lesson from the apostle.

(20) Augustine of Hippo

It seems to me that the sevenfold work of the Holy Spirit of which Isaiah speaks corresponds to the [seven stages in the Beatitudes].[12] But there is a difference in order. For [in Isaiah] the enumeration begins with the more excellent, but here [in the Beatitudes] with the lesser. For there it begins with **wisdom** and closes with the **fear of God**. But *the fear of the LORD is the beginning of wisdom* (Ps 111:10 = Sir 1:16). If we consider the listing a series that ascends gradually, **fear of God** is first, **piety** second, **knowledge** third, **fortitude** fourth, **counsel** fifth, **understanding** sixth, **wisdom** seventh. The **fear of God** corresponds to the lowly, of whom it is said, *Blessed are the poor in spirit* (Matt 5:3), that is, those who are not puffed up or proud, to whom the apostle says, *Do not become proud but stand in awe* (Rom 11:20), or in other words, "Don't be haughty." **Piety** corresponds to the meek. For whoever seeks in a reverent way honors Holy Scripture and does not judge what he does not yet understand and for this reason is receptive. This is what it means to be meek. Hence it is said, *Blessed are the meek* (Matt 5:5). **Knowledge** corresponds to those that mourn and have already learned from the Scriptures which evils they foolishly coveted as though good and useful but which hold them in bondage. **Fortitude** corresponds to those who are hungry and thirsty. For they strive earnestly to find joy in the things that are genuinely good, and seek eagerly to turn their love from earthly and corporeal things. Of them it is said, *Blessed are those who hunger and thirst after righteousness* (Matt 5:6). **Counsel** corresponds to the merciful, for this is the one remedy that allows us to escape great evils, that we forgive as we wish ourselves to be forgiven, and that we assist others as far as we are able, as we desire to be assisted when we are not able. Of them it is said, *Blessed are the merciful* (Matt 5:7). **Understanding** corresponds to the pure in heart. For when the eye is purged, one can behold what the bodily *eye has not seen nor ear heard, and has not entered into the heart of man* (1 Cor 2:9). Of them it is said, *Blessed are the pure in heart* (Matt 5:8). **Wisdom** corresponds to the peacemakers, in whom all things are now brought into order, no passion is in rebellion against reason, and all things obey the spirit of man while he himself obeys God. And of them it is said, *Blessed are the peacemakers* (Matt 5:9).

(21) Augustine of Hippo

When sins are forgiven in the sacraments, the house is cleaned out, but it needs an occupant, the Holy Spirit, and the Holy Spirit lives only in the humble of heart. God, you see,

---

12. Augustine has just explained how the Beatitudes set forth stages in the Christian life, beginning with humility.

asks, "Upon whom shall my Spirit rest?" And he answers the question, *Upon the humble and the quiet, and the one who trembles at my words* (Isa 66:2).... There are some proud people, however, who, once their sins have been forgiven, rely solely on the free choices of the human will for living a good life, and by that very pride they shut their doors in the Holy Spirit's face, and the house remains apparently cleaned up from the mess of sins, but vacant, with nothing positively good in it.... The Holy Spirit is presented to us as sevenfold in his activity, so that he may be in us **the Spirit of wisdom and understanding, of counsel and courage, of knowledge and piety, and of the fear of God**. Now set against this sevenfold good the opposite sevenfold evil: the spirit of folly and error, the spirit of rashness and cowardice, the spirit of ignorance and impiety, and the spirit of pride against the fear of God. These are seven wicked spirits; who are the other seven more wicked still?[13]

Another seven more wicked still are found in hypocrisy: one evil spirit of folly, another worse one of pretended wisdom; an evil spirit is the spirit of error, another worse one is the pretense of truth; an evil spirit is the spirit of rashness, another worse one is the pretense of counsel; an evil spirit is the spirit of cowardice, another worse one is the pretense of courage; an evil spirit is the spirit of ignorance, another worse one is pretended knowledge; an evil spirit is the spirit of impiety, another worse one is the pretense of piety; an evil spirit is the spirit of arrogance, another worse one is pretended reverence. Seven were not to be borne; who could put up with fourteen? So it necessarily follows that when you add to malice the pretense of truth, the last state of a person is worse than the first (cf. Matt 12:45).

(22) Augustine of Hippo

And Paul writes to Timothy, *For God did not give you a spirit of fear, but of courage, love, and self-control* (2 Tim 1:7). By this testimony of the apostle we ought, of course, to be careful that we do not think that we have not received the **spirit of the fear of God**. For it is undoubtedly a great gift of God, of which the prophet Isaiah says, **The spirit of wisdom and understanding, the spirit of counsel and fortitude, the spirit of knowledge and piety, the spirit of the fear of the Lord will rest upon him** (11:2-3). This is not the fear that led Peter to deny Christ; rather, we have received the **spirit of that fear** of which Christ himself says, *Fear him who has the power to destroy both soul and body in hell; yes, I say to you: Fear him* (Matt 10:28 and Luke 12:5). He said this in order that they would not deny him because of that fear by which Peter was thrown into confusion. For he wanted to take from us this fear when he warned, *Do not fear those who kill the body and afterward do not have anything they can do* (Luke. 12:4). We have not received the spirit of this fear, but the spirit of courage, love, and self-control.

---

13. Augustine is playing on the verse in Matt 12:45: "Then he [the unclean spirit] goes and brings with him seven other spirits more evil than himself, and they enter and dwell there."

(23) Gregory the Great

When our Redeemer came in the flesh, he *joined together the [seven] stars of the Pleiades* (cf. Job 38:31) because he possessed the operations of the sevenfold Spirit all at once, and they rested in him. Of him Isaiah promises: **A shoot will come out of the root of Jesse, and a flower shall arise from his root; and on him will rest the Spirit of the Lord, a spirit of wisdom and understanding, a spirit of counsel and strength, a spirit of knowledge and piety, and the spirit of the fear of the Lord will fill him** (11:1-3). Of him Zechariah says, *On a single stone there are seven eyes* (Zech 3:9), and again, *On a golden candlestick are seven lights* (Zech 4:2). No human being has possessed at one time all the operations of the Holy Spirit save only the mediator of God and men, whose is the same Spirit which has proceeded from the Father before all ages. Therefore, it is well expressed, *On a single stone there are seven eyes*. For it belongs to this stone to have seven eyes in the sense that at the same time it retains in operation every virtue of the Spirit's sevenfold grace. For one person receives prophecy, another knowledge, another powers, another kinds of tongues, another the interpretation of words, according to the distribution of the Holy Spirit (cf. 1 Cor 12:8-11); but truly to possess all the gifts of this same Spirit is possible for no one. But our Creator, when he took on our weakness, taught that by the power of his divinity he possessed at the same time all the virtues of the Holy Spirit; therefore, he may doubtless be said to have *joined the shining Pleiades*. But while he *joins the Pleiades*, he also *breaks the chain of Arcturus* (Job 38:31); because he has revealed that, having been made human, he had all the operations of the Holy Spirit, he relaxes the labor of the letter in the Old Testament so that each believer now may understand through the freedom of the spirit that which formerly he served in fear amidst so many difficulties.[14] Let blessed Job therefore hear, *Are you able to join the shining stars of the Pleiades?* This amounts to saying, "Indeed, you can have the lights of some of the virtues, but are you able to perform all the operations of the Holy Spirit? Therefore, you should ponder how I *join the Pleiades* in all the virtues, but refrain from your pride in a few."

11:6-9
The wolf shall graze with the lamb, the leopard shall rest with the kid, the calf and the bull and the lion shall graze together, and a little child shall lead them.

(24) Irenaeus of Lyons

Concerning these times[15] the prophet Isaiah foretells, **The wolf shall graze with the lamb, the leopard shall rest with the kid, the calf and the bull and the lion shall graze together, and a little child shall lead them . . .** (11:6-9). I am not unaware that some in-

---

14. Gregory's allegory depends on his equation of the northern star Arcturus with the "frigidity" of the law, and the Pleiades, rising in the east, with Christ and the freedom of the Spirit (see *Moral Commentary on Job* 29.73).

15. By "these times" Irenaeus refers to a millennial age of miraculous abundance and fertility, a doctrine he regarded as part of apostolic tradition.

terpreters try to apply these verses metaphorically to savage peoples who come from various nations and occupations, and who after their conversion live on good terms with the righteous. Even if conversion of this sort is now occurring among people from various nations who arrive at the same point of view on the faith, at the time of the resurrection of the righteous no less a change will take place in the case of the animals, as has just been said. For God is rich in all things, and it is necessary that at the restoration of creation all the wild beasts should obey and be subject to human beings, and return to the diet that God originally gave to them, as they had been subjected to Adam before his fall when they ate the earth's produce. Now is not the time to prove that the lion will feed on chaff; but such a diet indicates the abundance and the fertility of earth's fruits. For if an animal like a lion shall feed on chaff, imagine how great the harvest of the wheat itself will be, to provide the chaff to feed those lions!

(25) Cyril of Alexandria

The prophet now gives an extraordinary sign of the things he has been speaking of. He depicts the marvelous fulfillment of the prophecies in the coming of the Savior, and rightly so. Before the only-begotten Word of God became a human being like us, before *he was concerned with the descendants of Abraham, and was made like his brethren in every respect* (Heb 2:16-17), as it is written, the human race was divided into two peoples, the people of the Jews and those who *worshipped the creation rather than the Creator* (Rom 1:25). For *God was known in Judea* (Ps 76:1). The other peoples worshiped a great swarm of idols. They did not honor God as God but followed their own ways. *All have turned aside, together they have gone wrong; no one does good, not even one* (Rom 3:12, citing Ps 14:3).

The Jews, however, by the tutoring of the law, learned to live gentle lives and were instructed in the ways of justice, and practiced a way of life befitting human beings. The other peoples, that is, those who worshiped idols and did not have the guidance of the law, were given over to terrifying fantasies, and were undisciplined and arrogant.... For this reason the prophet compares some to a wolf, others to a leopard.... To those who were nurtured in these brutish customs and way of life, Christ brought an end to savagery and introduced a gentle and a holy life. They learned to honor a way of life befitting human beings, a life of meekness. For they believed in the words of Christ: *Take my yoke upon you and learn from me; for I am gentle and lowly in heart, and you will find rest for your souls* (Matt 11:29). Through faith they were able to cast off the ancient savagery, and to become gentle and meek and to display the way of life of God's saints. They came to be called fellow citizens with the saints and friends of God. In my view, this is what the prophet indicates to us by the various figures in this passage.

The wolf shall graze with the lamb, and the leopard shall rest with the kid (11:6). Through Christ the savage and the meek will be joined together, and those who are wholly lacking in holiness will be joined to the holy ones and to the saints. Insofar as Israel was under the tutoring of the law and learned forbearance, it was gentle and meek, and also holy, similar to a sheep or goat. Both of these animals are holy and pure and by nature tame. The wolf and the leopard, however, and also the lion, are by nature savage and unable to dwell together. But in Christ that is what happened. Jews and Greeks were gathered together with one another, sharing a single food, the evangelical and apostolic kerygma, under the care of the one *chief shepherd* (1 Pet 5:4) who knows how to graze his flock in a *good pasture and in a very rich place* (Ezek 34:14). . . .

And they will not hurt or be able to destroy anyone on my holy mountain (11:9). The **holy mountain** is the Church, lifted up on a high place in glory and adorned with sublime teachings. It is a community devoted to higher things. It is our practice to worship the Creator and Maker, not the creation. Nor do we number the divine Word, maker of all things, among created things, but give him the glory that is due him. **The universe has been filled with the knowledge of the Lord**, that is, filled with devotion toward him, as the wide and spacious **sea** is filled with its own **waters** (11:9). One can see that this is true. For where and by whom is the name of Christ not invoked? What race of men does not come under his sway? *Every knee bows before him, and every tongue confesses,* as it is written, *that Jesus Christ is God, to the glory of God the Father* (Phil 2:11).

And in that day there shall be a root of Jesse, and he will arise to rule the Gentiles; they will hope in him, and his rest shall be an honor (11:10). Little by little the spiritual meaning of what was spoken obscurely shines forth, and those things that were uttered through figures are clearly elucidated for eager listeners. For how it is that the wolf shall graze with the lamb, and the leopard rest with the kid, and the calf, ox, and lion eat husks together, and when it shall be that these things actually come to pass — that those who were once bellicose and cruel become docile and mild, and how they shall be fed abundantly along with those who are gentle and holy under one chief shepherd — all of this is made clear when it says, **and there shall be a root of Jesse** (11:10).

But to what is this referring and about whom is it spoken? It says that there will be a **ruler over the Gentiles** (11:10) and hope for those who have no hope, that is to say, the Gentiles will have hope. To them the most-wise Paul wrote: *Therefore remember that at one time you Gentiles, called the uncircumcision by what is called the circumcision, which is made in the flesh by hands — remember that you were at that time separated from Christ, alienated from the commonwealth of Israel, and strangers to the covenants of promise, having no hope and without God in the world. But now you who once were far off have been brought near in the blood of Christ* (Eph 2:11-13). But even if they were without hope, and, after the fashion of the world, did not know God — for they worshiped the works of their own hands — nevertheless, since they have been called through faith to the knowledge of Christ, they have been made subject to him, they have laid hold of him who is truly, and by nature, God, and have come to share in the hope of the saints.

Then it says: **his rest shall be an honor** (11:10). This can be understood in two ways. **Rest** can be taken to indicate the physical death that Christ willingly endured for our sake — not as though being done in by death, for he was life by nature, but rather causing as it were the flesh to rest for a while. To call that **honor** is surely correct. For the Savior of all, our Lord Jesus Christ, was glorified after he endured slaughter on behalf of the world, and voluntarily faced death for the life of all. When he was about to go to the precious and honorable cross, he prayed to his Father in heaven, *Father, glorify thy Son that the Son may glorify thee* (John 17:1). And again, *Now is the Son of man glorified, and in him God is* *glorified* (John 13:31). With respect to the madness of the crucifiers and their unholy and hostile undertaking, his passion was shameful and disgraceful, since they no doubt thought he suffered unwillingly. But since he came to life again after he had despoiled Hades, showing by this act that he is mightier even than death, we find that the final outcome is **honor** and glory for him. This, then, is what it means to say, **his rest will be an honor**.

Now if someone should wish to add another interpretation to these considerations, the sense of this passage would be as follows: Christ is not only a matter of hope for the Gentiles; he will actually be manifested in the course of time. That is to say, he will rise again not simply to rule over them, but also to bestow freely his **rest** among them as their **honor** and glory. For the mind of his saints is a hospitable dwelling place for the Lord. He abides with the worthy, and he rests with the holy souls of those who worship him. And that is an **honor** and a glory for those who receive him. For what is comparable to having God abide and dwell in our hearts? For once we receive him willingly, it is right to say that **his rest** in us **will be an honor**. For it is written: *If a man loves me, he will keep my word, and my Father will love him, and we will come to him and make our home with him* (John 14:23).

Isaiah 12

1 And you will say in that day:
I will bless you, O Lord,
   for you were angry with me,
and you turned away your wrath,
   and you had compassion on me.

2 Behold, the Lord is my God, my Savior;
   I will trust in him and will not be afraid,
because the Lord is my glory and my praise;
   and he has become my salvation.

3 And with joy you will draw water out of the springs of salvation. 4 And you will say in that day:

Sing hymns to the Lord,
   call his name out loud;
declare his glorious deeds among the nations;
   remember them, because his name has been exalted.

5 Sing hymns to the name of the Lord, for he has done exalted things;
   declare these things in all the earth.
6 Be glad and rejoice, O you who dwell in Sion,
   because the Holy One of Israel has been exalted in your midst.

Isaiah 12 is a short chapter and did not play a large role in early Christian biblical interpretation, apologetics, preaching, or worship. The excerpts from Theodoret and from Jerome represent common approaches. There are, however, certain features of the passage that endeared it to Christian interpreters, and over time it came to be used in Christian worship and was an inspiration for Christian artists and poets. The Hebrew of v. 2, **God is my salvation**, *was translated by the LXX (and versions dependent on the LXX) as* **my Savior**, *allowing a direct application to*

Isaiah 12

Christ. Further, the reference to drawing **water from the wells of salvation** evoked passages in the Gospel of John, for example: "If any one thirst, let him come to me and drink. He who believes in me, as the scripture has said, 'Out of his heart shall flow rivers of living water'" (John 7:37-39). Gregory of Nyssa interprets the water as spiritual drink. In medieval times the chapter entered Christian worship as a canticle in morning prayer ("Confitebor tibi, domine," from the opening words, **I will bless you, O Lord, or I will give thanks to you, O Lord**), in which it is used to this day. In the Utrecht Psalter, an illuminated Latin manuscript from the ninth century, Isaiah 12 is associated with the Transfiguration. Christ is pictured with Moses and Elijah, as well as Peter, James, and John, and below them is the Eucharistic **spring of the Savior** (12:3), from which flows water. Two men drink from the spring, and others are bringing cups and jars to be filled. The Florentine artist Fra Bartolommeo della Porta (1472-1517) used the words **Ecce Deus Salvator Meus** (Behold, God is my Savior, or My Savior is God [12:2]) as a legend in a painting that pictures Isaiah pointing to Christ. And the English poet Michael Drayton (1563-1631) has a metrical rendering of the chapter in his poem "Harmonie of the Church."

(1) Jerome

Earlier in the desert when Israel had gone up from the land of Egypt, and the Red Sea was dried up, she exulted: *We will sing to the* LORD, *for he has triumphed gloriously* (Exod 15:1) and what follows. Now that *the tongue of the sea of Egypt* has been struck and the *River*[1] dried up (Isa 11:15), destroyed, and humiliated, Israel praises the Lord and says: **I will give thanks to you, O Lord** (12:1), for I who merited your wrath and anger have been shown mercy. For you are **my Savior** (12:2), and I put no trust in idols, nor do I fear things that are not to be feared, for you are **my strength and my song, and have become my salvation** (12:2). . . .

With joy you will draw water from the springs of salvation (12:3). Earlier Isaiah called Christ *Emmanuel* (7:14), next *Swiftly Spoil and Quickly Plunder* (8:1), and then other names. Now he calls him **Savior**, so that it might not appear that when Gabriel announced to the Virgin, *And you shall call his name Jesus, for he will save his people from their sins* (Matt 1:21), he was speaking of someone else. He promises that water will be drawn from his springs, not from the waters of the river of Egypt which was struck,[2] nor from the waters of the river of Rezin[3] (8:5-6), but from the springs of Jesus. In the Hebrew language this is expressed with the word **Savior**. So he calls out in the Gospel: *If any one thirst, let him come to me and drink. He who believes in me, as the scripture has said, "Out of his heart shall flow rivers of living water." Now this he said,* according to the Gospel writer, *about the Holy Spirit, which those who believed in him were to receive* (John 7:37-39). And in another place in the Gospel he declares: *Whoever drinks of the water that I shall give him will never thirst; the water that I shall give him will become in him a spring of water welling up to eternal life* (John 4:13-14). We understand the **springs** of the **Savior** to

---

1. The Euphrates.
2. The reference is to Moses striking the water of the Nile with a rod (Exod 7:17ff.).
3. That is, the river where Rezin is king in Assyria, namely, the Euphrates.

be the evangelical teaching, about which we read in Psalm 68: *In the churches[4] bless the Lord our God from the springs of Israel* (Ps 68:26).

On that day you will say: Acknowledge the Lord, call upon his name; declare his glorious deeds among the nations; remember them, because his name has been exalted. Sing to the Lord, for he has done marvelous things; declare these things in all the earth (12:4-5). These things are taught by the apostles and by others of Israel to those who would believe among the Gentiles, that they might acknowledge only the Lord, and, abandoning idols, call upon his name. They will proclaim all his works to the unbelievers in order that they might know that only the Lord is lifted up, and to him alone is praise to be sung because he has done marvelous things, and in all the world his mercy is proclaimed.

Be glad and rejoice, O you who dwell in Zion, because the Holy One of Israel has been exalted in your midst. This text should first be construed literally. You who dwell in Zion, be glad and rejoice in your God. For he who previously was seen as your God, known only within the narrow confines of the land of Judah, is now known throughout the world. Rising from the dead, he will reign among the Gentiles, and the nations will call upon him and worship him. This applies no less to the Jews, for the prophet says that *the Lord extended his hand a second time to recover the remnant which is left of his people* (11:11), bringing back the exiles of Israel and gathering those from Judah who have been dispersed to the four corners of the earth. For the fertilizing of the gospel began from the **springs** of Israel by means of the apostles, who themselves were Jews.

It would be better, however, for us to interpret **Zion**, the watchtower set on the heights, as the Church, about which Psalm 51 sings: *Do good to Zion in thy good pleasure; rebuild the walls of Jerusalem* (51:18), so that an offering acceptable to the Lord may be made in the Church, a sacrifice of justice, and oblations and burnt offerings, and the calf which the most merciful father offered for his repentant son (Luke 15:23).

(2) Theodoret of Cyrus

The hymn, **I will bless you, O Lord** (12:1), is an acknowledgment of blessings received. Those who have been blessed know the source of their blessings and give thanks as they are able. This is clearly prescribed in the law: *Offer to God a sacrifice of thanksgiving* (Ps 50:14), and *He will glorify me with a sacrifice of praise* (Ps 49:23 LXX). **With joy you will draw water out of the springs of salvation** (12:3). He calls the Holy Scriptures the **springs of salvation** because those who firmly believe draw water from them **with joy**.

Sing hymns to the Lord, call his name out loud (12:4). These words can be applied to the company of the apostles and those from among the Jews who believed with them. They brought the divine teaching to the nations and encouraged one another to fulfill the exhortation of the Lord: *Go therefore and make disciples of all nations* (Matt 28:19).

Sing hymns to the name of the Lord, for he has done exalted things; declare these things in all the earth (12:5). They call on the whole world to participate in the joy

---

4. The term in Latin is *ecclesiis*, which could be read as "congregations" or "churches."

and exhort Zion in particular to sing a hymn of praise to their benefactor. Moreover, the text seems to me to allude not only to God's wondrous works, for example, to miracles, but also to the saving cross on which Christ was nailed. For recall the words of the Lord to the Jews, *When you have lifted up the Son of man, then you will know that I am he* (John 8:28), and *As Moses lifted up the serpent in the wilderness, so must the Son of man be lifted up* (John 3:14).

As for us who have believed in him, we turn our faces toward him. For as the Jews were able to neutralize the venom of the poisonous snake by looking at the bronze serpent (Num 21:9), so we are healed from the sting of sin by looking at him. We have enjoyed the fullness of his salvation, and have received the good things promised to us through the grace of the one who laid down his life for us. To the Father with the Son in union with the all-Holy Spirit, be glory now and always and for ages upon ages. Amen.

(3) Irenaeus of Lyons

The knowledge of salvation does not consist in believing in another God, nor another Father . . . but the knowledge of salvation consists in knowing the Son of God who is called and truly is "salvation" and **Savior** and "bringer of salvation" *(salutare)*. "Salvation," as in the passage: *I waited for your salvation, O LORD* (Gen 49:18). And again, **Behold, my God, my Savior, I will put my trust in him** (12:2). As for "bringer of salvation": *God has made known his salvation in the sight of the nations* (Ps 98:2). For he is indeed **Savior** as Son and Word of God; "bringer of salvation" as Spirit, for he says: *The Spirit of our countenance, Christ the Lord* (Lam 4:20 LXX). And "salvation" as being flesh: *The Word was made flesh and dwelt among us* (John 1:14). This knowledge of salvation John made known to those who repented and who believed in the *Lamb of God, who takes away the sins of the world!* (John 1:29).

(4) Gregory of Nyssa

When I read the Holy Scripture, I do understand eating to refer not only to physical nourishment, or to the satisfactions of the body. I realize that there is another kind of food that is analogous to bodily nourishment. This food is enjoyed by the soul alone. Wisdom, for example, exhorts the hungry: *Eat of my bread* (Prov 9:5). And the Lord says that those who hunger for this kind of food are happy: *If any one thirst, let him come to me and drink* (John 7:37). And the great Isaiah bids those who are able to grasp this sublime teaching, **Drink with joy** (12:3). There is also a prophetic warning against those who are worthy of punishment that they shall be afflicted with famine, but the famine is not a lack of bread and water, but a failure of the Word: *not a famine of bread, nor a thirst for water, but a famine of hearing the words of the LORD* (Amos 8:11).

Isaiah 13

1 A vision, which Esaias son of Amos saw against Babylon.

2 On a mountain in the plain raise a signal,
    raise up your voice to them, do not fear;
  encourage them with your hand;
    open, you rulers.
3 It is I who command and I lead them;
    [they have been consecrated,] and it is I who summon them.
  Mighty ones come to fulfill my wrath,
    at the same time rejoicing and reviling.

4 A voice of many nations on the mountains
    like that of many nations!
  A voice of kings
    and of nations gathered together!
  The Lord Sabaoth has commanded
    a heavily armed nation
5 to come from a distant land,
    from the utmost foundation of heaven —
  the Lord and his armed men —
    to destroy the whole world.

6 Wail, for the day of the Lord is near,
    and a destruction will come from God!
7 Therefore every hand will be weakened,
    and every human soul will be afraid;
8 and the elders will be troubled,
    and pangs will seize them, as of a woman in labor.
  And they will bewail one to another and be amazed,
    and they will change their face like a flame.

9 For behold, the incurable day of the Lord comes,
    a day of wrath and anger,
  to make the whole world desolate,
    and to destroy the sinners from it.
10 For the stars of heaven and Orion,
    and all the ornament of heaven,
    will not give light;
  and it will be dark when the sun rises,
    and the moon will not give its light.
11 And I will order evils for the whole world,
    and for the ungodly, their own sins;
  I will destroy the pride of transgressors
    and bring low the pride of the arrogant.
12 And those that are left will be more valuable than unsmelted gold,
    and man will be more valuable than the stone from Souphir.
13 For heaven will be enraged,
    and the earth will be shaken out of its foundations,
  because of the fierce anger of the Lord Sabaoth
    in the day when his wrath comes upon it.
14 And those that are left will be like a fleeing gazelle,
    or like a wandering sheep, and there will be no one to gather them,
  so that a man will turn to his own people,
    and a man will run to his own land.
15 For whoever is caught will be defeated,
    and whoever are gathered together will fall by the sword.
16 And they will strike down their children
    in front of them;
  and they will plunder their houses
    and take their wives.
17 See, I am stirring up the Medes against you,
    who do not take silver into account
    nor have any need of gold.
18 They will crush the arrows of the young men;
    and they will have no mercy on your children,
    nor will their eyes be sparing upon the children.
19 And Babylon, which is called glorious
    by the king of the Chaldeans,
  will be as when God overthrew
    Sodoma and Gomorra.
20 It will not be inhabited forever,
    nor will they enter it for many generations;
  nor will Arabs pass through it,
    nor will shepherds rest in it.
21 But wild animals will rest there,

and the houses will be filled with noise;
there sirens will rest,
and there demons will dance.
22 Donkey-centaurs will dwell there,
and hedgehogs will build nests in their houses;
it is coming quickly
and will not delay.

The ancient commentators, like modern biblical scholars, realized that chapter 13 began a new section of the book of Isaiah. Chapters 13–23 are composed of oracles to the nations, Babylonians, Moabites, Egyptians, and others. At the request of a certain Bishop Amabilis, Jerome wrote a little work on 13–23, the ten "visions" of Isaiah, which offered a historical interpretation of the visions (or oracles).[1] *Later, when he wrote his complete commentary on Isaiah (from which the excerpts in this volume are taken), he inserted his earlier work as Book 5. This he followed with two more books, 6 and 7, interpreting the same material allegorically, or in his words "tropologically" or "anagogically," to give the section a "spiritual interpretation."*[2] *We have provided a few excerpts from the opening verses of his historical commentary and from his spiritual interpretation of chapter 13. Cyril of Alexandria also realized that chapter 13 began a new section whose significance was largely historical, yet he believed that one could draw "spiritual insight" from the visions.*

Verses from Isaiah 13–23 are rarely quoted in the New Testament. In Mark 13:24 (cf. Matt 24:29) Jesus uses the imagery of Isa 13:10 when describing the end of time, and in 1 Cor 15:32 St. Paul cites 22:13, "Let us eat and drink, for tomorrow we die." Similarly, verses from chapters 13–23 are cited infrequently in early Christian literature. Consequently we have treated only chapters 13, 14, 16, 19, and 20, and those briefly.

There were, however, some passages in these chapters that did catch the attention of early Christian thinkers. For example, the verse, "How you are fallen from heaven, O Day Star, son of Dawn!" (14:12), was taken as a depiction of the fall of Satan by the ancients as well as by medievals, as the selection from Thomas Aquinas illustrates. The "swift cloud" that comes to Egypt (19:1) was taken to refer to Christ. And the description of Isaiah going about the city "naked and barefoot" (20:2) offered an opportunity to discuss the person of Isaiah. Aelred of Rievaulx, the 12th-century Cistercian spiritual writer, author of the Mirror of Love, *delivered for the monks in his community a series of homilies devoted to these chapters called "The Burdens of Isaiah." The term "burden" is a translation of the Latin* onus, *the word Jerome used to translate the Hebrew* maśśā' *(13:1), rendered in Greek as "vision" and in English as "oracle." Hence: "Onus Babylonis, quod vidit Esaias filius Amos"* **(the burden of Babylon which Isaiah the son of Amos saw)**. *In chapters 13 and 16 we have included excerpts from Aelred's work.*

---

1. Jerome, *Commentary on Isaiah*, Book 5 (CCSL 73:160.15-51).
2. Jerome, *Commentary on Isaiah*, Book 5, Preface, and Book 6, Preface (CCSL 73:159.1-14, 223.1-10).

Isaiah 13

(1) The Gospel according to Mark

And as he sat on the Mount of Olives opposite the temple, Peter and James and John and Andrew asked him privately, "Tell us, when will this be, and what will be the sign when these things are all to be accomplished?" And Jesus began to say to them, "Take heed that no one leads you astray. Many will come in my name, saying 'I am he!' and they will lead many astray. . . . And then if any one says to you, 'Look, here is the Christ!' or 'Look, there he is!' do not believe it. False Christs and false prophets will arise and show signs and wonders to lead astray, if possible, the elect. But take heed; I have told you all things beforehand. But in those days, after that tribulation, **the sun will be darkened, and the moon will not give its light** (13:10), and the stars will be falling from heaven, and the powers in the heavens will be shaken. And then they will see the Son of man coming in clouds with great power and glory. And then he will send out the angels, and gather his elect from the four winds, from the ends of the earth to the ends of heaven.

(2) Jerome

The burden of Babylon which Isaiah the son of Amos saw (13:1). The Hebrew term *maśśā'* can be understood as "burden" or "weight," and wherever it occurs as a heading, the pronouncements that follow are dominated by warnings. For that reason I am surprised that the Septuagint translators wished to use "vision" for such somber material. But that is a subject for another time; right now we need to turn to the present topic. Babylon was the capital city of the Chaldaeans, and its king was Nebuchadnezzar, who had conquered all the neighboring peoples even as far as Ethiopia and had laid waste to Judah and other regions. In the eleventh year of the reign of Zedekiah, king of Judah, he captured Jerusalem after laying siege to the city. He took Zedekiah into captivity in Antioch, which was then called Reblatha, and before his eyes he killed his sons and then put out his eyes. He took the blinded king in a cage like a wild animal to Babylonia, fulfilling the prophecy in Jeremiah: *You will go into Babylon, yet you shall not see it* (Ezek 12:13). The destruction of Babylon was prophesied to comfort and encourage the people of Judah. For just as Nineveh, the capital of Assyria, whose kings — Pul, Tiglath-pileser, Shalmaneser, and Sennacherib — had conquered the ten tribes, and then were ravaged by the Chaldeans and overthrown, so all the Babylonians who had defied God would be overcome by the power of the Medes and Persians. . . .

If we consider the historical circumstances of this prophecy, it refers to the Medes. For a few verses later Scripture says explicitly: **Behold, I am stirring up the Medes against them, who have no regard for silver and do not delight in gold** (13:17). Do not be troubled if the Medes who overthrew the Babylonians are called **my consecrated ones** (13:3), since Nebuchadnezzar, who acknowledged God's authority and destroyed faithless Jerusalem, was called servant[3] and dove by Jeremiah. Moreover, when he speaks of **my**

---

3. Jer 25:9; 27:6; 43:10.

mighty men who exult in my glory (13:3),[4] he shows that the Medes did not overthrow such a powerful kingdom by their own strength but by God's wrath. . . .

The phrase **to destroy the whole earth** (13:5) here does not mean that **the whole earth** will be devastated. It refers to the entire country of Babylon and the Chaldeans. It is customary in Holy Scripture to use the expression **the whole earth** to designate the region which is being spoken about. Those who do not understand the expression mistakenly refer it to the entire world. . . .

Like a hunted gazelle (13:14) refers to the people of Babylon and Chaldea who flee the advance of the Medes in terror, like a gazelle or a sheep before a roaring lion or a howling wolf. For they will have no defender, no prince, no sovereign to protect them. After Babylon was captured and the enemy army entered its gates, all the troops from other nations that had come to their aid returned to their own land. Those who could not flee were put to the sword; and all who tried to resist or appease the enemy could do little to help the besieged city, and they too lost their lives.

David was referring to the words **infants will be dashed in pieces before their eyes** (13:16) when he prophesied by the Spirit: *O pitiful daughters of Babylon! Happy shall he be who requites you with what you have done to us! Happy shall he be who takes your little ones and dashes them against the rock!* (Ps 137:8-9). So great will be the devastation of the city and the ferocity of the victor that even innocent children will not be spared, **the houses** of the rich **will be plundered and wives ravished** (13:16) before their husbands. . . .

Babylon will be wholly destroyed, and the place will be so desolate as to be unfit for herding cattle or pasturing sheep. Bedouins will not pitch their tents there, and weary shepherds whose flocks have wandered there will not use it as a place to rest. Within what remains of its walls and amidst the ruins dwell *ṣiyyim* (13:21), which the Septuagint translates as **beasts**. Others, however, think the Hebrew word *ṣiyyim* means demons or sirens.

* * *

The burden or **vision against Babylon which Isaiah son of Amos saw** (13:1). He saw, not with the eyes of flesh but with the eyes of the mind, what a huge, heavy weight Babylon imposes. And since Babylon, which in Hebrew is "Babel," means "confused" (it was there that the speech of those who built the tower was confused [Genesis 11]), spiritually it signifies the world which is inclined toward evil that confuses not only tongues, but also individual behavior and outlook. The king of Babylon is indeed Nebuchadnezzar, who rose up against the Lord and boasted in his heart: *I will ascend to heaven; I will place my throne above the stars of heaven; I will sit on the mount of the covenant toward the north; I will ascend beyond the height of the clouds, I will be like the Most High* (Isa 14:13-14). This is the one who showed the Lord all the kingdoms of the world and said to him: *All these things have been given to me, and I will give them to you if you fall down and worship me* (Matt 4:9). Further, in what follows the threat is never against Babylon, but against the world.

---

4. In place of the phrase **my proudly exulting ones**, Jerome's Latin text reads: "my mighty men who exult in my glory."

The Lord of hosts warns a warlike people that he will come from a distant place, even the height of heaven, to plunder the world. And again: **Behold, the inevitable day of wrath and anger is coming, to make the whole world desolate, to rid it of sinners** (13:9). And then **I will order evil for the whole world, and for the ungodly their own sins** (13:11). These texts show that everything said against Babylon pertains to the ruin and destruction of the world.

On a misty hill, or **on a level hill, raise up a signal** (13:2). As foes of Babylon the apostles, apostolic men, and teachers of the churches were urged to raise the sign of the Lord's cross, not in an inconspicuous place or in the depth of a valley, but on a **misty** or **level hill**. Another interpretation would be that this refers to the hidden sacraments of the Church, for Moses entered the darkness and mist that he might see and hear the voice of God. *For God made darkness his covering, clouds and mist around him* (Ps 18:11). Another interpretation teaches that we should rise to such heights of orthodox doctrines that, like the apostle Paul, we would be brought low and would cry: *I am unfit to be called an apostle, because I persecuted the church of God* (1 Cor 15:9). He also **raised up a signal on a level hill** when, humility having been thrust upon him, he said: *I decided to know nothing among you except Jesus Christ and him crucified* (1 Cor 2:2). The one who **came forth from the root of Jesse** among the nations, that he might gather the lost from Israel, has himself raised up this sign on the heights (cf. 11:1, 10).

(3) Cyril of Alexandria

The oracle concerning Babylon which Isaiah the son of Amos saw (13:1). The vision against Babylon and the oracles that follow, against the Edomites, Moabites, the Egyptians, and others, were proclaimed to encourage Israel. The significance of what is written there is primarily historical, yet for those with spiritual insight the section offers something more. It teaches that the things that happened in ancient times were beautifully transformed. What was once a dull image is transfigured, so that it is filled with spiritual depth.

Through blessed Moses God called Israel to know and worship the true God. Though Israel was given a law that showed what was good and honorable, it neglected the law and turned instead to human teachings. What is more, Israel stumbled into the pits of idolatry. Through the prophets God reproached the Israelites for their godlessness, saying: *This people draws near and venerates me with their lips, while their hearts are far from me. In vain they worship me and teach doctrines made by men* (29:13). And again he asked: *Why has my beloved done an abomination in my house?* (Jer 11:15 LXX). The term "abomination" here refers to idols. Because the Israelites recklessly turned toward foolish things by turning away from serving God and arrogantly lifting up their own minds against him, God handed them over to the neighboring peoples, meaning the Edomites, the Moabites, the Egyptians, and those from Philistia. In the end they suffered great hardship at the hands of the Babylonians, the cruelest people on earth. With impunity the Babylonians devastated the entire country of Judea and took most of the people into captivity in their own country.

At that time the blessed prophets proclaimed that those who provoke the God of all would suffer misfortunes. Yet although what had been announced beforehand actually did happen to the Israelites, they remained as hard-hearted and unbelieving as they had been previously and pursued a way of life alien to the law and offensive to God. However, after they had suffered hardships and calamities and other misfortunes visited on them by their enemies, the one God, in his mercy, announced to them that they would enjoy the most wonderful things imaginable. He promised that those who had been taken captive would be returned home, that they would be released from their harsh servitude, and that those who had once conquered them would be handed over to the hands of their enemies. Even if they had not heeded the prophet's admonitions, surely they would eagerly grasp these promises of good things to come. And buoyed by the hope that their desires would be fulfilled, they would offer devoted service to God and keep their minds firmly fixed on him.

Among the several peoples who devastated the country of the Jews at that time, the cruelest and most savage were the Chaldeans, who ruled Babylonia in those days. Hence the prophet addresses them first.

(4) Pseudo-Basil of Caesarea

The oracle concerning Babylon which Isaiah the son of Amos saw (13:1). The prophet is not speaking of a vision by the senses, something that can be seen with the eyes of the body, but rather something that is perceived by the mind. God enlightens the mind and gives it the ability to see, for example, what is going to happen to Babylon. The prophets do not speak in a state of ecstasy. When someone is possessed by an evil demon, his mind is not his own. What he claims to see he does not actually see; he sees only fantasies presented to him by demons. Those possessed by demons see rivers and mountains and beasts that are not present. They see colors that are not actually there, and have images of friends or strangers whom they do not really see. They are deranged and beside themselves; their minds are confused and darkened.

With the saints it was not so. For God himself promised, *I will multiply visions* (Hos 12:10). When God grants visions, he does not blind the mind but readies it to receive a vision. Then he enlightens and illuminates it by the presence of the Holy Spirit. For this reason the prophets are called "those who see," because the mind's sight is expanded by the presence of the Spirit that enlightens it. Therefore, *Who makes him seeing or blind?* (Exod 4:11). Clearly the one who sees is the prophet. With his clarity of mind he is able to anticipate what is to come. But the person whose eyes have been blinded by evil is not able to see the wonders beheld by the saints. For this reason the Lord said, *"For judgment I came into this world, that those who do not see may see, and that those who see may become blind"* (John 9:39).

(5) Aelred of Rievaulx

This holy prophet is so profound in his utterances, so transparent in his predictions of the future, and so joyful in his moral strictures that sometimes he seems as though he had been borne up to heaven itself and made privy to the very secrets of the divine counsels, and at other times as though sent down on a swift wing to the lower parts of the firmament, to reveal those heavenly mysteries; sometimes, descending on a light wing, he traverses the flat plains of behavior, and then again, as though he had been seized into paradise, he returns to us bearing ineffable words which it is not permitted to man to speak. In his oracles he so plainly reveals everything that is Christ's and the mysteries of the Church that he seems not so much to have predicted the future as to have narrated what had already happened. . . .

I thought it seemed good to pass over the intervening material [from the beginning of the book of Isaiah], in order to explore for your edification whatever the Spirit himself has intimated concerning the eleven "burdens" about which the prophet, at the Spirit's urging, has expounded. I declare that I am in all respects a debtor for the sake of your progress, both by virtue of my office [as abbot] and of my affection for you. But also, *necessity has been laid upon me; woe to me if I do not preach the gospel* (1 Cor 9:16). I especially do not doubt that whatever ability I possess in spiritual teaching or in the understanding of Scripture has not so much been given to me as transmitted through me for your sake. Nor is that in any way to be ascribed to my merits, since I am a sinner; neither to my learning, since as you know I am virtually unschooled; nor to study, nor to my own effort, since I rarely have leisure and am constantly engaged in business. Everything that God has committed to me, I therefore pass on to you, so that he who boasts, let him boast in the Lord (cf. 1 Cor 1:31; 2 Cor 10:17). Come then, good Jesus, and infuse the grace of your blessing into the bread which we have offered, let the poor eat and be filled, and let them exclaim with the prophet: *How sweet are your words to my taste, sweeter than honey in my mouth!* (Ps 119:103). Behold, I raise my hands, may you give me help, because without you I can do nothing. You who inspired holy Isaiah to write, inspire me, I pray, so that I may understand what he has written; because you have inspired him that I may believe: For *unless we believe, we will not understand* (7:9).

What do we think is signified by these "**burdens**"?[5] Well, there are burdens that weigh us down, and burdens that actually destroy us. Weakness weighs on us; iniquity then destroys us. Temptation weighs on us; damnation then destroys us. Therefore, the **burden of Babylon** (13:1) is presented first, then the burden of *the Philistines* (14:28), then the *burden of Moab* (15:1), after which the *burden of Damascus* (17:1), followed by the *burden of Egypt* (19:1), then the *burden of the wilderness of the sea* (21:1), the *burden of Duma*, the *burden of Arabia* (21:13), then the *valley of vision* (22:1) and the *burden of Tyre* (23:1), and finally the *burden of the beasts of the south* (30:6 Vg.).

The holy Isaiah is thus revealing here the suffering of certain cities and nations, or rather the people who are represented by these cities and nations. Nor is he silent as to the manner, the causes, and the substance of this suffering. He also includes a word con-

---

5. See the editor's note on the rendering of Latin *onus* as "burden" rather than "oracle."

cerning the happiness of those who are thus burdened by this suffering, namely, that it is for their salvation rather than for their destruction; for it is everywhere manifest that *power belongs to God; and that to you, O Lord, belongs mercy; because you render to each man according to his works* (Ps 62:12), distinguishing between day and night, between light and darkness, so that by contrast with the light the darkness may appear even deeper, and by contrast with the darkness the light itself may shine more brightly. And who would it be who judges and distinguishes between these two things, save he who says, *The Father judges no one, but has given all judgment to the Son* (John 5:22)? And again: *For judgment I came into this world, that those who do not see may see, and that those who see may become blind* (John 9:39). Because this discernment between the good and the wicked has come into being through the advent of our Lord and Savior, and with it the suffering of some and the deliverance of others, we see that the prophet's primary subject matter throughout this whole section of the book is the advent of the Lord himself. On which, note the words of Simeon: *Behold, this child is set for the fall and the rising of many in Israel, and as a sign of contradiction* (Luke 2:34).

What Simeon calls a "fall" is what Isaiah means by a **burden**. Isaiah describes the burdens in such a way that God appears to exert pressure on some, without overwhelming and destroying; others he destroys without first making them suffer; and yet others he makes to suffer and then overwhelms. Those on whom he exerts pressure he is "afflicting"; those whom he overwhelms he "abandons." There are thus some whom he afflicts without abandoning, as it is written: *God disciplines every person whom he loves* (Heb 12:6, citing Prov 3:12). Whence also the psalmist: *I will punish their transgressions with the rod and their iniquity with scourges; but I will not remove from him my steadfast love* (Ps 89:32-33). Of those whom he abandons without afflicting, the prophet observes, *They are not in trouble, as other men are; they are not stricken like other men* (Ps 73:5). And again: *And I abandoned them according to the desires of their hearts* (Ps 80:13 Vg.). And according to another prophet: *I will not punish your daughters when they play the harlot, nor your brides when they commit adultery* (Hos 5:14). Of those whom he abandons besides afflicting, God says through his prophet, *I crushed them, and they refused to accept correction* (Jer 5:3). When we begin to comment on these **burdens**, it will become very clear, God willing, just how affliction and abandonment occur. For the **burden of Babylon**, or of the *Philistines*, or *Moab*, can be so called depending on whether it is the **burden** by which they exert pressure, or the **burden** by which, in turn, they are weighed down; and similarly for the rest of the nations.

But now, if you please, let us examine the heading of the following passage:

The burden of Babylon which Isaiah son of Amos saw (13:1). You are well aware, brothers, that **Babylon**, which means "confusion," stands for the world, in which everything is thoroughly "confused," that is, blended together: where the good live with the wicked, and the condemned with the elect; the wheat with the chaff, the olive oil with the liquid that is skimmed off, the wine with the dregs; where so far as the goods of this world are concerned, the impious fares as well as the just; where humanity has nothing more than the beasts. But we also often understand **Babylon** to be just the city of the wicked, with its own king, to which none of the elect belong and from which none of the reprobate are excluded. We divide the reprobate into three groups or categories: one which still has things in common with the society and the works of the elect; a second which is now separated from their works and fellowship; and a third which is already quit of their bodies and is given over to eternal punishment. And they are all rightly regarded by the name of **Babylon**, both the groups taken separately, and the individual human beings in each of these groups.

The elect are clearly divided in a similar way into three orders: for some have not yet been called, such as the Jews and the pagans; others have been called but not yet justified, like Christians who are sinners; still others have been justified but not yet glorified, like the saints who are still yoked to the miseries of this life. Thus there are elect who have not yet been called; though predestination will have set them apart from **Babylon**, nevertheless, so long as they are blinded by Babylonian errors, they cannot at present evade the name of **Babylon**. And those whose reprehensible works now set them apart (though their calling and predestination shall eventually join them to the elect) are also afflicted with the shame of the name of **Babylon**. And so it can be said that Babylon is that entire universe of human beings, in which both the elect and reprobate are linked by the same errors and vices. **Babylon** is also the name given to a depraved and inscrutable heart, because it is confounded with vices and passions. The society of the wicked is also called **Babylon**, for which eternal confusion is being prepared.

Now a **burden of Babylon** refers to a "burden" by which the confused totality of the many is destroyed when their city is separated [into its elements]; a "burden" by which the city is unceasingly afflicted with the evils of this world; a "burden" by which the structure of vices and wicked passions in individual hearts is destroyed, like a city of confusion; and, finally, a "burden" after this life, by which the wicked alone will be burdened with eternal punishments. And that is the **burden of Babylon** that Isaiah son of Amos saw. . . .

Pray, brothers, that, following the Spirit's meaning, we may so describe these burdens that we may courageously endure the ones which merely weigh us down and may avoid the ones which would destroy us; and pray too that we escape the ones that would condemn us, by the help of him who wishes to be burdened with our burdens for our sake, Jesus Christ our Lord, who lives and reigns with the Father and the Holy Spirit, God, forever and ever. Amen.

Isaiah 14

₁And the Lord will have compassion on Iakob and will yet choose Israel, and they will rest on their own land; and the gioras [resident aliens] will be added to them, indeed, he will be added to the house of Iakob. ₂And nations will take them and bring them into their place, and they will obtain an inheritance and will be multiplied on the land of God for male and female slaves; and those who captured them will be captives, and those who dominated them will be dominated.

₃And it shall be on that day that God will give you rest from your pain and wrath and your hard slavery with which you served them. ₄And you will take up this lament against the king of Babylon, and you will say on that day:

    How the exactor has ceased,
        and the taskmaster has ceased!
5   God has crushed the yoke of sinners,
        the yoke of rulers.
6   Having struck a nation in wrath
        with an incurable blow,
    smiting a nation with a wrathful blow
        that spared no one,
(7)   he rested confidently.
7   The whole earth shouts with joy,
8   and the trees of Lebanon rejoiced over you,
        even the cedar of Lebanon, saying,
    "Since you fell asleep,
        the one who is to cut us down has not come up."
9   Hades beneath was embittered
        on meeting you;
    all the mighty ones who have ruled the earth
        rose up together against you —
    those who have roused from their thrones
        all the kings of the nations.

10 All will answer
    and say to you:
  "You too were taken even as we were,
    and you were counted among us!"
11 But your glory has gone down to Hades —
    your abundant joy;
  they will spread decay beneath you,
    and a worm will be your covering.

12 How is fallen from heaven
    the Day Star, which used to rise early in the morning!
  He has been crushed into the earth
    who used to send light to all the nations!
13 You said in your mind,
    "I will ascend to heaven;
  I will set my throne
    above the stars of God;
  I will sit on a lofty mountain,
    upon the lofty mountains toward the north;
14 I will ascend above the clouds,
    I will be like the Most High."
15 But now you will descend into Hades,
    and into the foundations of the earth.
16 Those who see you will marvel at you and say:
  "Is this the man who troubles the earth,
    shaking kings?"
17 The one who made the whole world desolate
    and overthrew the cities
    has not released those who are in misery.
18 All the kings of the nations have fallen asleep in honor,
    a man in his own house;
19 but you will be cast out on the mountains,
    like an abominable corpse,
  with many dead, those pierced with swords,
    who go down into Hades.
  As a cloak stained with blood will not be clean,
20   so neither will you be clean,
  because you have destroyed my land
    and killed my people.
  You will not remain forever,
    you evil seed!
21 Prepare your children to be slaughtered
    for the sins of your father,

so that they will not rise and inherit the earth
    and fill the earth with wars.

22And I will rise up against them, says the Lord Sabaoth, and will destroy their name and remnant and offspring. This is what the Lord says: 23And I will make Babylonia desolate so that hedgehogs will dwell there, and it will become nothing; and I will make it a miry pit for destruction.

24 This is what the Lord Sabaoth says:
   As I have said,
     so shall it be;
   and as I have planned,
     so shall it remain:
25 to destroy the Assyrians from my land and from my mountains;
    and they shall be trampled,
   and their yoke shall be removed from them,
    and their renown shall be removed from their shoulders.
26 This is the plan that the Lord has planned
    against the whole earth;
   and this is the hand that is raised up
    against all the nations of the world.
27 For what the holy God has planned,
    who will scatter it?
   And his hand that is raised up,
    who will turn it back?

28 In the year that King Ahaz died this word came:
29 May you not rejoice, all you foreigners,
    for the yoke of him who struck you is broken,
   for from the seed of snakes will come forth the offspring of asps,
    and their offspring will come forth as flying snakes.
30 And the poor will graze through him,
    and poor men will rest in peace;
   but he will wipe out your offspring with famine,
    and your remnant he will wipe out.
31 Wail, O city gates;
    let the troubled cities cry out — all the foreigners!
   Because smoke comes out of the north,
    and there is no way to live.

32 What will the kings of the nations answer?
   "The Lord has founded Sion,
    and the humble among the people
    will be saved through him."

Isaiah 14

The interpretation of this oracle was chiefly historical, though interspersed within the expositions one will find occasional moral or spiritual observations. However, Isa 14:3-21, originally a taunt song against an oppressive foreign king, usually taken to be the Babylonian king Nebuchadnezzar, took on a particular importance in early Christianity as one of the primary biblical texts on the fall of the evil angels, including Satan: **How you are fallen from heaven, O Day Star, son of Dawn!** *(14:12), as the Hebrew has it, or* **How is fallen from heaven the Day Star** *(lit. "Bringer of the Dawn"),* **who rises early in the morning!** *in the Septuagint. According to Luke 10:18, Jesus himself seems to presume this allegorical interpretation when he says that he has seen Satan "falling from heaven like lightning" (cf. also Rev 8:10, "a great star fell from heaven, blazing like a torch," and 9:1, "I saw a star fallen from heaven to earth, and he was given the key of the shaft of the bottomless pit"). The Greek term for "the bringer of the dawn" is the source of the Latin Lucifer in the Vulgate, which became a personal name for Satan in Western culture. The identification of the devil with the Day Star or Morning Star in 14:12 is documented in several of the selections below. Augustine takes the passage to refer not directly to Satan but to the members of his "body" (by analogy to the Church as the body of Christ), that is, the company of those who have turned from the light to darkness. John Cassian uses the fall of Satan as an occasion to discuss the vice of pride.*

We have also included a fascinating selection from Thomas Aquinas's Literal Exposition on Isaiah *dealing with the fall of Satan. In the "literal" interpretation of the passage Thomas presents the chapter as a series of taunts against Nebuchadnezzar, king of Babylon, on his arrival in hell (14:9). But as he makes clear at the end of the excerpt, it is Satan that he has in mind. Read in that light and with the other biblical passages Thomas cites to heighten the denunciation of Satan, Isaiah 14 becomes a stirring invective against the workers of evil.*

Early Christian interpreters also identified the Day Star with Christ himself on the basis of precedents in the New Testament: "I am the root and the offspring of David, the bright morning star" (Rev 22:16; cf. also Rev 2:28 and 2 Pet 1:19). Behind such passages in the New Testament may be Ps 109:3 (LXX): "From the womb, before the Day Star I begot you," though some commentators sought to distinguish Christ from the Day Star in order to assert his absolute preexistence. The identification of Christ as Morning Star survives in the "Exultet" sung during the Great Vigil of Easter: "May the Morning Star (Lucifer) which never sets find this flame still burning: Christ, that Morning Star, who came back from the dead, and shed his peaceful light on all mankind, your Son who lives and reigns forever and ever."

(1) Cyril of Alexandria

The Lord will again have compassion on Jacob and will again choose Israel (14:1). In this oracle God again promises to restore the hopes of the Israelites who had suffered and awakens in them a keen desire for the good things he has promised. Because the people had been driven almost to the breaking point by the harsh treatment of their captors, the prophet clearly announces that Babylon and all of Assyria will be laid waste and that the Israelites will return from captivity and cast off the yoke of servitude to which they were unaccustomed. Israel will not be rejected forever, nor be punished indefinitely for its sins. In due time the one whom God elected will be shown mercy and will be renewed in spirit.

They will return to **their own country** (14:1), he writes, and **aliens** (14:1) will go up with them. The term **alien** here means a native or an indigenous person, that is, a Babylonian. For many Babylonians had returned with the Israelites: some had been joined to them by marriage, and some were inclined to practice Israel's religion. Since the Israelites had remained in captivity for a long time, it is reasonable that not a few natives of Babylonia had become attached to them. **Aliens will join them**, it says, that is, indigenous Babylonians will follow and accompany them. **The peoples will take them and bring them to their place** (14:2). When Cyrus freed Israel, he gave orders to the governors that they be returned home safely and securely. Xerxes, who became king of Assyria after him, brought this about. Anyone who wants to have more detailed information about these matters can read the books of Ezra and Nehemiah, where there is a full and accurate account of these events.

They went up from Assyria to Judah at the time of Zerubbabel, son of Shealtiel of the tribe of Judah, head of the sacred order of Jeshua, son of Jozadak the high priest. Therefore, **the peoples will take them and bring them to their** land (14:2), and they will receive the inheritance that had been promised to them from on high. And what is more astonishing, those who once venerated idols, who had called innumerable things gods, **shall be multiplied in God's land as male and female slaves; they will take captive those who were their captors** (14:2). For the captors of Israel will be brought up with her, and when they arrive in Judah, they will take upon themselves the yoke of the law and enjoy a pleasant and safe captivity. They will call the maker of all things Lord and God.

This passage indicates that those who had overpowered Israel, brought them from Judah, and subjected them to their rule will themselves be made subject and become captives to Cyrus and the might of the Medes and Persians. On that day, the prophet tells the Israelites, you will be freed from **your pain and turmoil** (14:3), that is, from the divine wrath that was hanging over you. You will escape bitter servitude and be freed of your troubles.

So far we have discussed the plain sense of this passage. But it is possible to transform the surface meaning and discern a spiritual significance in what took place. For this passage also signifies that the Maker of all things had mercy on those who had been harmed by the power of evil. For he sent his own Son as redeemer in the name of the Lord, that is, not as one of the holy prophets but in his lordly glory. Christ, who was supported by the invincible weapons of the apostles, destroyed idolatry as one would destroy an arrogant and haughty city. For the apostles overcame the devil, rescued those who had been deceived by him and were held in servitude, and brought them back to the holy city, the spiritual Jerusalem — the Church. In God's land their numbers increased, and many became **male and female slaves** (14:2) of God. Those who had held others in captivity, compelled them to serve demons, taught others to practice evil, and held them in the net of destruction, now became captives themselves, for they were conquered by the preaching of the holy apostles and were brought under the rule of Christ. Christ became Lord of those who had come to the faith, for Christ is Lord of those who believe. Under Christ's lordship and the authority of his holy apostles they found rest from the harsh servitude that had once enslaved them.

(2) Theodoret of Cyrus

You will take up this taunt against the king of Babylon (14:4). The change in situation requires a change in speech. For here the divine prophet predicts what the Israelites will say after their liberation and their return from exile. The prophets use the language of tragedy to declaim the destruction of Babylonia.... It had imposed a heavy tribute on all its subjects, but now that its kingdom has been destroyed it must pay tribute to those it had oppressed....

When Assyrians were masters of the world, they reviled the God of all and burned the holy temple. Now their kingdom has been destroyed, and everyone rejoices at the ruin of the Babylonians, who had treated all the peoples with unremitting cruelty....

The Holy Scripture sometimes personifies things to make them clearer. Hence the prophet introduces Death (i.e., **Hades**)[1] (14:9) — which of course has no existence and is without substance — as an actual living person who possesses reason and opposes the King of Babylon....

Driven by his crazed mind, Nebuchadnezzar hoped to become divine. The prophet calls him the **Day Star** (14:12), not because he was the day star, but because he had the illusion that he was the day star. To show how swiftly his pomp and glory had disappeared, the prophet likens him to a morning star that has fallen to the earth....

The prophecy of Daniel also speaks to us about these things. First Nebuchadnezzar had a huge golden image made, and ordered everyone to worship it instead of God. Then the king said to those noble athletes: *Who is the god that will deliver you out of my hands?* (Dan 3:15).

The text also mentions a **mountain** (14:13) that is north of the land of the Assyrians (and Medes), that separates them from the Scythians, and that is the highest mountain in the whole world. No doubt it was from this mountain that Nebuchadnezzar thought he would attempt to ascend to heaven. He was not the only one to have this illusion; there was one who had taught him these things, namely, Satan. For these words apply not only to the boasting of the king of Babylon; they also refer to the one who truly fell from heaven, usurped the name of God, and deceived mankind. Isaiah says, **You shall go down to Hades, even to the foundations of the earth** (14:15), that is to say, to the depths of the earth.... He plundered the **cities** (14:17) and ravaged their land, and he showed no pity to his captors. Then he adds that the other **kings** (14:18) died peacefully in their own homes. You are no different, he says, from other men. Like other soldiers you will be cast on the ground as food for birds of prey and wild beasts....

These words, **Prepare slaughter for his sons because of the guilt of their fathers** (14:21), are addressed to Nebuchadnezzar. For those who succeeded him on the throne were destroyed by the Medes and Persians. The prophecy of blessed Daniel also instructs

---

1. Hebrew **Sheol**.

us in these matters. When Belshazzar raged against the holy vessels, this writing was inscribed on the wall: *Tekel, Parsin, Mene.* Holy Daniel interpreted it as follows: *Your kingdom will be given to the Medes and Persians* (Dan 5:25, 28). **"I will rise up against them," says the Lord of hosts, "and will destroy their name and remnant and seed," says the Lord** (14:22); that is, I will destroy them utterly....

This text shows that the prophet uses the names Assyrian and Babylonian to refer to the same people. In this way he stops talking about Nebuchadnezzar and his descendants who had been deprived of the kingdom, and he turns to Sennacherib. For it was his army that besieged Jerusalem, whose ruins are famous to this day. **And their yoke shall depart from them, and their glory shall be taken away from their shoulder** (14:25). **Yoke** means the servitude that the Assyrians imposed on their subjects.

The dissolution of the empire of the Assyrians and Babylonians brought relief to all the nations, since they had been the dominant power in the entire region of Asia and Egypt. Even the inhabitants of Europe, when they learned of their change of fortune, knew they would benefit from it. **For what the Lord has purposed, who will annul it? His hand is stretched out, and who will turn it back?** (14:27). Recall also what was said by blessed Moses: *I kill and I make alive; I wound and I heal; and there is none that can deliver out of my hand* (Deut 32:39).

Rejoice not, O Philistia (14:29). When Isaiah has finished the prophecy concerning Babylonia, he turns to the Philistines. The name **Philistia** is Hebrew; in Greek it is translated as Palestine.... The reference to the death of **Ahaz** (14:28) indicates the date of the prophecy....

Because he was an ungodly man, Ahaz received no help from God. For this reason he was an easy prey to all the neighboring peoples. Not only did the ten tribes in league with the Syrians overcome him, but the Philistines also joined with others in plundering his cities and villages. Nevertheless when the Philistines learned of his death, they rejoiced because they hoped to seize all the cities of Judah. The prophetic word, however, urges them not to rejoice that Ahaz's ungodliness had led to the fall of the kingdom against which they had fought....

The most excellent king Hezekiah was a godly man and enjoyed divine favor. For that reason he had put an end to the arrogance of the Philistines (2 Kgs 18:8). It is he who is referred to in the phrase the **young of the serpents** (14:29), not because he imitated their evil, but because he dealt as harshly with the Philistines as they had with the Israelites....

God will look after the Jews whom the Philistines despised, and he will deliver them as from an attack by wolves, and they will live **in peace** (14:30). These words refer to the deliverance from the Assyrians....

When all the other nations are in captivity, Zion will effortlessly triumph over those who made war on her. From these events you learn that the God of all will watch over Israel, and because of the piety of her inhabitants, he will deliver her from all her troubles.

14:12-21
How is fallen from heaven the Day Star, which used to rise early in the morning! He has been crushed into the earth who used to send light to all the nations! O Day Star, who arises at dawn . . .

(3) Origen of Alexandria

It is most clearly shown in this passage (14:12-22) that he who formerly had been Lucifer and who **arises at dawn** (14:12) has fallen from heaven. For if, as some suppose, he was a being of darkness, why is he said formerly to have been Lucifer, "the bringer of light"? Or how could he, who had in him no light at all, **rise at dawn**? Moreover, the Savior teaches us about the devil as follows: *I saw Satan fall like lightning from heaven* (Luke 10:18). So he once was light. Furthermore, our Lord, who is the truth, compared even the power of his own glorious advent to lightning, in these words: *For as the lightning shines from one end of heaven even to the other, so will be the coming of the Son of man* (Matt 24:27). Yet he also compares Satan to lightning and says that he **fell from heaven**, in order to show thereby that he had once existed in heaven and had had a place among the holy ones. He shows too that Satan had shared in this light in which all the holy ones share, by which they became *angels of light* (cf. 2 Cor 11:14) and for which the apostles are called *the light of the world* (Matt 5:14) by the Lord.

In this way, then, even Satan was once light, before he went astray and fell to this place, when **his glory was turned into dust** (14:11), which is the peculiar mark of the wicked, as the prophet also says. And so he is called the *prince of this world* (John 12:31), meaning our earthly habitation, for he also exercises his princely power over those who are obedient to this wickedness, since *this whole world* (and here I take *world* to mean this earthly place) *lies in the power of the evil one* (1 John 5:19), that is, in this apostate. That he is an apostate or fugitive the Lord also says in Job in the following words: *You will take with a hook the apostate serpent* (cf. Job 40:20), that is, the fugitive serpent. And it is certain that the serpent means the devil himself.

(4) Augustine of Hippo

The prophet Isaiah discloses this about the devil: **How he has fallen from heaven, Lucifer, who rises in the morning! He has been crushed to the earth, who used to send [light] to all the nations. You, however, said in your mind: "I will ascend to heaven; beyond the stars of heaven I will set my throne; I will sit on a lofty mountain above the lofty mountains to the north; I will ascend above the clouds, I will be like the Most High." Now, however, you shall descend into the netherworld** (14:12-15). This and what follows are understood to have been said to the devil under the figure of the king of Babylon. But most of what is said seems better suited to his "body" which he gathers together from the human race, and especially to those who stick to him out of pride by disobeying the commandments of God. As the one who actually was the devil was called a man in the Gospel, *An enemy man has done this* (Matt 13:28), so too one who was a man is called the devil, again in the Gospel: *Did I not choose you, the twelve, and one of you is a devil?* (John 6:70).

Just as Christ's body, the Church, is called Christ — as in the passage: *You are the offspring of Abraham,* immediately after Paul had said, *It was to Abraham and to his seed that the promises were made. It does not say, "And to offsprings," referring to many; but, referring to one, "and to your offspring," which is Christ* (Gal 3:29, 16), and in another passage: *For just as the body is one and has many members, and all the members of the body, though many, are one body, so it is with Christ* (1 Cor 12:12) — in the same way the devil's body, of which the devil is the head, that is, the company of the wicked, and especially those who **fall** away from Christ or from the Church as **from heaven**, is called the devil. Many things are said against him figuratively which suit the body and the members more than the head. **Lucifer,** who rose in the morning and **fell,** can be understood as the band of apostates from Christ and the Church, who were converted to darkness and abandoned the light they were carrying, just as those who are converted to God pass from darkness to light. That is to say, those who were in darkness have become light.

(5) John Cassian

Here is how we can grasp the power of the most grievous tyranny of pride. We see that the angel who, on account of his great splendor and beauty, was called **Lucifer** (14:12) was cast out of heaven for no other vice than this one, and that, having been wounded by the dart of pride, he fell from the blessed and sublime post of the angels into hell. If, then, a single instance of pride of heart was able to cast down from heaven to earth such great virtue, adorned with the privilege of such great power, the immensity of his downfall demonstrates what care it behooves us who are girded in frail flesh to exercise. But we shall be able to learn how to avoid the baleful position of this disease if we seek out the causes and the origin of his downfall. . . .

Clothed then in divine brightness and shining in the midst of the other supernal powers, thanks to the bounty of the Creator, he believed that he had acquired the splendor of his wisdom and the beauty of his virtue, with which he was adorned by the grace of the Creator, not as the latter's munificent gift but by the power of his own nature. Made proud on this account, as if he did not stand in need of the divine help to preserve this purity, he judged himself to be similar to God since, like God, he lacked nothing. That is to say, he relied on the power of his free will, believing that by it everything that pertained to the perfection of his virtue and to the continuance of his supreme blessedness would be supplied to him in abundance.

This thought alone was his first downfall. Because of it he was abandoned by God, whom he believed he did not need. At once he lost his balance; he tottered, fully aware of the frailty of his own nature, and lost the blessedness that he had enjoyed as a gift of God. And because *he loved the words of ruin* (Ps 52:4) with which he had declared, **I will ascend to heaven** (14:13), and *the deceitful tongue* (Ps 52:4) with which he asserted both of himself, **I will be like the Most High** (14:14), and of Adam and Eve, *You shall be as gods* (Gen 3:5), there *God shall destroy him forever, pluck him up and remove him from this tent* *and uproot him from the land of the living* (Ps 52:5). Then *shall the righteous fear, when they see* his downfall, *and they shall mock at him and say, "Behold the man who did not take God as his helper but trusted in the abundance of his wealth and prevailed in his vanity"* (Ps 52:6-7). These words could also quite rightly be directed to those who believe that they can attain to the highest good without the protection and help of God.

This then is the cause of the first downfall and the ultimate origin of the disease that, once again by way of him who had let himself be cast down, crept into the first man and produced the weaknesses and the wherewithal of all the vices. For in his belief that he could attain to the glory of the Godhead by his own free will and effort, he lost even that which was his by the grace of the Creator.

And so it is very clearly shown from scriptural examples and texts that, although the disgrace of pride is last in the order of battle, it is nonetheless first in terms of origin and is the source of all sins and misdeeds, and that, unlike the other vices, it does not do away merely with its opposite virtue — that is, humility — but is actually the destroyer of all the virtues together, and that it tries not only the middling and the small but in particular those who stand at the summit of strength.

14:13-14
You said in your mind, "I will ascend to heaven, I will set my throne above the stars of God."

(6) Cyprian of Carthage

Exaltation and puffing up, arrogance and proud self-importance, spring not from the teaching of Christ, who teaches humility, but from the spirit of the Antichrist, whom the Lord rebukes by his prophet: **You said in your heart, "I will ascend above the heights of the clouds, I will make myself like the Most High"** (14:13-14). And he added: **But you will go down into Hades, to the foundations of the earth, and those who look on you will marvel over you**[2] (14:15-16).

(7) Augustine of Hippo

The soul that turns away from God as away from the light of truth ends up in the North instead of in the South. Now the kingdom of the **North** is the kingdom of the devil, who announces, **I will set my throne in the North; I will be like the Most High** (14:13-14). Human hearts grow cold there, and once grown cold they cannot catch the flavor of spiritual things from that fire of divine wisdom. And so they start thinking only about bodies, to the extent of even looking for divinity in bodies, that is, in the sea, in the earth, in the air, and above all in the heavenly bodies, as in the moon or the sun or the stars. You see, the sense of sight takes first place among the senses of the body, and so whatever shines

---

2. Cyprian is referring to Satan.

for the eyes, especially if it also occupies the highest place in the cosmos, is considered great. But if anyone suggests to them that there is something great which *no eye has seen, nor ear heard, nor the heart of man conceived* (1 Cor 2:9; cf. Isa 64:4), they reply that there isn't anything which cannot be seen.

Such hearts, then, have grown cold; if they have grown cold, they are in the North; if they are in the North, they are under the dominion of the one who said, **I will set my throne in the North; I will be like the Most High.**

(8) John Cassian

Vainglory and pride are consummated without any action on the body's part. For what need is there of bodily activity when it comes to seeking praise or pursuing glory? They bring harm to the captive soul without bodily movement. What bodily action accompanied Lucifer's ancient pride? Was it not solely a matter of mind and thought? As the prophet declares, **You said in your heart, "I will go up to heaven, above the stars of God I will set my throne; I will ascend above the heights of the clouds, I will be like the Most High"** (14:13-14). He had no one to provoke him to this pride. It was in thought alone that his crime and his eternal ruin were perfectly achieved, especially since he did nothing to impose the tyranny he desired.

(9) John Chrysostom

I will set my throne on high (14:13). The less we are filled with pride the more we advance in virtue, for this more than anything else is virtue, to hold ourselves in check. Just as the sharper our sight is, the more fully do we realize how far we are from the sky, so the more we advance in virtue, so much more do we learn the difference between God and ourselves. This is no small part of true wisdom, to be able to know our own worth; for he knows himself best who accounts himself to be nothing. Hence we see that both David and Abraham, when they had reached the highest pitch of virtue, best displayed this trait. The one called himself *earth and ashes* (Gen 18:27), the other *a worm* (Ps 22:6). Likewise all the saints acknowledge their own wretchedness. For the one who is filled up with boasting is the very person who does not know himself. For that reason it is customary to say of the proud, "he does not know himself," or "he is ignorant of himself." And if he does not know himself, whom does he know? For as he who knows himself will know all things, so he who does not know himself will not know anything else.

It was just such a person who said, **I will set my throne on high** (14:13). For since he did not know himself, he was ignorant of everything else. This was not the case with Paul. He used to call himself *one untimely born* (1 Cor 15:8) and *the very least of all the saints* (Eph 3:8), and he did not consider himself to be worthy of the title of the apostles (1 Cor 15:9), even after having done so many good things.

(10) Thomas Aquinas

14:9-20 Hell below was in an uproar on meeting you. It stirred up the giants against you. All the princes of the earth are roused from their thrones, all the kings of the nations. 10All will answer and say to you: "You are wounded as well as we; you have become like us." 11Your pride has been brought down to hell, your carcass has fallen down, the moth spreads decay beneath you, and maggots will be your covering. 12How is fallen from heaven the Day Star *(Lucifer),* who used to rise early in the morning! You who wounded the nations fell to the earth. 13You said in your heart, "I will ascend to heaven; I will exalt my throne above the stars of God; I will sit in the mountain of the covenant, in the sides of the north. 14I will ascend above the heights of the clouds; I will be like the Most High." 15But you will descend to hell, to the depths of the pit. 16Those who see you shall bend down to you and look at you: "Is this the man who troubled the earth, who shook kingdoms?" 17Who made the world a wilderness and destroyed its cities, who would not release those who were in prison. 18All the kings of the nation sleep in glory, each one in his own house. 19But you are cast out of your grave as a useless branch defiled, and wrapped up with those who were slain by the sword. You have gone down to the bottom of the pit as a rotten carcass. 20You shall not keep company with them even in burial; for you have destroyed your land; you have slain your people. The seed of the wicked will never again be mentioned.[3]

Here we see how the dead in hell revile Nebuchadnezzar:[4] first, **the princes** and **the powers** (14:9); second, **others who see you** (14:16). . . .

The text presents their taunts, which are three in number, all referring to the punishment he is receiving. First, as to death itself, **You are wounded** (14:10) in death, by the force of divine power, as Psalm 88 says: *You have laid the proud low, like one who has been wounded* (Ps 88:11Vg.); then, as to the laying low in death, both spiritually, **your pride is brought down** (14:11), and physically, **your corpse has fallen** (14:11); then too, as to the suffering in death in hell, **and maggots will be your covering** (14:11). Here are contained all the pains of hell, as it says in Judith: *Fire and worms he will give to their flesh, that they may be consumed, and may feel pain forever* (Jdt 16:21 Vg.).

Second, they taunt him for the glory that he has lost. Then with respect to his royal dignity, **Day Star *(Lucifer)*** (14:12), because he was splendid among all other kings; **in the morning** (14:12), meaning sole ruler before all others; **cut down to the ground** (14:12), said with reference to being overcome in war. See Daniel 2: *You are the head of gold, O King; and after you shall arise another less than you* (Dan 2:38-39).

Third, he is taunted for his proud heart. Three things are mentioned: his arrogant thoughts, his perverted intention (**I will be like the Most High** [14:14]), and his futile ambitions (**But . . .** , [14:15]). His thought was arrogant because he had the idea of usurping

---

3. Because Thomas's Latin text is different from the Hebrew and the LXX in several details, we have provided a translation here.
4. Though the object of the taunts is Nebuchadnezzar, at the end of the section Thomas applies them to Satan.

what belonged to God, erring in the way of the Gentiles who thought that men could change into gods, and princes could become stars, as it says in 2 Macc 11: *Now that our father has been taken up among the gods* (2 Macc 11:23). He even intended to usurp God's place: **I will ascend to heaven, above the stars of heaven** (14:13), as if to say, "Just as I am above all the kings on earth, so too will I be above all the stars in heaven." He also sought to usurp divine worship: **I will sit**, as though receiving sacrifices, **on the mount of the covenant** (14:13) — that is, in the temple of God, which was on Mount Zion and in which was the covenant of the law — **in the northern parts** (14:13), that is, in Jerusalem, which was on the northern side of the mountain. Finally, he sought to usurp divine action as well: **above the height of the clouds** (14:14), as if he were to say like thunder and lightning....

Like the Most High (14:14): Here we see his perverse intention. See Ezekiel 28: Is it not true that you spoke and *you said, "I am God"* (Ezek 28:2)? **But ...** (14:15). In that word you can see that his intention was in vain. See Job 21: *into the depth of the Pit*, meaning, into the most brutal punishments. See Job 21: *They spend their days in prosperity, and in an instant[5] they descend into hell* (Job 21:13).

Those who see you (14:16): Here the text refers to the taunt of others gathered there. First it describes their encounter with him: All the others **who see you** in torments **will bend over you** (14:16), as if to say, "You will be so far below them that they will have to bend over because they want to look at you." See Wisdom 6: *But the mighty will suffer mighty torments* (Wis 6:6). Then the text describes their reproaches, of which there are three. He is first blamed because **he made the earth tremble** in wars, **he shook kingdoms** (14:16) by overturning their dominions, **he made the world like a desert** (14:17) by exiling its peoples, **he overthrew its cities** by destroying them; **for the captives he did not open their prison** (14:17), so that they could once again see the light. See Ezekiel 32: *they spread terror in the land of the living* (Ezek 32:25). Their second taunt has to do with the tomb in which he was laid, because he was exhumed by his son, who shredded his corpse into two hundred pieces and tied it to as many birds brought from every corner of the world, so that he could not rise again.[6] He is **polluted** (14:19) by the blood of those whom he had slain. Cf. Jeremiah 22: *With the burial of an ass shall he be buried* (Jer 22:19). Third, they taunt him with the damage that he inflicted on his kingdom. **You destroyed your land** (14:20), because the Babylonians would have kept their kingdom for a longer time had it not been for Nebuchadnezzar's sins: a people is punished for its ruler's faults; compare Proverbs 29: *A prince who is willing to listen to lies will have nothing but wicked men for ministers* (Prov 29:12).

This text can be applied in a spiritual sense to the devil. For example, **Who shook kingdoms** (14:16) refers to him as the executor of punishment and instigator of sin. His power has been diminished by Christ, and he will be utterly cast into hell on the day of judgment. He is the one who wanted to climb up to heaven and to match in equality the

---

5. Vg. *in an instant*; both the LXX and the Hebrew have *in peace*.
6. According to Jewish tradition, when Nebuchadnezzar died, his son feared that he had only disappeared, as he had done previously. To demonstrate that he was dead, his mutilated corpse was dragged through the streets.

majesty of God — according to an interpretation found in the *Gloss*.[7] Note above on the phrase **above the stars of God** (14:16) that the saints are compared in several ways to the stars: first, because of their number, cf. *Who determines the number of the stars* (Ps 146:4 Vg.) and *a thousand thousands served him, and ten thousand times ten thousand stood before him* (Dan 7:10); second, because of their location, cf. *the glory of the stars is the beauty of heaven* (Sir 43:9) and *our citizenship is in the heavens* (Phil 3:20); third, because of their different degrees, cf. *star differs from star in brightness* (1 Cor 15:41); fourth, because of their shining splendor, cf. *and those who turn many to righteousness, like the stars forever and ever* (Dan 12:3); fifth, because of their orderly motion, cf. *the stars in their courses fought against Sisera* (Judg 5:20) and *let all things be done* among you *decently and in order* (1 Cor 14:40); sixth, because of what is seen, cf. *like the morning star among the clouds* (Sir 50:6) and *it has not yet appeared what we shall be* (1 John 3:2); and seventh, because of the circular shape of the symbol, cf. *a woman appeared in heaven . . . and on her head was a crown of twelve stars* (Rev 12:1), in which the perfection of glory is signified.

---

7. A reference to the *Glossa ordinaria*, the standard medieval commentary on Scripture composed of excerpts from the fathers inserted in the margins.

Isaiah 15–16

15:1 The word against Moabitis.

    By night Moabitis will perish,
        for by night the wall of Moabitis will perish.
2 Grieve for yourselves, for Lebedon will perish!
        Where your altar is, there you will go up to weep:
    wail over Nabau of Moabitis!
On every head will be baldness,
    all arms will be cut in pieces.
3 In her highways gird yourselves with sackcloth and smite yourselves;
    on her housetops and in her streets
    wail, all of you, with weeping!
4 Because Hesebon and Eleale have cried out,
    her voice is heard as far as Iassa;
therefore the loins of Moabitis cry aloud;
    her soul will know.
5 The heart of Moabitis cries aloud within her as far as Segor,
    for she is a three-year-old heifer.
And on the ascent of Louith
    they will go up to you weeping;
by the way of Haroniim she cries aloud,
    "Destruction and an earthquake!"
6 The water of Nemrim
    will be desolate,
and her grass will fail,
    for there will be no green grass.
7 Even so, will she be saved?
    For I will bring Arabs to the valley,
    and they will take her.
8 For the cry has reached

the boundary of Moabitis of Agallim,
and her wailing
as far as the well of Ailim.
9 And the water of Remmon will be filled with blood;
for I will bring Arabs upon Remmon,
and I will remove the offspring of Moab and Ariel,
and the remnant of Adama.

16:1 I will send as it were creeping animals on the land:
is Mount Sion a desolate rock?
2 For you will be as a nestling taken away
from a bird that is flying, O daughter of Moab!
And then, O Arnon,
3 take further counsel,
and make for her
a shelter for mourning for all time.
They flee in darkness at noon,
they were astonished;
do not be taken away.
4 The fugitives of Moab
will sojourn with you;
they will be a shelter to you
from before a pursuer,
because your alliance has been taken away,
and the ruler who trampled on the land has perished.
5 Then a throne shall be restored with mercy,
and he shall sit on it with truth in the tent of Dauid,
judging and seeking judgment
and quickly procuring righteousness.

6 We have heard of the pride of Moab:
exceedingly proud he is;
you have removed his arrogance.
Your divination is not thus,
7 Moab shall wail,
for in Moabitis all shall wail.
You will take care of those who dwell in Adeseth
and you will not be ashamed.

8 The plains of Hesebon will mourn;
the vine of Sebama.
As you swallow up the nations,
trample down her vines as far as Iazer.
You will not come together,

>   you will not wander in the desert;
>   those who were sent have been forsaken,
>   for they crossed the desert.
> 9 Therefore I will weep as with the weeping of Iazer
>   for the vine of Sebama.
>   He has cut down your trees,
>   O Hesebon and Eleale;
>   because I will trample down your harvest and vintage,
>   and all things will fall.
> 10 And joy and gladness will be taken away
>   from your vineyards,
>   and in your vineyards
>   they will not rejoice;
>   and they will not tread out wine in the vats,
>   for the vintage has ceased.
> 11 Therefore my belly will resound
>   like a lyre upon Moab,
>   and my inward parts will be
>   like a wall that you have made new.

12 And it will be for your shame, because Moab has become weary at the altars; and she will enter the works of her hands in order to pray, but will not be able to deliver him.

13 This was the word that the Lord spoke against Moab at the time he also spoke. 14 But now I say, In three years of the years of a hired worker, the glory of Moab will be dishonored with all its great wealth, and it will be left very few in number and without honor.

These two chapters, an oracle against Moab, receive a mainly historical interpretation from the commentators who had to struggle with obscurities in the Hebrew original that were scarcely clarified by the Septuagint or the Latin version. Eusebius of Caesarea admits that spiritual or allegorical interpretation is "forced" and prefers to look for the fulfillment of the prophecies at the time of the invasion of the Assyrians and Babylonians. He does, however, think that some of the verses refer to historical fulfillment in the Christian era and are predictions of the Christian conversion of Israel's ancient enemy the Moabites, who lived in Transjordan. A passage of special interest is Eusebius's interpretation of Isa 16:5, in which he blends christological fulfillment with ecclesiological doctrine by equating the one for whom the throne is being prepared first with Christ and then with the Christian bishop, who is Christ's placeholder. Cyril's exposition is historical, and we have provided his introduction to the oracle. Eusebius's doubts about spiritual interpretation to the contrary, Aelred of Rievaulx took advantage of an anomalous Latin rendering of Isa 16:1 to compose a meditation on Christ as the Lamb of God, and on the age of mercy that succeeds the age of judgment, in which he also takes up the subject of the devil's rights over humanity, won by the fall of Adam (cf. Col 2:14).

Isaiah 15–16

(1) Eusebius of Caesarea

The inhabitants of Moab boasted of their own gods and ridiculed and mocked the God of Israel. This is why the prophetic word addressed a prophecy about them. Therefore the prophet began by naming their ignorance of God **night** and **darkness**: he threatened that destruction would come upon them in the **night**, saying, **By night the region of Moab will perish, for by night the wall of the region of Moab will perish** (15:1)... I think it is clear that the occasion of the present section is the destruction of the idolatry that prevailed among the Moabites, along with the prediction of other things that would happen in the future to the capital city itself and to the surrounding countryside, as well as to villages and cities. These things were fulfilled historically at the time of the invasion of the Assyrians and Babylonians, and in later times in connection with those who subsequently held power over the region of the Arabs. When God threatens that he **will bring the Arabs** (15:7) against them, that may refer to their neighbors the **Arabs** or to the Saracens who live in their midst, the very ones to whom the prophetic word says that he will hand over Moab. As for what would befall the other cities which lie in the region of Moab, I see no need to trouble ourselves, nor to waste time on the villages and areas mentioned in the prophecy.... For of those areas and villages that still exist today in the territory of what is now called Areopolis, it is redundant to elaborate the threats made against them, or their literal fulfillments during the times when they were under siege.

I also think that allegorical interpretation of these passages is forced, just as allegory was unnecessary earlier in the case of the prophecy concerning the Babylonians [13:1-22], when the prophetic word said that the "Medes" [cf. 13:17] would attack Babylon. So here too, when God reveals that he **will bring the Arabs** against the Moabites....

It should not be surprising that we have to work hard to gain much benefit from this prophecy. The prophecy predicts the destruction and abandonment of their idolatry, and foretells that they will come to know the God of the universe, when the churches would be established among them and those whom they once considered as gods were cast out. The prophetic word foretells this development when it says, **For Debon will perish, where your altar is**, and again: **Because your alliance has been taken away, and the prince who tramples underfoot has perished from the land** (15:2). In this passage he refers to the wicked demon that dwelt within the nation, like the prince of the kingdom of Persia, the prince of the kingdom of the Greeks, and the prince of the Babylonians. He says that this demon will perish, the one established in the city of the Moabites, from whom they thought they would gain help in encounters with their enemies, since it trampled down their souls and made them bow to the earth, so that they could neither rise up nor look up.

After the demon's destruction the prophet goes on to say, **A throne will be restored in mercy, and he will sit on it in truth in the tent of David, judging and seeking judgment and quickly procuring righteousness** (16:5).... Who is the one for whom [the throne] will be prepared but Christ, who is the one begotten *from the seed of David* (Rom 1:3)? The prophet is thus saying that someday among the Moabites there will exist the **throne** of Christ, on which **he will sit in truth in the tent of David**. The prophetic spirit used this manner of speaking to refer to the Church of Christ since it was also his custom to call Christ himself **David**, because Christ was begotten *from the seed of David according to the flesh* (Rom 1:3). Therefore he gives the name of **tent of David** to the Church, and **throne** to the presiding officer of the Church who sits on it and who actually possesses the **throne**, taking as it were the place of Christ.

The Acts of the Apostles will demonstrate that this text is spoken about the Church of the Gentiles. There James, the first bishop of Jerusalem, is recorded as saying: *Brothers, listen to me. Simeon has related how God first visited the Gentiles, to take out of them a people for his name. And with this the words of the prophets agree, as it is written, "After this I will return, and I will rebuild the dwelling of David, which has fallen; I will rebuild its ruins, and I will set it up, that the rest of men may seek the Lord, and all the Gentiles who are called by my name, says the Lord, who has made these things known from of old"* (Acts 15:13-18, citing Amos 9:11-12).

He clearly introduced the prophecy of the *dwelling* or **tent of David** as a way of mentioning the calling of the Gentiles. He says that this will happen not by types and symbols but in truth; for **the tent of David will be established** among the highly superstitious Moabites, and a **throne** would be set up on which the Church's presiding officer [the bishop] **will sit, judging and seeking judgment and hastening righteousness**. . . . Who would not be convinced of the fulfillment of this text once they had perceived with their own eyes the churches of God established and Christ's **throne** in them in Areopolis itself and its surrounding region, including the other cities of Arabia, in which of old the demons and their fearful works were no longer even spoken of by name?

(2) Cyril of Alexandria

An oracle concerning Moab (15:1). Once he has finished the prophecy concerning the Babylonians and the Philistines, the prophet turns to the Moabites. The oracle is addressed to their chief city, to the villages surrounding it, and to the entire kingdom.

The Moabites were a barbaric people who were hateful to God because they were wholly devoted to the worship of idols, and they put their trust in magic. They arrogantly scorned the glory of God and were especially hostile to the people of Israel. When the Israelites were delivered from the tyranny of the Egyptians and had come into the land of promise, Balak, who was king of the Moabites at that time, attempted to destroy the entire people. For it is written in the book of Numbers: *Then the people of Israel set out, and encamped in the plains of Moab beyond the Jordan at Jericho. And Balak the son of Zippor saw all that Israel had done to the Amorites. And Moab was in great dread of the people because they were many; Moab was overcome with fear of the people of Israel* (Num 22:1-3). What was Balak's evil plan? He arranged for Balaam, a false prophet and soothsayer, to come from Mesopotamia. Then he tells him: *Curse Israel; for I know that whomever you bless will be blessed, and whomever you curse will be cursed* (Num 22:6). So Balaam began to prepare his magical arts and to build an altar for sacrifices.

But Balak's hope was disappointed and his plans foiled. Balaam, who was supposed to curse Israel, unexpectedly blessed her (Num 23:7–24:19). After his first effort failed, he conceived another plan to harm the Israelites. He ensnared them with the charms of Moabite women, and they abandoned their love for God and bowed down before the Baal of Peor, an idol of the Moabites. For it is written in Numbers: *While Israel dwelled in Shittim the people began to play the harlot with the daughters of Moab. They invited the people to the sacrifices of their gods, and the people ate, and bowed down to their gods. So Israel yoked himself to Baal of Peor. And the anger of the* LORD *was kindled against Israel* (Num 25:1-3).

When God is at the side of Israel, she is strong and powerful. But then, after the Israelites had turned away from God's help, they wickedly and malevolently ridiculed the God of all. And they continued to do so, even when they suffered misfortune. The Moabites boasted and railed violently that the God, who had promised to save those who worshiped him, was able to do nothing.

Jeremiah bears witness to this when he says in a vision: *The horn of Moab is cut off, and his arm is broken. Make him drunk, because he magnified himself against the* LORD (Jer 48:25-26). And again: *Karioth*[1] *is taken and the strongholds have been seized together. Moab shall be destroyed and be no longer a people, because he magnified himself against the* LORD (Jer 48:41-42). The imperious Assyrians and Babylonians plundered Judah, and they captured the cities of Samaria. In response the Moabites again derided and reproached without restraint those who had been ravaged, and they continued to deride the glory of God. For this reason they were exterminated. Their cities with all the people and their homes were utterly destroyed, so that it appears as though they do not exist. The present vision concerning Moab gives an account of these things.

(3) Aelred of Rievaulx

16:1 **Send forth the Lamb, O Lord, the ruler of the earth,**
    from Petra of the desert to the mountain of the daughter of Zion.
2 **And like a bird taking flight and nestlings flying from the nest,**
    so will the daughters of Moab be at the ford of the Arnon.
3 **Form a plan, convene a council,**
    make like night your shade in the noonday,
Hide the outcasts, betray not the fugitives;
4 **My refugees will dwell among you, O Moab;**
    be a refuge to them from the destroyer.
The dust is no more, the wretched man has come to an end,
    he who trampled down the earth.
5 **And a throne will be prepared in mercy,**
    and he will sit on it in truth in the tent of David,
One who judges and seeks justice and is swift to do justice (16:1-5)[2]

---

1. Instead of the translation, *the cities,* the LXX transliterates the Hebrew word *Karioth*. This Hebrew word can be understood to refer to a specific city in Moab, or it can mean "cities."

2. We have prefaced this translation of Aelred of Rievaulx's twenty-eighth sermon on the "Burdens of Isaiah" with a translation of the Latin Vg. version of Isa 16:1-5 because of its numerous differences from the Hebrew.

God will come from the south, and the Holy One from a shaded and thickly wooded mountain (Hab 3:3 Vg.).

Behold, dearest brothers, our Lord Jesus suddenly bursts forth into the open, after having hitherto been hidden in this exceedingly thick forest of allegorical texts, when the prophet says, **Send forth the Lamb, O Lord, the ruler of the earth, from the rock[3] in the desert to the mountain of the daughter of Zion** (16:1). Truly *my beloved stands behind our wall, gazing through the windows and looking through the grills* (Song 2:9). Who does not know that the Lord Jesus must be sought in the Scriptures, since we hear him say in the Gospel, *You search the Scriptures [. . . and it is they that bear witness to me]* (John 5:39)? But between us and him, like a kind of wall, stands the mysteriousness of that very Scripture, with its coded words and symbolic narratives. Scripture's spiritual components, which have created this wall for us, vary our perception of him through the windows and grills by which he, the Beloved, offers himself to be *put on* (cf. Eph 4:24; 6:14; Col 3:10) by his lovers. We should therefore not doubt that the same One who is so openly disclosed in those texts that reveal him, also exists everywhere in those texts that conceal him.

So the text says, **Send forth the Lamb, O Lord, the ruler of the earth**. We have already noted in our introduction that the prophets spoke sometimes in narratives, sometimes in commands, and sometimes in prayers. Therefore the prophet perceived in the spirit that even the wise ones of the world would have to be subject to the power of the cross and by believing could be saved, though through the *folly* (1 Cor 1:18) of the proclamation. As Paul writes, *nevertheless I will destroy the wisdom of the wise, and the cleverness of the clever I will thwart* (1 Cor 1:19, citing Isa 29:14), and so on, which is also what is being expounded in this particular "burden." The prophet burns with desire, he protests the delay, he wants Christ to come immediately, to fulfill the promises, to manifest what has been announced beforehand. And having turned to the Father, he asks with passionate feeling for the advent of his Son: **Send forth**, he says, **the Lamb, O Lord, the ruler of the earth, from the rock in the desert to the mountain of the daughter of Zion**. This is the Lamb who spoke through Jeremiah, saying, *And I, like an innocent lamb brought to the slaughter* (Jer 11:19), and of whom Isaiah too says, *like a sheep he will be led to the slaughter, and like a lamb he will be dumb before the shearers* (53:7 Vg.). This is the one whom, when the Holy Spirit revealed him, the holy Baptist recognized and exclaimed, *Behold, the Lamb of God!* (John 1:29). This is the one of whom David sang, *He will rule from sea to sea, and from the river to the ends of the earth* (Ps 72:8).

From the rock in the desert to the mountain of the daughter of Zion: I think that by the **rock in the desert** he is referring to that cave cut from rock, either by the natural forces of the wilderness or by human effort, in which the fleeing Lot escaped the men of Sodom (cf. Gen 19:30). **From** this **rock**, he says in great wonder, the **Lamb** will come forth, because Moab was begotten in it,[4] and from his race Christ was

---

3. Aelred takes a significant liberty with the Latin text by construing the proper noun "Petra" (by which Jerome in his translation intended the Nabataean city south of the Dead Sea) as a common noun meaning simply "rock."

4. "The first-born [daughter of Lot] bore a son, and called his name Moab; he is the father of the Moabites to this day" (Gen 19:37).

born.[5] He is sent forth **from the rock in the desert to the mountain of the daughter of Zion**, because after he was born of the Virgin in Bethlehem, in his own person he visited Jerusalem, in which is Mount Zion in the literal sense of the word, or a "mountain" in the sense of "exaltedness," and in which is the glory **of the daughter of Zion** — that is, of the Synagogue — by which we understand the splendor of the temple. The Synagogue is allegorically called the **rock in the desert** because, after she was led forth from Egypt, she became a dweller in the desert for forty years *and drank from the spiritual rock which followed them* (1 Cor 10:4). She is therefore called the **rock in the desert** because she preserved the substance of the faith among those who were more perfect, even though many others perished from unbelief during the long years of their exile. From this **rock** too came the apostles, who proclaimed to the peoples of the nations the **Lamb**, *who takes away the sin of the world!* (John 1:29), so that he might rule over the whole world and so that the Church might be born from the synagogue, being, as it were, **the daughter of Zion**, she whose life is deep faith, sublime hope, and *the still more excellent way* of love (cf. 1 Cor 12:31). Therefore the Lord says in the Gospel, *Thus it is written, that the Christ should suffer and on the third day rise from the dead, and that repentance and the forgiveness of sins should be preached in his name to all nations, beginning from Jerusalem* (Luke 24:46-47).

Or surely we can also say that **the Lamb was sent forth as the ruler of the earth, from the rock in the desert to the mountain of the daughter of Zion**, when Christ passed over from the shadow of the law to the truth of the gospel; when he brought us **from the rock in the desert**, the symbol[6] of our redemption from which the Israelites drank, to the truth of his most holy Body and Blood; when the veil of the Letter was torn away and he disclosed the secret of its spiritual meaning, as shown in the pronouncements of the New Testament. **It will be, etc.** (16:2 Vg.), the text says. What is the meaning of this verse? When the Lamb shall be sent forth as ruler of the earth, from **the rock in the desert to the mountain of the daughter of Zion, like a bird taking flight and nestlings flying from the nest, so will be the daughters of Moab at the ford of the Arnon** (16:1-2). By **the daughters of Moab** you are to understand carnal and weak souls that have been deceived by the errors of the Moabites. **Arnon** is to be translated as "their enlightenment." **My refugees will dwell among you, O Moab** (16:4): In this passage, you should understand **Moab** to mean those who are wise, of whom we said above that the degree of their insight into worldly wisdom matched their prudent judgment in divine things — that is the Moab whose **fugitives came to Segor** (cf. 15:5). . . .

Such a man was the most blessed Cyprian, so too were Ambrose, Augustine, and Jerome, who applied everything that they had drawn from secular learning to the strengthening and progress of the Church. Of such a kind too were those who more effectively subdued heretics; so too were those who by their teaching protected whoever was vulnerable from the contagion of false apostles, under whose care, as if under maternal wings, the vulnerable were kept covered more securely, so that they might not be seduced

---

5. Ruth was a Moabite (Ruth 1:4) who married Boaz, from their union came Obed, and Christ was born of this line (Matt 1:5).

6. Latin *sacramentum*.

and seized by demons. Of this **Moab**, that is, the wise men of this world, Christ declares, **My refugees will dwell among you, O Moab; be a refuge to them from the destroyer** (16:4). He calls those who had previously been seduced and carried off by the devil his **refugees**; when the enemy had been defeated, he recaptured them as was the victor's right. The devil in turn, aggrieved at their recapture, stirred up heretics, incited philosophers, and sowed false teachings, all so that by deceiving simple-minded believers, he could gain satisfaction for the charge that had been levied on him. But until iniquity perished and the truth was revealed, those immature in the faith depended on those who were mature, and the mature were responsible for wisely providing a refuge of teaching and protection for the simple ones, against such destroyers. Therefore he says, **My refugees will dwell among you, O Moab; be a refuge to them from the destroyer** (16:4).

So that this might not seem too difficult to one who realizes the devil's power and craftiness, he goes on, **The dust is no more, the wretched man has come to an end** (16:4a Vg.).[7] The devil's teaching is compared to dust, which as it were comes to its end when, under the shining brilliance of the gospel, the world receives its saving teaching. The prophet eloquently calls the devil **the wretched one**, for whom damnation to eternal fire has been prepared in the future and in whose wicked breast a futile anxiety burns. For he ever labors and ever profits nothing, always thirsting for the souls of the elect but never able to subject them permanently to himself — universally judged to be all the more **wretched** because he, a spiritual and immortal being, has been overcome by those who are earthly and mortal. Truly **wretched** is he, for he is oppressed by angels and mocked by all, regarded with contempt by the mature and conquered by the weak. Therefore the prophet says, **The dust is no more, the wretched man has come to an end**. To this is added, **He who trampled down the earth has vanished** (16:4b Vg.).

Let us give thanks, dear brothers, to that Lamb who, **sent from the rock in the desert to the mountain of the daughter of Zion**, has snatched the earth away from the tyranny of the one who from the beginning **trampled it down**, that is, the devil. To be more precise, the **Lamb** has taken the one who had **trampled down** the earth and has laid him (meaning the devil) prostrate at the feet of him (meaning the human race) whom he had trampled down, by giving human beings *the strength to tread upon serpents and scorpions, and over all the power of the enemy* (Luke 10:19). And therefore the apostle says to those who believe, *God will soon crush Satan under your feet* (Rom 16:20). The **earth** in question is thus said to be the holy company of all the saints, that fertile and fecund earth which will soon bring forth fruit, *now thirty, now sixty, and now a hundredfold* (cf. Matt 13:23).

The ancient enemy was **trampling down** with the feet of his malice the human race, up to that marvelous coming of our Savior. The devil was able to impose his legal right of evil damnation even against the elect, because of the fault of that first deception [i.e., original sin]. But then he exceeded the *bond of indebtedness* (cf. Col 2:14)[8] from

---

7. In Isa 16:4 the Vg. reads "dust" *(pulvis)* for Hebrew "oppressor," and "wretched one" *(miser)* for Hebrew "destruction."

8. According to ancient tradition, after Adam and Eve had sinned, Adam signed a bond that gave the devil rights over human beings. This is the "bond of indebtedness" of Col 2:14. The devil pleaded his rights at the death of Christ, but the divine court said that Christ did not fall under the terms of the contract. Satan had overplayed his hand. The surety he had held legitimately for centuries could now be torn up.

Isaiah 15–16

which his power derived by laying impious hands on and bringing to his death the one human being in whom no reason for death could be found. Therefore the violator of the bond that had been signed lost the verdict that was owed him by right because, as an excessively greedy and unjust exactor of punishment, he usurped what was *not* owed to him. Therefore **he who trampled down the earth has vanished**. Thus *God canceled the bond which stood against us . . . setting it aside, nailing it to the cross. He disarmed the principalities and powers and made a public example of them, triumphing over them in him* (Col 2:14-15). Thus with the enemy defeated, *he led captivity captive, giving gifts to men* (Eph 4:8). *Therefore God has highly exalted him, and has given him a name that is above every other name* (Phil 2:9). Then began the fulfillment of what the prophet had foretold when he added to the foregoing text, **And he will be established on the throne of his mercy, and he will sit on it in truth in the tent of David, one who judges and seeks justice and is swift to do what is just** (16:5 Vg.). *Mercy and justice I will sing to you, O Lord* (Ps 100:1 Vg.).

Brothers, let us draw near in trust to the throne of mercy which he has established within, **in the tent of David**, meaning the Church; for now is the age of being merciful, which assuredly will follow the age of passing judgment.

Isaiah 19

1 A vision concerning Egypt.

   See, the Lord is sitting on a swift cloud
      and will come to Egypt;
   and the handiworks of Egypt will be shaken at his presence,
      and their heart will be dismayed within them.
2 And Egyptians will be stirred up against Egyptians,
      and a man will war against his brother,
      and a man against his neighbor,
      city against city, and province against province;
3 and the spirit of the Egyptians will be troubled within them,
      and I will scatter their counsel;
   and they will consult their gods and their images
      and those who speak out of the earth and the ventriloquists;
4 and I will deliver Egypt
      into the hands of men, cruel lords;
   and cruel kings will lord it over them.

   This is what the Lord Sabaoth says:
5 And the Egyptians will drink the water that is by the sea,
      but the river will fail and be dried up;
6 and the rivers and the canals of the river will fail,
      and every collection of water,
      even in every marsh of reed and papyrus,
      will be dried up.
7 And the green marsh grass,
      all that is around the river,
   and all that is sown by the river,
      will be dried up, blasted by the wind.
8 And the fishers will groan;

and all who cast hooks into the river will groan,
and those who cast seines and those who are anglers will mourn.
9 And shame will take hold of those who work the split flax
and those who work the linen.
10 And those who weave them will be in pain,
and all who make beer will be grieved,
and they will afflict their souls.

11 And the rulers of Tanis will be fools;
as for the wise counselors of the king,
their counsel will become foolish.
How will you say to the king,
"We are sons of sages,
sons of kings who were from the beginning"?
12 Where now are your wise men?
And let them also declare to you and say
what the Lord Sabaoth has planned against Egypt.
13 The rulers of Tanis have failed,
and the rulers of Memphis have been exalted;
and they will lead Egypt astray
tribe by tribe.
14 For the Lord has prepared for them
a spirit of error;
and they have led Egypt astray in all their works,
as the drunkard and the one who vomits
are led astray together.
15 And there will not be a work for the Egyptians
that will make head or tail, beginning or end.

16 But on that day the Egyptians will be like women in fear and in trembling before the hand of the Lord Sabaoth, which he will lay on them. 17 And the land of the Judeans will become a terror to the Egyptians. As for everyone who should mention it to them — they will fear because of the plan that the Lord has planned against it.

18 On that day there will be five cities in Egypt speaking the Chananite language and swearing in the name of the Lord. The one city will be called Asedek City.

19 On that day there will be an altar to the Lord in the land of the Egyptians, and a pillar to the Lord at its border. 20 And it will be a sign forever to the Lord in the country of Egypt, because they will cry to the Lord on account of those who oppress them; and the Lord will send them a man who will save them — judging he will save them. 21 And the Lord will be known to the Egyptians; and the Egyptians will know the Lord on that day, and will offer sacrifices and make vows to the Lord and repay them. 22 And

the Lord will strike the Egyptians with a great blow and heal them with healing; and they will return to the Lord, and he will listen to them and heal them.

23On that day there will be a way from Egypt to the Assyrians, and the Assyrians will enter Egypt, and the Egyptians will go to the Assyrians, and the Egyptians will serve the Assyrians.

24On that day Israel will be third among the Assyrians and among the Egyptians, blessed in the land 25that the Lord Sabaoth has blessed, saying, "Blessed be my people that are in Egypt and among the Assyrians, even Israel my heritage."

The church fathers were fascinated by the reference to the **swift cloud** *that* **will come to Egypt** *mentioned in v. 1. Drawing on other biblical passages that speak of clouds — for example, "baptized in the cloud" (1 Cor 10:1), the cloud at the Transfiguration (Matt 17:5), the verse in Ps 104:3, "you make the clouds your chariot" — they took the swift cloud to be a reference to Christ's human nature. Since Egypt had become Christian, it seemed natural to the church fathers to interpret the words* **the Lord will send a man to save them** *(19:20) with reference to the bringing of the gospel to Egypt, and* **an altar to the Lord in the midst of the land of Egypt** *(19:19) to signify the building of Christian churches in Egypt. Similarly,* **terror to the Egyptians** *(19:17) signifies that the Egyptians who once despised the* **land of Judah** *(19:17) are now filled with awe before the holy places in Jerusalem.*

(1) Cyril of Alexandria

A vision concerning Egypt (19:1). In this passage the prophet seeks to explain how the land of Egypt, which had worshiped many gods and lived in grievous error, was delivered from idolatry and came to worship God in faith. Because they did not know the one true God, the maker of all things, the Egyptians lived in deep darkness and worshiped created things. The best evidence of their folly was their skill in making their own gods. They filled their temples with idols, sculpted images of dumb animals, and set up altars on which to offer sacrifices to them. Yet, the greater the sin the more grace abounds (Rom 6:1). So healing is a particular boon to those who are seriously ill, and the divine and heavenly light shines most brightly on those whose hearts are veiled with darkness.

The prophet declares: **The Lord is sitting on a swift cloud and will come to Egypt** (19:1). Why does he depict the Lord riding on a swift cloud? Some of our interpreters take the **swift cloud** to be the holy flesh of the Lord, that is, the temple received from the Virgin. They liken it to a cloud because it is freed from all carnal passions and desires and floats high above the earth. For the holy body of our Savior Christ is pure and free of all earthly impurities. Others, however, take the **swift cloud** to signify the blessed Virgin. Indeed, there are a wide range of opinions as to the meaning of the words **sitting on a swift cloud**.

When the blessed prophets beheld the glory of God, they wrote about their visions in many ways. Isaiah is said to have seen *the Lord sitting upon a throne, high and lifted up*

(6:1). Standing about him in a circle were the heavenly powers singing hymns of praise to him, saying that *the whole earth is full of his glory* (6:1-3). And the all-wise Daniel saw the *ancient of days* sitting on a throne, and observed that *a thousand thousands served him, and ten thousands times ten thousand stood before him*. And he beheld one *like a son of man* coming *with the clouds* and the other things that are related there (Dan 7:9-13). Likewise Ezekiel, it is recorded, saw a *firmament*, and under it the seraphim. On the *throne* he saw a man, or *the likeness as it were of a human form, and upward from what had the appearance of his loins I saw as it were gleaming bronze, like the appearance of fire enclosed round about* (Ezek 1:22-27). In each of these visions God's glory is manifested and the mystery of Christ is elegantly alluded to.

Nothing therefore prevents us from seeing Christ in the **swift cloud** (19:1); indeed, it is helpful and necessary to do so. For the **cloud** is a figure of spiritual rain and dew and of saving Baptism. For St. Paul said that Israelites of the flesh *were baptized in the cloud and in the sea* (1 Cor 10:1). During the day the cloud hovered over those who were traveling through the deep wilderness, and at night a cloud of fire went before them. The name of Christ is written on each, for each bears the mystery of Christ, for justification and holiness come about through faith and Holy Baptism. For this reason, when the Lord went to Egypt to heal and transform the lives of the Egyptians, it was fitting that he be depicted spiritually as a **swift cloud**. There was no other way that the stain that had penetrated erring souls could be removed except through Holy Baptism, and the cloud is a type of Baptism.

With good reason the **cloud** is called **swift** [or **buoyant**]. In Baptism our sins were cast off, and through it, as though ridding ourselves of a heavy burden, we changed course and became, as it were, winged — capable of fixing our minds on things above and loving spiritual matters. . . .

In that day the Egyptians will be like women in fear and trembling before the hand which the Lord of hosts lays on them (19:16). Some interpreters give this passage the following interpretation. When the God of all visited the Egyptians, and led them from darkness into light, he delivered them from their attachment to idolatry, and they came to know the one who is truly God by nature, the maker of all things. For they believed in Christ, and they knew the Father through him and in him. As a result of their piety and fervent devotion, says the prophet, **the land of Judah will become a terror to the Egyptians** (19:17). For the term **terror** here means fear in the sense of religious awe. For they venerate the holy places of Jerusalem, the place where Christ was born, the cross which he bore for the world's salvation, and the tomb where he was laid and from which he rose and returned to the Father. In ancient times **the land of Judah** (19:17) was despised by the Egyptians, for the religious practices of the two countries were at odds with each other. The Egyptians worshiped the creation and the works of their own hands; the Israelites served the all-holy God, ordered their affairs according to his laws, and were scrupulous in practicing a God-pleasing way of life. Because the Egyptians are today devoted to the God of all, the land that was once despised has **become a terror**, that is, a place of awe to them, for Christ was born there, and as Scripture says, He has *called them out of darkness into his marvelous light* (1 Pet 2:9). . . .

For this reason it is not surprising to see **an altar to the Lord in the land of Egypt**

(19:19) and, in addition, **a pillar to the Lord at its border** (19:19). The **pillar** seems to me to signify a holy temple of God, that is, a church, perhaps the first of those that were built on the border, or a replica of the holy cross where the faithful have built a shrine. For the cross is used to ward off every assault of the devil and to protect ourselves from the attacks of demons. The cross is an unbreachable wall for us, and we glory in it as the true source of salvation. *Far be it from me to glory except in the cross of Christ* (Gal 6:14).

The remarkable things proclaimed long ago by the prophet have in these last times taken place, for today there is, in the words of the prophet, **an altar to the Lord** [in Egypt]. Indeed, there are so many altars in Egypt that they cannot be counted. And replicas of the cross are venerated by the inhabitants of Egypt, for they have believed in our Lord Jesus Christ. . . .

Moreover, the prophet promises that the Lord **will send them a savior** (19:20). Who is this man if not the Christ? He is the divine Logos, the only-begotten of God who appeared in human form to save not only the Egyptians but also the whole world.

(2) Theodoret of Cyrus

Behold, the Lord is sitting on a swift cloud and will come to Egypt (19:1). The account in the holy gospels confirms what is written in the prophecy. For an angel commanded Joseph to go down **to Egypt** with the child and his mother. The human nature which God took on is called a **cloud** because Christ's conception did not come about through the watering of marriage.

Then the prophet indicates what the effect of the Lord's advent will be. **And the idols of Egypt will tremble at his presence** (19:1). The facts confirm the prophecy. The error of polytheism was extinguished, and the one who rides **on a swift cloud** is worshiped by the Egyptians. And their **heart will faint within them** (19:1). Sometimes defeat is better than victory. In an earlier passage the prophetic word commands the nations to accept such a defeat. *Know, you peoples, and be conquered* (8:9). Here the prophet tells us that those who once opposed God and said openly, "I do not know the Lord," were conquered and now cry out, "I know the Lord." . . .

And the land of Judah will become a terror to the Egyptians (19:17). I think that the prophet here predicts that the Egyptians, after being delivered from error, received the apostolic preaching and were filled with awe at the **land of Judah**. For the Savior of the world was born in that land, he underwent his saving passion there, and the cross and tomb and the place of his ascension are located there. That is why today the Egyptians, as well as men and women from elsewhere in the world, go on pilgrimage to that land. . . .

In that day there will be an altar to the Lord in the midst of the land of Egypt, and a pillar to the Lord at its border (19:19). It is clear that by **altar** the prophet is speaking of our altar and by **pillar** he signifies the temple of God, namely, a church. Moreover, he uses the singular not the plural, since the apostle uses the singular when he speaks of the Church throughout the whole world, *which is,* he says, *the church of the living God*[1]

---

1. 1 Tim 3:15 refers to the Church as *the pillar.*

Isaiah 19

(1 Tim 3:15), and *on that rock I will build my church* (Matt 16:18). We also offer our prayers on behalf of the one holy catholic and apostolic Church. In this passage, by the one **altar** the prophet signifies the many altars, and by the one **pillar** the many houses of prayer.

19:1
Behold, the Lord is sitting on a swift cloud.

(3) Gregory of Nyssa

The God who once *spoke in the pillar of cloud* (Ps 99:7) later appeared in the flesh. So if someone should say that it is unworthy of God to speak to us through the flesh, he would hardly then go on to say that a *pillar of cloud* is worthy. For what is so great about a cloud that it should be judged worthy of the divine majesty? Yet if it was credible to the Jews that God should speak in a *pillar of cloud,* it should not be judged incredible that he spoke in flesh, especially since Isaiah signified the flesh by means of a **cloud**. For he says, **Behold, the Lord is sitting upon a swift cloud** (19:1). And the same prophet again calls those who accompany him **clouds** when he asks, *Who are these who fly as clouds?* (60:8). It seems he wished to show the kinship of the flesh of the Lord to the rest of human nature by means of the equivocal term **clouds**. Speaking about God who once spoke to mankind through a **cloud** but later through flesh, David says: [*He spoke to them in the pillar of cloud . . .*] *O Lord our God, you heard them. O God, you were merciful to them and vindicated all their pursuits* (Ps 99:8).

(4) John Chrysostom

When he was transfigured Christ said nothing; neither did Moses nor Elijah. But he who is greater than all, and wholly trustworthy, utters a voice out of the cloud. Why did he speak out of the cloud? God often appears in that way. *Clouds and thick darkness are round about him* (Ps 97:2). And he **is riding on a swift cloud** (19:1). And again: *who makes the clouds his chariot* (Ps 104:3); and *a cloud took him out of their sight* (Acts 1:9); and *like a son of man coming with the clouds* (Dan 7:13). God's voice comes from a cloud that they might believe it comes from God.

(5) The Venerable Bede

Isaiah says: **Behold, the Lord will ascend on a swift cloud and will come to Egypt; and the idols of Egypt will tremble at his presence** (19:1). The Lord ascended **on a swift cloud** to enter Egypt and overturn its idols when *the Word was made flesh and dwelt among us* (John 1:14). He took upon himself a body free of all stain of iniquity and in it entered the world so that he might destroy the cult of idolatry and display the true light of divinity to the shadowy and dark hearts of the nations. He who is not confined to a place willed to go from place to place by means of this **cloud**, his human nature. In it he who always remains invisible in his divinity willed to suffer mockery, scourging, and death. By means of it he who fills the heavens with the power of his divinity ascended into heaven and was crowned with the power of his resurrection. He lifted up this earth upon the wings of the wind when he elevated what he had taken from the earth — not only above all the expanse of the lower air, but even above the entire height of the upper air — and placed it at the right hand of the majesty of his Father.

Isaiah 20

₁In the year that Tanathan entered Azotos, when he was sent by Sarnan, king of the Assyrians, and waged war against Azotos and took it — ₂then the Lord spoke to Esaias, saying, "Go, and take off the sackcloth from your loins and untie your sandals off your feet"; and he did so, walking naked and barefoot. ₃And the Lord said, "Just as my servant Esaias has walked naked and barefoot for three years, there will be signs and portents to the Egyptians and Ethiopians, ₄because thus shall the king of the Assyrians lead away the captivity of Egypt and of the Ethiopians, young and old, naked and barefoot, uncovered — the shame of Egypt. ₅And the Egyptians, having been defeated, shall be ashamed because of the Ethiopians, in whom the Egyptians had trusted, for they were their glory. ₆And those who dwell in this island will say, 'See, we had trusted to flee to them for help, who could not be saved from the king of the Assyrians! And we, how shall we be saved?'"

This chapter gives us a precious detail about Isaiah's ministry as a prophet: he went about naked and barefoot for three years. This incident is interpreted as a sign of Isaiah's obedience to God's command and the strength of his character. In the early Church Isaiah, along with Elijah, Daniel, and John the Baptist, were seen as biblical examples of the ascetic life.

(1) Cyril of Alexandria

Tanathan the commander of the Assyrian forces took the city of Ashdod by force. Because Ashdod was close to Judah, the Israelites realized that they would undergo the same fate. Hence they sent an embassy to Egypt to help them meet the attack of the Assyrian forces. But God declares that their hope is vain, and makes clear to them that they will become booty for the Assyrians and for a time will be kept in exile. For the Egyptians themselves came under the power of the Assyrians and were subject to them for three years; during that time a large part of the population was forcibly taken into captivity, and only later were they allowed to return home. God then gives a command to the prophet. The appropriate and customary dress for captives is to go about naked and without shoes.

The captors have no reason to show any regard for their captives. Those who have fallen into such wretchedness, even if they were well born or from a good family, are clothed with the garment of suffering, not having proper clothes and certainly nothing luxurious and no opportunity for ease. They are forced to do whatever their captors wish.

The prophet then is ordered to **loose the sackcloth from his loins and take off his shoes** (20:2) and to walk through the center of Jerusalem naked and without shoes. This he did without giving any thought as to how he would look and without changing anything God had told him, even though the command was a grievous burden and he knew that he would be subject to ridicule.

This wise, decent, and virtuous man, crowned with grace, a model of devotion, took off his sackcloth [the mantle worn by a prophet], itself not a splendid garment but one that was coarse and shabby. He removed the shoes from his feet and went around in this fashion, that those who saw him would be amazed and would want to know why he had done this. They would realize that it is vain to put one's hope in men. It is better to seek good from above and to call on God, who is ready to help....

Therefore it is better to put one's hope in God than to trust in man. As the prophet Jeremiah put it: *Cursed is the man who trusts in man and makes flesh his arm.... Blessed is the man who trusts in the* LORD (Jer 17:5, 7). The word of the prophet always contains something of value. Even if the historical account does not have an obvious spiritual meaning, it nevertheless contains something that can be edifying. For St. Paul said that what *happened to them* of old had a typological meaning for us and *they were written down for our instruction* (1 Cor 10:11).

20:2-3
And he did so, walking naked and barefoot.

(2) Clement of Alexandria

The blessed John the Baptist, scorning the wool of sheep as smacking of luxury, chose *camel's hair* (Mark 1:6) as his dress, making himself an example of frugal and simple living. For he also *ate locusts and wild honey* (Mark 1:6), a sweet and spiritual diet, preparing for the unpretentious and austere ways of the Lord. How could he have possibly worn a purple robe when he had turned away from the pretension of public life and withdrawn to the serenity of the desert, where he had his commonwealth with God and was totally removed from pointless make-work, from fake goodness, and from petty small-mindedness? Elijah used a sheepskin mantle and fastened the sheepskin with a girdle made of hair (cf. 2 Kgs 1:8). And Isaiah, another prophet, went about **naked and barefoot** (20:2) and used to wear **sackcloth** (20:2), the garment of humility. And if you recall Jeremiah, he had only a *linen waistcloth* (Jer 13:1).

(3) Origen of Alexandria

Among the Jewish prophets, some were wise before receiving the gift of prophecy and divine inspiration, but others became wise after their minds had been enlightened by the actual gift of prophecy. They were chosen by providence to be entrusted with the divine Spirit and the words he inspired because their lives were so remarkable. They faced danger and death with great courage, freedom, even equanimity. It is only reasonable that prophets of the supreme God should be people of this type. . . .

Because they spoke the truth and freely rebuked sinners, *they were stoned, they were sawn in two, tempted, they were killed with the sword; they went about in skins of sheep and goats, destitute, ill-treated — of whom the world was not worthy — wandering over deserts and mountains, and in dens and caves of the earth* (Heb 11:37-38). They always kept their eyes fixed on God and on spiritual things unseen by the eyes of the senses and, for that reason, eternal.

The life of each prophet is recorded in the Bible. One need only mention the life of Moses (for there are also prophecies by him, which are to be found written in the law). Then there is the life of Jeremiah recorded in the prophecy that bears his name. And there is the life of Isaiah, who surpassed every ascetic practice when he went **naked and barefoot for three years** (20:3). Don't forget the vigorous lives of the young men, Daniel and his companions. One can read about how they drank water and subsisted on vegetables because they abstained from animal food (cf. Dan 1:11-16).

If you are able, take note of what happened before their time, how Noah prophesied and Isaac gave a prophetic blessing to his son, and Jacob said to each of the twelve: *Come, that I may tell you what shall come to pass at the last days* (Gen 49:1; cf. Gen 9:25-27, 27:27-29). These and countless others prophesied in the name of God and foretold what would happen at the coming of Jesus Christ.

(4) Gregory the Great

The law of God is rightly called manifold because when it takes full possession of the mind it consists of one thing: love. Nevertheless it kindles many actions and issues in countless different kinds of works. This diversity can be briefly displayed by going through and enumerating her good works in each of the saints individually. In Abel she presented chosen gifts to God and submitted to the brother's sword without resistance. She taught Enoch to live in a spiritual way among men and carried him away bodily from among men to a more sublime life. . . . In Isaiah she did not blush to be seen in the **nakedness of the flesh** as he went about preaching, and when the veil of the flesh was removed, he penetrated heavenly mysteries (6:1).

Isaiah 24

1 Look, the Lord is ruining the world and will make it desolate,
   and he will uncover its surface and scatter those who dwell in it.
2 And the people shall be like the priest,
   and the servant like the master,
   and the maid like the mistress;
 the buyer shall be like the seller,
   and the lender like the borrower,
   and the creditor like the one to whom he owes.
3 The earth shall be ruined with ruin,
   and the earth shall be plundered with plundering,
   for the mouth of the Lord has spoken these things.

4 The earth mourned,
   and the world was ruined;
   the exalted ones of the earth mourned.
5 And the earth behaved unlawfully
   because of those who inhabit it;
 because they transgressed the law
   and changed the ordinances —
   an everlasting covenant.
6 Therefore a curse will devour the earth,
   because those who inhabit it have sinned;
 therefore those who dwell in the earth will be poor,
   and few people will be left.
7 The wine will mourn,
   the vine will mourn,
   all who rejoice in their soul will groan.
8 The joy of the drums has ceased,
   the stubbornness and wealth of the ungodly have ceased,
   the sound of the lyre has ceased.

9 They felt shame, did not drink wine;
>   the strong drink became bitter to those who drank it.
10 Every city was made desolate;
>   he will shut up the house so that no one can enter.
11 Wail everywhere for the wine;
>   all the joy of the earth has ceased.
12 And cities will be left desolate,
>   abandoned houses will perish.
13 All these things shall be on the earth,
>   in the midst of the nations;
> just as when someone gleans an olive tree,
>   so shall people glean them,
>   even when the harvest has ceased.

14 These will cry aloud with their voice,
>   but those who are left in the land
> will rejoice together in the glory of the Lord.
>   The water of the sea will be troubled.
15 Therefore the glory to the Lord will be in the islands of the sea;
>   the name of the Lord will be glorious.
16 O Lord God of Israel,
>   from the wings of the earth
> we have heard wonders:
>   Hope for the godly one.
> But those who reject the law will say,
>   Woe to those who reject!
17 Fear and pit and snare
>   are upon you who dwell on the earth!
18 And it shall be that the one who flees from the fear
>   shall fall into the pit;
> and the one who gets out of the pit
>   shall be caught by the snare.
> Because windows have been opened out of heaven,
>   and the foundations of the earth will be shaken.
19 The earth will be troubled with trouble,
>   and the earth will be perplexed with perplexity.
20 The earth has bent over, and it will be shaken like a hut,
>   like the one who drinks too much and is intoxicated;
> and it will fall and will not be able to rise,
>   for lawlessness has prevailed upon it.

21 And God will bring his hand
>   against the ornament of heaven
>   and against the kings of the earth.

22 **And they will gather them together**
   and shut them up in a fortress and in a prison;
 through many generations
   will be their visitation.
23 **Then the brick will be dissolved,**
   and the wall will fall;
 because the Lord will reign
   in Sion and in Ierousalem,
 and before the elders he will be glorified.

Chapters 24–27 are sometimes called the Isaiah Apocalypse because this section speaks of a universal judgment and an eschatological banquet. Eusebius realized that chapter 24 of Isaiah inaugurated a new section of the book, and he understood it as a general prophecy that referred not to a single people but to a final judgment when God will **lay waste the earth** *(24:1). Cyril of Alexandria focuses on the phrase* **the glory of the Lord** *that occurs several times in the chapter (24:14, 15) and sees it as a reference to the Incarnation of Christ and the establishment of the Church throughout the world. Origen remarks that while the earth is offended by the sins of* **those who inhabit her** *(24:5), she rejoices when she sustains the righteous and most especially the Son of God (24:14). Ambrose interprets the* **windows** *of 24:18 to be the prophets who, before the Incarnation, proclaimed God's concern for humankind.*

Patristic interpreters have greater interest in chapters 25 and 26 than in 24 and 27, perhaps because of the mention of the feast on the "mountain of the Lord" (25:6), which was taken to refer to the Eucharist, and the allusion to the resurrection, "the dead shall live again" (26:19).

(1) Eusebius of Caesarea

Behold, the Lord will lay waste the earth and make it desolate (24:1). At the beginning of the book the prophet had a vision *concerning Judah and Jerusalem* (1:1). As the work progressed, he said many things about the surrounding nations and dealt with each one of them individually. Following this he sets forth this prophecy that applies to everyone. It is an oracle dealing with the whole world, for *the earth is the* LORD's *and the fullness thereof* (Ps 24:1). It is certain that the God who cares for all has ordained that the world will face the coming judgment of God *on that day when God judges the secrets of men* (Rom 2:16). If one looks closely at this passage, it is evident that its message is universal. It is addressed neither to Judah, nor Samaria, nor Tyre, nor Damascus, nor Babylon, nor to any other people. This oracle concerns the end of life and the judgment that is to be expected at the end of time. On that day all men will know what punishment the ungodly will receive after this present life and what good things have been stored up for the godly. . . .

When the bodies which were hidden in the earth will be revealed, those to be judged *will stand before the judgment seat* (Rom 14:10) of the great judge. All will be equal. The distinctions that held in this mortal life will no longer hold, for example, between those who had great glory or rank or birth and those who possessed few goods.

When they *stand before the judgment seat of Christ*[1] (Rom 14:10), there will be no distinctions.

As with the people, so with the priest (24:2). All will be equal, *for God shows no partiality* (Rom 2:11). For this reason Job said: *The small and the great are there, and the servant did not fear his master* (Job 3:19). In the same way the **slave** and the **master**, and **the maid** and the one considered **her mistress** (24:2) will stand as equals. Likewise, **the seller** with his many goods and **the buyer**. And the one who out of his wealth **lends** to those in need will be equal to the one who **borrows** (24:2) because of his poverty and also to the one whose need makes him a debtor.

(2) Cyril of Alexandria

I glorified you on earth, having accomplished the work which you gave me to do (John 17:4). Indeed, God the Father said to blessed Moses: *As I live, so lives my name, and all the earth shall be filled with the glory of the* LORD (Num 14:21). For all things are filled with Christ.... It is possible to understand the prophetic words, **the glory of the Lord shall be in the isles of the sea** (24:15), as a reference to the mystery of Christ and to interpret the passage as pointing to the salvation that comes through him. For those who are left on the earth (24:6) will rejoice together in the glory of the Lord. We were saved, *not because of deeds done by us in righteousness, but in virtue of his great mercy* (Tit 3:5), for no one is justified by the shadow of the law (cf. Gal 2:16). For the law is incapable of justifying us. The grace of holy Baptism delivered us from our sins, and, being enriched by its bounty, we rejoice in the hope of good things to come. We expect that we will be with Christ himself, who is the Father's **glory** (24:14-15).

When the preaching of the holy apostles went forth to every corner of the world under heaven, it led the nations away from the error of polytheism and brought them to the grace of Christ. The prophet says that **the water of the sea will be troubled** (24:14), that is, people living all over the world will be troubled. They are agitated because they have heard new things, and men had abandoned their ancient errors to turn to the knowledge of the truth. For that reason he declares: **The glory of the Lord will be in the islands of the sea** (24:15). By **isles** I think one can understand the holy churches of God, which are established in the world as islands in the sea. Christ holds them safe so that they can endure, indeed, overcome the tumult of this world. For they did not allow the waves of persecution to overwhelm them. Since **sea** is a figure for the nations (cf. Ps 104:25), it is possible to give the passage a figurative interpretation and refer it to the churches in which men and women stand in awe before **the glory** of God.

O Lord God of Israel, from the wings of the earth we have heard of wonderful things, and there is hope for the godly (24:16). Here the prophet speaks of those who are left on the earth and who rejoice in the glory of God. They are the ones dwelling **in the isles of the sea**, namely, in the churches that glorify the one God and say: **From the wings of the earth we have heard of wonderful things.** They believe in a good **hope**,

---

[1]. Instead of *judgment seat of God*, Eusebius's Greek text read *judgment seat of Christ*.

that is, the godly will be justified by him and will share in his abundant kindness. He likens spiritual teachers to **the wings of the earth**, for through their words we are lifted up on wings, leaving earthly things far behind and freeing ourselves from our earthly and carnal thoughts, and we find *our commonwealth in heaven* (Phil 3:20).

From these spiritual **wings** we have heard the **wonderful things** accomplished by Christ. For we have been instructed by the writings of the apostles and evangelists, and learning the miracles of the Savior, we have firm faith in them and are confident and bold to believe that the **hope** of **the godly** is beautiful. For we anticipate the kingdom of heaven and the glory and honors which have been *prepared for those who love God* (1 Cor 2:9; Isa 64:4). . . .

For the Lord will reign in Zion and in Jerusalem, and before the elders he will be glorified (24:23). **Zion** means high and lifted up and watchtower, and **Jerusalem** means vision of peace. The Church of Christ would be the true watchtower and vision of peace. For in it one is accustomed to dig deeply into the divine mysteries and the vision of peace. For we proclaim that Christ is peace, and we learn about him from the Holy Scriptures, where the all-wise Moses and also the holy prophets wrote about him. For when foul and impure idolatry is eliminated, when men no longer worship the creation, when the evil impulses that rule the world are **shut up in a fortress and in a prison** (24:22), and when **the wall**[2] (24:23) is destroyed and its foundations shaken, **the Lord will reign in Zion, and before the elders he will be glorified** (24:23).

The term **elders** (24:23) is used here to designate those who are mature in mind, the wise, who are able to see with the eyes of the heart the depth of the mystery of Christ. Wise John was addressing these when he said: *I write to you, fathers, because you know him who is from the beginning* (1 John 2:14). Those who know stand in awe, offer up praise to the divine glory which belongs to Christ, and confess that he is King and Lord of all. Christ will reign when the tyranny of the devil is wholly destroyed, for he *gave himself as a ransom for all* (1 Tim 2:6) and bore the precious cross for us: *Now is the judgment of this world, now shall the ruler of the world be cast out; and I, when I am lifted up from the earth, will draw all men to myself* (John 12:31-32). Therefore he will subject all on earth to his rule, and the prince of this world will be cast out.

24:5
The earth behaved unlawfully because of those who inhabit it.

(3) Origen of Alexandria

The earth is offended by those who inhabit it (24:5). I think that the earth sustains us like a mother, and she rejoices over good children and is pained by sinners. Indeed, *a foolish son is a grief to his father and bitterness to her who bore him* (Prov 17:25), and not only to this father and mother from whose seed we originate, but to that mother which is our true mother. God took *soil from the earth* and *formed man* (Gen 2:7). Thus, the earth

---

2. **The wall** is a reference to Satan.

Isaiah 24

is our mother. She rejoices when she sustains a righteous son. The earth rejoiced when she upheld Abraham, Isaac, and Jacob. She rejoiced at the advent of my Lord Jesus Christ, when she saw herself worthy of sustaining the Son of God. What need is there to speak of the apostles and prophets, since Isaiah says of the Lord's advent: **All the earth cries out with joy** (24:14)?

24:18
Because windows have been opened out of heaven

(4) Ambrose of Milan

Christ comes, and initially he is *behind the wall* (Song 2:9), in order to break down the hostility (cf. Eph 2:14) between body and soul by removing the wall which seemed to be a barrier to harmonious union. Then he *looks through the windows* (Song 2:9). Listen to the prophet as he says what the windows are: **Windows are opened from heaven** (24:18). By this he means the prophets, in whom the Lord showed concern for humankind before he himself would descend to earth. Even today, if any soul searches for him earnestly, she will deserve much mercy, because much is owed to the one who searches greatly. Therefore if any soul seeks him eagerly, she hears his voice from far away. Even though she inquires of others, she hears his voice before these others do. She sees him coming to her, leaping — that is, hurrying and running and bounding (cf. Song 2:8) over those who, because of a weak heart, are unable to receive his strength. Then, by reading the prophets and remembering their words, the soul sees the Lord looking through their riddles, but looking as if through a **window**, not yet as if present.

Isaiah 25

1 O Lord, my God,
   I will glorify you, I will sing hymns to your name;
because you have done wonderful things —
   an ancient, true plan. May it be so, Lord!
2 Because you have made cities a heap,
   fortified cities, so their foundations might fall;
the city of the ungodly will not be built forever.
3 Therefore the poor people will bless you,
   and cities of ill-treated persons will bless you.
4 For you have become a helper to every humble city,
   and a shelter to those who are dispirited because of poverty;
you will rescue them from evil persons —
   a shelter for the thirsty, and breath for ill-treated persons,
5 like fainthearted persons thirsting in Sion
   because of ungodly persons, to whom you delivered us.

6 On this mountain the Lord Sabaoth will make a feast for all nations:
   they will drink joy,
   they will drink wine,
7   they will anoint themselves with perfume.
(7) Deliver all these things to the nations on this mountain,
   for this counsel is against all the nations.

8 Death, having prevailed, swallowed them up,
   and God has again taken away every tear from every face;
the disgrace of the people he has taken away from all the earth,
   for the mouth of the Lord has spoken.
9 And they will say on that day,
   Lo, our God, in whom we were hoping;
   and we were glad in our salvation.

Isaiah 25

10 **Because God will give us rest on this mountain,**
  and Moabitis shall be trodden down
  as they tread a threshing floor with wagons.
11 **And he will send forth his hands,**
  as he himself brought him low to destroy him;
  and he will bring low his pride —
  things on which he laid his hands.
12 **And he will bring low the height of the refuge of your wall,**
  and it will come down all the way to the ground.

*The church fathers saw in the words **a plan formed of old** (25:1) a reference to Ephesians, where it is written that Christ was chosen "before the foundation of the world" (Eph 1:4) and that the Father "has made known to us in all wisdom and insight the mystery of his will, according to his purpose which he set forth in Christ as a **plan** for the fullness of time, to unite all things in him, things in heaven and things on earth" (Eph 1:9-10). Hence 25:1 was understood to refer to the Incarnation. The references to **wine** and myrrh (LXX) in 25:6 were seen as figures of the Eucharist and of Baptism. Cyril of Alexandria skillfully weaves into his exposition the accounts in Luke of Simeon and Zechariah, who rejoice at the coming of the Lord. Their songs, known in Christian tradition as the "Nunc Dimittis" and the "Benedictus," are used as canticles in Compline, the Church's night prayer, and in morning prayer. The words **he will swallow up death forever** (25:8) are alluded to in 1 Cor 15:54, and Cyril understands them in light of the belief in the resurrection of the dead mentioned in the Creed used in Baptism.*

(1) The First Epistle of Paul to the Corinthians

When the perishable puts on the imperishable, and the mortal puts on immortality, then shall come to pass the saying that is written: **Death is swallowed up in victory** (25:8). O death, where is thy victory? O death, where is thy sting?

(2) The Revelation to John

(a) Then one of the elders addressed me, saying, "Who are these, clothed in white robes, and whence have they come?" I said to him, "Sir, you know." And he said to me, "These are they who have come out of the great tribulation; they have washed their robes and made them white in the blood of the Lamb. Therefore are they before the throne of God, and serve him day and night within his temple, and he who sits upon the throne will shelter them with his presence. They shall hunger no more, neither thirst any more; the sun shall not strike them, nor any scorching heat. For the Lamb in the midst of the throne will be their shepherd, and he will guide them to springs of living water; and **God will wipe away every tear from their eyes** (25:8)."

(b) And I saw the holy city, new Jerusalem, coming down out of heaven from God, prepared as a bride adorned for her husband; and I heard a loud voice from the throne saying, "Behold, the dwelling of God is with men. He will dwell with them, and they shall be his people, and God himself will be with them; **he will wipe away every tear from their eyes** (25:8), and death shall be no more, neither shall there be mourning nor crying nor pain anymore, for the former things have passed away."

(3) Cyril of Alexandria

In this passage the prophet announces the kingdom of Christ. For he has said that *the LORD will rule on Zion and in Jerusalem, and he will manifest his glory before the elders* (24:23). Knowing that all these things would take place, the prophet is filled with great joy, and he pays tribute to the one who will accomplish these marvelous deeds in the words: **O Lord, my God, I will glorify you, I will sing hymns to your name; for you have done wonderful things, a faithful plan formed of old. May it be so, Lord** (25:1). He says **you have done** although he is referring to things that had not yet happened. This was to show that what is promised in the future will certainly and surely take place. For that reason he adds, **May it be so, Lord!** With the eyes of the mind the prophets saw the time of Christ's sojourn as though it were present. They knew what was to take place. The phrase **wonderful things, a faithful plan formed of old**, refers to the mystery of the Incarnation of the only Son and of the things that would happen all over the earth because of it. The most-wise Paul asserted: *We were saved in Christ, who was chosen before the foundation of the world and manifested at the end of the age* (Eph 1:4). Paul also said that the mystery of Christ is neither new nor recent; though he appeared only at the fitting time, God chose him before the foundation of the world (Eph 1:4, 9). This is the **faithful plan**, the certain decrees of God who has power over all things.

The **fortified cities** will be thrown down and become a **ruin** (25:2), and they will be razed to their foundations. There will be no hope of recovery because they will **never be rebuilt** (25:2). When we say that cities will be thrown down, we are not thinking of actual cities with people living in them. Rather, we have in mind evil powers, and, most of all, the city of Satan, which is called a **fortified city** (25:2; cf. Matt 12:25-32). It is the custom of Scripture to liken strong persons to towers or walls or cities. . . . Speaking through the words of the blessed prophet Jeremiah, God says, *a fortified city, a strong wall of bronze* (Jer 1:18; 4:5; 5:17; 8:14; 15:20). When Emmanuel appeared and enlightened the world, the unholy army of evil powers was destroyed. Satan was shaken to his very foundations, laid low, and will remain defenseless forever. Never again will he be raised up or revived. . . .

Israel was called to the knowledge of God through the tutoring of the law and was richly endowed with the things of God. It was delivered from Egypt and inherited the promised land. Although there were many other peoples living throughout the world, all were alien to spiritual matters and heavenly things. They had not tasted the gifts that come from God. They were, so to speak, spiritually naked and unclothed, enjoying neither divine **protection** nor **shelter** (25:4) from on high. They had neither the spiritual wealth that comes from virtue nor other things worthy of praise and admiration.

When Christ appeared and destroyed the devil's arrogance, he led the nations to God the Father, and they basked in the splendor of the true light and shared in his glory. As they came to know the splendor of the evangelical way of life, they offered hymns of thanksgiving to God the Father for these gifts.

Thus when the text says, you have carried out a **faithful plan formed of old, O Lord**, it means that *all things have been summed up in Christ* (Eph 1:10, 22), that those who lived *in darkness have seen a great light* (Isa 9:2; Matt 4:16), and the dominant powers of this age have been destroyed (cf. Col 2:15). Like strong and **fortified cities** the **impoverished people will glorify you** and whole cities will **glorify you** (25:3). You have become a **help to all** and a **shelter** (25:4) to those who were languishing in the emptiness of their ancestral traditions, and you saved them from wicked men.

There were also in Zion some **fainthearted men** who were, as it were, **thirsting** (24:5). Perhaps what the prophet is referring to are those in Israel who were thirsting for the coming of the Savior. They desired to see the Savior and Redeemer of all. One such person was the righteous Simeon. When he took the infant Jesus in his arms he said: *Lord, now lettest thou thy servant depart in peace, according to thy word; for mine eyes have seen thy salvation which thou hast prepared in the presence of all peoples, a light for revelation, and for glory to thy people Israel* (Luke 2:29-32).

And blessed Zechariah, the father of John the Baptist, being filled with the Holy Spirit, glorified God and cried out: *Blessed be the Lord God of Israel, for he has visited and redeemed his people, and has raised up a horn of salvation for us in the house of his servant David, as he spoke by the mouth of his holy prophets from of old, that we should be saved from our enemies, and from the hand of all who hate us; to perform the mercy promised to our fathers, and to remember his holy covenant, the oath which he swore to our father Abraham, to grant us that we, being delivered from the hand of our enemies, might serve him without fear, in holiness and righteousness before him all the days of our life. And you, child, will be called the prophet of the Most High; for you will go before the Lord to prepare his ways, to give knowledge of salvation to his people in the forgiveness of their sins, through the tender mercy of our God, when the day shall dawn upon us from on high to give light to those who sit in darkness and in the shadow of death, to guide our feet into the way of peace* (Luke 1:68-79). You can see then how a **faithful plan formed of old** of our God and Father was promised to the generations in ancient times. . . .

Then the prophet says, **the Lord of hosts will make** (25:6). He **will make** not only for the Israelites who are beloved and elect because of their fathers (cf. Romans 11), but for all peoples, that is, for everyone living on earth. What will he **make**? **They will drink joy**, he answers, **they will drink wine, they will be anointed with myrrh on this holy mountain** (25:6). By **joy** he means gladness because of the hope we have in Christ. For we will reign with him, and enjoying those things that are beyond thought and speech, will be filled with all delight. **Wine** refers to the mystical oblation, to the unbloody sacrifice which we celebrate in the holy churches. **Myrrh** signifies the anointing of the Holy Spirit. For wise John writes: *You have been anointed by the Holy One and have no need that someone teach you, and his anointing teaches you everything* (1 John 2:20-27). We were anointed especially with **myrrh** at the time of Baptism, and anointing is a symbol of the Holy Spirit. **Hand this on**, he says, **to the nations** (25:7). For his **plan** (25:1) is for all peoples. For the ancient law and the worship administered by angels was not simply given to all peoples, but only to the one people who are Israelites by blood. But the grace of Christ, and the calling through faith, and in addition sanctification through the Holy Spirit, and the mystery itself through the **plan** of God the Father, are for all **nations**. For Christ is the expectation of the **nations** and the voice of the holy one....

It is appropriate and necessary that at the time the "mystery" is handed over, the resurrection of the dead is included.[1] For at the time we make the confession of faith at Holy Baptism, we say that we expect the resurrection of the flesh. And so we believe. Death overcame our forefather Adam on account of his transgression, and like a fierce wild animal it pounced on him and carried him amidst lamentation and loud wailing. Men wept and grieved because death ruled over all the earth. But all this came to an end with Christ. Striking down death, he rose up on the third day and became the way by which human nature would rid itself of corruption. He became the firstborn of the dead, and the first fruits of those who have fallen asleep.

We who come afterward will certainly follow the first fruits. He turned suffering into joy, and we cast off our sackcloth. We put on the joy given by God so that we can rejoice and cry out: *O death, where is your victory?* (1 Cor 15:55). Therefore **every tear** is taken away. For believing that Christ will surely raise the dead, we do not weep over the dead, nor are we overwhelmed by inconsolable grief like those who have no hope (1 Thess 4:13). Death itself is a **reproach of the people** (25:8), for it had its beginning among us through sin. Corruption entered in on account of sin, and death's power ruled on earth....

They will say on that day, Lo, our God, in whom we were hoping; and we were glad in his salvation (25:9). You recognize the one who gives you not only joy to drink, but also wine, anointing those in spiritual Zion with myrrh. You recognize that he is true God and Son of God by nature although he appeared in the *form of a servant* (Phil 2:7), and by becoming man he became the source of salvation and life for all, being in all things like those on earth though *without sin* (Heb 4:15). The prophet indicates that they are all but pointing [to Christ] with the finger when they declare: **Behold, our God, in whom we have hoped, and we will rejoice in our salvation** (25:9). I think that this text applies especially to the Israelites who were instructed by the words of Moses and knew the holy prophets' predictions. They waited for the time of the coming of the Savior and Redeemer, the Lord Jesus Christ. Therefore, as I have already said, when Zechariah the father of John [the Baptist] prophesied in the Spirit, he said of Christ: *He has raised up a horn of salvation* (Luke 1:69). And when Simeon took the holy child in his arms, he said: *Behold, my eyes have seen the salvation which you have prepared before the face of all people* (Luke 2:30-31). Recognizing at that time what had been announced of old, the Savior and Redeemer who is the hope of all, they said, according to Isaiah: **Lo, our God**.

They confess that **God will give rest on this mountain** (25:10). It seems to me that here **mountain** refers to the Church, for it is there that one finds rest. For we heard the words of Christ: *Come to me, all who labor and are heavy laden, and I will give you rest* (Matt 11:28).

---

1. The creed handed over at Baptism included an article on the resurrection.

25:1
A faithful plan formed of old

(4) Theodoret of Cyrus

Having learned of these things long before they were to happen, the prophet composes a hymn to God, saying: **O Lord, my God, I will glorify you, I will sing hymns to your name; for you have done wonderful things, a faithful plan formed of old** (25:1). What you have ordained from on high, these things you have now made known by your deeds. As the divine apostle wrote: *The mystery hidden for ages and generations in God who created all things* (Eph 3:9; Col 1:26). And again: *But we impart a secret and hidden wisdom of God, which God decreed before the ages for our glorification* (1 Cor 2:7). And again: *For those whom he foreknew he also predestined to be conformed to the image of his Son* (Rom 8:29). And the Lord says in the gospels: *Come, O blessed of my Father, inherit the kingdom prepared for you from the foundation of the world* (Matt 25:34). And in the words of the prophet: **for you have done wonderful things, a faithful plan formed of old**. . . .

He calls **mountain** (25:6) the pinnacle of the knowledge of God. . . . This prediction is a portent of the mysteries of the knowledge of God. **Joy** (25:6) is mentioned because he predicts that **all nations** (25:7) will partake of the drink offered by God. This is in accord with the words the Master spoke to the holy apostles: *Go teach all nations, baptizing them in the name of the Father and of the Son and of the Holy Spirit* (Matt 28:19). These **nations** will also partake of the **mountain**, that is, the teaching of the knowledge of God. The following passage is also in accord with these ideas: **Deliver all these things to the nations on this mountain, for this is God's counsel for all the nations** (25:7). Although he had given the law only to Jews, the New Testament was not reserved for them alone. The salvation brought by the New Testament has been offered to **all the nations**.

25:6-7
On this mountain the Lord Sabaoth will make provision for all nations: they will drink joy, they will drink wine, they will anoint themselves with perfume. Deliver all these things to the nations on this mountain, for this counsel is against all the nations.

(5) Cyril of Jerusalem

Preserve this chrism free from stain, for it teaches all things, if it remains in you, as you have just heard the blessed John say, when he was meditating upon it (cf. 1 John 2:20-28). For this chrism is a holy and spiritual thing, the body's protection and the soul's salvation. Long ago the blessed Isaiah prophesied this when he said, **On this mountain the Lord will make provision for all: they will drink wine, they will drink joy, they will anoint**

themselves with perfume[2] (25:6). Now Isaiah calls the Church a **mountain** in other passages also, such as when he says, *In the last days the mountain of the* LORD'*s house shall be manifest* (2:2). And so that he might confirm you in this, listen to what he says about this **perfume** as mystical: **Deliver all these things to the nations, for the Lord's counsel is against all the nations** (25:7). Therefore, since you have been anointed with this holy **perfume,** keep it free from stain and without blemish in you, making progress through good works and being made well-pleasing to the author of your salvation, Christ Jesus, to whom be glory forever and ever. Amen.

25:8
He will swallow up death forever.

(6) Irenaeus of Lyons

Just as flesh is capable of being corrupted, so it can be freed of corruption. In the same way, just as it is able to die, so it can live. These two give way to each other; they cannot remain in the same place together. The one is driven out by the other, and when one is present the other is destroyed. Thus, if death, when it takes hold of a person, drives life out of him and shows him to be dead, how much more does life, when it takes hold of someone, drive out death and restore him as a living person to God? For if death brings mortality, why should the coming of life not revive him? As the prophet Isaiah writes: **Death, having prevailed, swallowed them up, and God has again taken away every tear from every face** (25:8). Thus the former life is expelled, since it was not given through the Spirit but rather through breath. For the *breath of life* which made man a *living being* (Gen 2:7) is one thing, and the *life-giving Spirit* which made him a *spiritual being* (cf. 1 Cor 15:45-46) is another. Because of this Isaiah declares, *Thus says God, the* LORD, *who created heaven and established it, who bolstered the earth and the things that are in it, and who gave breath to the people upon it and spirit to those who tread on it* (42:5). This means that *breath* is given to all people on the earth in common, while the *Spirit* is given specifically to those who trample down earthly desires. Thus Isaiah himself, distinguishing the things already mentioned, said, *For a spirit shall go forth from me, and I have made every breath* (57:16). With this he counts the Spirit as unique to God, that Spirit which in the last times he poured out on the human race through their adoption as sons (cf. Joel 2:28; Acts 2:17). At the same time he shows that *breath* is common to all of creation and is something created. For what is made is different from the one who made it. Therefore, *breath* is temporal, but the *Spirit* is eternal. *Breath* increases to a degree and, after remaining for a time, it then leaves its previous abode without breath. The *Spirit,* instead, pervades the person inside and out, since it always continues and never leaves him.

---

2. The Greek word translated "perfume" was also used in the early Church to refer to the oil of chrism used in Baptism and the anointing of the sick.

(7) Tertullian

For we shall be as angels (cf. Matt 22:30; Luke 20:36). Such will be the change in the flesh — but flesh raised up. Or else, if there is going to be no flesh, how shall it be clothed with incorruption and immortality? When it is then made into something else by that change, it will obtain the kingdom of God, being no longer flesh and blood, but the body which God will have given to it. And so the apostle rightly says, *Flesh and blood shall not obtain the kingdom of God* (1 Cor 15:50), for he attributes that to the change which follows on the resurrection. So if the word written in the Creator's scriptures is fulfilled, *O death, where is your victory,* or, *your striving? O death, where is your sting?* (1 Cor 15:54) — this is a word of the Creator, spoken by the prophet (Isa 25:8) — the kingdom itself will belong to him whose word will come to pass in the kingdom. Nor do we give thanks to any other god[3] than the God from whom he has accepted that word of exultation over death, that shout of triumph [*O death, where is your victory?*]. For God has enabled us to gain the victory over death.

(8) Augustine of Hippo

What does a chaste man want? That no lust whatsoever should stir his members against living chastely. He wants peace, but he doesn't have it yet. When he gets to that point where no lusts whatsoever rise up that need to be opposed, there won't any longer be an enemy to struggle against. Nor will there be any striving for victory because the victory over the vanquished enemy is already being celebrated. Listen to what the apostle says about that victory: *The perishable must put on imperishability, and the mortal put on immortality; then shall come to pass the saying that is written:* **Death has been swallowed up in victory** (1 Cor 15:53-55; Isa 25:8).

(9) Aelred of Rievaulx

I think that, without a doubt, the Lord's sweet yoke gives birth to whatever tranquility, peace, and joy is mine, but whatever toil, fatigue, or sluggishness I have comes from the remnants of worldly concupiscence. For under that yoke, which the prince of Babylon (i.e., confusion) placed upon my unlucky neck, my *strength was weakened, my bones* (Ps 31:10) were crushed. Although to some extent my bondage was broken, nonetheless not a little weakness lingers from that ancient oppression. Thus, the serenity of the sweetness which I now sometimes experience is often disturbed, until he who is a propitiation for all my iniquities also heals all my infirmities and, redeeming my life from ruin, crowns me with mercy and compassion, *when the perishable puts on the imperishable, and the mortal puts on immortality, then shall come to pass the saying that is written:* **"Death is**

---

3. Marcion, against whom Tertullian is writing, believed that the God of the Old Testament, the Creator, was a lesser god than the God revealed in Jesus Christ.

swallowed up in victory" (1 Cor 15:54 and Isa 25:8). In the meantime I have some consolation from the sweetness of this yoke and not a little struggle against my long-standing weakness.

25:9
Lo, this is our God.

(10) Irenaeus of Lyons

When that which is perfect comes, we shall not see another Father but the one we now desire to see. For *blessed are the pure in heart, for they shall see God* (Matt 5:8). Neither shall we look for another Christ and Son of God but for the one who was born of the Virgin Mary, who also suffered, in whom also we believe, and whom we love, as Isaiah says: **And they shall say in that day, Lo, this is our Lord and God in whom we have trusted, and we rejoice in his salvation** (25:9). And Peter says in his epistle, *Without having seen him you love him; though you do not now see him, you believe in him and rejoice with unutterable joy* (1 Pet 1:8). Nor do we receive another Holy Spirit besides the one who is with us and who cries, *Abba! Father!* (Rom 8:15; Gal 4:6). And in these things we shall advance and progress, so that we shall enjoy the gifts of God no longer *through a mirror or dimly but face to face* (1 Cor 13:12).

Isaiah 26

1 On that day they will sing this song on the land of Ioudas, saying:
   Look, a strong city;
      and he will make our salvation
      its wall and outer wall.
2 Open the gates,
      let a people enter that keeps righteousness
      and that keeps truth,
3 that lays hold of truth
      and that keeps peace.
   Because in you
4   have they hoped, O Lord, forever —
      the great, eternal God,
5 you who have humbled and brought down
      those who dwell in lofty places;
   you will cast down strong cities
      and bring them down to the ground,
6 and the feet of the gentle and humble
      will trample them.

7 The way of the godly has become straight;
      the way of the godly has also been prepared.
8 For the way of the Lord is judgment;
      we have hoped in your name
   and in the remembrance
9   that our soul desires.
   In the night my spirit rises early toward you, O God,
      because your ordinances are a light upon the earth.
   Learn righteousness, you who dwell on the earth,
10   for the ungodly one has come to an end:
   he will not learn righteousness on the earth,

>   he will not perform truth.
>   Let the ungodly one be taken away
>   so that he may not see the glory of the Lord.
> 11 O Lord, your arm is lifted up,
>   and they have not known it,
>   but once they realize it, they will be ashamed.
>   Jealousy will take hold of an uninstructed people,
>   and fire will now consume the adversaries.
> 12 O Lord our God, give us peace,
>   for you have granted us all things.
> 13 O Lord our God, take possession of us:
>   O Lord, we know no other besides you,
>   we name your name.
> 14 But the dead will not see life,
>   nor will physicians raise them up;
>   because of this you have brought them and destroyed them
>   and taken away all their males.
> 15 Increase evils on them, O Lord,
>   increase evils on the glorious ones of the earth.
>
> 16 O Lord, in affliction I remembered you;
>   with small affliction your chastening was on us.
> 17 And as a woman in travail is about to give birth
>   and cries out in her pangs,
>   so were we to your beloved
> 18   because of the fear of you, O Lord.
> (18) We conceived and travailed and gave birth;
>   we produced a wind of your salvation on the earth,
>   but those who dwell on the earth will fall.
> 19 The dead shall rise, and those who are in the tombs shall be raised,
>   and those who are in the earth shall rejoice.
>   For the dew from you is healing to them,
>   but the land of the ungodly shall fall.
>
> 20 Go, my people, enter your chambers,
>   shut your door;
>   hide yourselves for a little while
>   until the wrath of the Lord has passed.
> 21 For look, the Lord from his holy place
>   brings his wrath upon those who dwell on the earth;
>   the earth will disclose its blood
>   and will not cover the slain.

The interpretation of this chapter is particularly rich. The church fathers took the words **The dead shall live, their bodies shall rise** *(26:19), to refer to the resurrection of the dead. Tertullian cites this verse, as well as passages from other prophets, to show that the vision of the dry bones of Ezekiel 37 is not to be understood allegorically. Rather, the prophets envisioned the resurrection of the body. The* **dew** *(26:19) was understood to be God's life-giving power, and in some cases was identified with the Holy Spirit, the "life-giver," as in the words of the Nicene Creed: "We believe in the Holy Spirit, the Lord and Life-giver." Some took the* **strong city** *(26:1) to signify the Church, and others related* **my soul yearns for thee** *(v. 9) to passages in the Scriptures that speak of spiritual longing for God, for example, "my soul thirsts for the living God" (Ps 42:2). At 26:10 the Septuagint reads* **glory of the Lord** *for the Hebrew* **majesty of the Lord,** *and some commentators saw this as a reference to the beatific vision when, in Augustine's words, God will "show himself to those who love him." Gregory of Nyssa explains that when the Scriptures use the word "see," as here,* **see the glory of God,** *"see" means "possess." Augustine observes that the words,* **Take possession of us, Lord** *(26:13), mean that God possesses and is possessed, for he cultivates us as his soil. Augustine cites 26:12,* **O Lord our God, give us peace, for you have given us all things**, *at the very end of his* Confessions, *to depict "the peace with no evening" (1 Thess 3:16), when "the most beautiful order of very good things" will have come to fulfillment and God "will rest in us."*

(1) The Gospel according to Matthew

But when you pray, **go into your room and shut the door** (26:20) and pray to your Father who is in secret; and your Father who sees in secret will reward you.

(2) Cyril of Alexandria

Once Moab is trampled under foot, that is to say, when idolatry has been wholly abolished, those who are freed from error and have come to the light of the truth will see God with an interior vision. They will know the God of all who is our Savior and Redeemer. Through him are all things, and in him are all things, and for our sake he became like us in every way. Accompanied by a lyre, they will sing this song in praise of God: **We have a strong city which is our salvation** (26:1). For our Lord Jesus Christ is indeed like a **strong** and invincible **city**, well fortified with towers, and in him we put our hope. He welcomes those who have fled Satan's tyranny, and he cares for his own. Hence he asserted: *My sheep hear my voice, and they follow me; and I give them eternal life, and no one shall snatch them out of my hand* (John 10:27-28).

Our Savior then is a like a **strong** and secure **city** that is surrounded by two **walls** and in every way secure. For a well-protected city is not encircled by only one wall. In addition to the large **wall** that surrounds it there stands another wall enclosing the inner **wall**. For that reason it is fitting that those who sing this song about the Church of our Savior say: **Behold, we have a strong city which is our salvation.** For *the gates of hell will not prevail against it* (Matt 16:18), as the Savior said. It is protected by a double **wall**, by the host of the holy angels and by the most high God, who is its

outer wall. Its strength comes from these heavenly beings and the one who is himself the Lord of all powers.

It might also be noted that in the Holy Scriptures Christ is sometimes called **Judah** (26:1), because he came from the tribe of Judah. As Jacob said: *Judah, your brothers shall praise you* (Gen 49:8). This hymn then is sung in the land of **Judah**, the city of Christ which is the Church.

Since our Lord Jesus Christ is known throughout the world and there is a **strong city which is our salvation** (26:1) the Holy Spirit speaking through the prophet's voice commands the holy teachers, that is, the apostles and evangelists: **Open the gates** (26:2). That is, explain to those who stand at the door that one enters through faith and that one must pass through the awesome sacrament, so that a people may enter who is **righteous and holds to the truth** (26:2). For the divine and saving gospel instructs believers in a righteousness that is greater than that of the law. The faithful stand firm in the truth, for the gospel did not introduce a form of worship based on types and shadows, as in the ancient law, but *worship in spirit and in truth* (John 4:24). This then is the truth we possess, a truth that is not satisfied with shadows, but only with the reality of Christ who is the truth.

This **truth keeps peace** (26:3). How and in what way? When Christ comes to us the ancient enemy is destroyed, and, once we have been liberated from his devious ways, we are free to serve God with an unshakeable faith. St. Paul confirmed this when he wrote: *Therefore, since we are justified by faith, we have peace with God through our Lord Jesus Christ* (Rom 5:1). When we worshiped the creation and clung to our carnal desires, we were at enmity with God. But now we are called friends and live in **peace** with God. To him alone do we say: "We know no other God but you. We call upon your name, and we are adorned with the crown of the marvelous life according to the gospel." So great is this honor that even in this life we might say what the saints of God say: "On you, Lord, we have hoped until the end of the age. Our hope in God will never end, and we will exult in God forever."

The blessed prophet Jeremiah was pointing to the evangelical way of life and righteousness in Christ when he urged the lovers of truth, *Stand on the roads and ask for the eternal ways of the* LORD, *and find where the good way is and walk in it, and you will find purification for your souls* (Jer 6:16). The *roads* and *ways of the* LORD are the words of the holy prophets and the law of Moses, which foreshadowed the mystery of Christ in shadows and types. By examining these *ways* we learn the path of truth, that is, the way of life discovered in Christ. And when our souls follow this way of life, we will find true purification through the Spirit. Hence Isaiah asserts that **the way of the godly is straight** (26:7). How can it not be **straight** without curves and hills, for we are justified by faith and through Holy Baptism we are marvelously cleansed? . . .

The prescience of the saints is remarkable. They even anticipate objections to their teaching. For example, they say that the life-giving Spirit will revive the earth's inhabitants. Yet death still has power over human beings. Hence one can imagine someone saying: "What value do these proclamations of the prophets have for us? Where is the life-giving Spirit? **Those who dwell on the earth will fall**" (26:18). In answer they reply: **The dead shall live again** (26:19) by the grace of God, as the apostle Paul said: *Our Lord Jesus*

Christ tasted death for everyone (Heb 2:9); indeed, he rose on the third day and became the *first fruits of those who have fallen asleep* (1 Cor 15:20), and the root of those who are being restored to life. In him human nature has begun to put off corruption and we possess eternal life with a certain hope. For the dead will most assuredly be restored to life, and the power of death will be wholly destroyed. However, since the time of the resurrection is not yet present, human nature is still subject to death. In Christ, however, death has been weakened and in due time will lose its power over us. Are then the life-giving words of the prophet, **that the inhabitants of the world fall**, shown to be false? Surely not, for he affirms: **The dead shall live again, and the bodies in the tombs will be raised** (26:19).

And how will this happen? **The dew from you is healing for them** (26:19), says the prophet. The **dew** signifies the life-giving energy and power of the Spirit through which, according to David, the dead will be raised. For he sings to God: *When thou hidest thy face, they are dismayed and return to the dust. When thou sendest forth thy Spirit, they are created; and thou renewest the face of the earth* (Ps 104:29-30). The life-giving **dew** is the Holy Spirit of the Father through the Son, through whom earthly bodies receive the gift of incorruption.

(3) Jerome

When Moab is demolished and only dust remains and all the enemies of Christ are at his feet, then this **song will be sung in the land of Judah** (26:1). As we understand Zion and Jerusalem to refer to the heavenly city, so we interpret **Judah** to refer to the heavenly land that belongs to this city.

For the saints, who did not want to sing a **song to Judah** in a strange land, ask: *How shall we sing a song to the LORD in a foreign land?* (Ps 137:4). I think the song referred to in this passage is that song mentioned elsewhere in the Scriptures which the saints were urged to sing: *O sing to the LORD a new song!* (Ps 96:1). It will, however, be followed by this song: **The city of our strength, the Savior** (26:1).

What city is this? The city situated on a mountain that cannot be hid about which it is said, *There is a river whose streams make glad the city of God* (Ps 46:4). And again: *Glorious things are spoken of you, O city of God* (Ps 87:3). This city's founder is the one about whom the Father said: He built my city. Indeed, the city of our strength is the Savior, that is, Jesus.

[Salvation] is set up **in it as a wall and outer wall** (26:1). The city has a double fortification, a **wall** of good works and a **bulwark** of true faith. For a wall of faith is not sufficient; faith must be confirmed by good works. According to the prophet this **wall** and **outer wall** or surrounding wall are constructed of living stones taken from the earth.

26:1
Look, a strong city; and he will make our salvation its wall and outer wall.

(4) Didymus the Blind

By God's abundant grace we are able to bring forth the fruits of the Spirit, for the Lord encircles us with a **wall** of fire that illuminates and protects us and consumes our enemies who seek to destroy us. Hence we are able to raise a shout of victory and point to the invincible city: **Behold, the strong city which is our salvation** (26:1).

(5) Gregory the Great

Often in Holy Scripture, because of the rampart of his protection, the incarnate Lord is called a **wall**, as the prophet says about the holy Church: **A wall and a bulwark shall be set there** (26:1). He is a **wall** for us who surrounds us by guarding us on every side. The **bulwark** of our wall was all the prophets who, before the Lord appeared in the flesh, were sent to build up the faith by prophesying. Therefore in the holy Church the Lord was placed as **a wall** for us and the prophets were its **bulwark** because their words were a support for the faith of those whom he perfectly protects. Thus the **wall** is placed first, and then the **bulwark** is added because we who were called from the nations would by no means have accepted the sayings of his prophets if we had not first recognized the Lord.

26:9
**My spirit yearns for you in the early morning,
because your ordinances are a light.**

(6) Athanasius of Alexandria

So great is the love of the saints that they never cease offering uninterrupted and continual sacrifice to the Lord. They thirst for him and ask again and again to drink of him. As David sang, *O God, you are my God, I seek you, my soul thirsts for you; my flesh faints for you as in a dry and weary land where no water is. So I have looked upon you in the sanctuary* (Ps 63:1-2). And Isaiah the prophet says, **My spirit yearns for you in the early morning, because your ordinances are a light** (26:9). And another says, *My soul is consumed with longing for your ordinances at all times* (Ps 119:20); and again the psalmist says, *For your ordinances have I hoped, and I will keep your law continually* (Ps 119:43-44). Yet another cries out in faith: *My eyes are ever toward the* LORD (Ps 25:15). And another joins in: *Let the meditations of my heart come before you at all times* (Ps 19:14). And Paul also urges, *At all times give thanks; pray without ceasing* (1 Thess 5:17-18). Those who are continually engaged in prayer, waiting wholly on the Lord, resolve, *Let us press on to know the* LORD; *his going forth is sure as the dawn; he will come to us as the showers,* *as the spring rains that water the earth* (Hos 6:3). For not only does he satisfy them in the morning; he gives them as much to drink as they ask, he gives them abundantly according to the multitude of his loving-kindness, granting to them at all times the grace of the Spirit. And what they thirst for he identifies in the words: *He who believes in me* (John 7:38). For *as cold water is pleasant to a thirsty soul* (Prov 25:25), according to the proverb, so to those who believe in the Lord, the coming of the Spirit is better than all refreshment and joy.

(7) Ambrose of Milan

Since the abundance of the Church's grace and the precious reward of faithfulness beckon us, let us anticipate the rising sun and run to meet it at daybreak, before it says, *See, here I am* (58:9). The *Sun of Justice* (Mal 4:2) wants to be anticipated and looks forward to it. Listen to the way in which he looks forward, and how he desires to be anticipated: *To the angel of the church in Pergamum*, he says, *Repent then. If not, I will come to you soon. . . . To the angel of the church in Laodicea*, he says, *Be zealous and repent. Behold, I stand at the door and knock; if anyone hears my voice and opens the door, I will come in to him* (Rev 2:12, 16 and 3:14, 19-20). He will be able to come in. Indeed, locked and bolted doors were not able to stop him when he had risen with his body. He appeared suddenly and unexpectedly in the apostles' inner room (cf. John 20:19). But he longs to experience the ardor of your devotion, whereas he had already tested the apostles. Or perhaps he anticipates you in time of persecution, but when it is peaceful, he wishes to be anticipated. In any event, be sure to get up before the sun whom you see. *Awake, O sleeper, and arise from the dead, and Christ shall give you light* (Eph 5:14). If you get up before this sun rises, you will receive Christ shining on you. He shines on you beforehand in the secret of your heart; he shines on you as you say, **My spirit keeps vigil before you at night** (26:9). He will make the morning light shine in splendor during the night hours, if you meditate upon God's words. When you meditate, there is light, and when you see the light — not of day, but of grace — you will declare: **Your ordinances are a light** (26:9). Later, when the day finds you still meditating on the divine words, and when the pleasant work of praying and singing psalms has delighted your mind, again you will say to the Lord Jesus, *You make glad the going forth of the morning and the evening* (Ps 65:8).

(8) Gregory the Great

Holy desires increase when they are not fulfilled. Yet if delay causes them to slacken, this means the desires were not genuine. Whoever has been set on fire strains to reach the truth. For this reason David said: *My soul thirsts for the living God. When shall I come and behold the face of God?* (Ps 42:2). And he urges us: *Seek his face always* (Ps 105:4). Hence the prophet also said: **My soul yearns for you in the night, and in my spirit and my inner being I watch for you in the morning** (26:9).

26:10
Let the wicked be taken away so that he may not see the glory of the Lord.

(9) Irenaeus of Lyons

For behold, says Isaiah, *the day of the* LORD *comes, cruel, with wrath and fierce anger, to make the earth a desolation and to destroy its sinners from it* (13:9). Again he asks: **Let him be taken away so that he may not see the glory of God** (26:10). And when these things are done, he says, *God will remove men far away, and those that are left shall multiply in the earth* (6:12). *And they shall build houses and inhabit them; they shall plant vineyards and eat of them themselves* (65:21). For all these and other words were unquestionably spoken in reference to the resurrection of the just, which takes place after the coming of Antichrist and the destruction of all peoples under his rule. At the time of the resurrection the just will reign on the earth, growing stronger by the vision of the Lord. Through him they shall grow accustomed to know the **glory** of God the Father, and in the kingdom they shall enjoy fellowship and communion with the holy angels and kinship with spiritual beings.

(10) Gregory of Nyssa

So great is the promise in the beatitude, *Happy are the pure in heart, for they shall see God* (Matt 5:8), that it transcends the utmost limit of happiness. What else could one desire after such a good? For one possesses all things in the one that is seen. According to the usage of the Scripture, "to see" means "to possess." For example, the passage, *May you see the good things of Jerusalem* (Ps 128:5), means, "May you find the good things of Jerusalem." Similarly, in the passage, **Let the wicked be taken away so that he may not see the glory of the Lord** (26:10), the prophet uses the phrase **not see** to mean "not share in."

Therefore the person who sees God possesses by seeing all the things that are good: life without end and free of corruption, undying happiness, endless reign, unceasing joy, true light, spiritual and sweet speech, unapproachable glory, continuous rejoicing, in short everything good. So magnificent is the promise of happiness.

(11) Augustine of Hippo

The death of the body is everlasting punishment; the death of the soul is the absence of God. Do you want to know what the death of the soul is? Listen to what the prophet says: **Let the wicked be taken away that he may not see the glory of the Lord** (26:10).

(12) Augustine of Hippo

Is the wicked person also going to see God, the one of whom Isaiah writes, **Let the wicked be taken away that he may not see the glory of God** (26:10)? Both the godless and the godly will see God in that form.... When the Lord was in the flesh he was seen not only by the good but also by the wicked. He spoke among the good and the wicked and was visible to all of them, hidden as God, revealed as a human being. As God he rules men, as a man he is visible among men.... He said: *I will show myself to him* (John 14:21). When did he say that? When he was still visible among men. When did he say that? When he was visible to those who did not love him.

It would make no sense to say that he was going to show himself to those who loved him if there had not been a time when they could not see him. So because the form of God was being kept in reserve, the form of man was being shown; by speaking to men in the form of man and being visible for all to see, he showed himself to all, both good and bad, while keeping himself in reserve for those who loved him.

When then is he going to show himself to those who love him? After the resurrection of the body, when the **godless will be taken away lest he see the glory of God** (26:10). For *when he appears, we shall be like him, because we shall see him just as he is* (1 John 3:2). That is what is meant by eternal life. That is, everything we are talking about amounts to nothing in comparison with that life. What does it matter that we are alive? What does it matter that we are in good health? What really matters is that we shall see God. That is eternal life. Christ said that himself. *Now this is eternal life, that they should know you, the one true God, and Jesus Christ whom you have sent* (John 17:3).

(13) John Chrysostom

O how blessed, thrice blessed, indeed many times more are those deemed worthy to see the **glory of the Lord**. The prophet was speaking about this when he said: **Let the wicked be taken away that he not see the glory of the Lord** (26:10). May God grant that not one of us be taken away or excluded from seeing God's **glory**. For if one day we will not enjoy it, it is time to say of ourselves, "Would that we had not been born" (cf. Job 3:3). For why do we live? Why do we breathe? What are we if we are deprived of that vision, if we are never able to behold our Lord? If those who do not see the light of the sun endure a life more bitter than any death, what do they endure who are deprived of the light that shines from God's face?

26:12
O Lord our God, give us peace, for you have granted us all things.

(14) Augustine of Hippo

The time when our external enemy the devil will be under our feet is when the internal enemy, covetousness, has been healed, and we shall be living in **peace**. What sort of **peace**? The sort that *eye has not seen, nor ear heard* (1 Cor 2:9). What sort of **peace**? The sort that no imagination can conceive and no quarreling intrude on. What sort of **peace**?

The sort about which the apostle said: *And the peace of God which surpasses all understanding will guard your hearts* (Phil 4:7). About this peace the prophet Isaiah prays, **O Lord our God, give us peace, for you have given us everything you promised** (26:12). You promised Christ; you have given him to us. You promised his cross and the shedding of blood for the forgiveness of sins; you have given them to us. You promised his ascension, and the sending of the Holy Spirit from heaven; you have given them to us. You promised us a Church spread throughout the world; you have given it. You promised there would be heretics to try us and put us through our paces, and that the Church would triumph over their errors; you have given this. You promised the abolition of the idols of the heathen; you have given it. **O Lord our God, give us peace, for you have given us everything you promised.**

(15) Augustine of Hippo

Lord God, give us peace, for you have given us all things (26:12), the peace of quietness, the peace of the sabbath, a peace with no evening (2 Thess 3:16). This entire most beautiful order of very good things will complete its course and then pass away; for at creation there was both morning and evening. The seventh day has no evening and has no ending. You sanctified it to abide everlastingly. After your *very good* works which you made while remaining yourself in repose, you *rested the seventh day* (Gen 1:31; 2:2-3). This utterance in your book foretells for us that after our works which, because they are your gift to us, are *very good,* we also may rest in you for the sabbath of eternal life. There also you will rest in us, just as now you work in us. Your rest will be through us, just as now your works are done through us. But you, Lord, are always working and always at rest. Your seeing is not in time, your movement is not in time, and your rest is not in time. Yet your acting causes us to see things in time, time itself, and the repose which is outside time.

26:13
O Lord our God, take possession of us.

(16) Augustine of Hippo

Receive this rich guest, the Spirit of God. Your space will be widened, not narrowed. . . . When Scripture proclaims, *The love of God has been poured out* (Rom 5:5), that very pouring out signifies spaciousness. So don't be afraid of being squeezed out; receive this guest, and don't let him be one of those passing guests. For if he departs he will not be able to give you anything. Let him come and take up residence in you, and you will see what he has given. Be his, don't let him leave you, don't let him move on from there; hold on to him altogether, and say to him, **Lord our God, take possession of us** (26:13).

(17) Augustine of Hippo

Our happiness will consist in possessing God. How should we understand this? We shall possess him, yes; but will he not also possess us? Certainly he will, for Isaiah urges, **Take possession of us, Lord** (26:13). God both possesses and is possessed, and all this is for our benefit; for although we possess him in order that we may be happy, the converse is not true; he does not possess us in order that he may be happy. He possesses us, and he is possessed by us, to no end other than our happiness. We possess him, and he possesses us, because we worship (*colimus*) him and he cultivates (*colit*) us.[1] We worship him as the Lord God, and he cultivates us as his soil. That we worship him goes without saying, but what evidence have we that he cultivates us? His own words prove it: *I am the vine; you are the branches. My Father is the vinedresser* (John 15:5, 1).

(18) Augustine of Hippo

David was a mighty warrior. Relying on his Lord he waged all his wars, and with the Lord's help he laid low all his enemies in accordance with the orders he had been given. But he prefigured another who would be strong of hand in defeating other enemies, namely, the devil and his angels. These are the enemies against which the Church wages victorious warfare. How does the Church defeat them? By patient endurance, for it was also by patient endurance that our king himself vanquished the devil. The devil raged, Christ suffered. The raging enemy was defeated, the suffering Christ conquered. By the same patient endurance Christ's body, the Church, vanquishes its enemies. The Church needs to be strong of hand in order to conquer, but Christ's body is his temple and his house and his city, and he who is head of the body is the dweller in the house and the sanctifier of the temple and the king of the city. As all the former — body, temple, house, city — are truly what the Church is, so is Christ head, sanctifier, dweller, and king: all these. What, then, can we vow to God except to be God's temple? We can offer nothing more pleasing to him than the prayer found in Isaiah: **Take possession of us** (26:13). In the transference of earthly properties a householder gains something when he acquires rights of ownership, but with the Church it is different. The property itself gains by being possessed by such an owner.

26:14
But the dead will not see life, nor will physicians raise them up.

(19) Gregory the Great

The prophet said, **The dead shall not live, the giants shall not rise up again.**[2] Whom does he call **the dead** except sinners? And whom does he refer to as **giants** other than

---

1. Augustine plays on the Latin word *colo*, which means to till the soil and to worship God. The closest one can come in English would be to translate: "We offer our cult to God, and God cultivates us."
2. Where the LXX has "physicians," the Vg. has "giants."

those who take pride in sin? Now the former **do not live** because by sinning they have lost the life of righteousness. The latter also cannot **rise up again** after death because, since they are swollen with pride after their transgression, they do not have recourse to the remedies of penitence. Thus it is written again, *A man who wanders from the way of understanding will rest in the assembly of the dead* (Prov 21:16). For whoever abandons the way of righteousness, to whom is he joined except to the number of the proud spirits?

26:18
We conceived and travailed and gave birth; we have conceived and brought forth the spirit of salvation on the earth.

(20) Augustine of Hippo

Even now let us rejoice in whatever way we can in this hope based on the promises of one who is most faithful, until that most abundant joy arrives when we *shall be like him, because we shall see him as he is* (1 John 3:2), and our joy nobody will take from us. Of this hope we have received already the gracious pledge given freely, the Holy Spirit, who works in our hearts the unutterable groanings (Rom 8:23) of holy desires. **For we have conceived**, as Isaiah says, **and brought forth the spirit of salvation** (26:18). And *when a woman is in labor,* the Lord says, *she has sorrow, because her day has come; but when she has brought forth, there is great joy, because a human being has been born into the world* (John 16:21). This will be the joy that nobody will take away from us; on the day when we are brought forth into the eternal light **conceived** by this faith. But for now let us fast and pray, while it is still the day for **bringing forth**.

26:18-20
The dead shall rise . . . for the dew from you is healing for them.

(21) Tertullian

Certainly, if it were only figuratively that the people of Israel complained about their dispersion and the destruction of their hope[3] — plaintively crying out in exile — it would be reasonable for God to console their figurative despair with a figurative promise. But since the people had not yet suffered any harm from being in dispersion, and the hope of resurrection had often languished among them, their faith in the resurrection was shaken. For it is evident that bodies disintegrate at death. So God was shoring up that faith which the people were pulling down.

And yet, even if Israel's mourning at that time was occasioned by some dismay at their present condition, it would not follow that the purpose of the revelation must be understood in the fashion of a parable. Rather, it is a testimony to the resurrection given

---

3. Tertullian is commenting on the vision of the valley of dry bones in Ezekiel 37.

to raise them up toward the hope of eternal salvation and the restoration that will inevitably follow and to turn their minds away from their present affairs. The other prophets make this same point: *Ye shall go forth* — from the tombs — *as calves let loose from halters, and ye shall tread down your enemies* (Mal 4:2-3) and again, *Your heart shall rejoice, and your bones shall grow like grass* (66:14) — because the grass also is refashioned from the disintegration and dissolution of the seed.

To get to the point: if it is claimed that the image of the resurrection of the bones applies specifically to the condition of Israel, why is that same hope proclaimed not only to Israel but to all the nations? I mean of course the hope of restoring and breathing life into their remains and of awakening the dead from their tombs? For it is said about all peoples: **The dead shall live and arise from the sepulchers, for the dew which is from thee is healing to their bones** (26:19). Also in another place, *All flesh shall come before me to worship, says the* LORD (66:23). When? When the fashion of this world begins to pass away. For just before that he had said, *For as the new heaven and the new earth, which I am making, remain before me, says the* LORD, *so shall your offspring stand* (66:22). Then also will be fulfilled what he says next, *And they shall go forth* — speaking about their tombs — *and see the limbs of the people who have transgressed against me; for their worm shall not die, their fire shall not be quenched, and they shall become a spectacle to all flesh* (66:24) — that flesh which has been raised and come forth from the sepulchers will be worshiping the Lord for this gift.

(22) Gregory of Nyssa

How does the prophet seek healing from God? He says: *Have mercy upon me, O* LORD, *for I am weak; O* LORD, *heal me, for my bones are troubled* (Ps 6:2). Isaiah says to God: **The dew that is from you is healing to them** (26:19). Again, the prophetic words attest that the conversion of those wandering in error is God's work. For *they went astray in the wilderness in a thirsty land*, says the psalmist, and he adds, *he led them by a straight way, till they reached a city to dwell in* (Ps 106:4, 7 LXX). And *when the Lord turned again the captivity of Zion* (Ps 126:1). Similarly, Paul states that it is the business of God to give comfort to the afflicted: *Blessed be the God and Father of our Lord Jesus Christ, who comforts us in all our affliction* (2 Cor 1:3-4).

(23) Ambrose of Milan

Holy Job, after experiencing this life's miseries, and overcoming all adversity by his virtuous patience, foresaw his recompense for present evils in the resurrection when he said, *You shall raise up this body of mine which has suffered many evils* (Job 19:26 LXX). Isaiah also, proclaiming the resurrection to the people, said that he is the herald of the Lord's message, for we read: *For the mouth of the* LORD *has spoken, and they will say on that day* (25:8-9). What the mouth of the Lord declared the people should say is set forth later on, where it is written: **Because of fear of you, O Lord, we have been with child and have** brought forth the Spirit of thy salvation which thou hast poured forth upon the earth. **They that inhabit the earth shall fall, they shall rise that are in the graves. For the dew which is from you is health for them, but the land of the wicked shall perish. Go, my people, enter your chambers, and shut your doors behind you; hide yourselves for a little while until the Lord's wrath is past** (26:18-20).

How well did he, with the word **chambers**, signify the tombs of the dead, in which we are hidden for a short time, so that we may be ready for God's judgment which shall claim the right of the anger due for our wickedness. Therefore, he who is hidden is alive. He is at rest, as though he has withdrawn himself from our midst and retired, lest this world's distress envelop him with tighter snares. Through the prophets' voices the heavenly oracles promise that the joy of the resurrection is reserved for the dead and that the health of their limp bodies will be restored by divine **dew**. And **dew** is an appropriate symbol since it brings growth to all of the earth's seeds. What wonder is it, then, if the dust and ashes of our exhausted body become vigorous by the richness of celestial **dew** and if our limbs are refashioned and connected together again by receiving this vital moisture?

(24) Didymus the Blind

Those who live virtuously and are practiced in the contemplative life are *united in the same mind and the same judgment* (1 Cor 1:10). One might say that by their union they constitute a single heaven which drops down spiritual **dew**. Yet each one gives forth his own **dew**, just as that holy teacher Moses said: *May my teaching drop as the rain, my speech distil as the dew* (Deut 32:2).

However, although this **dew** is given by the heavens, that is, by virtuous and contemplative men and women, that **dew** is also given by the Lord of the heavens, as one learns from the inspired word of Isaiah: **The dead shall live, those in the tombs shall be raised, and those in the earth shall sing for joy. For the dew from you is healing for them** (26:19). And since **those in the earth** will rejoice in the spiritual **dew** with its healing power, one should also say that the dead who are raised and come forth from their tombs will also share in this **dew**, especially when the imperfect passes away and they are able to behold the truth face to face. Then they will not see in part nor through a mirror (1 Cor 13:12), but will behold in his fullness the Christ who has overcome death.

(25) Augustine of Hippo

The prophet Isaiah predicts: **The dead will rise, and those who were in the tombs will rise, and all who are in the earth shall rejoice; for the dew from you is health for them; but the land of the ungodly will fall** (26:19). The whole first part of this passage is concerned with the resurrection of the blessed. But the words **the land of the ungodly will fall** are rightly understood to mean that the destruction of the ungodly following their condemnation has to do with their bodies. And if we wish to examine more carefully

Isaiah 26

what is said about the resurrection of the good, then we would refer to the first resurrection the statement that **the dead will rise**, while the words that follow, **and those who were in the graves will rise**, would be referred to the second resurrection.[4] Now if we ask about those saints whom the Lord is to find alive here, the next statement may be appropriately assigned to them. **And all who are in the earth will rejoice; for the dew from you is health for them**. I take it that **health** in this passage is rightly understood to signify immortality; for **health** in the fullest sense is **health** which is not continually restored by food — by daily remedies, as it were.

26:20
Go, my people, enter your chambers, shut your door.

(26) Gregory the Great

Isaiah enjoins, **Enter your chambers, and shut your doors**. We go into our **chambers** when we enter the recesses of our minds; we **shut the doors** when we restrain illicit desires. When our consent opened these doors of carnal concupiscence, it forced us to the countless evils of our corrupt state. Thus, now we groan under the weight of mortality, even though we came to this point by our own free will, since the justice of the sentence against us demands that what we have done willingly, we should endure against our will.

---

4. The "first resurrection" is the resurrection of the soul in this life, that is, coming alive in faith. Being brought from unbelief to righteousness, says Augustine, is being brought from death to life. The "second resurrection" is the resurrection at the end of time (*City of God* 20.6).

Isaiah 28

1 Ah, the crown of pride,
    the hired workers of Ephraim,
the flower that has fallen from its glory
    on the top of the stout mountain —
    those who are drunk without wine!
2 See, the wrath of the Lord is a strong and harsh thing,
    like hail rushing down where there is no shelter;
violently rushing down like a great flood that sweeps a country,
    it will give rest to the land.
3 With hands and feet the garland of pride will be trampled —
    the hired workers of Ephraim.
4 And the flower that has fallen from its glorious hope
    on the topmost of the lofty mountain
will be like an early fig;
    the one who sees it will want to eat it up
    before he takes it into his hand.

5 In that day the Lord Sabaoth will be the garland of hope,
    which is woven of glory, to what is left of my people.
6 They will be left for a spirit of judgment —
    for judgment and strength in forbidding anyone to destroy.

7 For these have gone astray with wine,
    they went astray because of strong drink;
the priest and the prophet lost their senses because of wine,
    they were shaken up as a result of the drunkenness of strong drink;
    they went astray: this is an omen.
8 A curse will devour this counsel;
    for this counsel is for the sake of greed.

9 To whom did we declare evil things,
    and to whom did we declare a message?
  Those who are weaned from milk,
    those pulled away from the breast?
10 Expect affliction upon affliction,
    hope upon hope,
    yet a little, yet a little,
11 because of contempt from lips,
    through a different tongue;
  because they will speak to this people,
12 saying to them,
  "This is the rest for the hungry,
    and this is the destruction";
  yet they would not hear.
13 And the oracle of the Lord God will be to them
    affliction upon affliction,
    hope upon hope,
    yet a little, yet a little,
  in order that they may go and fall backward;
    and they will be in danger, and crushed, and taken.

14 Therefore hear the word of the Lord, you afflicted men
    and rulers of this people that is in Ierousalem.
15 Because you have said, "We have made a covenant with Hades,
    and agreements with death;
  if a rushing storm passes through,
    it will not come to us;
  we have made falsehood our hope,
    and in falsehood we will be sheltered";
16 therefore thus says the Lord,
  See, I will lay for the foundations of Sion
    a precious, choice stone,
  a highly valued cornerstone for its foundations,
    and the one who believes in him will not be put to shame.
17 And I will turn judgment into hope,
    and my mercy will become weight balances;
  and as for you who trust vainly in falsehood,
    I tell you that the tempest will not pass you by,
18 lest it also take away your covenant of death.
  And your hope regarding Hades will not remain:
    if a rushing storm comes,
    you will be trampled down by it.
19 When it passes by, it will take you;
    early, early in the day it will pass by,

and at night it will be an evil hope;
    learn to hear.
20 We are in straits and unable to fight,
    and we ourselves are too weak to be mobilized.
21 He will rise up as a mountain of ungodly people,
    and he will be in the valley of Gabaon;
with wrath he will do his deeds — a deed of bitterness!
    But his wrath will deal strangely,
    and his bitterness will be strange.
22 And as for you, may you not rejoice,
    nor let your bonds become strong;
because I have heard from the Lord Sabaoth
    of deeds finished and cut short,
    which he will perform upon the whole land.

23 Give ear and hear my voice;
    pay attention, and hear my words.
24 Will the plowman plow the whole day?
    Will he prepare the seed prior to working the land?
25 When he has leveled its surface,
    does he not then sow small dill and cumin,
and again sow wheat and barley
    and spelt in your borders?
26 And you will be instructed by the judgment of your God,
    and you will rejoice.

27 For the dill is not purified with harshness,
    nor will a cart wheel roll over the cumin;
but the dill is shaken with a rod,
28   and the cumin will be eaten with bread.
For I will not be angry with you forever,
    nor will the voice of my bitterness trample you.
29 And these wonders came forth from the Lord Sabaoth;
    take counsel, lift up a vain appeal.

For early Christian commentators, the most significant feature of this chapter was v. 16: **See, I lay for the foundations of Zion a precious, choice stone.** *Following St. Paul (Rom 9:32-33) and 1 Peter (1 Pet 2:6-8), the* **stone** *was taken to be Christ. Also in v. 16 the phrase* **who believes in him will not be put to shame** *caught their interest. Origen uses the passage as an occasion to discuss the nature of faith in Christ. Perhaps the most imaginative interpretation of the* **stone** *is found in a beautiful passage from Gregory of Nyssa's oration on the Baptism of Christ. He relates the* **stone** *of 28:16 to the stone Jacob removed from the well where he met Rachel (Gen 29:1-12). The stone over the well points to the "water of salvation," that is, Baptism. Not all, however, took the* **stone** *to refer to Christ, and in the final selection Theodoret criticizes those interpreters (most* *likely Theodore of Mopsuestia) who referred it to King Hezekiah. Besides this verse, chapter 28 was seldom cited in early Christian writings. For that reason the selections focus on the one passage that did receive extensive commentary.*

(1) The Letter of Paul to the Romans

[a] They have stumbled over the stumbling stone, as it is written, **Behold, I am laying in Zion a stone that will make men stumble, a rock that will make them fall; and he who believes in him will not be put to shame**

[b] For a man believes with his heart and so is justified, and he confesses with his lips and so is saved. The scripture says, **No one who believes in him will be put to shame.**

(2) The First Letter of Peter

Come to him, to that living stone, rejected by men but in God's sight chosen and precious; and like living stones be yourselves built into a spiritual house, to be a holy priesthood, to offer spiritual sacrifices acceptable to God through Jesus Christ. For it stands in scripture: **Behold, I am laying in Zion a stone, a cornerstone chosen and precious, and he who believes in him will not be put to shame** (28:16). To you therefore who believe, he is precious, but for those who do not believe, *The very stone which the builders rejected has become the head of the corner* (Ps 118:22), and *A stone that will make men stumble, a rock that will make them fall* (Isa 8:14); for they stumble because they disobey the word, as you were destined to do.

(3) Irenaeus of Lyons

Daniel, foreseeing his advent, said that a *stone, cut out without hands* (Dan 2:34), came into this world. For this is what *without hands* means, that [Jesus'] coming into this world was not by the operation of human hands, that is, of those men who practice stonecutting. Joseph took no part in it, but Mary alone cooperated with the prearranged plan. For this stone from the earth derives existence from the power and the wisdom of God. Hence Isaiah also declared: **Thus says the Lord, Behold, I am laying in Zion for a foundation a stone, precious, elect, the chief, the cornerstone, to be held in honor** (28:16). So then, we understand that his advent in human nature was not by the will of a man but by the will of God.

(4) Origen of Alexandria

Take note of what Paul says: *If you confess with your mouth that Jesus is Lord, and believe in your heart that God raised him from the dead, you will be saved* (Rom 10:9). Some take this to mean that even if a person is lacking in the benefits of good works, even if someone does not practice virtue, simply because he believed he would not perish and would be saved and gain salvation, though he would not attain the glory of beatitude.

But should the text not be understood to mean that whoever genuinely *confesses with the mouth* without feigning that Jesus is Lord, and *believes in his heart,* would also confess that he is subjected to the lordship of Wisdom, and Righteousness and Truth, and to everything Christ is? Such a person confesses that mammon is no longer his lord (cf. Matt 6:24), that he is no longer under the lordship of greed, unrighteousness, unchastity, or lying. For if one *confesses* once and for all *that Jesus Christ is Lord,* he declares that he is no longer a slave to any of these things.

Further, by *believing in* his *heart that God raised* Jesus *from the dead,* it is surely the case that he believes him to be raised for his justification (Rom 4:25). What would it profit me to know and believe that God raised Jesus from the dead if he was not raised within me? If I do not *walk in newness of life* (Rom 6:4), nor flee the old habit of sinning, Christ is not yet raised from the dead within me. The following words are in accord with this: For Scripture promises that **everyone who believes in him will not be put to shame** (28:16). This is written in Isaiah. If everyone who believes in him will not be put to shame, and everyone who sins is ashamed, as Adam sinned and was ashamed and hid himself (Gen 3:8), so anyone who wears the shame of sin would seem not to believe.

(5) Ambrose of Milan

The foundation of justice is faith, for the hearts of the just dwell on faith, and the just man that accuses himself builds justice on faith. For his justice becomes evident when he confesses the truth. So the Lord said through Isaiah: **I will lay a stone for a foundation in Zion** (28:16). This means that Christ is the **foundation** of the Church. For Christ is the object of faith to all; but the Church is, as it were, the form that justice takes. The justice of all is found in her. For she prays in common for all, she works in common for all, she is tested in the temptations of all. Whoever denies himself is a just man and is worthy of Christ. For this reason Paul said that Christ is the foundation so that we might construct the works of justice (cf. 1 Cor 3:9-15). Faith is the foundation. If our works are evil, they are without justice, but if good, they are just.

(6) Ambrosiaster

Scripture says in the words of Isaiah: **Everyone who believes in him will not be put to shame** (28:16). When, on the day of judgment, all things will be weighed and all contrivances and false teachings will be unmasked, then those who believe in Christ will dance for joy. For they will see that what they believed is true (and what was considered foolish will be thought wise). They will discover that those who were once looked on with disdain as foolish are now admired and reckoned prudent. For there will be certain proof where there is recompense and condemnation.

(7) Jerome

I had said to you, he says, **Hear the word of the Lord, you scoffers** (28:14), or "you leaders who oppress my people": "don't **make a covenant with death, or an agreement with hell** (28:18). You who condemn my precepts have **made a lie your hope** (28:15). In your boasting, or rather in your despair, you say, **We are protected by a lie** (28:15)." But *the LORD is gracious and merciful, slow to anger and abounding in steadfast love* (Exod 34:6; Ps 145:8), and even though you do not want it, he says that he will send to **Zion a chosen stone, tested, and precious, a cornerstone** (28:16). The apostle was speaking about this when he said: *Like a skilled master builder I laid a foundation* (1 Cor 3:10). And again: *For no other foundation can any one lay than that which is laid, which is Jesus Christ* (1 Cor 3:11). This indeed is the true **stone**. Note that the text uses the word **foundation** twice, just as in Leviticus man is twice called "man."[1] It is the **cornerstone** because it joined the people of the circumcision and the people of the Gentiles, about which it is also said in the psalm, *The stone which the builders rejected has become the head of the corner* (Ps 118:22). These are the builders and workmen who are here called **scoffers** and **leaders of the people in Jerusalem** (28:14). In Daniel we also read that this *stone was cut out* of the mountain *by no human hand and filled the whole earth* (Dan 2:34-35), meaning that the dispensation of the divine seed took on a human body, and the fullness of divinity dwelt in it bodily (Col 1:19). On this **stone**, which is also called *rock*, Christ built his Church (Matt 16:18). According to the Hebrew version, he laid a **sure foundation** in which the **one who believes will not be ashamed** (28:16) or, according to the Hebrew, will **not be in haste**.

(8) Gregory of Nyssa

Not only do the gospels, written after the crucifixion, proclaim the grace of Baptism, but before the Incarnation the ancient Scripture everywhere prefigured the pattern of our regeneration, not clearly representing its form, but foreshadowing in figures God's abundant love. As the Lamb was anticipated and the cross foretold, so too Baptism was shown forth in actions and in words. Let us recall some of the types for those who are interested in learning. . . .

Hagar, Abraham's servant girl (whom Paul interprets allegorically in writing to the Galatians [4:21-31]), was driven from her master's house by Sarah's anger — it is hard for a lawful wife to put up with a servant who is suspected of having relations with the master of the house. So Hagar, abandoned and desolate, wanders about the desert with the infant Ishmael at her breast. When her food ran out and she feared death, especially the death of her child, because her water skin was empty, unexpectedly an angel appears and shows her a well of living water (Gen 21:19). Drawing water from the well, she saves Ishmael.

---

1. In Lev 15:2 both the Hebrew and the LXX repeat the word "man," and this is rendered into English as *any man*: "Say to the people of Israel, When any man has a discharge from his body, his discharge is unclean."

This then is a type filled with spiritual meaning. For from earliest times it was by means of water that salvation came to someone who was perishing, and this water was not there previously but was given out of grace by an angel. . . .

When Jacob was looking for a bride, he met Rachel unexpectedly at the well (Gen 29:1-12). A great stone was placed over the well, and it required many shepherds to roll it away to provide water for them and their flocks. Jacob, however, moves the stone away by himself and waters the flocks of his betrothed. This stone is a type pointing to what is to come. For what is the stone lying over the well but Christ himself? For of him Isaiah says: **I will lay for the foundation of Zion a stone that is precious, costly, chosen** (28:16). And Daniel also says: *A stone was cut without hands* (Dan 2:34, 45)

Just as it is new and uncommon that a stone should be cut out of a rock without a stonecutter and other tools for cutting stone, so it is a thing beyond imagining that an unwedded Virgin should give birth to a child. Over the well, then, was lying the spiritual stone Christ, concealing in the depth of the mystery the washing of regeneration that needed much time — one might say a long rope — to bring it to light. And no one was able to move the stone except Israel [Jacob], who signifies the mind that sees God. He draws up the water and also gives drink to the sheep of Rachel. That is, he reveals the hidden mystery and gives water to the flock of the Church.

(9) Augustine of Hippo

By dying Christ showed you what you are going to suffer, no matter what; by rising again he showed you what, if you live a good life, you are going to receive. This is what *one believes with the heart unto justice, makes confession of with the mouth unto salvation* (Rom 10:10). But you are afraid to confess it because people might taunt you with it. I am not talking about those who don't believe because even they believe it inwardly. But if those who are ashamed to confess it should taunt you with it, listen to what comes next: *For scripture says,* **Nobody who believes in him shall be put to shame** (Rom 10:10-11, citing Isa 28:16). Think about this, hold to it. This is food not for the belly but for the mind.

(10) Augustine of Hippo

Jacob saw a ladder in a dream, and on the ladder he saw angels ascending and descending. He anointed the stone which he had placed at his head (Gen 28:10-22). You have heard that Christ is the Messiah. Jacob did not place the stone which he anointed to come and adore it. That would have been idolatry, not a sign pointing to Christ. Insofar as it was a sign, its purpose was to point to Christ. A stone was anointed, but not that it should be made into an idol. But why was a stone anointed? **See, I will place in Zion an elect and precious stone, and whoever believes in him shall not be put to shame** (28:16). Why was the stone anointed? Because the name Christ comes from the word that means "anointing" *(chrisma)*.

Isaiah 28

(11) Cyril of Alexandria

The prophet says, **Hear the word of the Lord, you men who are afflicted, who rule this people in Jerusalem** (28:14). What does he command them to hear? **I am laying as foundations in Zion a costly choice stone, a cornerstone, a precious stone for its foundations** (28:16). He calls our Lord Jesus the stone that is chosen, beautiful, and **precious**, for it stands out because of its divine glory and magnificence. For he became the **foundation**, and the support, and the immoveable base of the spiritual **Zion** which is the Church. This he makes clear by saying that the **foundation** had been laid by the Father (cf. Eph 2:20-21).[2] He asserts that it is a **cornerstone** because through faith two peoples, Israel and the Gentiles, have been joined in a spiritual union. For in the corners of a building two walls always come together, and where they meet they are fused into one.

He says that the **one who believes in him will not be ashamed** (28:16). See how he puts believers at ease and proclaims the deliverance of the gospel to the afflicted. **O afflicted ones** (28:14), he says, **I will lay the chosen stone as foundation for Zion** (28:16). And what good is that? **Who believes in him will not be ashamed** (28:16). This means that the heavy yoke of the law will be removed and the unspiritual and ineffective shadow of the law will pass away. In its place they will receive grace through faith, and in Christ the righteousness whose burden is light. **And I will make judgment into hope, and mercy will be like a balance** (28:17). As the Savior himself said, *The Father judges no one, but has given judgment to the Son, that all may honor the Son, even as they honor the Father* (John 5:22-23). This the apostle Paul understood when he wrote: *For we must all appear before the judgment seat of Christ, so that each one may receive good or evil, according to what he has done in the body* (2 Cor 5:10). On that day we expect that the **judgment** will be merciful and fitting for each person in accord with what one has done. This too is the meaning of the phrase **the mercy** of the judge **will be like a balance** (28:17). The judgment will be fair and equitable and in accord with one's good deeds.

(12) Theodoret of Cyrus

It is beyond comprehension how someone could apply this prophecy to Hezekiah.[3] The Holy Scriptures forbid us from putting our trust in a man. *Put not your trust in princes*, say the Scriptures, *nor in sons of men in whom there is no salvation* (Ps 146:3). Or again: *Cursed is the man who hopes in man* (Jer 17:5). And again: *It is better to trust in the LORD than to trust in man* (Ps 118:8). But in this passage the prophetic oracle praises the one who puts his trust in this stone. The **cornerstone** (28:16) is our Lord Christ, *who has made us both one* (Eph 2:14), who has joined in himself those who came from the

---

2. Isaiah presents the oracle as a word from the Lord God, hence Cyril understands it to be spoken by God the Father, who lays the foundation that is Christ.

3. Theodoret has in mind commentators such as Theodore of Mopsuestia, who rejected the christological interpretation of this verse.

Gentiles and those who came from Israel to make us one people. He has also been called the **foundation** (28:16). *For no other foundation,* [the apostle] stresses, *can anyone lay than that which is laid, which is Jesus Christ* (1 Cor 3:11). For since the leaders of the ten tribes threatened to bring down the kingdom of David, he wishes to show that it is invincible and prophesies that the stone taken from it would be hewn without human hands. This stone has become a great mountain that covers the world.

Isaiah 29

1 Ah, city of Ariel,
    against which Dauid waged war!
  Gather crops year by year;
    for you will eat with Moab.
2 For I will greatly distress Ariel,
    and her strength and wealth shall be mine.
3 And like Dauid I will surround you;
    I will lay ramparts around you
    and set up towers around you.
4 Then your words shall be brought low to the earth,
    to the earth shall your words sink;
  your voice shall be like those who utter sounds from the earth,
    and your voice shall be weak near the ground.

5 But the wealth of the ungodly shall be like dust from a wheel
    and like flying chaff.
  And it shall be like an instant, suddenly,
6   from the Lord Sabaoth;
  for there shall be a visitation
    with thunder and earthquake and a great voice,
    a rushing storm and a devouring flame of fire.
7 And the wealth of all the nations —
    as many as marched against Ariel,
    and all that went to war against Ierousalem,
    and all who were gathered against her and were distressing her —
  shall be like one who dreams in his sleep.
8 And they shall be like those who hunger and eat in their sleep,
    and after rising, their dream is vain;
  and just as a thirsty person dreams that he is drinking
    and after rising is still thirsty,

and his soul has hoped for something vain,
  so shall the wealth of all the nations be,
    as many as have marched against Mount Sion.

9 Be faint and amazed,
    get a drunken headache —
  not from strong drink
    nor from wine!
10 Because the Lord has made you drink
    with a spirit of deep sleep;
  he will close their eyes
    and those of their prophets and of their rulers —
    the ones who see the hidden things.

11 And all these sayings shall become for you like the words of this sealed book. If they give it to a learned man, saying, "Read these things," then he will say, "I cannot read it, for it is sealed." 12 And this book will be given into the hands of an unlearned man, and one will say to him, "Read this," and he will say, "I am not learned."

13 The Lord said:
  These people draw near me:
    they honor me with their lips,
    while their heart is far from me,
  and in vain do they worship me,
    teaching human precepts and teachings.
14 Therefore look, I will proceed
    to remove this people.
  I will remove them and destroy the wisdom of the wise,
    and the discernment of the discerning I will hide.

15 Ah, those who make plans deeply,
    and not through the Lord!
  Ah, those who make plans in secret,
    and their works will be in darkness!
  And they will say, "Who has seen us
    and who will know us or the things we do?"
16 Shall you not be regarded as the potter's clay?
  Shall the thing formed say to the one who formed it,
    "You did not form me";
  or the thing made to the one who made it,
    "You made me with no understanding"?

17 Is it not yet a little while,
    and Lebanon shall be changed like Mount Chermel,

and Mount Chermel shall be regarded as a forest?
18 On that day the deaf shall hear
the words of a scroll,
and as for those who are in the darkness
and those who are in the fog:
the eyes of the blind shall see.
19 And the poor shall be glad with joy because of the Lord,
and those despairing among people shall be filled with joy.
20 The transgressor has failed,
and the arrogant has perished,
and those who transgress wickedly have been utterly destroyed —
21 even those who cause people to sin in word.
And they will make all those who reprove in the gates a cause of stumbling;
and they have turned aside the just among the unjust.

22 Therefore this is what the Lord says concerning the house of Iakob, which he set apart from Abraam:

Iakob shall not be ashamed now,
nor shall Israel now change his face.
23 But when their children see my works,
because of me they will sanctify my name;
they will sanctify the Holy One of Iakob,
and will fear the God of Israel.
24 And those who wander in spirit will know understanding,
and those who grumble will learn to obey,
[and the faltering tongues will learn to speak peace].

Isaiah 29:13, **These people honor me with their lips, but their heart is far from me,** *is cited by Jesus in a dispute with the Pharisees in Matthew 15. In answer to the charge of the Pharisees, "Why do your disciples transgress the tradition of the elders" [by not washing their hands before they eat], Jesus responded: "And why do you transgress the commandment of God for the sake of your tradition?" (Matt 15:1-3). Then Jesus says, "So, for the sake of your tradition, you have made void the word of God," and cites* **This people honors me with their lips.** *. . . Early Christian interpreters follow the lead of the Gospel of Matthew, and Isaiah 29 becomes an occasion to mount a polemic against Jewish interpretation of the Bible. We have provided a rather long passage from Origen's commentary on Matthew illustrating the direction interpretation took. This is one of the more striking examples of how passages from the prophet Isaiah, when read in the context of conflict between Christians and Jews over the interpretation of the Bible, served to legitimate harsh language about Jewish perfidy. Elsewhere Origen interprets the phrase* **sealed book** *to mean that the Old Testament will be understood only if the seal is broken by the divine Word. Augustine and Gregory of Nyssa use the words,* **They honor me with their lips, while their hearts are far from me** *(29:13), to accent the importance of interior prayer: prayer springs from the heart, not from the lips, and in Augustine's words, "we draw near to God by love." Taking a* *quite different approach, Origen observes that there are occasions when confession with the lips is what counts, namely, when one is called on to be a martyr. Then it is not enough that one hold Christ in one's heart; one must make confession of one's faith publicly. Several writers deal with the meaning of the elusive term* **Ariel** *(29:1).*

(1) The Gospel according to Matthew

You hypocrites! Well did Isaiah prophesy of you when he said: **This people honors me with their lips, but their heart is far from me; in vain do they worship me, teaching as doctrines the precepts of men (29:13).**

(2) The Letter of Paul to the Romans

But who are you, a man, to answer back to God? **Will what is molded say to its molder, "Why have you made me thus?" (29:16)**

(3) The First Letter of Paul to the Corinthians

For the word of the cross is folly to those who are perishing, but to us who are being saved it is the power of God. For it is written, **I will destroy the wisdom of the wise, and the cleverness of the clever I will thwart (29:14).**

(4) Eusebius of Caesarea

The Jews hold that the unfortunate city mentioned in this passage, **Ariel** (29:1), is Jerusalem. More specifically they contend that the altar which stands before the temple is called **Ariel**, as is clear in Ezekiel where, at the end of the description of the city, he says: *These are the dimensions of the altar by cubits (the cubit being a cubit and a handbreadth); its base shall be one cubit high* (Ezek 43:13). And then he adds: *And the altar* (ariel) *four cubits, and from the altar projecting upward, four horns, one cubit high. And the altar shall be twelve cubits long by twelve broad* (Ezek 43:15-16). They also say that **Ariel** is to be interpreted as "lion of God," since the altar was God's altar, and all the living sacrifices offered on it were consumed. This is the reason it received the name **Ariel**. In Hebrew the passage reads, **the city against which David waged war** (29:1). But Aquila has translated it as **fortified town of David,** and Symmachus as **the fortified city of David**. The city belonged to the Philistines before David subdued them and drove them from it. For this reason one can reconcile the Hebrew with the translation of the Septuagint. The passage would refer to the city against which David waged war when it was under the Philistines. This expression is used instead of "the city which he defended" or "the city for which David is said to have gone to war." Accordingly the present text can properly be understood as follows. After speaking about its previous rulers, *the crown of their pride* (28:1-3), he now prophesies about what Jerusalem is going to undergo on account of its transgressions.

(5) Jerome

The word I have translated **Woe** is *hoi* in Hebrew. It is vocative, and hence it means not that **Ariel** "wept," but that **Ariel** is *addressed*. In the present passage, however, it does refer to lamentation. **Ariel** means "lion of God." Aquila interpreted the term as "town," basing his translation on the Hebrew word *cariatha*, meaning "small **city**" (a similar word in Syriac means "village"), hence a town constructed of wood [rather than stone] is called *Cariatharim*. In an earlier text we read: *How the faithful city of Sion has become a harlot!* (1:21). There the Hebrew uses the term for small city, which, if we were to put Aquila's translation into Latin, would be *civitatulum*. Jerusalem is called **Ariel**, lion of God, because it was once very strong. Some, however, think that **Ariel** refers to the temple of God which was in Jerusalem.

29:9
**Be faint and amazed, get a drunken headache —
not from strong drink nor from wine!**

(6) John Cassian

But there is another surfeiting (or dissipation, Luke 21:34) that is no less dangerous and a spiritual drunkenness that is harder to avoid [than actual drunkenness], as well as a concern and a worldly anxiety that frequently seize hold of us even after we have perfectly renounced all our property and are abstaining completely from wine and rich foods and, in fact, are living in the desert.[1] About these things the prophet commands: **Purge yourselves, you who are drunk, and not with wine** (29:9). And another one calls out: **Be astonished and wonder, waver and reel; be drunk, and not with wine; be moved, and not with drunkenness** (29:9). Consequently the wine of this drunkenness must be, according to the prophet, *the fury of dragons* (Deut 32:33 LXX). Listen to what root this wine proceeds from: *From the vineyards of Sodom*, he says, *is their vine, and from Gomorrah their shoots* (Deut 32:32). Do you also want to know the fruit of this vine and the seed of that shoot? *Their grape is a grape of gall, a cluster of bitterness for them* (Deut 32:32).

Unless we have been completely purged of every vice and unless we have abstained from a surfeit of all the passions, our heart will be weighed down — not with a drunkenness from wine or any abundance of every kind of food but with a drunkenness and a surfeiting that is far worse. That worldly cares can sometimes beset even us who are involved in none of this world's activity is clearly demonstrated from the rule of the elders.

---

1. Cassian is writing to his fellow monks.

29:11
And all these sayings shall become for you like the words of this sealed book.

(7) Origen of Alexandria

It is not peculiar to Isaiah that the words of the book should be **sealed** (29:11). Obviously the book of Isaiah cannot be read by someone who does not know how to read (29:12). But even if someone can read, the book cannot be understood because it is **sealed**. What is true of Isaiah is true of every book of the Bible; it can be opened only by the Word who closed it, for *he shall shut, and none shall open* (22:22; Rev 3:7). And when he opens it, its meaning will be clear. This is why it is said, *He shall open, and none shall shut*. . . .

I take it that something similar is intended in the case of the book mentioned by Ezekiel in which had been *written lamentation and a song[2] and woe* (Ezek 2:10). For the whole book contains the *woe* of those perishing, and the *song* of those being saved, and the *lamentation* of those in between.

And John too, when he speaks of eating the one scroll on which there is writing *on the front and the back* (cf. Rev 5:1), considered the whole Scripture as one book which is *sweet* at first when one chews it but then becomes *bitter* (Rev 10:10) as one gets to know it better and realizes that one is seeing oneself in it.

(8) Origen of Alexandria

Take care that not only *when Moses is read* but also when Paul is read *a veil is not placed over* our *heart* (2 Cor 3:15). For it is evident, if we do not listen attentively, if we are not zealous in study and intent on understanding, that not only are the writings of the law and the prophets covered with a heavy *veil*, but the writings of the apostles and the gospels as well.

I fear that out of excessive negligence or dullness of heart, the divine books will not only be veiled but also **sealed** (29:11). For **If a book is put in the hands of a man who cannot read to be read, he would say that he does not know how to read; if it is put into the hands of a man who can read, he would say that it is sealed** (29:11-12). From this we learn that we must not only be zealous in studying the sacred writings, but we must also pray to the Lord *day and night* (Josh 1:8) that the lamb *of the tribe of Judah* (Rev 5:5) may come, and taking the *sealed book,* be worthy to open it. For this is the one who, *opening the scriptures,* kindles the hearts of his disciples so that they ask, *Was not our heart burning within us when he opened to us the scriptures?* (Luke 24:32). Even now may he grant to open to us what it was that inspired his apostle to say: *But the Lord is the Spirit, and where the Spirit of the Lord is there is freedom* (2 Cor 3:17).

---

2. Instead of *mourning,* the LXX reads *a song.*

(9) Jerome

In the Apocalypse there is a book sealed with seven seals. If you would give this book to a person who knows how to read, he would say, **I cannot read it because it is sealed** (29:11). How many people are there today who consider themselves learned, yet the Scriptures are a sealed book to them. They cannot open it unless the one who *has the key of David, who opens and no one shall shut, who shuts and no one opens* (Rev 3:7), opens it. In the Acts of the Apostles the holy eunuch (or rather "man," as the Scripture calls him) who was reading Isaiah was asked by Philip: *Do you understand what you are reading?* He answered: *How can I unless someone guides me?* (Acts 8:30-31). I — if I may be permitted to speak of myself for a moment — am neither holier nor more diligent than this eunuch who came from Ethiopia, that is, from the ends of the world, on pilgrimage to the temple. He left the royal quarters and had such great love of divine things that he even read the Holy Scriptures while riding in his chariot. Nevertheless, though he held the book in his hand and was able to form the words of the Lord in his mind and speak them with his tongue and sound them with his lips, he did not know him whom — without knowing it — he worshiped in the book. Then Philip came and showed him Jesus, who was hidden beneath the letter. What an extraordinary teacher! The eunuch believed and was baptized in the same hour and became one of the faithful and a saint, no longer a disciple but a master.

(10) Theodoret of Cyrus

Here the prophet displays their disobedience, resistance, and lack of understanding. However, the divine text anticipates something else. Formerly neither the Jews nor the Gentiles were able to understand the prophecies concerning the Lord: the former because they were *veiled* (2 Cor 3:12-16) and locked under a **seal** (29:11), and the latter because they did not know the prophetic writings. However, after the Master's appearance, the **seals** were removed, and historical events confirmed the words of the prophets. Many Jews understood the meaning of the prophecies, and the Gentiles have understood the writings that speak of devotion to God and now read the Bible. For those who did not believe, however, it remains sealed.

It was the Lord himself who first removed the **seals** of the prophecy. When he entered the synagogue he took up the prophet Isaiah and read: *The Spirit of the Lord is upon me, because he has anointed me to preach good news to the poor. He has sent me to proclaim release to the captives and recovering of sight to the blind* and what follows. Then he adds: *Today this scripture has been fulfilled in your hearing* (Luke 4:18-21).

(11) Symeon the New Theologian

Things that are sealed and locked up, unseen and unknown by all men, only the Holy Spirit can open ... *God is Spirit* (John 4:24), invisible, immortal, inaccessible, ineffable.

He makes those who are born of him to be like the Father who brought them into being. Only their bodies may be seen and touched, but in other ways they are known to God alone and know only him; or, rather, they wish to be *known by God alone* (Gal 4:9) and strive always to behold him and long to be seen by him.

Put another way: just as the illiterate cannot read books as those who are literate can, so those who have refused to keep the commandments of Christ by practicing them will not one day — like those who have meditated on them, kept them, and shed their blood for them — be judged worthy to receive the revelation of the Holy Spirit. The person who takes a sealed and closed book cannot see what is written in it, nor can he understand its subject as long as **the book remains sealed** (29:11), even though he may have learned all the wisdom of the world. So it is that someone who . . . has learned all the divine Scriptures by heart will never be able to know and perceive the mystical and divine glory and power hidden in them without keeping all God's commandments and being helped by the Paraclete. The Paraclete will open to him the words as one opens a book, and will mystically show him the glory contained in them. Even more, along with the eternal life that makes them gush forth, he will reveal the good things of God hidden in them, things that are veiled and completely invisible to those who despise and neglect them.

29:13
They honor me with their lips, while their hearts are far from me.

(12) Irenaeus of Lyons

The Lord said: *The scribes and Pharisees sit on Moses' seat; so practice and observe what they tell you, but not what they do; for they preach, but do not practice. They bind heavy burdens, hard to bear, and lay them on men's shoulders, but they themselves will not move them with their finger* (Matt 23:2-4). He does not condemn the law of Moses. He urged that it be observed while Jerusalem was still standing. But he censured those who taught the law but were without love. For this reason they were unrighteous with respect to God and to their neighbors. As Isaiah said: **This people honors me with their lips, but their heart is far from me. In vain do they worship me, teaching human doctrines and precepts** (29:13). He does not call the law of Moses **human precepts**, but the traditions of the elders which they created. By upholding these they rejected the law of God, and for this reason did not submit to the Word. Here is what Paul wrote about this matter: *For, being ignorant of the righteousness that comes from God, and seeking to establish their own, they did not submit to God's righteousness. For Christ is the end of the law, that every one who has faith may be justified* (Rom 10:3-4).

(13) Origen of Alexandria

On one occasion [in his disputes with the Pharisees], when Jesus wished to meet the arguments of the Jews concerning the traditions of the elders with words from the prophets, he cited a passage from the book of Isaiah that reads as follows: **And the Lord said: These people draw near with their mouth, etc.** (29:13ff.). Matthew has not, however, written out the full text. Because this passage is cited in the Gospel, it should be interpreted to the best of our ability, and that means taking note of what precedes it. Only that way can we understand the section in the Gospel taken from the prophet.

Here then is the passage in Isaiah from its beginning: **Be faint and amazed, get a drunken headache — not from strong drink, nor from wine! Because the Lord has made you drink with a spirit of deep sleep; he will close their eyes and those of their prophets and of their rulers — the ones who see the hidden things. And all these sayings shall become for you like the words of this sealed book. If they give it to a learned man, saying, "Read these things," he will say, "I cannot read it, for it is sealed." And this book will be given into the hands of an unlearned man, and one will say to him, "Read this," and he will say, "I am not learned." The Lord said: These people draw near me,** and what follows down to the words, **Woe to those who make plans in secret, and their works will be in darkness** (29:9-15)!

I have taken the words in the Gospel and added to them some of the verses that come before and some which follow to show how the Word threatens to **close the eyes** of those people who are **amazed and have a drunken headache, and are drunk with a spirit of deep sleep**. He threatens also to blind the eyes of their prophets and their rulers who profess to see **what is secret**. That threat was realized, I think, after the coming of the Savior among that people. For all the words of the entire Scriptures, and in particular the book of Isaiah, have become for them like the **words of a sealed book**.

The expression **sealed book** is used of a book that has been locked in obscurity and does not become transparent. It is equally obscure to those who are unable to read at all because they do not know their letters, and to those who claim to know their letters but do not understand the meaning of what is written. For that reason he goes on to add this: when the people have become brutalized by their sins and maddened with rage against him, they will **become drunk with a spirit of deep sleep** which the Lord will make them to drink, so as to be unworthy to see. He will also **close the eyes of their prophets and of their rulers who claim to see the hidden things** of the mysteries in the divine Scriptures. And when their eyes are closed, the prophetic words shall be **sealed** to them and hidden. This will happen to the people who do not believe in Jesus as the Christ.

When the words of the prophets have become for them **like words of a sealed book**, not only to those who do not know how to read but also to those who claim to know, it was then that the Lord said that the people of the Jews **draw near to God with their mouth only**. He says that they **honor** him only **with their lips** because **their heart** out of unbelief is **far** from the Lord.

(14) Origen of Alexandria

Only those who fight on behalf of genuine religion are *the chosen race, the royal priesthood, the holy nation, God's own people* (1 Pet 2:9). The rest of humankind, when faced with the persecution of religious people, do not even make a show of willingness to die for their faith or to prefer death rather than deny their faith and live. And each one of those who wish to be members of the chosen race is convinced that at all times, when attacked by those who claim to be polytheists but are atheists in disguise, one must listen to God who says, *You shall have no other gods before me* (Exod 20:3) and *Make no mention of the names of other gods in your hearts, nor let such be heard out of your mouth* (Exod 23:13).

Moreover, such persons *believe in God with the heart to righteousness, and with the mouth make confession unto salvation* (Rom 10:10). They understand that they are not justified until they believe in God so firmly that their hearts remain unmoved and that they are not saved until their word corresponds to their inner conviction.

Those who suppose that it is enough to attain the *end* (cf. Rom 10:4; 1 Cor 1:8) in Christ by *believing in the heart to righteousness* (Rom 10:10), and not adding the words *confessing with the mouth to salvation,* deceive themselves. Indeed, I would go so far as to say that it is better **to honor God with the lips when the heart is far from God** (29:13) than to honor him with the heart and not *confess with the mouth to salvation* (Rom 10:10).

(15) Gregory of Nyssa

What is the meaning of this verse? That in the sight of God who hears the *sighs too deep for words* (Rom 8:26) the relation of the soul to the truth is more precious than pretty phrases. For words can be used in an opposite sense when the tongue is put at the service of the speaker's will. But the disposition of the soul is open to God, who knows all our secrets.

(16) Augustine of Hippo

The verse of the psalm, *be angry and sin not* (Ps 4:4), can signify penance. Turn your anger against yourself for your past misdeeds, and in the future sin no more. Speak out loud the things you say *in your hearts* (Ps 4:4). Hence the meaning of the psalm is: what you say aloud, echo also in your hearts, and do not be the kind of people described in the words: **With their lips they glorify me, but their heart is far from me** (29:13).

(17) Augustine of Hippo

Even though no one can escape from God who is everywhere present, there are people who are far from God. Otherwise scripture would not have said: **This people honors me with its lips, but its heart is far from me** (29:13). Being far from God does not mean being distant in location, but being unlike God. What would it mean to be unlike God? A bad life and corrupt morals. For if we draw near to God by living virtuously, we withdraw from God by our evil actions. The same person, while standing in the same place, may approach God by loving him or withdraw from him by loving sin. The feet make no move whatsoever, yet one is able to come near or to withdraw. The feet that carry us on this journey are our affections. Everything depends on our affections, on our love. The more we love the closer we are; the less we love the more distant we become. When we look at two things that are unlike, don't we often say: "This one is far removed from that one"? Or suppose we are comparing two people, or two horses, or two coats, and someone asserts: "This coat is very much like that one," or "this person resembles that one." What does someone say who does not agree? "Oh no, they are miles apart." What does that expression "miles apart" mean? It means: "This one is unlike the other." The two may be standing side by side, yet they are far apart. You might even find two wicked people, two of a kind as to their way of life and behavior. And even though one may be in the east and the other in the west, it is as though they are side by side. Or think about two just persons, one in the east, the other in the west. Though far distant from each other, they are close to one another because they are in God. But on the other hand, suppose one is just and the other wicked; then even if they are shackled with the same chain, they are a great distance from one another.

If, then, we move away from God by being unlike him, we also come close to him by being like him. What kind of likeness is this? It is being in the likeness in which we were created, which we spoiled by our sin, which we receive again when our sins are forgiven. This likeness is renewed in us inwardly in our minds. So the image of our God is engraved anew on the coin which is our soul so that we my return to his treasury.

(18) Gregory the Great

Since some people are faithful in confessing their faith but not in living the faith, this is what the voice of Truth says: *Not everyone who says to me, "Lord, Lord," shall enter the kingdom of heaven* (Matt 7:21). And he asks: *Why do you call me "Lord, Lord" and do not do what I tell you?* (Luke 6:46). Paul adds his voice: *They profess to know God, but they deny him by their deeds* (Tit 1:16). And John: *He who says "know him" but disobeys his commandments is a liar* (1 John 2:4). So it is that the Lord complains of his own ancient people: **This people honors me with their lips while their hearts are far from me** (29:13). So also the psalmist writes: *They flattered him with their mouths and lied to him with their tongues* (Ps 78:36). . . . Let no one then believe that faith without works suffices for him, for we know what is written: *Faith without works is dead* (Jas 2:20).

29:16
Will what is molded say to its molder, "Why have you made me thus?"

(19) Augustine of Hippo

The apostle poses a question for him as an objection when he says: *And so you say to me, "What complaint still remains? For who can resist his will?"* (Rom 9:19). Let us suppose that this objection is made to us. What else, then, ought we to answer but what the apostle answered? If such questions trouble us also, because we too are human beings, we ought all together to listen to him as he inquires, *Who are you, O human being, to answer back to God?* **Does the pot say to him who fashioned it, "Why did you make me that way?"** (29:16). *Or does the potter not have the power to make from the same lump of clay one vessel for honor and another for dishonor?* (Rom 9:20-21; cf. Isa 45:9).

If this lump were so positioned in the middle that, as it merited nothing good, so it merited nothing bad, it would seem with good reason to be an injustice that vessels were made from it for dishonor. But the whole lump fell into condemnation because of the one sin through the free choice of the first human being. Therefore, that vessels are made from it for honor is not due to its righteousness, because no righteousness preceded grace, but to the mercy of God. That a vessel is made for dishonor, however, is not to be attributed to the injustice of God — heaven forbid that there should be any injustice in God! — but to his judgment. Whoever holds this along with the Catholic Church does not argue against grace in favor of merits but sings to the Lord of his mercy and judgment (cf. Rom 11:33), so that he does not ungratefully reject his mercy or unjustly accuse his judgment.

Isaiah 35

1 Rejoice, O thirsty desert!
    Let the desert be glad
      and let it blossom like a lily!
2 And the deserts of the Jordan
    shall blossom and be glad.
    And the glory of Lebanon has been given to it,
      as well as the honor of Carmel;
    and my people shall see the glory of the Lord
      and the loftiness of God.

3 Be strong, you weak hands
    and feeble knees!
4 Give comfort,
    you who are faint of heart and mind!
    Be strong, do not fear!
    Look, our God is repaying judgment,
      yes, he will repay:
      he himself will come and save us.

5 Then the eyes of the blind shall be opened,
    and the ears of the deaf shall hear;
6 then the lame shall leap like a deer,
    and the tongue of stammerers shall be clear.
    Because water has broken forth in the wilderness,
      and a ravine in a thirsty land;
7 the dry place shall turn into marshlands,
    and in the thirsty land there shall be a spring of water;
    the joy of birds shall be there —
      a bed of reed and marshlands.

8 A pure way shall be there,
    and it shall be called a holy way;
  and the unclean shall not pass by there,
    nor shall be there an unclean way,
  but those who have been dispersed shall walk on it,
    and they shall not go astray.
9 And no lion shall be there,
    nor shall any of the evil beasts come up on it
  or be found there,
    but the redeemed shall walk on it.
10 And those gathered together because of the Lord shall return,
    and come to Sion with joy;
  everlasting joy shall be above their head;
    for upon their head shall be praise and gladness,
  and joy shall take hold of them —
    pain and sorrow and sighing have fled away.

According to the church fathers Isaiah 35 describes how all things are made new in Christ — creation is renewed, bodily ailments are healed, and believers are granted spiritual discernment. In the Septuagint 35:2 reads, **the deserts of the Jordan shall blossom,** *and this suggested that the passage is referring to Christ's baptism in the Jordan and the new life that blossomed through him. The verse* **the eyes of the blind shall be opened, and the ears of the deaf shall hear** *(35:5) refers to Christ's miracles, because he "healed every disease and bodily affliction" (Eusebius). But these words, according to the church fathers, can also refer to spiritual things, for those who know Christ perceive the true God, and, like those who are healed of diseases, glorify the God of Israel. Some commentators took note of the sentence,* **He will come and save us** *(35:4), and understood it to mean that we are saved "not by ourselves" but by God. The final verse,* **pain and sorrow and sighing have fled away** *(35:10), was taken to refer to the ultimate consummation of all things when Christ hands over the kingdom to the Father (1 Cor 15:24) and when "God will wipe away every tear from their eyes" (Rev 7:17).*

(1) The Gospel according to Matthew

"Go and tell John what you hear and see: the blind receive their sight and the lame walk, lepers are cleansed and the deaf hear, and the dead are raised up, and the poor have good news preached to them. And blessed is he who takes no offense at me."

(2) Eusebius of Caesarea

The Word says that new plants **shall blossom** (35:1). There will be beautiful flowers, as it is said in the Song of Songs, *flowers appear on the earth* (Song 2:12), *the mandrakes give forth fragrance* (Song 7:13). The text explains which particular **desert** (35:1) is meant when

Isaiah 35

it says, **the desert places of the Jordan shall be glad** (35:2). The gospel confirms this, for *in the river Jordan* (Matt 3:6) John first proclaimed the kingdom of heaven. Because worship according to the Mosaic law was no longer to be practiced in Jerusalem, the prophet announces the baptism of repentance and the washing of rebirth. When our Savior and Lord, Jesus the Christ of God, was baptized by John in the Jordan, he ratified the preaching of John and confirmed the sacrament of rebirth in his own person. And the **desert** that formerly was waterless and barren has become the Church of God through the rite of purification and the washing of rebirth in the **Jordan**, and she baptizes and proclaims the kingdom of God. The Church of God, which once was a desert, observes the practice of Baptism throughout the whole world. Therefore the Word exhorts her to rejoice and **be glad**, and to **blossom** like the fragrant **lily** (35:1).

To the Church also has been given the **glory of Lebanon** and the **majesty of Carmel** (35:2). Earlier texts indicated that **Lebanon** is the altar of sacrifice and the temple in which *the sacrifices with their lebanon*[1] (i.e., frankincense; Lev 6:15) and offerings were made according to the law. As for **Carmel**, this has often been construed symbolically as the people of the circumcision. It is prophesied that the **majesty** that belonged to the ancient people and the **glory** of the temple in Jerusalem are to be given to the **desert** of old, I mean the church of the Gentiles. Then the text says, **my people**, that is, no longer Israel, but **my people shall see the glory of the Lord** (35:2). This promise is made to the new people, inasmuch as they will receive the first coming of the Savior. Moreover, they **shall see** his second and glorious appearance and will behold his **majesty**.

Next the prophet proclaims that the passions of the soul will be changed by the illumination of the Savior: **Strengthen the weak hands, and make firm the feeble knees** (35:3). Symmachus translated this: **Be strong, slack hands and weak knees; be resolute, tell the uncomprehending, "Be strong, do not fear."** Aquila and Theodotion both translated this similarly, namely, that the text encourages the Savior's disciples and apostles to **strengthen the weak** souls among the Gentiles and to **support the knees** of those who have grown shaky. But the Word also enjoins them to address those who once had a fearful heart with the words, **Be strong, do not fear!** (35:4). For even if persecutors make threats, provoke fear, and inflict pain and torture, you who once were **of a fearful heart** ought not to **fear**, since you possess strength and power, having **your God** (35:4) with you for all time. Hence according to Symmachus's translation the text reads: **Do not be afraid. Behold, your God, the vengeance of retribution, shall come; the Lord himself shall come and save you.** When you have been instructed in this fashion, you who once had **a fearful heart, be strong,** and **fear not** (35:4).

Having predicted these things and plainly announced God's coming, the text also adds signs and evidence of his deeds, saying, **Then the eyes of the blind shall be opened, and the ears of the deaf shall hear; then the lame man shall leap like a deer, and the tongue of the stammerers speak clearly** (35:5-6). This was manifestly fulfilled at the time of the coming of our Savior Jesus Christ (cf. Matt 11:2-5; Luke 7:18-23), when the things mentioned here came to pass, and he healed every disease and bodily affliction by his divine power. However, Christ healed not only the body; his teaching also

---

1. *Lebanon* is a Greek word for "frankincense."

healed the illnesses of the soul. Even now, throughout the whole world and among every nation, those who through hardness of heart and blindness once marveled at lifeless and immobile statues as though they were gods have had the eye of their souls illuminated by his light and their sight restored. Now they spurn their ancestral superstitions and acknowledge the one true God alone. And those who once neither heard nor heeded the divine Scriptures have, by his grace, been instructed in the inspired sayings, and those who were hobbled in the spiritual life have **leapt like a deer** (35:6) when they made the teachings of the Scriptures their own. These are the ones whom the prophecy in the previous chapter had compared to a **deer**. And the **tongue of the stammerers** (35:6), which Satan had bound (cf. Luke 13:16) to keep them from confessing the true God, has learned to speak **clearly** (35:6) and coherently. One might even say that the **stammerers** among the wise men of this age (cf. 1 Cor 1:20) have dared to think and speak the truth about God.

At the time the vision of this prophecy was fulfilled, **waters shall break forth in the ancient desert** (35:6). Now this water is the water of the Jordan, about which it had just been said, **the desert places of the Jordan shall be glad** (35:2). This symbolizes the washing of rebirth and the sacrament of the New Covenant; as for the **streams** (35:6), they represent the evangelical words of the Savior. . . .

The text says: **And a pure way shall be there, and it shall be called the Holy Way** (35:8). This refers to the way that leads to the thrice-blessed heavenly city of God (cf. Heb 12:22), which the Savior built when he said, *I am the Way* (John 14:6). The salvific Word, who leads those making their way to the Father and directs them to the kingdom of God, prophesies that besides other good things, it will be granted to the desert that **the unclean shall not pass** (35:8) by this way. It further says that **the dispersed shall walk on it** (35:8). Who would those be if not people in ancient times who had wandered away from God and strayed from the truth? Now they are once again on the move, and once they have found the good and true path, they will travel on it.

And **no lion shall be there** (35:9), that is, on the way just mentioned, nor shall any evil beast come up on it or be found there (35:9). For since he said, *I am the Way* (John 14:6), how could anything evil be found there? Nor will *the way of a serpent on a rock* be found there, according to Solomon (Prov 30:19). For it says, **the redeemed shall walk there** (35:9), whom he himself has *ransomed*[2] *by the price of his own blood* (1 Pet 1:18-19), and **those who have been gathered by the Lord shall walk on it**.[3] Neither through the prophet nor through any human zeal, but through the Lord himself, **the redeemed and those who have been gathered shall walk** on this way. On it they will come at last to the thrice-blessed *heavenly Zion,* concerning which the apostle says, We *have come to Mount Zion and to the city of the living God, the heavenly Jerusalem* (Heb 12:22). Therefore it is said, They shall **come to Zion with joy** (35:10). No one wishes to arrive at the Zion of which it is said, *a year of recompense of judgment of Zion, and her streams shall be turned*

---

2. This same word, which can be translated either "redeemed" or "ransomed," is used both in 35:9 and in 1 Pet 1:18.

3. Eusebius's text inserts the clause **those who have been gathered by the Lord** between **the redeemed** and **shall walk there.**

into pitch (34:8-9). Therefore it is necessary to distinguish different Zions though they bear the same name. First there is the earthly one, which is subjected to threats, and second the heavenly, to which **the redeemed and those who have been gathered by the Lord shall come** (35:10), about whom it is said, **Everlasting joy shall be upon their heads** (35:10). For those who have become victors in the great struggle will be wrapped with a crown of joy, as the apostle plainly uttered: *There is laid up for me the crown of righteousness* (2 Tim 4:8). Therefore it was said, **Everlasting joy shall be upon their heads**, and again, **Joy will take hold of them**, that is, of those who proceed without deviating on the way of salvation and by it arrive at the thrice-blessed goal. For those who are worthy of the crown shall enjoy eternal life in the kingdom of heaven, and **sorrow and sighing shall flee away** (35:10).

35:1-2
The wilderness and the dry land shall be glad.

(3) Theodoret of Cyrus

The wilderness and the dry land shall be glad, the desert shall rejoice and blossom; like the crocus it shall blossom abundantly, and rejoice with joy and singing. The glory of Lebanon shall be given to it, the majesty of Carmel and Sharon (35:1-2). He calls the wilderness **thirsty** (35:1) because it had not received the prophetic watering, and a **desert** (35:1) because it had not been cultivated by God. He exhorts it to **blossom like the lily** (35:1). The **bloom of the lily** is a figure of the purity that comes about in Baptism through the Holy Spirit. The prophet announces that the desert will **bloom** because it has been irrigated by the streams **of the Jordan**. For it was these streams that first received the grace of the Holy Spirit, and the words of the text are a foreshadowing of Holy Baptism. The prophet further says that **the glory of Lebanon** and **the majesty of Carmel** will be transferred to the **desert**. Judea is often called **Carmel**, for of old she had received the testimony of the prophets. The Scripture also calls Jerusalem **Lebanon**: *A great eagle with great wings and long pinions came to Lebanon and took the top of the cedar* (Ezek 17:3). Here Lebanon is Jerusalem, Babylon the eagle, and the top of the cedar the heir of the kingdom (cf. Ezek 17:12).

(4) Gregory of Nyssa

What shall we make of that oracle of Isaiah, which cries to the wilderness: **The wilderness and the thirsty land shall be glad, the desert shall rejoice and blossom like the lily; and the desert places of the Jordan shall blossom and rejoice** (35:1-2)? It is clear that good tidings of joy were not spoken to a lifeless object. He figuratively addresses, as though to the desert, the soul that is thirsty and without provisions, just as David also said, *My soul thirsts for thee like a parched land* (Ps 143:6) and *My soul thirsts for God, for the strong living God* (Ps 42:2). So also the Lord declares in the gospels: *If anyone thirsts,* *let him come to me and drink* (John 7:37). To the woman of Samaria he added: *Every one who drinks of this water will thirst again, but whoever drinks of the water that I shall give him will never thirst* (John 4:13-14).

35:3-4
He will come and save you.

(5) Irenaeus of Lyons

The Lord himself who is *Immanuel* from the *virgin* (7:14) is the sign of our salvation, since it was the Lord himself who saved us. We were not able to save ourselves. Hence when St. Paul speaks of human weakness he says: *For I know that nothing good dwells within me, that is, in my flesh* (Rom 7:18), indicating that the *good* of our salvation is not from us but from God. And again: *Wretched man that I am! Who will deliver me from this body of death?* (Rom 7:24). Then he introduces the deliverer: *Thanks be to God through Jesus Christ our Lord!* (Rom 7:25). Isaiah declares this as well: **Strengthen the weak hands, and make firm the feeble knees. Say to those who are of a fearful heart, "Be strong, fear not! Behold, your God will come with vengeance, with the recompense of God. He will come and save you"** (35:3-4). In this we see that we are saved not by ourselves but by the help of God.

(6) Augustine of Hippo

This text, **He will come and save you** (35:4), hints at a great and significant mystery. Christ was going to come in the flesh — not just anyone, not an angel, not an ambassador, but **He will come and save you**. It wasn't just anybody who was going to come. Yet how was he going to come? He was going to be born in mortal flesh, to be a tiny infant, to be laid in a manger, wrapped in cradle clothes, nourished on milk; he was going to grow up, and finally even to be put to death. So in all these marks of humility there is indeed a pattern of extreme humility. Who is showing this humility? Someone very exalted. How exalted? Don't inquire on earth; soar even beyond the stars. When you reach the heavenly host of angels, you will hear from them, "Go beyond us too." When you reach the *thrones or dominions or principalities or authorities* (Col 1:16), you will hear, "Go beyond us too; we too have been made." *All things were made through him* (John 1:3). Soar beyond the whole of creation. Whatever has been made, whatever has been set up, whatever is changeable, whether with or without a body, soar beyond it all. You cannot yet do it by seeing. Soar on the wings of faith; arrive at the Creator. With faith going ahead of you, arrive where it is leading you; arrive at the Creator.

Isaiah 35

35:5-6
Then the eyes of the blind shall be opened.

(7) Leo the Great

When *in Christ God was reconciling the world to himself* (2 Cor 5:19), when the Creator himself was wearing the creature which was to be restored to the image of the Creator, and when the divinely miraculous works had been accomplished as the spirit of prophecy had once predicted, **Then the eyes of the blind shall be opened, and the ears of the deaf unstopped; then shall the lame man leap like a deer, and the tongue of the dumb speak clearly** (35:5-6).

35:6
Then the lame shall leap like a deer.

(8) Origen of Alexandria

When one sees the transformations that have come about among those who have come into the Church, one might say that those who were formerly **dumb** learned to speak the Word of God, and the **lame** learned to walk. For the prophecy of Isaiah was fulfilled not only in physical matters but also in spiritual things. **Then shall the lame man leap like a deer, and the tongue of the dumb speak clearly** (35:6). Unless the expression, **shall the lame man leap like a deer,** is accidental, we would say that those who were formerly lame and now through the power of Jesus **leap like a deer** are with good reason compared to a deer. The **deer** is a clean animal and hostile to serpents and cannot be injured by their venom. And because the **dumb** learned to speak, the words are fulfilled that say: **And the tongue of the dumb speak clearly.**

Also the words, *Hear, you deaf* (42:18), were fulfilled, as well as those addressed to the blind: *Look, you blind, that you may see!* (42:18). Now the blind see when they look at the world, see the great beauty of the things that were created, and are lifted up to behold the Creator. When they behold that *since the creation of the world his invisible nature has been clearly perceived in the things that have been made* (Rom 1:20), they see clearly and perceive with understanding. When the multitudes beheld these things, *they glorified the God of Israel* (Matt 15:31). They glorify him because they are convinced that he is the one God. For he is not the God of the Jews only but also of the nations. Let us then go up to the mountain where Jesus has established his Church and bring those who wish to go up with us, the **deaf**, the **blind**, the **lame**, the maimed, and many others, and cast them at the feet of Jesus that he may heal them. Then the multitudes will be astonished.

(9) Cyril of Jerusalem

In the power of the Holy Spirit *Peter and John went up to the temple at the hour of prayer, the ninth hour* (Acts 3:1), and in the name of Jesus they healed the man at the Beautiful Gate who had been lame from his mother's womb for forty years, that what was spoken by the prophet might be fulfilled: **Then shall the lame man leap like a deer** (35:6).

35:8
A pure way shall be there, and it shall be called a holy way.

(10) Cyril of Alexandria

The prophet calls life lived according to the power of the gospel a **pure way** (35:8). The phrase can also signify the purification that comes through the Holy Spirit. For the Spirit removes the stain that had penetrated the souls of men, forgives our transgressions, and makes us clean. The **way** then is **holy** (35:8) and **pure** and for that reason is said to be inaccessible to those who are not yet cleansed. Only those who have been made rich through the cleansing of Holy Baptism are able to live according to the gospel.

No lion shall be there, nor shall any other evil beast come on it (35:9), that is, on the **pure way**. Once the inventor of sin, like a wild beast, preyed on human beings by afflicting them with evil spirits. His power, however, was stripped from him by Christ, he was driven away from the flock of believers, and his oppressive regime was dismantled. On this **pure way** they **walk** (35:9), they who have been **redeemed** (35:9) by Christ and who **have been gathered** through faith into a spiritual bond. For they have abandoned the old path, and they have turned off and arrived at Zion, the Church where they find **everlasting joy** (35:10) on earth and in heaven. For they sing praise to the God who saves. There will be **joy and gladness** (35:10), and in Christ all their yearnings will be satisfied and they will know nothing of **sorrow and sighing** (35:10). Those who have been called to such a glorious hope will inherit eternal life, possess splendor from on high, and rule with Christ. How can they have any part in grief? What will there be to grieve over? They will rejoice and enjoy all good things, for the one God will scatter and destroy the **evil beasts** (35:9).

35:10
Pain and sorrow and sighing have fled away.

(11) Tertullian

Everlasting joy, says Isaiah, **shall be upon their heads** (35:10). There is nothing **everlasting** until after the resurrection. **And sorrow and sighing**, he continues, **shall flee away** (35:10). The angel echoes the same to John: *And God will wipe away every tear from their eyes* (Rev 7:17), that is to say, from the same eyes that formerly wept and might one day weep again if God's compassion did not dry up every tear that flows. And again: *God will wipe away every tear from their eyes, and death shall be no more* (Rev 21:4). And there will no longer be corruption, because it has been driven away by incorruption as death is driven away by immortality. If **sorrow and sighing** and mourning and death itself assault us with afflictions of soul and body, how shall they be removed except by removing the things that cause them, namely, the afflictions of soul and body? Will there be adversities in the presence of God? Or attacks of the enemy when you are close to Christ? Will the devil assail you when the Holy Spirit is near and the devil with his angels *is cast into the lake of fire* (Rev 20:10)? Where will be necessity, or fortune or fate? What plague will harm those who after being raised have been pardoned? Or what wrath for those reconciled to God after grace? What weakness after strength, or infirmity after being made whole?

(12) John Chrysostom

When the prophet says, **sorrow and sighing shall flee away** (35:10), he is speaking of the place where there will be great joy, peace, love, delight, and mirth; where there is eternal life, unspeakable glory, and inexpressible beauty; where there are eternal tabernacles and the untold splendor of the King and those good things which *no eye has seen, nor ear heard, nor the heart of man conceived* (1 Cor 2:9; Isa 64:4); where there are spiritual bedchambers and celestial apartments (cf. John 14:2); where there are virgins bearing bright lamps (Matt 25:1-3) and guests in wedding garments (Matt 22:11-13); where many are the possessions of our Lord (cf. Matt 3:17) and the storehouses of the King.

(13) Augustine of Hippo

When *he has handed over the kingdom to God and the Father* (1 Cor 15:24), that is, when he has brought those who believe and live by faith, for whom he now makes intercession as mediator (Rom 8:34), to that contemplation which we are sighing and yearning to attain (Rom 8:23, 26), and when **weariness and weeping are at an end** (35:10), then he will no longer intercede for us to God and the Father since he has handed over the kingdom. He said as much in the words: *These things have I spoken to you in comparisons; the hour will come when I shall speak to you in comparisons no more, but shall tell you openly about the Father* (John 16:25), that is, there will be no more comparison when there is direct vision face to face. That is what he means by *I shall tell you openly about the Father*, as though to say, "I shall show you the Father openly." He uses the word *tell*, presumably, because he is the Word. He goes on to say, *In that day you will ask in my name, and I do not say that I will beg the Father for you, for the Father himself loves you, because you love me and have believed that I come forth from the Father and have come into this world; again, I am leaving the world and going to the Father* (John 16:26-28).

(14) Augustine of Hippo

Hope is necessary for us in our exile from God; it consoles us on the journey. When the traveler finds walking on the road wearisome, he puts up with the fatigue precisely because he hopes to arrive. Rob him of any hope of arriving, and straightaway his strength for walking is broken. So also the hope which we have here is appropriate to those who are in exile and on a journey. Listen to the apostle himself: *We groan inwardly as we wait for adoption as sons* (Rom 8:23). Where there is still groaning, we cannot yet say there is the bliss of which Scripture says, **Sorrow and groaning**[4] **shall flee away** (35:10).

---

4. This word can be translated as either "groaning" or "sighing." The words in the Latin text for groaning in 35:10 and Rom 8:23 are cognates, and this led Augustine to refer to the Romans passage.

Isaiah 40

1 Comfort, O comfort my people,
    says God.
2 O priests, speak to the heart of Ierousalem,
    comfort her,
because her humiliation has been fulfilled,
    her sin has been done away with;
because she has received from the Lord's hand
    double that of her sins.

3 A voice of one crying out in the wilderness:
    "Prepare the way of the Lord,
    make straight the paths of our God.
4 Every valley shall be filled up,
    and every mountain and hill be made low;
all the crooked ways shall become straight,
    and the rough place smooth ways.
5 Then the glory of the Lord shall appear,
    and all flesh shall see the salvation of God,
    because the Lord has spoken."

6 A voice of one saying, "Cry out!"
    And I said, "What shall I cry?"
All flesh is grass,
    all the glory of man is like the flower of grass.
7 The grass has withered, and the flower has fallen,
8   but the word of our God remains forever.
9 Go up on a high mountain,
    you who bring good tidings to Sion;
lift up your voice with strength,
    you who bring good tidings to Ierousalem,

> lift it up, do not fear;
> say to the cities of Ioudas,
> > "See, your God!"
> 10 See, the Lord comes with strength,
> > and his arm with authority;
> > see, his reward is with him,
> > and his work before him.
> 11 He will tend his flock like a shepherd,
> > and gather lambs with his arm,
> > and comfort those that are with young.
> 12 Who has measured the water with his hand,
> > and heaven with a span,
> > and all the earth by handful?
> > Who has weighed the mountains with a scale,
> > and the forests with a balance?
> 13 Who has known the mind of the Lord,
> > and who has been his counselor to instruct him?
> 14 Or with whom did he consult, and he instructed him?
> > > Or who showed him judgment?
> > > Or who showed him the way of understanding?
> 15 If all the nations have been accounted as a drop from a jar
> > and as the sinking of a balance,
> > they will also be accounted as spittle.
> 16 Lebanon is not enough for burning,
> > nor are all the quadrupeds enough for a burnt offering.
> 17 And all the nations are as nothing,
> > and they have been accounted as nothing.

> 18 To whom have you likened the Lord,
> > or with what likeness have you likened him?
> 19 Has an artisan made an image,
> > or has a goldsmith, after casting gold,
> > gilded it — prepared a likeness of it?
> 20 For an artisan chooses wood that will not rot,
> > then inquires wisely how he should set up his image
> > and what to do so that it will not topple.

> 21 Will you not know? Will you not hear?
> > Has it not been declared to you from the beginning?
> > Have you not known the foundations of the earth?
> 22 It is he who holds the circle of the earth,
> > and those who dwell in it are like grasshoppers;
> > who has set up heaven like a vault,
> > and stretched it out like a tent to live in;

Isaiah 40

23 who has appointed rulers to rule for naught,
   and has made the earth as nothing.

24 For they will not sow, nor will they plant,
   neither will their root take root in the earth;
  he blew upon them, and they withered,
   and a tempest will carry them off like brushwood.

25 Now therefore to whom did you liken me
   and will I be made equal? said the Holy One.
26 Look up on high with your eyes and see:
   Who has exhibited all these?
  He who brings out his ornamentation by number;
   he will call them all by name;
  because of abundant glory
   and by might of strength,
   nothing has escaped you.

27 For do not say, O Iakob,
   and why have you spoken, O Israel,
  "My way was hidden from God,
   and my God has taken away my judgment and has withdrawn"?
28 And now, have you not known? Have you not heard?
  God everlasting,
   God who prepared the ends of the earth,
  will not hunger or grow weary —
   nor is there searching of his understanding —
29 giving strength to those who hunger
   and sorrow to those who are not grieving.
30 For youths will hunger,
   and the young will be weary,
   and the chosen will be powerless;
31 but those who wait for God shall change their strength,
   they shall grow wings like eagles,
  they shall run and not be weary,
   they shall walk and not hunger.

Chapter 40 of Isaiah introduces a different literary style and assumes a different historical context from the earlier chapters. Modern biblical scholars presume that this and succeeding chapters must have been written by someone other than the prophet Isaiah, who lived in the eighth century B.C. Chapters 40–55 are usually regarded as a distinct unit and the product of a single author. This anonymous figure is conventionally given the name of "Second Isaiah," and he lived, it is supposed, near the end of the Babylonian exile in the sixth century B.C.

The church fathers also recognized that this section of Isaiah differs from what went be-

fore. Eusebius says that it introduces a new subject matter, and Cyril of Alexandria says that the prophet now shifts to the time of Christ. The history of Hezekiah's reign is now left behind, and the prophetic text envisions a more expansive historical horizon. The remaining twenty-seven chapters of the book of Isaiah contain some of the most quoted and beloved passages in the Old Testament. In the gospels the mission of John the Baptizer, the "forerunner," was seen as announced in Isaiah's cry to prepare the way of the Lord (40:3). Many other events in the gospels were regarded as heralded in Isaiah 40–66. These chapters also became the occasion to reflect on the otherness and transcendence of God (i.e., to contrast God's eternity with the finitude of human beings who are **grass that withers** [40:6]), on the Church's universal mission, and on the eschatological consummation of history. Hilary takes **Who has measured the earth with the palm of his hand?** (40:12) as complementary to "I am that I am" (Exod 3:14), while Exodus depicts God as "existence" (esse), Isaiah emphasizes God's infinite power. Following St. Paul (Rom 11:33-36), Basil and Chrysostom take **Who has known the mind of the Lord?** (40:13) to refer to Christ.

(1) The Gospel according to St. Luke

In the fifteenth year of the reign of Tiberius Caesar, Pontius Pilate being governor of Judea, and Herod being tetrarch of Galilee, and his brother Philip tetrarch of the region of Ituraea and Trachonitis, and Lysanias tetrarch of Abilene, in the high priesthood of Annas and Caiaphas, the word of God came to John the son of Zechariah in the wilderness; and he went into all the region about the Jordan, preaching a baptism of repentance for the forgiveness of sins. As it is written in the book of the words of Isaiah the prophet: **The voice of one crying in the wilderness: Prepare the way of the Lord, make his paths straight. Every valley shall be filled, and every mountain and hill shall be brought low, and the crooked shall be made straight, and the rough ways shall be made smooth; and all flesh shall see the salvation of God** (40:3-5).

(2) The Letter of Paul to the Romans

O the depth of the riches and wisdom and knowledge of God! How unsearchable are his judgments and how inscrutable his ways! **For who has known the mind of the Lord, or who has been his counselor?** (40:13). Or who has given a gift to him that he might be repaid? (Job 35:7) For from him and through him and to him are all things. To him be glory forever. Amen.

(3) The First Letter of Peter

Having purified your souls by your obedience to the truth for a sincere love of the brethren, love one another earnestly from the heart. You have been born anew, not of perishable seed but of imperishable, through the living and abiding word of God; for **All flesh is like grass, and all its glory like the flower of grass. The grass withers, and the flower**

fails, but the word of the Lord abides forever (40:6-8). That word is the good news which was preached to you.

(4) Cyril of Alexandria

The word of the prophet now shifts to the time of Christ, and makes an explicit prophecy of the grace that comes from him. This is neither inappropriate nor anachronistic. Admittedly, less highly trained readers of Scripture may ask why the prophet uses the words of Hezekiah to make a prediction about Christ that has to do with us. We offer the following explanation: now that he has given an account of the last conquest of the land of the Jews and of the residents of Jerusalem (ch. 39), in a timely way the word of the prophet begins to discuss the **comfort** (40:1) that comes from God.

Let me briefly clarify this. There had been any number of attacks against Jerusalem, and the land of the Jews had often been laid waste at the hand of the Assyrians and other barbarian neighbors of theirs. The most recent conquest had been carried out by Nebuchadnezzar during the reign of Jechoniah, when Israel was led off captive to the land of her conquerors. She was released from captivity during the reign of Cyrus, returned to Judea, rebuilt the temple, and dwelt there without being dispersed until our Savior's advent.

After the last conquest, when the Babylonians took all the wealth of the kings of Judah and returned to their own land, the text speaks of the spiritual **comfort** that would be given later with the coming of Christ. Those who serve the holy gospel are urged to say, **Comfort, comfort my people, says God** (40:1). Now the **comfort** that brings salvation came about through Christ and was first extended to the people of Israel, as his own words say plainly: *I was sent only to the lost sheep of the house of Israel* (Matt 15:24). Therefore the text says, **O priests,**[1] O ministers of the temple and Christ's words, **speak to the heart of Jerusalem** (40:2), that is, give an appropriate word of **comfort** to the listeners. For the law laid a burden on everyone by teaching through shadows and types. It did not bring its listeners what is essential for the education of mind and heart; it presented only a kind of external knowledge of the mere words, and that with difficulty. But now the saving gospel has been proclaimed, and the Holy Spirit has shown the law's deeper meaning and introduced a spiritual understanding. For it was the Holy Spirit who implanted words in the saints and burned them into the innermost recesses of their minds. For example, David the psalmist said: *I have hidden your words in my heart, that I might not sin against you* (Ps 119:11). The Savior also said to his holy apostles: *Put the word in your hearts* (Luke 9:44; 21:14), which refers to the saving word that comes from him.

When the gospel is preached to the mind and the heart, by the cooperation of the Holy Spirit, indeed with the Spirit doing everything whatsoever, faith will follow, according to the Sacred Scriptures. For God says through one of his holy prophets, *Behold, the days are coming, says the* LORD, *when I will make a new covenant with the house of Israel and the house of Judah, not like the covenant which I made with their fathers when I took*

---

1. The LXX of 40:1 adds **O priests** to the Hebrew.

them by the hand to bring them out of the land of Egypt, my covenant which they broke, and I disregarded them, says the LORD. *But this is the covenant which I will make with the house of Israel after those days, says the* LORD: *I will put my law within them, and I will write it upon their hearts* (Jer 31:31-33). And St. Paul writes to his readers, *You yourselves are our letter, known and read by all men; and you show that you are a letter from Christ delivered by us, written not with ink but with the Spirit of the living God, not on tablets of stone but on tablets of human hearts* (2 Cor 3:2, 3).

Comfort them (40:3). What do these words mean? That God's wrath toward them has ceased. **Because her humiliation has been fulfilled** (40:2). He says that she has been humbled sufficiently, and her sin has been pardoned. **That she has received from the Lord's hand double that of her sins** (40:2). Does this mean that God punished beyond what was necessary, and imposed penalties disproportionate to the crime, in fact twice as great? How is that to be understood? How can it be reconciled with the text that says, *The Lord shall not impose punishment twice on the same one in affliction* (Nah 1:9 LXX)? How, then, are we to understand these words of Isaiah? Consider the case of a father who loves his children and is very compassionate. After he has punished his son, he becomes rather sorrowful because he thinks the punishment was excessive. He feels that way, of course, because he loves his children dearly. Because he is a father his affection for them is very deep. In the same way, the text says, **she has received from the Lord's hand double that of her sins**: though Jerusalem had been charged with grave and intolerable deeds, she is not punished in proportion to what she had done. *The Lord is merciful and gracious, slow to anger and abounding in steadfast love. He does not deal with us according to our sins, nor requite us according to our iniquities* (Ps 103:8, 10).

A voice of one crying out in the wilderness: "Prepare the way of the Lord, make straight the paths of our God . . ." (40:3-5).

The prophet has said that Israel has been redeemed, Jerusalem has been pardoned for her **sins**, and she will be **comforted** (40:1-3). Now, on the heels of what has just been said, he brings to light the time of **comfort**, the coming of our Savior, whose forerunner, the inspired John the Baptist, appeared in the desert of Judea and cried out, saying, **Prepare the way of the Lord, make straight a highway for our God** (Mark 1:3 and parallels; Isa 40:3). The blessed Zechariah, who was the father of John, had also foreseen this in the Spirit and prophesied, *And you, child, will be called a prophet of the Most High; for you will go before the Lord to prepare his ways* (Luke 1:76). And the Savior said about him, *He was a burning and shining lamp, and you were willing to rejoice for a while in his light* (John 5:35). Now Christ is the *sun of righteousness* (Mal 4:2) and the true light, but the Holy Scripture compares the blessed Baptist to a lamp. In comparison to the divine light and its transcendent brightness, the human mind, though it be filled with light and wisdom, may well be likened to a mere lamp.

What does it mean to order, **Prepare the way of the Lord**, and why must **his paths be made straight**? He explains this when he says: **Every valley shall be filled up, and every mountain and hill be made low; the crooked ways shall become straight, and the rough places plain** (40:4). By the Spirit's power this has happened spiritually. In ancient times the evangelical way of life was not yet known, and many struggled to live virtuous lives. Their minds were dominated by worldly desires and subverted by alien movements of the flesh. But when the Word became man — that is, flesh — he destroyed sin in the flesh and overthrew *the principalities and powers* (Col 2:15) and the cosmic rulers of this world. He showed us a smooth and well-traveled way to piety that is neither steep nor hilly nor precipitous, but level like a plain. All the curves have been made straight. Not only this, but also **the glory of the Lord shall be revealed, and all flesh shall see the salvation of our God, because the Lord has spoken** (40:5). He was the only-begotten Word of God, inasmuch as he existed as God and was begotten ineffably of God the Father, in the majesty of the godhead, *above all rule and authority and power and dominion, and above every name that is named, not only in this age but in that which is to come* (Eph 1:21). He himself is the Lord of Glory. Though in ancient times we did not know him, now we have come to know him and see his glory. But when he became a man like us, he showed himself to us by sojourning among us. At the same time, in power, actions, and glory he was equal to God the Father, sustaining all things through the word of his power, performing miracles with ease, reproving creation, raising the dead, and working the rest of his marvels effortlessly. **The glory of the Lord**, then, **has been revealed**, and **all flesh has seen the salvation of God** (40:5; cf. Luke 3:6), that is, the salvation of the Father. For he sent his Son from heaven to be our savior and redeemer. Since the law brought nothing to perfection, and the ancient sacrifices were "types" that could not wipe away sin, we are made perfect in Christ, and, now that the stain of sin is removed, we have been honored with the spirit of adoption.

It was God's intention that the grace revealed in Christ was to come upon **all flesh** (40:1), that is, everyone, for the term **flesh** signifies humanity. However, if some human beings should seem to have no share in salvation, the prophet's word would not be falsified. For God honored us by desiring our salvation; he did not wish that his will be frustrated by the indifference of those who have been called. The prophet rightly adds, **the Lord has spoken** (40:5), so that nobody should think that he is simply stating his own opinion or perhaps just blurting out what occurs to him. To the contrary: he has announced ahead of time God's intention and what will surely take place in the future.

For those who truly love God there is no other way to attain the salvation offered by God than to think and do what is precious and pleasing to him. Those who wish to live in accord with their high calling must live a holy and virtuous way of life, adorning themselves with the glorious deeds of Christ's example as with a crown. They must despise the temptations of this life and spurn the pomp and circumstance of this transitory state. For the works of human beings are no more than **grass** (40:6) and stubble. Those who love God must make a dwelling place for the **Word of God** (40:8), that is, the Logos of God the Father, in their minds and hearts, for he dwells in our hearts by faith. When we have been endowed with the Holy Spirit, we are able to possess him within ourselves. This is the great treasure that leads to eternal life. The living Word of God, who preserves life and gives life, abides forever. And those who obey God's command will reap a great reward, everlasting life: *Truly, truly, I say to you, if any one keeps my word, he will never see death* (John 8:51).

The passage that begins, **Go up on a high mountain, you who bring good tidings to Sion** (40:9-11), is directed to the ministers of the life-giving proclamation, not just to the holy apostles and the evangelists but to the whole company of those who throughout history have presided over their flocks and guided the spiritual life of the faithful. It tells them how they can become lovers of God, speak out clearly, and share in the God's supreme glory. How can one proclaim the glory and salvation of God to the whole world timidly and cautiously and be hidden from sight? One should be lifted up and visible to all, on a mountaintop, and speak boldly with a clear and confident voice. This the inspired disciples earnestly wished when they beseeched the God who governs the universe: *And now, Lord, look upon their threats and grant to thy servants to speak thy word with all boldness* (Acts 4:29). **Lift it up, do not fear**, the prophet urges. **Say to the cities of Judah, "Here is your God!" See, the Lord comes with strength, and his arm with authority** (40:9-10).

By adding the sentence **See, the Lord comes with strength**, the prophet indicates that the hope of Christ's coming will soon be fulfilled. Though he is not yet present, the Redeemer will come soon, indeed he is already at the door. For the prophet has, as it were, told them to stretch out their hands and point to the promised one. But he does not come like one of the prophets, nor like a suppliant; he will come with commanding authority, power, and divine sovereignty, as the text indicates: **He comes with strength, and his arm with authority** (40:10).

The inspired prophets prayed for someone to come who was from God and, at the same time, from among the people. When the Savior and Lord of the universe came, he did not offer prayers of supplication as though he needed to receive something. Rather, like a true Son, he apportioned the Father's gifts with a dignity befitting a free person. He gave gifts to those who believe in him, and accomplished everything by his own power and authority. Though Christ came for our sake and endured death on the cross for us, the mystery of God's eternal plan also bore fruit for him. For the text says: **His reward is with him, and his work before him** (40:10). And he names as his **reward** the fruit that comes from dying according to the flesh. For he declared, *Truly, truly, I say to you, unless a grain of wheat falls into the earth and dies, it remains alone; but if it dies, it bears much fruit* (John 12:24). And again: *And I, when I am lifted up from the earth, will draw all men to myself* (John 12:32). As Paul too says, *He endured the cross, despising the shame* (Heb 12:2); *therefore God has highly exalted him and bestowed on him the name which is above every name, that at the name of Jesus every knee should bow, in heaven and on earth and under the earth, and every tongue confess that Jesus Christ is Lord, to the glory of God the Father* (Phil 2:9-11). This is what the inspired David also foreknew and sang in the Spirit, for he says to him, *All the nations that thou hast made shall come and bow down before thee, O Lord* (Ps 85:9 LXX).

Thus his sojourn among us bears fruit abundantly. The nations followed, and he **shepherded** them as **flocks** under his care and **gathered them as lambs in his arms** (40:11). Through the regeneration of the Spirit who comes down from above, those who believe in him have been re-created like newborn **lambs** to newness of life. Therefore they desire *spiritual milk* (1 Pet 2:2), having been nourished at first like infants, but then advancing to the maturity and the fullness of Christ. The **lambs** were **shepherded**, and those who were **pregnant with young** were cared for. The **lambs**, being newly born, signify the Gentiles. Those **pregnant with young** would seem to be those who have already given birth to the Word as it had been known from the teaching of the law and the predictions of the prophets. For Christ saved not only the Gentiles but the Israelites by blood, to whom in particular the Word was sent. Though they had no certain knowledge of the mystery, those who were confirmed in faith were comforted.

The passage, **Who measured the water with his hand** (40:12-14), attempts to display the transcendence and incomprehensibility of God's wisdom by invoking things which are beyond the reach of human beings, even beyond the heavenly powers. Who cannot be overcome by the ineffable mystery of Christ and of God's plan for mankind? Paul seems to me to be using Isaiah's words when he exclaims: *O the depth of the riches and wisdom and knowledge of God! How unsearchable are his judgments and how inscrutable his ways!* **For who has known the mind of the Lord?** (Rom 11:33-34; Isa 40:13). Are not Paul's words very close to Isaiah's? For the reality of God is deep and unfathomable. Just as we are totally unable to measure the oceans with our hands, to mark off the heavens with a span, to hold the whole earth within our grasp, or to weigh the mountains in scales and the hills in a balance, in the same degree, we cannot comprehend the mind of the Lord. This is confirmed in his own words, spoken through his holy prophet: *For my ways are not your ways, for as the heavens are higher than the earth, so are my ways higher than your ways and my thoughts than your thoughts* (55:8-9). And he asks: **With whom did he consult so that he instructed him?** (40:14). Or who **showed him judgment** (40:14), that is, righteousness or right judgment, and **the way of understanding** (40:14)? If he is truly Wisdom that grants wisdom to every mind, and the one who imparts the light of understanding to every rational creature, how could he need someone else, or how could anyone give counsel to him or find fault with him?

How good it is that the prophet said these things to his hearers! Even today we still hear unbelievers impudently ask, "What need was there for the Word of God to come among us, to put on the flesh and its filth? Why does he wish to save earthly creatures in this way, especially since it is said that God is able to do whatever seems good to him? What purpose did it serve for God to become man?" With such absurd opinions they impiously misrepresent and disfigure the plan of salvation and wage war against the splendor of this mystery. The prophet cuts off their futile arguments with the words of this passage; the wisdom and the understanding of God, he asserts, are incomprehensible. Indeed, God is himself Wisdom and Understanding in the most exalted and purest sense. In this way, then, the prophet dismisses the speeches of unbelievers who find fault with the dispensation of the only-begotten in the flesh.

40:3
Prepare the way of the Lord; make straight the paths of our God

(5) Origen of Alexandria

As he who is uniquely the Son of God uses a word since he is none other than the Word (for he himself was *the Word in the beginning, the Word with God, the Word that was God* [John 1:1]), so John, the servant of that Word, if we understand the Scripture rightly, is none other than the **voice**, yet he uses his **voice** to point to the Word.

Because he understood the prophecy spoken by Isaiah concerning himself, he does not say that he is a *voice crying in the wilderness*, but a *voice of one crying in the wilderness* (John 1:23; Isa 40:3), of the one who stood and cried, *If anyone thirst, let him come to me and drink* (John 7:37-38; cf. Isa 55:1), of the one also who said, **Prepare the way of the Lord; make straight his paths; every valley shall be filled up, and every mountain and hill shall be made low, and the rough places smooth ways** (40:3-5; Luke 3:4-6; John 1:23).

As it is written in Exodus that God says to Moses, *Behold, I have made you the God of Pharaoh, and Aaron your brother shall be your prophet* (Exod 7:1), so one must understand the situation of God the Word in the beginning and of John to be somewhat analogous, although not alike in every way. For John was the voice of that Word, capable of pointing him out and revealing him. . . .

Earlier in this commentary [on John], when we were explaining how we should understand that the Son of God is the Word, we set forth the thoughts that had come to us at that point; now we must try to understand how John was the **voice** that alone was able to speak in a manner worthy of the Word that was announced. For John *came for a witness, as a man sent from God . . . that he might bear witness to the light, that all might believe through him* (John 1:6-7).

We will understand this especially if we recall what was earlier said in our exposition of the passages, *That all might believe through him* (John 1:7) and *This is he of whom it is written, "Behold I am sending my angel before your face, who will prepare your way before you"* (Matt 11:10; Mal 3:1). It is also proper that the text says, not that he is the **voice of one** "speaking" **in the desert**, but **of one crying in the desert**. For one who "cries out," **Prepare the way of the Lord**, also "says" it, but the same person could say it without actually crying out.

But he cries out and shouts that even those who are far from the speaker may hear, and that those who are hard of hearing may understand the magnitude of what is said. For it is proclaimed in a loud voice, reaching those who have turned away from God and those who have lost the keenness of their hearing. For this reason too *Jesus stood and cried, saying, "If anyone thirsts, let him come to me and drink"* (John 7:37). John too *bore witness to him and cried out* (John 1:15). Hence God commands Isaiah to cry out with the voice **of one saying, "Cry." And I said, "What shall I cry?"** (40:6).

But even if the words of those who pray are not spoken aloud but only in the heart, rather than cried out and shouted, God still hears those who pray thus. For God asked Moses, *Why do you cry out to me?* (Exod 14:15), even though, according to the book of Exodus, he had not cried out audibly. Yet Moses cried out mightily to God in prayer with that voice which is heard by God alone. For this reason also David says, *I cried to the Lord with my voice, and he hearkened to me* (Ps 77:1).

Now the **voice** of one who cries in the **desert** is necessary for the soul deprived of God and destitute of truth — for what greater **desert** can there be than for a soul to be deprived of God and of all virtue? — because when a soul follows a **crooked** path, it is in need of teaching and must be exhorted to **make straight the way of the Lord** (40:3).

(6) Gregory the Great

He sent them ahead of him to every city and place where he himself was to come (Luke 10:1). The Lord follows his preachers. Preaching comes first, and then the Lord comes to the dwelling places of our hearts; words of exhortation precede, and by means of them Truth is received by hearts. This is why Isaiah addresses preachers: **Prepare the way of the Lord, make straight the paths of our God** (40:3). And the psalmist orders, *Make a way for him who rises in the west* (Ps 68:4). The Lord rose in the west because he manifested his glory by rising from the place where he underwent his passion. He rose in the west because by rising he trampled death underfoot. We make a way for him who rises in the west, then, when we preach his glory to your hearts, so that he himself, coming afterward, may enlighten them by the presence of his love.

(7) Ambrose of Milan

If we hold fast to those things that are worthy of the Son of God, we will understand that the Word of God, in the incomprehensible and ineffable mystery of the depth of his majesty, was sent to present himself in such a way that we could know him. For we were able to lay hold of him not only when he *emptied himself* (Phil 2:7) but also when he dwelt in us, as it is written: *I will dwell in them* (2 Cor 6:16). Elsewhere it is written that God said: *Come, let us go down and confuse their language* (Gen 11:7). Of course God does not descend from a place, for he says: *I fill heaven and earth* (Jer 23:24). The Word of God descends when he enters our hearts, as the prophet enjoined: **Prepare the way of the Lord, make his paths straight** (40:3). We do this so that, as he promised, he may come with the Father and take up residence in us. It should be clear, then, what is meant when we say Christ comes to us.

40:6-7
All flesh is grass, and the glory of man is like the flower of the grass.

(8) Origen of Alexandria

Because we have been enlightened by this command from the Lord,[2] when the flame of illicit envy burns our mind and heart, his words teach us to say: If I wish to be envied by the wicked, or if I should envy those who do evil, take note of what the psalm says next: *They will soon fade like grass, and like green herbs they will soon wither* (Ps 37:2). Would you like to be strengthened by a similar counsel of another prophet? Listen also to what Isaiah pronounces about all fleshly glory: **All flesh is grass, and all its glory like the flower of the grass** (40:6). And would you like to see some examples of how the **glory** of the **flesh** is the **flower of the grass**? Consider him who ruled thirty years ago, how his

---

2. *The commandment of the Lord is pure, enlightening the eyes* (Ps 19:8).

reign flourished; gradually he **withered** (40:7) like the **flower of the grass**, then another came after him, and another and yet another, each of them in turn leaders and rulers; and all their honor and glory not only **withered** like a **flower** but were scattered by the wind like dry dust, so that not a trace was left.[3] Other people are made arrogant by their wealth, or are swollen with their accomplishments; some of them eager to be praised for an artificial goodness, others eager to be cursed for their implacable cruelty. If someone should think of envying the empty projects of such people, let him first go to their corpses — that is, if he can find them, because in some cases not even this is possible. Then he will find out how **all flesh is grass, and all its glory like the flower of the grass. The grass has withered, and its flower has fallen** (40:6-7). But for the man who does not love the little flowers of the flesh, nor live carnally, but loves the word of God and lives by it, listen to what he may hope for: **The word of the Lord remains forever** (40:8).

As for the text itself that says, **like grass they will soon fade** (Ps 37:2), referring of course to the wicked, I do not think it is idle to ask why it compares them to **grass**, since there are surely other things to which the wicked could be compared. **Grass** is the food of dumb and irrational animals. Perhaps, therefore, the text is alluding to all who are stupid and ignorant, and who live contrary to reason and to the wisdom of God — the sort who follow in the wake of those who are leaders in evil. They may be said to feed on the life and deeds of the wicked, to whom they are obedient, and the text has therefore compared the wicked to **grass**. No wise man would take his example from such people. Like a wise man who hears the word of God and does it (cf. Matt 7:24) is he who eats the bread that comes down from heaven (John 6:33); Jesus is his food, in that he is fed by his words and lives by his commands. In a similar way, those who stand out for their wickedness become like grass for those who submit to them or who try to compete with them in their evildoing.

(9) Gregory of Nyssa

In the Song of Songs the bride says: *My beloved is mine, he pastures his flock among the lilies until the day dawns and the shadows flee* (Song 2:16-17). This means that I saw face to face the one who always remains who he is and who for my sake shone forth in human form from my sister the synagogue. In him I rest, and in me he finds a dwelling place. For he is the *good shepherd* (John 10:14; Isa 40:11) who does not shepherd his flock among grass, but nourishes his sheep with pure lilies. They no longer feed on grass because grass is the proper nourishment for unreasoning animals. Since man is a reasonable creature, he is nourished by the true Word. If, however, he is satisfied with such a thing as grass, he will become grass. **All flesh is grass** (40:6) as long as it is flesh. But if a person becomes spirit by being born of the Spirit (cf. John 3:6), he no longer grazes upon grass, but he will be nourished by the Spirit, who is signified by the purity and fragrance of the lily. Such a person will be a pure and fragrant lily by being changed into the food that he eats. . . . Those who are nourished by lilies, that is, those whose souls have been fattened by pure

---

3. Origen is referring to Emperor Septimius Severus (146-211), who was succeeded by a string of short-lived rulers.

Isaiah 40

and fragrant nourishment, have turned away from every deceitful and illusory appearance that people hold on to in this life. They become children of light and children of the day (cf. 1 Thess 5:5) because they see things as they really are.

(10) Augustine of Hippo

A Christian sees a poor proletarian, moaning and groaning at his daily drudgery, and perhaps he asks himself, "What's the good of my having become a Christian? Has it made me any better off than that fellow who isn't, than that guy who doesn't believe in Christ, than that so-and-so who blasphemes my God?" The psalm warns him, *Do not put your trust in princes* (Ps 146:3). Why do you take pleasure in the flower of the field? **All flesh is grass**, says the prophet (40:6). He doesn't merely say it, he shouts it. The Lord cries out to him: **Shout!** he says. And he answers: **What shall I shout? All flesh is grass, and all the honor of the flesh as the flower of the field. The grass has withered, the flower fallen** (40:6-7). So has everything perished then? Heaven forbid! **But the word of the Lord abides forever** (40:8). Why take pleasure in grass? Look, the grass has perished. Do you want to avoid perishing? Hold fast to the Word.

40:8
The word of our God remains forever.

(11) Augustine of Hippo

The more progress we make in God, so much the more do voices[4] diminish, and the Word grow in us (cf. John 3:30). Why, indeed, do we have voices, except to help us understand something? If we enjoyed fullness of understanding, we wouldn't need voices. If we could see one another's thoughts, would we need any language with which to talk to each other? So there is going to be a time when we shall see the Word as he is seen by the angels, and there will be no need of voices. If we could see one another's thoughts, would we need any language with which to talk to each other? So there is going to be a time when we shall see the Word as he is seen by the angels, and there will be no need of voices. After all, there will be no evangelizing to be done when we all see the Word itself. All time-bound things will pass away because the voice is of the flesh, is of the hay; now **the splendor of the flesh is like flowers in the grass; the grass has dried up, the flowers have fallen; but the Word of the Lord abides forever** (40:6-8). The more we make progress toward understanding, the less need there will be for voices by which we are led toward understanding, as John himself said, *He must increase, but I must decrease* (John 3:30). As the Word grows, the voice diminishes. What do I mean, "as the Word grows"? The Word itself, after all, doesn't grow, but we grow in him, we who make progress in him, we who increase in him, until we no longer find voices necessary.

---

4. Augustine is contrasting Christ the Word and John the "voice," as in John 1:23: *I am the voice of one crying in the wilderness.*

40:12
Who has measured the water with his hand, and heaven with a span, and all the earth with the palm of his hand?

(12) Hilary of Poitiers

Nothing is more characteristic of God than being *(esse)*. For that which is cannot come to an end at a certain time, nor can it have a beginning. He who exists eternally in perfect happiness could not have not existed at some time in the past, nor could he ever not exist at some time in the future. For what is divine cannot have come into being, nor ever cease to be. Hence, since God's eternity is in no way separable from God himself, it was proper that he revealed only this about himself, that he is, when he said, *I am that I am* (Exod 3:14) and this is evidence of his perfect eternity.

To show that God is infinite, the words *I am that I am* were sufficient. But we also needed to know the working of his majesty and power. For though it is characteristic of the one who abides eternally to have no beginning, there are other biblical texts in which the eternal and holy God speaks of himself in other ways: **Who holds the heaven in his palm, and the earth in his hand?** (40:12). And again: *Heaven is my throne and the earth is my footstool; what is the house which you would build for me, and what is the place of my rest?* (66:1).

According to this text, the whole **heaven** is held in the **palm**, and the whole **earth** is grasped in his **hand**. Now, even though the Word of God is edifying to a devout person who reads it casually, it contains a deeper meaning for those who meditate on it patiently and do not read it hurriedly. For the **heaven** held in God's **palm** is God's throne, and the **earth** that is grasped in his **hand** is the footstool beneath his feet. Of course this does not mean that throne and footstool refer to someone who is sitting upon a throne, as though God exists in space and has a body. Throne and footstool, **palm** and **hand**, are used to signify God's infinite power.

By these things we learn that God is recognized in everything that is born or created as being within them and also outside of them, at once transcendent and immanent, surrounding all and infusing all. The **palm** and **hand** which hold things display the power by which he controls things outside of him, and the throne and footstool indicate things external to him that are subject to him who is at the same time within them. He resides within what is outside, and contains what is within, and wholly contains everything that is within him and outside of him. Since he is infinite he is related to all things, nor is anything that exists not in him.

Because of its zeal for the truth, my mind delighted in these edifying thoughts about God. For there is nothing more fitting to be thought of God than that he far transcends our powers of comprehension. The more the mind strives to comprehend him to any extent, the more the mind realizes the boundless infinity that lies beyond its grasp. I had learned this through my own experience, but it was confirmed by the prophet's words: *Whither shall I go from thy Spirit? Or whither shall I flee from thy presence? If I ascend to heaven, thou art there! If I descend to hell, thou art there! If I take the wings of the morning and dwell in the uttermost parts of the sea, even there thy hand shall lead me, and thy right hand shall hold me up* (Ps 139:7-10). There is no place without God, nor is there any place that is not in God. He is in heaven, he is in hell, and he is beyond the seas. He is within all things, yet he contains all things. Though he possesses all and is possessed by all, he is not in anything nor is he not in all things.

(13) Gregory of Nyssa

What is man compared with the divine nature? Which saint's words shall I quote to prove that human nature is held in low esteem? According to Abraham, human nature is *dust and ashes* (Gen 18:27); according to Isaiah, **grass** (40:6). David does not actually call it grass but *as grass*. For Isaiah says, **All flesh is grass**, and David, *Man is as grass* (Ps 37:2). Ecclesiastes says it is *vanity* (Eccl 1:2), St. Paul, *misery* (cf. Rom 7:24). For the whole human race bemoans its fate in the words the apostle uses for his own person. Such is man.

But what is God? How shall I name that which can neither be seen nor heard, nor comprehended by the heart? By which words shall I make known his nature? Where among the things we can know can I find a likeness of this greatest good? What new words can I coin so as to describe the wholly inexpressible? I have heard the divinely inspired Scriptures disclose marvelous things about the transcendent nature; yet what are they compared with that nature itself? For even if I were capable of grasping all that Scripture says, yet that which it signifies is always more. For when we breathe in air to fill the space that is in each of us, one will receive more air, the other, less. Yet he who takes in much has not absorbed the whole element into himself; but he has only taken from the whole as much as he could, while the whole is still there.

So it is also with the words spoken about God in Holy Scripture, which are expounded to us by men inspired by the Holy Spirit. If measured by our understanding, they are indeed exalted above all greatness; yet they do not reach the majesty of the truth. **Who has measured heaven with a span, and water with his hand, and all the earth in his palm?** (40:12). Do you see with what majestic words he describes the transcendent Power? Yet what are they compared with the reality? For despite these magnificent terms the prophet's words show but part of the divine energy. He does not name the power itself from which springs this energy, to say nothing of the nature which comes from this power; nor would he name it. Rather, by these words he rebukes those who attempt some representation of the Divinity; for, speaking in the person of God, he asks, **To whom have you likened me?** (40:18 and 46:5).

Man is esteemed as nothing, as *ashes* and **grass** and *vanity* among the things that exist, yet he becomes akin to this great Majesty that can neither be seen nor heard nor thought; he is received as a son by the God of the universe.

(14) Gregory of Nyssa

It behooves prudent and temperate people to believe what God has said, but not to ask about the modes and causes of actions, inasmuch as they are beyond us. Let it be said to busybodies, "Show me by your reason the essence of things visible. Tell me by what skill he fashioned his handiwork in its polymorphic variety." Though you were to search out that sort of thing, you will still find yourself at a loss and distressed that you don't understand the transformation wrought by rebirth, though you may know the reason for birth.[5] If the essence of things visible is a dream and a delusion to you, and universal knowledge fails, do not be upset if you don't know the reason for creation and for the correction of decay. The same One is fashioner both of the first creation and of the second re-creation. He knows how his own handiwork, once it has undergone decomposition, will come together again and be restored to its original constitution. If this will require wisdom, the source of wisdom lies in him; if power is wanted, he will not need a collaborator or assistant. According to the voice of that wisest of prophets, he it is who **measured the water with his hand, and** the great expanse of **heaven with a span, and the earth with the palm of a hand** (40:12). Think about the images, the works, the signs that are provided of his ineffable power. They induce us to despair at our total inability to conceive anything worthy of God's nature. He is, and is said to be, almighty.

40:13
Who has known the mind of the Lord,
and who has been his counselor to instruct him?

(15) Basil of Caesarea

When the blessed Paul writes, *for from him and through him and to him are all things* (Rom 11:36), he is clearly referring to the Lord, as should be evident to anyone who looks carefully at the sense of the passage. The apostle had just quoted the prophecy of Isaiah: **Who has known the mind of the Lord, or who has been his counselor?** (40:13). Then he goes on to say: *for from him and through him and to him are all things.* That the prophet is speaking about God the Word, the craftsman of all creation, we learn from his previous words: **Who has measured the water with his hand, and marked off the heaven with a span, and all the earth with the palm of his hand? Who has weighed the mountains with a scale, and the forests with a balance? Who has known the mind of the Lord, and who has been his counselor?** (40:12-13).

This **who** is not a mystery; it refers to someone quite unique, as in the following passages: *Who will rise up for me against the wicked?* (Ps 94:16). Or: *What man is there who desires life?* (Ps 34:12). Or: *Who shall ascend the hill of the* LORD*?* (Ps 24:3). All these questions, including **Who has known the mind of the Lord, or who has been his counselor?**, have the same answer: *For the Father loves the Son, and shows him all that he himself is doing* (John 5:20). It is he who sustains the earth and holds it in his hand. He has set all things in order and brings them into harmony. He has put the mountains in their place and measured the waters and arranged all things in their proper order. He encompasses the expanse of the heavens with only a small part of his power, which the prophet

---

5. The context of this selection is a discussion of the resurrection in an Easter sermon.

in his figurative language calls a **span** (40:12).⁶ It is right, then, that the apostle says: *For from him and through him and to him are all things* (Rom 11:36).

All things that exist, then, come *from him* according to the will of God the Father. Through him things endure over time and are maintained, for he created all things and gives to each what is needed for its well-being. Therefore all things are oriented to him, looking with irresistible longing and inexpressive desire to the Creator and Sustainer of life, as it is written: *The eyes of all place their hope in you* (Ps 145:15), and *All look to thee* (Ps 104:27), and again, *Thou openest thy hand, thou satisfiest the desire of every living thing* (Ps 145:16).

(16) John Chrysostom

When you hear the words "one" and "no one"⁷ and similar terms, you should not lessen the glory of the Trinity, but through these expressions learn the distance that separates God from the creation. For it is written elsewhere: **Who has known the mind of the Lord?** (40:13; Rom 11:34). We have already shown that the Son and the Spirit are not excluded from such knowledge, when we cited the testimony that says: *For who knows a man's thought except the spirit of the man which is in him? So also no one comprehends the thoughts of God except the Spirit of God* (1 Cor 2:11). And the Son has also said: *No one knows the Son except the Father, or the Father except the Son* (Matt 11:27). And in another place: *Not that any one has seen the Father except him who is from God; he has seen the Father* (John 6:46). In short, the Son indicates that he knows the Father fully and gives the reason for such knowledge. What is the reason? He is from him. And the proof that he is from him is that he knows him fully. Thus he knows him intimately — because he is from him, and the sign that he is from him is that he knows him intimately. For it is not possible to know fully something superior even if the gap between them is small.

40:15
If all the nations have been accounted as a drop from a jar, and as the sinking of a balance....

(17) Ambrose of Milan

Why does God, without whose will the smallest sparrow does not fall, and by whom the very hairs of our heads are numbered (cf. Matt 10:29-30), say through Isaiah, **all the nations are accounted like a drop from a bucket and the weight of a balance, and will be accounted as spittle** (40:15)? Shall all the nations therefore perish like a drop from a bucket and like spit, and serve no purpose? However, our God has not held all the nations as worthless, since he said to Abraham, *In you all the nations of the earth will be blessed*

---

6. The space one can span with the thumb and the little finger.
7. "One" in reference to the "one God," and "no one" in the sense of "no other God."

(Gen 12:3). And through David, he said to his Son, *I will make the nations your inheritance* (Ps 2:8), and elsewhere, *All the nations will serve him* (Ps 72:11). It is also written that he offered his Son for *every* nation, to save sinners. How then should one understand the divine utterance in the present text?

When we contemplate the heavenly creatures, which are indeed numerous, and the heavens, which are vastly greater than earth, so that many would consider the earth no greater than a pinpoint in comparison; when, as I say, we contemplate the ranks of angels, archangels, principalities and powers, thrones, dominions (cf. Col 1:16), thousands, tens of thousands, millions of thousands, by comparison with these, the **nations** appear to be no more than a **drop from a bucket** (40:15), the merest drop of the heavenly fullness. The Gentiles indeed are like a drop that falls from that heavenly fullness. How could they be considered great when the earth itself, on which the nations exist, is but a slight part of the universe?

40:26
Look up on high with your eyes and see.

(18) Origen of Alexandria

Lift up your eyes (John 4:35) occurs in many places in Scripture when the divine Word invites us to lift up and elevate our thoughts, to turn our sight from its fixation on things below to higher things, as is written in Isaiah, **Lift up your eyes on high and see. Who has made all these things known?** (40:26).

The Savior, when he was about to speak the Beatitudes, lifted up his eyes to the disciples and said, *Blessed* are such and such (Matt 5:2-12). No true disciple of Jesus, nor one who rests in Abraham's bosom, has his sight fixed on things below. The rich man in torment *lifted up his eyes* (Luke 16:23) and saw Abraham and Lazarus in his bosom. Further, after Jesus restored the health of the woman *who was bent over and completely incapable of looking up* (Luke 13:11), she was no longer bent over and incapable of looking up and was able to lift up her eyes.

On the other hand, anyone who is overcome by passions, dominated by the flesh and preoccupied by material things, has not obeyed the command to **Lift up your eyes**. As a consequence such a person will not see the fields, even if they be *already white for harvest* (John 4:35). In truth, no one who does the works of the flesh has lifted up his eyes.

Isaiah 41

1 Be dedicated to me, O islands;
   for the rulers will change strength;
 let them approach and speak together,
   then let them declare judgment.

2 Who has roused righteousness from the east,
   called it to its feet and it will go?
 He will place it before nations
   and astonish kings;
 and he will place their swords in the earth,
   and their bows like brushwood that is driven out.
3 And he will pursue them,
   and the way of his feet will pass through in peace.
4 Who has wrought and done these things?
   The one calling her from the beginning of generations
   has called her.
 I, God, am first,
   and for the things that are coming, I am.
5 The nations saw and became afraid,
   the ends of the earth drew near and came together,
6 each deciding to help
   his neighbor and his brother.
 And he will say:
7 The artisan man has become strong,
   also the smith as he smites with the hammer
   while at the same time striking.
 At some time he will say, "The seam is good";
   they have strengthened them with nails,
   they will set them up and they will not be moved.
8 But you, Israel, my servant,

> Iakob, whom I have chosen,
>> the offspring of Abraam, whom I have loved;
> 9 you whom I took hold of from the ends of the earth,
>> and I called you from its mountain peaks,
> and I said to you, "You are my servant,
>> I have chosen you and not forsaken you";
> 10 do not fear, for I am with you,
>> do not wander off, for I am your God,
>> who has strengthened you,
> and I have helped you,
>> and I have made you secure
>> with my righteous right hand.

> 11 See, all who oppose you
>> shall be ashamed and disgraced;
> for they shall be as though they were not,
>> and all your adversaries shall perish.
> 12 You shall seek them,
>> but you shall not find
>> the men who shall treat you violently;
> for they shall be as though they were not,
>> and those who war against you shall not be.
> 13 Because I am your God,
>> who holds your right hand;
> who says to you, "Do not fear,
> 14   O Iakob, O small Israel."
> I have helped you, says God
>> who redeems you, O Israel.
> 15 Look, I made you as the threshing wheels of a cart,
>> new and saw-shaped;
> and you shall thresh mountains,
>> and grind hills to powder
>> and make them like dust.
> 16 And you shall winnow them and a wind shall take them,
>> and a tempest shall scatter them.
> But you shall rejoice in the holy things of Israel.

> 17 And the poor and needy shall be glad,
>> for they shall seek water, and there will be none;
>> their tongue has been dried up from thirst.
> I the Lord God, I the God of Israel,
>> will listen and will not forsake them.
> 18 But I will open rivers on the mountains,
>> and fountains in the midst of the plains;

I will make the wilderness into marshlands,
and the thirsty land as watercourses.
19 I will put in the dry land a cedar,
and a box tree and a myrtle,
and a cypress and a white poplar,
20 so that together they may see and know,
and consider and understand,
that the hand of the Lord has done all these things,
and the Holy One of Israel has exhibited them.

21 Your judgment draws near, says the Lord God;
your counsels have drawn near, says the King of Iakob.
22 Let them draw near and declare to you
the things that will happen;
or speak of the former things, what they were,
and we will apply our mind
and know what the last things will be —
and tell us the things that are coming.
23 Declare the things that are coming at the end,
and we will know that you are gods;
do good and do harm,
and we will wonder as well as see.
24 Because whence are you?
and whence is your work?
From the earth.
They have chosen you as an abomination.

25 But I stirred up the one who is from the north
and the one who is from the rising of the sun;
they shall be called by my name.
Let rulers come; and like potter's clay —
even as a potter treading clay —
so shall you be trodden down.
26 For who shall declare the things that were from the beginning,
so that we might know them,
and the former things,
and we will say that they are true?
There is none who foretells,
nor any who hears your words.
27 I will give dominion to Sion,
and I will comfort Ierousalem on the way.
28 For from among the nations, behold no one;
and from among their idols, there was none who declared.
And if I should ask them, Whence are you?

>   they will not answer me.
> 29 **For they are the ones who make you**
>   **and those who lead you astray are vain.**

*Like other chapters of this section of Isaiah, chapter 41 emphasizes God's transcendence and universal sovereignty. It also attacks idolatry. This chapter was not, however, cited widely in the early Church. Eusebius's commentary is devoted to the spread of the gospel to the Gentiles. He also sees the character of the Church outlined in certain passages. Origen observes that **righteousness** (41:2) is **called**, that is, "addressed," hence righteousness is personified and refers to Christ. Accordingly he interprets the passage in light of 1 Cor 1:30, which says that Christ is "wisdom, righteousness, sanctification, and redemption," a much loved text among early Christian writers. Another selection from Origen relates the **judgment** and **counsels** of the Lord (41:21) to Rom 11:33, "how unsearchable are his judgments," and discusses the incomprehensibility not only of God but also of created things. The words **I, God, am first, and for the times that are coming, I am** (41:4) were sometimes conflated with 44:6 ("I am the first and the last") and 46:9 ("For I am God, and there is no other"), and comments on these verses can be found in the excerpt from Gregory of Nyssa in chapter 44.*

(1) Eusebius of Caesarea

So you, Jacob, shall understand these things.[1]

But since the Savior of the universe, who did not consider the salvation of the whole human race secondary, spoke [in the previous chapter] about what had to do with you, now he addresses what has to do with the other nations, the Gentiles, all of whom he invites to hasten toward the knowledge of God. Therefore he says, **Be dedicated to me, O islands, for the rulers will change their strength** (41:1). Instead of this, Symmachus has, **Serve me, O islands; and let the nations change their strength**; and according to Aquila and Theodotion, **Keep quiet before me**. The command is thus given to **the islands to keep quiet** and be silent, so that they may listen to the divine address and the saving proclamation. The prophet constantly refers to the churches from all the nations as **islands** because, as it were, of the bitter salt water of the evil life flowing all around them. Whereas earlier he said, *Those who wait on God will change their strength* (40:31), here he asserts, **For the leaders will change their strength** (41:1), or, according to Symmachus, **and let the nations change their strength**. While the message in the previous chapter was proclaimed to *those who wait* for him, he now commands this same thing to **the islands** and to **the nations** . . . so that they might convert from their past way of life and make a change toward a better one. Then this follows: **let them approach**, he says, **and let them speak together** (41:1), by which he means, "**Let the nations approach** me, I who am God, **and let them speak together** my words when they are gathered in the same

---

1. By "Jacob" Eusebius here understands the Jewish people of Isaiah's time, and his reference to Jacob is based on the prophet's mention of the name in the preceding chapter (40:27). In Eusebius's interpretation chapter 41 now turns to prophecy meant for the Gentiles.

place, namely, in my Church." And what those who are so summoned are supposed to **speak**, he says next: **Then let them declare judgment** (41:1). For he wants those **nations** who have learned the word of **judgment** to themselves go on to **declare** it to others.

And to those who are to learn this, he also gives the command that they should know **who has roused righteousness from the east** (41:2). For the work of **righteousness** involved the calling not only of the Jews but also of the rest of the nations to the knowledge of God. . . .

Who is the one who has done all of these things but the God who is over all? Therefore the text reads as follows: **He called her**, namely, **righteousness, the one who is calling her from the beginning of generations, I, God, am first, and in the times to come, I am** (41:4). In Symmachus's translation: **I the Lord am first, and with the last, I am**. For he himself was known even to the first people long ago, those who **from the beginning** became friends of God, and he is the one in whom later the church of the nations has believed. Hence the text says, **The nations saw and were filled with awe** (41:5). The text bears witness that no ordinary help comes to the nations once they put aside their former polytheistic blindness and know the one who has said: **I the Lord am first, and in the times to come, I am. And they saw and became afraid** (41:4-5). Then they were on the way to wisdom: *The fear of the* LORD *is the beginning of wisdom* (Ps 111:10). But also **the ends of the earth trembled** (41:5): For it is marvelous how foreign peoples, even those at the farthest distance from the land of the Jews, the only place in ancient times where God was known, have received the knowledge of God. They **trembled** at the righteousness of God, they hurried to receive his favor, in keeping with the declaration, **let them draw near and speak together** (41:1). But in that passage they were commanded to gather together and **to speak**, that is, to glorify God, whereas here the text says, **they drew near and came together, each deciding to help his neighbor** (41:5-6). For those who were summoned to come saved not only themselves but also their neighbors, according to the laws of the love of humanity. Therefore, since they wished to serve their **neighbor** and their **brothers** and acquaintances who were still in error, they said these things to them.

Since this **offspring of Abraham** (41:8) has been scattered throughout the whole world, he adds the following: **whom I took hold of from the ends of the earth, and I called you from its mountain peaks** (41:9). . . . This refers to the Diaspora of the Jewish people, the people who first were deemed worthy of his call, as the apostle Paul showed to the Jews when he said, *It was necessary that the word of God should be spoken first to you. Since you thrust it from you, we turn to the Gentiles* (Acts 13:46). Thus, to those who heeded the call and accepted the word of the gospel, he addresses the words, **whom I took from the ends of the earth, and I called you from its mountain peaks**. For in the apostolic age there were a great many among the Jews who accepted the word of Christ, not only in the land of Judea but also among the other nations. . . .

Finally, the text encourages the elect to preach the gospel fearlessly to all nations, just as the Savior does in the gospels when he says, *Lo, I am with you always, to the close of the age* (Matt 28:20). Then the text adds, **Do not fear, for I am with you, do not wander off, for I am your God, who has strengthened you; I have helped you, and I have made you secure with my righteous right hand** (41:10). . . .

Therefore, the prophet maintains, you should endure patiently the persecutions which your enemies inflict on you, averting your eyes from the end that awaits them (41:11-12), and staying confident that my promise is not deceptive when I proclaim to you **that I, the Lord, am your God, and I will hold your right hand, who says to you, "Do not fear, I will help you"** (41:13-14). The Septuagint itself does not contain the words **I will help you, do not fear, you worm Jacob,** though they are found in the other Greek translations.[2] The Jacob who is here called a "**worm**" is the same person who above was called "**chosen**" — **Jacob, whom I have chosen** (41:8) — because, like a worm, "Jacob" has slipped into the cities of unbelieving nations and destroyed the entire errant system of polytheism, and has completely driven out the demonic influence in the minds of men. The apostolic preaching is also **worm**-like in its unpretentious and unlettered character. Thus the Savior too compared himself to a worm: *I am a worm and no man, scorned by men and despised by the people* (Ps 22:6).... And the text adds: **Behold, I have made you as the threshing wheels of a cart, new and saw-shaped** (41:15). This shows the power of the One who makes them strong: though they differ in no way from a **worm**... nevertheless, like the wheels of a threshing sledge, they thresh and crush into chaff the demonic idol-making of godless foreign nations as though they were reeds. Therefore the text continues: **you shall thresh mountains, and level hills** (41:15); **mountains** and **hills** symbolize the hostile powers which of old are raised up against the knowledge of God....

After its prophecy about the apostles, the text changes the subject to the conversion of the Gentiles.

In the present prophecy (41:17-18) the text expounds how it was fulfilled in the present age in the churches of God established by the apostles throughout the world. In the past the souls of the Gentiles were impoverished and in need of the knowledge of God. They possessed not a drop of life-giving drink, so that their tongues and their speech were parched. Because they had no share in the moisture of the saving word, they obtained a marvelous benefit when they were filled by heavenly favor with **springs** and **rivers** (41:18) and every kind of living water, so that they enjoy the water that was spoken of above: *and they drink water from the springs of salvation* (12:3). And they drink from the *springs of Israel,* as is mentioned in the text which says, *Bless God in the great assembly, the* LORD, *O you who are of Israel's fountain* (Ps 68:26). This would refer to the Holy Spirit, which springs up in the Church of God, the *assembly,* and rains down living waters, in former times from the Old Testament, and in this time from the new teaching of the gospel. There are also **rivers** that flow unfailingly and flood the ancient **desert** (41:18), **rivers** which have their origin in the great river of which is said, *the river whose streams make glad the city of God* (Ps 46:4), and *the river of God is full of water* (Ps 65:9).

And it is possible to see in **the dry land** (41:18) the Church of God, composed of souls flourishing from so much water and raised aloft, represented in this passage as plants that require a large supply of water to exist.

---

2. Eusebius's LXX text of 41:14 lacked the Hebrew words that the RSV translates as *you worm, Jacob,* which the translation at the head of the present chapter has rendered as **O small Israel**. As is often his practice, Eusebius treats the several Greek versions, including the LXX, as a composite text if it suits his interpretive purposes.

If it had not been God and **the hand of the Lord** (41:20) that worked the conversion of the Gentiles, through his apostles, how could the churches of God have existed in that great Gentile wasteland? Or how could spiritual waters have existed in it, surging throughout the earth to cultivate the souls of what previously were desolate and arid Gentiles? Or how could speech based on reverence for God enable the growth of tall and lofty products, on the one hand rooted deep in the earth (standing for mortal life), and on the other hand raised on high, so as to reach as far as the kingdom of heaven and to fix their hopes there? Hence they are compared to trees that flourish and grow skyward.

In this passage (41:24-26) the prophet is pointing to **the one who is from the rising of the sun** (41:25), who is Christ and his righteousness, as he revealed earlier in the passage that read, **Who roused righteousness from the east** (41:2), which he also indicated has been given to the nations. But **the one who is from the north** (41:25) is the people from the Gentiles, who of old were in the north, as it says, *From the north will be poured out evil upon all those who dwell on the earth* (Jer 1:14). This people from the Gentiles **I stirred up from the north,** so that evil will no longer exist in it; I will also summon the one **from the rising of the sun,** the Christ of God. To which he adds, **They shall be called by my name** (41:25). Their identity is disclosed in what follows: **Let rulers come** (41:25), meaning either the angels who stand guard over his kingdom, his agents in overthrowing godless error, or the leaders and overseers of his church. . . .

To this the prophet adds, **I will give rule to Zion, and I will comfort Jerusalem on the way** (41:27). The meaning is this: "Know, O men, that to my Church (which is here called **Zion** and **Jerusalem**) I myself will give universal rule, and I will invite my church and show it the way."

41:2
Who has roused justice from the east,
called it to its feet and it will go?

(2) Origen of Alexandria

The prophets say that Christ is living justice,[3] and we know that the apostle said that Christ is *justice, sanctification, redemption, and wisdom* (1 Cor 1:30). Perhaps the apostle was taught by the prophets, for he knows that justice is personified and alive. What is this justice? The Only-Begotten of God. The teaching that Christ is justice, living justice and justice itself, did not begin with the apostle. Rather, you will find it from the mystery revealed to us in the words of the prophets and confirmed in the present reading. **For who,** he asks, **has roused justice from the east and called it to its feet?** (41:2). He summoned **justice.** It is obvious that **justice** is personified if it is addressed. Now the Father called Christ to sojourn among us for the sake of our salvation and to descend to us from heaven, for *No one ascends into heaven save the Son of man, who has come down from*

---

3. The Greek term translated "righteousness" in the *NETS* can be also rendered as "justice"; so also in 1 Cor 1:30.

heaven (John 3:13). He called him from the east: not the geographical east, but the "east" of true light. Therefore it is written, **Who has roused justice from the east, and called it to its feet?** The Father called the Son, or, to be strictly accurate, the Father called a personified **justice to its feet**, that is, in the incarnation of his own Son. Therefore we adore the stool under his feet, as it is written: *Adore the footstool under his feet* (cf. Ps 110:1). Thus the flesh of the Lord takes on the dignity of the godhead.

41:4
I, God, am first, and for the things that are coming, I am.

(3) Cyril of Alexandria

He declares that he is **God the first** (41:4) and that there is no second God after him. What does that mean? There is one God of all whose existence had no beginning. It was he who called all things into existence. He is the **first** and only God, without beginning, the maker of all things, and there will never be any other God in the unending ages to come. He alone is God. When the **nations** beheld Christ and the righteousness he brought, they all beheld his glory with the eyes of the mind. For the text says that those from the **ends of the earth**, that is, from all over the earth, **became afraid** (41:5). They were gathered **together and drew near**, no longer remaining far off and alien because of sin. By a spiritual relationship they were gathered together with a single mind in the one faith. This is apparent from the words of the text, **drew near and came together** (41:5). When they tasted of the Lord and understood his goodness and were amazed at the beauty of the truth, they did not keep the gift to themselves; rather, they generously reached out and **each decided to help his brother** and friend (41:6). . . .

In this way the Gentiles were initiated into the mysteries and taught to know that God is the maker of all things, that everything is subject to him and to his divine commands. All things came to be in the beginning, and what was brought into existence was fixed permanently in the good. Finally, as one might expect, he encourages those ministers through whom he would instruct the Gentiles in the evangelical oracles. He shows that they are wise and courageous and bring to mind the virtue of the holy fathers. To show the love he has for them he says: **But you, Israel, my servant, Jacob, whom I have chosen, the offspring of Abraham, whom I have loved** (41:8). This refers to Israelites who believed in Christ, of whom one might say the first fruits were the holy disciples. He states that their fathers were **chosen and beloved** (41:8), as if to say, "You who are from the noble race, so honored and beloved by me, from the blood of Abraham, emulate the splendid virtue of your fathers and become imitators of their piety."

He also says that he **took hold of Abraham and called him from the ends of the earth**, or **from its mountain peaks** (41:9), because it was from the far-off land of the Chaldeans that he was called to Judea. For he heard God saying: *Go from your country and your kindred and your father's house to the land that I will show you* (Gen 12:1). He spoke as though addressing all of Israel, **I said to you, "You are my servant"** (41:9), for he is called firstborn. He was, as I have said, **chosen and not forsaken by God** (41:9). He heard, **Do not fear** and **Do not wander off. For I am your God, who has strengthened you** (41:10). He learned through the law that *God is one and one Lord* (Deut 6:4) and alone ought to be worshiped, that he was **helped** by him, that is, by his **right hand** (41:10) who is the maker, his power, that is, the Son. And he was **made secure** (41:10) and safe from all snares. He conquered the Gentiles and inherited their land.

41:21-23
Your judgment draws near, says the Lord God; your counsels have drawn near.

(4) Origen of Alexandria

It is not just difficult, the apostle Paul says, to search out the judgments of God, it is impossible. However much someone advances in his search, and works with ever more focused zeal, even helped by the grace of God and illuminated in his perception, he will be unable to plumb the depths of what he is examining. For no created intelligence has the possibility of arriving at the absolute knowledge of a thing. Once it has found some part of what it seeks, it then turns to something else that needs examination. And once it has come to *that*, it will discern still more things which require study.

Therefore, Solomon, that wisest of men, contemplating the nature of things in his wisdom, wrote, *I said, "I will be wise," but wisdom was far from me. That which is, is far off, and deep, very deep; who can find it out?* (Eccl 7:23b-24). But Isaiah knew that the beginnings of things could not be found by a mortal nature, not even by natures that are more divine than human,[4] since they are nevertheless creatures that have been made. Knowing, therefore, that not any of them could know the beginning or the end, he said: **Speak of the former things, what they were, and we will know that you are gods, or declare to us the things that are coming, and we will know that you are gods** (41:22-23).[5] For a Hebrew teacher[6] passed on a tradition of this kind: no one could understand the beginning or the end of everything, save only the Lord Jesus Christ and the Holy Spirit. He used to say that in the figure of the vision, Isaiah saw that the seraphim were only two in number, and that they covered the face of God with two of their wings, and their feet with two others, and with the remaining two wings flew and cried out to one another, *Holy, holy, holy, the* LORD *of hosts, the whole earth is full of your glory* (6:2-3). That the seraphim alone had their wings over the face of God and over their feet must be seen as declaring that neither the host of the holy angels, nor the holy thrones, nor dominions, nor principalities, nor powers (cf. Col 1:16) can know the absolute beginning of everything and the end of the universe. Rather, it must be understood that these holy ones whom we have mentioned here are spirits and virtuous powers that are very close indeed to the absolute beginning, and grasp more about the beginning than others are able to do.

---

4. Here Origen is thinking of the angels.
5. Origen conflates vv. 22 and 23 and duplicates in v. 22 the clause **we will know that you are gods** from v. 23.
6. Origen means a Jewish-Christian teacher.

Nevertheless, however much these virtuous powers have learned from what the Son of God and the Holy Spirit have revealed, however much they were able to grasp, and however greater the higher powers are than the lower ones, nevertheless they are unable to understand absolutely everything, for it is written: *Most of the works of God are concealed* (Sir 16:21).

It is therefore desirable that each person should always *extend* himself to the utmost of his abilities *to what lies ahead, forgetting what lies behind* (Phil 3:13), both to better deeds and to a perception and understanding which are purer, through our Lord Jesus Christ, to whom be glory forever and ever.

Isaiah 42

1 Iakob is my servant, I will lay hold of him;
    Israel is my chosen, my soul has accepted him;
  I have put my spirit upon him;
    he will bring forth judgment to the nations.
2 He will not cry out or send forth his voice,
    nor will his voice be heard outside;
3 a bruised reed he will not break,
    and a smoking wick he will not quench;
    but he will bring forth judgment for truth.
4 He will blaze up and not be overwhelmed
    until he has established judgment on the earth;
    and nations will hope in his name.

5 Thus says the Lord God,
    who created heaven and established it,
    who bolstered the earth and the things that are in it,
  and who gave breath to the people upon it
    and spirit to those who tread on it:
6 I the Lord God have called you in righteousness,
    and I will take hold of your hand and strengthen you;
  I have given you as a covenant to a race,
    as a light to nations,
7   to open the eyes of the blind,
  to bring out from bonds those who are bound,
    and from the prison house those who sit in darkness.
8 I am the Lord God, this is my name;
    my glory I will not give to another,
    nor my excellences to the graven images.
9 As for the things that were from the beginning,
    see, they have come;

    also new things,
        which I myself will declare;
  and before they sprang forth,
      they were made plain to you.

10 Sing to the Lord a new song,
      [you, his dominion]!
  Glorify his name from the end of the earth,
      you who go down to the sea and sail it,
      you islands and those who inhabit them.
11 Rejoice, O desert and its villages,
      O homesteads and those who inhabit Kedar.
  Those who inhabit Petra will rejoice,
      they will shout from the tops of the mountains.
12 They will give glory to God,
      they will declare his excellences in the islands.
13 The Lord God of the powers will go forth
      and crush the war;
  he will stir up jealousy
      and shout against his foes with strength.

14 I have been silent.
      Shall I even always be silent and hold back?
  I have endured like a woman in labor,
      I will amaze and wither at once.

15 And I will turn rivers into islands,
      and dry up marshlands.
16 And I will lead the blind
      by a road they have not known,
  and I will make them tread paths
      they had no knowledge of.
  I will turn the darkness into light for them,
      and the crooked places into a straight path.
  I will do these things,
      and I will not forsake them.
17 But they turned away backwards!
  Be ashamed with shame,
      you who trust in the graven images,
  who say to the cast images,
      "You are our gods."

18 Hear, you that are deaf;
      and you that are blind, look up to see!

19 And who is blind but my servants,
    and deaf but they who lord it over them?
    Even God's slaves have become blind.
20 You have often seen, but not observed;
    your ears are open, but you have not heard.

21 The Lord God has willed to be justified
    and to magnify praise.
   And I saw,
22   and the people were plundered and spoiled;
   for the snare was in the secret rooms everywhere,
    as well as in houses where they hid them;
   they have become plunder,
    and there was no one to rescue the prey,
    and no one to say, "Restore!"
23 Who is there among you that will give ear to these things,
    that will listen for the things to come?
24 Who gave Iakob for spoil,
    and Israel to those who plunder him?
   Was it not God, against whom they have sinned,
    and they would not walk in his ways,
    nor hear his law?
25 So he brought upon them the anger of his wrath,
    and war overpowered them,
    as did those who were burning them all around.
   And they — each of them — did not know,
    nor did they take it to heart.

Chapter 42 is cited in the New Testament and was popular among the church fathers. A principal attraction was Second Isaiah's first Servant song, the opening lines of which are spoken by the heavenly voice in the account of the Baptism of Jesus in the synoptic gospels (Matt 3:17). Later in Matthew (Matt 12:18-21) the full passage (42:1-4) is cited after the Evangelist reports that when many people followed Jesus to be healed, Jesus told his disciples "not to make him known." The text as cited in Matthew, however, differs significantly from the Septuagint version, which does not have the words "my beloved with whom my soul is well pleased" (Matt 12:18). But other terms in the text, for example, **servant and chosen** *(42:1) and the phrase* **put my spirit upon him** *(42:1), confirmed that the passage referred to Christ, God's beloved Son. The presence of the names of "Jacob" and "Israel" in the LXX of 42:1 (but not in the Hebrew) required the interpreters to connect these names with Jesus.*

The chapter also offered opportunities to reflect on trinitarian themes, because of the identification of the Servant with Jesus and the references to the Spirit (42:1). The words **Glorify his name from the end of the earth** *(42:10) invited discussion of the spread of the Church in all the world, one of the dominant themes in early Christian interpretation of Isaiah. Verse 8,* **my glory I will not give to another**, *was invoked by the anti-Nicene bishop Eunomius to show that only* *the Father possessed glory and what glory the Son received came from the Father. In an astute analysis of the text, Gregory of Nyssa demonstrates that God's glory was given not to the Son but to the **graven images** mentioned in the second part of the verse.*

(1) The Gospel according to Matthew

And many followed him, and he healed them all, and ordered them not to make him known. This was to fulfill what was spoken by the prophet Isaiah: **Behold, my servant whom I have chosen, my beloved with whom my soul is well pleased. I will put my Spirit upon him, and he shall proclaim justice to the Gentiles. He will not wrangle or cry aloud, nor will any one hear his voice in the streets; he will not break a bruised reed or quench a smoldering wick, till he brings justice to victory; and in his name will the Gentiles hope** (42:1-4).

(2) Eusebius of Caesarea

Immediately after the refutation of the idolaters (41:29), the prophet includes a prophecy about Christ and, following that, one about the calling of the Gentiles. To understand this passage best, however, it is worth noticing that neither the name of Jacob nor of Israel is found in the Hebrew, nor in other translations. But Symmachus has the following reading: **Behold my servant, I will embrace him; my chosen one, in whom my soul is well pleased** (42:1). And Aquila has, **Behold my servant, I will help him.** Now in an earlier passage, the band of apostles was named **Jacob** and **Israel**, in the text which says, *But you, Jacob, my servant, Israel, whom I have chosen, the offspring of Abraham, whom I have loved* (41:8). But here a mightier personage has been introduced without being named, lest he be counted among those already referred to in 41:8 as *Jacob* or *Israel* or *the offspring of Abraham*. This is plainly said of the Christ of God, as the Evangelist[1] testifies: **I have put my spirit upon him, and he will bring forth judgment to the nations** (42:1), and a few lines later, **and nations will hope in his name** (42:4). Neither of these could be said of the band of the apostles. Perhaps for that reason the prophet has omitted the names of **Jacob** and **Israel**. There is no one else who could be here called **servant of God** and **chosen one**. Therefore he continues, **my soul has accepted him** (42:1). He alone is the **chosen** of God, he in whom the **soul** of God is said to delight, consistent with the practice of sacred Scripture in using the word "soul" for God, since it also habitually describes him in anthropomorphic fashion as having feet, hands, fingers, and eyes.

    I have put my spirit upon him, and he will bring forth judgment to the nations (42:1). This fits with what was prophesied much earlier in the book of Isaiah regarding the one who would come *from the root of Jesse* (11:1). Similarly, **chosen** (42:1) could not be attributed to the apostles, since only to him has it been said, *my servant whom I have*

---

1. Eusebius means Isaiah.

chosen (Matt 12:18) and also the passage *the Spirit of God rested only on him* (Isa 11:2). *For in him the whole fullness of deity dwells bodily* (Col 2:9). *The Spirit* given to the one who came *from the root of Jesse* (Isa 11:1) is the same as the Only-begotten Word of God, as the apostle Paul also indicated when he said, *The Lord is the Spirit* (2 Cor 3:17). Therefore, as the one who alone contains the Father's **Spirit**, he accomplishes everything that follows, proclaiming universal judgment to the nations, so as to prepare everyone for God's future judgment. Thus it is said, **he will bring forth judgment to the nations** (42:1).

The next verses indicate that he passed his human life gently and quietly, so that he did not even allow those whom he cured to make news about him public. This is why it is written, **He will not cry out or send forth his voice, nor will his voice be heard outside,** but **a bruised reed he will not break** (42:2-3). For he would live his mortal life so quietly and discreetly that he would not grieve the ordinary person, or someone lowlier and weaker than all the rest, who is likened to a **reed** because of his weakness. But **a smoking wick he will not quench** (42:3) or, according to Symmachus, **a dim wick he will not quench**, which is what Aquila also has, and, according to Theodotion, **a dim wick of hemp he will not quench**. We might say that a **smoldering wick**[2] represents someone whose body and soul have been puffed up and inflated, and set smoldering. The one who is prophesied here was said to inhibit and to keep such a person from his pride. And this is in fact what happened with the Christ of God when he sojourned in his mortal life: he neither burdened the poor and oppressed, nor courted the high and the mighty; but toward all men he was *gentle and lowly in heart* (Matt 11:29).

With the truth and by his free speech, he presented everyone with the facts of the judgment of God and did not stop until, like a beacon, he **blazed up** (42:4) by means of his resurrection from the dead, which the prophetic text presented figuratively in saying, **he will blaze up and not be broken** (42:4). For those who contrived his death attempted to **break** and to **quench** him, since this mortal race by its very nature is **broken** by death. But him they were unable to **break**. He is the only one who has ever proven stronger than death, and it is therefore appropriately said of him, **he will blaze up and not be broken**. Then the text continues, **until he has established judgment on the earth; and in his name the nations will hope** (42:4). After his resurrection, therefore, he shone forth over the whole cosmos like a beacon. Nor has he ceased to exercise authority over the earth, but does so through the administration and the judgment of his church, which he passed on to his disciples.

(3) Cyril of Alexandria

Earlier God had promised: *I shall give dominion to Zion* (41:27). What kind of governance that would be the prophet now makes clear. The ruler and teacher who is here commissioned for the spiritual Zion, that is, the Church, does not refer to the governance at the time of the prophecy, but to what happened in the present time. The Word born of the

---

2. Eusebius alludes here to the form in which Matt 12:20 quotes Isa 42:3 LXX.

Virgin was always King and Lord of the universe, but after his Incarnation he became the proper and distinctive measure of humanity. That he became like us we believe without any doubt. Therefore, even though he is said to receive power over everything, this should be taken as referring to his dispensation in the flesh, not to the divine majesty by which he is known as the Lord of the universe.

He calls him by the names of **Jacob** and **Israel** inasmuch as he came into being, according to the flesh, from the blood of Jacob, who was also given the name of **Israel**. He says that he **will help him** and calls him **chosen** (42:1). For the Father worked together with the Son, who accomplished his great deeds as though by his own power. The Son is also truly **chosen** because he is handsome and *more beautiful than all the sons of men* (Ps 45:2), and welcomed as the beloved. For God the Father took pleasure in him, as he says in the Gospel: *This is my beloved Son, with whom I am well pleased* (Matt 3:17). That the Son has been anointed in a human manner, and is said to participate in the Holy Spirit, though he himself gives the Spirit and sanctifies the creation through him, the Father makes plain in the words of the prophet: **I have put my spirit upon him** (42:1). When he was baptized, the Spirit came down upon him from heaven, in the form of a dove, and rested upon him. If he received the Spirit at the time of his baptism as a human being, this should be understood in the same way one understands other things that happened to him as a human being. For it was not as God that he was made holy when he received the Spirit, since he himself, as I said, is the one who *makes* holy. Rather, he appeared as man for the sake of our salvation. He was anointed, therefore, **to bring forth judgment to the nations** (42:1). The judgment he pronounces on them is just. For he made them righteous by his condemnation of Satan, who tyrannized over them. He himself taught us this when he said: *Now is the judgment of this world, now shall the ruler of this world be cast out. And I, when I am lifted up from the earth, will draw all men to myself* (John 12:31-32). He sentenced to destruction the one who had oppressed the world, and by his holy **judgment** he also saved those led astray.

But **he has not cried out**, the text says, **nor will he send forth his voice, nor will his voice be heard outside** (42:2). For the Lord and Savior of the universe sojourned among us in great lowliness and humility, without making a sound, as it were, and doing wrong to no one. He came in silence and quietness, so as **not to break a bruised reed, nor to quench a smoking wick** (42:2), meaning that he did not lift his foot against those who were lowly and had long been accustomed to enduring suffering.

42:1
He will bring forth judgment to the nations.

(4) Augustine of Hippo

When we read in the prophetic books that God is to come to pronounce the last judgment, we do not need any indication more specific than the mention of the judgment to realize that it is Christ who is meant. The Father, of course, will judge, but he will execute judgment through the coming of the Son of man. Though the Father will not be manifest he will be present, for the Father *judges no one, but has given all judgment to the Son* (John 5:22). The Son, on the other hand, will manifest himself as a man who is to judge, because it was as a man that he was judged. This is confirmed by a passage in the prophet Isaiah, where God uses the names of **Jacob** and **Israel** to indicate Christ, who assumed his body from their descendants. The passage reads: **Jacob is my servant, I will lift him up; Israel is my chosen one; my Spirit has taken him to himself. I have given my Spirit to him; he will bring forth judgment to the nations. He will not cry out, nor will he cease to speak, nor will his voice be heard outside. He will not break a crushed reed, and he will not quench a smoking wick; but he will bring forth judgment in truth. He will shine and will not be overwhelmed, until he has established judgment on the earth. In his name the nations will put their hope** (42:1-4).

It is true, indeed, that the Hebrew has **my servant** in place of **Jacob** and **Israel**, but the Septuagint translators preferred to make the meaning more explicit, namely, that the prophecy refers to the *form of a servant* (Phil 2:7), in which the Most High showed himself in utter humility. To signify him they used the name of the man from whose stock Christ took the *form of a servant*.

According to the testimony of the Evangelist, *the Holy Spirit was given* to him under the form of a dove (Matt 3:16). He **brought forth judgment to the nations** (42:1) because he foretold the judgment to come which had been hidden from them. In his meekness he did not **cry out**, nor did he **cease from speaking the truth** (42:2). But his voice was not, and is not, **outside** (42:2), because those who are **outside** and do not listen to him are cut off from his body. He did not **break** nor **quench** those very Jews who persecuted him, although they were like a **bruised reed** because of their lost innocence, and like a **smoking wick** that had lost its light. Rather, he spared them, since he came to be judged by them before he came to be their Judge. Of course, he **brought forth judgment in truth** when he foretold the time of punishment for those who persist in sin. His face **shone** on the mount, and his fame **shone** throughout the whole world. He was not **broken** or crushed because neither in his own person nor in his Church has he yielded to the efforts of persecutors who have sought to eliminate his Church.

42:5
Who gave breath to the people upon it and spirit to those who tread on it.

(5) Irenaeus of Lyons

Just as flesh is capable of being corrupted, so it can be freed of corruption. In the same way, just as it is able to die, so it can live. These two give way to each other; they cannot remain in the same place together. The one is driven out by the other, and when one is present the other is destroyed. Thus, if death, when it takes hold of a person, drives life out of him and shows him to be dead, how much more does life, when it takes hold of someone, drive out death and restore him as a living person to God? For if death brings mortality, why should the coming of life not revive him? As the prophet Isaiah says: *Death, having prevailed, swallowed them up, and God has again taken away every tear from every face* (25:8). Thus the former life is expelled, since it was not given through the Spirit but rather through breath. For the *breath of life* which made man a *living being* (Gen 2:7) is one thing, and the *life-giving Spirit* which made him a *spiritual being* (1 Cor 15:45-46) is another. Because of this Isaiah said, **Thus says the Lord God, who created heaven and established it, who bolstered the earth and the things that are in it, and who gave breath to the people upon it and spirit to those who tread on it** (42:5). This means that **breath** is given to all people on the earth in common, while the **Spirit** is given specifically to those who trample down earthly desires. Thus Isaiah himself, distinguishing the things already mentioned, said, *For a spirit shall go forth from me, and I have made every breath* (57:16). With this he counts the Spirit as unique to God, that Spirit which in the last times he poured out on the human race through their adoption as sons (cf. Joel 2:28; Acts 2:17). At the same time he shows that **breath** is common to all of creation and is something created. For what is made is different from the one who made it. Therefore, **breath** is temporal, but the **Spirit** is eternal. **Breath** increases to a degree and, after remaining for a time, it then leaves its previous abode without breath. The **Spirit**, instead, pervades the person inside and out since it always continues and never leaves him.

(6) Ambrose of Milan

The Holy Spirit too has been given, because it is said: *And I will pray the Father, and he will give you another Counselor* (John 14:16), and the apostle says, *Therefore whoever disregards this, disregards not man but God, who gives his Holy Spirit to you* (1 Thess 4:8). Isaiah also shows that the Holy Spirit has been given, and the Son. **Thus says the Lord God, who created heaven and established it, who bolstered the earth and the things that are in it, and gave breath to the people upon it and spirit to those who walk on it** (42:5). And to the Son: **I the Lord God have called you in righteousness, and I will take hold of your hand and strengthen you; and I have given you as a covenant to a race, a light to nations, to open the eyes of the blind, to bring out from their bonds those who are bound** (42:6-7). When therefore the Son has been sent and given, the Spirit too has been sent and given, and thus they have a single divinity, a single work.

42:7
**To bring out from their bonds those who are bound,
and from the prison house those who sit in darkness.**

(7) Origen of Alexandria

The soul is contemplative by nature and is able to know the things that are and to search them out. If we see that the soul has become subject to the devil or even to his angels and wholly in bondage to the hostile powers, we will to a certain extent understand what it means to be held in captivity and who it is that has taken it captive. But if we take refuge in Christ who through the prophet Isaiah proclaimed *release to the captives* (61:1), we will be liberated from captivity even though he has kept us in bondage until now. For Jesus came **to bring out from their bonds those who are bound, and from the prison house those who sit in darkness** (42:7).

42:8
I am the Lord God, this is my name; my glory I will not give to another, nor my excellencies to the graven images.

(8) Gregory of Nyssa

Eunomius says: [The Son] does not partake of the status of the one who begot him nor share with any other the Father's essence or kingdom; rather, he became glorious and the *Lord of glory* (1 Cor 2:8) as a result of his begetting and *receiving glory from the Father* (2 Pet 1:17). He does not participate in his glory, for the glory of the Almighty is incommunicable, as he himself says, **My glory I will not give to another** (42:8).

These are his deadly potions which only those whose spiritual senses are well trained can recognize. But the deadly evil of his words is disclosed in their conclusion. For Eunomius argues: "Because [the Son] *receives glory from the Father* (2 Pet 1:17), he does not participate in his glory, for the glory of the Almighty is incommunicable, as he himself says: **My glory I will not give to another** (42:8)."

Who is this "other" to whom God has said he will not give his glory? The prophet speaks of God's adversary, and Eunomius applies the prophecy to the only-begotten God himself! When the prophet, speaking in the person of God, said, **My glory I will not give to another**, he then added, **nor my excellencies to graven images** (42:8). For men were deceived into offering worship and adoration due to God alone to his adversary and into venerating the enemy of God in carved images and many other kinds of idols made by men. But the one who takes pity on human depravity and heals the sick foretold through the prophet the love God would show in the "latter days" by abolishing the veneration of idols, saying, "When my **truth** (42:3) will be manifest, **my glory will no longer be given to another, nor my excellencies to graven images** (42:8). For when they come to know my glory, they shall no longer be in bondage to those who by nature are not gods."

Everything the prophet says in the person of the Lord about the power of the adversary, these things God's foe applies to the Lord himself who uttered these words through the prophet!

(9) Gregory of Nyssa

Blessed are those who hunger and thirst for God's justice, for they shall be satisfied (Matt 5:6). Does this mean that someone who has desire for justice is to be blessed, whereas if someone has the same yearning for temperance or wisdom or prudence[3] or some other

---
3. Gregory is thinking of the cardinal virtues: justice, prudence, temperance, and courage.

kind of virtue, the Word does not call that blessed? Perhaps the saying can be understood in this way. Justice is numbered among the virtues. It is the custom of the Sacred Scripture, however, to deal with the whole by referring to the part, as when it explains the divine nature through names. For example, the prophecy says: **I am the Lord** (42:8) — the prophet speaking in the person of God. And: *This is my name forever, and my memorial from generation to generation* (Exod 3:15). And again in another place: *I am who I am* (Exod 3:14). And again: *I am merciful* (Exod 22:27). There are thousands of other names befitting God used by Holy Scripture to signify God's sublime nature. For that reason it is correct to say that when it mentions one, the whole list of names is implicitly included though only one is mentioned. For it could hardly be true that when he is called "Lord" he is not all these other things as well. All the attributes are implied by the one name. From this we conclude that the inspired Word is able to comprehend many things through a part. So also in the beatitude. When the Word says that hungering for justice is to be blessed, he indicates by this that everyone who hungers for prudence, courage, temperance, and every other kind of virtue is blessed.

42:10
Sing to the Lord a new song. . . . Glorify his name from the end of the earth.

(10) Cyril of Alexandria

The newness of the song is appropriate to the newness of its subject, as it is written: *Therefore, if anyone is in Christ, he is a new creation; the old has passed away, all things have been made new* (2 Cor 5:17). Through the mediation of the all-wise Moses, Israel in the flesh had been redeemed from the oppression of the Egyptians. The Israelites were liberated from the labor of making bricks, from the fruitless striving after worldly pursuits, the ferocity of the overseers, and the inhumanity of their rulers. They passed through the middle of the sea, they ate manna in the desert, they drank water from the rock, they crossed the Jordan on dry feet, and were brought into the Promised Land.

But in our case, all things are new and incomparably better than the things of old. For we have been liberated from spiritual slavery rather than from physical bondage. We have been released from the defilements of fleshly addictions, rather than from worldly pursuits. We did not flee Egyptian slave drivers, nor a tyrant who, while wicked and savage, is yet a man like us. Instead we fled the evil and impure demons that were thronging together for sinful purposes, and the chief of the flock, Satan himself. We too passed through a kind of sea, the flood of this present life, its turbulence, and its futile distractions. We ate the spiritual bread, the bread from heaven that gives life to the world. We drank water from the rock, delighting in the streams of Christ, which are spiritual. We crossed the Jordan when we were judged worthy of holy Baptism, we came into the land promised and fit for the saints, which the Savior himself speaks of when he says, *Blessed are the meek, for they shall inherit the earth* (Matt 5:5).

In short, to celebrate the new state of affairs **a new song** (42:10) was necessary, on the basis of **his dominion**, that is, what happened under him and when we came under his rule. The **song**, which is the worship and praise due to him, was sung not only throughout the land of the Jews, but even **from the end of the earth**, that is, the whole world under heaven. For of old God was known in Judea, and his name was great only in Israel. But since we have been called through Christ to the knowledge of the truth, heaven and earth are full of his glory. This is what the psalmist also says: *The whole earth will be filled with his glory* (Ps 103:24 LXX). Who are they who are ordered to **glorify his name from the end of the earth**? Who are they who raise songs to him, and are moved to form a chorus, and gather in assembly for a spiritual sacrifice? Who are they **who go down to the sea and sail it, the islands and those who inhabit them** (42:10)? This is a reference, I believe, to the holy apostles. For it was not just in Judea that they preached Jesus and the grace that comes through him; they also crossed the sea and preached the gospel in the lands of the Gentiles. They traveled as far as Illyricum and beyond, so that there was not an island or its inhabitants that had not heard the holy preaching.

The words of this prophecy have thus had a historical fulfillment. But one could also understand them in another way. The inspired Scriptures often compare this world, or human life, to the sea, as the psalmist sings: *This is the sea, great and wide; here are serpents without number, creatures great and small* (Ps 103:25 LXX). Human life is likened to a sea, perhaps because of the unsteadiness of life in the sea, its perpetual up and down, its great turmoil. Those who sail this kind of sea without drowning have learned to swim, that is, who have kept themselves from worldly preoccupations. Enjoying the help that comes from God and ever mindful of Christ's spiritual gifts, they give him praise and glory. **The islands** (42:15) are thus the churches that have been saved in this spiritual sea and that welcome those tossed by the storms of the evil spirit. The churches and those who dwell in them worship Christ. When we speak of churches, we also of course mean the holy worshipers in them. Finally, this too should be known: they can be called **islands** because they are like so many villages and cities set amidst a great and expansive desert.

(11) Jerome

The one who had just said, **Behold, the former things have come to pass, and new things I now declare; before they sprang forth, they were made plain to you** (42:9), and had promised that he would say what they did not know, now proclaims what these **new things** are (42:9). He commands the apostles and the apostolic generation to sing a new song, not in the oldness of the letter, but in the newness of the spirit (cf. 2 Cor 3:3). And not only in the Old Testament, but also in the New; and his praise will penetrate to the ends of the earth. *Its rising is from the end of the heavens, and its circuit to the end of them* (Ps 19.6). The voice of the apostles went throughout all the earth, and to the ends of the world their words. Or according to the Septuagint, *Praise his name to the ends of the earth* (Ps 48:10), that throughout the whole world Christ's name might be announced to the Gentiles. The next words testify to the identity of those who ought to sing a new song, when the text speaks of **those who go down to the sea** and set sail on it, or **the fullness of the sea** (42:10). When Jesus saw the apostles repairing their nets on the shore along the

Sea of Gennesareth, he called and sent them on the great sea. From catchers of fish he made them into fishers of men, who preached the gospel from Jerusalem as far as the Dalmatian coast and Spain. In a short time they even captured the very power of the city of Rome. Now they did indeed **go down to the sea** and sail on it, enduring the storms and persecutions of this world. By **the islands and their inhabitants**, understand either the diversity of the nations or the multitude of the churches.

The desert, he notes, **and its cities will lift their voice** (42:11). We have already discussed this. On the one hand, the text says that **the desert and its cities will rejoice**, and **Kedar**, which was formerly an uninhabited area across from Arabia of the Saracens, and also the residents of **Petra** (42:11),[4] which is the city of that name in Palestine. In that case the text means that races which had previously been "deserted" by the knowledge of God and bound by the errors of idolatry will be converted to the praises of the Lord. If, on the other hand, **Kedar** is interpreted to mean "darkness," and since according to the apostle the *rock* [*petra*] is Christ (1 Cor 10:4), then the text also anticipates all those who believe, so that those who once were in darkness but now believe in the Lord and Savior shall proclaim from the tops of the mountains and preach Christ openly. Of these it was said earlier, *Go up on a high mountain, you who preach the good news to Zion. Lift up your voice, you who preach the good news to Jerusalem* (40:9). And I will put his glory in the islands, of which we spoke earlier. And the prophetic speech describes the glorious coming of the Savior, of whom the apostle Paul speaks: *Awaiting the illumination of the glory of the great God and Savior, our Lord Jesus Christ* (Tit 2:13). And he compares him to an exceedingly courageous man, who will fight against his adversaries to rouse up zeal. He is also the one who is prophesied in the song of Deuteronomy: *They have stirred me to jealousy with what is no god; they have provoked me with their idols. So I will stir them to jealousy with those who are no people; I will provoke them with a foolish nation* (Deut 32:21). He will raise his voice and will cry out against his enemies, openly reproving their infidelity and saying when he cries out, **For a long time I have held my peace, I have kept still and restrained myself** (42:14), or, as the Septuagint has it, **I have been silent; shall I even always be silent?** This was in order that what Solomon said might be fulfilled: *A time to be silent, a time to speak* (Eccl 3:7).

Here then is the sense of the text: "For a long time I endured your lapses. But my silence in the past in no way means I will continue to be silent. And as a woman giving birth brings forth her infant into the light, and makes open what had been closed within the womb, so I will now express my sorrow; and the disregard I had previously exercised over your crimes, I will now set aside. And I will shatter your plans. And all at once I will gather up the whole race, and all the pride of the mountains and the arrogance of your hills and the grass, of which was said earlier, *Truly the people is grass* (40:7). That is, I will turn both leaders and common people back into wilderness."

---

4. For the reading **Sela** in 42:11, the LXX and the Vg. read **Petra**.

Isaiah 43

1 But now thus says the Lord God,
      he who made you, O Iakob,
      he who formed you, O Israel:
   Do not fear, for I have redeemed you;
      I have called you by your name, you are mine.
2 And if you should pass through water, I am with you;
      and rivers shall not overwhelm you;
   and if you should go through fire, you shall by no means be burned,
      the flame shall not consume you.
3 Because I am the Lord your God,
      the Holy One of Israel, who saves you.
   I have made Egypt and Ethiopia and Soene
      your exchange on your behalf.
4 Because you have become precious in my sight,
      you have been glorified and I have loved you,
   and I will give many people on your behalf,
      and rulers on behalf of your head.
5 Do not fear, because I am with you;
      I will bring your offspring from the east,
      and from the west I will gather you;
6 I will say to the north, "Bring them,"
      and to the south, "Do not hinder;
   bring my sons from a land far away
      and my daughters from the ends of the earth —
7 all who have been called by my name.
   For I prepared him in my glory,
      and I formed and made him."

8 And I have brought forth a blind people,
      and their eyes are likewise blind,

      and they are deaf, though they have ears!
9 All the nations have gathered together,
      and rulers will be gathered from among them.
  Who will declare these things?
      Or who will declare to you
      the things that were from the beginning?
  Let them bring their witnesses,
      and let them be justified and speak truths.
10 Be my witnesses;
      I too am a witness, says the Lord God,
      and the servant whom I have chosen,
  so that you may know and believe
      and understand that I am.
  Before me there was no other god,
      nor shall there be any after me.
11 I am God,
      and besides me there is none who saves.
12 I declared and saved, I reproached,
      and there was no stranger among you.
  You are my witnesses;
      I too am a witness, says the Lord God.
13 Even from the beginning
      there is also no one who rescues from my hands;
      I will do it and who will turn it back?

14 Thus says the Lord God,
      the one who redeems you, the Holy One of Israel:
  For your sake I will send to Babylon
      and stir up all who are fleeing,
      and the Chaldeans will be bound in ships.
15 I am the Lord God, your Holy One,
      the one who exhibited Israel as your king.
16 Thus says the Lord,
      who provides a way in the sea,
      a path in the mighty water,
17 who has brought out chariots and horses
      and a mighty throng together;
  they have lain down and will not rise,
      they have been quenched like a wick that is quenched.
18 Do not remember the former things,
      or consider the things of old.
19 Look, I am doing new things that will now spring forth,
      and you will know them;
  and I will make a way in the wilderness

and rivers in the dry land.
20 The wild animals of the field will praise me,
    sirens and the daughters of ostriches;
because I have provided water in the wilderness,
    and rivers in the dry land,
to give drink to my chosen race,
21   my people whom I have acquired
    to set forth my excellences.

22 I have not called you now, O Iakob,
    nor have I made you weary, O Israel.
23 There are no sheep for me from your burnt offering,
    nor have you glorified me with your sacrifices,
nor have I made you tired with frankincense,
24   nor have you bought me incense with silver,
nor did I desire the fat of your sacrifices;
    but in your sins and iniquities
    I have stood before you.

25 I am, I am
    the one who blots out your transgressions,
    and I will not remember them at all.
26 But as for you, do remember, and let us be judged;
    you state your transgressions first, so that you may be justified.
27 Your ancestors first,
    also their rulers, transgressed against me.
28 And the rulers defiled my holy things,
    and I gave Iakob to destroy him,
    and Israel for a reproach.

Isaiah 43 is a celebration of God's universal redemption as foreshadowed in the deliverance of Israel out of exile. The mention of east, west, north, and south (43:5-6) signals that the redeemed will come from the four corners of the earth. Those who were once "no people" have been "called out of darkness" to become "God's people" (1 Pet 2:9-10). Two texts from St. Paul — God "was pleased to recapitulate all things in him [Christ]" (Eph 1:10) and "if anyone is in Christ, he is a new creation" (2 Cor 5:17) — set the theme for the interpretation: the ancient beauty of human nature is renewed in Christ. The prophet's invocation of the deliverance from Egypt to interpret the return from exile prompted Christian interpreters to extend the typology to embrace the Incarnation and the calling of the Gentiles. Cyril of Alexandria's commentary has been used to provide a nearly continuous exposition on the whole chapter. Note also his interest in themes of repentance and forgiveness at verse 25, **I am the one who blots out your transgressions.**

Apparently some members of Augustine's congregation in Hippo wanted to know why the animal sacrifices of the Old Testament had been abandoned. In a sermon Augustine draws extensively on this chapter, in particular the words, **Do not remember the former things.** . . .

Look, I am doing new things *(43:18-19), to contrast the unique sacrifice of Christ with the bloody sacrifices of ancient times.*

(1) The First Letter of Peter

But you are a **chosen race** (43:20), a royal priesthood, a holy nation, God's own **people** (43:21), that **you may declare the wonderful deeds** (43:21) of him who called you out of darkness into his marvelous light. Once you were no people but now you are God's people; once you had not received mercy but now you have received mercy.

(2) Cyril of Alexandria

This text moves one to break out in wonder at the mercy of God. By nature God is good and he is the Creator of the universe, and even if, for the sake of cleansing us from sin, he imposes his wrath on us — which is only just — he is soon moved to mercy. For the one who strikes the blow is the same one who heals the wound and dispenses with the scourge. He restores to favor those who repent, and raises up those who have fallen. He extends a saving hand to those overcome with suffering, delivers them from their troubles, and restores them to happiness.

Notice how he forgives offenses so that they are forgotten and promises to erase sins by the forgiveness that only God can give. He brings about a new beginning, a time when they will be led to happiness. Consider the text from the book of Psalms: *Oh that today you would hearken to his voice! Harden not your hearts, as in provocation* (Ps 94:7-8 LXX). Just as the *today* of the psalm represents a new start in time, the **now** (43:1) of the present text adds the subject of forgiveness to what has already been said. He leads them to the beginning of the way and of the future things that God will do. Therefore, he neither allows them to be completely deprived of happiness, nor does he make their rejection permanent. He removes fear of every kind and grants them confidence to partake of every good thing. It is God who transforms their condition into something incomparably better.

For I redeemed you (43:1), the text says. The manner of the redemption is made plain by the all-wise Paul in speaking about Christ, the Savior of us all, when he says that the God and Father was pleased *to recapitulate all things in him, things in heaven and things on earth* (Eph 1:10). In him there is universal redemption, in him absolution and forgiveness of past deeds, and through spiritual kinship with him and sanctification we reach maturity and are lifted up to communion with our God and Father.

Therefore he says, **I have called you by name** (43:1). Which name? The name by which we are called is **you are mine**, for we are Christ's. His is the fair name by which we have been called. . . .

God also promises invincible help that makes one invulnerable to every temptation. **Rivers** and **water** and **fire** (43:2) symbolize the various kinds of temptations. It is written that *all who desire to live a godly life in Christ Jesus will be persecuted* (2 Tim 3:12).

Isaiah 43

And Christ himself said to those who believed in him, *In this world you have tribulation* (John 16:33). **But if you should pass through water**, he promises in this passage, **I am with you** (43:2). For when Christ is present, nothing can harm those who are his.... Christ himself teaches the same thing using an illustration or a simile: *Every one then who hears these words of mine and does them will be like a wise man who built his house upon the rock; and the rain fell, and the floods came, and the winds blew and beat upon that house, but it did not fall, because it had been founded upon the rock* (Matt 7:24-25), and the rock was Christ (1 Cor 10:4)....

I will bring your offspring from the east, and from the west I will gather you (43:5). The only-begotten Word of God appeared to the inhabitants of our world in human form, that is, he became man. When he became man, he brought true and perfect knowledge of God to the Greeks and Jews whose many and varied offenses had led them to rebel against the Creator of the universe. His purpose was to gather them together, through faith and sanctification, in spiritual unity, so that they might be perfected in friendship with him and through him to be joined to the God and Father....

He promises to the company gathered from the Gentiles and from the Jews, that is, to the Church, that he will gather them all from the east and the west, and from the **north** and from **Libya**,[1] or the south, by which one is to understand every region under heaven. That is what is meant by **east** and **west**, **north** and **south**. In saying **to the north, "Bring them," and to the south, "Do not hinder"** (43:6), he wishes us to understand that he will not allow hostile and wicked spirits to offer any spiritual opposition to those who come to him. For wicked Satan, like a cruel and proud tyrant of old, dominated the inhabitants of the earth, and with his evil henchmen he would not allow them to see the truth or to turn to God. But Christ has brought an end to his rule and has made smooth the way to salvation. He has removed every obstacle that stood in the way.

By calling them **sons** and **daughters** (43:6) who come from the four corners of the earth, the text makes clear that at the time of Christ's coming the favor of adoption was given to everyone through the sanctification of the Holy Spirit (cf. Rom 8:15-16; Gal 4:6). That he did not gather a single people, but called all peoples, is clear from the words of the text: **all who have been called by my name** (43:7). For we are called Christians, or the people of God. Recall how Peter wrote to those who had been called: *But you are a chosen race, a royal priesthood, a holy nation, God's own people, that you may declare the wonderful deeds of him who called you out of darkness into his marvelous light. Once you were no people but now you are God's people* (1 Pet 2:9-10).

All things have become new in Christ, as Paul has confirmed in writing: *Therefore, if anyone is in Christ, he is a new creation* (2 Cor 5:17). He also writes to those who have been called to newness of a spiritual kind, *Do not be conformed to this world but be transformed by the renewal of your mind, that you may prove what is the will of God, what is good and acceptable and perfect* (Rom 12:2). For we have been renewed in Christ, through sanctification, returning to the ancient beauty of our nature, which was made in the image of [God]. Casting off the oldness of sin and every kind of vice, we have put off the old man, who had been corrupted by being drawn to error, and have put on the new man,

---

1. Cyril's text read **Libya** in place of **south**.

who has been renewed according to the image of the one who created him (cf. Col 3:9-10). Only in Christ has our refashioning and what is called the new birth occurred. We did not get it from corruptible seed but through the Word of the living and eternal God. The people, then, who has been gathered from the four corners of the world **and called by my name** is not another people, but rather the very one which **I have prepared in my glory, and formed, and made** (43:7). One may say that the glory of the God and Father is the Son, through whom and in whom he is glorified, as it is written, *I glorified you on the earth* (John 17:4), which is plainly said about him. For we have been assured, as I said, that those who believe in him have been formed by him, and have the beauty of the divine nature shining brightly in their souls, by virtue of conformity to him. The inspired psalmist said something of this sort: *A generation to come shall proclaim to the* Lord*, and a people yet unborn will praise the* Lord (Ps 102:18). . . .

You are my witnesses (43:10), he declares, "that I alone am the God of the universe, that none existed before me, and that none will exist after me. I alone am the one who saves, as I proclaimed to you of old, and what was said then I have brought to fulfillment. For **I saved** you in Christ; **I reproached** you and was no stranger among you (43:12). Over the course of time, the people of Israel forgot the sacred oracles, those delivered by that supremely wise man Moses, and they became devoted to pleasure rather than to God. Then, when an accounting was made for their laxity, they were sometimes put in danger by invasions of their enemies. In such times of affliction, they sought help by calling upon the one who was always their deliverer. **I reproached** them when I said through the voice of Jeremiah, *But in the time of their trouble they say, "Arise and save us!" But where are your gods that you made for yourself? Let them arise, if they can save you, in your time of trouble* (Jer 2:27-28). So I often reproached you who are of the blood of Israel, and you have often learned by experience that I was not among you as a **strange god** (43:12). For none of them saved you; it is I alone who save you. Therefore **be my witnesses** (43:10, 12), and I will be my own witness, says the Lord God."

This then is the point of the text: *Every one who acknowledges me before men, I also will acknowledge him* (Matt 10:32). "**You are my witnesses**, then, that I exist **from the beginning** (43:13), that is, I am the one who **from the beginning** until now has predicted the future, and who is able effortlessly to save those who thirst for kinship with me. For I save in such a way that **no one** whatsoever **can deliver from my hand** the person whom I have once chosen." Hence he adds, **There is no one who rescues from my hands; I will do it and who will turn it back?** (43:13). "For I brought about the calling of the Gentiles," he says, "I saved those who had wandered away." And who will change this, or make it not so? That no one can seize from the hand of God those whom he has saved, the Savior confirms when he says, *My sheep hear my voice, and I know them, and they follow me; and I give them eternal life, and they shall never perish, and no one shall snatch them out of my hand. My Father, who has given them to me, is greater than all, and no one is able to snatch them out of my Father's hand* (John 10:27-29). This is exactly what is written in Isaiah: **there is no one who rescues from my hands** (43:13). . . .

I who exhibited Israel your king (43:15). This can be understood in two ways. On the one hand, he may be saying, "I am the one who exhibits *myself* as your king, by many signs and by power and might beyond telling." On the other hand, possibly he is indicating something different: throughout the divine Scriptures, our Lord Jesus Christ is called "Israel" and also "Jacob," as is the practice of David in the Psalms, in the sense that he comes from the seed according to the flesh of those just named. "Therefore," he says, "**I am the one who exhibits your king** from the blood of Jacob and Israel."

This text contains an exceptional demonstration of providence. It has already spoken of a partial liberation in which, as I said, Israel was brought back from Babylon to Judea. Then it necessarily lifts the promise toward something incomparably greater by mentioning the future liberation through Christ. His redemption is neither partial nor limited to a single people, as formerly, but more universal and for every nation under heaven. Because the mystery of Christ is wonderful in its extraordinary display of God's economy and his great gentleness toward us, no one could doubt it once he has known it. For being God by nature and from God the Father, the only-begotten One shone forth and *emptied himself, taking the form of a servant* (Phil 2:7), to set free from the devil's tyranny those who were in his hold and to subject them to his own scepter. So then, the text has mentioned in this place a liberation to come in due season, a partial one which has been given only to those of the blood of Israel, and another which is universal and general, the liberation through Christ, by which our God and Father has saved the whole world....

Someone may ask, "If the ruler of Egypt is pursuing Israel by his own choice, why is the God of the universe himself said to lead out the **horses** and **chariots** and their **host?**" (43:17). We answer in the words said to Pharaoh by the God who rules the world: "*But for this purpose have I let you live, to show you my power, so that my name may be declared throughout all the earth*" (Exod 9:16). Historically speaking, that seems to fit the text.

But I have another answer as well. Those who have chosen to live virtuously, who flee the devil's servitude, avoid earthly pursuits, and desire to rid themselves of impurity, these the evil one surely persecutes, but God saves them in a marvelous way. He makes the flood of the present life passable, brings them across by his ineffable power, and does not allow them to be swept away by the temptations of this life. He lifts them above the carnal waves, and as he calms the **sea** (43:16), so he quiets the various temptations that beset them. And so those who have been in a desert, that is, are possessed of a pure and calm internal disposition, are able to eat the bread from heaven and to drink the water from the rock, that is, to become partakers of Christ, and to cross the Jordan and advance into the Promised Land. A person who is spiritual will understand fully what I am saying.

Previously, in bringing before the people of Israel knowledge of their coming deliverance, he had directed the narrative of events toward what was incomparably better, by speaking of salvation through Christ, when he said that he had **exhibited Israel as your king** (43:15). In the same way, when in the current passage he appropriately mentions the Red Sea, the waves of the Jordan, and the passage of the Israelites, he is again pointing us toward the mystery of Christ. Therefore he admonishes, **Do not remember the former things, or consider the things of old** (43:18). The reference to what is incomparable means that whatever is less is forgotten. Its brilliance tones down whatever is not itself as brilliant, even though it may have been prior in time. This is something of what the all-wise Paul meant when he said, *Now we know in part; when the perfect comes, the imperfect will pass away* (1 Cor 13:9a, 10). Great and beyond words are the things accomplished by

God through the all-wise Moses, but the things done by the might and excellence of our Savior exceed them. For through him and by him a host of nations throughout the whole world has been saved. Therefore he all but tells them to forget the first things. Instead he directs the mind toward things that are utterly superior and splendidly glorious.

He says, **I will make a way in the wilderness** (43:19). By **wilderness** is understood the dry and fruitless mass of nations, like thorns, because of the total absence of men who were pious and worthy, and knew how to act wisely. For so the psalmist says, *They have all turned away, they are all alike corrupt, and among them there is no one who does good, not even one* (Ps 14:3). In this **wilderness**, then, appeared a way that brought those who walked on it to the true knowledge of God, and to a holy and pure life, and to the knowledge of every good thing. We say that this **way** is either the divine and saving preaching of the gospel, or perhaps Christ himself. For we have heard him say plainly, *I am the Way* (John 14:6). But there was not just a **way in the wilderness, rivers** (43:19) were also shown, with spiritually beneficial waves which could intoxicate those who were in that wilderness. We say that these **rivers** are the ministers of the evangelical and apostolic oracles. Of these rivers the inspired David says: *The rivers have raised their voices* (Ps 92:3 LXX). Elsewhere he adds, *Their voice has gone throughout all the earth, and their words to the ends of the world* (Ps 19:4). The **rivers** that are named here should be understood as the leaders of the people, who can faithfully and conscientiously hand on the mysteries, and who can sprinkle with pious language those who come to Christ in faith. . . .

Then he says, **I have not called you now, O Jacob** (43:22). The reference to **now** must be understood to mean that "I called you *not* when you were sacrificing, or offering up cattle and sheep, when you might have thought to have gained forgiveness as a reward for your offering. Rather, when you were sunk in your sins and bound by your defilements — for you had worshiped the gods of Egypt — *then* I judged you deserving of mercy and love." Thus his grace is the gift of gentleness and the fruit of his love of humanity. Redemption comes by way of love. "For," he says, "the **sheep of your burnt offering** meant nothing to me, nor **did you worship me with your sacrifices** (43:23). How could what was totally unacceptable and vainly offered be a form of worship? You did not serve me in your sacrifices. For the one who pursues goodness, who does deeds notable for their virtue, who bends his neck to my will and follows the sacred oracles — this is the sort of person who may be said to serve God above all things. But the one who makes the altar thick with the smoke of incense, or offers up cattle or sheep, without carrying out what is truly good, such a person does not render genuine worship." . . .

Consider again how God did not endow worship according to the law with the power to free people from the impurity they had incurred. The blood of bulls and goats could not take away sins (cf. Heb 10:4), and the shadow of the law was of no use to them. For no one is justified by the law, according to the voice of the inspired Paul. About himself and the other apostles, or at least those from the circumcision, he writes in a letter, *We ourselves, who are Jews by birth and not Gentile sinners, yet who know that a man is not justified by works of the law but through faith in Jesus Christ, even we have believed in Christ Jesus, in order to be justified by faith in Christ, and not by works of the law, because by works of the law shall no one be justified* (Gal 2:15-16). "Do not," he warns, "think that by **sacrifice** (43:24) and smoke you can make yourself free from the indictment for your wickedness.

Rather, know that **I am the one who removes your sins, and I shall by no means remember them** (43:25)." For we have been justified not by the deeds of righteousness which we did, but by the great mercy of him who wills to forget our offenses. This, and this alone, will save human beings, whose minds are feeble and easily drawn to everything forbidden by the law. For, it is said, from his youth the mind of man inclines toward evil (cf. Gen 8:21). Quite rightly, therefore, the inspired David said, speaking of human failings, *If you, O LORD, mark iniquity, who shall stand? Because with you is forgiveness* (Ps 130:3-4).

The God of the universe feels compassion, his will is favorably disposed, he practices an amnesty appropriate to him as God, he puts away the accusations and lapses of which they have been convicted. Yet he does not let those on whom he has shown mercy actually know the grace of the one who justifies them. Let us see if we can learn what purpose this divine reticence serves, and why God does it out of his care for the saints. Now the blessed David says in one place, *I know my iniquity, and my sin is always before me* (Ps 51:3), and in another that *I will declare my iniquity and meditate upon my sin* (Ps 37:19 LXX). But God says, "I will forget your guilt. **But as for you, do remember, and let us be judged; you state your transgressions first, so that you may be justified**" (43:26). For it is written, *The just man accuses himself, taking the part of the prosecutor* (Prov 18:17 LXX). And again: *Do not be ashamed to confess your sin* (Sir 4:26). This was the command which the proud Pharisee did not keep, who in the Savior's parable prays in the synagogue, ignorant that he is gravely ill and swollen with his own vanity, *O God, I thank you that I am not like the rest of men, greedy, unjust, or even like this tax collector. I fast twice a week, I give tithes of all that I get* (Luke 18:11-12). This man could not bear to speak of his own sins. He is therefore judged as arrogant and a liar, for no one is spotlessly pure; we all have fallen often. The tax collector knew this and confessed his sinfulness. For he stood and struck his breast, saying, *God, be merciful to me, a sinner* (Luke 18:13). The one who has been justified is he who confessed his failings and, so that he might be cleansed, did not hide the shameful filth that clung to him.

43:2
If you should go through fire, you shall by no means be burned, the flame shall not consume you.

(3) Origen of Alexandria

Before the coming of my Lord Jesus Christ it was impossible for anyone to go to the place where the tree of life was located because one could not pass by those who guarded the way to the tree of life. For *[God] placed the cherubim and a flaming sword which turns about to guard the way to the tree of life* (Gen 3:24). Who could make a way past? Who is able to get someone by this flaming sword? Just as no one was able to make a way in the sea except with God's help and the pillar of fire and the pillar of light sent by God, and no one was able to cross the Jordan without Joshua [in Greek, Jesus] (Josh 3:16) — for this Jesus was a type of the real Jesus — so Samuel was not able to pass by the flaming sword, nor was Abraham.

That is why Abraham was seen by the person who was being punished (Luke 16:23). He was in torment, and raising his eyes he saw Abraham — though from far off — and he also saw Lazarus in his bosom. The patriarchs and prophets and all men waited for the coming of my Lord Jesus, for he was the one to open up the way. *I am the way* (John 14:6). *I am the door* (John 10:9). He is the way that leads to the tree of life. That is to say, **if you go through fire, the flame will not consume you** (43:2). What fire? *He placed the cherubim and a flaming sword which turns about to guard the way to the tree of life* (Gen 3:24). That is why the blessed, somewhat surprisingly,[2] are waiting in the netherworld. They were prevented from going to the place where the tree of life is, where the paradise of God is located, where God is the gardener, and where the blessed and the elect and the saints of God are to be found.

43:10
Before me there was no other God.

(4) Irenaeus of Lyons

God is one and the same who rolls up the heavens as a book and renews the face of the earth; he made the things of time for man, so that coming to maturity in the passage of time, he may produce the fruit of immortality. Through his kindness he also bestows eternal things on him *that in the ages to come he may show the exceeding riches of his grace* (Eph 2:7). This God was proclaimed by the law and the prophets, and Christ confessed him as Father. He is the Creator and the God over all, as Isaiah says: **I too am a witness, says the Lord God, and the servant whom I have chosen, so that you may know and believe and understand that I am. Before me there was no other god, nor shall there be any after me. I am God, and besides me there is none who saves** (43:10-11). And again: *I myself am the first God, and I am in the things to come* (Isa 41:4). This is not said in vanity, nor arrogantly, nor boastfully. Since it is impossible to come to a knowledge of God without God, he teaches men through his word to know God. To those who are ignorant of these matters, and for this reason imagine they have discovered another Father, one can rightly say, *You err, because you do not know the Scriptures nor the power of God* (Matt 22:29).

43:12
You are my witnesses; I too am a witness, says the Lord God.

(5) Origen of Alexandria

For God is my witness, whom I serve with my spirit in the gospel of his Son (Rom 1:9). God is a witness for his saints, because they are also witnesses of God according to the word of the prophet: **You shall be my witnesses, and I am a witness, says the Lord** (43:12). More-

---

2. Their true home was heaven.

Isaiah 43

over, the Savior says to his disciples: *You will be my witnesses in Jerusalem and in Samaria and to all the ends of the earth* (Acts 1:8). Accordingly it is written: *Everyone who confesses me, I will also confess him before my Father* (Matt 10:32).

43:19
Look, I am doing new things that will now spring forth. . . .

(6) Augustine of Hippo

Though the true sacrifice is owed to the one true God, various models of it were sketched beforehand in offerings of incense and victims. Divine providence, by foretelling in many ways what was going to be accomplished in one way, would show how great this true sacrifice would be. For besides the other things that were foretold as going to come about in Christian times, this too was prophesied. All the things that were previously offered to God in various sacrifices were to be totally changed.

"So why were they laid down," you ask, "if they were due to be changed?" O my dear sick man, don't start giving the doctor advice about how you are to be cured. . . . Some things were good for the benefit of the human race in earlier times, other things are good in later times. . . . Among many other things the prophet Isaiah, whose volume I have in my hand, inquires — what does Isaiah say? **There is no cause for you to be mindful of ancient things or to call old things to mind** (43:18). There you are, brothers and sisters, already the abolition of the old ways is evident.

Here is what the text means. "I will do new things which were not there before, so that you can understand the things that were there before." An animal used to be slaughtered, blood poured out, and by means of the blood God was being placated. But was God really being placated by means of the blood, and does God really hanker after blood, and does God really take delight in the smoke of sacrifices, or does the one who created all things, who gives you all things, really have a craving for the smell of incense or other aromatic spices? Far be it from you to believe that! It's your devotion that he feeds on, and that indeed for your benefit, not for that of the one you are serving as his slave.

Every human slave of a human lord and master serves his master for his master's benefit, and again the master takes care of his slave for his slave's benefit. It's not like that with God. Those who serve him serve him for their benefit, not for his. And am I perhaps saying this from myself? Listen to the prophet:[3] *I said to the Lord* — what? *It is you who are my Lord* — why? *Since you have no need*, he [the psalmist] says, *of my good things* (Ps 15:2 Vg.). There you have an unconditional statement, there's nothing you can have any hesitation about; God has no need of your good things. So stop believing that your God is in need of such sacrifices, but ask yourself what lesson they are teaching, what they mean.

Previously blood used to be shed by animal victims, because the blood foretold what was to be shed by the one true victim, the blood of your Lord, the blood that is the

---

3. The church fathers called the psalmist a prophet.

price paid for you, the blood by which the bond of your debt would be cancelled (cf. Col 2:14), by which, that is, the old staleness of your sin would be eliminated. It has happened, it has been shed, he himself is being offered. *Let the day now breathe, and the shadows withdraw* (Song 2:17; 4:6). **There is no cause for you to be mindful of ancient things or to call old things to mind. For I will do new things which will spring up now, and you will understand** (43:18-19). Now at last we can understand why those things came before which were foretelling things to come. They all point to Christ, they all have their end in Christ. **I will do**, he says, **new things which will spring up now, and you will understand** (43:19). Before all these new things came about, the old ones were being practiced and not being understood.

What comes next? **I will make a way in the wilderness** (43:19). In which wilderness? That of the nations, of course, where there was no worship of the true God. **I will make a way in the wilderness, and streams in the dry places.** Nowhere among the nations were the prophets ever read; now their writings are flooding all the nations. You can see the **streams in dry places. The beasts of the field shall bless me** (43:20). What are the **beasts of the field** if not the Gentiles? **The beasts of the field shall bless me, and the siren daughters of ostriches** (43:20). Some godless souls, daughters of demons, shall bless me. How, if not by forsaking the devil and being converted to Christ?

43:25-26
I am, I am the one who blots your transgressions,
and I will not remember them at all.

(7) Ambrose of Milan

One whose sins have been forgiven by Christ rightly says, *Repay your servant, and I will live and keep your words* (Ps 119:17). Repaid by the Lord, he has no cause for despair. The Lord came to save the world, not to destroy it. He does not remember the injury we have done him, but he remembers the good. As it is written in the prophetic book: **I am, I am the one who blots out your transgressions, and I will not remember them at all. But as for you, do remember, and let us be judged; you state your transgressions, so that you may be justified** (43:25-26). . . .

Why am I afraid to confess? Why do I shrink from reciting my sins? Why do I fear making mention of my disgrace to one all of whose judgments are sweet? What would be harsh in others is delightful in Christ. In Christ there is only sweetness, because he is sweet. *Taste and see how good the* LORD *is* (Ps 34:8). His judgment of the one who confesses his sins is kind and gentle, because he said: **I am, I am the one who blots out your transgressions, and I will not remember them at all. But as for you, do remember, and let us be judged; you state your transgressions, so that you may be justified** (43:25-26). Moreover, to the one who repents he promises: *There will be more rejoicing in heaven over one repentant sinner than over ninety-nine righteous persons who need no repentance* (Luke 15:7). If the Lord's judgments are so sweet, we must make an effort to claim the harvest of his sweetness. . . .

Isaiah 43

David was often encouraged by heavenly oracles to hope that his faith and his merits would be rewarded. For example, it is recorded that God said to him through the prophet Nathan: *I took you from the pasture, from following the sheep, that you should be prince over my people Israel; and I have been with you wherever you went and have cut off all your enemies from before you* (2 Sam 7:8-9). And a little further he says: *I will give you rest from all your enemies* (2 Sam 7:11). David replied: *Who am I, Lord God, and what is my house, that you have brought me this far, since you have loved me in this way? For I, O Lord, am least of all and yet you make your promises extend to the house of your servant into the distant future* (2 Sam 7:18-19). And yet further he adds: *And now, O Lord God, you are God, and your words are true, and you have promised this good thing to your servant. Now therefore may it please you to bless the house of your servant that it may continue forever before you; for you, O Lord God, have spoken, and with your blessing the house of your servant will be blessed forever* (2 Sam 7:28-29).

By this oracle and by others, David was encouraged not to lose hope. Firm in the prophetic faith, he called upon the Lord to remember his promises. Not that it is God's way to forget, for he fulfills the promises that he makes to his saints. He forgets our iniquities but remembers his promises. As it is written: **I am, I am the one who blots out your transgressions, and I will not remember them at all. But as for you, do remember, and let us be judged** (43:25-26).

He wants us to forget whatever threats he made to sinners if one day they take another path. He also wishes to be called upon so that anyone who has aimed at the rewards he promises to virtue, and who has fought well, will receive the fruits of his effort. Indeed, it is altogether fitting to demand the prize, as Scripture says: *I have fought the good fight, I have finished the race. Hence there is laid up for me the crown of righteousness* (2 Tim 4:7-8). This is not a mark of arrogance, but of faith. For it reminds us that God cannot deceive us. So too David tells the Lord to remember his word which was the ground of our hope, that we might renounce hopes oriented to the earth and cling to what is heavenly.

Isaiah 44

1 But now hear, O Iakob my servant,
    and Israel whom I have chosen!
2 Thus says the Lord God who made you,
    and who formed you from the womb:
  You will still be helped, do not fear, O Iakob my servant,
    and the beloved Israel whom I have chosen.
3 Because I will provide water in their thirst
    to those who walk in a dry land;
  I will put my spirit on your offspring,
    and my blessings on your children.
4 And they shall spring up like grass in the midst of water,
    and like a willow by flowing water.
5 This one will say, "I am God's,"
    and this one will call out in the name of Iakob,
  yet another will inscribe, "I am God's,"
    in the name of Israel.

6 Thus says God, the King of Israel,
    who delivered him, God Sabaoth:
  I am first and I am after these things;
    besides me there is no god.
7 Who is like me? Let him stand, let him call,
    and let him make ready for me,
    inasmuch as I have made man forever;
  and let them declare to you
    the things that are coming
    before they come.
8 Do not cover yourselves;
    did you not give ear from the beginning
    and I declared it to you?

> You are witnesses
>> whether there is a god besides me;
>> and they were not formerly.

9All who fashion and carve are vain — those who do the things that are in their mind, which will not profit them. But they will be put to shame, 10all who fashion a god or cast useless things; 11and all from where they came have withered and are mute from among men. Let them all assemble and stand together; let them be disgraced and put to shame together.

12Because the artisan sharpened the iron, he fashioned it with an ax and bored it with a gimlet, he fashioned it with his strong arm; he also will become hungry and weak and will not drink water. 13Having chosen a piece of wood, the artisan set it up with a measure and arranged it with glue; he made it like the form of a man, like human beauty, to set it up in a house. 14He cut this wood from the forest, which the Lord planted and the rain made grow, 15so that it might be for people to burn. And taking part of it, he warmed himself; and they burned the pieces and baked bread on them. But the rest they fashioned into gods and they worship them. 16Half of it he burned up in the fire; and after roasting meat over it, he ate it and was satisfied. And having warmed himself he said, "I am pleased, for I have been warmed and have seen the fire!" 17The rest he made into a graven god and worships it; and he prays, saying, "Rescue me, for you are my god!"

18They did not know how to think, because they were blinded so as not to see with their eyes and understand with their heart. 19And he has not considered in his heart, nor regarded in his soul, nor known in his mind, that half of it he burned in the fire, and that he baked bread on its coals and roasted meat and ate, and that the rest of it he made into an abomination and they are worshiping it. 20Know that their heart is ashes, and they are going astray, and no one is able to deliver his soul. See, will you not say, "There is a lie in my right hand"?

> 21 Remember these things, O Iakob,
>> and Israel, for you are my servant;
>> I formed you as my servant,
>> and you, Israel, do not forget me.
> 22 For see, I have blotted out your transgressions like a cloud,
>> and your sins like darkness;
>> return to me, and I will redeem you.

> 23 Rejoice, O heavens, because God has had mercy on Israel;
>> blow the trumpet, O foundations of the earth;
>> shout for joy, O mountains,
>>> the hills and all the trees that are in them!

> Because God has redeemed Iakob,
> > and Israel will be glorified.
>
> 24 Thus says the Lord, who redeems you,
> > who forms you from the womb:
> I am the Lord, who accomplishes all things;
> > I alone stretched out heaven,
> > and I bolstered the earth.
> 25 Who else will scatter the signs given by ventriloquists
> > and the divinations from the heart,
> turning the wise backward,
> > and making their counsel foolish,
> 26 and confirming the words of his servant,
> > and proving true the counsel of his messengers?
> The one who says to Ierousalem, "You shall be inhabited,"
> > and to the cities of Judea, "You shall be built,"
> > and her deserts shall arise;
> 27 who says to the deep, "You will become desolate,
> > and I will dry up your rivers";
> 28 who tells Cyrus to be wise, and says,
> > "He shall carry out all my wishes";
> who says to Ierousalem, "You shall be built,
> > and I will lay the foundations of my holy house."

Interpretation of this chapter in the early Church focused primarily on verses that spoke about God's oneness, for example, **I am first and I am after these things; besides me there is no god** *(44:6), and* **I alone stretched out heaven** *(44:24). If taken to refer to the Father alone, they seemed to pose a challenge to the Christian profession of the divinity of the Son. Selections from Tertullian, Eusebius, Athanasius, and Gregory of Nyssa address this interpretation. As the selection from Gregory's* Against Eunomius *shows, a defender of the faith of Nicea (with its confession of the Son as "of one being with the Father") had to develop highly subtle expositions of these texts because they were vulnerable to an Arian interpretation. The chapter also speaks of repentance and forgiveness, a theme to which a passage from Origen's* Commentary on Romans *alludes. It also contains two references to God's creative power extending to life in the womb, which provoked the anonymous late-fourth-century Latin writer known as Ambrosiaster to reflect on the origin of the soul. Finally, a number of commentators deal with the historical references to the end of the Babylonian exile, to Cyrus, and to the rebuilding of Jerusalem and the temple, which Christian interpreters understood to be fulfilled both in the actual rebuilding of Jerusalem and in the foundation of the Church. Many of these themes are summarized in the initial selection from Cyril of Alexandria, which covers the opening verses of the chapter.*

Isaiah 44

(1) Cyril of Alexandria

Previously God had charged the Israelites with apostasy, for having withdrawn their love for him and serving those who were no gods, when he said, *Your fathers and your leaders sinned against me, and the leaders polluted my holy places* (43:27-28a). Now he fittingly continues with the above words, **Now hear, O Jacob my servant, Israel whom I have chosen. You will still be helped** (44:1-2), for he permits them neither to remain in apostasy, nor to fall into despair, nor to lose hope in him. Rather, he proclaims gentleness to them, restores them because of his unfailing love of humankind, and turns them toward repentance. And he lets it be understood that those who sinned were not utterly lost, nor had Israel perished root and branch, because he is merciful and makes straight the way of salvation.

Identifying himself as Lord and God, the one who creates and shapes from the womb, he declares that Israel had erred in applying the name of divinity to others and in thoughtlessly bestowing the glory of dominion on those who are not gods. God says that Israel did not know the Creator, the one who has brought into being something that had not existed on earth, a human being. For God, the Creator and Maker, reproaches for their ingratitude those who turn from loving him.

For it is the height of absurdity for us to offer supreme honor to our parents according to the flesh (as the law of God requires of us) if we do not at the same time, through total obedience, give the Creator of the universe the praise and honor that are due to him — more even than to our parents. This is what he says through one of his prophets: *A son honors his father, and a servant his master. If then I am a father, where is my honor? And if I am a master, where is my fear? says the* LORD *Almighty* (Mal 1:6). For he is at the same time "Lord," having the whole of creation under his yoke and service — as the psalmist says somewhere, *Everything is yours* (Ps 24:1) — and "Father," as the Creator and Maker who brings everything into being. Therefore the obedience appropriate to sons and the fear appropriate to servants must be rendered to God, returning what is justly due. So when God says that he is Creator and Maker, that is a way of saying we owe him veneration, as the one who is the author of being itself and the source of existence for what had not previously existed.

When he says to sinners, **You will still be helped** (44:2), he encourages confidence that a store of gentleness and love of humanity has been reserved for them, even though they have been guilty of many undeniable faults. And he would stop at nothing in order to save them, if they were to choose to return to the better and nobler way, and to what was consistent with his laws.

The words **Israel** and **Jacob** (44:1) seem to name the company of the holy apostles, understood as a single person, for they are all in Christ. Notice how he says that this person is **beloved** and **chosen**, although in what way is not clear to everyone, since he would never have called "beloved" and "chosen" those who had rejected faith in him. Since, being "Jacob" and "Israel" by blood, they have become honored and choice vessels, and have been called to the sacred service of proclaiming the gospel, he thought it necessary to crown them with such splendid names, inasmuch as they would be like lights in the world, bearing the word of life and initiating the whole world under the sun into the divine mysteries.

Then he commands, **Be not afraid** (44:2), which means: "Be brave and strong, hard and high-spirited, laughing at the efforts of your persecutors, and have firm faith in God. For many opposed the sacred tidings, and an unholy host will rise up to resist your words. But," he adds, "rise above cowardice, lethargy, and weakness." For **I will provide water for those who walk in a dry land** (44:3). Sweet and life-saving it is when travelers in a desert encounter springs of water; but it is far more desirable for those grown weary in pursuit of genuine devotion to be sprinkled with divine and spiritual rivers. This means the encouragement given by the Holy Spirit by which the human mind, temporarily weakened, is renewed and emboldened with courage. In my view the water that this text promises God will give **to those who walk in a dry land** signifies the Holy Spirit. The Savior himself said that according to Scripture, *"Rivers of living water will flow from within him." He said this about the Spirit that those who believe in him were going to receive* (John 7:38-39). Just as water is life-giving and makes plants and grasses grow, so the working of the Holy Spirit imitates the life-giving power of water. The power of the Spirit enabled the existence and well-being of everything. The spiritual creation enriches growth in everything that is good, and urges it forward in spiritual increase.

That the water promised **for those who walk in a dry land** represents the life-giving power and working of the Holy Spirit, the spiritual consolation that comes from him, the next passage will make clear: **For I will put my spirit on your seed, and my blessings on your children** (44:3). We say that the **seed** and **children** of the holy apostles are those who have been called to the knowledge of the truth and to spiritual regeneration: the apostles have begotten them anew not by mortal seed but by the word of the living and abiding God, and the working of his Holy Spirit. The blessed Paul therefore writes to those who have been called through him, *Even if you should have countless guides to Christ, yet you do not have many fathers, for I begot you in Christ Jesus through the gospel* (1 Cor 4:15). Everywhere we will find that God calls **children** those who believe in him through the apostles' efforts, so he says, **I will put my spirit on your seed, and my blessings on your children**. We hold that the **blessings** that God provides to the saints are the variety of spiritual gifts. To one has been given a word of wisdom, to another a word of knowledge, and the like (cf. 1 Cor 12:8). The all-wise Paul writes, *Each of you has his own gift from God* (1 Cor 7:7).

Then the text goes on to explain what sort of benefit comes from these **blessings**: **They shall spring up like grass in the midst of water, like a willow by flowing water** (44:4). Grasses and plants that grow in waterless places grow up very slowly, and once grown, promptly wither. But the ones that are nourished by flowing streams and a supply of life-giving water flourish abundantly, such as the perpetually green willow tree, which always grows alongside springs and rivers. Irrigated by spiritual streams and enriched by their fruits, the text says, they will confess that they know God alone and will be inscribed with the name of the God who called them. When the text states, **This one will say, "I am God's,"** and **this one will cry out**, and **another will write** (44:5), it is referring to the many who come to God because of their faith in Christ. For it is not a single nation that will be called, but the entire mass of peoples under the sun, all of whom will confess that they have become God's, and the name of the Savior himself, the Redeemer, will be inscribed on them. They are furthermore known by the **name of Jacob**, that is, the portion and inheritance of God. For, it says, the Lord's people *became his lot, Israel, the portion of his inheritance* (Deut 32:9). Therefore, let us who have believed boast at becoming God's lot and the portion of the Savior of us all, Jesus Christ.

After he has mentioned the knowledge of Christ in the passages just read, the prophet now changes his discourse to another necessary topic. At the time when the inspired prophet Isaiah was composing his words for us, the king who ruled them hated God, and his people lived amidst unbearable vices. "God" and "religion" were whatever appealed to each person. God composed a necessary exhortation for them, wrapped in well-formed arguments. Now that they have been delivered from the worship of many gods and its attendant ills, he then exhorts them to turn to the knowledge of the truth and to acknowledge his glory by reminding them of his incomparable power. Therefore, he writes, **Thus says the Lord, the King of Israel, who delivered him, God Sabaoth** (44:6). That is, he wants them to know that God is the Lord of hosts and, having recovered from their drunkenness, recognize that he saved them from the tyranny of the Egyptians, when he did wonders by his power and revealed his awesome might. . . .

For this reason he not only proclaimed himself Lord and God, but in addition he says, **who delivered him** (44:6), calling to their remembrance the wonderful things he had done for them.

Know then, he announces, that **I, God, am first and I am after these things, and none is God besides me** (44:6). For God is the first principle, the beginning of the universe. He himself has no beginning, and through him everything has been brought into being. He himself did not come into being by some agent; rather, he is and he will be. For this is his very name and his eternal remembrance unto ages of ages (cf. Exod 3:14). There was no other God before him, nor will there be one after him. God is by nature one, and there is no other besides him.

Such an exhortation was utterly to the point for people who had denied him, and who had fallen through great want of understanding into supposing that there were many gods. He shows that there is no other God when he says, **Who is like me?** (44:7). Which of those whom you suppose wrongly to be gods would be equal to my glory and power? By what kind of mighty act did you come to believe that they are gods? **Let him stand** if he is my equal. **Let him make ready** if he can equal my nature, my strength, my glory. **Let them call** those whom they choose from among the so-called gods, **inasmuch as I have made man forever** (44:7), for, he maintains, "I created the heavens and what is in them, with the companies of the countless holy spirits that venerate and worship me. **Inasmuch as I have made man** on the earth" and, in the words that follow, "**forever**, let them show me one who is equal to me." With the clause **Inasmuch as I have made man**, he shows that he is the fashioner, and the gods falsely so-called are nothing whatsoever. What person among those who worship them did those "gods" ever bring into being? Again: "I am known to be the fashioner, the creator of the universe, the one who has the knowledge of all things. Inquire among those whom you call gods, **let them declare to you the things that are coming before they come** (44:7)." Only to the one who is God by nature is there knowledge of the things that are already past and of those yet to come. If none of those gods falsely so-called has such knowledge, it is obvious that those who lack God's knowledge could not themselves be God.

44:6
I am the first and I am after these things; besides me there is no god.

(2) Tertullian

Therefore there is one God, the Father (cf. 1 Cor 8:6), and **besides him there is no other** (cf. 44:6). The one who says this is not denying that there is a Son; rather, he is denying that there is another god. The Son is not another god in addition to the Father. Moreover, if you look at the context of statements like this, you will discover that their meaning has to do with makers and worshipers of idols. The point is to drive out the multitude of false gods by proclaiming the oneness of the divine, the one God who nevertheless has a Son. Because the Son is indivisible and inseparable from the Father, he must be accounted as in the Father even though his name is not mentioned. Suppose that he *had* mentioned him by name; then he would have distinguished the Son as separate, by saying something like this: "Besides me there is none other except my Son." Then indeed he would have made the Son another God by having distinguished him from those others who are no gods. Imagine the sun saying, "I am the sun, and besides me there is none other except my sunbeam." Would you not regard that as gratuitous, as though the sunbeam were not already included in the sun? And so the statement that **besides himself there is no other god** (cf. 44:6) was spoken on account of the idolatry both of the Gentiles and of Israel. It is also addressed to the heretics, who manufacture idols with words as the Gentiles do with their hands — that is, creating another God and another Christ. Therefore, even when pronouncing himself as "one," the Father was serving the Son's interest, lest Christ should be believed to have come from some other god besides the one who had already asserted, **I am God, and there is none other besides me** (cf. 45:5; 44:6). God reveals himself as "one," but with a Son, with whom he **alone has spread out the heaven** (44:24).

Indeed, they also seize on this saying as evidence that he is one without remainder: **I alone**, he says, **have spread out the heaven** (44:24). The point, however, is that he is alone with respect to other heavenly powers. In this way the text erects a barrier against the imaginings of the heretics who hold that the world was constructed by angels and hostile powers. Such heretics make the Creator himself either an angel or a being unwittingly set up from without, for the making of the world. Or if, according to their interpretation, he **alone spreads out the heaven**, why do these heretics perversely exclude that unique Wisdom who says, *When he prepared the heaven, I was present with him* (Prov 8:27)? And if Isaiah has said, *Who has known the mind of the* LORD, *and who has been his counselor?* (40:13), evidently he means "besides Wisdom who *was present with him*." In him, however, and with him, Wisdom fashioned the universe, though not in ignorance of what he was doing. But "besides Wisdom" means "besides the Son," who is *Christ, the Wisdom and the Power of God* (1 Cor 1:24), as the apostle says, he who alone knows the mind of the Father. For *who knows the things which are in God, except the Spirit which is in him?* (1 Cor 2:11) — not which is outside him! There was then one who caused God to be not alone [i.e., solitary], except in the sense that he is alone with respect to other gods.

But if we agree with the heretics, the Gospel will also be denied a hearing because it indicates that all things were made by God through the Word, and that *without him was nothing made* (John 1:3). For, if I am not mistaken, it is also written elsewhere: *By his Word were the heavens established, and all their powers by his Spirit* (Ps 33:6). Moreover, the one who is Word, Power, and Wisdom will himself be the Son of God. Thus if all things are by the Son, when he also **spreads out the heaven** (44:24), he does not spread it out alone, save through that Reason by which he is alone with respect to other gods. And so in the passage he goes on to say of the Son: **Who else has cast down the tokens of the ventriloquists, and divinations from the heart, turning the wise backward, and making their counsel foolish, establishing the words of his Son**[1] (44:25-26a), namely, in the pronouncement, *This is my Son, my Beloved, listen to him* (Matt 3:17; Luke 9:35). Thus by attaching a reference to the Son, he himself is the interpreter of how he **alone has spread out heaven** (44:24), that is, alone with his Son, even as he is one thing with his Son. And further, it will be the Son's voice [which says], **I alone have spread out heaven** (44:24), because *by the Word were the heavens established* (Ps 33:6): with the assistance of Wisdom, heaven was prepared by the Word, and because all things were made by the Word, it is fitting as well to say that the Son **alone has spread out the heaven**, because he alone ministered to the working of the Father. He also it will be who says, **I am the first, and for the things to come after, I am** (41:4; cf. 44:6). Clearly the Word is the first thing of all: *In the beginning was the Word* (John 1:1), and in that beginning he was brought forth by the Father. The Father, however, had no beginning, since he was brought forth by no one, being unborn. The one who was always singular cannot be regarded as the first nor ranked in numerical order.

(3) Basil of Caesarea

There is one God the Father; one, the only-begotten Son; one, the Holy Spirit. We affirm each of the persons distinctly, and if one wishes to number them together, one should not be carried away by thoughtless counting and fall into a polytheistic way of thinking. For we do not add them in counting from one to many. It is improper to say one, two, three, or first, second, third. For **I, God, I am the first and the last** (44:6). We have never heard of a second God. When we worship God we confess the unique character of each person, and hold fast to the "monarchy"[2] without splitting up the mystery of God into separate parts. For we contemplate, as it were, God the Father and God the Only-begotten as one form reflecting (as in a mirror) the identical divinity. For the Son is in the Father, and the Father is in the Son (cf. John 10:30). For what the one is the other is, and what the other is the one is. And in this way they are one. According to the distinction of persons they are one and one; but according to the unity of nature the two are one.

---

1. Tertullian's Latin version apparently read "his son" for the LXX's "his servant." The Greek term can be rendered as either "servant" or "child."

2. That there is a single principle *(archē)* in the Holy Trinity, namely, the Father.

(4) Gregory of Nyssa

Let us not fall into the same error [as those who worshiped many gods] — we who have been taught by Scripture to revere the true divinity, and have learned to consider everything created as external to the divine nature, and to worship and venerate only the uncreated nature, which has neither beginning nor end. This is how the great Isaiah, in his sublime voice, speaks about these divine matters: when, speaking in the person of God, he declared, "**I am first and I am after these things** (44:6; cf. 42:4; 48:14 LXX), no deity existed before me and none will exist after me." This great prophet knew the mystery of the religion of the gospel more perfectly than anyone else: he gave voice to that astonishing miracle of the Virgin and proclaimed the Good News of her child's birth by clearly referring to the name of her Son (7:14). Because the Holy Spirit was present in him, he was able to give himself wholly to the truth. He proclaimed the nature of God clearly, that is to say, that which truly "is" must be distinguished from that which "comes into being." Speaking in the person of God, he made this plain: "**I am first and I am after these things**, no deity existed before me and none will exist after me." Since, then, there is neither a God-before-God, nor a God-after-God (because what comes after God is the creation, and there is nothing beyond God, and "nothing" certainly cannot *be* God, or, better, nothing transcends God save God himself in his eternal blessedness) — since, then, as I say, the inspired voice that spoke through the prophet's mouth was the voice of God, we learn from it the teaching that the divine nature is single, continuous with itself, and indivisible. Though God is proclaimed as trinity, no past or future is imputed to it, and none of its attributes is "older" or "younger."

Because this is God's voice, it matters not whether you say that the words are those of the Father or of the Son. In either case the teaching is orthodox. For if it be the Father that says this, he bears witness that the Son does not come after him (for if the Son is God, and whatever comes after the Father is *not* God, then it is clear that the passage testifies that the Son is in the Father and not after the Father). If, on the other hand, someone should grant that this is the voice of the Son, the assertion that "nothing existed before me" clearly teaches that the one who is contemplated as *in the beginning* (John 1:1) is conceived with the eternity of that beginning.

*   *   *

The word of Holy Scripture tells us that one mark of true divinity is what Moses was taught when he heard the voice from above say, *I am who am* (Exod 3:14). Therefore we think that the one thing we must hold as truly divine is what is perceived as eternal and infinite in its being, and regardless of how it is contemplated, it remains always the same, neither increasing nor diminishing. As a result, if someone should say that once God existed but now he does not, or that now he is but once he was not, we would judge both expressions to be equally irreligious. For both mutilate the meaning of God's eternity in a similar way, being cut short by nonexistence in one direction or the other: whether we put his nonexistence before his existence, or whether we judge that his existence ends in nonexistence — it is all the same. No amount of noisy argument about God's nonexistence, whether "first of all" or "last of all," can make amends for such impious views concerning the divine.

For this reason we hold that the view that the One who truly "is" could ever be said not to be is a denial and a repudiation of his actual divinity. For the One who revealed himself to Moses through the light of the burning bush gives his name as "Being" when he says, *I am who am*. And Isaiah, serving as an instrument of the One who spoke in him, says in the person of the One who is, **I am the first and I am after these things** (44:6), the two statements being understood to mean the eternity of God. . . .

And the great John, the Evangelist, when he proclaims the only-begotten God in his prologue, safeguards his account in every way, so that there is no chance of attributing non-being to the One who is. For he says that he *was in the beginning* and *was with God and was God*, and was *light* and *life* and *truth*, and at all times everything that is good and never lacking anything good, for he *is* the fullness of every good and is *in the bosom of the Father* (John 1:1, 4, 14, 18). So then: Moses lays down the law for us in his characterization of true divinity when he says that we know nothing of God but this, that *he is* (for that is the meaning of *I am who am*). And for his part, Isaiah cries out in his preaching that "being" is utterly unbounded: God's being is delimited neither by a beginning nor by an end, for he says, **I am the first and I am after these things** (44:6). In neither of these clauses does he set a limit to God's eternity, so that those who look to the beginning find no indication from what time he has come to be, and after what time he ceased to be; nor if we turn our thoughts to the future do we cut short by any boundary the procession of "being" toward eternity.

44:22
I have blotted out your transgressions like a cloud, and your sins like a darkness.

(5) Origen of Alexandria

Who shall bring any charge against God's elect? It is God who justifies. Who is to condemn? It is Christ Jesus, who died; yes, who was raised from the dead, who is at the right hand of God, who indeed intercedes for us (Rom 8:33-34).

It seems to me that when he asks, *Who shall bring any charge against God's elect?* he is speaking of the devil. For there is no one so chosen and so great that the devil would not dare to accuse, except him alone *who committed no sin* (1 Pet 2:22), who also said, *Now the ruler of this world is coming, and he finds nothing in me* (John 14:30). But although he may practice his wicked intention, what good will it do the accuser since God is the one who justifies, and who **wipes out the iniquities of his elect like a cloud, and their sins like a mist** (44:22), and makes their former sins *white as snow and as pure as wool* (1:18)? Moreover, since Christ died for them, indeed also was resurrected from the dead and stands at the right hand of the Father interceding for them, who is able to condemn them? Immediately prior to this section he noted that the *Holy Spirit intercedes for us with sighs too deep for words* (Rom 8:26). Here he says, "Christ Jesus, who died and was raised from the dead, himself intercedes for us. God, who handed over his own Son for us (Rom 8:32), justifies the elect. Is there anyone who would dare to condemn him?"

44:24
Thus says the Lord, who redeems you, who forms you from the womb. I am the Lord, who accomplishes all things; I alone stretched out heaven. . . .

(6) Eusebius of Caesarea

Having given a refutation of idolatry in the previous passage, the text speaks as though idolatry would cease among those who had benefited from the prophetic teaching and makes promises about the return from captivity in Babylon. For since they were handed over to the Babylonians when they were idolaters, and Jerusalem herself underwent siege and total destruction during the time of the Assyrians because of the outrages committed in the city, he prophesies to its residents that they who had suffered would have freedom from ills if they ceased from error. This was fulfilled in the time of Cyrus, the first king of the Persians. That is why he even mentions Cyrus by name, who would appear astonishingly two centuries later[3] and would liberate the Jewish people from captivity and give permission for them to reconstruct the temple in Jerusalem.

Therefore, in the present passage, on the grounds of such good tidings, the text tells **the heavens** and **the foundations of the earth** and **the mountains and hills and all the trees** (44:23) to hymn and praise God. Following which he also adds: **Thus says the Lord, who redeems you, who forms you from the womb** (44:24). Who this is **who forms from the womb** the book of Jeremiah teaches, where it says, *And the word of the LORD came to me saying, "Before I formed you in the womb I knew you, and before you came forth from your mother I consecrated you"* (Jer 1:4-5). In adding this word of the Lord, the prophet plainly teaches that he is the one who forms bodies conceived in the womb. Then, since he had hinted to them that they would return from the exile, he appropriately named himself as the one who **redeems**. If those to whom this was said were rather corporeal in their disposition, he rightly reminds them that he himself is the one who **forms** them **from the womb**, and then adds, **I am the Lord, who accomplishes all things**, or according to the other translations, **who has made all things**. And first he says, **I alone stretched out heaven**, then **I bolstered the earth**. For *everything was made through him, and without him not one thing came into being* (John 1:3). He **stretched out heaven alone, and bolstered the earth**, by the will and command of the Father. For *he spoke and they came into being, he commanded and they were made* (Ps 32:9 LXX). Therefore, in Proverbs it is said of his person, *When he made ready the heavens, I was alongside him* (Prov 8:27). He *was alongside* the Father when he *made ready* by means of his willing and commanding, and he served him when the Father summoned him to work, by fulfilling in action what the Father had decreed. Therefore he asserts, **I alone stretched out heaven and**

---

3. Eusebius assumes that the prophecy of Isaiah was written in the 8th century B.C.

bolstered the earth. Now the earth being firm and hard, so that the whole world is immovably established, it is rightly said to have been **bolstered**; but **the heaven**, inasmuch as it been unfolded, has been thoroughly **stretched out**. Therefore it is written in another text, *you stretched out the heavens like a tent* (Ps 104:2).

What things so great a Lord teaches, he goes on to ask: **Who else will scatter the signs given by ventriloquists and divinations from their heart?** (44:25). This means that at a later time all the divinations and the oracles of those who long ago were called gods will be scattered by his power. At that time, too, those who are considered the **wise** of this age **I will turn back** (44:25), he says, and will show their so-called wisdom to be **foolish**. This is how I interpret this passage: of **my beloved servant and chosen** (44:1-2), I mean my anointed [Christ], about whom so much of the preceding has been spoken, **I will confirm his words**, and **of his messengers**, that is, the apostles, disciples, and evangelists, I will make **their counsel prove true**. I who will do this declare and proclaim even now that I will cause Jerusalem to be rebuilt, following its first destruction yet to come at the hands of the Babylonians, so that **the cities of Judah will be inhabited** and their **deserts shall arise** as in the beginning.

(7) Athanasius of Alexandria

When the prophet says of the creation, **I alone stretched out the heaven** (44:24), it is evident to everyone that in the term **alone** [or **only**] is also signified the Word of the **Only**[4] through whom *all things were made, and without him was nothing made* (John 1:3). Therefore if things came to be through the Word, and he says **I alone**, with the **alone** is to be understood the Son through whom the **heaven** came to be. So if it is said "one God" and **I alone** and "I the First," in the terms "one" and **alone** and "First" is understood the Word coexisting as the radiance in the light. And this cannot be understood of any other than the Word alone. For all other things came to subsist out of nothing through the Son and are wholly from him. But the Son himself is from the Father by nature and his true offspring.

(8) Ambrosiaster

I think there is something ignoble about saying that souls are produced along with bodies, with the result that soul would be born from soul, something that is quite contrary to the soul's character. If it is the case that the individual heavenly powers were created and other created things were born from them, is it believable that other souls are born from the single soul of Adam? This way of thinking will not do because only God is simple [i.e., not made up of parts] and capable of bringing things into being. This power was not granted to others. So mysterious is this truth with respect to our Savior that it is considered unbelievable not only by pagans or Jews, but even by some who consider themselves Christians, for the Photinians and the Arians reject this belief. . . .

---

4. That is, the one God.

The prophet Zechariah writes, *you who form the soul of man in him* (Zech 12:1). Isaiah does not disagree with this when he says, **Thus spoke the Lord God, who made you and formed you in the womb** (44:24). If, therefore, the soul is fashioned in the womb, it is imparted to a body that has already been formed. As all the individual members that make up the body are said to be formed in the body; and as water, which has no shape, seems to be given form when it is put into a vessel; so the soul, whose nature is incorporeal and simple, is "formed," as it were, in the body, when it vivifies the individual parts of the body. Moses has expressed this more clearly when he warns, *whoever shall strike a pregnant woman and she shall have a miscarriage, if it shall have been formed, let him give a life for a life; but if it shall have been unformed, he shall pay a money fine* (Exod 21:22-23). This demonstrates that the soul did not exist before the form. And so if the soul is given to a body already formed, it is wrong to contend that the soul is born by being derived along with the semen when the body is conceived. Besides, if soul comes into being from soul along with the semen, many souls are lost every day, when semen from some type of flow does not produce a birth.

44:28
. . . who says to Jerusalem, "You shall be built," and I will lay the foundation of my holy house."

(9) Didymus the Blind

Consider whether the house whose foundation has been laid and the temple that has been rebuilt is the glorious Church, concerning which the apostle says to his disciple Timothy, *If I am delayed, you may know how one ought to behave in the household of God, which is the church of the living God, the pillar and the bulwark of the truth* (1 Tim 3:15). This interpretation has also been suggested by the prophetic voice of Isaiah, when he declares, **who says of Jerusalem, "She shall be built," and "I will lay the foundation of my holy house"** (44:28). As to when this will happen, can it be other than when all who have heard the gospel through perfect faith and virtue shall be *built upon the foundation of the apostles and prophets, Jesus Christ himself being the cornerstone, into a holy temple in the Lord, into a dwelling place* of the Trinity (Eph 2:20-22)?

Isaiah 45

1 Thus says the Lord God to my anointed, Cyrus,
    whose right hand I have grasped
so that nations will obey before him;
    and I will break through the strength of kings,
I will open doors before him —
    and cities shall not be closed:
2 I will go before you
    and level mountains,
I will break in pieces doors of bronze
    and break off bars of iron,
3 and I will give you dark treasures,
    I will open for you hidden, unseen places,
so that you may know that I am the Lord God,
    the God of Israel, who calls your name.
4 For the sake of my servant Iakob,
    and Israel my chosen,
I will call you by my name
    and receive you, but you did not know me.
5 Because I am the Lord God,
    and there is no other god besides me,
    and you did not know me,
6 so that they who are from the rising of the sun
    and from its going down
may know that there is no one besides me;
    I am the Lord God, and there is no other.
7 I am the one who has prepared light and made darkness,
    who makes peace and creates evils;
    I am the Lord who does all these things.

8 Let heaven rejoice from above,

> and let the clouds shower down righteousness;
> let the earth bring forth mercy,
> > and let it bring forth righteousness as well;
> > I am the Lord who created you.

9 What better thing have I formed like potter's clay?
> Shall the plowman plow the earth?
Shall the clay say to the potter, "What are you doing,
> since you are not working, nor do you have hands"?
10 It is like the one who says to his father, "What will you beget?"
> and to his mother, "With what are you in labor?"
11 Because thus says the Lord God, the Holy One of Israel,
> the one who has made the things that are coming:
Ask me about my sons and about my daughters,
> and command me concerning the works of my hands.
12 I made the earth
> and humankind upon it;
I bolstered heaven with my hand,
> I commanded all the stars.
13 I have raised him with righteousness,
> and all his paths shall be straight;
he shall build my city
> and turn back the captivity of my people,
not with ransom or with gifts,
> said the Lord Sabaoth.
14 Thus says the Lord Sabaoth:
Egypt has worked hard,
> as has the commerce of the Ethiopians.
And the lofty men of Seboin shall come over to you,
> and they shall be your slaves;
> > they shall follow behind you bound in handcuffs.
They will worship you and pray in you,
> because God is in you;
and they will say,
> "There is no god besides you."
15 For you are God and we did not know it,
> O God of Israel, Savior.
16 All who oppose him shall be ashamed and disgraced,
> and they shall go in shame.
> Dedicate yourselves to me, you islands!
17 Israel is being saved by the Lord
> with everlasting salvation;
they shall not be ashamed or disgraced
> > forever.

18 Thus says the Lord,
      who made heaven —
   this is the God who displayed the earth and made it,
      he himself marked its limits;
   he did not make it to be empty
      but to be inhabited:
   I am, and there is no other.
19 I have not spoken in secret,
      nor in a dark place of the earth;
   I did not say to the offspring of Iakob,
      "Seek a vain thing."
   I am, I am the Lord,
      speaking righteousness
      and declaring truth.

20 Assemble yourselves and come,
      take counsel together,
      you who are being saved from among the nations!
   They did not know —
      those who lift up the wood, their graven image,
   and pray as if to gods
      that do not save.
21 If they will declare it,
      let them draw near,
   so that they may know together
      who made from the beginning
      these things that are to be heard.
   Then it was declared to you,
      I am God and there is no other besides me,
      there is no righteous one or savior except me.

22 Turn to me and you shall be saved,
      you who are from the end of the earth!
   I am God, and there is no other.
23 By myself I swear,
   "Verily righteousness shall go forth from my mouth;
      my words shall not be turned back,
   because to me every knee shall bow
      and every tongue shall confess to God,
24 saying, Righteousness and glory shall come to him,
      and all who separate themselves shall be ashamed."
25 By the Lord shall they be justified,
      and all the offspring of the sons of Israel
      shall be glorified in God.

Isaiah 45 offered Christian interpreters a rich variety of material for comment, beginning with the very opening words, in which the Persian king Cyrus is hailed as God's "anointed," that is, as Messiah. The derivation of "Christ" from the Greek word for "anointed one" or "messiah" was a natural invitation to a christological interpretation, as many of the following selections illustrate. In the first stages of Christian appropriation of the Cyrus prophecy, its popularity even led to an apparently spontaneous emendation in which an iota *was inserted in Cyrus's name* (Kyros) *to yield the Greek title* Kyrios (= Lord), *so that Irenaeus and Lactantius, for example, could construe 45:1 as actually meaning, "Thus says the Lord to his Christ, the Lord." Even after this inventive reading had to be abandoned, a long stream of typological interpretations continued to flow, as documented below. The Vulgate rendering of 45:8, for example, inspired the Introit of the Fourth Sunday of Advent and the refrain of the lovely Advent chant, "Rorate coeli desuper, et nubes pluant Iustum," "Drop down dew, you heavens, and rain forth the Just One." The Hebrew version and the LXX read "righteousness" (or "justice"); the Vulgate rendering,* iustus *("just one"), invited a christological interpretation.*

Those engaged in writing full-scale commentaries, such as Jerome, Eusebius, Cyril, and Theodoret, also acknowledged the literal application of the prophecy to Cyrus. Eusebius was particularly interested in the accuracy of the prophecy as a description of Cyrus's capture of Babylon in 539 B.C. (see also his comment on 44:28 in the previous chapter). But he declared the kingship of Christ as well when he came to 45:13, thanks to a variant Greek reading that inserted the word "king" into the prophecy about "one raised up in righteousness." 45:7, **I am the one who has prepared light and made darkness, who makes peace and creates evils**, *prompted significant discussion because it seems to say that God was the origin of evil. Because of its importance we have included three excerpts, from Origen, Augustine, and Gregory the Great. The direction of interpretation was set by Origen, who said that God did not create evil in the proper sense of the term. This passage (and its parallels, such as "If you have received good things from the Lord, should you not also accept evil?" [Job 2:10]) means that when the good things of this world made by God are used contrary to God's intention, they become evil. The question,* **Does the pot say to him who fashioned it, "Why did you make me that way?"** *(45:9), alluded to by St. Paul in Rom 9:20-21, also seemed to imply that God creates things for dishonor, and Augustine discusses the problem in connection with the passage from Romans. Verses 23-24 at the end of the chapter seems to have inspired the "Christ hymn" in Paul's letter to the Philippians (Phil 2:9-11), and Origen calls attention to the similarity of language.*

(1) Letter of Paul to the Romans

But who are you, a man, to answer back to God? **Will what is molded say to its molder, "Why have you made me thus?"** (45:9). Has the potter no right over the clay, to make out of the same lump one vessel for beauty and another for menial use?

*   *   *

Why do you pass judgment on your brother? Or you, why do you despise your brother? For we shall all stand before the judgment seat of God, for it is written, **As I live, says the Lord, every knee shall bow to me, and every tongue shall give praise to God** (45:23).

(2) Letter of Paul to the Philippians

Therefore God has highly exalted him and bestowed on him the name which is above every name, that at the name of Jesus **every knee should bow**, in heaven and on earth, and **every tongue confess** (45:23) that Jesus Christ is Lord, to the glory of God the Father.

(3) Cyril of Alexandria

It is said that the great and mighty Cyrus read this prophecy, and was exceedingly pleased at the things foretold by God about him, and was of such a mind that even in the cities and lands under his hand he caused the glory of the Lord to break forth, confessing openly that the one who alone was worshiped by the Judeans was God, even the Lord of all. It seems to me that the meaning of the predictions of the prophet is plain enough, but let us consider the passage carefully to clarify, as far as possible, what seems murky and difficult. He calls Cyrus by the name **anointed** (*christos*, 45:1), not because he was one of the holy men who could be given the name. To be sure, the term was used, but because it was customary to anoint with oil those who were called to rule, even if some were not holy and venerable. For we find that the holy prophets said to some of those who were brought forward for kingship: *The Lord anointed you to be king over Israel* (Ps 45:7). Therefore Cyrus, as a king, is the Anointed. His authority, however, came from God. Though he was raised to exceptional glory, by calling him **anointed** the prophet makes clear that he is king by God's anointing and decree. The prophecy says that **he grasped his right hand** (45:1). This too is a certain sign of God's help, as it has been said by the saints in the book of Psalms: *Thou dost hold my right hand and guide me with thy counsel* (Ps 73:23-24).

He asserts that God held his **right hand** to indicate that the nations also will be obedient to him, that is, they will be subjected and give way to him, and the might of kings will be thoroughly broken. For they say that there were seven kings under this supreme king of the Babylonians. That cities would voluntarily open up before him and nothing would prevent Cyrus from overcoming the power of his enemies is made clear in what is said: **Cities shall not be closed. I will go before him and level the mountains** (45:1-2), that is, everything will lie open and accessible, and nothing will stand in his way. Even if someone should come out against you and like a **mountain** meet your forces, this too I shall **level** as though it were pitiful, unimposing, and unresisting. **I will break in pieces doors of bronze and shatter bars of iron and give you hidden treasures, and open for you unseen places** (45:2-3). They say that after the capture of the city the Babylonians streamed down into dark caves, especially the nobles, who, fearing death, went down like snakes into every cave and clefts of the rocks. Yet they did not remain undetected. For some showed them to Cyrus, and he ordered that torches be lit to drag these terrified people out of the crevices and punish them severely. Others say that he emptied the treasuries of the Babylonians which were hidden underground.

"So you will be so renowned and acclaimed and know that **I am the Lord God who calls you by name, the God of Israel for the sake of my servant Jacob and Israel my chosen** (45:4). For this I have called you," he says. "I alone am God, and I have honored you with great glory, in order that you might help my servant Israel. Though I called you," he adds, "and crowned you with such honors, you did not realize that I am God, and there is no god besides me. For you knew me not. It is as though someone would say: you did not gain such glory as compensation for illustrious deeds as those who are devout. Rather, I have honored you even though you did not know my divinity and excellence, nor were you among those who worship me, but I honored you that **those from the rising of the sun to its setting may know there is no other god besides me** (45:6). For if I chose, he says, to deliver my own, I was able to do it even through those who did not know my glory, that all the world would clearly know that there is no god besides me. For I am the Lord of hosts, the Master of every nation and race, and I incline even the hearts of those who are not my own to my designs. I am the Lord God, who made light and created darkness, day and night, or rather, light for the redeemed and darkness for those who are lost. For the one rejoices because he was set free from his bonds, but the other dwells in unending misery. **I am the one who prepared light and darkness, who makes peace and creates evils** (45:7). This passage too should be understood in accord with what I just said: peace for the redeemed and evils, that is, miseries, or things that bring about every kind of misery, for those cruel and savage people who assailed Israel.

45:1
Thus says the Lord God to my anointed, Cyrus, whose right hand I have grasped. . . .

(4) Irenaeus of Lyons

Isaiah the prophet declares, **Thus says the Lord God to my anointed, to the Lord,**[1] **whose right hand I have grasped, so that the nations will obey before him** (45:1). The prophet therefore says that the Son of God is also called "Christ" ["anointed"] and King of the nations, that is, of all men. And that Christ may be called, and really is, Son of God and King of all, David expresses in this way: *The LORD said to me, "You are my son; today I have begotten you; ask of me, and I will give you the nations as your inheritance, and for your possession the ends of the earth"* (Ps 2:7-8). It was not to David that these words were said, because he did not exercise his power over the nations or over the world, but only over the Jews. It is therefore clear that the promise made to **the anointed** (45:1) one to rule over the ends of the earth is proper to the Son of God, whom David himself confesses as his Lord: *The LORD said to my Lord, "Sit at my right hand"* (Ps 110:1) etc., as we

---

1. See the editorial introduction to this chapter of Isaiah.

have already noted. In effect, David says that the Father entrusts everything to the Son, just as we have shown above in the case of Isaiah, when he says, **Thus says God to my anointed, to the Lord, . . . so that the nations will obey before him.** It is the same promise in both prophets: he will be a king. Therefore, God's words are addressed to one and the same person, namely, to Christ, the Son of God. Since David affirms, *The LORD said to me*, we must declare that neither David nor any other prophet speaks in his own person; rather, the Spirit of God, assuming a shape and a form appropriate to the person in question, speaks sometimes in the name of Christ, sometimes in the name of the Father.

(5) Lactantius

That Christ would ascend to God the Father after his passion and resurrection, David has confirmed in Psalm 108 [*sic*] in these words: *The LORD said to my Lord, "Sit at my right hand, until I have placed your enemies under your feet"* (Ps 110:1). Since this prophet was himself a king, whom could he call his "Lord," who would sit at God's right hand except Christ the Son of God, who is *King of kings and Lord of lords* (Rev 19:16)? This is what Isaiah says more plainly: **Thus says the Lord God to Christ my Lord, whose right hand I have grasped, so that the nations would obey before him, and I will break the strength of kings, I will open gates before him, and cities will not be closed. I will go before him and level the mountains, and I will break in pieces the doors of bronze and shatter the bars of iron. And I will give you hidden and invisible treasures, so that you may know that I am God, who calls you by name** (45:1-3). Then, because of the virtue and fidelity which he has shown to God while on earth, *to him has been given kingship, honor, and power, and all peoples, tribes, and languages serve him, and his power will be eternal: it will never pass away and his kingship will never be destroyed* (Dan 7:14).

Now this can be understood in two ways. On the one hand, he already has perpetual power: since all peoples and languages venerate his name, confess his majesty, follow his teaching, imitate his virtue, he possesses *power and honor,* for all the tribes of the earth obey his precepts. On the other hand, when he shall come again in glory and power, to judge every soul and to restore the just to life, then he really will obtain rule over the whole world. Then, when every evil has been purged from human life, what the poets call a Golden Age will arise, an age of justice and peace.

(6) Eusebius of Caesarea

"What I have done and willed," says God in this verse, "**Cyrus** the king of the Persians will bring to pass in fact. Therefore I have named him **the anointed** *(christos),* because he was appointed by me for kingship." All of those appointed as kings among the Hebrews were called "anointed ones." "Having found Cyrus a good steward *of my counsel* (46:11), I even now proclaim that **I will grasp him by his right hand** (45:1) to keep him from being conquered by a stronger enemy. I will subject to him as many peoples as are ruled among the nations. Through him **I will break through the strength** of the ruling power of all other nations. Having made them all docile and tame before his feet, I will surrender to him the gates of cities and make them all subject to him, so that no opposition whatsoever survives."

"Let Cyrus himself hear this prediction, since he has been deemed worthy of what the text says about him. Therefore, he is to know now how **I will go before you and level the mountains and break in pieces the doors of bronze** (45:2) and will bring out what has been locked away as though by unbreakable **bars of iron**. Before you I will spread the hidden and **unseen treasures** (45:3) that had been stored inside them, once the property of other kings, so that you may know by historical fulfillment who I am that so many years beforehand inscribed your name in the prophetic writings, as it were, on eternal monuments. . . ."

(7) Jerome

I know that not only many Latin but also Greek commentators misinterpret this chapter, thinking that what is written is this: **Thus says the Lord to Christ my Lord** (45:1). As such the passage is understood in accord with what we read elsewhere: *The LORD rained on Sodom and Gomorrah brimstone from the LORD* (Gen 19:24) and *The LORD said to my Lord* (Ps 110:1). But the text does not read *kyrio,* which signifies "Lord," but it says "to Cyrus," who in Hebrew is called "Koresh," king of the Persians, who conquered Babylon and the Chaldaeans. . . . This Cyrus has been given the title *christus,* that is, the **anointed** of the Lord. This title was the distinctive sign of royal sovereignty among the Jews, just as among us the crown and the purple are given only to emperors. The rulers of the Hebrews were anointed with perfume. For that reason Saul was called *the LORD's anointed* (1 Sam 24:6). And in the Psalms we read: *Touch not my anointed ones; do my prophets no harm* (Ps 105:15).

God grasped and held the **right hand** (45:1) of Cyrus, that no one would be able to resist his strength. We can read of the history of the great Cyrus in Book 8 of Xenophon and see also what is found in the prophet Isaiah. Which city did not lie open before him? Which kings did not submit to him? Which walls once thought invincible did not succumb to his siege? Hence God addresses Cyrus directly: "**I will give you treasures, the hidden wealth of all the cities** (45:3). For you, who first worshiped idols, now recognize the favor of the one God, especially when you learned that long before you were born your name was foretold." Even Josephus in Book 11 of his *Jewish Antiquities* said that Cyrus had surely read a prophecy that mentions himself, and therefore the Jews as friends of God have great love for him. "However, I granted you these things **for the sake of my servant Jacob and Israel my chosen, and I will call you by your name** (45:4), as I called Abraham, Isaac, and Jacob. And much earlier I foretold about Isaac and Josiah.[2]

"You, Cyrus, were not considered the Christ; rather, you were a likeness of him whom you preceded as a type and image. You, moreover, **did not know me** (45:4), that is to say, you worshiped idols, not God. **I equipped you** with power; I made you the victor

---

2. The births of both Isaac and Josiah were foretold before they occurred (Gen 17:16 and 1 Kgs 13:2).

over many **nations**, and **you did not recognize** your helper." I am astonished at the foolishness of readers who apply this text to Christ, through whom the world has been reconciled to God.

(8) Theodoret of Cyrus

The Holy Scripture uses the expression **anointed** (45:1) to designate not only those who have been consecrated by being anointed but also those who have been set apart by the one God for a certain task. So when mentioning the patriarchs who lived before the law, Scripture orders: *Touch not my anointed ones* (Ps 105:15). In the present passage he calls Cyrus **anointed** to indicate that God anointed Cyrus as king so that he might destroy the power of the Babylonians, deliver the Jews from captivity, and rebuild God's temple.

Through these words God teaches that he established Cyrus as king and gave him the authority to rule his empire and that he will smooth his way before him. This is what is meant by the expression: **I will level the mountains and break in piece doors of bronze** (45:2). The next verse, **I will give you dark treasures** (45:3)..., refers to the treasures of the Babylonians that Nebuchadnezzar and other kings had gathered together and hidden. **That you may know that I am the Lord God** (45:3) means that since the beginning of time and many generations previously I had given you the name which you bear. And to identify the God who has done this he adds, **the God of Israel** (45:3). Because those who had gone astray thought there were many gods, he reveals himself through those who worshiped him.

Then he explains the reason for such high regard. **For the sake of my servant Jacob, and Israel my chosen, I will call you by my name and receive you** (43:4). It is my name that I will give you, he says, the name[3] that I will take when I assume human nature. To you I have given it first. The prophetic oracle clearly indicates that it is the only-begotten Word of God who says these things. For he is the one who is most especially called **anointed**, that is, Christ.

Cyrus was of course a worshiper of idols. Although he had received his rule (and much assistance) from the one God, he did not know the one who had bestowed these good things on him. In spite of his error, God had found him worthy of his goodness and had used him as his instrument to punish the Babylonians and to deliver Israel.

Some copies of this text, however, read as follows: **You Israel did not know me** (45:4). But I have found the word **Israel** neither in the Hebrew text nor among other translations, nor in the Septuagint or in the Hexapla.[4] And as far as the sense of the verse is concerned, it is clear that it is not Israel who is being reproached for not knowing God, but Cyrus.

---

3. That is, Christ or "anointed one."
4. The edition of the Old Testament produced by Origen of Alexandria. It included the Hebrew text, the Hebrew text transliterated into Greek characters, and four Greek versions, LXX, Aquila, Symmachus, and Theodotion, arranged in parallel columns.

(9) Hesychius of Jerusalem

This text not only refers to the king of the Persians who was called by God and authorized the building of ancient Jerusalem, but also to the faithful people, who became truly **anointed** (45:1) by the unction of Baptism. **Cyrus** is an image of the people of the Gentiles who believed, for he was led by the **hand** (45:1) of God, and all the **nations** (45:1) followed him in turn.

(10) Venerable Bede

According to the mystical sense, King **Cyrus** signifies the Lord and Savior both by name and by deeds. We learned this not from our own inferences but from the extremely clear words of Isaiah, who spoke in the person of the Lord: **I made you a likeness, and you did not recognize me** (45:4). For God made him a **likeness** to his own Son — even though Cyrus by no means knew God first. God made him a **likeness** because the Lord gave him the title **his anointed** [*christus*], and because the Lord arranged that **Cyrus** — which is interpreted "Heir" — should be **called** (45:4) long before he was born. God the Father made **Cyrus** a **likeness** to our Lord and Savior, who, by a circle of preaching apostles, **subjected** the necks of all the **nations** as well as the lords of these states, and who put the authors of secular wisdom under his domination (Ps 2:8).... The Lord, therefore, made **Cyrus** a **likeness** to his only-begotten, divine Son and our Lord, Jesus Christ.

45:2
I will go before you and level the mountains, I will break in pieces doors of bronze and break off bars of iron.

(11) John Cassian

Although the causes of the eight principal passions are recognized by everyone as soon as they have been set forth by the teachings of the elders, until then they are not known by everyone even though we are all hurt by them and they are found in everyone. But we are confident that we can explain them somewhat if, through your prayers, that word of the Lord is also addressed to us which was uttered through Isaiah: **I will go before you and I will humble the powerful of the earth. I will smash bronze gates and I will break iron bolts. And I will open to you hidden treasures and concealed secrets** (45:2-3). Then the word of God will precede us and first humble the powerful of our earth — that is, these same harmful passions that we wish to subdue and that claim dominion for themselves and a most cruel tyranny in our mortal body — and it will make them submit to our investigation and our exposure. And, breaking open the gates of ignorance and smashing the bolts of the vices that shut us out from true knowledge, it will lead us to our concealed secrets and, according to the apostle, it will, once we have been enlightened, reveal to us *the hidden things of darkness and make manifest the counsels of hearts* (1 Cor 4:5).

Isaiah 45

Thus, penetrating the dark shadows of our vices with the most pure eyes of our soul, we shall be able to expose them and to bring them into the light, and we shall be in a position to disclose their causes and natures both to those who are free of them and to those who are still under their sway. In this way, according to the prophet,[5] we shall pass through the fire of the vices that burn our minds most terribly and immediately be able to pass unharmed as well through the waters of the virtues that extinguish them (cf. Ps 66:12), and, bedewed with spiritual remedies, we shall deserve, thanks to our purity of heart, to be led to a place of refreshment and perfection.

45:7
I am the one who has prepared light and made darkness, who makes peace and creates evils; I am the Lord who does all these things.

(12) Irenaeus of Lyons

There is one God the Father, who has made ready the good things that belong to him for those who desire fellowship with him and persevere in obedience to him. For the ringleader of the apostasy, the devil, however, and those who rebelled with him, he has made ready an *eternal fire* (Matt 25:41). Those who are on his *left hand* (Matt 25:41) will be sent there. This is what the prophet meant when he wrote: **I am a jealous God, making peace and creating evils** (45:7). For those who repent and turn to him, he makes peace and friendship, bringing them into union with him. For those who do not repent and who flee his light, he makes ready an eternal fire and *outer darkness* (Matt 8:12) that indeed are **evils** for those who fall into them.

(13) Origen of Alexandria

Let us briefly consider in light of the Holy Scriptures the question of good and evil, and see how we should reply to [Celsus's] remark: "How can it be that God should make what is evil? And how can he be incapable of persuading and admonishing men." According to the divine Scriptures, good in its proper sense[6] has to do with the virtues and with virtuous actions, and evil in its proper sense designates their opposites. It is enough to cite the words of Psalm 34: *Those who seek the LORD will lack no good thing. Come, children, listen to me, I will teach you the fear of the LORD. What man is there who desires life and loves to see good days? Keep your tongue from evil, and your lips from seeking deceit. Depart from evil, and do good* (Ps 34:10-14). The words *Depart from evil, and do good* refer neither to physical good or evil things, as they are called by some, nor to external things, but to good and evil of the soul. The one who has abandoned evil in this sense, and has done good actions of this kind because he desires the true life, will certainly possess it. And the

---

5. The church fathers regularly referred to the psalmist, David, as "the prophet."
6. Good and evil refer to moral and immoral actions, not physical evil such as sickness.

one who *loves to see good days* of which the Logos is the *sun of righteousness* (Mal 4:2) will attain them, since God delivers him out of this present evil world and from the evil days which Paul mentioned when he said: *redeeming the time because the days are evil* (Gal 1:4).

Using the terms more loosely, one could say both that physical and external things that contribute to a life according to nature are considered good, and those contrary to this bad. In this sense Job says to his wife: *If we have received good from the Lord's hand, should we not bear up under evil?* (Job 2:10). In the Holy Scriptures God is also represented as saying: **I am the one who makes peace and who creates evils** (45:7), while in another place it is said of him: *Evil has come down from the Lord to the gates of Jerusalem, a noise of chariots and horsemen* (Mic 1:12-13). These passages have disturbed many readers of Scripture because they are not able to discern what it means by the terms "good" and "evil." No doubt this is the reason why Celsus posed this difficulty: "How can God make evil?" . . .

Our response is that God did not make evils, or evil in the proper sense, or the actions which result from it. For if God had made what is truly evil, how could the message of his judgment be preached with confidence, for it teaches that the wicked will be punished for their evil deeds in proportion to the sins they have committed, and those who have lived virtuous lives or done virtuous deeds are blessed and will be honored by God. I am quite aware that some claim that evil has its origin in God and cite certain texts from the Bible in support of their views. But they are unable to give a coherent account of how the Scriptures are to be understood in this way. For while the Scriptures blame sinners and approve of those who do what is right, they nevertheless include some passages, though few in number, that seem to confuse unlearned readers of the Holy Scriptures. . . .

If then the term is used in the strict sense, God did not make evil. But evils, which are few in number when compared to the order of the universe, have resulted from God's primary works that had another intention, as spiral shavings and sawdust are a consequence of the primary works of a carpenter, and as the debris around buildings, for example, the dirt that falls off the stones and plaster, appears to be the work of the builders.

(14) Augustine of Hippo

Our opponent[7] contends, "God himself speaks through the same prophet and says, **I am God, making good and creating evil**" (45:7). And so he does, for he is the God of whom the apostle says, *You see then the goodness and the severity of God* (Rom 11:22). His severity is evil for those worthy of damnation, because it inflicts the evil of damnation upon them. Since it is just, it is found to be good in another sense, for everything just is good. How elegantly this fellow thinks he weighs and distinguishes words, though he does not know what he is saying! He wants to turn into an accusation that this text puts things in

---

7. Most likely a Marcionite or someone who believed that the God of the Old Testament was a lesser god who made the world, and hence the evil in it.

such a way that it does not say, "making good and evil," or "creating good and evil," or "creating good and making evil," but **making good and creating evil** (45:7). He tries to show that what is made is outside the maker, but what is created is made within the creator and proceeds from him. Thus the God of the prophets would seem to have been at some time the maker of a good external to himself, but the creator of evil is, as it were, evil by nature and brought forth from himself what he created.

If we consider these words in terms of the usual way human beings speak, not only the children that one generates from oneself, but also magistrates and cities and other things which do not proceed from the one who brings them forth — that is, they are made exterior to the agent — are said both to be made and to be created. If we examine how the Holy Scriptures attacked by him usually speak, "to make" is the same as "to create," though "to give birth to" is distinguished from them. For the sake of verbal clarity and not for any real difference, one could say, **making good and creating evil** (45:7), though one equally well could, say **creating good and making evil**.

If the prophetic spirit had wanted there to be some distinction here, these words would be much more aptly interpreted if we understand that for something to be made means that, if it were not made, it would not exist at all. On the other hand, for something to be created means that something that already existed is erected or constituted. Thus we say that magistrates and cities are created. After all, when magistrates are created, those who were already counted among the ranks of human beings are raised to positions of honor, and the wood and stones from which cities are constructed surely were already there in existence, but had not yet, by their arrangement and assemblage, taken on that appearance of things which we see in cities. And when this happens, we say that cities are created.

What the Greeks call "create" *(ktizein)*, our writers translate at times as "create" *(creare)*, at times as "set up" *(constituere)*, and at times as "establish" *(condere)*, which most often has the same meaning as "make" *(facere)* in our literature. We find both that *God made man in the image of God, and God created man imperishable* (Wis 2:23). And if at times some difference is expressed, the difference I mentioned is more correctly found there. That is, one "makes" what previously did not exist at all; whereas, to "create" is to erect something from things that already existed by setting them in order.

Therefore, this passage speaks of God **creating evil** (45:7) because by the disposition of his severity he changes into evil for sinners what was made good by his bountiful goodness. Hence the apostle Paul declares: *We are the good odor of Christ in every place, both for those who were being saved and for those who were perishing, to the one group the odor of life unto life, but to others the odor of death unto death* (2 Cor 2:15-16).

(15) Gregory the Great

If we have received good at the hand of the LORD, *should we not also accept evil?* (Job 2:10). By *good* he means God's good gifts, either temporal or eternal; by *evil* he means the scourgings of the present about which the Lord spoke through the prophet's mouth: **I am the Lord, and there is no other; forming light and creating darkness; making peace**

and creating evil (45:7). This passage does not mean that evil, which does not subsist of its own nature, is created by the Lord; it means that the Lord presents himself as creating evil when the things created good by God are perverted by us and he turns them into a scourge. By the pain they inflict these same things become evil for those who have sinned, even though by nature they are good. For humans poison means death, but for a snake it means life.

By excessive love for present things we kept our distance from love of the Creator, and the perverse soul, captive to love of created things, separated itself from fellowship with the Creator. Consequently the soul was smitten by the Creator by means of those things that it mistakenly preferred to the Creator, so that man, proud man, who did not hesitate to commit sin, might find punishment for his correction, and more quickly ponder what he had lost when he discovered that what he had sought brought only grief. So it is well said: **Forming light and creating darkness** because when the darkness that accompanies grief was created in external things, the light of the mind is kindled by interior instruction. **I make peace and create evil**, for peace with God is restored when things that were made good were not desired in the way they were intended to be, and turned into scourges which are evil for us. For by our sin we set ourselves at odds with God; hence it is right that we should return to his peace by scourges. For when things that were made good become grief for us, the mind of one who has been chastened will in humility return to peace with God. So it is that blessed Job calls these scourges *evil* because he realizes with what disquiet they smite the good condition of health and tranquility.

45:8
Drop down dew, you heavens, and let the clouds rain down the just one; let the earth open and bud forth a savior (Vg.).[8]

(16) Jerome

Two interpretations are given of this passage. Some think that it relates directly to what preceded, namely, that Cyrus released the captives, and **heaven** and **earth** (45:8) rejoiced. He speaks by metonymy, using heaven and earth to signify those who dwell in heaven and on earth.

Others separate this passage from what went before and wish to say that the subject matter of the prophecy is the beginning of the coming of the Lord. In this case **clouds** (45:8) would be understood in the sense used earlier in Isaiah, *I will command the clouds that they rain no rain upon it* (5:6), that is, on the vineyard of Israel. The truth of God came to the clouds that they might **rain down the just one** or justice; **the earth was opened and brought forth a savior** (45:8). The Psalms also sing about this: *Truth will spring up from the earth, and righteousness will look down from the heaven* (Ps 85:11).

---

8. For this verse see the editor's introduction to chapter 45.

(17) Leo the Great

To undo the bonds of sin and death the almighty Son of God, who fills all things and contains all things, wholly equal to the Father and co-eternal in one essence from him and with him, took on human nature, and the Creator and Lord of all things deigned to become a mortal. He chose for his mother one whom he had made, who while remaining a virgin brought him forth in human form, that without the pollution of human seed there might be a new man of purity and truth.

Though the birth of Christ is marvelous, for he was born of the Virgin's womb, his nature does not differ from ours. He who is true God is also true man, neither his divine nor human nature being a deception. *The Word became flesh* (John 1:14) by exalting the flesh, not by becoming less divine. He tempered his power and goodness, so that in taking on our nature he exalted it and in sharing it did not lose his power.

When Christ was born, according to the prophecy of David, *Truth sprang out of the earth, and righteousness looked down from heaven* (Ps 85:11). In his nativity Isaiah's prophecy is also fulfilled: **Let the earth bring forth salvation, and at the same time let righteousness spring up** (45:8). For the earth of human flesh was cursed by the first to sin, but in giving birth the Blessed Virgin brought forth a seed that was blessed and free from the fault of our race. We trail his spiritual origin in our rebirth. For everyone who is reborn, the water of Baptism is like that of the Virgin's womb, since the same Holy Spirit fills the baptismal font who first filled the Virgin. So the sin her holy conception cancelled, this mystical washing now takes away.

(18) Hymn: "Rorate coeli"

> *Refrain:* **Drop down dew, you heavens, from above, and let the clouds rain the Just One** (45:8).

> Be not very angry, O Lord,
> And remember no longer our iniquity;
> Behold, the city of the Holy One is become deserted;
> Zion is become a desert, Jerusalem is desolate,
> The house of your holiness and of your glory,
> Where our fathers sang your praises.

> *Refrain:* **Drop down dew, you heavens, from above, and let the clouds rain the Just One.**

> We have sinned, we have become as though unclean,
> And we have all fallen like leaves:
> And our iniquities like the wind have carried us away;
> You have hidden your face from us,
> And you have crushed us in the hand of our iniquity.

Refrain: **Drop down dew, you heavens, from above, and let the clouds rain the Just One.**

Behold, O Lord, the affliction of your people,
And send forth him who is to come:
Send forth the Lamb, the ruler of the earth,
From Petra of the desert to the mountain of the daughter of Zion (16:1 Vg.):
That he may take away the yoke of our captivity.

Refrain: **Drop down dew, you heavens, from above, and let the clouds rain the Just One.**

Be comforted, be comforted, my people (40:1):
Your salvation will come quickly:
Why with grief are you consumed, for sorrow has stricken you?
I will save you, be not afraid, for I am the Lord your God,
The Holy One of Israel, your Redeemer.

Refrain: **Drop down dew, you heavens, from above, and let the clouds rain the Just One.**

45:9
Shall the clay say to the potter, "What are you doing?"

(19) Augustine of Hippo

Paul the apostle asks: *Who are you, O human being, to answer back to God?* **Does the pot say to him who fashioned it, "Why did you make me that way?"** (45:9). *Or does the potter have the power to make from the same lump of clay one vessel for honor and another for dishonor?* (Rom 9:20-21). If this lump were so positioned in the middle that, as it merited nothing good, so it merited nothing bad, it would seem with good reason to be an injustice that vessels were made from it for dishonor. But since the whole lump fell into condemnation because of the one sin through the free choice of the first human being, that vessels are made from it for honor is not due to his [Adam's] righteousness, because no righteousness preceded grace, but to the mercy of God. That, however, a vessel is made for dishonor is not to be attributed to the injustice of God — heaven forbid that there should be any injustice in God! — but to his judgment, so that he does not ungratefully reject his mercy or unjustly accuse his judgment.

45:13

I have raised him up a king[9] with righteousness, and all his paths shall be straight; he shall build my city and turn back the captivity of my people....

(20) Eusebius of Caesarea

What sort of **king** could this be? Some will say that it is Cyrus, the Persian king, of whom the text has spoken previously [45:1] ... and whom history proves fulfilled this verse as well. Others would say it applies to Zerubbabel, who came of royal stock from the tribe of Judah and the Davidic succession, because he led the return of those who came back to Judea from Babylon and rebuilt the temple, as Haggai and Zechariah prophesied: *The hands of Zerubbabel have laid the foundation of this house; his hands shall also complete it* (Zech 4:9). But besides these, someone else might refer this text to the Christ of God, *whom the Father raised from the dead* (Acts 3:15), *having loosed the pangs of death* (Acts 2:24), and whom the Father appointed as **a king with righteousness**, so that he could speak the truth when he said, *I was made king by him upon Zion, his holy mountain* (Ps 2:6 LXX). Of Christ alone were **all his paths** truly **straight**, and he himself **built** the true **city** of God, concerning which he has made this pronouncement: *Upon this rock I* **shall build** *my church, and the gates of Hades shall not prevail against it* (Matt 16:18). This is truly the **city** which is made of *living stones* (1 Pet 2:5), the indestructible **City** of God, which stretches *from the rising of the sun to its setting* (Isa 45:6), and embraces all the nations with the godly polity; but also, only the Christ of God overturned the **captivity** of souls, when he liberated them from the error and slavery of the demons.

45:14

They will worship you and pray in you, because God is in you.

(21) Gregory of Nyssa

No one initiated in the divine mysteries needs to be told that prophets, evangelists, disciples, and apostles confess that the Lord is God. For who does not know that in the forty-fifth psalm the prophet proclaims in word that Christ is God: *anointed by God* (45:1). Further, who is not aware that in a number of places Isaiah openly announces the divinity of the Son, as, for example, when he asserts: **The Sabaeans, men of stature, shall come over to you, and they shall be your slaves; they shall follow behind you bound in fetters, and shall pray to you, because God is in you and there is no God beside you; for you are God** (45:14). What other God is there who has God in himself and is himself God except the Only-Begotten, let those say who have no regard for prophecy? As for the interpretation of the name Emmanuel (Matt 1:23) or the confession of Thomas (John 20:28)

---

9. "King" appears in several ancient Greek versions of 45:13, thus opening the verse to messianic interpretation, both among Jewish and Christian commentators. Eusebius of Caesarea eschews his previous historical application of Isaiah 45 to Cyrus and sees v. 13 as a prophecy of Christ.

or the sublime utterances of John which are evident even to those outside of the faith — of these I will say nothing.

I do not think it necessary to bring forth in any detail the words of Paul since they are well known. He not only calls the Lord, God, but great God and God over all when he wrote to the Romans: *Whose are the fathers, and of whom, according to the flesh, Christ came, who is over all, God blessed forever* (Rom 9:5). And writing to his disciple Titus, he said: *According to the appearing of the glory of our great God and Savior Jesus Christ* (Tit 2:13). And to Timothy he speaks plainly: *God was manifested in the flesh, justified in the Spirit* (1 Tim 3:16).

45:23
To me every knee shall bow, and every tongue shall confess to God.

(22) Origen of Alexandria

Kneeling is necessary when someone is going to reproach himself before God for his sins, making supplication for healing and forgiveness of sins. Kneeling is a symbol of someone who is abject and submissive, as Paul says, *For this reason I bow my knees before the Father, from whom every family in heaven and on earth is named* (Eph 3:14-15). There is also a spiritual kneeling which means that a creature falls down before God *at the name of Jesus* and humbles himself before God. The apostle intimates this in the phrase, *That at the name of Jesus every knee should bow, in heaven and on earth and under the earth* (Phil 2:10). . . . The verse in the prophet says the same thing, **To me every knee shall bow** (45:23).

Isaiah 46

1 Bel has fallen, Dagon has been crushed,
    their graven images have become for beasts and cattle;
you carry them bound
    as a burden for the weary
2 and the hungry as well as for the feeble
    who has no strength,
who will not be able to be saved from war,
    but themselves have been led captive.

3 Hear me, O house of Iakob
    and everyone who is left of Israel,
you who are being carried from the womb
    and trained from the time you were a child.
4 Until your old age I am,
    and until you grow old, I am;
I bear with you,
    I have made and I will set free,
    I will take up and save you.

5 To whom have you likened me?
    See, act with cunning,
    you who are going astray!
6 Those who contribute gold from a bag
    and silver in a balance
    will set it on a scale;
and after hiring a goldsmith, they made handiwork,
    and bowing down they worship them!
7 They carry it on their shoulders and go,
    and if they set it up, it stays in its place;
    it will not move.

> And whoever cries out to him, he will not listen;
>> he will not save him from evils.
>
> 8 Remember these things and groan,
>> repent, you who have gone astray,
>> turn in your heart;
> 9 and remember the former things of old;
>> because I am God, and there is no other besides me,
> 10 declaring the last things first, before they happen,
>> and at once they came to pass;
>> and I said, "My whole plan shall stand,
>> and I will do all the things I have planned,"
> 11 calling a bird from the east,
>> and from a far country those concerning whom I have planned.
>> I have spoken and brought it;
>> I have created and made it.
>
> 12 Hear me, you who have ruined your heart,
>> you who are far from righteousness:
> 13 I brought near my righteousness,
>> and I will not delay the salvation that comes from me;
>> I have provided salvation in Sion,
>> to Israel for glorying.

Isaiah 46 elicited various comments from the fathers. The celebration of the one God in the verse, **I am God, and there is no other besides me** *(46:9), evoked theological commentary from Cyril of Alexandria and from Origen. See also comments at 41:4 and 44:6. The commentaries of Theodoret and Jerome provide contextual interpretations, although the selection from Jerome moves into overtly Christian readings as well. Augustine notices the mention of the heart in 46:8 and relates the text to the parable of the Prodigal Son returning to himself, to his heart. He also speaks of finding Christ in the heart. Origen and Jerome highlight the metaphorical meaning of "heart." John Cassian sees in the words,* **My whole counsel shall stand** *(46:10), an allusion to the Lord's Prayer, "Thy will be done."*

(1) Theodoret of Cyrus

After having spoken about God, given support to those who believe, and confounded unbelievers, the prophet now foretells the destruction of idols. **Bel has fallen, Nebo has been crushed** (46:1). Instead of "Nebo," some manuscripts have **Dagon**, who was an idol of the Philistines. Some people equate this **Bel** with Kronos.[1] Then the prophet speaks of

---

1. Jerome echoes this statement when he says that the Latins call Bel "Saturn" (= Kronos). The link, as Eusebius and Cyril of Alexandria say, is the eating of human flesh.

idols in general. **Their graven images have been made into beasts and cattle** (46:1). For they not only made idols resembling human beings, they also made idols that resembled **beasts and cattle**. In particular, the Egyptians worshiped representations of monkeys, of dogs, of lions, of sheep, and of crocodiles, and the Akaronites even had an image of a fly, and others worshiped figures of bats. Earlier in his book the prophet had already denounced such practices (2:20). Here he predicts the destruction of all these idols: **Lift them off that were a heavy burden for the weary, the feeble, the hungry, and the exhausted** (46:1-2). Like other burdens that need to be carried because they cannot move themselves, inanimate idols weigh heavily on those who bear them. So impotent are they that they are unable, unlike men, to flee in time of war. . . .

With the words **To whom have you likened me?** (46:5) he is clearly mocking the impotence of idols. And since he has already mentioned those made with wood (45:20), he now discusses those made of things more precious than wood, that is, gold and silver. Many people have much higher regard for gods made of gold or silver. Men, he says, collect gold and silver, hire a goldsmith, weigh the statue crafted by him, and then honor it as a god. Yet it cannot move by its own feet, and if others do not carry it, it stands still. Nor can it give any aid to those who worship it.

(2) Jerome

You who were lifted from the womb (46:3). The text teaches that the Israelites were carried from Egypt by God like children or infants, like someone taken from the belly of the mother or from the womb of a pregnant woman. This does not mean that the ineffable and incomprehensible majesty of God has a belly or a womb or feet and hands or other bodily members. Rather, the text teaches that we learn that God's affections are expressed in our language. Moreover, in the Septuagint version of Psalm 110, the same idea is expressed in the person of God himself: *From the womb before the Morning Star, I have begotten you* (Ps 109:3 LXX). . . . The sense is: "I have begotten you as an infant, and I bore you in my belly and in my womb, and I will watch over you until old age, not my old age, but yours." By this he teaches the Israelites that they will be preserved by divine mercy. The Creator of all cares for his creatures, and *a good shepherd lays down his life for his sheep* (John 10:11). The hireling, whose own the sheep are not, flees when he sees a wolf. Because I made and gave birth to children, I will look after them and carry them. The words **You who have been lifted from the womb and trained from the time you were a child until your old age** (46:3-4) indicate that though they had meditated on the law, they had no knowledge of God but worshiped images of men and animals. Hence they had to be trained from childhood. Even more they needed the reproach of the prophet through whom God said: **To whom have you likened me, and to whom have you made me equal?** (46:5). They offer **gold** and **silver** and hire a maker of statues to form an idol. They worship the works of their hands and **carry them on their shoulders** (46:7). Once they are **set up** and made stable, they are not able to move them, and they are of no benefit to those who worship them. But enough of this, let us go on to set forth the hidden mercy of Christ.

Because I bore and carried you, the text says, you are preserved from infancy to old age not by your merits but by my goodness. Give up the idols you have made, and return to the worship of the one God. Repent and weep over your sin which holds you back. Set in place a new foundation so that you are not suddenly swept off your feet by the winds of idolatry. **Return to your heart** (46:8), that is, to your mind. Those who worship idols are like one who has lost his senses and strikes against wood or stones. Keep in mind that **from the beginning** (46:10) of the world **there is no God besides me** (46:9). No one is able to know the future unless I announce through the prophets what is to happen, so that when I bring to pass what was predicted, I prove my *divinity* by *divining* the future. The secret that had been unknown to all previous ages, that is, my will and counsel, I now declare **shall stand** (46:10), so that when you see it fulfilled, you will know that there is no God save he who not only knows the future but commands that it will happen. I am the one who **calls a bird from the East** — whom the Hebrews identify as Cyrus, the Persian king, or as Darius the Mede — **and the man of my counsel from a far country** (46:11), to fulfill **my whole counsel** (46:10) against Babylon and the Chaldeans.

Or else, as we are convinced is true, this refers to our Lord and Savior, of whom Balaam also prophesied: *A star shall arise from Jacob, and a man from Israel* (Num 24:17) whose name is the East[2] and whom the Magi from the East came to adore. For he is the one who says in the Psalms, *O God, I wish that I may do your will* (Ps 40:8), the same one of whom the Father has spoken here in Isaiah. And he has given a proof of his promise by his deed.

What we have cited from the Hebrew as **the man of my counsel**, the Septuagint translators have rendered as **those concerning whom I have planned** (46:11). Therefore we could also understand by those **birds called from the East** (46:11) the ministering angels of God, who traverse the whole world at his command and are his ministering spirits sent for the salvation of those who believe. Of them the psalmist sings: *You who make the winds your messengers, and burning fire your ministers*[3] (Ps 104:4).

46:4
Until your old age I am, and until you grow old, I am; I bear with you, I have made and I will set you free, I will take up and save you.

(3) Augustine of Hippo

O Lord our God, *under the covering of your wings* (Ps 61:4) we set our hope. Protect us and bear us up. It is you who will carry us; **you will bear us up** from our infancy **until old age** (46:4). When you are our firm support, then it is firm indeed. But when our support

---

2. Jerome is basing his interpretation on a play on words in Latin. His translation of the prophecy of Balaam, which was popular among the early Christians, reads *A star shall arise (orietur)* ... (Num 2:17), hence Jerome's assertion that Christ's name is "the East" (Latin *Oriens*).

3. A more literal translation of the Latin rendering of Ps 104:4 makes its relevance to Jerome clearer: "You who make the *spirits* your *angels*. . . ." (*Qui facis angelos tuos spiritus. . . .*)

rests on our own strength, it is infirmity. Our good is life with you forever, and because we turned away from that, we became twisted. Let us now return to you that we may not be overturned. Our good is life with you and suffers no deficiency; for you yourself are that good. We have no fear that there is no home to which we may return because we fell from it. During our absence our house suffers no ruin; it is your eternity.

46:8
Remember these things and groan, repent, you who have gone astray, turn in your heart.

(4) Augustine of Hippo

Recall how the Prodigal Son went off and lost his way, the one who said to the father who was looking after him, *Give me the sum that falls to me* (Luke 15:12). Look how he went off, look how he squandered it all, look how he fed swine, look how he was left penniless. He preferred his own company, and this took him a long way away from his father. You see, in preferring his own company he didn't even remain in his own company. If you fall away from your God, you very soon fall away from yourself too, and turn your back even on yourself. That's why such people are told, **Come back, transgressors, to the heart** (46:8), come back to yourselves, so that you may be able to come back to the one who made you. So it was with this young man when he began to be in want, having forsaken his father, being forsaken now by himself; what does the text say about him? *And returning to himself, he said . . .* (Luke 15:17). Because he says that he *returned to himself,* it is evident that previously he had even turned his back on himself.

(5) Augustine of Hippo

Turn back in your heart (46:8), and if you are believers, you will find Christ there; he himself is speaking to you there. Yes, here I am, shouting my head off; but he, in silence, is doing more teaching. I am speaking by the sound of these words; but he is speaking inwardly by the awe in your thoughts. So may he infiltrate my words in your minds, because I dared to say, "Live good lives in order not to die a bad death." So there you see, because there is faith in your hearts, and Christ is there, he too has the task of teaching you what I am eager to trumpet out loud.

(6) Augustine of Hippo

Christ is most certainly your king. Living, he is your king; slain, he is still your king. Now he has risen, and in heaven he is your king. But he will come again, and then woe betide you, for he is your king. Go on, folks, go on speaking about justice but refusing to judge rightly; if you are unwilling to judge rightly, rightly will you be judged. Your king is alive; he dies no more, nor will death ever have dominion over him again (Rom 6:9). He is coming, so **return to your hearts, you transgressors** (46:8). He will come indeed, so correct yourselves before he comes, forestall him by coming into his presence confessing. Yes, come he will, and he is your king. Remember the title over his cross. Even if you no longer see it in writing, it is valid still; it cannot now be read on earth, but it is preserved in heaven. What does the title of this psalm [Psalm 57 LXX] say? *For the end, as a title for David himself that is not to be tampered with.* That title written over the cross is inviolable. Christ is your king because Christ is the universal king: *the kingship is the Lord's, and he will hold sway over the nations* (Ps 21:29 LXX). If, then, he is your king, listen: before he comes, he says to you, "I am still speaking, not judging as yet. I shout my warnings to you like this because I do not want to strike you with my judgments." So then, men and women, *If you truly speak about justice, judge rightly in your own case* (Ps 57:2 LXX).

(7) Augustine of Hippo

He who for us is life itself descended here and endured our death and slew it by the abundance of his life. In a thunderous voice he called us to return to him, at that secret place where he came forth to us. First he came into the Virgin's womb where the human creation was married to him, so that mortal flesh should not forever be mortal. Coming forth from thence *as a bridegroom from his marriage bed, he bounded like a giant to run his course* (Ps 18:6). He did not delay, but ran crying out loudly by his words, deeds, death, life, descent, and ascent — calling us to return to him. And he has gone from our sight that we should **return to our heart** (46:8) and find him there. He went away and, behold, here he is. He did not wish to remain long with us, yet he did not abandon us. He has gone to that place which he never left, *for the world was made by him* (John 1:10); and he was in this world, and *came into this world to save sinners* (1 Tim 1:15). To him my soul is making confession, and he is healing it, because it was against him that it sinned.

(8) Gregory the Great

It is well said by the prophet: **Return, transgressors, to your heart** (46:8). For if they returned to the heart, they would not be captivated by empty words. For what is closer to us than our hearts? Is anything nearer to us than that which is within us? And yet, when the heart is distracted by evil thoughts, it wanders far from us. So when the prophet urges the sinner to return to his heart, he is sending him on a long journey. For the more he is distracted by external things, the more he is unable to find it within him to return to himself.

46:9
I am God, and there is no other besides me.

(9) Origen of Alexandria

Now that we have discussed these matters in order and as briefly as possible, it remains for us, following the plan we set out at the beginning,[4] to refute those who think that the Father of our Lord Jesus Christ is a different God from the one who gave Moses the law and sent the prophets, the God of Abraham, Isaac, and Jacob. For it is essential that we be grounded first in this teaching of our faith. . . .

Consider then that Jesus indicates that those who pray should say, *Our Father, who art in heaven* (Matt 6:9). What else does he seem to be saying except that God is to be sought in the better things of our world, that is, in his own creation? When, too, he gives excellent precepts on swearing oaths, saying that we must swear *not by heaven, for it is the throne of God, nor by the earth, for it is his footstool* (Matt 5:34-35), is he not in full agreement with the prophet's words: *Heaven is my throne and the earth is my footstool* (66:1)? And when he casts out of the temple those who are selling *oxen and sheep and doves*, turning over the tables of the money changers and saying, *Take these things away; you shall not make my Father's house a house of trade* (John 2:14, 16), he was most certainly saying that his Father is that God to whose name Solomon had erected the magnificent temple.

Again, the saying, *Have you not read what was said to you by God, "I am the God of Abraham, and the God of Isaac, and the God of Jacob?" He is not God of the dead, but of the living* (Matt 22:31-32), teaches us clearly that he called God the God of the patriarchs because they were holy and alive, *the God of the living*. This is the same God too who had said through the prophets, **I am God, and there is no god besides me** (46:9). If the Savior, knowing that the one written about in the law is the God of Abraham, and that this is the same one who declares, **I am God, and there is no god besides me**, should recognize as Father this God who is unaware that there is another god above him (for this is what the heretics[5] think), then the Savior makes the absurd mistake of declaring as "Father" one who does not know that there is a higher god. In that case God is not ignorant but is actually deceiving us when he asserts, **There is no god besides me**, and we have a much greater absurdity that the Savior professes his Father to be a liar. All of this leads us to conclude that the Savior knows no other Father except God the maker and creator of all things.

---

4. Of his work, *On First Principles*.
5. Origen is referring to the Gnostics.

46:10
I will do all the things I have planned.

(10) John Cassian

Thy will be done, on earth as it is in heaven (Matt 6:10). There can be no greater prayer than to desire that earthly things should deserve to equal heavenly ones. For what does it mean to say, *Thy will be done, on earth as it is in heaven* if not that human beings should be like angels and that, just as the will of God is fulfilled by them in heaven, so also all those who are on earth should do not their own but his will? No one will really be able to say this but he who believes that God regulates all things that are seen, whether fortunate or unfortunate, for the sake of our well-being, and that he is more provident and careful with regard to the salvation and interests of those who are his own than we are for ourselves.

And of course it is to be understood in this way — namely, that God's will is the salvation of all, according to the text of the blessed Paul: *Who desires all to be saved and to come to the knowledge of the truth* (1 Tim 2:4). Of this will the prophet Isaiah, speaking in the person of God the Father, also says: **All my will shall be done** (46:10). When we say to him then, *Thy will be done, on earth as it is in heaven,* we are praying as follows: Father, just as those who are in heaven are saved by the knowledge of you, so also are those who are on earth.

(11) Cyril of Alexandria

When God sees that they [the Israelites] have been overcome by deception, darkness, and terrible ignorance, he again has pity on them, and bids them cast, as it were, a glance with the mind's eye to what once was, to turn from their present evils to better things, and to repent, not with the lips alone but in the heart. For this kind of repentance is truly worthy of praise.

For they certainly could learn from what was said earlier, that the making of idols is a most ridiculous thing. From those things that are found in him by nature and are most fitting of God, he attempts to have them understand that he alone is the God of all. For he claims, "I am the one who knows all things, making things known even before they happen, and who brings to fulfillment that which was proclaimed. For I affirm that what I will comes to be, and what I think is never in vain." This too is certain evidence of the invincible power that befits God.

Men who have received the highest honors and reached the pinnacle of power, when they set before themselves a goal and try to carry it off, learn that their plans are seldom if ever successful. For many unexpected things intervene, and unwelcome delays undercut them. But who can stand in the way of God's will or frustrate the plans of the holy God? Who can turn back his upraised hand? Therefore, as evidence that he is truly God by nature, it is most fittingly said of him: **My whole plan shall stand, and I will do all the things I have planned** (46:10).

46:12
Hear me, you who have ruined your heart.

(12) Origen of Alexandria

The inner man has a heart. **Hear me, you who have lost your heart** (46:12). The heart that belongs to the body cannot be lost. But when a person neglects to cultivate his spiritual life and his capacity to think atrophies from lack of use, we may fairly say that he has **lost his heart**. It is to such a person that the words of the text are addressed: **Hear me, you who have lost your heart**. . . . Since all of these elements of the physical body are found in the inner man, have no doubt that the same is true of the blood when physical blood is mentioned; as with the other parts of the body, it too is in the inner man. This is the blood which is poured out from the soul of the sinner. And indeed we read, *For the blood of your souls there will be a reckoning* (Gen 9:5 LXX). He did not say simply "your blood," but "the blood of your *souls*." And there is this saying: *His blood I will require at the watchman's hand* (Ezek 33:6). What kind of blood does God require *from the watchman's hand* but that which has been poured out from the sinner? In this way the heart of a heedless man is lost, and so it is said, **Hear me, you who have lost your heart**.

Isaiah 48

1 Hear these things, O house of Iakob,
    who are called by the name of Israel,
    and who came forth out of Ioudas;
who swear by the name of the Lord God of Israel,
    remembering it, not with truth or with righteousness,
2 and clinging to the name of the holy city,
    and leaning on the God of Israel;
    the Lord Sabaoth is his name.

3 The former things I have moreover declared,
    and they went out from my mouth and came to be heard;
    suddenly I did them and they came to pass.
4 I know that you are unyielding,
    and your neck is an iron sinew
    and your forehead brass,
5 and I declared to you the things of old,
    before they came upon you I made them to be heard by you;
do not say, "The idols did them for me,"
    and do not say, "The graven and the cast images commanded me."

6 You have heard all things,
    and you yourselves have not known.
But I have also made to be heard by you, from now on,
    the new things that shall come to pass;
    yet you did not speak.
7 They are happening now, not long ago;
    in former days you did not hear of them;
    do not say, "Yes, I know them."
8 You have neither known nor understood,
    nor did I open your ears from the beginning.

For I knew that betraying you would betray,
> and that even from the womb you would be called a transgressor.

9 For my name's sake I will show you my wrath,
> I will bring my glorious deeds upon you,
> so that I may not utterly destroy you.
10 See, I have sold you, not for silver;
> but I delivered you from the furnace of poverty.
11 For my own sake will I do this to you,
> because my name is being profaned,
> and my glory I will not give to another.

12 Hear me, O Iakob,
> and Israel, whom I call:
> I am the first,
> and I am forever.
13 And my hand laid the foundation of the earth,
> and my right hand bolstered heaven;
> I will call them,
> and they will stand together.
14 And all of them will be gathered and hear.
> Who has declared these things to them?
> Because I love you,
> I have performed your will on Babylon,
> to do away with the offspring of the Chaldeans.
15 I have spoken, I have called,
> brought him, and made his way prosperous.
16 Draw near to me and hear these things!
> From the beginning I have not spoken in secret;
> when it happened I was there,
> and now the Lord has sent me and his spirit.

17 Thus says the Lord who delivered you,
> the Holy One of Israel:
> I am your God,
> I have shown you how to find
> the way in which you should go.
18 And if you had heard my commandments,
> your peace would have become like a river,
> and your righteousness like a wave of the sea;
19 your offspring would have become like the sand,
> and the descendants of your womb like the dust of the earth.
> Now neither will you be utterly destroyed,
> nor will your name perish before me.

20 Go out from Babylon, fleeing from the Chaldeans,
　　proclaim a voice of joy and let this be heard,
　report it to the end of the earth;
　　say, "The Lord has delivered his slave Iakob!"
21 Even if they are thirsty, he will lead them through the desert;
　　he will bring forth water for them out of a rock;
　a rock will be split and water will flow
　　[and my people will drink].

22 "There is no rejoicing," says the Lord, "for the ungodly."

Certain verses in this chapter caught the interest of the early commentators. Cyril of Alexandria takes the words **I am the first, and I am forever** *(48:12), as an occasion to discuss the transcendence of God. God is the "one who is" (Exod 3:14), who by nature is before all things, eternal and without end, whose essence is beyond knowing. Ambrose of Milan found the phrase* **Because I love you, I have performed your will** *(48:14), suggestive of the difference between obedience that flows from love and that which stems from fear. The sentence,* **The Lord has sent me and the Spirit** *(48:16), was taken to refer to the Holy Trinity, but interpreters recognized the sentence was ambiguous. Is "Spirit" joined with Lord as the subject of the sentence, or is it the object of the verb "send"? Taking it as subject suggests that the Father and the Spirit sent the Son; as object, that the Father sent the Son and the Spirit. In the selections below Augustine reads the verse the first way, and Origen the second. Augustine uses the verse* **There is no rejoicing for the ungodly** *(48:22) to help explain the words of the psalmist, "Rejoice, you just" (Ps 97:12). True joy is to be found not in the pleasures of the cup or the table or the bed but in the Lord.*

48:12
Hear me, O Iakob, and Israel, whom I call: I am the first, and I am forever.

(1) Cyril of Alexandria

God reminds Israel of the honor and glory bestowed on them, as well as the mercy and love shown them. They were worthy of the highest privileges, for they alone had been called from among all the nations to have intimate fellowship with God and become God's portion and lot. Therefore inspired Moses cried out: *The heaven of heavens belongs to the* Lord *your God. The* Lord *has chosen you from all the nations to be his people* (Deut 10:14; 7:6). And again: *When the Most High divided the nations, when he separated the sons of Adam, he fixed the bounds of the people according to the number of the sons of God, and his people Jacob became the portion of the* Lord, *Israel his allotted heritage* (Deut 32:8-9).

　　It was necessary then that those who were honored, elected, and selected to be God's chosen lot should not turn away from God's law nor disappoint the God who loved them and bestowed on them the best and most desirable things. But these poor folk forgot what they had received and became mired in idolatry, forsaking the true God to worship the elements of the universe.

However, God again had compassion on them. He called them to obedience, saying, **Hear me** (48:12), so that they might choose to become what they once were and to enjoy continuous good fortune. Even though it was late in the day, he decreed that they would be free of condemnation and delivered from the bonds of servitude. Though they had worshiped the host of heaven, forsaking the Creator, and worshiped things that had been brought into existence by him, he instructs them again in the divine mysteries. As blessed Paul wrote: *Though by this time you ought to be teachers, you need someone to teach you again the first principles of God's word. You need milk, not solid food* (Heb 5:12).

When he says, **I am the first, and I am forever** (48:12), the prophet indicates that God is the "one who is" (Exod 3:14). He is before all things, and his essence is, by nature, beyond knowing. Who can be conceived as prior to the **first**? Just as nothing can be conceived prior to that which is truly the **first** and the beginning, so it is not possible to image another **first** than the **first**. Therefore the God of all is before all things and exists for endless ages. What sort of end does one have who has no beginning? Can there be an end to divine glory?

The company of so-called gods, that is, the elements of the universe, cannot be considered **first**, nor can they be eternal in the way God is eternal. For the stars, the sun and the moon, even the heavens, came into being, and will one day come to an end. In every way they are inferior to the glory of God. This passage speaks truly when it says: **my hand laid the foundation of the earth, and my right hand bolstered heaven** (48:13). How can what has been made contend as though equal with the one who created it? How can it struggle against its framer? This is demonstrably absurd. Indeed, it is the height of impiety to worship the creation rather than the Creator (cf. Rom 1:25), to turn away from the one who always exists and is **first** and to attribute the name and dignity of the truly divine to things that were made in time or to their works. They worship what their *fingers have made* (31:7), as it is written.

The text also says that God the Father calls the Son his **hand** and **right hand** (48:13). We find him called **hand** in the Holy Scriptures. Therefore inspired Moses asserts: *Your right hand, O Lord, glorious in power, your right hand, O Lord, shatters the enemy* (Exod 15:6). And blessed David: *Let your hand be strong, your right hand lifted up* (Ps 89:13).

48:14
Because I love you, I have performed your will on Babylon. . . .

(2) Ambrose of Milan

How I love your law, O Lord! It is my meditation all the day (Ps 119:97). This is the voice of one who is diligent and zealous to know the law. The law teaches the perfection of human beings, which is the point of this entire psalm. The psalmist knew that the greatest commandment in the law is to *love the Lord our God with our whole heart and with our whole mind* (Deut 6:5; Mark 12:30). Therefore, he devotes himself to instructing us, as well as those whom he wishes to be perfect, to imitate him, and he exclaims, *How I love your law, O Lord!* Charity grows from this affirmation, since it calls as witness the very one to whom the gift of love is given. In this way it invokes the fullness of love, not merely its appearance. This is what Peter did when he insisted, *Lord, you know that I love you* (John 21:15). But whoever loves the Lord loves his law, like Mary who, loving her son, carried all his words[1] in her heart with maternal affection (cf. Luke 2:19). It is written, **Because I love you, I have done your will** (48:14). Christ recognized Peter's love, and therefore entrusted Peter [with the Church] so that he might shepherd his flock and do the Lord's will. The one who loves does willingly the things that are commanded, while the one who is fearful does them out of compulsion. Thus the Lord approves more when his servants carry out their tasks willingly, rather than being forced. For this reason he frees us from slavery, so that we might offer him our free will rather than obedience out of necessity.

48:16
And now the Lord has sent me and his spirit.

(3) Origen of Alexandria

That the Savior and the Holy Spirit were sent by the Father is made clear in Isaiah when, speaking in the person of the Savior, it is said, **And now the Lord has sent me and his Spirit** (48:16). It must, however, be recognized that this passage is ambiguous. Either God sent, and also the Holy Spirit sent the Savior,[2] or as we understand it, the Father sent both, the Savior and the Holy Spirit.

(4) Origen of Alexandria

Isaiah declares: **And now the Lord sent me and his spirit** (48:16). This passage is ambiguous. Does it mean that the Father and the Holy Spirit sent Jesus, or that the Father sent Christ and the Holy Spirit? In my view the second interpretation is correct. First the Savior had been sent, then the Holy Spirit was sent, and in this way the prophet's saying might be fulfilled; and, to insure that the fulfillment of the prophecy should also be made known to posterity, the disciples of Jesus recorded what had happened.

(5) Augustine of Hippo

If both Son and Holy Spirit are sent to where they already are,[3] the question arises what can really be meant by this sending of the Son or of the Holy Spirit — the Father alone is

---

1. Ambrose's text apparently read *omnia verba eius* ("all his words") rather than *omnia verba haec* ("all these words [or things]"). The Latin *verba* can mean either things or words, and with the addition of "his" it seems more correct to translate it as "words" rather than "things."

2. The LXX text can be read as **The Lord and his Spirit sent me** or **The Lord sent me as well as his Spirit**. Because the Greek word for Spirit *(pneuma)* is neuter, it can be either the subject or the object of the verb "sent."

3. Because God is wholly everywhere at the same time.

nowhere said to have been sent. About the Son the apostle writes, *When the fullness of time had come, God sent his Son, made of a woman, made under law, to redeem those who were under the law* (Gal 4:4). He *sent his Son, made of a woman* — by *woman* of course, as presumably every Catholic knows, he did not intend to suggest loss of virginity, but merely difference of sex according to the Hebrew idiom.[4] So then, by saying that *God sent his Son, made of woman,* he shows plainly enough that it was in being made of a woman that the Son was sent. Thus inasmuch as he was born of God he already was in this world; in that he was born of Mary he was sent and came into the world.

Furthermore, he could not be sent by the Father without the Holy Spirit. On principle, when the Father sent him, that is, made him of woman, he cannot be supposed to have done it without his Spirit. And in any case there is the clear testimony of the answer given to the Virgin Mary when she asked the angel, *How shall this happen? The Holy Spirit shall come upon you, and the might of the Most High shall overshadow you* (Luke 1:34-35), and Matthew says, *She was found to be with child of the Holy Spirit* (Matt 1:18). There is even a prophecy of Isaiah in which Christ himself is to be understood as saying about his future coming, **And now the Lord, and his spirit, has sent me** (48:16).

(6) Theodoret of Cyrus

It is the prophet who speaks here. I do not speak in my own name, he says, but as one who has been sent by the God of all and the all-holy Spirit. He clearly shows that there is another being referred to besides the person of God [the Father]. . . . For he says: **The Lord sent me and his spirit** (48:16). Often he speaks of the one God. For example: *I am the first, and I am forever* (48:12). And: *Before me there was no other god, nor shall there be any after me* (43:10). He also speaks of the properties of the persons, sometimes of the Son and the Father, sometimes of the Father and the Holy Spirit. So on the subject of the Son and the Father, he said: *Because God is in you, and there is no god besides you* (Isa 45:14). And on the subject of the Father and the Spirit: **The Lord sent me and his spirit** (48:16).

48:22
"There is no rejoicing," says the Lord, "for the ungodly."

(7) Augustine of Hippo

Make merry, you just (Ps 97:12). It is possible that when the faithful hear the invitation to *make merry* their minds turn to feasting, they prepare cups and look forward to the season of roses: all this because the psalm urged, *Make merry, you just.* But notice the next words: *in the Lord.* It bids us, *Make merry, you just, in the Lord.* You are looking forward

---

4. The word *mulier* ("woman" or "wife"), which is the term used in the Latin translation of Gal 4:4, is usually contrasted with *virgo*.

to the merrymaking of springtime; but you have the Lord as your gladness, and the Lord is with you all the year round, for with God there is no marking of time. You have him at night, and you have him by day. Be upright of heart, and there will always be good cheer for you from the Lord. What the world calls good cheer does not merit the name. Listen to the prophet Isaiah: **There is no joy for the wicked, says the Lord** (48:22).[5]

What the impious call rejoicing is no true rejoicing. What kind of joy must he have experienced himself, the man who deprecated such joy? Let us believe him, brothers and sisters; he was only a man, but he had known both sorts of joy. He was certainly familiar with the joys of the cup since he was human; he knew the joy of the table; he knew the joy of the bed; he knew all these worldly, sensuous joys. He knew them all, yet took it upon himself to declare, **There is no joy for the wicked, says the Lord**. This is not a man's statement: The Lord says it; from the Lord's truth we hear that **there is no joy for the wicked**. They think they are rejoicing, but the Lord — not man — says that **there is no joy for the wicked**.

After observing what passes for joy, another prophet says: *I have never craved the human light of day* (Jer 17:16 LXX). You show me a different light of day, you teach me about a different dawn, you flood me with a different gladness, you give me an inkling of something different in my inmost self, and so you have saved me from craving the human light of day. Isaiah was undoubtedly used to seeing people drinking, indulging themselves, frequenting theaters and shows; he saw his whole world abandoned to licentiousness and all kinds of frivolity; and yet he kept shouting, **"There is no joy for the wicked," says the Lord**.

---

5. The Septuagint reads **joy** for **peace**.

Isaiah 49

1 Hear me, O islands,
 pay attention, O nations!
 After a long time it shall stand,
 says the Lord.
 From my mother's womb he called my name,
2 and made my mouth like a sharp sword,
 and under the shelter of his hand he hid me;
 he made me like a chosen arrow,
 and in his quiver he sheltered me.
3 And he said to me, "You are my slave,
 Israel, and in you I will be glorified."
4 But I said, "I have labored vainly,
 and I have given my strength in vain and for nothing;
 therefore my judgment is with the Lord,
 and my toil before my God."

5 And now thus says the Lord,
 who formed me from the womb to be his own slave,
 to gather Iakob and Israel to him;
 I will be gathered and glorified before the Lord,
 and my God shall become my strength.
6 And he said to me,
 "It is a great thing for you to be called my servant
 so that you may set up the tribes of Iakob
 and turn back the dispersion of Israel.
 See, I have made you a light of nations,
 that you may be for salvation to the end of the earth."

7 Thus says the Lord who delivered you,
 the God of Israel:

"Sanctify him who despises his own soul,
    who is abhorred by the nations, the slave of rulers;
kings shall see him, and rulers shall stand up
    and worship him for the Lord's sake,
because the Holy One of Israel is faithful,
    and I have chosen you."

8 Thus says the Lord:
In an acceptable time I have listened to you,
    on a day of salvation I have helped you;
I gave you as a covenant to nations,
    to establish the land,
    and to inherit a desert heritage;
9 saying to those who are in bonds, "Come out,"
    and to those who are in darkness that they be revealed.
And they shall feed in all their ways,
    in all the paths shall be their pasture;
10 they shall not hunger or thirst,
    neither shall burning heat nor sun strike them down,
but he who has mercy on them will comfort them,
    and through springs of water will lead them.
11 And I will turn every mountain into a road,
    and every path into a pasture for them.
12 Lo, these come from far away,
    these from the north, and these from the sea,
    but others from the land of the Persians.

13 Rejoice, O heavens, and let the earth be glad;
    let the mountains break forth with joy,
    and the hills with righteousness.
Because God has had mercy on his people,
    and he has comforted the humble of his people.

14 But Sion said, "The Lord has forsaken me,
    the Lord has forgotten me."
15 Will a mother forget her child,
    so as not to have mercy on the descendants of her womb?
But even if a woman should forget these,
    yet I will not forget you, said the Lord.
16 See, I have painted your walls on my hands;
    and you are continually before me.
17 And soon you will be built by those by whom you were destroyed,
    and those who made you desolate will go forth from you.
18 Lift up your eyes all around and see them all;

look, they have gathered and have come to you.
As I live, says the Lord,
    you shall clothe yourself with all of them,
    and put them on like a bride's ornament.

19 Because your desolate and spoiled and ruined places
    will now be crowded on account of your inhabitants,
    and those who swallow you up will be far away from you.
20 For your sons whom you have lost
    will say in your ears:
"The place is too narrow for me;
    make a place for me so that I may settle."
21 Then you will say in your heart,
    "Who has begotten me these?
But I was childless and a widow,
    so who has reared these for me?
But I was left all alone,
    so from where have these come to me?"

22 Thus says the Lord:
Look, I am lifting up my hand to the nations,
    and I will lift my signal to the islands;
and they shall bring your sons in their bosom,
    and your daughters shall they lift on their shoulders.
23 And kings shall be your foster fathers,
    and the women who rule, your nurses.
On the face of the earth they shall worship you,
    and they shall lick the dust of your feet.
Then you will know that I am the Lord,
    and you shall not be put to shame.

24 Will anyone take spoils from a mighty one?
    And if one should take a captive unjustly, shall he be saved?
25 Thus says the Lord:
If one should take a mighty one captive,
    he will take spoils;
and by taking them from a strong one
    he will be saved.
And I will judge your cause,
    and I will rescue your sons.
26 And those who afflicted you shall eat their own flesh,
    and they shall drink their own blood like new wine, and be drunk.
Then all flesh shall perceive

> that I am the Lord who rescued you,
> who assists the strength of Iakob.

It was customary among the church fathers to interpret **islands** *(49:1; RSV translates* **coastlands***) to refer to the churches in the midst of a stormy sea. In the first verse of chapter 55, for example,* **islands** *is paired with* **nations***, hence Cyril takes the text to refer to the churches of the Gentiles who had turned from idolatry to worship the true God.* **From my mother's womb he called my name** *(49:1) was understood to refer to the Lord's birth from the Virgin Mary, and* **my name** *to the name Christ Jesus. Cyril uses this passage as an occasion to discuss the significance of the Incarnation. The phrase* **chosen arrow** *(49:2) was frequently taken as a reference to Christ, and several texts illustrate that interpretation.* **Chosen arrow** *was in turn related to the words in the Song of Songs, "I am wounded with love" (Song 2:5). Gregory of Nyssa uses the phrase* **made me . . . a servant** *(49:5) to discuss how the Scriptures refer to the divine Word of God when he has become man. Some had claimed that the verse "the* LORD *created me" (Prov 8:22) meant that the Word was not fully divine, but Gregory shows that in this passage as elsewhere the term* **servant** *(and like expressions) refers to Christ's human nature.* **That you may be for salvation to the ends of the earth** *(49:6) is quoted by Augustine in a sermon on the Feast of Epiphany, celebrating the revelation of the gospel to the nations and the coming of the Magi from distant places to worship the infant Jesus. Jerome, in an interesting comment on the term* **Zion** *(49:14), and hence Jerusalem, indicates that for early Christian readers the term had four distinct senses.*

(1) The Acts of the Apostles

The next Sabbath almost the whole city gathered together to hear the word of God. But when the Jews saw the multitudes, they were filled with jealousy, and contradicted what was spoken by Paul, and reviled him. And Paul and Barnabas spoke out boldly, saying, "It was necessary that the word of God should be spoken first to you. Since you thrust it from you, and judge yourselves unworthy of eternal life, behold, we turn to the Gentiles. For so the Lord commanded us, saying,

> **I have set you to be a light for the Gentiles, that you may bring salvation to the uttermost parts of the earth.** (49:6)

And when the Gentiles heard this, they were glad and glorified the word of God; and as many as were ordained to eternal life believed. And the word of the Lord spread throughout all the region.

(2) The Second Letter of Paul to the Corinthians

Working together with him, then, we entreat you not to accept the grace of God in vain. For he says, **At the acceptable time I have listened to you, and helped you on the day of salvation** (49:8). Behold, now is the **acceptable time**; behold, now is the **day of salvation**.

(3) The Revelation to John

Then one of the elders addressed me, saying, "Who are these, clothed in white robes, and whence have they come?" I said to him, "Sir, you know." And he said to me, "These are they who have come out of the great tribulation; they have washed their robes and made them white in the blood of the Lamb. Therefore are they before the throne of God, and serve him day and night within his temple; and he who sits upon the throne will shelter them with his presence. **They shall hunger no more, neither thirst any more; the sun shall not strike them, nor any scorching heat** (49:10). For the Lamb in the midst of the throne will be their shepherd, and **he will guide** them to **springs of living water** (49:10); and God will wipe away every tear from their eyes.

(4) Cyril of Alexandria

Since he has already encouraged Israel with exhortations and admonitions, he now turns his spiritual message to the nations, and makes clear once again the mystery of Christ. For through Christ they abandoned their brutish and base life to embrace the way of life that is most dear to him and to be enlightened with the true light. They came to certain knowledge of the one who is by nature truly God, the nature that rules all things. He calls out to the **islands** (49:1), which we understand to be the churches of Christ. For they lie as it were in the midst of the sea surrounded by the fierce waves and stormy waters of the present life, buffeted by unbearable attacks and persecutions and afflictions brought upon them by truth's enemies and those who fight against God's call. The Scriptures speak often of such **islands**, as, for example, David in the psalm: *The LORD is King. Let the earth rejoice, and the many islands be glad* (Ps 97:1). When Christ came to rule over the whole earth and everything was given into his hands, the churches throughout the world rejoiced and were filled with joy.

It should be clear from what follows in this passage that the prophet is referring to the churches of the Gentiles with the word **islands**. For he adds, **pay attention, O nations!** (49:1). And immediately after, **hear me, O islands**. Then he says, **After a long time it shall stand, says the Lord** (49:1). He promises that the Savior of us all, Jesus Christ, will be shown forth. The Word who is God will dwell with those on earth in human form. That the prophecy does not refer to events at the time it was written is clear from the words, **After a long time** what had been **shall stand**.

He declares what will happen by mentioning the person of the Savior who says, **From my mother's womb he called my name** (49:1). A great and profound mystery is hidden in these words and can only be understood if one has been enlightened from above, as happened when it was revealed to blessed Peter that Jesus was *the Christ, the Son of the living God* (Matt 16:16-17). The Word was and is God, of equal glory, sharing the throne of God the Father, coexistent and coeternal (cf. John 1:1). The names which he had by nature before his Incarnation are "God," "Wisdom," "Light," "Life," and "Might," and others besides these found in the Holy Scriptures. When he humbled himself, *being born in the likeness of men and being found in human form* (Phil 2:7-8), he received a name like other names, "Christ" and "Jesus," or "God with us." The expression "with us" signifies that he shared our life. For it is written, *Look, the virgin shall conceive and bear a son, and you shall name him Emmanuel* (7:14).

The blessed Gabriel revealed the mystery to the holy Virgin, the Theotokos, when he said, *Do not be afraid, Mary, for you have found favor with God. And behold, you will conceive in your womb and bear a son, and you shall call his name Jesus. For he will save his people from their sins* (Luke 1:30-31; Matt 1:21). Have these two — the blessed angel and the prophet — spoken things that are not in agreement with each other? Of course not. For the holy prophet, relating mysteries by the Spirit, announced that God would come among us and so named him from his divine nature and his sojourn in flesh. But the blessed angel gave him a name based on what he would do, for he saved his own people (Matt 1:21). For this reason he is called Savior. When he submitted to a birth according to the flesh for our sake, the angelic hosts proclaimed this good news to the shepherds, saying: *Be not afraid; for behold, I bring you good news of a great joy which will come to all the people; for to you is born this day in the city of David a Savior, who is Christ the Lord* (Luke 2:10-11). Thus, he is *Emmanuel*, because he who is by nature God came to be with us, that is, became man; and he is *Jesus* because, in order to save those on earth, he had to be God and become man.

When he came forth **from his mother's womb** (49:1) and was born from her according to the flesh, he was given the name Jesus Christ. The name Christ was not suitable to God the Word before his birth according to the flesh. How could he be called Christ, since he had not yet been anointed? Only when he had come from his mother's womb as a human being did he receive a name befitting one born according to the flesh.

He says that he has made his **mouth like a sharp sword** (49:2). How true this is, for somewhere it is written about him, indeed the prophet Isaiah himself says, *He shall be girded with righteousness around the waist, and bound with truth around the sides, and with breath from his lips he shall do away with the ungodly* (11:5, 4b). The divine and heavenly proclamation, the gospel which was spoken through the mouth of Christ, became a sharp and keen-edged sword against the devil's tyranny, doing away with *the rulers of this present darkness* and *the spiritual hosts of wickedness* (Eph 6:12). He dispersed the fog of deceit and shined the rays of the knowledge of God into the hearts of all. He transformed those on earth into a godly community and made them lovers of holy habits. He pruned away the sin of the world, justifying the ungodly by faith, filling those who turn to him with the Holy Spirit, and making them sons of God. He instills in them a healthy mind, well equipped to engage the enemy, giving them *the sword of the Spirit, which is the word of God* (Eph 6:17). Now they rise up against those who were once their masters and run *for the prize of the upward call* (Phil 3:14) with no obstacle standing in the way. The prophet Isaiah makes clear that the spiritual teaching given by Christ puts an end to the devil's tyranny over those on earth when he states, *On that day God will bring his holy and great . . . sword against the dragon, . . . the crooked serpent — and he will kill the dragon* (27:1).

The prophet continues: **Under the shelter of his hand he hid me** (49:2). Though he speaks in a way befitting human things, it is not difficult for those with understanding to see in these words that the Son cannot be divided from God the Father even though he

Isaiah 49

became man. He says he is **under the shelter of his hand** to indicate that his ineffable and invincible nature remains intact even when he became like us in other respects. For no one can overpower the all-powerful hand, and, as I said, the Word is not measured by the limits of his humanity. He remains the all-powerful Word of God the Father and the Lord of hosts. When he became man, the Father, respecting the power of the mystery, confirms the Incarnation and through the lyre of the psalmist says: The enemy shall not outwit him, the wicked shall not humble him. I will crush his foes before him and strike down those who hate him. My faithfulness and my steadfast love shall be with him (Ps 89:22-24).

Take note of what the prophet, speaking in a human way, puts into the mouth of the one who for our sake became like us: **Under the shelter of his hand he hid me; he made me**, he says, **like a chosen arrow, and in his quiver he sheltered me** (49:2). Now there have been many **arrows** of God, hidden as it were in a quiver for a time by God's foreknowledge, each brought forth at the right moment. But the **arrow** chosen above all is Christ, hidden in a **quiver** as I have said by the Father's foreknowledge. He was known before the world's foundation (cf. Eph 1:4), and he appeared among us when the whole world was on the verge of destruction. Captive to evil spirits and ensnared in sin, it had grown decadent and corrupt by worshiping *the creature rather than the Creator* (Rom 1:25). This **chosen arrow** routs Satan himself and his evil hosts. Likewise, he destroys the profane adversaries of his sacred teachings, the enemies of Truth. But in wounding he brings health and salvation. Hence the passage in the Song of Songs where the smitten bride says, *I am wounded with love* (Song 2:5).

Then the prophet has the Father speak to Christ: **You are my bond servant, Israel, and in you I will be glorified** (49:3). *O the depth of the riches and wisdom and knowledge of God!* as it is written (Rom 11:33). For the Son was and is free, as one who springs ineffably from the nature that rules over all. But he heard the Father saying, **You are my bond servant**. The Word, though free by nature, assumes the role of **bond servant** through the Incarnation, being seen in the flesh, so that you might realize that he was born from a woman in time according to the flesh. He also calls the one who is born **Israel** because his birth according to the flesh is from the blood of Israel.

But he also says, **In you I will be glorified** (49:3). The God of the universe is glorified *through* the holy prophets, but not *in* them. But in Christ he is glorified in a new and unique way, for he is glorified *in* him. When Christ is glorified, the Father is glorified in him. We see the Father conspicuously displayed in him by means of his divine attributes, his all-embracing power and energy, his holiness and righteousness, and his abundant loving-kindness. In him the divine takes a form we can grasp. Christ said, *He who has seen me has seen the Father* (John 14:9). And the all-wise Paul declared that the one who begets is glorified in the face of Christ (1 Cor 3:18). Therefore, [God] says, **in you I will be glorified**. As it is written, *Every knee in heaven and on earth and under the earth will bow down before the Son, and every tongue confess that Jesus Christ is Lord, to the glory of God the Father* (Phil 2:10-11).

49:1
From my mother's womb he called my name.

(5) Origen of Alexandria

The observant reader of sacred Scripture can find [titles for Christ] in the prophets that are similar to [those found in the New Testament]. For example, Christ calls himself a **chosen arrow** (49:2) and a **servant of God** (49:3) and **light of the nations** (49:6). Isaiah speaks as follows: **From my mother's womb he called my name, and he made my mouth like a sharp sword, and he hid me under the shelter of his hand. He made me like a chosen arrow and hid me in his quiver. And he said to me, "You are my servant Israel, and in you I will be glorified"** (49:1-3).

And a little further he asserted: **And my God shall become my strength. And he said to me, "It is a great thing for you to be called my servant so that you may establish the tribes of Jacob and turn back the dispersion of Israel. See, I have made you a light of the nations, that you may be for salvation to the end of the earth"** (49:5-6). And in Jeremiah he likens himself to a lamb as follows, *I was like an innocent lamb led to the slaughter* (Jer 11:19).

[Christ] applies these and similar titles to himself. And in the gospels, in the apostles, and throughout the prophets, we could collect thousands of such titles by which the Son of God is called: either from those who wrote the gospels and set forth their own idea of what he is, or from the apostles who glorify him based on what they have learned, or from the prophets who announced his future coming in advance and used different names to proclaim what was true about him.

49:2
He made me like a chosen arrow.

(6) Origen of Alexandria

If there is anyone anywhere who has ever burned with unwavering love for the Word of God; if there be anyone who, as the prophet says, has received the sweet wound of this **chosen arrow** (49:2); if there be anyone who has been pierced through and through by the lovable javelin of the knowledge of him, so as to long for him by day and by night, to be unable to speak of anything else, to refuse to hear anything else, to know not how to think anything else, to have no inclination to desire or want or hope for anything else except him — this is the soul that deservedly says, *I have been wounded by love* (Song 2:5), and has received the wound from him of whom Isaiah says, **He established me as a chosen arrow, and hid me in his quiver** (49:2).

It is right and proper for God to smite souls with a wound like this, to transfix them with spears and darts like these, and to hurt them with these saving wounds, so that, since *God is love* (1 John 4:8), they too may say for themselves: *I have been wounded by love*. And in truth the Bride in this love-story-like drama says that the wounds she has sustained are those of love. Moreover, a soul that in a similar way burns with desire for God's Wisdom — a soul, I mean, that is able to discern the beauty of Wisdom — can say: *I have been wounded by* Wisdom. Further, yet another soul, one that perceives the grandeur of the Word of God and has wondered at his power, can say: *I have been wounded by* Strength — such a soul as he that shouted: *The LORD is my light and my salvation, whom then shall I fear? The LORD is the strength of my life, of whom then shall I be afraid?* (Ps 27:1). But again another soul, burning with love of his justice, and perceiving the justice of his dispensations and his providence, surely says: *I have been wounded by* Justice. And another that sees the immeasurable greatness of his goodness and his goodwill says similar things. What includes all of these, however, is that wound of love by which the Bride proclaims she has been wounded. . . .

(7) Gregory of Nyssa

The bride praises the archer's marksmanship because his arrow had hit her directly. *My soul is wounded with love,* she says (Song 2:5). These words indicate that the arrow has penetrated to the depth of her heart. The archer who shoots this arrow is love, for we have learned from the Holy Scriptures that *God is love* (1 John 4:8) and sent his **chosen arrow** (49:2), the only Son, to those who are being saved, smearing its triple-tipped point with the Spirit of life. The tip of the arrow is faith, for by it God introduces the archer into the heart along with the arrow. As the Lord says: *I and the Father are one, and will come and make our dwelling place with him* (John 14:23).

Then the soul, buoyed up as it ascends by divine help, sees within itself the sweet arrow of love with which she was wounded; she boasts of her wound and says, *I am wounded with love.* O beautiful wound and sweet blow by which life makes its way within, penetrating by opening for itself a door and an entrance. As soon as the bride receives the arrow of love, the imagery shifts from archery to nuptial delight.

(8) Gregory of Nyssa

And what is the triad of arrows (cf. 2 Sam 18:14) that strikes the middle of the enemy's heart and brings death to the *last enemy* (1 Cor 15:26)? In order to grasp the significance of this arrow, take note of Isaiah's prophecy where it is said in the person of the Lord, **He has made me as a chosen arrow, and in his quiver he has exalted me** (49:2). This arrow is *the living Word of God,* and *is more piercing than any two-edged sword* (Heb 4:12). Now Christ is the Word, and the mystery of the Trinity is confessed by this name. This word teaches us about the one who anoints, the one who was anointed, and by what he was anointed. For if any one of these is omitted, the name of Christ, that is, the one who is anointed, loses its meaning.

Whenever this name is **exalted in our quiver**, that is, when it takes up residence in our soul through faith (for the soul is the quiver of the Word), then it destroys the one who rises up against us and pursues us. For he met his end on the tree.[1]

---

1. Satan, who was vanquished by the cross.

(9) Ambrose of Milan

The Church advances joyfully to other resting places such as the cross of Christ and his tomb. In these the Church is wounded, but with the wound of love. Christ received a wound, but what he freely imparted is perfumed ointment, what he disbursed is fruit. The Church has partaken of this fruit and says, *His fruit was sweet to my taste* (Song 2:3). And so that you may know that this fruit is the Lord, just before this it says, *As an apple tree among the trees of the wood, so is my beloved* (Song 2:3). We likewise confess this wound when *we preach Christ crucified* (1 Cor 1:23), and what's more, *we are a sweet odor to God* (cf. 2 Cor 2:15) since the cross of Christ is *a stumbling block to Jews and folly to Gentiles* but to us it is *the power and wisdom of God* (1 Cor 1:23). The Church is wounded with this wound of love when she preaches the death of her Savior. In short, the one who does not believe denies, while the one who loves, confesses. The Manichee denies, the Christian confesses. It is written, *A wound from a friend is more beneficial than kisses freely given by an enemy* (cf. Prov 27:6). Therefore the Church beautifully says, *I am wounded with love* (Song 2:5). Let us expose ourselves to this good wound, let us expose ourselves to the **chosen arrow** (49:2). This arrow is Christ, who says, **He made me like a chosen arrow**, and thus it is good to be wounded by this **arrow**. This journey is not to an ordinary resting place, and not all can say that they are wounded with love. The apostles affirmed it when they preached Christ and were stoned on his behalf. Paul said it when on three occasions he was beaten with rods (cf. 2 Cor 11:25), and he argued day and night to the Gentiles that Christ ought to be adored. The martyrs also say it: they were wounded for Christ, and since they merited being wounded for his name, they love him all the more.

49:5
And now thus says the Lord, who formed me from the womb to be his own servant.

(10) Gregory of Nyssa

In response to those who quote the passage from Proverbs, *the LORD created me* (Prov 8:22), and claim that it makes a strong case that the Creator and Maker of all things was created, one should say that the only-begotten God was *made* many things for us. For he was the Word and was made flesh; he was God and was made man; he was without a body and was made a body. Further, he was made *sin* (2 Cor 5:21), and a *curse* (Gal 3:13), and a *stone* (Acts 4:11), and an *axe* (Matt 3:10), and *bread* (John 6:32-33), and a *lamb* (John 1:29), and a *way* (John 14:6), and a *door* (John 10:7), and a *rock* (1 Cor 10:4). He was none of these things by nature, but he became them for us during his sojourn among us.

Just as he is the Word who was made flesh for our sake and God who was made man, so he is the Creator who was made a creature for our sake. As he said through the prophet: **Thus says the Lord, who formed me from the womb to be his servant** (49:5). And through Solomon he also said: *The LORD created me the beginning of his ways, for his* *works* (Prov 8:22). For the whole creation is servant, as the apostle says (Rom 8:22-23). Therefore the one formed in the womb of the Virgin according to the word of the prophet is the **servant**, not the Lord. That is, it refers to the man according to the flesh in whom God was revealed. Likewise the one who was *created the beginning of his ways* (Prov 8:22) is not God but the man in whom God was revealed in order to renew for mankind the way of salvation which had been corrupted. Since we recognize two things in Christ, the one divine, the other human, the divine by nature, the human when he sojourned among us as a man, we attribute that which is eternal to the godhead, and that which is created we ascribe to his human nature. As he was **formed in the womb as a servant** according to the prophet, so according to Solomon he was revealed in flesh by means of this servile creation. So, when some contend, "If he always was, he was not begotten, and if he was begotten there was a time when he was not," they should learn that one should not ascribe to his divine nature those attributes that belong to his birth in the flesh.

49:6
**See, I have made you[2] a light for the nations,
that you may be for salvation to the end of the earth.**

(11) Origen of Alexandria

He claimed that he was the *light of the world* (John 8:12; 9:5), and we must examine other titles similar to this one, since it seems to me that some are not only similar but identical. There are *the light of men, true light,* and *light of the nations. Light of men* is found at the beginning of the present Gospel[3] where it says: *That which came into being in him was life, and the life was the light of men, and the light shines in the darkness, and the darkness has not overcome it* (John 1:4-5). Further, in the same passage it is written: *He was the true light that enlightens every man coming into the world* (John 1:9). *Light of the nations* is found in Isaiah, which I have already cited: **See, I have made you a light to the nations, that you may be for salvation to the end of the earth** (49:6).

(12) Augustine of Hippo

Recently we celebrated the day on which the Lord was born of the Jews. Today we are celebrating the day on which he was worshiped by the Gentiles.[4] *Salvation is from the Jews* (John 4:22), but **this salvation reaches to the ends of the earth** (49:6). On that day the shepherds worshiped him, on this one the Magi. To those the message was brought by angels, to these by a star. Both learned about him from heaven, when they saw the King of

---

2. Some versions of the LXX include the additional phrase **covenant for the race**.
3. Origen is expounding the Gospel of John.
4. Feast of Epiphany.

heaven on earth, so that there might be *glory to God in the highest, and on earth peace to people of goodwill* (Luke 2:14).

For he is our peace, who made both into one (Eph 2:14). Already from this moment, by the way he was born and proclaimed, the infant is shown to be that cornerstone (cf. Ps 118:22); already from the first moments of his birth he appeared as such. He began at once to tie together in himself two walls coming from different directions, bringing the shepherds from Judea, the Magi from the East; *so that he might establish the two in himself as one new man, making peace; peace for those who were far off, and peace for those who were near* (Eph 2:15, 17). Thus it is that those hurrying from nearby on the very day, and those arriving today from far away, marked two days to be celebrated by posterity, and yet both saw the one light of the world.

(13) Theodoret of Cyrus

The Lord shares a common nature with all human beings, but Israel is his own people to whom he is very close. Since he came to Israel, but also shone his light on the Gentiles through the apostles, he declared: I have given you to them because of the promise made to their fathers, but through you I will enlighten the Gentiles and bring salvation to all men — this is what is meant by **to the end of the earth** (49:6) — and I will bring to completion the **agreements** (49:6) I made with their fathers. Some interpreters translate **covenant** as **agreement**.

49:8
Thus says the Lord: In an acceptable time I have listened to you, on a day of salvation I have helped you. . . .

(14) Origen of Alexandria

As the sufferings of Christ abound, so also through Christ does comfort abound (2 Cor 1:5). Let us then gladly accept the sufferings of Christ so that they may abound in us — if we desire the abundant comfort received by all who mourn (cf. Matt 5:4), though perhaps not in equal measure. For if the comfort were given in equal measure to all, it would not have been written: *As the sufferings of Christ abound in us, so also through Christ does our comfort abound.* They who *share in the sufferings will also share in consolation* (2 Cor 1:7), in proportion to the sufferings that they share with Christ. This you learn also from him who with full conviction said: *For we know that as you share in the sufferings, you will also share in the comfort* (2 Cor 1:7).

Moreover, God says by the prophet: **In an acceptable time I have heard you, and in the day of salvation I have helped you** (49:8). What time could be more acceptable than when, because of our faith toward God in Christ, we are brought in procession under guard in the world and led away to die — in triumph, however, rather than in defeat? For the martyrs in Christ *disarm with him the principalities and powers, triumphing over* *them in him* (Col 2:15). As they share in his sufferings, so also they share in the great victory won by his sufferings. By that I mean his triumph over the principalities and powers that soon you will see vanquished and put to shame. What other day could be for us such a **day of salvation** as the day we are delivered from this life?

(15) Augustine of Hippo

If anyone asserts that faith merits the grace of doing good actions, we cannot deny it; in fact, we most gratefully admit it. For we want these brothers of ours, who boast much of their good works, to have this faith by which they might obtain the love that alone truly produces good works. But love is so much a gift of God that it is called God (1 John 4:8). Those, then, who have the faith by which they obtain justification have come through the grace of God to the law of righteousness; for this reason Scripture says, **I heard you at an acceptable time, and I helped you on the day of salvation** (49:8; 2 Cor 6:2). Hence, in those who are being saved through the choice of his grace, God as a helper *produces the willing and the action in accord with goodwill* (Phil 2:13), *because for those who love God all things work out for the good* (Rom 8:28) — and if all things, then certainly the love itself that we obtain by faith in order that we may love through his grace him who first loved us (cf. 1 John 4:19) so that we might believe in him and so that by loving him we might do good works, which we did not do in order that we might be loved.

49:9
Say to those who are in bonds, "Come out,"
and to those who are in darkness that they be revealed.

(16) Eusebius of Caesarea

He also commands him to say **to those who are in bonds**, that is, those *caught in the chains of their sins* (Prov 5:22), **"Come out"** (49:9). To these he announced forgiveness, the manner of rebirth conforming to their deeds. Thus to those **who are in bonds**, he says, **"Come out,"** and **to those who are in darkness**, he adds, **be filled with light** (49:9). For *we were all children of wrath* (Eph 2:3) and *once were in darkness, but now . . . are light in the Lord* (Eph 5:8). Then he preaches the good news to those freed from their previous bonds and from their former darkness, saying, **And they shall be fed in all their ways, in all the paths shall be their pasture.** The ways and paths that the ancient men of God traveled are the inspired Scriptures. Those who have obtained the divine promise feed on them and enjoy this godly and spiritual food since they have found this good pasture. As it is said: *The LORD is my shepherd, I shall not want; he makes me lie down in green pastures. He leads me beside still waters* (Ps 23:1-2).

(17) Cyril of Alexandria

That which had resisted being conquered — Death! — was conquered, corruption was made into something new, the seemingly invincible evil routed. The relentless and insatiable desire of Hades for yet more dead had no one to welcome, and learned — much to its regret — what it had never had to learn before. For now Hades no longer had the power to snatch those who are yet dying, it had to vomit forth those whom it had already caught, and by the power of our Savior it was left to endure splendid isolation. For Christ came **saying to those in bonds, "Come out," and to those in darkness, "see the light of day"** (49:9). And after he *preached to the incredulous spirits in Hades* (1 Pet 3:19), he mounted up victorious, raising his own *temple* (John 2:19-21) as a kind of *first fruits* (1 Cor 15:20) of our hope. He led the way for our nature to rise from the dead and for us to be showered with other good gifts.

49:14
But Zion said, "The Lord has forsaken me, the Lord has forgotten me."

(18) Jerome

I have often said that in the Sacred Scriptures "Jerusalem" and **Zion** can be interpreted in four different ways. First, among the Jews **Zion** refers to that city over which the Lord wept in the Gospel, *O Jerusalem, Jerusalem, killing the prophets and stoning those who are sent to you* (Matt 23:37). And elsewhere he says, *But when you see Jerusalem surrounded by armies, then know that its desolation has come near* (Luke 21:20). Second, the assembly of believers, that is, those who are established in the Lord's peace and as a tower of virtues, is properly called **Zion**. So it is said, *On the holy mount stands the city he founded; the LORD loves the gates of Zion more than all the dwelling places of Jacob* (Ps 87:1-2). . . . Third, the host of angels, dominions, and powers, as well as everything else established to serve God is called Jerusalem. Concerning this Jerusalem, the apostle remarked, *But the Jerusalem above is free, and she is our mother* (Gal 4:26). And in another place it is written, *But you have come to Mount Zion and to the city of the living God, the heavenly Jerusalem* (Heb 12:22). The fourth meaning of "Jerusalem" is that place which the Jews and judaizing Christians (according to the Apocalypse of John [Rev 21:10-22:5]) think is a gilded and bejeweled city in the heavens whose outer limits and huge size are described in the last part of Ezekiel (Ezekiel 47-48). They do not, however, understand the passage.

Since there are these several meanings, we must now carefully consider which **Zion** among the four said, **The Lord has forsaken me, the Lord has forgotten me** (49:14). Without doubt, the congregation of believers, which was among the Jews before and was forsaken by the Lord, recites these words and complains with weeping that it was deserted, bereft of the Lord's help. God responds to them using a metaphor from nature: If it could happen that a mother should forget her own child and not turn in mercy to the fruit of her womb, then I also will forget you. I will say something more: Even if she should forget, overpowering the laws of nature by hardness of heart, still I will not forget my creature. I will always cherish the lives of my saints in my heart. Know this, you who think yourselves completely forsaken, you are written down **on my hands, painted there. Your walls remain continually before my eyes** (49:16). From this we learn that it is not the Jerusalem in the region of Palestine that is being talked about, since it is the least hospitable place in the whole province. It is studded with rocky peaks and suffers such drought that it must rely on rains from heaven and dig deep wells to alleviate the paucity of water. But to the one in the hands of God it says, **Your builders outstrip your destroyers** (49:17), or, according to the Septuagint, **And soon you will be built by those who destroyed you.** Destroyed by Jews, it was rebuilt by Jews. She who was deserted on account of the scribes and Pharisees has been gathered together from Jews as well as from Gentiles as a result of the preaching of Christ's apostles. It continues, **those who destroyed you and those who made you desolate will go forth from you** (49:17). Mischievous teachers, see to it that you do not follow the commands and traditions of men but the law of God (cf. Mark 7:8).

She is addressed as she lifts her eyes round about and sees the sons who have been gathered to her. The Lord says about them, *Lift up your eyes, and see how the fields are already white for harvest* (John 4:35). And to make us confident, he adds: **As I live, says the Lord**, (which, in the Old Testament, is the typical expression for an oath), **you shall clothe yourself with all of them, and put them on like a bride's ornament** (49:18). Blessed is he who has such merit, such virtue, that he may be called an ornament of the Church. I believe that the text indicates different spiritual graces which adorn the bride's beauty. Psalm 44 [45] sings about this, *At your right hand stands the queen in gold, clothed with rich variety* (Ps 45:12b). They who had first been deserted and fallen into desolate ruins will be restored with the coming of the gospel of Christ and will have such a multitude of inhabitants as not to be able to hold them all.

49:15
Will a mother forget her child, so as not to have mercy on the descendants of her womb?

(19) John Chrysostom

Though God is affronted he is still Father, though provoked to anger he remains fond of his children. This alone he seeks — not to take vengeance when we affront him but to see you repent and call on him. Would that we were fervid in our affections as his love is kindled toward us. This fire seeks only a beginning, and if you allow it a tiny spark, you will kindle a roaring fire of goodness. It is not because he is affronted that his anger is kindled, but because you are the one who has affronted him and been alienated from him. For if we who are sinners, when our children affront us, are distressed, how much more is God, who cannot bear being affronted, filled with anger at your offense? If we love by nature, how much more intense is the love of the one whose tender affection is beyond nature. **For even if a mother forget the children of her womb, yet I will not forget you** (49:15).

49:16
See, I have painted your walls on my hands; you are continually before me.

(20) Ambrose of Milan

Only in the soul is the fullness of wisdom, the fullness of devotion and justice, for all virtue comes from God. **Behold, Jerusalem, I have painted your walls** (49:16). Your soul is painted by God, and it is in the soul that one finds the shining grace that attends the virtues and the luster of true devotion. That soul is well painted in which shines the imprint of divine operation. That soul is well painted in which resides the splendor of grace and the reflection of its paternal nature. Precious is that picture which in its brilliance is in accord with that divine reflection.

Adam before he sinned conformed to this image. But after his fall he lost that celestial image and took on one that is terrestrial. Let us flee from this image which cannot enter the city of God, for it is written: *In thy city, O Lord, thou shall bring their image to nothing* (Ps 72:20 LXX). An unworthy image does not enter there; no sooner does it enter than it is excluded, because we read: *There shall not enter into it anything common, nor he who practices abomination and falsehood* (Rev 21:27). He in whose forehead is written the name of the Lamb will find entrance there.

Our soul, therefore, is made to the image of God. In this is man's entire essence, because without it man is nothing but earth, and into earth he shall return (cf. Gen 3:19). Hence, in order to convince you that without the soul the flesh is nothing, Scripture says: *Do not be afraid of those who kill the body but cannot kill the soul* (Matt 10:28).

(21) Ambrose of Milan

Do not remove God's law from your heart and adhere to the law of sin. Do not inscribe in your senses the devil's enticements and erase God's commandments. **See**, he says, **I have painted your walls on my hands** (49:16). The Lord says this to Jerusalem, that is, to the soul eager for tranquility and peace, the soul which he made in his own image (cf. Gen 1:26). Do not remove the heavenly image and put in its place an image of death. You have renounced the world's inheritance; guard Christ's testimonies since in these there is joy and exultation.

49:20
This place is too narrow for me; make a place for me so that I may dwell [in it].

(22) Gregory of Nyssa

When I see you crowding together here with your families for the celebration,[5] I am reminded of the prophetic oracle that Isaiah proclaimed long ago, speaking in anticipation of the Church blessed with many lovely children: *Who are these that fly like clouds and like doves with their young to me?* (60:8). And in addition to this he says: **The place is too narrow for me; make a place for me to dwell in** (49:20). The power of the Spirit prophesied these things about the populous Church of God which in later times would fill the whole world from one end of the earth to the other.

---

5. Gregory is preaching on the festival of the Baptism of Christ.

Isaiah 50

1 Thus says the Lord:
   Of what kind was your mother's bill of divorce
      with which I sent her away?
   Or to which creditor
      have I sold you?
   Look, for your sins you were sold,
      and for your transgressions I sent away your mother.
2 Why was it that I came and no man was there?
      I called, and there was none to answer?
   Is not my hand strong to deliver?
      Or am I not strong to rescue?
   Look, by my threat I will make the sea desolate,
      and the rivers I will make deserts;
   and their fish shall be dried up because there is no water,
      and they will die by thirst.
3 And I will clothe heaven with darkness,
      and make its covering like sackcloth.

4 The Lord gives me
      the tongue of instruction,
   that I may know in season
      when it is necessary to speak a word.
   He assigned it to me in the morning,
      he added to me an ear to hear.
5 And the instruction of the Lord opens my ears,
      and I do not disobey nor contradict.
6 I have given my back to scourges,
      and my cheeks to blows,
   but I did not turn away my face
      from the shame of spittings.

7 **And the Lord became my helper,**
   therefore I was not disgraced;
  but I have set my face like solid rock,
   and I realized that I would not be put to shame,
8   because he who justified me draws near.
  Who is the one who contends with me?
   Let him confront me at once.
  Yes, who is the one who contends with me?
   Let him draw near me.
9 Look, the Lord helps me;
   who will harm me?
  Look, all of you will become old like a garment,
   and as it were a moth will devour you.

10 Who among you is the one who fears the Lord?
   Let him hear the voice of his servant.
  Those who walk in darkness —
   they have no light;
  trust in the name of the Lord
   and lean upon God.
11 Look, all of you kindle a fire
   and make a flame stronger.
  Walk by the light of your fire
   and by the flame you have kindled.
  Because of me, these things came upon you:
   you shall lie down in sorrow.

Isaiah 50 contains the third "servant song," and the church fathers interpreted v. 6, **I gave my back to scourges, and my cheeks to blows,** *with reference to Christ's passion. Today 50:4-7 is often read as the Old Testament reading for Palm Sunday prior to the reading of the passion account from one of the synoptic gospels. Ancient commentators took the phrase* **know when it is necessary to speak a word** *(50:4) to depict Christ's silence before Pilate. They observed, however, that the prophet later indicates that there would be a time when Christ would no longer be "silent" (62:1) — when the apostles went into the world to preach the gospel. In the same spirit Cyril of Alexandria takes* **I do not disobey nor oppose** *(50:5) as a prophecy of Christ's obedience to the Father reflected in his statement during his agony in the Garden of Gethsemane, "Not as I will, but as thou wilt" (Matt 26:39). Ambrose, on the other hand, saw 50:4 as a piece of ancient wisdom and related it to the saying in Sirach, "A wise man will be silent until the right moment" (Sir 20:7). The sage knows when to keep silent and when to speak. Others were intrigued by the phrase* **an ear to hear** *(50:4); several play on the metaphor of ear to signify either those who heard and heeded the teaching of Jesus or those who understood the fuller sense of the Scriptures. In a sermon to the newly baptized Cyril of Jerusalem reminds his hearers that they were anointed on the ears (as well as the forehead, nostrils, and breast) and cites the word of Jesus: "He who has ears to hear, let him hear" (Matt 11:15). For Bernard of Clairvaux* **a ready ear** *(50:4)* *signified obedience, a necessary preparation, he observes, for the vision of God. Origen, always as imaginative as he is insightful, suggests that **walk by the light of your fire** (50:11) means that the sinner kindles his own fire of perdition by his sins.*

(1) The Gospel according to Matthew

Then they **spat in his face**, and **struck him** (50:6); and some slapped him, saying, "Prophesy to us, you Christ! Who is it that struck you?"

(2) Jerome

Against those who think that the Lord is not able to deliver his people from captivity, he makes his case with many examples (50:2). He made a way for his people through the Red Sea, he dried up the waters of the Jordan, and made the rivers in Egypt so foul the fish were killed (Exod 7:21). He made darkness so dense in Egypt that the heavens seemed covered with a thick sack (Exod 10:22-23). Certainly he was able to deliver his people from danger. Or as the text has it: **I came and no man was there; I called, and there was none to answer** (50:2). This we are able to say, because he who accomplished such great wonders, who makes the heaven and the earth and the sea serve at his command, also would have been able to escape the cross, as he says in the Gospel: *Do you think that I cannot appeal to my Father, and he will at once send me more than twelve legions of angels?* (Matt 26:53)....

Jewish interpreters distinguish the next section (50:4-11) from what came previously and refer it to the person of Isaiah because he said that he had received the word from the Lord to urge on a weary and wayward people and call them back to salvation. And in the fashion of children who are instructed in the **morning** (50:4), he heard from the Holy Spirit what he was to say and obeyed. And when he was asked by the Lord, *Whom shall I send, and who will go to this people?* he responded to him, *Here am I! Send me* (6:8). For he had said: *Hear the word of the* LORD, *you rulers of Sodom. Give ear to the law of God, you people of Gomorrah* (1:10). So heavy were his trials that he was exposed not only to verbal abuse but also to physical violence. Nevertheless he did not shrink before God's command, but acted as it was said of Ezekiel, *Behold, I have made your face hard against their faces, and your forehead hard against their foreheads. Like adamant harder than flint I have made your face* (Ezek 3:8-9), and stood up to all their blows.

Those who interpret the text in this way use every means at their disposal to turn the prophecy away from Christ and misunderstand it by distorting its interpretation. Even if this passage is taken to refer to Isaiah, there are many other passages that refer to Christ so clearly that they shed his bright light on the eyes of everyone. However, it is my view that these things are to be referred to the person of the Lord as at the end of the previous book[1] (50:2-3). For he assumed a body at the time of the Incarnation and received **a tongue of one who had been taught**, and knew when **he ought to speak** (50:4) and when

---

1. Jerome's commentary was divided into books.

Isaiah 50

to be silent. Moreover, though silent during his passion, he now speaks throughout the whole world through the apostles and apostolic men.

50:1
Thus says the Lord: Of what kind was your mother's bill of divorce with which I sent her away? Or to which creditor have I sold you? Look, for your sins you were sold, and for your transgressions I sent away your mother.

(3) Origen of Alexandria

The apostle observes: *You were bought with a price* (1 Cor 7:23). But listen to what the prophet says: **You have been sold for your sins; and for your iniquities I have sent away your mother** (50:1). You see then that we are all creatures of God, but each one has been **sold for his sins and by his iniquities** and has set himself apart from his Creator. We belong to God; in fact, we have been created by him. But we have become slaves, sold into bondage for our sins. However, when Christ came, *he redeemed us* (Gal 3:13) who had been serving that master to whom we had sold ourselves because of our sin. And so it seems that he has claimed his own whom he had created. He has acquired as aliens those who by sinning had sought a foreign master for themselves. But perhaps it is correct to say that Christ redeemed us, he who gave his own blood as the price for us.

50:4
The Lord gives me the tongue of instruction, that I may know in season when it is necessary to speak a word. He assigned it to me in the morning, he granted to me an ear to hear.

(4) Eusebius of Caesarea

After doing such marvelous things in the time of your ancestors, why, asks Christ, was I not able to deliver myself (and the bodily instrument I had taken for the sake of mankind) out of your hands? The answer is that it was the good pleasure of the One who is over all, the Lord most high, my Lord and Father. So, calling him Lord, I said: **The Lord, the Lord gives me a tongue of instruction that I may know when it is necessary to speak a word** (50:4). Of course even when being accused *I kept silent,* and though false testimony was brought against me *I did not answer* (cf. Mark 14:61). This I was doing at the behest of the Father, for it was necessary *to become obedient to him even unto death* (Phil 2:8). This is why I kept silent, enduring abuse on your behalf, knowing well that the time will come in which I shall *no longer be silent* (62:1). But I will receive from the Father **a tongue of instruction** to be used at the fitting time **when it is necessary to speak a word** (50:4). May that time come when I shall establish my churches throughout all the inhabited world. Then I will no longer be silent, but will shout to all the nations within hearing and make my Father known. At the promised time he will give me those who have **ears for hearing** (50:4) and are able to understand my teaching. In the hours of the **morning** (50:4) these ears are always at my side taking in my **instruction**. For my Lord himself will open those who are my ears and are always at my side being instructed.

(5) Cyril of Jerusalem

First you were anointed on the forehead[2] to free you of the shame the first transgressor carried with him everywhere so that you might *with unveiled face behold the glory of the Lord* (2 Cor 3:18). Then you were anointed on the ears that you might have ears ready to hear the divine mysteries about which Isaiah said: **The Lord gave me an ear for hearing** (50:4). And in the Gospel the Lord Jesus urged: *He who has ears to hear, let him hear* (Matt 11:15). Then on the nostrils, that when you receive the sacred ointment you might say: *We are to God the aroma of Christ among those who are being saved* (2 Cor 2:15). After this on the breast, that *having put on the breastplate of righteousness, you might stand against the wiles of the devil* (Eph 6:14, 11). Just as, after his Baptism and the coming of the Holy Spirit, Christ went forth to vanquish the adversary, so you might, after Holy Baptism and the mystical chrism, having put on the whole armor of God, stand against the power of the adversary and vanquish it, saying, *I can do all things in him who strengthens me* (Phil 4:13).

(6) Ambrose of Milan

Is there anything more important to learn than to be silent? For only if we learn silence do we know how to speak. I do not want to be condemned by my own voice before someone else's voice acquits me. For it is written: *By your words you shall be condemned* (Matt 12:37). Why should one be in a hurry to risk condemnation by speaking, when by keeping silent you build confidence? I have seen many folks fall into sin by speaking, few, however, by keeping silent. Silence is much more demanding than speaking. Many speak because they don't know how to keep silent, and rarely does one keep silent even when nothing is gained by speaking. So wisdom is found in knowing how to keep silent. For the wisdom of God said: **The Lord gave me the tongue of instruction, that I may know when it is necessary to speak a word** (50:4). He is surely wise who has learned from the Lord when he should speak, as is said well in the Scripture: *A wise man will be silent until the right moment* (Sir 20:7).[3]

(7) Cyril of Alexandria

It would not be unreasonable, indeed it is appropriate, to apply these words (vv. 4-5) to the chorus of the holy apostles, or to all those who trust in our Lord Jesus Christ and have

---

2. Cyril is addressing the newly baptized during Easter week.
3. One of Ambrose's examples is Susanna, who was silent before her accusers (Susanna 35).

been instructed by the Spirit, who bountifully filled their minds with light and understanding. They have partaken of the divine gifts and were able to perceive the depth of the inspired Scripture with the pure eyes of the mind, and have learned to practice the good life of the gospel and to apply themselves to holy wisdom.

So, lifting their voices in songs of thanksgiving, they say that they have been given a **tongue of instruction** (50:4). That is, they are able to speak as those who have been taught and to explain the divine mysteries without reproach and to know when and how one should use words of exhortation. And this they did, for in their hearts they had a sound and faultless knowledge of faith in Christ. When people were drawn to the holy gospel, they offered one word to one person and another to another, each word suitable to that particular person. To those who are *babes* they supplied the word of simple instruction like *milk* (1 Cor 3:1-2), but to those who were mature, having attained *the measure of the stature of the fullness of Christ* (Eph 4:13), they offered hearty fare. This then is what is meant by **tongue of instruction**, the charisma to know **when a word needs to be spoken** (50:4).

They say that they **have been assigned in the morning** (50:5), that is, the brightness of the day, the illumination of the divine and spiritual light, the rising of the morning star, have been put in their minds and hearts. This we know from what blessed Paul has written: *Giving thanks to the Father, who has delivered us from the power of darkness and transferred us into the kingdom of his beloved Son in light* (Col 1:12-13). For *the god of this world has blinded the minds of unbelievers to keep them from seeing the light of the gospel of Christ* (2 Cor 4:4).[4] But the *son of righteousness* (Mal 4:2) has risen among us, illuminating the mind with divine light so that we might be and be called children of the light and of the day (cf. Eph 5:8).

Then he adds: **He granted me an ear to hear, and the instruction of the Lord opens my ears** (50:4-5). When we came to faith in Christ we were richly illuminated by him, for we were given the addition of an **ear**, that is, a faculty of hearing unlike anything we had previously. When the Jews read the law, they do not go beyond the shadow but are satisfied only with the types. For, as it is written, the *unspiritual man does not receive the gifts of the Spirit of God* (1 Cor 2:14). For we believe that the *law was a custodian* (Gal 3:24), and when we hear the things of Moses, we understand them with a different kind of hearing, transposing the types into the truth, the shadow becoming an occasion to contemplate spiritual things. Therefore we have been given an additional **ear**. For being formed by Christ, that is, by the proclamation of the gospel, and being initiated into the mysteries through him, he teaches us to understand the law spiritually. He spreads open, so to speak, the **ears** of those who believe in him, a belief Israel did not have. The Lord Jesus Christ said to them: *You search the Scriptures, because you think that in them you have eternal life; and it is they that bear witness to me; yet you refuse to come to me that you may have life* (John 5:39-40). Wise and divine Paul also writes about them: *Whenever Moses is read a veil lies over their minds that remains unlifted, because only through Christ our Lord and Savior is it taken away* (2 Cor 3:14-15).

---

4. Cyril does not cite the passages from Colossians and 2 Corinthians verbatim.

50:5
And the instruction of the Lord opens my ears,
and I do not disobey nor contradict.

(8) Cyril of Alexandria

When the Savior was conversing with Pilate he maintained: *You would have no power over me unless it had been given you from above* (John 19:11). In another passage when addressing the Father who is in heaven, he said: *Father, if it be possible, let this cup pass from me; nevertheless not as I will but as thou wilt* (Matt 26:39). The child does not oppose his Father. *The Son humbled himself, though he was God, becoming obedient unto death, even death on a cross* (Phil 2:7-8). That is why he said through the prophet Isaiah: **I do not disobey nor oppose** (50:5).

(9) Bernard of Clairvaux

Since the sense of sight is not ready, let us rouse our hearing, let us put it to work, let hearing grasp the truth. Happy is the person to whom the Truth testifies saying: "When his ear heard, he obeyed me. I am worthy to see if before seeing I was found obedient. I will look at him confidently if I have already learned to serve him with obedience. How happy the one who said: **The Lord opened my ear, and I did not disobey nor turn my back** (50:5). Here is a model of willing obedience and an example of great patience. The one who does not oppose responds freely, and the one who does not turn his back perseveres. Both are necessary, for *the Lord loves a cheerful giver* (2 Cor 9:7) and *whoever perseveres to the end will be saved* (Matt 10:22). How I wish the Lord would open my ear, that the word of truth would enter my heart and cleanse my eye to be ready for that happy vision. Then even I could say to God: *Your ear has heard the preparation of my heart* (Ps 9:38 Vg.[5]). Then I, along with others who are obedient, will hear from God: *You are clean because of the word I spoke to you* (John 15:3). However, not all who hear are cleansed, but only those who are obedient: *Happy are those who hear and keep the Word* (Luke 11:28). This is the kind of hearing he asks for when he commands, *Hear, O Israel* (Deut 6:4). This is also the kind of hearing he offers who says: *Speak, Lord, your servant hears* (1 Sam 3:10). And this is the response of one who says: *Let me hear what God the Lord speaks within me* (Ps 85:8).

---

5. Bernard's rendering of Ps 9:38 departs from the Vg. in reading *the preparation of* my *heart* instead of *the preparation of* their *heart.*

50:6
I gave my back to scourges, and my cheeks to blows, but I did not turn away my face from the shame of spittings.

(10) Origen of Alexandria

Then they spat in his face, and struck him; and some slapped him, saying, "Prophesy to us, you Christ! Who is it that struck you?" (Matt 26:67-68). They were resentful of Jesus' words, *I tell you, in a little while you will see the Son of man seated at the right hand of the power of God* (Matt 26:64), and dared to spit in his face. They thought they could show he was lying, for he could not endure the reproach of being spat on — he who claimed to sit at the right hand of power and would come again on the clouds. For they did not know the oracles of the prophet Isaiah, who prophesied these things about him, speaking in the person of the Lord and Savior himself: **Did I come and no man was there? I called, and there was none who obeyed. Is my hand not strong enough to deliver, or I to rescue? Look, by my threat I will make the sea desolate and the rivers deserts, and their fish shall be dried up because there is no water, and they will die of thirst. And I will clothe the heaven with darkness, and make its covering like sackcloth. The Lord gives me the tongue of instruction, that I may know when it is necessary to speak a word. He assigned it to me in the morning, he granted to me an ear to hear. The instruction of the Lord opens my ears, and I do not disobey or contradict. I gave my back to scourges, and my cheeks to blows. I did not turn away my face from the shame of spitting, and the Lord became my helper** (50:2-7).

All who belong to the Church believe that it is Christ who says: **The Lord gave me a tongue of instruction** (50:4) and the other things I have cited. It seemed appropriate then to include the rest of the passage to show that the prophecy about being **spit upon** and **beaten** referred to that most glorious person. . . .

He is the one who **clothed the heaven with darkness, and made its covering like sackcloth** (50:3). Receiving from the Father the **tongue of instruction**, he knew **when to speak the word** that God had entrusted to him. And the Father **granted to him an ear** that he might hear more than other hearers; the instruction of the Father opened his ear because he believed the Father who sent him and did not **contradict** him, and by his work taught meekness and praiseworthy humility to those who desired to learn. This work consisted in his teaching by what he did, offering his back to **scourges and his cheeks to blows, and not turning his face away from the shame of spittings** (50:6), that he might deliver us who deserved to suffer such shameful things by suffering them himself. He did not die for us to spare us from dying, but that we might die for ourselves; and he was pummeled for us and spat upon, so that we who deserved to suffer such things would not suffer them on account of our sins but for the sake of righteousness and with gratitude. For Paul comments that the Savior *humbled himself and became obedient unto death, even death on a cross* (Phil 2:8). If someone wanted to enumerate how many ways Christ humbled himself, it would not be inappropriate to go beyond what Paul has expounded and to say that *he humbled himself and became obedient unto* **blows**, to **the shame of spittings**, and **scourges**, and death. For the sake of all these things *God has ex-*

alted him. For he exalted him not only because he died for us, but also because of the **blows**, the **spittings**, and the rest.

(11) Athanasius of Alexandria

Even our Lord and Savior Jesus Christ accepted suffering, for he wished to teach men how to suffer. Thus when he was struck, he endured it patiently; and *when reviled, he reviled not in return; and when he suffered, he threatened not* (1 Pet 2:23); but **he gave his back to scourgings, and his cheeks to beatings, and he turned not his face from spitting** (50:6); and at last he consented to be led to death. In the measure that we behold in him the image of all that is entirely perfect and immortal, we all, following these examples, can indeed tread on serpents and scorpions and on all the power of the enemy.

(12) Cyril of Jerusalem

Realizing that people would not believe the sufferings to which Christ the Son of God and the *arm of the* LORD would be subject, the prophet asked: *Who has believed our report?* (53:1). But that those who are being saved would not disbelieve, the Holy Spirit, speaking in the person of Christ, had written earlier (the one who spoke then would himself later undergo these things): **I gave my back to scourges** — *after having him scourged, Pilate handed him over to be crucified* (Matt 27:26) — **and my cheeks to blows, but I did not turn my face away from the shame of spittings** (50:6). It was as if he had said: "Knowing beforehand that they would pummel me, I didn't turn my cheeks aside. For how shall I give my disciples courage to face death for the sake of truth if I myself am anxious about this? I said: *He who loves his life will lose it* (John 12:25). If I loved my life, who was I to teach them without practicing what I taught?" Since he was God he endured these sufferings at the hands of men, that afterward when we suffer such things at the hands of men for his sake we might not be ashamed. You see that the prophets wrote clearly of these things beforehand.

(13) Ambrose of Milan

Christ goes before that we may follow after him. The Word goes before; Christ is the beginning. Therefore Wisdom says: *The* LORD *created me the beginning of his ways* (Prov 8:22). We should note that Christ is the beginning and the end of his ways. I have no misgivings if some were to ask: Are you asserting that Christ was created? To which I respond: Yes, in the sense that he is said to be *made (factum), born (factum) of a woman, born (factum) under the law* (Gal 4:4). I call him "created" insofar as he took on flesh and was born of a virgin. He was created that he might redeem creatures, and made man that he might deliver men from eternal death. He was created that he might show me the ways leading to eternity by which human beings might be able to return to the kingdom of

God. Therefore, because he is the *beginning of the ways of God* (Prov 8:22), let us follow this beginning. First he embarked on the way of the New Covenant, so that he might make smooth the path of genuine devotion. If we fast, he fasted before us. If we suffer wrongs in the name of God, he first suffered wrongs for our redemption. **He offered his neck to the scourge, his cheeks to blows** (50:6). He mounted the cross to teach us not to fear death. He went before us, as he commanded Peter: *Follow me* (John 21:22), and Peter finished the course because he followed Christ.

(14) Cyril of Alexandria

The sole aim of the one who suffered was to carry out the good will of the Father to its end. For Christ said: *I have come down from heaven not to do my own will, but the will of my Father who sent me. And this is the will of the One who sent me, that I should lose nothing of all that he has given me, but raise it up at the last day* (John 6:38-39). Therefore to procure life for those who believe on him, he did not spurn the injuries, the **scourges**, or the trial of **spittings** (50:6), although he was God by nature and the true Lord. Then as man he says: **The Lord became my helper, therefore I was not disgraced; but I have set my face like solid rock, and I realized that I would not be put to shame, because he who justified me draws near** (50:7-8). So he speaks in human fashion, as I mentioned, in a way appropriate to the measure of his *emptying* (Phil 2:7). Moreover, he seems to intimate darkly through these words the punishment that fell upon those who mistreated him. For, he says, **The Lord became my helper** (50:7). It is as though he should say: **When I gave my back to scourges and my cheeks to blows** and underwent the sufferings of the cross, **the Father became my helper**. For he helped him, and did not grant that his own Son be wholly disgraced and shamed.

50:11
Walk by the light of your fire and by the flame you have kindled.

(15) Origen of Alexandria

We find in the prophet Isaiah that the fire by which each person is punished is of his own making. For he orders: **Walk in the light of your fire and in the flame which you have kindled for yourselves** (50:11). These words seem to indicate that each sinner kindles for himself the flame of his own fire and is not cast into a fire which had been kindled previously by someone else or had existed before him. The food and the material to kindle it are our sins, which the apostle Paul calls *wood, hay, and straw* (1 Cor 3:12).

Isaiah 51

1 Hear me, you that pursue what is righteous
    and seek the Lord.
  Look to the solid rock that you hewed,
    and to the hole of the pit that you dug.
2 Look to Abraam your father
    and to Sarra who bore you;
  because he was but one, then I called him,
    and blessed him, and loved him, and multiplied him.
3 And I will comfort you now, Sion;
    I comforted all her desolate places,
  and I will make her desolate places
    like the garden of the Lord;
  in her they will find joy and gladness,
    confession and the voice of praise.

4 Hear me, hear, my people,
    and you kings, give ear to me;
  because a law will go out from me,
    and my judgment for a light to nations.
5 My righteousness draws near swiftly,
    my salvation will go out,
    and the nations will hope in my arm;
  the islands will wait for me
    and hope in my arm.
6 Lift up your eyes to heaven,
    and look at the earth beneath;
  because heaven was strengthened like smoke,
    and the earth will become old like a garment,
    and those who live on the earth will die like these things;

but my salvation will be forever,
      and my righteousness will not fail.

7 Hear me, you who know judgment,
      my people, you in whose heart is my law;
   do not fear the reproach of men,
      and do not be dismayed by their contempt.
8 For just as a garment it will be devoured by time,
      and like wool it will be devoured by a moth;
   but my righteousness will be forever,
      and my salvation for generations of generations.

9 Awake, awake, O Ierousalem,
      put on the strength of your arm!
   Awake, as at the beginning of a day,
      like a generation of long ago!
   Are you not 10 she who made desolate the sea,
      the water, the abundance of the deep;
   who made the depths of the sea a way of passage
      for those being delivered
11   and those who have been ransomed?
   For by the Lord they shall be returned
      and come to Sion with joy
      and everlasting gladness;
   for gladness and praise shall be upon their heads,
      and joy shall take hold of them;
      pain and sorrow and sighing have fled away.

12 I am, I am he who comforts you.
   Acknowledge of whom you were cautious;
      you were afraid because of a mortal man
      and a son of man, who have dried up like grass.
13 And you have forgotten God who made you,
      who made heaven
      and laid the foundations of the earth.
   And always, all the days, you feared
      the face of the fury of the one who was oppressing you;
   for just as he planned to do away with you,
      and where now is the fury of the one who was oppressing you?
14 For when you are saved,
      he will not stand nor linger.
15 Because I am your God,
      who stirs up the sea and makes its waves to sound —
      the Lord Sabaoth is my name.

16 I will put my words in your mouth,
    and shelter you under the shadow of my hand,
 by which I established heaven
    and laid the foundations of the earth.
 And he will say to Sion,
    "You are my people."

17 Awake, awake!
    Stand up, O Ierousalem,
 you who have drunk from the hand of the Lord
    the cup of his wrath,
 for you have drained dry and emptied
    the cup of ruin, the goblet of wrath.
18 And there was none who comforted you
    from among all your children whom you have borne,
 and there was none who took hold of your hand,
    not even from among all your sons, whom you have raised.
19 These two things are set against you
    — who will grieve with you? —
 ruin and destruction, famine and sword —
    who will comfort you?
20 Your sons are the ones perplexed,
    who lie down at the head of every street
    like a half-cooked beet;
 who are full of the wrath of the Lord,
    made feeble by the Lord God.

21 Therefore hear, you who are humbled,
    who are drunk, but not with wine:
22 Thus says the Lord God,
    who judges his people:
 See, I have taken from your hand
    the cup of ruin, the goblet of wrath,
    and you shall not continue to drink it any longer.
23 And I will put it into the hands
    of those who have wronged you and humbled you,
 who have said to your soul,
    "Bow down, that we may pass by";
 and you put your back level to the ground,
    outside, for those who were going by.

Several themes appear in the exposition of chapter 51, most notably God's grace and mercy. Cyril's discussion of the opening verses is a good illustration of how certain words in a text suggested the direction of interpretation. In this chapter Cyril notes the conjunction of **righteous-**

ness and **salvation** in v. 5, terms that are central to the presentation of Christ in the New Testament. **Righteousness**, says Cyril, refers to the "grace that justifies," for we are "justified [made righteous] in him not through righteous deeds but 'by his great mercy'" (1 Pet 1:3). Similarly, the prophet speaks of **salvation** because Christ came into the world "not to condemn it, but that it might be saved through him" (John 3:17). The mention of Sarah who gave birth in old age offers an occasion to discuss God's power. But perhaps the most original comment on Abraham and Sarah is by Gregory of Nyssa, who observed that, because human beings are divided into male and female, both Abraham and Sarah are mentioned by the prophet as the **rock** from which the Israelites were hewed (51:1-2) so that both men and women might have a model of the virtuous life appropriate to their sex. **Lift up your eyes to heaven** (51:6) prompts Gregory the Theologian to meditate on the order and harmony of the universe. In the words **do not fear the reproach of men** (51:7), Origen finds encouragement for Christians who face persecution; Augustine sees the saying as useful advice for a bishop.

(1) Cyril of Alexandria

The holy prophets always use the language of visual and sensory images to signify spiritual things beyond the senses. Surely then, if Isaiah says **Zion** (51:3), he is not thinking of the earthly city. Rather, one should understand **Zion** to mean the spiritual city, the Church of the living God. For how else can one understand the prophet's words actually to have been fulfilled? God promised to comfort her, but this did not happen to the earthly city. On the contrary, we see that the city has been stripped bare and destroyed. Therefore the prophet's words have come to pass among the great number of believers, that is, the Church of the living God. For what does he say just before this? As **I called Abraham** and made him the father of many nations though **he was but one** (51:2), so also **I will comfort you, Zion**. The **comfort** spoken of in this passage is the promise that brings gladness and implants a *firm hope* (2 Cor 1:7) in those who hear it. For God certainly gathers together those called in faith not to a desolate or barren place (cf. Jer 2:31), but to a kind of **garden** (51:3), filled with trees and flowers and luxuriant beautiful plants and the spiritual fruit of **joy and gladness, confession and the voice of praise** (51:3). Understand, then, that he promises to free them from worship according to the law and from resting their hopes in an earthly garden and to fill them with spiritual fruit, what the prophet calls the **garden of God**. For long ago the law of Moses commanded them to sacrifice oxen and sheep and to bring to God turtledoves and wheaten flour soaked in oil. But one can no longer approach the one God through such things, as Christ himself says: *God is spirit, and those who worship him must worship in spirit and truth* (John 4:24). Adoration *in spirit and truth* and offering of the spiritual worship have a sweet fragrance, spiritual **joy**, and the **gladness** of hope in Christ. For we are convinced that Christ *will change our lowly body to be like his glorious body* (Phil 3:21). We shall be with him and rule with him, formed as children of God, possessing in abundance his divine and life-giving Spirit (cf. John 6:63; 1 Cor 15:45). We offer him spiritual fruit, **confession**, and hymns of thanksgiving. *For such sacrifices are pleasing to God* (Heb 13:16)....

My righteousness draws near swiftly, my salvation will go out, and the nations

will hope in my arm; the islands will wait for me and hope in my arm (51:5). He does not allow the zeal of those who have been called to wither because of injustices, nor does he say that their hope will be delayed long. Rather, in this verse he declares that the promise is at hand. Something similar is said by God through the voice of Habakkuk: *Yet a little while, yet a little while, he will surely come, he will not delay* (Hab 2:3). The hopes for good things dissolve with delay and procrastination, even when our hope is intense. Therefore in this passage he asserts that **his righteousness draws near** (51:5). If we understand these words to refer to the person of God the Father, we say that the Son is called **his righteousness**. For we are justified in him, not through righteous works we have done, *but by his great mercy* (1 Pet 1:3). He came *into the world, not to condemn it, but that it might be saved through him* (cf. John 3:17). The world is saved in no other way than through *great mercy*. For he affirms, *I am the one who blots out your transgressions, and I will not remember them at all* (Isa 43:25). He also says, *And you, Israel, do not forget me. For see, I have blotted out your transgressions like a cloud, and your sins like darkness* (Isa 44:21-22). David too sings, and says to him, L ORD, *thou wast favorable to thy land; thou didst restore the fortunes of Jacob. Thou didst forgive the iniquity of thy people; thou didst pardon all their sin* (Ps 85:1-2). Therefore, in the righteousness of God the Father — that is, in Christ — we have been saved and made holy, cleansed from the filth of evil.

But if it be Christ himself who declares, **My righteousness draws near swiftly** (51:5), the **righteousness** mentioned in this passage should be understood to refer to the grace that justifies, the evangelical and heavenly proclamation of the gospel. Through the gospel we have come to know the God-pleasing way of **righteousness** and have been led to the best and noblest deeds, as it is said in the Psalms: *Your law is a lamp to my feet, and a light to my path* (Ps 119:105). Quite rightly he mentions **righteousness** and **salvation** (51:5), for he rescues us from every evil, frees us from the chains of death, and brings us to eternal life. But he promises something else, for he says: **the nations will hope in my arm** (51:5). Moreover, he affirms that **the islands will wait for** him (51:5). . . . The nations did not know the Lord, *having no hope and without God in the world*, as blessed Paul said (Eph 2:12). In times past they were weak and cast down, but after receiving **my arm**, they gained the unexpected **hope** of salvation. Often Holy Scripture calls the Son the **arm** of the Father, for he is God's power. If, however, someone wishes to understand the **arm** to be the arm of the Son himself — in whom rests the hope of the nations called to salvation — one can see that his power is extraordinary and worthy of God. By his power *he will crush Satan* (Rom 16:20) and the rulers of this world, and through it he saved the Gentiles. For Jesus himself asked, *How can one enter a strong man's house and plunder his goods, unless he first binds the strong man? Then indeed he may plunder his goods* (cf. Matt 12:29). And David said, *Thou hast brought down the proud as one that is wounded; thou didst scatter thy enemies with thy mighty arm* (Ps 88:11 LXX). Therefore Christ is the hope and way of salvation not only for Israel but also for all the nations. It is for him that **the islands will wait** (51:5). In my opinion, he calls the Gentile churches **islands** because they are like islands in the midst of the sea, pummeled by the turbulence of history as if by waves. Their endurance merits high praise. For *endurance produces character, and character produces hope, and hope does not disappoint us* (Rom 5:4-5). Those who **wait for** God are pleasing to him because they have persevered and endured and become the beneficiaries of his mercy and providential care. For it is written: *I waited patiently for the LORD, and he inclined to me* (Ps 40:1).

(2) Theodoret of Cyrus

Hear me, you that pursue what is righteous and seek the Lord (51:1). In this section Isaiah turns away from unbelievers to address the faithful, whom he calls lovers of God and of righteousness. He comforts them because they are few in number, and he exhorts them to focus on their ancestors. He reminds them of Abraham and Sarah and the countless descendants who came from them. This same point is made in the holy gospels: *Fear not, little flock, for it is your Father's good pleasure to give you the kingdom* (Luke 12:32). Thus Isaiah urges, **Look to the solid rock out of which you were hewn, and to the hole of the pit from which you were dug** (51:1).[1] He calls Abraham's old age **solid rock** and Sarah's not **pit** but as **the hole of the pit**, because she was barren. Scripture says, *It had ceased to be with Sarah after the manner of women* (Gen 18:11). Likewise the divine apostle comments, *In hope he believed against hope, that he should become the father of many nations* (Rom 4:18): *against hope* because of his old age and Sarah's condition — for she was sterile — and *in hope* of the divine promise. Paul also says, *He did not consider his own body, which was as good as dead because he was about a hundred years old, or the barrenness of Sarah's womb. No distrust made him waver concerning the promise of God, but he grew strong in his faith as he gave glory to God, fully convinced that God was able to do what he had promised* (Rom 4:19-21). After commanding, **Look to the solid rock out of which you were hewn, and to the hole of the pit from which you were dug** (51:1), Isaiah clarifies what he means in what follows: **Look to Abraham your father and to Sarah who bore you; because he was but one, then I called him, and blessed him, and loved him, and multiplied him** (51:2). "Nothing," says the Lord, "stands in the way of my power: not that the one who was called was unique, nor the old age that weighed on him, nor Sarah's inability to bear children. The people grew as I had willed it. Therefore do not disbelieve, for though you are few in number, I will make you more numerous than all others."

51:1
Look to the solid rock that you hewed.

(3) Eusebius of Caesarea

This seems to point to that same **rock** which received the Lord's body, in which *Joseph dug the cavern in his own new tomb* (Matt 27:59-60). From this, the passage moves to the example of Abraham and Sarah, who, like a **rock**, were barren, without fruit, childless. Even in their old age, when they were sterile, God promised them descendants *like the stars of heaven in number* (Exod 32:13). Thus he adds: **he was one, then I called him, and**

---

1. Theodoret's text reads **out of which you were hewn** rather than **which you hewed**.

loved him, and multiplied him (51:2). Therefore, just as I did this with Abraham, do not despair, since a great hope for salvation will come to all people from this **rock, which you yourselves hewed**. So do not forget the promise to Abraham which I gave to all nations in peace for the sake of the **rock**. Therefore the **rock** is the cave *which Joseph had hewn* for a tomb. But the divine apostle also calls Christ himself the **rock**: *And the rock was Christ* (1 Cor 10:4). And since they mutilated Christ's body when they laid hands on him at the time of his passion and brought about his death through trickery and cunning, therefore Isaiah commands, **Look to the solid rock that you hewed, and to the hole of the pit that you digged** (51:1). The Savior himself teaches this in the Psalms when he says, *They have pierced[2] my hands and my feet — I can count all my bones* (Ps 22:16-17). Perhaps **the hole of the pit** suggests the wound in his side, out of which *came blood and water* (John 19:34).

51:2
Look to Abraham your father and to Sarah who bore you.

(4) Gregory of Nyssa

Perfection for human beings consists in always moving forward in goodness. It seems to me that Scripture is a good counselor in this matter. For the divine voice beckons somewhere in the prophecy of Isaiah: **Look to Abraham your father and to Sarah who bore you** (51:2). This word is addressed to those who have strayed from the way of virtue. They are like seafarers who are blown far off course from the route leading to the harbor, and are brought back on course by an unmistakable sign, a lighthouse tall enough to be seen from a distance or the top of a mountain peak; in the same way those led by a misguided mind to stray on the sea of life return directly to the harbor of the divine will by following the example of Abraham and Sarah. Since human beings are divided into male and female and the choice between living virtuously or not is set before each equally, Scripture provides a model appropriate to each so that by observing the one who is fitting for each, Abraham for men, Sarah for women, each may have their own examples of the virtuous life.

51:5
And the nations will hope in my arm.

(5) Theodoret of Cyrus

My righteousness draws near swiftly, my salvation will go out, and the nations will hope in my arm; the islands will wait for me and hope in my arm (51:5). He calls his power **arm**, for the great proof of divine power is that he conquered the whole world

---

2. Eusebius makes a connection between the psalm and the passage from Isaiah because the Greek term for "pierce" and "dig" is the same.

Isaiah 51

through the cross, through dishonor, through death; that he established fishermen, tax collectors, shoemakers, as teachers of philosophers and rhetors. He cultivated the entire world through twelve men, and through only a few people he filled all the land and sea with the divine proclamation.

51:6
Lift up your eyes to heaven, and look at the earth beneath.

(6) Gregory the Theologian

Let us listen to the divine voice that orders, **Lift up your eyes to heaven above and to earth below** (51:6), and seek to know the laws of creation. Heaven and earth and sea, indeed this whole cosmos, is the great and celebrated sign by which God is revealed in a silent proclamation (Ps 19:1-4). As long as it remains well ordered and at peace with itself, keeping within the limits proper to its nature, and one thing does not contend against another, nor anything overstep the bonds of love by which the Logos, the craftsman, has bound together the whole, then it is truly called a cosmos, a thing of unapproachable beauty, beyond which nothing more splendid or excellent can be imagined. But when it ceases to be at peace, it ceases being a cosmos. Are not the heavens, being so ordered as to impart light to the air and rains to the earth, governed by the law of love? Do not the earth and the air, the one giving food, the other breath to all living things, and so preserving life, imitate parental love?

51:7
Do not fear the reproach of men, and do not be defeated by their contempt.

(7) Origen of Alexandria

I would wish that during the whole of the present trial[3] you would remember the great reward prepared in heaven for those who are persecuted and mocked *for justice's sake* (Matt 5:10) and *on account of the Son of man* (Luke 6:22). Be *glad and rejoice* and exult, as did the apostles when they were *accounted worthy to suffer reproach for his name* (Acts 5:41)! And if you should happen to feel your soul seized with dread, let the *mind of Christ* that is *in us* (cf. 1 Cor 2:16 and Phil 2:5) say to it when it wants to disturb that mind, *Why art thou sad, O soul? And why dost thou trouble me? Hope in God, for I will give praise to him* (Ps 42:5). O that our soul may not be troubled, but that even before the courts, before the swords ready to behead us, our soul should be preserved by the peace of God which *passes all understanding* (Phil 4:7), and be tranquil in the thought that those who are *away from the body* (2 Cor 5:8) live with the Lord of all (cf. 2 Cor 5:8)!

---

3. The persecution under Maximinus Thrax in A.D. 235.

But if we are not the kind that can always preserve tranquility, at least we should not allow our troubled soul to show itself and become obvious to unbelievers. In this way we can still justify ourselves before God, saying to him: *My God, my soul is troubled within myself* (Ps 41:7). Reason, too, invites us to remember the word spoken in Isaiah: **Do not fear the reproach of men, and do not be defeated by their contempt** (51:7). God manifestly watches over the movement of the heavens and the stars and over all the animals and plants of all kinds on the earth and in the sea. Through his divine art they are brought to perfection in birth, development, nourishment, and increase. So it would clearly be absurd for us to close our eyes to this and not look to God, and to have regard rather for men and to fear them — men who will soon die and be delivered up to the punishment which they deserve.

(8) Augustine of Hippo

Many people fawn on us,[3] many think ill of us and revile us. The ones who fawn on us put us in greater danger than the ones who revile us. The bowing and scraping of people, after all, tickles our pride, while their slanders and abuse give our patience exercise; on the one side I fear a fall, on the other I am strengthened and fortified. **Do not dread**, says one of God's servants to me, **the insults of men** (51:7); and the Lord Jesus Christ promises, *Blessed shall you be when people curse you, and speak every kind of evil against you falsely on my account* (Matt 5:11). For if anyone speaks evil and speaks the truth, they are not in fact speaking evil because they are speaking the truth; but they do speak evil when they speak falsely. But what did the Lord promise us? *Rejoice and exult, because your reward is abundant in heaven* (Matt 5:12). The person who speaks ill of me increases my wages, the one who flatters me is trying to reduce my wages.

(9) Theodoret of Cyrus

Do not fear the reproach of men, and do not be defeated by their contempt. For just as a garment they will be devoured by time, and like wool they will be devoured by a moth; but my righteousness will be forever, and my salvation for generations of generations (51:7-8). The Lord enjoins this in the divine gospels: *Do not fear those who kill the body* (Matt 10:28); and *Have no fear of them* (Matt 10:26); and *Blessed are you when men revile you and persecute you and utter all kinds of evil against you falsely on my account. Rejoice and be glad, for your reward is great in heaven . . .* (Matt 5:11-12). Likewise here the prophetic passage showed that while those who **reproach** and abuse the preachers of the truth are like **garments** and **wool** that are consumed **by a moth**, the **salvation** and **righteousness** of those **reproached** is indestructible and infinite.

---

3. As bishops.

51:23
And I will put it into the hands of those who have wronged you and humbled you, who have said to your soul, "Bow down, that we may pass by."

(10) Gregory the Great

Isaiah says of unclean spirits: **There are those who have said to your soul, "Bow down, that we may walk over you"** (51:23). The soul stands upright when it desires the things of heaven and does not bend down to what is low. When evil spirits see it standing in an upright condition, they cannot **walk over** it. Walking over it means scattering unclean desires in front of it. Therefore they order, **Bow down, that we may walk over you.** If the soul does not cast itself down by desiring what is low, their wickedness has no power over it. They are unable to pass over it because they are terrified when one stands against them firmly upright, with their mind on the things of heaven.

Isaiah 52:1-12

1. Awake, awake, O Sion!
    Put on your strength, O Sion,
   and put on your glory,
    O Ierousalem, the holy city;
   the uncircumcised and unclean
    shall no longer continue to pass through you.
2. Shake off the dust and rise up,
    sit down, O Ierousalem;
   take off the bond from your neck,
    O captive daughter Sion!

3Because this is what the Lord says: You were sold for nothing, and not with money you shall be redeemed. 4Thus says the Lord: Formerly, my people went down into Egypt to reside there as aliens, and they were led by force to the Assyrians. 5And now, why are you here? This is what the Lord says, Because my people were taken for nothing, you marvel and howl. This is what the Lord says, Because of you, my name is continually blasphemed among the nations. 6Therefore my people shall know my name in that day, because I myself am the one who speaks: I am here,

7. like springtime upon the mountains,
    like the feet of one bringing glad tidings of a report of peace,
    like one bringing glad tidings of good things;
   because I will make your salvation heard,
    saying to Sion, "Your God shall reign."
8. Because the voice of those who watch over you was lifted up,
    and with their voice they shall rejoice together;
   because eyes shall look at eyes
    when the Lord will have mercy on Sion.
9. Let the desolate places of Ierousalem
    break forth together in joy,

>   because the Lord has had mercy on her
>   and has delivered Ierousalem.
> 10 And the Lord shall reveal his holy arm
>   before all the nations;
>   and all the ends of the earth shall see
>   the salvation that comes from God.
>
> 11 Depart, depart, go out from there
>   and touch no unclean thing;
>   go out from the midst of it, be separated,
>   you who carry the vessels of the Lord.
> 12 Because you shall not go out with confusion,
>   nor shall you go in flight;
>   for the Lord will go before you,
>   and the Lord God of Israel
>   is the one who gathers you together.

In this chapter, as elsewhere, the ancient commentators take **Zion** *and* **Jerusalem** *to signify the Church. The phrase in v. 1,* **put on your strength,** *to which the LXX adds,* **put on your glory,** *reminded interpreters of Rom 13:14, "put on the Lord Jesus Christ," who is the glory of God. Israel's deliverance from captivity is seen as a foreshadowing of Christ's deliverance of mankind from the bondage to sin. The verse quoted (somewhat freely) by St. Paul in Rom 10:15,* **like springtime upon the mountains are the feet of one proclaiming a report of peace** *(52:7), invited discussion of the mission of the apostles. Some writers, following Isaiah, highlight the term* **peace,** *which does not appear in Paul. The most beautiful of the selections we have chosen is that of Origen of Alexandria, who relates this passage to Jesus' washing of his disciples' feet. When our feet are "washed and cleansed and dried by Jesus' hands," says Origen, they become beautiful. Leo the Great saw* **before all the nations** *and* **all the ends of the earth** *(52:10) as fulfilled in the coming of the Magi from the East to offer gifts to Christ, and Augustine understands* **touch no unclean thing** *(52:11) to be an admonition not to consent to sin.*

(1) The Letter of Paul to the Romans

But how are men to call upon him in whom they have not believed? And how are they to believe in him of whom they have never heard? And how are they to hear without a preacher? And how can men preach unless they are sent? As it is written, **How beautiful are the feet of those who preach good news** (52:7). But they have not all obeyed the gospel; for Isaiah asks: LORD, *who has believed what he has heard from us?* (53:1).

(2) Cyril of Alexandria

When you hear **Zion** and **Jerusalem** (52:1) in this passage, do not think that it refers solely to the city built from stone. Rather, the prophet is referring to the company of those who have been called through faith, that is, the Church formed from both Jews and Gentiles. When the prophet twice says **awake** (52:1), he offers great comfort. For just as the all-wise Paul said, *Where sin increased, grace abounded all the more* (Rom 5:20), so though the penalty is harsh, God's comfort is equal to the sins, indeed, it is greater than the sins. God commanded Jerusalem to put on her **strength** and, with it, her **glory** (52:1). **Strength** may refer to the actual doing of good works when, for example, a person goes about the task at hand with youthful enthusiasm. And what is **glory** other than the *Lord of glory* (Jas 2:1) who is Christ? The holy psalmist speaks about Christ when he urges, *Awake, my glory* (Ps 57:8). In another place, speaking about all who believe in Christ, the psalmist declares, *Thou art the glory of their strength* (Ps 89:17). How we shall put on **glory** and **strength**, the all-wise Paul shows us clearly: *Put on the Lord Jesus Christ, and make no provision for the flesh, to gratify its desires* (Rom 13:14). He also says, *For as many of you as were baptized into Christ have put on Christ* (Gal 3:27). Furthermore, the prophet Isaiah introduced the Church as a woman beautifully adorned when he said, *My soul shall exult in the Lord, for he has clothed me with the garment of salvation, he has covered me with the robe of joy* (61:10). Therefore, Christ is the most fitting garment for every holy person; he is the robe of spiritual joy that provides us with **strength** and **glory**.

Isaiah calls the Church a **holy city** (52:1). It was not made **holy** through the rites of the law (*for the law made no one perfect* [Heb 7:19]), but we become perfect by being conformed to Christ, by sharing in his divine nature, and by participation in the Holy Spirit. Through the Spirit we have been *sealed for the day of redemption* (Eph 4:30), washed of all impurity and cleansed of every blemish. For we have been justified through faith in him (cf. Rom 3:26) and are rich with every assurance from him. We have been fortified with grace from Christ, who defended us by fighting off the assaults of the devil and putting down Satan's rebellious minions. Isaiah teaches us this when he says to **Zion**, that is, to **Jerusalem**, the Church of the living God: The **uncircumcised and the unclean shall no longer pass through you again** (52:1).

The prophet can also be understood to be speaking about the historical events of his own day. The nations dwelling around Jerusalem were **uncircumcised** and considered **unclean** (52:1) since they did not know the true God nor had they been tutored by the law. Moreover, they seemed to be more powerful than the Israelites and were able to invade their country and bring it into subjection.

From such contingent historical events we may fashion the spiritual meaning. The array of demons, the lords of darkness, and, along with them, that impure Satan, are able to bring into subjection those souls that are not yet under God's sway. Hence they are able **to pass through them** (52:1), for nothing hinders or helps them. But since we have been made God's own, we have God's glory and power, and the demons' advantage has disappeared. For it is written, *The angel of the* LORD *encamps around those who fear him, and delivers them* (Ps 34:7). Thus, in a spiritual reading of the text, **the uncircumcised** and **the unclean** would be the opposing powers who are loathsome, impure, filthy, and evil.

Isaiah 52:1-12

Isaiah shows what kind of praise befits the saints. He teaches clearly that Jerusalem shall put on the **strength** of her arm (cf. Luke 1:51) and **glory** (52:1). First he exhorts Zion to **shake off the dust**, then to **rise up, sit down**, and **take off the bond from** her **neck** (52:2). In my view, here **dust** can refer to an earthly mind and impure desires. Just as those who lie on the ground become covered with **dust** and dirt, in the same way those whose minds are sinful, focused upon earthly things, become filled with impure and carnal thoughts. Since we have been called to spiritual friendship with our Lord Jesus Christ, and since we wish to put him on as **strength** and **glory**, we must first **shake off** any earthly thoughts and cleanse our mind. This is what Paul means when he urges us to strip off *the old nature which is corrupt through deceitful lusts* and *to put on* the new nature which is restored according to the image of its Creator (Eph 4:22, 24). When we have done this, we have stood up, that is, we have a well-ordered mind and a steady heart. What is said here is echoed in the passage where God commanded through one of the prophets: *Stand up yourself, Zion* (cf. Jer 31:21). In another passage the holy David sang, *He set my feet upon a rock, making my steps secure* (Ps 40:2).

The book of Psalms also says, *God sits on his holy throne* (Ps 47:8), that is, his kingdom is always firm and secure, for it is inappropriate to understand anything said about God in a bodily way. Now, when someone is seated, that is, when his mind is firm and resolute, he **takes off the bond** from around his **neck**, for everyone is bound by the chains of his own sins. We had been subject to the yoke of sin, bound by Satan himself, but in Christ we have been freed. In Christ *the bonds are burst*, as it is written, *and their yoke is cast off* (Ps 2:3). When our mind is free of these constraints, we are able to do the good. In another passage the God of all says to us through one of the prophets, *And you shall be free, and you shall leap like calves freed from their bonds. And you shall tread down the wicked, for they will be like ashes under your feet* (Mal 4:2-3).

After saying that Zion was captive, the prophet thinks it necessary to mention the hardships that always befall those who are taken into captivity. The Israelites were carried away into captivity, and no one offered to redeem them, for they were like prizes in a contest, the fruit of war and a cruel invasion. By force and against their will they were taken into slavery. Hence the God of all says that he will be their ransom. Satan had seized the human race, and holding the whole world captive he oppressed it terribly and subjected it to his cruelty. But the only-begotten Word of God became man and conquered Satan on our behalf. Christ came into the house of the strong man and bound him fast (cf. Mark 3:27), seizing his vessels and making everything on earth his own. Thus, after being seized, **we were redeemed** (52:3). Now Christ took us back to himself not simply by an act of will; rather, he crushed the force of Satan and routed his army by divine power. We were not bought by silver or anything of that kind, but by the power of Christ the Savior of us all. He is the good shepherd who *laid down his life for his own sheep* (John 10:11) and saved us by his own blood (cf. Rom 5:9). For *by his bruise we were healed, and made to bear infirmity on account of our sins* (53:5). We have been set free, and we have thrown off the yoke of sin and the oppression of the devil. . . .

Because of your laxity, says God, I am despised **among the Gentiles** (52:5). I cannot endure this calumny, nor will I allow my glory to be blasphemed. On that day when I will take on flesh to shine on those dwelling on earth, those who embrace the faith will be my people, and whether they come from the Jews or from the Gentiles they will know my **name** (52:5). The prophet says **name** instead of glory. This is customary in the Holy Scriptures. For it is written, *A good name is to be chosen rather than great riches* (Prov 22:1). We who have been called by him know his glory and draw near to him as to Christ the Savior and Judge of all, not as to a mere man. For even though the Word became flesh, we believe that he is God by nature and begotten ineffably from God the Father and above every created thing. He surpasses the thrones of heaven (cf. Col 1:16) and rules over all things. His right hand is all powerful, and out of his gracious will he has chosen those whom he has begotten. In all things he is preeminent. But the Jews were not disposed to believe these things. They consider him to be merely human, like us, not God incarnate. Hence they inquired: *Who are you? And who do you claim to be?* (John 8:53). They also said: *It is not for a good work that we stone you, but for blasphemy; because you, being a man, make yourself God* (John 10:33). He asserts that those who will be called *to the knowledge of the truth* (1 Tim 2:4) shall know my glory. For he is the one who, through the prophets, says: **I am here** (52:6). God the Lord has appeared to us, as all-wise Paul[1] teaches: *In many and various ways God spoke of old to our fathers by the prophets; but in these last days he has spoken to us by a Son, whom he appointed the heir of all things, through whom also he created the world* (Heb 1:1-2). One should observe here that God the Father brought all things into being through the Son, and in these last times he has spoken to us, not through another Son who was born from a woman, as the heretics teach, but through the one and only Son, the Word, who is the creator of the ages and who took on flesh and became a human being for our sake. Therefore he says, **Here am I, like springtime upon the mountains** (52:6-7), and spring is the season of beauty.

What is the spiritual meaning of **springtime**? What happens when **spring** appears on the **mountains**? The plants crown themselves with new flowers, and what was once barren and lifeless gives birth, as we read in the Song of Songs: *My beloved speaks and says to me: "Arise, my love, my fair one, and come away; for lo, the winter is past, the rain is over and gone. The flowers appear on the earth, the time of singing has come"* (Song 2:10-12). For when winter is past, spring appears on the earth in all its brilliance as a nursemaid to flowers and the mother of ripe fruit. This same thing happens in us spiritually. For that rebel, the serpent, tormented the earth with storms, and made it lifeless and barren. *For there is not one who does good, no, not one. They have all gone astray; they are all alike corrupt* (Ps 14:3). But when the Only-Begotten appeared in the flesh, he became **like springtime upon the mountains** (52:7) for us. For we who were withered because we had rid our souls of the lovely flowers of virtue were brought back to life in him and were filled with spiritual fruit. Hence it is possible to say, in the words of the Song of Songs: *Let my beloved come to his garden and eat its choicest fruits* (Song 4:16). Therefore, Christ is **like springtime upon the mountains, like the feet of one proclaiming a report of peace, like one proclaiming good news** (52:7).

When sin intervened between us and God, we became separated from him and distant from the Lord. By rising up against God's laws and defying the Lord's will we became God's enemies. But Christ, our *peace* (Eph 2:14), appeared and removed the sin that stood

---

1. The early Church considered St. Paul the author of the Epistle to the Hebrews.

Isaiah 52:1-12

between us and God. He united us with the Father through himself and prepared us for friendship with God. *For through him we have obtained access* (Rom 5:1). Therefore, says Isaiah: just as someone might come swiftly and without delay to say that the enemy had been captured, promising **peace** and **proclaiming good news** (52:7), so the Savior of all visited the world in flesh, and became the author of our **peace** with God the Father. For he stripped Satan of his power and destroyed his armies. Hence we are now able to share in the good, and because we believe in him and know and do his will, we hope to share fully in the heavenly good. For the Savior's munificence is boundless.

In this passage [52:7] the prophet again uses the name **Zion** to refer not to the earthly city but to the holy Church, which he has established from two peoples. For it is written, *Rejoice, O Gentiles, with the people* (Rom 15:10; Deut 32:43). And it is said that Christ *has made us both one and has broken down the dividing wall of hostility by abolishing the law of commandments and ordinances* (Eph 2:14-15). When the gospel was preached and its truth made known, the effectiveness of the law's shadow, that is, access to God through the offering of animal sacrifices, came to an end. For this reason **Zion** is to be understood as the Church, which, as the Scripture says, Christ presented to himself *without spot or wrinkle . . . holy and without blemish* (Eph 5:27).

The phrase **make her salvation heard** (52:7) means that it was noised abroad. For the power of the gospel was not hidden from anyone living on earth; no one remained ignorant of the salvation through Christ. For through the psalmist's lyre it is said, *Hear this, all peoples! Give ear, all inhabitants of the world!* (Ps 49:1). When the sound of the gospel went forth, the demons were forgotten, and in a remarkable way the news that the demonic rule had ended was prominently and conspicuously broadcast to all. Thus the divine and heavenly gospel was heard by everyone, bringing salvation to those who acknowledged the appearance of Christ.

But what is the power of this preaching? **Zion, your God shall reign** (52:7). Long before our Savior's earthly sojourn, Satan ruled over us through sin, and he imposed a perverse and tyrannical servitude on those who dwelled on earth. But since the ruler of all, the Lord, has shined his light on us, we have broken our chains and thrown off the yoke of that ancient and imperious enemy. Now we are subject to God's royal power, and God the Father rules us through the Son. This is a cause for celebration. As David sings: *The* LORD *rules; let the earth rejoice* (Ps 97:1) and *Sing praises with a psalm! God reigns over the nations* (Ps 47:7-8). The Savior himself called us to this when he summoned: *Come to me, all who labor and are heavy laden, and I will give you rest. Take my yoke upon you* (Matt 11:28-29).

Because we were subject to a cruel tyrant and oppressed by the yoke of sin, our situation was desperate. But the power of the holy gospel brought the good news of the kingdom of Christ, and we came under its sway. This was proclaimed in the words: **Zion, your God shall reign** (52:7). How he will be a king and in what way he will rule is immediately made clear: **The voice of those who watch over you is lifted up** (52:8). **Those who watch over you** are the holy disciples, or those who initiate others into the mysteries and persuade the elect to walk uprightly, that is, to do the good, and to cling to Christ with love, and to confess the true and dependable faith in him. These are the good shepherds who keep watch over the flock for the chief shepherd, Christ, and fend off the assaults of wild beasts. Of these he says: **Their voice will be lifted up** (52:8), that is, they will be heard everywhere. And elsewhere Isaiah exclaims: *Get you up to a high mountain, O Zion, herald of good tidings; lift up your voice with strength, O Jerusalem, herald of good tidings. Lift up your voice! Be not afraid!* (40:9).

The preaching of the apostles has gone out into the world, bringing happiness to all. Those who have been called received the word and rejoiced greatly when they saw the fruits of their initiation into the divine mysteries. For Isaiah says: **And with their voice they shall rejoice together** (52:8). For, he says, when they speak a great multitude will be initiated into the mysteries, and those who have been instructed will turn to the faith without looking back. What joy for those who have been charged with teaching the faith, as St. Paul writes to those who came to believe in Christ through him: *My joy and my crown!* (Phil 4:1).

That many responded to the invitation of those who taught the mysteries and then were initiated into the mysteries of the saints, can be seen from the holy and divinely inspired Scripture. For the holy disciples spoke to the Jewish people in Jerusalem, as it is written in the Acts of the Apostles: *There were added that day about three thousand souls* (Acts 2:41). Indeed, we read that St. Paul and blessed Silas, who were imprisoned together, were singing hymns to God in the middle of the night. A holy angel who was keeping guard over the prison loosed all their chains. This terrified the jailer, and he wanted to kill himself, but Paul cried out: *Do not harm yourself, for we are all here* (Acts 16:28). Amazed at this miracle, the jailer was baptized, with his whole household (Acts 16:33). Is this not a cause for rejoicing? For it is written: your **eyes shall look at eyes when the Lord will have mercy on Zion** (52:8). What will they see, except Christ, the Lord of salvation, who took on flesh? The psalmist testifies to this when he declares: *God shines forth; our God comes, he does not keep silence* (Ps 50:2-3). For Isaiah said: **With their voice they shall rejoice together**. With your own eyes you will see him on that day **when the Lord will have mercy upon Zion**, bestowing his grace and abundant heavenly joy on all through faith.

(3) Eusebius of Caesarea

The words **Put on your strength, O Zion, and put on your glory, O Jerusalem** (52:1) can be referred to the soul, which has vast power and strength. It also has great **glory**, because it was *made in the image of God* (Gen 1:26-27). God wishes it to become a holy city so that **the uncircumcised and unclean shall no longer pass through** (52:1) it. **Uncircumcised** means foreign or alien, and **unclean** refers to an idolater. Therefore, if your soul is to respond to the exhortation to **rise up** and become a **holy city** of God, this word of Scripture says to you, "Neither the idolater nor the foreigner shall come into you." . . .

In ancient times the Word spoke to the prophets of his sojourn among men (cf. Heb 1:1). Hence this passage mentions that the apostles would preach the gospel to all nations. St. Paul understood the meaning of this prophecy and paraphrased it in his letter to the Romans: *How beautiful are the feet of those who announce good things, who proclaim peace!* (Rom 10:15). . . . The prophetic spirit marvels at the **feet** (52:7) of these heralds of the gospel, the feet by which they ran around the world, making their way from one nation to another. Their **feet** were beautiful because they had been cleansed by the Savior who washed them (John 13:1-17), and they are said to run upon the **mountains** because their evangelical message was noble and sublime. When they proclaimed **peace**, they were announcing the good news that men could have **peace** with God (cf. Rom 5:1). This peace they preached *to those who are far off, and to those who are near* (Eph 2:17), showing forth the Christ of God *who has made us both one, and has broken down the dividing wall of hostility in his flesh* (Eph 2:14). Moreover, when Paul sent letters to the churches, he wrote, *Grace and* **peace** *to you* (Rom 1:7; 1 Cor 1:3). And the **good news** that was preached was truly good, for it was the blessings the Savior bestowed through the preaching of the Gospel. He proclaimed the gospel to Zion, that is, to the godly commonwealth and to the apostolic choir. When the prophet says, **Your God shall reign** (52:7), this means that the kingdom of heaven was announced to all men. . . .

Here Scripture calls the disciples and apostles of our Lord **watchmen** (52:8). For since the prophets of Israel were called **watchmen** of the people of the circumcision, so now our Savior's apostles are clearly **watchmen** and guardians of the new and youthful Zion, the Church of God and the godly commonwealth. Those who saw the Savior with their own eyes and heard him with their own ears lifted up their voice for all the Gentiles to hear. They were filled with the spiritual and compassionate joy which God had bestowed on us in Zion and in the ancient desert places that were delivered by his saving redemption.

Some think that the earthly Jerusalem is the city of God, but I believe that Jerusalem is the godly commonwealth that was announced when the prophet spoke of the desert places of old. In this passage Isaiah says that now the desert places are filled with gladness and rejoicing because of God's mercy. . . .

Isaiah next [52:10] presents an oracle that follows on what he had said earlier about Jerusalem: **The Lord shall reveal his holy arm before all the nations; and all the ends of the earth shall see the salvation that comes from God** (52:10). Here you see how through these things the preaching of the gospel brings promises to the nations. For he declares that God **shall reveal his holy arm** — that is, God the Word — **before all the nations; and all the ends of the earth shall see the salvation that comes from God**. Therefore, whenever the prophet speaks to Zion and to Jerusalem, what is said is to be referred to the calling of the nations. For the holy way of life, at times found among the Jews and at times among the nations, is called Zion and Jerusalem. For so great a city of God has always existed among men. Therefore, when one is speaking about God's calling of the nations and his setting aside men and women for himself, it makes no difference whether you call it Zion or Jerusalem.

The disciples were not forced to go to the nations. Rather, they freely and zealously accepted the command *to make disciples of all nations in his name* (Matt 28:19). This is why the text says, **Because you shall not go out with confusion, nor shall you go in flight** (52:12). They journeyed with complete serenity, carrying with them what Christ had said to them: *Behold, I am with you always, even to the end of the age* (Matt 28:20). Isaiah hints at this when he promises: **For the Lord will go before you, and the Lord God of Israel is the one who gathers you together** (52:12).

52:7
How beautiful[2] upon the mountains are the feet of one bringing glad tidings of a report of peace. . . .

(4) Theodoret of Cyrus

This passage was fulfilled when those who were dwelling in Jerusalem received word that the captives would be released. But the ancient events were types that receive their fuller meaning in the holy apostles. For their **feet**, which had been washed by the hands of the Savior, were **beautiful** (52:7). He gave them strength to go throughout the world bringing the good news of God's peace that men might enjoy what God promised. **Because I will make your salvation heard, saying to Zion, "Your God shall reign"** (52:7). This oracle too refers to the holy apostles, for they proclaimed the kingdom of our God and Savior. . . .

The prophetic passage exhorts those who believe to separate themselves from unbelievers. **Separate yourselves, you who carry the vessels of the Lord** (52:11). **Vessels** means those who are deemed worthy of election. The Lord spoke about the blessed Paul in this way when he addressed Ananias, *Go, for he is a chosen vessel of mine to carry my name before nations and kings and the sons of Israel* (Acts 9:15). And the divine apostle himself says, *If any one purifies himself from what is ignoble, then he will be a vessel for noble use, consecrated and useful to the master of the house, ready for any good work* (2 Tim 2:21). . . .

When the Romans were about to march against Jerusalem, all who had received the gospel fled to other cities, for they knew the misfortunes that were to befall her. The Lord himself exhorted them to do this: *When*, he observes, *you see Jerusalem surrounded by armies, then know that its desolation has come near* (Luke 21:20), and again, *Then let those who are in Judea flee to the mountains; let him who is on the housetop not go down to take what is in his house* (Matt 24:16-17). Since they knew beforehand what was to happen, they withdrew to escape the destruction that would accompany the siege of the city. The Savior himself guided them, leading them to the nations so that they might gather the Church from among the nations.

Since we too have learned these things, let us flee unfaithfulness, let us hold fast to the faith, let us keep the divine commandments and travel the straight road with the Lord Jesus as guide for our journey, to whom be glory with the Father in the unity of the Holy Spirit, now and forever. Amen.

(5) John Chrysostom

The prophet of old proclaimed: **How beautiful are the feet of them that bring good tidings of peace** (52:7). To show how precious **peace** is, he added: **that brings glad tidings of good things**. This peace Christ also declared to be marvelous when he said: *Peace I leave with you, my peace I give to you* (John 14:27). And we should do everything to enjoy this **peace**, at home and in church. For in church the presiding minister gives the **peace**.

---

2. The word translated "springtime" in the *NETS* can also mean "beautiful."

For this **peace** is a sign of the peace given by Christ. You should receive it eagerly from the heart before taking communion.

(6) Origen of Alexandria

What was Jesus doing when he washed the disciples' feet? Was he not, by washing their feet and drying them with the towel with which he had girded himself, making them **beautiful** before they went out to **proclaim good news** (52:7)? I think that what was spoken prophetically about his apostles — **How beautiful are the feet of those who proclaim good news** (52:7) — was fulfilled when Jesus washed the disciples' feet. And if he makes the **feet** of the disciples **beautiful** by washing them, what shall we say of the true beauty found in all those who have been baptized by Jesus with the Holy Spirit and fire?

Once the feet of those proclaiming **good news** became **beautiful**, that is, they were washed and cleansed and dried by Jesus' hands, they were able to walk on the holy way and travel on the one who said, *I am the Way* (John 14:6). For whoever has had his feet washed by Jesus — and only that one — travels on the living way that brings one to the Father. Feet that are defiled and still unclean have no place on this way. This is why Moses had to loose the sandals from his feet. The place he had come to and where he was standing was holy ground (Exod 3:5). This was also true of Joshua the son of Nun (Josh 5:15).

52:10
The Lord has bared his holy arm.

(7) Leo the Great

The day, dearly beloved, on which Christ the Savior of the world first appeared to the nations must be celebrated among us with holy worship; and today [the Feast of Epiphany] the joys that existed in the breasts of the three Magi will be entertained in our hearts. When they were aroused by the sign and leading of a new star, which they believed to have been promised, they fell down in the presence of the King of heaven and earth. . . . And though the narrative which is read to us from the Gospel [Matt 2:1-12] properly records those days on which the three men, who had neither been taught by the prophets' predictions nor been instructed by the law's testimony, came from the furthest parts of the East to acknowledge God, yet we behold this same thing more clearly and abundantly carried on now in the enlightenment of all those who are called. Hence Isaiah's prophecy is fulfilled: **The Lord has bared his holy arm before the eyes of all the nations; and all the ends of the earth shall see the salvation of our God** (52:10). And again: **those to whom it has not been announced about him shall see, and that which they have not heard they shall understand** (52:15).

Therefore when we see men devoted to worldly wisdom and far distant from belief in Jesus Christ brought out of the depth of their error and called to the knowledge of the true Light, it is undoubtedly the brightness of divine grace that is at work; and whatever of new light illumines the darkness of their hearts comes from the rays of the same star. And so it both moves and lead the minds it visited with its splendor to the adoration of God. And if we wish to know more particularly how their threefold gift is also offered by all who come to Christ with the feet of faith, is not the same offering also realized in the hearts of true believers? For whoever acknowledges Christ the King of the universe offers gold from the treasure of his heart; and whoever believes the Only-Begotten of God to have united man's true nature to himself offers myrrh; and whoever confesses him in no way inferior to the Father's majesty worships him with frankincense.

52:11
Depart, depart, go out from there and touch no unclean thing.

(8) Origen of Alexandria

Isaiah orders: **Separate yourselves, you who carry the vessels of the Lord, and go out from the midst of them. Separate yourself** from earthly deeds; **separate yourself** (52:11) from worldly lust. *For all that is in the world,* according to the apostle, *is the lust of the flesh and the lust of the eyes, which is not from God* (cf. 1 John 2:16). Therefore, when you have **separated yourself** from all these things, devote yourself to God as a *firstling* calf;[3] sin should not work through you, and malice should not impose its yoke on you, but be different and set apart only for priestly uses, delivered up as a firstling calf. Be set apart and separated as holy *cups* and holy *censers* (cf. Exod 25:29) used only for service in the temple and for the ministry of God. Set yourself apart and remove yourself from every pollution of sin, and be separated and removed for service in the temple of God as is the holy garment of the high priest. For in the temple of God one *meditates on the law of God day and night* (Ps 1:2) and *greatly delights in his commandments* (Ps 112:1). Therefore, *Be holy, says the* LORD, *for I am holy* (Lev 20:7).

(9) Augustine of Hippo

The Donatists[4] tell us, "Listen to what the prophet says." **Depart, depart, go out from there and touch no unclean thing** (52:11). "How," they say, "are we to tolerate bad people for the sake of peace, when we are ordered to depart and go out from them, lest we should touch anything unclean?" We understand this departing spiritually; they take it literally and materially. For I too cry out, and God uses us, and whatever sort of instrument is at hand, to care for you. We too cry out and say to you: **Depart, go out from there and touch no unclean thing** — but with the touch of the heart, not bodily contact. What else does touching anything unclean mean but consenting to sin? And what else

---

3. The "firstling" of a cow or a sheep or a goat was "holy" (Num 18:17).
4. The Donatists were members of an early Christian schismatic group that held that the Church was composed of holy people and that sacraments administered by priests who were impure were invalid.

does going out from there mean but taking on the task of rebuking the bad — insofar as this can be done — and taking account of each person's status and position, without damage to peace? . . .

When Scripture thunders at us that we must withdraw from the wicked, this means only that we are asked to withdraw in our hearts. For we commit a greater evil by setting ourselves off from the good than we would in fleeing contact with the bad. . . . My dear brothers and sisters, there are those among your acquaintances who are still weighed down with love of the world — misers, perjurers, adulterers, devotees of vain spectacles, people who consult astrologers, temple oracles, augurs, soothsayers, drunkards, profligates, whatever kind of bad persons you know. As far as you can, show your disapproval, and so depart in your hearts; at the same time try to convince them of their wrongdoing, and in that way separate yourself from them. Do not go along with their ways and so avoid touching anything unclean.

Isaiah 52:13–53:12

52.13 See, my servant shall understand;
    and he shall be exalted and glorified exceedingly.
14 Just as many shall be astonished at you
    — so shall your appearance be without glory from men,
    and your glory be absent from men —
15 so shall many nations be astonished at him,
    and kings shall shut their mouth;
because those who were not informed about him shall see,
    and those who did not hear shall understand.

53.1 Lord, who has believed our report?
    And to whom has the arm of the Lord been revealed?
2 He grew up before him like a child,
    like a root in a thirsty land;
he has no form or glory,
    and we saw him, and he had no form or beauty.
3 But his form was without honor, failing beyond all men;
    a man being in calamity and knowing how to bear sickness;
because his face is turned away,
    he was dishonored, and not esteemed.

4 This one bears our sins
    and suffers pain for us;
and we accounted him to be in trouble
    and calamity and ill-treatment.
5 But he was wounded because of our transgressions,
    and has been weakened because of our sins;
upon him was the discipline of our peace,
    by his bruise we were healed.
6 All we like sheep have gone astray;

a man has strayed in his own way,
    and the Lord gave him over to our sins.

7 And he, because he has been ill-treated,
    does not open his mouth;
  like a sheep he was led to the slaughter,
    and as a lamb is silent before the one shearing it,
    so he does not open his mouth.
8 In his humiliation his judgment was taken away.
    Who will describe his generation?
  Because his life is being taken from the earth;
    he was led to death on account of the transgressions of my people.
9 And I will give the wicked for his burial
    and the rich for his death;
  because he committed no transgression,
    nor was deceit found in his mouth.

10 And the Lord desires
    to cleanse him from his blow.
  If you give an offering for sin,
    your soul shall see a long-lived offspring.
  And the Lord wishes to take away
11   from the pain of his soul,
  to show him light
    and fill him with understanding,
  to justify a righteous one who is serving many well;
    and he himself shall bear their sins.
12 Therefore he shall inherit many,
    and he shall divide the spoils of the strong;
  because his soul was given over to death,
    and he was reckoned among the transgressors;
  and he bore the sins of many,
    and because of their sins he was given over.

Isaiah 52:13–53:12, the fourth of the prophet's Servant Songs, is cited or alluded to numerous times in New Testament passages dealing with Jesus' ministry and passion. Not surprisingly, when interpreting Isaiah 52–53, patristic authors develop and deepen the reflection on Christ's suffering and death. This passage is also one of those that gave rise to the view that Isaiah was an evangelist as well as a prophet. What is said here of the "servant" is taken to be a description, in anticipation, of what happened to Christ during his passion. Cyril of Alexandria cites Philippians 2 at the very beginning of his exposition to alert the reader that his commentary will interpret Isaiah with the help of St. Paul. But he also weaves together texts from the gospels with verses from the prophetic oracle, giving his readers a fuller and more graphic depiction of Christ's suffering. We have included a number of passages from sermons of Augustine that treat the suf-

fering Servant, one of which draws out the implications of the metaphor of **root** *(53:2). The Servant, like the root, was without beauty, yet from the root grew a beautiful tree, the Church. Origen relates the* **lamb** *(53:7) to the Lamb of God in the Gospel of John (John 1:29), the innocent lamb who was sacrificed in Jeremiah (Jer 11:19), and the "little lamb" who is slain in Revelation (Rev 5:6). 53:8,* **Who will describe his generation?**, *was given two interpretations, as Cyril shows in his* Commentary. *It could refer either to the eternal generation of the divine Logos from God the Father or to the mystery of Christ's human birth of a woman. As Augustine says in a sermon preached on Christmas Day, he was begotten of the Father as God without a mother, and born as a human being of a mother without a father. Basil of Caesarea takes the passage to mean that we cannot know the essence of God. Gregory of Nyssa cites* **nor was there any deceit in his mouth** *(53:9) to say that Christ could obliterate evil because he was without sin.*

(1) The Gospel According to Matthew

And when Jesus entered Peter's house, he saw his mother-in-law lying sick with a fever; he touched her hand, and the fever left her, and she rose and served him. That evening they brought to him many who were possessed with demons; and he cast out the spirits with a word, and healed all who were sick. This was to fulfill what was spoken by the prophet Isaiah, **He took our infirmities and bore our diseases** (53:4).

(2) The Gospel According to Luke

And he said to them, "When I sent you out with no purse or bag or sandals, did you lack anything?" They said, "Nothing." He said to them, "But now, let him who has a purse take it, and likewise a bag. And let him who has no sword sell his mantle and buy one. For I tell you that this scripture must be fulfilled in me, **And he was reckoned with transgressors** (53:12); for what is written about me has its fulfillment."

(3) The Gospel According to John

When Jesus had said this, he departed and hid himself from them. Though he had done so many signs before them, yet they did not believe in him; it was that the word spoken by the prophet Isaiah might be fulfilled: **Lord, who has believed our report, and to whom has the arm of the Lord been revealed?** (53:1).

(4) The Acts of the Apostles

But an angel of the Lord said to Philip, "Rise and go toward the south to the road that goes down from Jerusalem to Gaza." This is a desert road. And he rose and went. And behold, an Ethiopian, a eunuch, a minister of the Candace, queen of the Ethiopians, in charge of all her treasure, had come to Jerusalem to worship and was returning; seated in his chariot, he was reading the prophet Isaiah. And the Spirit said to Philip, "Go up and join this chariot." So Philip ran to him, and heard him reading Isaiah the prophet, and asked, "Do you understand what you are reading?" And he said, "How can I, unless some one guides me?" And he invited Philip to come up and sit with him. Now the passage of the scripture which he was reading was this: **As a sheep led to the slaughter or a lamb before its shearer is dumb, so he opens not his mouth. In his humiliation justice was denied him. Who can describe his generation? For his life is taken up from the earth** (53:7-8). And the eunuch said to Philip, "About whom, pray, does the prophet say this, about himself or about someone else?" Then Philip opened his mouth, and beginning with this scripture he told him the good news of Jesus. And as they went along the road they came to some water, and the eunuch said, "See, here is water! What is to prevent my being baptized?" And he commanded the chariot to stop, and they both went down into the water, Philip and the eunuch, and he baptized him.

(5) The Letter of Paul to the Romans

But how are men to call upon him in whom they have not believed? And how are they to believe in him of whom they have never heard? And how are they to hear without a preacher? And how can men preach unless they are sent? As it is written, *How beautiful are the feet of those who preach good news!* (52:7). But they have not all obeyed the gospel; for Isaiah says, **Lord, who has believed what he has heard from us?** (53:1). So faith comes from what is heard, and what is heard comes by the preaching of Christ.

(6) The Letter of Paul to the Romans

For I will not venture to speak of anything except what Christ has wrought through me to win obedience from the Gentiles, by word and deed, by the power of signs and wonders, by the power of the Holy Spirit, so that from Jerusalem and as far round as Illyricum I have fully preached the gospel of Christ, thus making it my ambition to preach the gospel, not where Christ has already been named, lest I build on another man's foundation, but as it is written, **They shall see who have never been told of him, and they shall understand who have never heard of him** (52:15).

(7) The First Letter of Peter

Servants, be submissive to your masters with all resepct, not only to the kind and gentle but also to the overbearing. For one is approved if, mindful of God, he endures pain while suffering unjustly. For what credit is it, if when you do wrong and are beaten for it you take it patiently? But if when you do right and suffer for it you take it patiently, you have God's approval. For to this you have been called, because Christ also suffered for you, leaving you an example, that you should follow in his steps. **He committed no sin; no guile was found on his lips** (53:9). **When he was reviled, he did not revile in return** (53:7); when he suffered, he did not threaten; but he trusted to him who judges justly. He himself **bore** our **sins** (53:11) in his body on the tree, that we might die to sin and live to righteousness. **By his wounds** you **have been healed** (53:5). For you were straying like sheep, but have now returned to the Shepherd and Guardian of your souls.

(8) Cyril of Alexandria

When he says, **See, my servant shall understand** (52:13), God the Father openly speaks about Christ, the Savior of us all. Understand that the **servant** — or rather, the slave — is the Son, because even though he was God and Lord of all, the Word took the *form of a servant* (Phil 2:7) and entered into the limitations of humankind. *He did not count equality with God a thing to be grasped, but emptied himself . . . being born in the likeness of men. And being found in human form, he humbled himself . . .* (Phil 2:6-8). Therefore, when he became man and humbled himself, he was without doubt called slave since he had taken on the form of slavery. But the prophet says, **He shall understand**, by which he means that he will do all things with understanding and wisdom and will speak in a way befitting God. This indeed was a work of wisdom befitting God — that the only-begotten Word of God took on flesh on behalf of others. He became a beggar among us on earth, in order that we might become rich from his poverty, and by believing in him we might be washed of sin's defilement since the law given through Moses *cannot take away sins* (Heb 10:11). By the death of his own flesh, he destroyed death (cf. Heb 2:14). He overturned destruction, and he fashions anew those overpowered by death so that they become incorruptible. He makes those on earth citizens of heaven and, through himself, unites those who had long ago strayed to God the Father. *He proclaims release to the captives, and recovery of sight to the blind* (Isa 61:1). *He heals the brokenhearted* (61:1; cf. Ps 147:3). He emptied Hades and freed them from Satan's oppressive rule.

Therefore he says, **my servant shall understand**. For everything done for our sake was done with understanding and wisdom. According to the psalmist, *In wisdom he made all things* (cf. Ps 104:24). Because of this, he says that **he shall be exalted and glorified exceedingly** (52:13). We praise him as God and Lord, and we call him both Savior and Redeemer. This we believe to be true. But, in order that the Word from God the Father be entirely true and blameless, he adds: **Just as many shall be astonished at you — so shall your appearance be without glory from men, and your glory be absent from men** (52:14). Those who have witnessed his appearance and were perceptive enough to discern with eyes of understanding the greatness of the divine power present in him are astonished at the divine economy. One such person was the prophet Habakkuk, who said, *Lord, I have heard your report, and I was afraid. I have considered your works, and I was astonished* (Hab 3:2). Those who do not perceive his glory have remained faithless and foolish, judging him to be without glory and honor. They call him a Samaritan, a glutton and drunkard, born of fornication, a sinner (cf. Matt 11:19). Therefore, **as many**

Isaiah 52:13–53:12

shall be astonished at you — so shall your appearance be without glory from men, and your glory be absent from men (52:14).

And the following also was to happen: **so shall many nations be astonished at you, and kings shall shut their mouth** (52:15). . . . Since most kings fear God, offering glory to the King of the universe, they **shall shut their mouth**, that is, they shall say nothing harsh, nothing that maligns Christ's glory. The divine, holy, and saving announcement, that is, the gospel, will not be with those among whom **his appearance** was **without glory**, but rather with those who **shut their mouth**, who have been amazed at his glory. Isaiah showed this plainly when he said that **those who were not informed about him shall see, and those who did not hear shall understand** (52:15). The Israelites had been informed about Christ through the law and the prophets, and the Gentiles knew nothing. But, the prophet says, *they shall see the salvation that comes from him* (52:10). Those who had not at all heard the mysteries about him will understand them, that is to say, they have come to faith. Faith provides the root to nurture understanding because it is the beginning of true devotion and brings life to those who receive it. Thus the prophet Isaiah said, *If you do not believe, neither shall you understand* (7:9).

Lord, who has believed our report? And to whom has the arm of the Lord been revealed? We announced before him, like a field, like a root in a thirsty land (53:1-2). The prophets speak often about the Savior of all. They were unceasing in their exhortations and wisely announced that God the Word would come in human form at the opportune time and would work miracles befitting God. These things he does to call those who have wandered back to the straight path and make the ungodly righteous by faith. . . .

When they say, **We saw him, and he had no form or beauty** (53:2), they are telling us the state and condition in which they beheld the one being proclaimed, they are presenting things clearly. For, they say, he is like **a man in calamity** who nobly **bears sickness** (53:3), that is, affliction, which means to suffer evil. They contemplated the Savior's **face** (53:3) when he was downcast: he was confused and terrified since he was about to suffer death upon a tree, and he said, *Now my soul is troubled* (John 12:27), and *My soul is very sorrowful, even to death* (Mark 14:3-4), and *And what shall I say, "Father, save me from this hour"? No, for this purpose I have come to this hour* (John 12:27). One of the holy Evangelists says that when *the time was at hand* (cf. Matt 26:18; Rev 1:3; 22:10) when he was about to suffer, *he began to be sorrowful and troubled* (Matt 26:37). Indeed, although the only-begotten Word of the Father is God by nature, and hence incapable of suffering, bodily pain, and other things of that sort, he accommodated himself to just those kinds of things, and when tempted he was not immune to pain, but in every way he showed that he had become like us. When he was seen on the earth, he was not a shadow and phantom, as some think; he was really and truly a human being.

His face, the prophet says, **is turned away** (53:3). The phrase **is turned away** means "was put to shame." **He was dishonored, and not esteemed** (53:3), for Pilate sent Jesus to Herod, but Herod, *treating him with contempt, sent him back* (Luke 23:11). He **did not esteem** him to be Jesus, and **his face was dishonored**. That is, he was spat upon and Pilate's soldiers beat him, saying, *Prophesy to us, you Christ! Who is it that struck you?* (Matt 26:68). **He was dishonored** in other ways also, when he endured torments from whips and the blows from the guards (cf. Mark 14:65). Through the voice of Isaiah he says, *I gave my back to scourges, and my cheeks to blows, but I did not turn away my face from the shame of spittings* (50:6). Therefore, it seems, as I have said, that the holy prophets clearly saw the Son through a vision given by the Holy Spirit. That is, he was not beyond human shame, for the time was at hand that he must suffer, in order that he might destroy death by the death of his own flesh and bear the world's sin.

This one bears our sins and suffers pain for us; and we accounted him to be in trouble and calamity and ill-treatment. But he was wounded because of our transgressions, and has been weakened because of our sins; upon him was the discipline of our own peace, by his bruise we were healed. All we like sheep have gone astray; a man has strayed in his own way, and the Lord gave him over to our sins (53:4-6). Our Lord, Jesus Christ, *endured the cross, despising the shame* (Heb 12:2), *became obedient to the Father unto death* (cf. Phil 2:8), and bore the Jews' impiety, in order that *he might take away the sin of the world* (cf. John 1:29; Rom 11:27), since neither the written law nor worship according to the law was able to accomplish this, for *the blood of goats and bulls* was unable *to take away sin* (cf. Heb 10:4). But he *suffered outside the gate*, as Paul says, *in order to sanctify the people through his own blood* (Heb 13:12). He did not suffer on behalf of himself — that was in no way necessary — but on behalf of everything under heaven. The all-wise Paul testifies to this when he writes about God the Father: *He did not spare his own Son but gave him up for us all, in order that he might give us all things with him* (Rom 8:32).

And somewhere, through the psalmist's lyre, Christ says to God the Father in heaven, *Sacrifices and offerings thou hast not desired, but a body hast thou prepared for me; in burnt offerings and sin offerings thou hast taken no pleasure. Then I said, "Lo, I have come. I desired to do thy will, O God," as it is written of me in the roll of the book* (Ps 39:7-9 LXX; cf. Heb 10:5-7). For since worship according to the law was of no benefit to mortals for taking away their sins — inasmuch as God did not desire the sacrifice of oxen and the slaughter of sheep — the true *Lamb who takes away the sin of the world* (John 1:29) offered himself as a sweet perfume on our behalf. Therefore, since his flesh endured death, he freed everything under heaven from death and sin. For the one who was more worthy than all suffered on behalf of all, in order that he might possess and rule all things.

Again, Paul will confirm this since he writes: *For to this end Christ died and lived again, that he might be Lord both of the dead and of the living* (Rom 14:9), and also this: *He died for all, that those who live might live no longer for themselves but for him who for their sake died and was raised* (2 Cor 5:15). Therefore the prophet rightly says that he was **a man in calamity, knowing how to bearing sickness**, whose **face is turned away**, who **was dishonored, and not esteemed. This one bears our sins and suffers pain for us; and we accounted him to be in trouble and calamity and ill-treatment** (53:3-4). Consider with me again how skillfully the prophet develops his message in this passage. He imagines those who have not known the mystery of Christ and believe that he suffered so that his own sins might be taken away. For **we accounted him to be in trouble and calamity and ill-treatment**, the prophet says, that is, we thought his suffering was sent by God because of certain sins and because of this sin he was **in trouble and calamity and ill-treatment**. But this is not the case at all; rather, **he was wounded because of our**

Isaiah 52:13–53:12

transgressions, and has been weakened because of our sins (53:5). Thus the prophet gives other reasons which make it clear that he who did not know sin suffered for the sake of our salvation and life.

Long ago we were divided into factions because of *hostility* toward God (Eph 2:14, 16), since we fought against his holy laws, did not accept the yoke of obedience, and refused to serve him. But it was necessary, he says, to discipline with a whip those who had risen to such a height of arrogance. For it was only after we were free of evil that hostility would come to an end and we would be at peace with God (cf. Eph. 2:14-16) by submitting our neck to him and striving to do what pleases him. But this **discipline** (53:5) — which ought to have been placed upon those who had sinned, that is, the enemies of God, in order that they might be reconciled with him — came upon Christ instead. This, I think, is the meaning of the phrase, **upon him was the discipline of our peace**. Isaiah very wisely confirms the text's meaning when he immediately adds, **by his bruise we were healed**. He has suffered, the prophet said, on our behalf, for **all we like sheep have gone astray; we have turned everyone to his own way, and the Lord gave him over to our sins** (53:6). We have gone astray, turning away from the living God and following after our own desires. But the Lord of all things, that is, God the Father, **gave him over to our sins**, in order that he might deliver us from judgment and save those who have faith. Knowing this, Christ himself says, *For God so loved the world that he gave his only Son, that whoever believes in him should not perish but have eternal life* (John 3:16)....

Who will describe his generation? (53:8). This passage can be understood in two ways. As God the Word he was born of God the Father. The manner of his birth was ineffable and wholly beyond our understanding. He was not begotten in bodily fashion, but in a manner befitting a spiritual and incorporeal nature. Light shone from light, and life came forth from life. We believe firmly that he was truly begotten of the being of God the Father, but it is not ours to say how.

Moreover, though he was God by nature, he lowered himself so that he might be *emptied* for our sake. He *took on the form of a servant* (Phil 2:7) and was born in human fashion of a woman, not, however, according to the laws of human nature. His coming forth was not from a man and a woman; rather, it was an unusual and mystical coming forth far beyond our powers of description. To the holy virgin it was said: *The Holy Spirit will come upon you, and the power of the Most High will overshadow you; therefore the child to be born will be called holy, the Son of God* (Luke 1:35). Since it is believed that the mystery of his human birth did not happen in a natural way, the prophet says, **Who will describe his generation?**

When the text says that **his life is taken**, it means **lifted up**,[1] because his life, that is, the way he lived as a human being among us, was more sublime than any other life on earth. Although he appeared as a man among us, he was the only one to **commit no sin, nor was deceit found in his mouth**, something no one else on earth could accomplish. For no one else was blameless. The word **taken** (i.e., **lifted up**) can also refer to the existence of the Only-Begotten without flesh, that is, before he became man for our

---

1. Cyril is playing here with two Greek words, *airetai* ("taken"), which occurs in the text, and *epairetai* ("lifted up"), which is his interpretation of its meaning.

sake. That life was unlike anything human beings know. Though his birth according to the flesh was strange and wonderful, his divine life transcends every human measure. . . .

Then **your soul shall see a long-lived offspring** (53:10), that is, you will be companions of those who have been preserved for eternal life, the saints who have become rich in the hope of life everlasting. For the Greeks had no notion of the resurrection of the dead, and the mystery was not believed until now. They say that the breath in our nostrils is smoke, and when this has been quenched, everything will turn out to be ashes, and the spirit will be dispersed like a man spread out over a vast area. But among those nourished by the Church, the resurrection of the dead is a firm hope. God promises the Gentiles, since they had chosen the retribution of their souls, to offer Christ, who chose to suffer for their sins. Paul makes clear what sort of debt we have when he writes: For *one has died for all, that those who live might live no longer for themselves but for him who for their sake died and was raised* (2 Cor 5:14-15). Surely then we owe him still more, our own life. Because of this Christ says, *If any man would come after me, let him deny himself and take up his cross and follow me* (Matt 16:24). Whoever denies himself will spend his life not in pleasure, but rather in that life deemed to be of Christ, a holy and blameless life, like the one St. Paul wrote about: *For I through the law died to the law, that I might live to God. I have been crucified with Christ; it is no longer I who live, but Christ who lives in me; and the life I now live in the flesh I live by faith in the Son of God, who loved me and gave himself for me. I do not nullify the grace of God* (Gal 2:19-21). . . .

Consider, therefore, how Paul gave himself for sin, dedicating his own life to the one who suffered for him. We have heard Christ warn those who know him well, *He who loves father or mother more than me is not worthy of me; and he who loves son or daughter more than me is not worthy of me* (Matt 10:37). The mother and father of a person are the origin and cause of his physical existence, but the God and Father of all gave new life to those who were under the rule of death and wasting away like grass. He renewed them for immortal life without corruption through Christ in the Spirit, crowning them with eternal and everlasting life. Therefore one's love for God should be greater even than love for one's parents. To love Christ with one's whole soul and heart (cf. Matt. 22:37) and to follow his commands and holy oracles, while clinging to an upright and blameless faith in him, is to **give an offering for sin** (53:10). Therefore, **your soul shall see a long-lived offspring** (53:10).

For **the Lord wishes to take away from the pain of his soul, to show him light and fill him with understanding** (53:11). Christ became *very sorrowful, even to death* (Matt 26:38; Mark 14:34) before the precious cross, as the holy Evangelists have written. But when he came to life again after he had dwelt in Hades for three days, then he beheld his own human nature transformed into incorruptibility and *the good will* (cf. Eph 1:5, 9) of God the Father spread through the entire earth. He also saw that the multitude of the Gentiles were enlightened as they abandoned their ancient and habitual wandering after other gods and were called to knowledge of him and the Father. He had scorn for the pain of his suffering and gave victory to the believers. In his goodness after he had been raised from the dead, he rejoiced over the world's salvation and life, and said to the holy disciples, *All authority in heaven and on earth has been given to me. Go therefore and make dis-*

ciples of all nations, baptizing them in the name of the Father and of the Son and of the Holy Spirit (Matt 28:18-19). Therefore, **if you give an offering for sin**, you yourselves will be partners of **long-lived offspring** (53:10), that is, of the saints. For God the Father **wishes to take away from the pain of his soul** (53:11); he wishes to transform the pain of Christ on the cross into joy by showing him those who were in darkness — that is, those who had wandered after other gods — changed into light. To these people the all-wise Paul wrote, *For once you were darkness, but now you are light in the Lord* (Eph 5:8). His aim is that they be formed **with understanding** (53:11). The all-wise Paul teaches us about this when he says: *And we all, with unveiled face, beholding the glory of the Lord, are being changed into his likeness from one degree of glory to another; for this comes from the Lord who is the Spirit* (2 Cor 3:18). But those who are sinful, serving the creature rather than the Creator (cf. Rom 1:25), have a malign heart and faulty understanding, which Jeremiah spoke about: *Behold, neither your eyes nor your heart are good* (Jer 22:17 LXX). But when they receive faith in Christ, they are transformed spiritually into his divinity and made exceptionally beautiful. The all-wise Paul writes to some of these: *My little children, with whom I am again in travail until Christ be formed in you!* (Gal 4:19).

By his understanding, that is, by his own divine wisdom, God the Father wishes to mold the faithful to Christ and to display his image through sanctification in the Spirit. *Those whom he foreknew he also predestined to be conformed to the image of his Son . . . and these he also called* (Rom 8:29-30). From the two peoples, God is said *to create one new man* (cf. Eph 2:15). God the Father, I think, wishes **to justify a righteous one who is serving many well; and he himself shall bear their sins** (53:11). But no one should think that the **righteous one who is serving many well** (53:11) is any other than our Lord, Jesus Christ. For, as Christ himself emphasizes, *he came not to be served but rather to serve* (Matt 20:28), in accordance with the economy of the Incarnation. This seems to refer to the service Paul wrote about, because with regard to the law and the New Covenant he says, *For if there was splendor in the dispensation of condemnation — since Moses' face had splendor — the dispensation of righteousness must far exceed it in splendor* (2 Cor 3:9). Christ is a blameless and **righteous one who is serving many well**. Although the *Word was God; he took the form of a servant* (cf. John 1:1; Phil 2:7), not in order that he himself might benefit his own nature but rather share it with us, and as it were exercising among us that ministry by which we have been saved. . . .

(9) Eusebius of Caesarea

See, my servant shall understand; and he shall be exalted, glorified, and lifted up very high (52:13). Since the New Testament says, *He humbled himself and became obedient unto death, even death on a cross; therefore God has highly exalted him and bestowed upon him the name which is above every name* (Phil 2:8-9), the present prophecy is clearly expressing the very same thing when it says, **See, my servant shall understand; and he shall be exalted, glorified, and lifted up very high**, which refers to his resurrection after his death and his ascension and exaltation into heaven. And in the passages that follow, Isaiah presents his humiliation *unto death* (Phil 2:8) when he asserts: **We saw him, and**

he had neither form nor beauty. But his form was despised and marred beyond the sons of men (53:3), and again: **He was despised and rejected. He bears our sins and suffers torment for us** (53:3-4), and again: **Like a sheep he was led to the slaughter, and like a lamb before the shearer he is dumb and does not open his mouth. In his humiliation his punishment was exacted; who shall declare his generation — that his life is taken from the earth, he was led unto death by the lawless ones among my people** (53:7-8). So when his humiliation and his death were presented in this fashion, the prophetic spirit was first predicting his posthumous exaltation and giving priority to the happy outcome rather than to the suffering which preceded it. This is confirmed by the text which says, **Behold, my servant will understand**, or, according to Aquila, **Behold, my servant will gain understanding** (52:13). He fittingly calls him **servant** because of the *form of the servant which he took* (Phil 2:7), for *he who was in the form of God*, meaning God the Word, according to St. Paul, *took the form of a servant and was found in the likeness of men* (Phil 2:7). But this **servant and child of God** *was filled with* all *wisdom* and knowledge (Luke 2:40) and contained the Word of God in himself. Therefore it is said, **He will gain understanding**, but also **he will be exalted and glorified and lifted up** (52:13). All of this was fulfilled concerning the humanity of our Savior because of its union with God the Word.

53:1
And to whom has the arm of the Lord been revealed?

(10) Augustine of Hippo

Pray, then, that he will not let you go, but will lead you to the very end. How does he lead? By constantly admonishing, constantly giving you his hand. **To whom has the arm of the Lord been revealed?** (53:1). By giving us his Christ, he gives us his hand; in giving his hand, he gives his Christ. He leads us to his way by leading us to his Christ; he leads us in his way by leading us in his Christ. But Christ is the truth. *Lead me in your way*, then LORD, *and I will walk in your truth* (Ps 86:11), in him who declared, *I am the Way, the Truth, and the Life* (John 14:6). If you lead us along the way and in the truth, where else but to life will you bring us? You lead us in him, and to him. *Lead me in your way,* LORD, *and I will walk in your truth* (Ps 86:11).

53:2-3
He grew up before him like a child, like a root in a thirsty land. . . . But his form was without honor, failing beyond all men.

(11) Augustine of Hippo

A prophecy, my dearest brothers and sisters, was made about our Lord and Savior a long time before him: **he will come up like a sapling, and like a root in thirsty ground** (53:2).

Why like a root? For this reason: **He has no fine appearance, nor honor** (53:3). He suffered, he was humiliated, he was spat upon; he had no beauty; he appeared as a mere man, though he was God. In the same way a **root** is not beautiful, but contains within itself the potentiality of its beauty. Consider, my friends, observe the mercy of God. You notice a beautiful tree, such a pleasure to look at with its thick foliage and abundant fruit, and you admire it. It's delightful to pick some of its fruit, to sit in its shade and rest from the heat. You admire that whole display of beauty. If you are shown its roots, you don't find any beauty in them. Don't despise what has been tossed aside; that's where what you so admire comes from. **Like a root in thirsty ground** (53:2). Now observe the splendor of the tree.

The Church has grown, the nations have come to believe, the rulers of the earth have been conquered by the name of Christ, that they themselves may be conquerors in the whole wide world. They have placed their necks under the yoke of Christ. They used previously to persecute Christians on behalf of idols; now they persecute idols on behalf of Christ. Everyone is running to the Church for help, in all their afflictions, in all their distress. That grain of mustard seed has grown, it has become greater than all herbs. The birds of the sky, the high and mighty ones of the world, come and rest in its branches (Matt 13:31-32; Luke 13:19).

Where does all this beauty come from? It has arisen from goodness knows what kind of **root**, and it's a beauty that is world famous. Let's look for its **root**. He was spat upon, he was humiliated, he was flogged, he was crucified, he was wounded, he was despised. You can see there's **no fine appearance** here; but the glory of the **root** comes to the fore in the Church. So the prophet is describing the bridegroom in that despised, dishonored, and rejected figure. But now you have the tree to look at, which has sprung up from that **root** and filled the wide world. **A root in thirsty ground**.

(12) Augustine of Hippo

Now we are walking by faith, then it will be by sight. What does "by sight" *(in specie)* mean? *His form was a beautiful sight (speciosa)*[2] *beyond the sons of men* (Ps 45:2 Vg.). Because *in the beginning was the Word, and the Word was with God, and the Word was God* (John 1:1). *Whoever loves me,* he says, *keeps my commandments, and whoever loves me, shall be loved by my Father, and I myself will love him* (John 14:21). And what will you give him? *And I will show myself to him* (John 14:21). There will be sight when he does what he said, *And I will show myself to him*. There you will see God's impartiality, there you will read the Word without a book. So *when we see him as he is* (1 John 3:2), our journey will be over. After that we will rejoice with the joy of the angels. Now we are still on the way. What is the way? It is faith. For the sake of your faith Christ became **deformed** (53:2), yet Christ remains beautiful. When we have come to the end of our journey, *his form* will be *seen as a beautiful sight beyond the sons of men* (Ps 45:2 Vg.).

But how is he seen now, in faith? **And we saw him, and he did not have any beauty nor comeliness, but his face was abject, and his bearing** [i.e., his strength] **deformed . . . a**

---

2. Drawing on the term *speciosa* in Ps 45:2, Augustine plays on the double meaning of the Latin *species*, sight and beautiful.

man beset with calamity and knowing how to bear infirmities (53:2-3). It is Christ's deformity that gives form to you. For if he had been unwilling to be **deformed**, you would never have gotten back the form you lost. So he hung on the cross **deformed**; but his deformity is our beauty. Therefore in this life let us hold fast to the **deformed** Christ. What do I mean the **deformed** Christ? *Far be it from me to glory except in the cross of our Lord Jesus Christ, through whom the world has been crucified to me, and I to the world* (Gal 6:14). That is the deformity of Christ. Have I ever spoken to you about anything except that way? This is the way to believe in the crucifix. We carry the sign of this deformity on the forehead.

53:4
This one bears our sins and suffers pain for us.

(13) *The Apostolic Constitutions*

You [O bishops] are the voice of God and witnesses of his will, who bear the sins of all and intercede for all.... For you are imitators of Christ the Lord, and just as *he bore the sins of us all on the tree* (1 Pet 2:24) at his crucifixion — the blameless for those worthy of punishment — so also you ought to make the sins of the people your own. For it is said concerning the Savior in Isaiah: **Thus he bears our sins and suffers for us** (53:4). And again: **He himself bore the sins of many and was handed over for their transgressions** (53:12). So, just as you are a pattern for others, so also you have Christ as your pattern. Therefore, as he took upon himself the sins of all of you, so you ought to take upon yourselves the sins of the laity. For do not think that the episcopacy is an easily managed and light burden.

53:5
And by his bruise we were healed.

(14) Theodoret of Cyrus

This is a new and strange way of healing: the physician underwent the operation, but the sickly patient obtained the healing.

53:7
Like a sheep he was led to the slaughter, and as a lamb is silent before the one shearing it, so he does not open his mouth.

(15) Irenaeus of Lyons

When Philip discovered the eunuch of the queen of Ethiopia reading the words that had been written, **Like a sheep he was led to the slaughter, and as a lamb is silent before the shearer, so he opened not his mouth; in his humiliation his judgment was taken away**

(53:7-8), and the other things the prophet related about his passion and his coming in the flesh, and how he was dishonored by those who did not believe him, Philip easily persuaded him to believe in him, that he was Christ Jesus, who was crucified under Pontius Pilate and suffered what the prophet had predicted, and that he was the Son of God who gives eternal life to all. As soon as Philip had baptized him, the eunuch departed. For nothing other than Baptism was lacking to him who had already been instructed by the prophets. He was not ignorant of God the Father, nor of the rules as to how one should live. But he did not know of the coming of the Son of God. When he learned of this, in a brief space of time he went his way rejoicing to be the herald in Ethiopia of Christ's coming. Philip had to exert little effort with this man because he had already been trained in the fear of God by the prophets.

(16) Augustine of Hippo

We have been singing, *God will come openly, our God, and he will not keep silent* (Ps 50:3). This scripture foretold that Christ as God would come to judge the living and the dead. When he first came to be judged, it was in a hidden manner; when he comes to judge, it will be openly. How hidden he was then, you can tell from what the apostle writes: *For if they had known, they would never have crucified the Lord of glory* (1 Cor 2:8). He kept silent then when he was being interrogated, as the gospel tells us, in order to fulfill the prophecy of Isaiah which says: **Like a sheep he was led to the slaughter, and like a lamb before the shearer he was without voice, so he opened not his mouth** (53:7). But then he will *come openly and will not keep silent* (Ps 50:3). The reason it says that he will not keep silent when he judges is that he kept silent when he was judged. After all, as regards those words of his which were necessary for us, when did he ever keep silent? He did not keep silent through the patriarchs, he did not keep silent through the prophets, he did not keep silent through the mouth of his own body.

And if he were silent now, he would still be speaking through the Scriptures, wouldn't he? The reader goes to the lectern, but it is Christ who is not silent. The preacher explains the text; if he holds forth what is true, it is Christ speaking. If Christ were silent, I myself wouldn't be saying all this to you now. Nor has he been keeping silent through your mouths. When you were singing, he was speaking. He's not silent. What we have to do is hear him — but with the ears of the heart, because it's easy to hear with these fleshly ears. We ought to hear with the kind of ears the master himself was looking for when he said, *Whoever has ears to hear, let him hear* (Matt 13:9). When he said that, were there any standing in front of him without a pair of ears on their head? They all had ears, but they didn't all have ears to hear, that is, to obey, to take to heart.

(17) Origen of Alexandria

Even though the Father calls it a "great thing" for him to become a servant, it is actually something quite modest in comparison to his becoming an innocent **sheep** and a **lamb**

(53:7). For the Lamb of God became like an innocent sheep led to the slaughter, in order that he might *take away the sin of the world* (John 1:29). He who grants everyone the ability to speak is likened to a sheep dumb **before his shearers**, because by his death we have all been purified. Like a magical charm his death is an antidote against the powers of evil and the sin of those wishing to receive the truth. For the death of Christ has done in the powers who make war on the human race, and by its ineffable power has delivered the life of every believer from the hold of sin.

So that the whole world may be without sin, he takes away sin until every enemy is destroyed, death being the last. This is why John said as he pointed to him: *Behold, the Lamb of God, who takes away the sin of the world!* (John 1:29). He is not the one who is going to take it away but is not yet taking it away; nor is he the one who has already taken it away but is not still taking it away. The "taking away" is at work in every single being in the world, until the sin of the entire world shall have been taken away and the Savior hands over to the Father a kingdom prepared to be ruled by the Father (1 Cor 15:28) in which there is no sin and again all the things of God wholly and in every way will find a place. When this happens, the saying will be fulfilled, *God shall be all in all* (1 Cor 15:28).

(18) Origen of Alexandria

If we examine John's declaration about Jesus when he points to him and exclaims, *This is the Lamb of God, who takes away the sin of the world!* (John 1:29), from the perspective of the mystery of the appearance of the Son of God in a body for the life of men, we will recognize that the lamb is none other than the man he became. For **he was led as a sheep to the slaughter, and was dumb as a lamb before its shearer** (53:7), saying, *I was an innocent lamb being led to be sacrificed* (Jer 11:19).

This is why in the Apocalypse, too, a little lamb is seen *standing as though slain* (Rev 5:6). According to ineffable teachings, this is the Lamb which was slain as an expiation for the whole world. To carry out the Father's great love for humankind, the Lamb offered himself as a victim on behalf of the world and purchased us with his own blood from him who had taken possession of us when we had sold ourselves by our sins. The one who led this Lamb to sacrifice was God in man, the great high priest (cf. Heb 8:1). This he made known to us when he asserted: *No one takes it from me, but I lay it down of my own accord. I have power to lay it down, and I have power to take it again* (John 10:18)

Other sacrifices, of which those of the law are a symbol, are like this sacrifice. Among those sacrifices that are like this sacrifice one should include the shedding of the blood of the valiant martyrs. It is not without reason that the disciple John saw them standing beside the heavenly altar. *But who is wise and will understand these things? Who is discerning and will know them?* (Hos 14:9). . . . We hold then that the death of the holy martyrs destroys the evil powers. Their endurance and their confession even to the point of death, and their zeal for true devotion, blunt, as it were, the sharp point of the treachery of their enemies against their victims.

Isaiah 52:13–53:12

(19) Augustine of Hippo

The truth sounded forth through the apostles: *their sound went forth into all the earth, and their words to the ends of the wide world* (Ps 19:3-4), *Christ, our Passover, has been sacrificed* (1 Cor 5:7). This had previously been foretold by the prophet: **Like a sheep he was led to be slaughtered, and like a lamb in the presence of his shearer he was without voice, thus he did not open his mouth** (53:7). Who is this? Obviously the one about whom he goes on to say, **In humility his judgment was taken away. His generation, who shall relate?** (53:8). I can see this model of such humility in a king of such power and authority. Because this one, who is like a lamb not opening its mouth in the presence of the shearer, is himself *the Lion from the tribe of Judah* (Rev 5:5). Who is this, both lamb and lion? He endured death as a lamb; he devoured it as a lion. Who is this, both lamb and lion? Gentle and strong, lovable and terrifying, innocent and mighty, silent when he was being judged (cf. Mark 15:5), roaring when he comes to judge.

Or perhaps both in his passion lamb and lion, and also in his resurrection lamb and lion. Let us see him as a lamb in his passion. It was stated a moment ago: **Like a lamb in the presence of his shearer he was without voice, thus he did not open his mouth** (53:7). Let us see him as a lion in his passion: Jacob said, *You have gone up; lying down you have slept like a lion* (Gen 49:9). Let us see him as a lamb in his resurrection: the book of Revelation, when it was talking about the eternal glory of virgins, declared, *They follow the Lamb wherever he goes* (Rev 14:4). The same book of Revelation says, what I mentioned just now, *The Lion from the tribe of Judah has conquered, to open the book* (Rev 5:5). Why a lamb in his passion? Because he underwent death without being guilty of any iniquity. Why a lion in his passion? Because in being slain, he slew death. Why a lamb in his resurrection? Because his innocence is everlasting. Why a lion in his resurrection? Because everlasting also is his might.

Who is this lamb and lion? How can you ask who he is if this is what he was before: *In the beginning was the Word*; if this is where he was before: *and the Word was with God*; if this is what sort of Word he was: *and the Word was God*; if this is the kind of power he had: *all things were made through him*; if this is what he became: *and the Word was made flesh* (John 1:1, 3, 14)? If you want to know how he was either from the Father without a mother, or from his mother without a father, **Who shall declare his generation?** (53:8).

Begotten from all eternity, co-eternal with his begetter; remaining the Word, becoming flesh; creator of all times, created at the appropriate time; the prey of death, the predator of death; *deformed in posture beyond the sons of men* (53:3), *handsome in figure beyond the sons of men* (Ps 45:2); **knowing how to bear infirmity** (53:3), and how to bear it away; so sublime that he could do lowly things; so lowly that he could do sublime things; the God of man, and a man who is God; both firstborn and creator of the firstborn (Col. 1:15-16; Heb 12:23); only son, and also brother of many (Heb 2:11-12); born of the Father's substance, and made a partner with the adopted children (Gal 4:5-6); both Lord of all, and slave of the many.

This is the lamb *who takes away the sins of the world* (John 1:29); this is the lion who has conquered the kingdoms of the world. We were asking who this one is; let us ask who those are for whom this one died. Was it perhaps for the just and holy? That's not what the apostle says, but rather that *Christ died for the ungodly* (Rom 5:6); not of course so that they might remain ungodly, but so that the ungodly might be justified by the death of the just, and that by the shedding of sinless blood, the liability of sin might be cancelled.

(20) Gregory the Great

Abel, Isaiah, and John lived at different times. They were separated in time but not in what they preached. Abel offered up a lamb for sacrifice, typifying the passion of our Redeemer (Gen 4:4). Of him Isaiah says: **as a lamb is silent before its shearer, so he does not open his mouth** (53:7). And John exclaims: *Behold, the Lamb of God, who takes away the sin of the world!* (John 1:29). Behold, they were sent at different times indeed, and yet they were one in thinking that the redeemer was innocent. They spoke of the same Lamb, John by pointing to him, Isaiah by foreseeing him, and Abel by offering him. The one whom John set forth by pointing to him and Isaiah proclaimed in his words, Abel held as a type in his hands.

53:8
Who will describe his generation?

(21) Basil of Caesarea

What arrogance, what haughtiness of those who think that God's essence could be discovered! They almost surpass the boasting of the one who said: *I will set my throne above the stars* (14:13).[3] For their challenge has to do neither with the stars nor with the heavens; they claim to be able to penetrate the essence of the God of the universe.

Let us inquire where this clever idea comes from. Is it a matter of common opinion? Hardly, for that tells us only that God exists, not what he is. Is this a teaching of the Holy Spirit? What teaching? And where is it found? Did not the great David, to whom God had revealed mysteries and hidden things, of his wisdom clearly confess that such knowledge is beyond our reach, when he said: *The knowledge of you is a matter of wonder to me; it is overwhelming. I am not able to reach it* (Ps 139:6)? And Isaiah, who had a vision of the glory of God (6:1), what did he reveal to us of the divine essence? He was the one who in his prophecy bore witness to Christ, saying: **Who will describe his generation?** (53:8). As for Paul, that *chosen instrument* (Act 9:15) who had *Christ speaking in him* (2 Cor 13:3), who *was caught up in the third heaven, who heard words that cannot be told which man may not utter* (2 Cor 12:4), what teaching did he leave us concerning the essence of God? When he looked closely at the specifics of the economy, he became dizzy contemplating its unfathomable depth. And this is what he exclaimed: *O the depth of the riches and the wisdom and knowledge of God! How unsearchable are his judgments and how inscrutable his ways!* (Rom

---

3. The reference is to Satan. See chapter 14.

11:33). If these things are inaccessible to those who have reached the measure of Paul's knowledge, what kind of hubris drives those who claim to know the essence of God?

(22) Augustine of Hippo

Rejoice, all Christians; it is the birthday of Christ. Born of his mother, he commended this day to the ages, while born of his Father he created all ages. The one birth could have no mother, while the other required no man as father. In sum, Christ was born both of a Father and of a mother; both without a father and without a mother; of a Father as God, of a mother as man; without a mother as God; without a father as man. Therefore, **who will recount his generation?** (53:8), whether that one without time or this one without seed; that one without beginning or this one without precedent; that one which never was not or this one which never was before or after; that one which has no end or this one which has its beginning in its end?

Rightly therefore did the prophets foretell that he would be born, while the heavens and the angels announced that he had been. The one who holds the world in being was lying in a manger; he was simultaneously speechless infant and Word. The heavens cannot contain him, a woman carried him in her bosom. She was ruling our ruler, carrying the one in whom we are, suckling our bread. O manifest infirmity and wondrous humility in which was thus concealed total divinity! Omnipotence was ruling the mother on whom infancy was depending; was nourishing on truth the mother whose breasts it was sucking. May he bring his gifts to perfection in us, since he did not shrink from making his own our tiny beginnings; and may he make us into children of God, since for our sake he was willing to be made a child of man.

53:9
He committed no transgression, nor was deceit found in his mouth.

(23) Gregory of Nyssa

When all things are subjected to him, then the Son himself will also be subjected to him who put all things under him, that God may be all in all (1 Cor 15:28).[4] I first will set forth in my own words the general sense of what Paul has written, then I will quote the words of the apostle in which the ideas I have presented are stated. What then is the point the divine apostle is making in this text? That at some time evil will recede into non being and be completely eradicated and that God's perfect goodness will enfold in itself every rational being, and nothing God has made will be cast out of his kingdom. This will come to be when all the evil mixed in with what exists has been consumed, like dross, by the purifying fire, and everything God has made will be as it was at the beginning, before evil entered the world.

---

4. This excerpt is taken from an essay on 1 Cor 15:28.

Paul indicates that this happens in the following way: the pure, perfect divinity of the only Son entered into human nature, which is subject to death. The human Christ came to be from the mingling of the divine with human nature as a whole, a kind of *first fruits* (1 Cor 15:20) from the one *lump of dough* (Rom 11:16), and by this all humanity was attached to the godhead. In him all evil was completely obliterated since he did not commit sin — as the prophet says, **nor was there any deceit in his mouth** (53:9) — and in him death, which follows sin, was also totally wiped out, since there is no other cause of death except sin (Rom 5:12). Thus both the obliteration of evil and the dissolution of death had their beginning in him.

(24) John of Damascus

Our Lord Jesus Christ was without sin, for **he committed no transgression** (53:9), *he who takes away the sin of the world* (John 1:29), **nor was deceit found in his mouth** (53:9). He was not subject to death, since *death came into the world through sin* (Rom 5:12). He dies, therefore, because he took on himself death on our behalf, and offers himself as a sacrifice to the Father for our sake. For we had sinned against him, and he had to receive the ransom for us so that we would be delivered from condemnation! God forbid that the Lord's blood should have been offered to the tyrant. Therefore, when death approached and gulped down the bait of his body, it was snared by the hook of his divinity. After tasting his sinless and life-giving body, death is destroyed, and vomits up again everything he had swallowed long ago. For just as darkness disappears with the coming of light, so corruption is driven away by the assault of life. Life comes to all, but death to the destroyer.

Isaiah 54

1 Rejoice, O barren one who does not bear;
   break forth and shout,
   you who are not in labor!
  Because more are the children of the desolate woman
   than of her that has a husband,
   for the Lord has spoken.
2 Enlarge the site of your tent
   and of your curtains;
  make it firm, do not hold back;
   lengthen your cords and strengthen your stakes.
3 Because you must spread out to the right and to the left,
   and your offspring will inherit the nations
   and will inhabit the cities that have become desolate.

4 Do not fear because you were put to shame,
   neither feel disgraced because you were reproached;
  because you will forget your ancient shame,
   and the reproach of your widowhood you will not remember.
5 Because the Lord is the one who makes you,
   the Lord Sabaoth is his name,
  and the one who delivered you is the very God of Israel,
   he shall be called thus in all the earth.
6 The Lord has not called you
   as a forsaken and faint-hearted woman,
  nor as a woman hated from youth,
   your God has said.
7 For a brief moment I forsook you,
   but with great mercy I will have mercy on you.
8 With a little wrath
   I turned my face away from you,

but with everlasting mercy I have had mercy on you,
  the Lord who delivered you has said.

9 From the water at the time of Noe, this is my oath:
  Just as I swore to him at that time
    that I would no more be angry at the earth because of you,
  nor as a threat to you
10   would I remove the mountains,
    nor would the hills be shifted,
  so neither shall the mercy that comes from me to you fail,
    nor shall the covenant of your peace be removed,
    for the Lord said he would be merciful to you.
11 O humbled and unsteady one,
    you have not been comforted;
  see, I am preparing for you charcoal as your stone,
    and sapphire as your foundations.
12 And I will make your battlements of jasper,
    and your gates of crystal stones,
    and your enclosure of precious stones;
13 And I will make all your sons taught by God,
    and your children to be in great peace.
14 And in righteousness you shall be built;
    keep away from injustice, and you shall not be afraid,
    and trembling shall not come near you.
15 See, guests shall approach you through me,
    and flee to you for refuge.
16 See, I create you,
    not as a smith who blows the coals,
    and produces a vessel for work.
  But I have created you not for destruction, to ruin
17   every perishable vessel.
  I will not make it prosper against you —
    and every voice that shall rise against you in judgment.
  You will defeat all of them,
    and those who are held by you shall be in sorrow.
  There is a heritage for those who do service to the Lord,
    and you shall be righteous to me, says the Lord.

The interpretation of this chapter was set by St. Paul, who quotes the opening passage, **Rejoice, O barren one who does not bear,** *in Galatians 4. The words are spoken, according to Paul, to the "Jerusalem above," not to the "present Jerusalem" (Gal 4:26). Accordingly the text was understood to refer to the Church, the new Jerusalem, and, in particular, to the Church gathered from the nations. This is of course a major theme of the interpretation of Isaiah in the early Church, as can be seen in the exposition of 2:1ff., 25:6, 60:1ff., and other passages. Cyril takes his cue from the* *phrase* **inherit the nations** *(54:3), which he takes to be the Gentiles who have become part of the Church, and he understands the phrase* **enlarge the site of your tent** *(54:2) quite literally to mean that a new temple had to be constructed, the Church, to make room for the many people who would embrace the gospel. By contrast the ancient tabernacle was a small structure with a narrow courtyard. Other commentators also focus on the Church. For example, Gregory the Great allegorizes the descriptive terms for the new Jerusalem.* **Jasper** *(54:12), a green stone, signifies the "inner greenness" of believers,* **engraved stones** *their "holy works."*

(1) The Letter of Paul to the Galatians

Now Hagar is Mount Sinai in Arabia; she corresponds to the present Jerusalem, for she is in slavery with her children. But the Jerusalem above is free, and she is our mother. For it is written, **Rejoice, O barren one who does not bear; break forth and shout, you who are not in travail; for the children of the desolate one are many more than the children of her that is married** (54:1).

(2) The Gospel according to John

It is written in the prophets, **And they shall all be taught by God** (54:13). Every one who has heard and learned from the Father comes to me.

(3) Jerome

[In Isaiah 53] the prophet had spoken of the birth of the Savior, the course of his life and his works, his suffering on the cross, and the glory of his resurrection, when, *laying down his life, he* [i.e., the Savior] *saw a long-lived offspring, and with his understanding justified many, and divided the spoils of the strong, and prayed for sinners* (53:10-12), so that they might have an opportunity for repentance. Now [in ch. 54] the prophet turns to the calling of the nations and describes fully those who are going to believe in Christ. The apostle Paul interprets this passage in relation to Sarah and Isaac and refers it to the "church" which the people in former times served at Mount Sinai, and to Hagar with their children. He cites the following words of Isaiah: **Rejoice, O barren one who does not bear; break forth and shout, you who are not in travail, for the desolate has more children than she who has a husband** (54:1). And then he adds at once: *Now we, brethren, like Isaac, are children of promise. But as at that time he who was born according to the flesh persecuted him who was born according to the Spirit, so it is now. But what does the scripture say? "Cast out the slave and her son; for the son of the slave shall not inherit with the son of the free woman"* (Gen 21:10). *So, brethren, we are not children of the slave but of the free woman* (Gal 4:28-31).

So Paul, the *chosen instrument* (Acts 9:15), drawing on the testimony of Isaiah that is before us, refers it to the sons of promise and to the Church gathered from both peoples, the Gentiles and the Jews. The Gentiles, however, did not have God as husband, nor did they receive the law and the prophets, and for that reason, following earlier interpretations, I say that the Church of the Gentiles is **desolate**. For about it we read, **Rejoice, desolate one** (54:1), and so on. Jeremiah also wrote about this, speaking in the person of God: *She is left desolate who bore seven; her soul faints. Her sun goes down while it is still midday* (Jer 15:9). And in Samuel: *The barren has borne seven, and she who had many children is forlorn* (1 Sam 2:5). And in the Psalms: *He gives the barren woman a home, making her the joyous mother of children* (Ps 113:9).

(4) Cyril of Alexandria

As we have seen from the beautiful description in the previous section, the Lamb of God, that is, Christ, bore the precious cross for us and offered himself as a sacrifice for the world. Now the text announces that he will **inherit** (54:3) many, and the prophecy will be fulfilled in those given to him as an inheritance by God, that is, the **nations**. As the Son said somewhere through the psalmist's lyre: *The LORD said to me. "You are my Son, today I have begotten you. Ask of me, and I will make the nations your inheritance, and the ends of the earth your possession"* (Ps 2:7-8). Note that he says **nations**, not nation. For the number of the **nations** is many more than that of the Israelites, who are only one people. He considers it fitting to liken the multitude of the **nations** to a barren and rejected woman, that is, a desolate woman. And he commands her: **Rejoice, O barren one who does not bear** (54:1).

But perhaps someone will ask: Why does he call the many, the Church gathered from the nations, **barren**? He had already indicated that there were many more who lived in error, *worshiping the creature rather than the Creator* (Rom 1:25), than those who were redeemed through Moses and hence numbered among the inheritance of God. For the Scripture says, *When the Most High apportioned the nations and divided up the sons of Adam, he fixed the boundaries of the peoples according to the number of the angels of God; and his people Jacob became the portion of the LORD, and Israel was the line of his inheritance* (Deut 32:8-9). Why does he call the one who has many children and is fruitful **barren**? Because there was no one who knew the God of all and who in knowledge and virtue was reckoned among God's children. One might say that there was no one among the Gentiles who was reborn of water and the Spirit. They were corrupted and given to earthly things, as the psalmist declares: *The wicked are alienated from God from birth, they go astray from the womb* (Ps 57:4 LXX). Sinners born of sinners, they had *no hope,* as wise Paul says (Eph 2:12). That is to say, they were **barren** with respect to God, and gave birth to no one who could have been considered God's children in faith and virtue.

But notice that she is ordered to **cry out and shout** (54:1). It is customary when women are on the birth stool for their nurses to urge them to cry out with a vehement, piercing cry, so that helped by their cries they may be fully dilated and push the baby from the womb. This is what is meant by **cry out and shout.** Begin to give birth, he orders, as one who is in labor with many children; cry out continually with the cry of one

Isaiah 54

who is giving birth. Be filled with joy as the mother of countless people, be filled with spiritual joy. God makes clear the meaning of the present text when he says: **the children of the barren woman are more than of her that has a husband** (54:1).

It is the custom in the Sacred Scriptures to call a widow **desolate**. The multitude of the nations was widowed because it did not share in the wealth of the Word that sows the seeds of all knowledge and zeal for godliness. For the Word was like a husbandman who brought forth truth in intellectual creatures. Through him all kinds of spiritual fruit were implanted in the holy angels and in ourselves. But before the coming of the Savior she was a widow, unfruitful and hence without children. But now that she has received through faith the bridegroom from heaven, she has more children than the one who had a husband, that is, the synagogue of the Jews, whom God led by all-wise Moses to spiritual fellowship and kinship and made her the mother and nurse of many. But since the coming of Christ, she who was childless was, as Jeremiah says, blessed with many children.[1]

Then the text commands: **Enlarge the site of your tent and of your curtains** (54:2). When she welcomed the Word from heaven, that is, the Bridegroom, she had to extend her courtyard in length and width and strengthen her **stakes**. By this we understand that the Church of the Gentiles is impregnable. **Lengthen her cords** (54:2) indicates that in comparison to the former tent with its narrow courtyard, the holy churches are magnificent and commodious. Hence in this figure one is to see a type of the Church of the nations that spreads abundantly in all directions.

The twelve tribes had a tent made of animal skins, surrounded by courtyards on four sides to indicate the four parts of the world. It was a hundred cubits in length and fifty in width.[2] This is why he orders, **spread out to the right and to the left** (54:3), that is, put your stakes down everywhere. For the Church of the nations is spacious, grand, and beautiful and spread throughout the world. Thus when the temple in Jerusalem was raised after first being destroyed by the Assyrians, the God of all asked: *Who is left among you that saw the house in its former glory? And how does it look now? Is it not in your sight as nothing? I live, says the* LORD, *and the latter splendor of this house shall be greater than the former* (Hag 2:3, 9). For the temples, that is, churches, that have been built throughout the world are greater and more splendid than the temple that was in Jerusalem, because in them one will find the sacred altar to the glory of Christ. **Enlarge then the site of your tent and of your curtains. Your offspring will inherit the nations, and you will inhabit the cities that have become desolate** (54:3).

The Church of the Gentiles has become the mother and nurse of many holy and good men. She has given birth to many teachers and leaders of the people, and many nations have found guides who hand on the true mystical word and are not lacking in pastoral skills. To those who practice the marvelous and glorious life the Savior promised as an inheritance that he would be their shepherd in the coming age. In distributing money to the one who had doubled what he received he said: *Take charge of ten cities*, and to another, *Take charge of five* (Luke 19:17-18). Therefore, **your offspring will in-**

---

1. It is not clear what text Cyril has in mind.
2. See Exodus 27.

herit the nations (54:3). It is fitting in this regard, as I have already said, for the leaders of the Church to rejoice with great joy: *He subdued peoples under us, and nations under our feet. He chose our heritage for us* (Ps 47:3-4). The only fitting inheritance for Christ is to rule others. For this reason he ordered them to call no one "Rabbi": *You have one teacher*, Christ (Matt 23:8). But since he is the true light (cf. John 1:9), he calls his holy apostles lights, and because he is by nature the one true Son, he gives authority to those who believe in him and enjoy the dignity of sonship to call God Father. So also he is the teacher of all, and because he has a heavenly inheritance, he crowns his holy ones with his own glory. Because they became coworkers with him and genuine leaders of the people, they won many and presented to him those who had worshiped creatures rather than him and did not know the most excellent way of life. This is how one should understand **inhabit desolate cities** (54:3). So it will be, he says, that the multitude of his offspring will fill the **desolate cities**, because the cities that are already inhabited will not be sufficient for them.

54:1
Rejoice, O barren one who does not bear.

(5) Irenaeus of Lyons

It is our task to expound clearly and accurately the meaning of things spoken in figures in accord with the pattern of the faith. . . . For example, we should not be silent as to how God made the Gentiles who were without hope of salvation *fellow heirs, members of the same body and partakers [of the promise]* with the saints (Eph 3:6); and should explain how it is that *this mortal flesh shall put on immortality, and this corruptible flesh shall put on incorruption* (1 Cor 15:54); and should teach how it happened *that there is a people who was no people, and she is beloved who was not beloved* (Hos 2:23); and in what sense he says that **she who was desolate has more children than she who had a husband** (54:1; Gal 4:27). For in reference to these points and others of a like nature, the apostle exclaims: *O the depth of the riches both of the wisdom and knowledge of God! How unsearchable are his judgments, and his ways past finding out!* (Rom 11:33).

(6) Origen of Alexandria

When the *fullness of time had come* (Gal 4:4), the law began to be *weakened by the flesh* (Rom 8:3), and in the wake of its weakness came death. But when the letter died, those who had lived like a married woman under the authority of her husband believed in Christ and were wedded to the Spirit. Those, however, who from among the Gentiles believed in the Lord had not lived under this husband, that is, under the power of the law, and did not have the word of the law as a husband. In the book of Isaiah here is a testimony to this, namely, that those who were of the circumcision lived under the authority of a husband, and the Gentiles had no husband: **Rejoice, O barren one who does not** bear; break forth and shout, you who are not in labor; for the children of the desolate woman are more than of her that has a husband (54:1). He says that the desolate one has more children than the one who has a husband because many more believed from among the Gentiles than from among the Jews. He indicates that the one who had a husband was the synagogue that had the law. But the desolate one, without ties, who lived without the authority of the law, is the multitude of the Gentiles. She was unfruitful and could bring forth no offspring from the word of the law.

(7) Augustine of Hippo

Let that prophecy be fulfilled in which Isaiah addresses your[3] Church in your name. He speaks to your Church, to your holy city, to that barren woman whose children are multiplying: **Many are the children of the forsaken one, more than of her who has a husband** (54:1). And to her the summons is sent, **Rejoice, you barren woman, you who are childless, break out and cry aloud, you who bear no children; for many are the children of the forsaken one, more than of her who has a husband** (54:1), more than those of the Jewish race which has a husband and was given the law.

Your children outnumber those of the nation that had a king it could see. Your king is hidden, and by that invisible bridegroom you bear many children. To the Church are the words addressed, **Many are the children of the forsaken one, more than of her who has a husband**; and the prophet continues, **Widen your encampment and stretch out your tent; do not hold back. Lengthen your guy ropes and drive your pegs in firmly; spread further and further, to the right and to the left** (54:2-3). Hold the good people at your right, hold the bad at your left, until the winnowing fork comes into play (cf. Matt 3:12). But claim all the Gentiles as your possession. Let both good and bad be invited to the wedding, and the wedding feast be filled with guests, for the servants' job is to invite people, the Lord's prerogative to sort them out (cf. Matt 22:1-14).

Spread further and further, to the right and to the left. Your descendants will inherit the nations, and will people deserted cities (54:3) — deserted they have been by God, deserted by the prophets, deserted by the apostles and deserted by the gospel, but they are populated by demons. **Your descendants will people the deserted cities. You have nothing to fear, for you will prevail; you need feel no shame that you were once abhorred** (54:3-4). So although you are forced to admit, **The strong pounced upon me**, you need not be ashamed. Though in former days the Christian name was outlawed, and it was a stigma and a disgrace to be a Christian, **you need feel no shame that you were once abhorred, for you will forget your confusion forever, and no longer be mindful of the stigma of your widowhood. For I am the Lord, and I create you. The Lord is his name, and he who has rescued you will be called the Lord God of Israel and the God of all the earth** (54:4-5). *Do you, Lord God of hosts, God of Israel, set yourself to visit all nations.* This I pray, *set yourself to visit all nations* (Ps 58:6 Vg.).

---

3. The Church of the Gentiles.

(8) Augustine of Hippo

Some commentators call Isaiah an evangelist rather than a prophet, because in the midst of his indictment of wrongdoing and his teaching concerning justice, and among his predictions of the disasters that were to come upon a sinful people, he made many more prophecies about Christ and the Church than the other prophets. That is, he spoke about the king and the city he founded. But because I am determined to keep my book within bounds, I shall quote here only one of many passages. He says, speaking in the person of God the Father: [Augustine then cites in its entirety 52:13–53:12].

So far about Christ. Now let us listen to what he says about the Church in what follows, which concerns the Church: **Rejoice, O barren one who does not bear; break forth and shout, you who are not in labor! Because more are the children of the desolate woman than of her that has a husband....** [Augustine cites 54:1-5.] This will have to suffice. There are a number of points in it that demand explanation; but there are, in my judgment, enough points in the passage so plain that even our opponents are forced to recognize their meaning, even though it goes against their will.

54:12-13
I will make your battlements of jasper, your gates of crystal stones, and your enclosure of precious stones; I will make all your sons taught by God, and your children to be in great peace.

(9) Gregory the Great

Peter the apostle regarded the minds of the faithful as strong in the faith when he said: *And like living stones be yourselves built into a spiritual house* (1 Pet 2:5). The Lord spoke about these stones of the holy Church through Isaiah: **I will make your battlements of jasper, your gates of engraved stones, and your borders of precious stones; all your sons will be taught by God** (54:12-13). Almighty God made the **battlements** of the holy Church **jasper**, a green stone, because he strengthened his preachers' minds with love of inner greenness, so that they might despise everything transitory, desire nothing in this world which is finite, and disdain all earthly joys as barren. Thus the shepherd of the Church himself, when calling his hearers to pastures of eternal greenness, says about God: *By his great mercy we have been born anew to a living hope through the resurrection of Jesus Christ from the dead, and to an inheritance which is imperishable, undefiled, and unfading, kept in heaven* (1 Pet 1:3-4).

The gates of this holy Church are made of **engraved stones**, which signify those through whose voice we enter into eternal life. They are **engraved stones** because, when they displayed in themselves the holy works which are divinely commanded, it is as if they held within themselves **engraved stones**. The **gates** would not be **engraved**, but rather plain, if they spoke up without exhibiting holy works in themselves. Whenever they show that their lives conform to their words, they are **gates** — since they lead inward — and **engraved stones** — since by their manner of life they are an example of what they

Isaiah 54

say to others. We see that all the **borders** of this holy Church are set in **precious stones** when we see the faithful being strong in faith and charity. In order to show who these **stones** were, Isaiah added: **all your sons will be taught by God.**

(10) Augustine of Hippo

The surest sign that you have been taught of God is that you put into practice what you have been **taught by God** (54:13). In this way all who have been called according to God's purpose (Rom 8:28) are **taught by God**, as we read in the prophets. But those who know what they ought to do and do not do it have not yet learned it from God through grace, but through the law; they have not learned it through the Spirit, but through the letter. Many seem, nonetheless, to do what the law commanded out of a fear of punishment, not out of a love of righteousness. Such is the righteousness that the apostle called his own righteousness, which comes from the law as a commandment, but not as a gift. If it were a gift, it would not be called our righteousness but God's because it becomes ours only insofar as we receive it from God. After all, he says, *That I might be found in him, not having my own righteousness derived from the law, but that which comes through faith in Jesus, a righteousness that comes from God in faith* (Phil 3:9).

Isaiah 55

1 You who thirst,
    go to water;
  and as many of you as have no money,
    go, buy and drink wine and fat,
    without money and without price.
2 Why do you set a price with money
    and your labor for that which does not satisfy?
  Hear me, and you shall eat good things,
    and your soul shall revel in good things.
3 Pay attention with your ears,
    and follow my ways;
  listen to me,
    and your soul will live in good things.
  I will make with you an everlasting covenant,
    the sacred things of Dauid that are sure.
4 See, I have given him as a testimony among the nations,
    a ruler and commander for the nations.
5 Nations that did not know you shall call upon you,
    and peoples that do not understand you shall flee to you for refuge,
  for the sake of your God, the Holy One of Israel,
    because he has glorified you.

6 Seek God, and when you find him, call upon him;
    and whenever he should draw near you,
7 let the wicked forsake his ways,
    and the lawless man his plans,
  and let him return to the Lord, and he will have mercy,
    because he will abundantly forgive your sins.
8 For my plans are not like your plans,
    nor are your ways like my ways, says the Lord.

Isaiah 55

9 But as heaven is far from the earth,
    so is my way far from your ways
    and your notions from my thought.

10 For as rain or snow comes down from heaven,
    and will not return until it has soaked the earth,
  and brought forth and blossomed
    and given seed to the sower and bread for food,
11 so shall my word be, whatever goes out from my mouth;
    it shall not return
  until whatever I have willed is fulfilled,
    and I will prosper your ways and my commandments.

12 For you shall go out with joy,
    and be taught with happiness;
  for the mountains and the hills shall leap forth
    as they welcome you with happiness,
    and all the trees of the field shall clap with their branches.
13 And instead of the brier shall come up a cypress;
    and instead of the nettle shall come up a myrtle;
  and the Lord shall be for a name,
    and for an everlasting sign, and shall not fail.

The excerpts in this chapter develop several themes. The opening words, **go and buy without . . . money and without price,** *offered a way of speaking about the grace of Christ as a gift freely offered to which the response is faith. The mention of* **wine** *(55:1) suggested to Cyril that the passage was speaking about the wine of the Eucharist. Tertullian takes the link between the* **sacred things of David** *and the* **nations** *(55:3-4) to signify that the promises to David were fulfilled in Christ, through whom the worship of the one God was brought to the nations spread all over the world. Some writers focus on the words,* **Seek God, and when you find him, call upon him** *(55:6). Gregory of Nyssa interprets this verse to mean a continual seeking: in his words, "seeking the Lord is one's entire life." Augustine quotes Sir 24:29, "Those who eat me will be hungry still, and those who drink me will be thirsty still," to emphasize that we "seek God's face always" (Ps 105:4). With God we are always seekers, for God is always more than we imagine or desire, and our yearnings are never satisfied. Each finding gives way to a more intense seeking, and the closer we are to God the more ardent our desire. See also #6 in chapter 7.*

(1) The Acts of the Apostles

And we bring you the good news that what God promised to the fathers, this he has fulfilled to us their children by raising Jesus; as also it is written in the second psalm, "Thou art my Son, today I have begotten thee" (Ps 2:7). And as for the fact that he raised him from the dead, no more to return to corruption, he spoke in this way, **I will give you the holy and sure blessings of David** (55:3).

(2) Cyril of Alexandria

Divine David, illuminated by the torch of the Spirit, composed choral songs to God, saying of Christ the Savior of all: *How wide is your mercy, O God! The children of men hope in the shadow of your wings. They feast on the abundance of your house, and you give them drink from the river of your delights. For with you is the fountain of life* (Ps 36:7-9). And in another place: *There is a river whose streams make glad the city of God* (Ps 46:4). And through the prophet the Son, who is the fountain of all good things, the life-giving stream which flows out from the being of the Father, promises: *Behold, I will extend peace to them like a river, and the glory of the nations like an overflowing stream* (66:12).

The prophet Zechariah[1] also says: *A fountain shall come forth from the house of the* LORD, *and it will water the valley of reeds* (Joel 3:18). In the Scriptures we often find that the Word of God is called a fountain or a river. For this reason, when speaking to the Jews, Jesus said of himself: *If anyone thirst, let him come to me and drink. He who believes in me, as the scripture has said, "Out of his heart shall flow rivers of living water"* (John 7:37-38). And when he spoke to the Samaritan woman again, he declared: *Everyone who drinks of this water will thirst again, but whoever drinks of the water that I shall give him will never thirst; the water that I shall give him will become in him a spring of water welling up to eternal life* (John 4:13-14).

Therefore he says that if someone thirsts, let him go to Christ, let him **drink**. Receiving in abundance the consolation of the Holy Spirit and grace and the purest spiritual teaching, he does not have to lay out **money** to purchase something but without paying enjoys the abundant generosity of the one who welcomes him. He moves, or **goes** (55:1), as the text says, from one place to another, that is, from error to knowledge of the truth. **Buy and drink, without money and without price** (55:1). How will they buy and receive a gift without silver? By faith! For by faith we receive grace as a gift from Christ, paying nothing perishable and transient. *For I said to the* LORD, *according to the psalm, "You are my Lord, for you have no need of my goodness"* (Ps 16:1). In place of gifts and precious things we offer our confession of faith in him. Therefore this **drink** and the abundant gift of graces from him are acquired **without money or price**.

What is it we merit and what kind of drink do we receive? **Wine** and food, and in addition **fat** and grain. Most assuredly the abundant gifts of Christ bring joy to the soul. For the **wine** he gives is spiritual wine, and **fat** the nourishment that brings health and strength. It is possible that this passage also hints at the sacrament of Christ. Those who drink the living water, that is, the grace poured out through the Holy Spirit, partake of Christ. They **buy** this through faith and have a part in the **wine** and **fat**, that is, the holy body and blood of Christ.

---

1. Cyril mistakenly says Zechariah, but the passage actually comes from the prophet Joel.

Isaiah 55

55:1
You who thirst, go to the water; and as many of you as have no money, go, buy and drink wine and fat, without money and without price.

(3) Clement of Alexandria

Let us not be enslaved nor become like swine, but rather, as true *children of light* (Eph 5:8), let us lift up our eyes and look to the light. . . . Let us repent and move from ignorance to knowledge, from foolishness to wisdom, from debauchery to self-restraint, from unrighteousness to righteousness, from ungodliness to God. It is a high adventure to join oneself to God. There are many noble things to be enjoyed by lovers of righteousness, that is, by us who seek eternal salvation that God himself hints at through Isaiah: *There is an inheritance for those who do service to the* LORD (54:17). This inheritance is good and lovely. It is neither gold, nor silver, nor clothing — all earthly things the moth consumes and the thief whose eye is dazzled by worldly wealth steals (cf. Matt 6:19-20). Rather, it is that treasure of salvation toward which we must hasten as lovers of the Word. Then noble works will go with us borne on the wing of truth. God's eternal covenant entrusts us with this inheritance and bestows on us an everlasting gift. He is the father who loves us dearly, the true father, who never ceases to exhort, admonish, train, and love us. Nor does his salvation ever come to an end, for he gives us wise counsel: **Be righteous, says the Lord. You who thirst, go to the water; and as many of you as have no money, go and buy, and drink wine without money** (54:17–55:1). He invites us to the washing, to salvation, to illumination, all but crying out and saying, "I give you the land, the sea, and the heavens, my child, and all the living things in them." Only, O child, thirst for your Father; God will be shown to you **without price**. The truth is not for sale. He gives you creatures that fly and swim and make their way on the earth. All these things the Father has created that you may enjoy them with thanksgiving.

(4) Ambrose of Milan

Anyone who has not been fed by Christ is hungry. Let us then purchase the nourishment needed to ward off famine. Let no one hold back because he is poor, let no one **without money** be afraid. Christ does not ask for money but faith, something more valuable than money. Indeed, Peter, who had no money, was able to buy him. *Silver and gold I do not have,* he said, *but what I have I give you. In the name of Jesus Christ, arise and walk* (Acts 3:6). And the prophet Isaiah gives the invitation, **All who are thirsty, come to the water, and you that have no money, come, buy, and drink and eat without money and without the price of the wine** (55:1). For he who paid for us with the price of his blood did not ask a price from us, because he redeemed us not with gold or silver but with his precious blood (1 Cor 6:19-20). Your debt then is the price that has purchased you. Even if he does not ask for it, you are still in his debt. Buy Christ for yourself, then, not with what few possess, but with what all are capable of but few offer because of fear — yourself. What Christ claims from you belongs to him. He gave his life for all, he offered himself to death for all.

(5) Theodoret of Cyrus

You who thirst, go to the water (55:1). Through holy Baptism we are *justified by his grace as a gift,* according to the holy apostle, *through the redemption which is in Christ Jesus* (Rom 3:24). This is what is hinted at in the prophetic word: **And as many of you as have no silver, go, buy and eat; come, buy and drink without silver** (55:1). The Holy Scripture often refers to justice as **silver.** *The words of the* LORD *are pure words, silver refined in a furnace on the ground* (Ps 12:6). As for those who live with iniquity, *they are called refuse silver, for the* LORD *has rejected them* (Jer 6:30). The merciful Lord, however, has promised to those who do not possess what is called **silver,** that is, righteousness, to give them freely of the water that is thrice desired.[2] For he does not demand a reckoning of their former sins from those who approach most holy Baptism, but he promises to grant them forgiveness of their sins.

(6) Gregory the Great

And [Job's sons] would send and invite their three sisters to eat and drink with them (Job 1:4). The sons call their sisters to the feast because the holy apostles proclaim the joys of heavenly refreshment to weak hearers. When the apostles see their souls starved of the food of truth, they nourish them with the banquet of God's word. And so it is well said: *to eat and drink with them,* for Sacred Scripture is sometimes solid food for us, and sometimes drink. It is food in the more obscure passages, since it is broken into pieces when it is explained and swallowed after being chewed. It is drink in the more straightforward parts since it is absorbed just as it is found. The prophet [Jeremiah] understood Sacred Scripture to be food which should be broken up by explaining when he wrote, *The children begged for bread, but there was no one to break it up for them* (Lam 4:4 Vg.). This means that those who are weak asked that the more substantial passages of Holy Scripture be broken up by explanation, but no one could be found to explain it to them. The prophet saw the Sacred Scripture as drink when he said: **All who thirst, come to the waters** (55:1). If the plain commandments had not been drink, the Truth would not himself have cried out, *If anyone thirst, let him come to me and drink* (John 7:37).

(7) Gregory the Theologian

From the day you were changed,[3] all the ancient marks were effaced, and the same form of Christ was put on all of you. Do not shirk from confessing your sin since you know how John baptized.[4] For if you endure the shame of the present you will escape future shame, for shame is also a part of future punishment. Prove that you really hate sin by

---

2. Because the person being baptized was immersed three times.
3. Gregory is speaking about Baptism.
4. Requiring that people who came to him confess their sins.

making a public example of it and triumphing over it as worthy of contempt. Do not reject the remedy of exorcism, nor be discouraged because it stretches out for such a long time. This too is a touchstone of your sincerity with respect to grace. What does your effort add up to when compared with the Queen of Ethiopia, who came from the end of the world to see the wisdom of Solomon (1 Kings 10:1)? But look, *here is someone greater than Solomon* (Matt 12:42), as those who see things clearly say. Don't shrink from taking a long journey, or sailing the broad sea, or passing through fire if that stands in the way, or anything else great or small that prevents you from reaching the gift. But that is not the way things are. What you desire is yours without effort or trouble. How foolish to put off the gift. Isaiah invites you with these words: **You who thirst, go to the water, and whoever has no silver, come, buy and drink wine without paying** (55:1). How swift his goodness! How easy the transaction! You buy simply by wanting it. God accepts your desire as a great price. He thirsts to be thirsted for; he gives those who wish something to drink; he considers it an act of generosity when one asks for generosity; his munificence pours from his hand; for him giving brings greater pleasure than others have in receiving. So let us not be condemned by asking for too little or for something that is unworthy of the giver. Happy is the one from whom Jesus asks for a drink, as he did from that Samaritan woman, for he *gave her a spring of water welling up to eternal life* (John 4:14).

55:3
I will make with you an everlasting covenant.

(8) Tertullian

I now will lay out appropriate passages from the Creator's scriptures of things that were prophesied to happen after Christ's coming. For events were found to have taken place as ordained that would not have happened had the coming of Christ not preceded them. Take note that since that time all the nations are looking up from the depths of human error toward God the Creator and toward his Christ. No one would be so bold as to deny that this was prophesied.

At the beginning of the Psalms you will find this promise of the Father: *You are my son, today I have begotten you. Ask of me, and I will make the nations your heritage, and the ends of the earth your possession* (Ps 2:7-8). You cannot claim that David rather than Christ is his son; or that the *ends of the earth* were promised to David, who reigned over the single nation of the Jews alone, rather than to Christ who has now taken the whole world captive by faith in his gospel. So also Isaiah said: *I have given you as a covenant for the human race, for a light to the nations, to open the eyes that are blind,* that is, those who are in error, *to loose from their bonds those that are bound,* that is, to set them free from sins, *and from the cell of the prison,* which is death, *those who sit in darkness,* the darkness of ignorance (42:6-7). If these things are happening through Christ, they could not have been prophesied of any other person than him. For it is because of him that they are taking place.

Isaiah also writes in another place: **See, I gave him as a testimony to the nations;**

nations that have not known you shall call upon you, and people shall take refuge with you (55:4-5). Even though the prophet had just said, **I will make for you an eternal covenant, the religious and faithful things of David** (55:3), this verse cannot be taken to refer to David. It means that Christ is understood to have come from David by carnal descent because of the lineage of the virgin Mary.

In the psalm when he swears an oath to David, *Of the fruit of your body I will set on your throne* (Ps 132:11), it is this promise that he has in mind. Whose body is this? David's own? Certainly not. David could not have given birth. Nor was it his wife's body. For if that had been so, he would not have said, *of the fruit of your body,* but "of the fruit of your wife's body." So it is that by mentioning David's body he indicated that it was the fruit of the body of one of his descendants that was to be the flesh of Christ. This had its flowering out of Mary's womb. That is why he mentions only the fruit of the body, making a special point of emphasizing *body*. For he wanted to stress that it was the body alone without a husband. In that way he referred the body back to David as the head of the race and the father of the family. Because it was impossible for him to refer that *body* to the husband of the Virgin, he referred it back to the forefather. So it is that this New Covenant, which is found today in Christ, must be the one that the Creator promised when he spoke of the **sacred and faithful things of David** (55:3). These are the things of Christ because Christ is from David. . . .

It is in Christ, then, that one finds the **holy and faithful things of David**. It was he, not David, whom God set up as a **testimony to the nations** (55:4); he it was whom he made prince and commander to the nations, not David, who commanded only Israel. Today it is Christ **upon whom the nations that have not known him call**, and peoples today **take refuge** (55:5) in Christ of whom they had heard nothing in former times. You cannot say that an event will take place in the future when it is staring you in the face now.

55:5
Nations that have not known you shall call upon you.

(9) Leo the Great

Now that we have been instructed in these mysteries of divine grace,[5] dearly beloved, let us celebrate with an informed joy the day of our first fruits and the beginning of that call to the nations. Let us give thanks to the merciful God who, as the blessed apostle said, *made us worthy of a share in the lot of the saints in light, who has snatched us from darkness and the power of darkness, and transferred us to the kingdom of his beloved Son* (Col 1:12-13). For, as Isaiah prophesied, *the people who walked in darkness have seen a great light. A light has arisen for those who were living in the realm of the shadow of death* (9:2). Concerning these, the same prophet also said to the Lord: **Nations that have not known you shall call upon you, and peoples that did not know you shall flee to you** (55:5).

---

5. This passage is taken from a sermon preached on the Feast of Epiphany.

Abraham saw this day and *rejoiced* (John 8:56). He rejoiced when he realized that the children of his faith would be blessed *in his seed, which is Christ* (Gal 3:16). By believing he foresaw that he would become the *father of many nations* (Rom 4:18), *giving glory to God and knowing full well that what God promised he is capable of doing* (Rom 4:20-21).

55:6-7
Seek God, and when you find him, call upon him.

(10) Jerome

Seek the Lord while he may be found, that is, while you are in the body, when you have an opportunity for penance. Seek him not in a place but in faith. How God is to be sought is said clearly in another place. *Know the Lord in goodness, and seek him with simplicity of heart, because he is found by those who do not put him to the test; and he manifests himself to those who do not distrust him* (Wis 1:1-2). Because we know what is said about sinners, *Those who are far from you will perish* (Ps 73:27), let us say to the Lord: *Where can I go from your spirit? Or where can I flee from your presence? If I ascend to heaven, you are there; if I make my bed in Sheol, you are there* (Ps 139:7-8). Let us call upon him since he is near, that our faults and our sins will depart from us. For he draws near to those who draw near to him, and, filled with joy, he runs to meet the son who has returned after a long time (cf. Luke 15:20). *For it is good to cleave to God* (Ps 73:28).

Moses alone was able to approach near to God. Through Jeremiah God said: *I am a God who is near, not far off* (Jer 23:23 LXX). I draw near to those who draw near to me in faith, and turn away from those who separate themselves far from me in infidelity. For that reason it is said to the believers: *Draw near to God and he will draw near to you* (Jas 4:8). However, lest we think this is sufficient, he adds: *Resist the devil, and he will flee from you* (Jas 4:7) about whom he said: *Your adversary the devil, like a roaring lion, prowls around looking for someone to devour. Resist him, steadfast in faith* (1 Pet 5:8-9).

While there is still time for penitence, it is not enough **to seek the Lord to find him, nor to call upon him while he is near** (55:6), unless one gives up on evil ways and thoughts that turned one away from God. Then we can return to the Lord who is merciful to us, to the gentle Father who is filled with compassion. Having turned from our former ways, we hear the words: *Happy are those whose transgressions are forgiven and whose sins are covered* (Ps 32:1).

(11) Gregory of Nyssa

A time to seek, and a time to lose (Eccl 3:6). What is it I should seek if I wish to grasp the opportune moment? Prophecy shows what to seek when it urges, *Seek the* Lord *and be strong* (Ps 105:4). And again, **Seek the Lord, and when you find him, call upon him** (55:6). And, *Let the hearts of those who seek the* Lord *rejoice* (Ps 105:3). From these words I know that something is to be sought, and yet finding it is to seek it forever. For it is not one thing to seek, and another to find. The reward of seeking is to be found in the seeking itself.

Do you want to know the opportune time to seek the Lord? The simple answer is: all your life. In this matter alone the time to devote oneself to seeking the Lord is one's entire life. For there is no certain moment or fixed time that is good for seeking the Lord. That is a seeking that goes on continuously and without interruption — that is the truly opportune time. For it is said, *my eyes are always toward the* L{\sc ord} (Ps 25:15). Haven't you noticed how the eye searches diligently for its object, and allows itself no rest nor pause until it finds what it is seeking? By adding the word *always* the psalmist indicates the continuous and unceasing nature of the search.

(12) Augustine of Hippo

The God whom we are seeking will help us, I confidently hope, to get some fruit from our labors and to understand the meaning of the text in the holy psalm, *Let the heart of those who seek the* L{\sc ord} *rejoice! Seek the* L{\sc ord} *and be strengthened; seek his face always* (Ps 105:3-4). Now it would seem that what is always being sought is never being found, and in that case how is the heart of the seekers to rejoice and not rather grow sad, if they cannot find what they are looking for? He does not, you see, say, "Let the heart of those who find," but *of those who seek the* L{\sc ord} *rejoice.* And yet the prophet Isaiah testifies that the Lord God can be found provided he is sought, when he implores, **Seek the Lord, and as soon as you find him, call upon him, and when he draws near to you, let the godless man forsake his ways and the wicked man his thoughts** (55:6-7). So if he can be found when he is sought, why does it say, *Seek his face always*? Does he perhaps have to be sought even when he has been found? That is how incomprehensible things have to be searched for, in case the man, who has been able to find out how incomprehensible the thing is for which he is looking, should reckon that he has found nothing.

Why then look for something when you have comprehended the incomprehensibility of what you are looking for, if not because you should not give up the search as long as you are making progress in your inquiry into things incomprehensible, and because you become better and better by looking for so great a good, which is both sought in order to be found and found in order to be sought? It is sought in order to be found all the more delightfully, and it is found in order to be sought all the more avidly. This is how we might also take the words of Wisdom in the book of Ecclesiasticus [Sirach]. *Those who eat me will be hungry still, and those who drink me will be thirsty still* (Sir 24:29). They eat and drink because they find, and because they are hungry and thirsty they still go on seeking. Faith seeks, understanding finds; which is why the prophet says, *Unless you believe, you shall not understand* (Isa 7:9). And again understanding still goes on seeking the one it has found, for *God gazed down upon the sons of men,* as we chant in the sacred psalm, *to see if there is any who is understanding or looking for God* (Ps 14:2).

55:12
And all the trees of the field shall clap with their branches.

(13) Origen of Alexandria

A great audience is gathered to watch you who are engaged in conflict and are called to martyrdom. We might compare it to the vast crowd that gathered to watch the conflict between famous popular wrestlers. As you fight you may say no less than Paul: *We are become a spectacle to the world, to angels and to men* (1 Cor 4:9). The whole world, and all the angels of the right and the left,[6] and all men, both those who belong to God's portion (Deut 32:9) and the rest, will be watching us as we fight for Christianity. Either the angels in heaven will rejoice over us, and *the rivers will clap their hands together, and the hills sing for joy* (Ps 98:8), and **all the trees of the plain shall clap their branches** (55:12), or, which God forbid, those who rejoice will be the powers of darkness that delight in evil.

---

6. The phrase "angels of the right and left" may refer to the good and bad angels.

Isaiah 56

1 This is what the Lord says:
 Keep judgment, do righteousness,
 for my salvation has drawn near to arrive,
  and my mercy to be revealed.

2 Happy is the man who does these things,
  the person who holds them fast,
 who keeps the sabbaths so as not to profane them,
  and watches his hands so as not to do wrong.

3 Let not the foreigner who clings to the Lord say,
  "So then the Lord will separate me from his people";
 and let not the eunuch say,
  "I am a dry tree."
4 This is what the Lord says:
 To the eunuchs, as many as keep my sabbaths,
  and choose the things that I want,
  and hold fast my covenant,
5 I will give to them, in my house and within my wall,
  an esteemed place,
  better than sons and daughters;
 I will give them an everlasting name,
  and it shall not fail.

6 And to the foreigners who cling to the Lord,
  to serve him, to love the name of the Lord,
  so that they may be his male and female slaves —
 and as for all who keep my sabbaths so as not to profane them,
  and hold fast my covenant —
7 I will bring them into my holy mountain,

and make them joyful in my house of prayer;
their burnt offerings and their sacrifices
will be acceptable on my altar;
for my house shall be called a house of prayer
for all the nations —
8 said the Lord, who gathers the dispersed of Israel —
for I will gather to him a gathering.
9 All you wild animals that live in the fields,
all you wild animals of the forest, come here, eat!
10 Observe that all have become totally blind,
they have not learned how to think;
they are all silent dogs,
they will not be able to bark;
dreaming in bed,
loving to slumber.
11 The dogs are shameless in their soul,
not knowing satisfaction.
They are evil,
not knowing understanding.
They have all followed their own ways,
each in the same manner.

According to the synoptic gospels, when Jesus drove the money changers from the temple he cited 56:7, **My house shall be called a house of prayer for all nations***. But in the early Church the passage in chapter 56 that particularly stood out was the mention of* **eunuchs** *(56:4), who are not excluded from participation in the covenant people of God. In the Torah, eunuchs were excluded "from entering the assembly of the* LORD*" (Deut 23:1). But, according to the oracle in this chapter, on the day of God's deliverance not only those who keep the Sabbath, but also* **eunuchs** *(56:4) who hold fast to the covenant and* **foreigners** *(56:3) will be welcomed. Indeed, they will be given a place in God's* **house . . . better than sons and daughters** *(56:5). The passage in Isaiah is speaking about physical eunuchs, that is, males who have been castrated, but in the New Testament Jesus speaks of those who have made themselves eunuchs for the sake of the kingdom of heaven (Matt 19:12). As Christians pondered this chapter, the question arose whether Isaiah was speaking about actual eunuchs or those who abstained from sexual relations to give themselves fully to serving God.*

In the second century, Julius Cassian, once a follower of the Gnostic Valentinus, appealed to the blessing of eunuchs in Isaiah 56 to support his rejection of marriage and procreation. The selection from Clement of Alexandria responds to Julius's interpretation of the passage. In the fourth century, when asceticism was on the rise, a Christian monk named Jovinian denied that virginity was a higher state than marriage. In support he argued that the eunuchs mentioned in Isaiah 56 were actual eunuchs, not spiritual eunuchs, that is, ascetics. Hence the text does not mean that those who have chosen celibacy should be ranked higher in the kingdom than those who marry. In his Commentary on Isaiah *Jerome, a fierce critic of Jovinian, argues that the passage refers to eunuchs for the sake of the kingdom. Augustine, in his treatise* On Holy Virginity, *a defense of the life of consecrated virginity and a complement to his treatise* On the Good of Marriage, *also defends a "spiritual" reading of the text.*

The excerpt from Jerome is given first (after the passage from the Gospel of Mark) because it is taken from his commentary and deals with other verses in the chapter than the verses on **eunuchs**. *The excerpts from Clement and Augustine deal only with the meaning of the passage on* **eunuchs**.

(1) The Gospel according to Matthew

The disciples said to him, "If such is the case of a man with his wife, it is not expedient to marry." But he said to them, "Not all men can receive this saying, but only those to whom it is given. For there are eunuchs who have been so from birth, and there are eunuchs who have been made eunuchs by men, and there are eunuchs who have made themselves eunuchs for the sake of the kingdom of heaven. He who is able to receive this, let him receive it."

(2) Gospel according to Mark

And they came to Jerusalem. And he entered the temple and began to drive out those who sold and those who bought in the temple, and he overturned the tables of the money-changers and the seats of those who sold pigeons; and he would not allow any one to carry anything through the temple. And he taught, and said to them, "Is it not written, **My house shall be called a house of prayer for all nations**? But you have made it a den of robbers."

(3) Jerome

Thus says the Lord: "Keep judgment, and do justice, for soon my salvation will come, and my justice be revealed" (56:1). The seventy have written "mercy" instead of **justice**, and others have done likewise. After the conclusion of the prophecy about the Gentiles, who are to be changed from the *thorn* and the *brier* into the *cypress* and the *myrtle* (55:13) at the coming of the Word of God, Isaiah tells the hearers of that time to do everything that is right, and to prepare themselves for the coming of the Savior, since he is himself the **justice** and the **mercy** (56:1) of God. For if the thoughts of the saints are judgments (cf. Prov 12:5), and we ought to *have faculties trained to distinguish good from evil* (Heb 5:14), then why should we not guard judgment at all times, lest in judgment we show partiality to a poor man, or be frightened by the power of a rich man? Let us rather judge the great and the small alike, since we know, according to Moses, that judgment is of the Lord, who judges those who judge (Deut 1:17). This is in accordance with what we read in the psalm, *God stood in the congregation of the gods; and in their midst he passes judgment on the gods* (Ps 82:1). What is said in our text, **keep judgment, and do justice** (56:1), is similar to what is found in another passage, *Blessed are they who guard judgment, who do justice at all times* (Ps 106:3), such that they *justly follow what is just* (Deut 16:20 Vg.). Nevertheless, by the term **justice** I think every virtue is meant, because whoever does justice is said to have fulfilled in turn all the virtues that follow and adhere to it. To the extent that you have one, you have them all, and to the extent that you lack one, you lack them all. That is what the fifteenth psalm also expresses, *He who walks blamelessly, and does justice* (Ps 15:2). And in another place it is written, *Learn justice, you who dwell on the earth* (Isa 26:9 Vg.). Moreover, the Savior, *who was made our justice, sanctification, and redemption* (1 Cor 1:30), is himself the mercy of God, as the words of the saints testify, *God sent forth his mercy and his truth* (Ps 57:3).

Happy is the man who does this, and the son of man who will hold it fast, who keeps the sabbath, not profaning it, and keeps his hand from doing any evil. LXX: Happy is the man who does these things, the person who holds them fast, who keeps the sabbaths so as not to profane them, and watches his hands so as not to do wrong (56:2). Such a man can say with the apostle, *When I was a child, I spoke like a child, I thought like a child, I reasoned like a child; when I became a man, I gave up childish ways* (1 Cor 13:11). He pursues blessedness in the present by forgetting the past and straining toward the future (cf. Phil 3:13), until he should attain *to the unity of the faith, to the knowledge of the Son of God, to mature manhood, to the measure of the age of the fullness of Christ* (Eph 4:13). To him can be applied that psalm, *Blessed is the man who walks not in the counsel of the ungodly* (Ps 1:1). This is the man, and the son of the inner man, about whom it is often said in Leviticus, *a man, a man* (Lev 17:8 Vg.). He is blessed in that he is the first to do these things, and he will hold fast to these things, that is, to the judgment, justice, and the salvation of the Lord, which are soon to be revealed to all the Gentiles. Thus he not only does what is commanded, he holds onto it with a clenched fist, and he **keeps the sabbath, not profaning it** (56:2). Now as to the Sabbath which the Lord commanded to be observed, the following phrase shows what it is: **and keeps his hand from doing any evil** (56:2). For it is of no use to sit around on the Sabbath, or to lie there and long for a feast. On the contrary, if one is trying to do good, let him abstain from evil, let him have a perpetual Sabbath, a cessation, that is, from iniquity, let him do only those things that pertain to the soul's salvation, and let him undertake no servile work. For *everyone who commits sin is a slave to sin* (John 8:34). We, however, were called to the freedom with which Christ has endowed us (cf. Gal 5:1), so that we do not by any means *labor for the food which perishes* (John 6:27). Rather, drawing near to the Lord, let us say with the prophet, *But for me it is good to cleave to God* (Ps 73:28). Let us be one spirit with him, and let us keep the Sabbath with delight (cf. Isa 58:13), lest we be of the six days in which the world was made. For the apostles were not of those days, and the Lord said to them, *If you were of the world, the world would love its own; but because you are not of the world, but I chose you out of the world, therefore the world hates you* (John 15:19).

Let not the foreigner who has joined himself to the Lord say, "The Lord will surely separate me from his people"; and let not the eunuch say, "Behold, I am a dry tree." LXX: Let not the foreigner who clings to the Lord say, "So then the Lord will separate me from his people"; and let not the eunuch say, "I am a dry tree" (56:3). Those who understand this passage in a lowly manner insist that these words really do refer to proselytes from the Gentiles and to eunuchs. For foreigners, if they take upon themselves the law of God and are circumcised, as well as eunuchs are not beyond salvation. For the eunuch who belonged to Queen Candace was not idle even while on a journey. He sought out an interpreter for what he was reading and found Christ whom he sought (Acts 8:27-38).

Some believe that this passage is directed against Jews who boast of the nobility of their race, who say that they are the sons of Abraham, and who think that those who have seed in Zion and relatives in Jerusalem are blessed (cf. Matt 3:9; Luke 3:8; John 8:39-59). We understand the passage to be referring to the same people mentioned above who were called to faith in the gospel. For the *thorn* and *brier* (*konyzēn* and *stoibēn* in Greek) have been changed into trees, that is, into the *cypress* and the *myrtle* (55:13). So if they draw near to the Lord, they ought not to despair; neither should they think that they are separated from the people of God. For all who have been *baptized into Christ have put on Christ* (Gal 3:27). It is not the Jew and the heathen, the circumcised and the uncircumcised (cf. Col 3:11) to whom the command is given in the song of Deuteronomy, *Rejoice, you gentiles, with his people* (Deut 32:43 Vg.). *People* here refers to the people of God, that is, the people of the Jews whom he had previously made his own. But the Gentiles will come from the east and the west and rest in the bosom of Abraham (cf. Matt 8:11; Luke 16:22-23). This is what John the Baptist said as well, *And do not presume to say to yourselves, "We have Abraham as our father"; for I tell you, God is able from these stones to raise up children to Abraham* (Matt 3:9). As there is no distinction among proselytes, and men and women alike are called to salvation, so also there is no distinction among eunuchs *who have made themselves eunuchs for the sake of the kingdom of heaven* (Matt 19:12). Both sexes are received. For they have put to death their members on earth — fornication, impurity, passion, and evil desire — until they come to *maturity* (Eph 4:13), and say with the apostle, *we know no one according to the flesh; even though we once knew Christ according to the flesh, we know him thus no longer* (2 Cor 5:16). Therefore they can in no way be understood to be among the eunuchs whom the spirited poet describes:

> Unfortunate youths mutilated by the sword,
>   and emasculated. . . .[1]

On the contrary, they are the ones to whom the Lord referred in the Gospel, *who have made themselves eunuchs for the sake of the kingdom of heaven* (Matt 19:12). Such were the apostles. When they were astonished at how high the barrier had been set, they said, *Who then can be saved?* The Savior replied, *He who is able to receive this, let him receive it* (Matt 19:25, 12). So even the apostle bears witness that there is no command from the Lord about becoming actual eunuchs, that is, someone without sexual experience. Rather, having obtained mercy from the Lord, his advice, as it were, is that all be like himself. *For*, he says, *the appointed time has grown very short; from now on, let those who have wives live as though they had none* (1 Cor 7:29). Whoever has been called away from the bonds and duties of marriage is truly a servant of Christ.

---

1. Lucan, *On the Civil War* 10.133-34.

Isaiah 56

For thus says the Lord: "To the eunuchs who keep my sabbaths, who choose the things that please me and hold fast my covenant, I will give in my house and within my walls a place and a name better than sons and daughters; I will give them an everlasting name which shall not be cut off." LXX: **Thus says the Lord: To the eunuchs, as many as keep my sabbaths, and choose the things that I want, and hold fast my covenant, I will give to them, in my house and within my wall, an esteemed place, better than sons and daughters; I will give them an everlasting name, and it shall not fail** (56:4-5). He is speaking of two different groups of people, the proselytes and the eunuchs. First he speaks about the eunuchs to whom he sets forth precepts for living, and he promises them future rewards. After them he comes to the proselytes, to whom he promises similar things. So he tells the eunuchs, who cried out in despair, **Behold, I am a dry tree** (56:3), not to think that they are under the curse pronounced to the infertile, *Cursed is the infertile man who does not produce seed in Israel* (cf. Exod 23:26; Deut 7:14). "**If**, he says, **they keep my sabbaths, and they choose from my precepts** the things that please me, and not the things that I allowed because of the weakness of my hearers, **and if they hold fast my covenant**, or testament, in all good faith, **I will give to them a place in my house**, in my temple, **and within the walls** of my unshakeable city, **and a name that is better than sons and daughters**, that will not be consigned to oblivion" (56:4-5). We have mentioned above who the eunuchs are: they are the ones who make their business the things of God. The book of Wisdom, which is entitled "of Solomon," says to them, *Blessed is the barren woman who is undefiled, who has not entered into a sinful union; she will have fruit when God examines souls. Blessed also is the eunuch whose hands have done no lawless deed, and who has not devised wicked things against the Lord; for special favor will be shown him for his faithfulness, and a place of great delight in the temple of the Lord* (Wis 3:13-14). This barren woman is fertile even though she is a virgin; this eunuch makes an assault on the kingdom of heaven, and puts forth a great effort to grasp it. He keeps the Sabbath to such a degree that he never practices sexual intercourse. He has chosen the things that please the Lord and offers more than what is commanded; he does not seek *concession* as an apostle of the Lord (1 Cor 7:6), but only to do his will. He keeps the everlasting covenant of the Lord, so that he does not *devote himself to prayer only for a spell and then return to the same thing again* (1 Cor 7:5-6).[2] Rather, he knows that there is waiting for him the best place in the house of the Lord, which is the Church of the Lord. For *in the Father's house there are many mansions* (John 14:2). Whoever is a eunuch, and does all the things that are written, will have the best place within his walls. In that way the tower of the Lord may be built, and he will be ranked among the priests and will have many spiritual sons rather than sons of the flesh.

The church histories relate that John the Evangelist, whom Jesus loved the most, was such a eunuch. He reclined on Jesus' breast (John 13:23). While Peter walked more slowly, John ran to the Lord, borne aloft on the wings of virginity. Immersing himself in the mysteries of divine generation, he dared to say what all the ages did not know: *In the*

---

2. Jerome is playing with Paul's language in 1 Corinthians 7 about a married person devoting himself to prayer and then "returning" to his wife for sexual intercourse. The eunuch for the sake of the kingdom devotes himself wholly to prayer.

beginning was the Word, and the Word was with God, and the Word was God. He was in the beginning with God (John 1:1-2). Therefore, let all the scoffing of the Jews be set aside and mockery cease; a eunuch can open up the kingdom of heaven, for chastity lies not in weakness of the body but in resoluteness of will.

And the foreigners who join themselves to the Lord, to minister to him, to love the name of the Lord, and to be his servants, every one who keeps the sabbath, and does not profane it, and holds fast my covenant — these I will bring to my holy mountain, and make them joyful in my house of prayer. LXX: **And to the foreigners who cling to the Lord, to serve him, to love the name of the Lord, so that they may be his bondmen÷[3] and bondwomen — and as for all who keep my sabbaths so as not to profane them, and hold fast my covenant — I will bring them into my holy mountain, and make them joyful in my house of prayer** (56:6-7). After the eunuchs, he passes to the foreigners, whom he had mentioned first, and he promises them rewards as well. For if they serve him, and pass from obligatory service to the love of his name, then they are truly his servants. Such was the apostle Paul, who writes in the beginning of his letter, *Paul, a servant of Jesus Christ* (Rom 1:1). Moses was also a servant of God (cf. Num 12:7; Heb 3:5). However, as to what is added in the LXX, **and bondwomen**, we have marked it with an *obelus* (÷). For in spiritual gifts there cannot be any difference due to sex, since *in Christ Jesus there is neither male nor female* (Gal 3:28; Col 3:11). Rather, all who are in him are one. Of the Sabbath and the everlasting covenant we have spoken above. Whoever, then, does these things God will lead to his holy mountain and will cause them to rejoice in his house of prayer. This holy mountain, to which, according to Isaiah as well as the prophet Micah, a great number of Gentiles will stream at the end of time (Isa 2:2; Mic 4:1), can be understood to signify either the true teaching that confesses the Trinity, or the Lord himself. The house of prayer is the Church, which is dispersed throughout the whole world; it is not the temple of the Jews, which was restricted to the narrow confines of the land of Judea.

(4) Clement of Alexandria

In his book *Abstinence* or *Chastity* Julius Cassian says this: "Let no one say, seeing that we have these parts, the female being shaped this way and the male body that way, the one to receive and the other to give seed, that sexual intercourse is therefore condoned by God. For if this arrangement were made by God toward whom we tend, he would not have blessed eunuchs; nor would the prophet have said: **eunuchs are not an unfruitful tree** (56:3), using the tree to signify someone who chose to emasculate himself of such an idea." . . .

---

3. As he explains below, Jerome here indicates with the sign called the *obelus* that the word **bondwomen** is contained in the LXX but is missing from the Hebrew. The *asteriskos*, an "x" with four dots set between the legs of the "x," was used to indicate passages absent from the LXX but found in the Hebrew. The use of these textual signs originated with the work of the Alexandrian philologists who prepared the editions of the Greek classics. Origen introduced them into Christian scholarship in his edition of the Old Testament known as the Hexapla, and Jerome followed Origen's practice.

In response the Lord gives the following promises: **Let the eunuch not say, "I am a dry tree." The Lord says this to eunuchs: If you keep my sabbaths and do all the things I command, I will give you a better place than sons and daughters** (56:3-5). For a eunuch is not justified merely because he is a eunuch, and certainly not because he keeps the Sabbath, if he does not keep the commandments. Further on the prophet addresses those who are married in this way: *My chosen ones shall not labor in vain nor bear children for a curse, because they are an offspring blessed by God* (65:23). For whoever begets children and rears them and trains them in the Lord, just as for someone who begets children by means of the true instruction, a reward is laid up, as also for the chosen seed. But those who hold that procreation is a curse do not realize that the Scripture speaks against them.

A eunuch, then, does not mean one who has been castrated or someone unmarried, but one who does not produce truth. Once he was a **dry tree** (56:3), but if he obeys the word and **keeps the sabbaths** (56:4) by refraining from sins and observing the commandments, he will receive greater honor than those who are instructed in word alone and fail to live by what is right. *Little children,* our teacher says, *yet a little while and I am with you* (John 13:33). This is why Paul, addressing the Galatians, says: *My little children, with whom I am again in travail until Christ be formed in you* (Gal 4:19). And again he writes to the Corinthians: *For though you have countless instructors in Christ, you do not have many fathers. For I became your father in Christ through the gospel* (1 Cor 4:15). So when it reads that *a eunuch will not enter the church of God* (Deut 23:1), this refers to someone who is unproductive and unfruitful in life and in word. But those who *have made themselves eunuchs* free of sin *for the sake of the kingdom of heaven* (Matt 19:12) by fasting from the things of the world will be blessed.

(5) Augustine of Hippo

Who are the eunuchs God speaks of through the prophet Isaiah when he asserts that he will give them an **esteemed place in his house, much better than the one his sons and daughters have** (56:5)? They must be those who have *made themselves eunuchs for the sake of the kingdom of heaven* (Matt 19:12). However, there are actual eunuchs who serve kings and rich people. They have castrated themselves and cannot have children. When they become Christians and keep God's commandments yet have the view that they would have married had they been able to, they are equal in God's house to the rest of the faithful who married and had children in a legitimate union and raised them in the fear of God, teaching them to put their hope in God. But they are not to be given a **better place than that of the sons and daughters** (56:5). For they remained unmarried not because they were strong spiritually but because they had a physical impediment.

To be sure, one could claim that this prophecy had reference to actual eunuchs. But even this error supports our argument. For God did not prefer those eunuchs to those who have no place in his house, but to those who have the place deserved for those who marry and have children. When he says, **I will give them a much better place** (56:5), he shows that married persons will be given a place too, though a much inferior one.

Let us then grant that it was foretold that there would be actual eunuchs in God's house, although there were none among the people of Israel. For we see that they became Christians though they did not become Jews. Let us also grant that the prophet was not speaking about those who did not seek marriage because they had chosen to be celibate and made themselves eunuchs for the sake of the kingdom of heaven. But is there anyone so demented and opposed to the truth that he would believe that those who are actual eunuchs have a more honored place than those who are married — and then go on to claim that those who choose to be celibate and who shun marriage by disciplining their bodies, "castrating" their bodies not literally but by cutting desire at the root, and following a heavenly and angelical way of life while living in this mortal life, that such people deserve only the same merit as those who are married?

Would a Christian contradict Christ when he praises those who make themselves eunuchs not for this age but for the kingdom of heaven, and hold that this is advantageous for the present life but not for the life to come? This is like saying that the kingdom of heaven has reference to this earthly life in which we are now living. . . . Even though the Church which exists in the world is sometimes called the kingdom of heaven, the reason it is called this is that it exists for the future life. Although it has a *promise for the present life and also for the life to come* (1 Tim 4:8), in all its good works it looks *not to the things that are seen but to the things that are unseen; for the things that are seen are transient, but the things that are unseen are eternal* (2 Cor 4:18).

The Holy Spirit certainly did not keep silent in the face of those impudent, mindless, and stubborn claims. In fact he spoke forcefully, clearly, and firmly against their ferocious onslaught and provided his flock with an unassailable fortification. He said: **I will give to them in my house and within my wall an esteemed place, better than that of sons and daughters** (56:5). But to prevent someone who is carnally minded from thinking that these words offer hope for some type of temporal benefit, he immediately adds: **I will give them an eternal name, and it shall never fail** (56:5). It is as if he had said: "Why in your spiritual blindness do you ignore this? . . . Why do you promise benefits only in this life for those who are holy persons who embrace celibacy? **I will give them eternal name.** . . . And if by chance you take **eternal** to mean "long lasting," I can add more, pile it on, press it down: **and it shall never fail**. What more do you want? What more can you say? Whatever that may be, it indicates that **an eternal name** will be given to eunuchs. And this signifies a unique and special honor that they will not share with others, even though they will have a place in the same kingdom and in the same house. Perhaps it is called a **name** to distinguish those to whom it is given from the rest.

Isaiah 60

1 Shine, shine, O Ierousalem; for your light has come,
   and the glory of the Lord has risen upon you.
2 Look, darkness and gloom
   shall cover the earth upon the nations;
  but the Lord will appear upon you,
   and his glory will be seen upon you.
3 Kings shall walk by your light,
   and nations by your brightness.

4 Lift up your eyes round about,
   and see your children gathered together;
  look, all your sons have come from far away,
   and your daughters shall be carried on shoulders.
5 Then you shall see and be afraid
   and be amazed in your heart,
  because the wealth of the sea and of nations and of peoples
   shall change over to you.
  And there shall come to you
6   herds of camels,
  and the camels of Madiam and Gaiphar
   shall cover you.
  All those from Saba shall come,
   bringing gold;
  and they shall bring frankincense,
   and announce the good news of the salvation of the Lord.
7 And all the sheep of Kedar shall be gathered to you,
   and the rams of Nabaioth shall come to you;
  and acceptable things shall be offered on my altar,
   and my house of prayer shall be glorified.

8 Who are these that fly like clouds,
    and like doves with their young?
9 The islands waited for me,
    and the ships of Tharsis among the first,
to bring your children from far away,
    and their silver and gold with them,
because of the holy name of the Lord,
    and because the Holy One of Israel is glorious.
10 And foreigners shall build up your walls,
    and their kings shall attend to you;
for because of my wrath I struck you down,
    but because of my mercy I loved you.
11 And your gates shall always be opened —
    day and night they shall not be shut —
to bring to you the power of nations,
    and kings who are being led away.
12 For the nations and kings
    that will not serve you shall perish,
    and the nations shall be made desolate with desolation.
13 And the glory of Lebanon shall come to you,
    with cypress and pine and cedar together,
    to glorify my holy place.
14 The sons of those who humbled and provoked you
    shall come to you with dread;
you shall be called City of the Lord,
    Sion of the Holy One of Israel.
15 Because you have become forsaken and hated,
    and there was none who helped;
and I will make you an everlasting gladness,
    a joy for generations of generations.
16 You shall suck the milk of nations,
    and you shall eat the wealth of kings;
and you shall know that I am the Lord who saves you
    and rescues you, the God of Israel.

17 And instead of bronze I will bring you gold,
    instead of iron I will bring you silver;
instead of wood I will bring you bronze,
    instead of stones, iron.
And I will appoint your rulers in peace,
    and your overseers in righteousness.
18 And injustice shall no more be heard in your land,
    nor destruction or wretchedness within your borders;
rather, your walls shall be called Salvation,

and your gates Sculpture.
19 And the sun shall not be
    to you as a light by day,
    nor shall the rising of the moon
    give light to you at night;
    but the Lord will be to you an everlasting light,
    and God will be your glory.
20 For your sun shall not go down,
    and your moon shall not fail;
    for the Lord will be to you an everlasting light,
    and the days of your mourning shall be fulfilled.
21 Your people shall all be righteous,
    and they shall inherit the land forever,
    guarding their plant,
    the works of their hands, for glory.
22 The smallest one shall become thousands,
    and the least, a great nation;
    I the Lord will gather them in due time.

The opening verses of this chapter are read on the Feast of Epiphany when the Church celebrates the proclamation of the gospel to all peoples of the world, signified by the three wise men from the East who came to worship the newborn babe. Early Christian commentators interpreted Isaiah 60 as a prophecy of the manifestation of the light of Christ to the nations. Cyril observes that the prophet speaks with such vividness that the passage reads more like a depiction of what has already happened than what is to come at the end of the age. Though this interpretation of Isaiah 60 was not found in the New Testament, it was widespread in the early Church and became part of the liturgical tradition. Most of the church fathers believed that the christological interpretation of the Old Testament should not be restricted to those passages that were cited or alluded to in the New Testament.

Jerome says that the words **Lift up your eyes round about, and see; they all gather together, they come to you** *(60:4 in the Hebrew version) were first addressed to the Church which was gathered in Zion through the apostles. In the Septuagint version of Isa 60:17 the word* **taskmasters** *was translated into Greek as* episkopoi, *meaning "overseers," which in Christian usage became the name for the office of the bishop; this prompted Clement of Rome and Irenaeus to speak about the character of a faithful pastor or bishop, and their line of interpretation became quite common. Verses 19-20, which begin,* **The sun shall not be to you as a light by day**, *received two different interpretations. In one, the passage was taken eschatologically to refer to the end of time, when the heaven and earth will pass away. But in the other interpretation, writers took it to mean, as Ambrose put it, that there are some people "for whom it is always day" because Christ is always present to them.*

(1) The Revelation to John

And I saw no temple in the city, for its temple is the Lord God the Almighty and the Lamb. And the city has **no need of sun or moon, for the glory of God is its light** (60:19), and its lamp is the Lamb. By its light shall the nations walk; and the kings of the earth shall bring their glory into it, and its gates shall never be shut by day — and there shall be no night there; they shall bring into it the glory and the honor of the nations.

(2) Cyril of Alexandria

It is as though the promise that Israel will be saved had already been fulfilled! The prophetic message, as it were, skips forward to the time when we knew great joy. Raising his voice to the heights, the prophet proclaims: **Shine, shine, O Jerusalem; for your light has come** (60:1). Note that the divine light that comes from God shines on the Israelites before it shines on other nations. It is also clear that when the prophet asserts, **your light has come**, he is referring to the light that has come through Christ. He all but says that Christ, who was long ago predicted by the law and the holy prophets, was already present among them and now at the end of the age has shone on all who dwell on earth.

He calls the one who appeared **the glory of the Lord** (60:1), for Christ **has risen** like a kind of sun shining all around with divine and spiritual light to bring the radiance of the true knowledge of God to those who are eager to believe. He is the glory of God the Father. Indeed, in him and through him and with him God is glorified. In his own nature he is a living portrait of the one who begot him. Since we have known the Son, through him and in him we have seen the majesty of the Father, the incomparable glory and the surpassing excellence that befit God alone. Christ himself said somewhere, *Father, glorify thy Son that the Son may glorify thee* (John 17:1). In this way, the glory of God the Father has appeared among us.

Then, setting Israel apart from all other nations as especially honored by God and as God's own portion, he adds: **Look, darkness and gloom shall cover the earth upon the nations** (60:2). This does not mean that Christ has shone forth in the world with the intent to spread darkness over the nations. It means rather that the world has been illuminated, and he has cast out the darkness of the ancient error. Very frequently those who translated Holy Scripture did not give the proper rendering of the tenses. Thus they wrote **shall cover** instead of **covers**. When Christ shone on the Israelites before other nations, the multitude of the nations was still overcome with darkness and grace had not yet been brought to them. That is why it says, **Behold**, it has been covered with **darkness** and **gloom**. Though the darkness of ignorance and deceit covered all the lands of the Gentiles, **the Lord will rise upon you** (60:2). On them he shone, as the text indicates, and his **glory** first appeared to them through his marvelous works, his signs and wonders. Since he was God, he worked wonders among them, raising the dead from their graves, giving sight to the eyes of the blind, cleansing lepers with a simple gesture, rebuking demons with authority, and, in general, using every means to confirm that he is God in truth and the Son of God by nature.

Kings shall walk by your light, and nations by your brightness (60:3). The prophet again links the calling of the nations to the visitation of the Israelites. For if they slight the Redeemer, and turn away from his love and bring ruin on themselves, God will not be deprived of worshipers. Instead he will cast his net for others, for nations and kings, to come to him by faith. He then says that **kings and nations shall walk by the brightness** given to you, that is, by the light of Christ. Where will they go? To salvation by faith, of course, to a noble and blameless life, to knowing and confessing the One who is by nature truly the Creator and Fashioner of the world. For the nations worshiped *the creature rather than the Creator* (Rom 1:25), venerating trees and stones. But once they had been illuminated by the light given to them, they walked the straight and royal road and did not stumble over anything lying in the way. Though they were children of the night and of darkness (cf. 1 Thess 5:5), they slipped past all obstacles on the path as though it were bright as day.

Lift up your eyes round about . . . (60:4-7). This passage is arranged with understanding and skill. It tells the Good News about the call of the nations, the union of the two peoples in Christ, and the transition from the shadow of the law to spiritual worship. In Christ all things are new and the old things have passed away. *He himself created one new man in place of the two, so making peace, and reconciled both to the Father in one body* (Eph 2:15-16). He predicts all this and maintains that the spiritual Jerusalem, that is, the Church, is initially composed of Jews, for they were the first to believe.

This passage refers to the Church, for the preaching of the holy gospel draws believers from every nation and land under heaven and persuades them to come to a kind of well-fortified city, to grace through faith, to the nourishment given the saints, that is, to the Church. So also in another place the prophet said: *It shall come to pass in the latter days that the mountain of the house of the* LORD *shall be established as the highest of the mountains, and shall be raised above the hills; and all the nations shall flow to it, and many peoples shall come, and say: "Come, let us go up to the mountain of the* LORD*, to the house of the God of Jacob; that he may teach us his ways and that we may walk in his paths"* (2:2-3).

The children of Jerusalem will be not only Israelites by blood but also people from every nation and land called to the light of truth through faith. As the most-wise Paul writes, *Not all who are descended from Israel belong to Israel, and not all are children of Abraham because they are his descendants; but . . . the children of the promise are reckoned as descendants* (Rom 9:6-8). And to holy Abraham God said, *I have made you the father of many nations* (Rom 4:17). Accordingly, Isaiah speaks as though the multitude had already been gathered from the nations and was worshiping Christ.

He beckons, **Lift up our eyes round about** (60:4), that is, look around the whole inhabited earth and from its every region you shall see your children hastening to you, they who were once far from you, not only geographically but in mind and heart. For example, one of the holy prophets said to those who were running away from the knowledge of the one true God: *Remember the* LORD *from afar, and let Jerusalem come into your mind* (Jer 51:50). Furthermore, the most-wise Paul wrote concerning Christ, *He came and preached peace to you who were far off and peace to those who were near* (Eph 2:17). He also wrote to those from the Gentiles, *Remember that you were at that time separated* *from Christ, alienated from the commonwealth of Israel, and strangers to the covenants of promise, having no hope and without God in the world. But now in Christ Jesus you who once were far off have been brought near in the blood of Christ* (Eph 2:12-13). Those who were wholly ignorant of the one true God are said to be far off, that is, distant in mind and heart, as I have already mentioned. But behold, they **have come** (60:4), as the text indicates, that is, they would soon be called, and they hearkened to the gospel at once and made their approach to God through faith without labor or hardship or sweat.

They **shall be carried on the shoulders** (60:4). This expression of course is drawn from human experience. For newborn children are accustomed to being nursed and seek comfort within their mothers' arms and upon their breasts. Here it is applied to those who have been called to leave the folly of the Greeks and are healed and abundantly nourished through the sacraments. Such is the case for those who are called from the deception of the Greeks, whose errors are gently healed by the Church's teachers. At first they do not take the difficult road, but they are gradually led to drink milk until little by little they ascend to *mature manhood, to the measure of the stature of the fullness of Christ* (Eph 4:13). Moreover, the holy apostles were commanded to *baptize all nations in the name of the Father and of the Son and of the Holy Spirit, and to teach them to observe everything they had been commanded* (Matt 28:19-20). In their readiness to do this, as skilled teachers they laid nothing unduly burdensome on those who first came to faith. To the Gentiles they wrote: *For it has seemed good to the Holy Spirit and to us to lay upon you no greater burden than . . . that you abstain from unchastity and from what is strangled and from blood* (Acts 15:28-29). The most excellent Paul also wrote to others: *I fed you with milk, not solid food; for you were not ready for it; and even yet you are not ready* (1 Cor 3:2). Solid food belongs to the mature, to those whose sensibilities of the heart have been trained through habit to discern good and evil. That is why it says that your **sons and daughters shall be carried on the shoulders** (60:4).

60:4
Lift up your eyes round about, and see your children gathered together; look, all your sons have come from far away, and your daughters shall be carried on shoulders.

(3) Jerome

The words, **Lift up your eyes round about, and see; they all gather together** (60:4), are addressed to the Church which first was gathered in Zion by the apostles. In the Acts of the Apostles we read that there were devout men in Jerusalem from all over the world who received the word of God. Whether in a foreign language or in their own tongue, they heard other men speaking or they themselves spoke to others (Acts 2). And they were instructed to lift up their eyes round about, as the Lord had also commanded the apostles, saying: *Lift up your eyes, and see how the fields are already white for harvest* (John 4:35). *For out of Zion* — not Mount Sinai — *shall go forth the law, and the word of the Lord God from Jerusalem* (Isa 2:3).

Zion was also instructed with uplifted eyes to behold her own sons who are gathered together and come from afar. For to her is said: *Rejoice greatly, O daughter of Zion; speak forth, O daughter of Jerusalem; for lo, I come and I will dwell in the midst of you, says the LORD. And many nations shall join themselves to the LORD in that day, and shall be my people; and I will dwell in the midst of you* (Zeph 3:14; Zech 2:10-11). Now we are the children who come to the Lord from afar, since at one time we were strangers to the *covenant of God and his promises, having no hope and without God in the world* (Eph 2:12). What does the apostle say: *You who once were far off have been brought near* (Eph 2:13)?

And your daughters shall be nursed at your side (60:4). This signifies that the souls of those who are nurslings in Christ or are little children in Baptism suck the milk of the apostles. Concerning them the apostle Peter also writes: *Like newborn babes, they long for the pure spiritual milk* (1 Pet 2:2). To these little children and nurslings the apostle Paul also was speaking: *My little children, with whom I am again in travail until Christ be formed in you!* (Gal 4:19). And in another place: *Like a nurse taking care of her children, so being affectionately desirous of you, we were ready to share with you not only the gospel of God but also our own selves* (1 Thess 2:7, 8).

60:8
Who are these that fly like clouds, and like doves with their young?

(4) Tertullian

There is a gate which opens to heaven and a way which leads us there, laid down by Christ. When Amos says of him, *Who builds up his ascent into heaven* (Amos 9:6), he surely does not mean for himself alone, but for those who are his own who will be with him. *And you shall bind them upon you*, it is said, *like adornment upon a bride* (Isa 49:18). So the Spirit marvels at those who by that ascent are making their way to heavenly kingdoms, saying: **They fly like hawks, as the clouds fly, and as the nestlings of doves, toward me** (60:8). This means that they fly in simplicity, like doves. For we shall be taken up *in the clouds to meet the Lord* (1 Thess 4:17), the apostle promises, when that son of man of whom Daniel speaks (Dan 7:13) comes on the clouds; and we will be with the Lord always, for he is both on earth and in heaven. And because some have no gratitude for either promise,[1] he calls upon even the elements to bear witness: *Hear, O heaven, and give ear, O earth* (Isa 1:2). For my part, although the Scripture did not hold out to me the hand of heavenly hope (giving me sufficient reason to expect this promise too), nevertheless, because I am already in possession of earthly grace, I should also expect something from heaven, from God who is the God of heaven and of earth. I believe that the Christ who promises higher things is the Christ of him who had also promised more lowly things, of God who by small things had given proof of things greater, who also had reserved for Christ alone this proclamation of a kingdom unheard of — if it was unheard of — so that earthly glory should be spoken of by servants, but heavenly glory by God himself.

1. Earthly and heavenly.

60:17
I will appoint your princes in peace, and your overseers in righteousness.

(5) Clement of Rome[2]

Therefore, having received their instructions, and having been fully assured through the resurrection of our Lord Jesus Christ, and having believed in the word of God, with the full assurance of the Holy Spirit, the apostles went forth preaching the good news that the kingdom of God was coming. Therefore, preaching in each region and city, testing their first converts by the Spirit, they established bishops and deacons over those who would believe. And this is nothing new, for it has been written about bishops and deacons for many years; thus the Scripture says in one place, **I will establish their bishops in righteousness, and their deacons in faith** (60:17).

(6) Irenaeus of Lyons

Isaiah speaks about the presbyters who care for the Church when he writes: **I will give your princes in peace, and your bishops in righteousness** (60:17). And the Lord also said concerning them: *Who then is the faithful manager, good and wise, whom the Lord has set over his household to give them their food at the proper time? Blessed is that servant whom the Lord when he comes will find doing things so* (Matt 24:45-46). Paul then teaches us where one will find such a person when he says: *And God has appointed in the church first apostles, second prophets, third teachers* (1 Cor 12:28). Hence where the gifts of God have been placed, there we are to learn the truth, namely, from those who stand in the succession of the apostles, where the way of life is upstanding and irreproachable, and whose word is unadulterated and incorrupt. For these also are the guardians of our faith in the one God who created all things; and they help us to grow in love of the Son of God, who accomplished such marvelous things on our behalf. They expound the Scriptures with confidence, neither blaspheming God, nor dishonoring the patriarchs, nor despising the prophets.

60:19-20
And the sun shall not be to you as a light by day, nor shall the rising of the moon give light to you at night.

(7) Origen of Alexandria

If we wish to examine the passage *the days of the blameless* (Ps 37:18) in order to discern its more profound spiritual meaning, we can say that the evil days are the days of this age,

---

2. See the introductory comments concerning the LXX text of Isa 60:17 and the interpretations of Clement and Irenaeus.

about which was written, *because the days are evil* (Eph 5:16). But other days are good, the *days of the blameless, whom God knows* (Ps 37:18), whose inheritance remains forever. So when the righteous receive the inheritance of life eternal, they will obtain *what no eye has seen, nor ear heard, nor reached the heart of man, what God has prepared for those who love him* (1 Cor 2:9). These are the *days of the blameless*, on which the sun will not set nor night intervene. But the *sun of righteousness* (Mal 4:2) who knows no night, whose light is eternal, will give light, as it is written: **The Lord himself will be an everlasting light for them** (60:19).

(8) Ambrose of Milan

There are some people for whom it is always day. They are the ones for whom Christ is always present. For he commands: *Walk while you have the light* (John 12:35). This is the day which Abraham saw, the day of the forgiveness of sins, about which you read: *This is the day the LORD has made; let us rejoice and be glad in it* (Ps 118:24). They are the holy ones on whom the sun never sets, because the Lord is their light, as it is written in the Scriptures: **The Lord will be their everlasting light** (60:19).

(9) Jerome

Everything said in this chapter must be referred to the end times, when heaven and earth will pass away and the sun and moon will cease from their service and the Lord himself will be a perpetual light. We believe that those things will exist in a spiritual sense, but the millennialists[3] assert that they will be fulfilled in a fleshly sense. Our disagreement with them is over the nature of the promises, not over the timing. To the millennialists we must briefly respond that, if the sun sets at midday for false prophets and sinners and, on the other hand, the sun of righteousness rises for those who fear the Lord, is he not always speaking to the saints when he declares: *I am the light of the world* (John 8:12), *which shines in darkness, and the darkness comprehended it not* (John 1:5)?

The sun shall not smite by day, nor the moon by night (Ps 121:6), because **the Lord will be our everlasting light, and the days of mourning shall be ended** (60:20). This does not refer to those who mourn at the destruction of Jerusalem, but for those who rejoice over the building of the Church. For *blessed are those who mourn, for they shall be comforted* (Matt 5:4); and blessed are those who weep, for they shall laugh (cf. Luke 6:21). *Blessed are those who hunger and thirst for righteousness, for they shall be satisfied* (Matt 5:6), so that, after they have been satisfied with the flesh of the Lord, they may *overflow with the Word of God and address their verses to the king* (Ps 45:1).

---

3. Christians who believed that there would be a kingdom established on earth before the final consummation (the figure of a thousand years is based on Rev 20:1-10).

(10) Cyril of Alexandria

Some would like us to interpret these verses [60:19-20] as follows: At the end of the age when those who were lying in the earth are raised and Christ the Savior of all comes down from heaven with his holy angels in the glory of the Father, there will be no need for the splendor of the heavenly bodies. For there will be new heavens and a new earth, and we will await the fulfillment of his promises, as it is written. The Savior himself said something of this sort: *In those days the sun will be darkened, and the moon will not give its light* (Matt 24:29). The glory of the Savior will be sufficient illumination. This interpretation is a good one and fits the sense of what comes immediately before. But I think that these verses can have another meaning.

Both the light of the sun and the light of the moon are useful and necessary for the eyes of the body. But at night the sun's light gives way to the light of the moon, and during the day the moon gives way to the sun. Each in turn steps aside for the other to shine. The divine and eternal light, so says the text, which the Savior of all implants in the hearts of believers through the Holy Spirit and through those who know how to expound the sacred mysteries, is unquenchable, unceasing, and always shining. So there is no need for the sun or the moon to provide illumination or vision to each mind. The mind is not enlightened by sensible light; the illumination of the Holy Spirit suffices, and by its brilliance one is able to behold the glory of Christ and to perceive his likeness to the Father who begot him, a likeness that is clearly a matter of being, and indeed to know with certainty the most excellent way of life. For the Savior became an eternal light for us, as he makes clear when he claims: *I am the light of the world* (John 8:12), and again, *As long as I am in the world, I am the light of the world* (John 9:5), and *Who follows me will not walk in darkness, but will have the light of life* (John 8:12).

60:21-22
Your people shall all be righteous, and they shall inherit the land forever, guarding their plant, the works of their hands, for glory. The smallest one shall become thousands. . . .

(11) Jerome

When the days of grief have come to an end and sadness has turned to joy, the people of Zion will all become righteous, not for a brief time, but forever; and because they are righteous, they will possess the land of the meek. One should not be surprised that to receive the good things that have been promised, they will possess the land of the meek and the land of the living, which the Prophet longed for when he said: *I believe that I shall see the goodness of the* LORD *in the land of the living!* (Ps 27:13), since it is the shoot of the Lord's planting, the work of his hands that God might be glorified. For, he warns, *Every plant which my heavenly Father has not planted will be rooted up* (Matt 15:13). Or, if one

Isaiah 60

follows the Septuagint, the people will care for the planting of God and the work of the Lord's hands, and the glory of the Creator will be preserved.

Concerning this good planting God speaks through Jeremiah: *I planted you a choice vine, wholly of pure seed* (Jer 2:21), which in Isaiah is called the vineyard of Sorech, that is, a choice vine (5:2). And because St. Paul was conscious of the power of Christ that spoke through him, he was able to say, *Be imitators of me, as I am of Christ* (1 Cor 11:1). Hence he told the Corinthians: *I planted, Apollos watered, but God gave the growth* (1 Cor 3:6). For *they are planted in the house of the Lord, they flourish in the courts of our God* (Ps 92:13).

Then the **least shall become thousands** (60:22) and will hear from the Lord: *You shall have authority over five or ten cities* (Luke 19:19, 17). The result is that he will be called ruler of a thousand men. And he who had said as an apostle, *I am the least of all the saints, to whom this grace was given* (Eph 3:8), will become prince of a great nation in heaven when at the appointed time the Lord *sends forth his angels, and they will gather for him all the saints from one end of heaven to the other* (Matt 24:31). He was speaking not only about Israel but also about the Gentiles, whom he indicated when he said: *And I have other sheep that are not of this fold; I must bring them also, so there shall be one flock, one shepherd* (John 10:16). Moreover, this he will do **quickly** (60:22), so that, after all hope has been lost, they may then be gathered together into a mighty nation. Although we see these things partly fulfilled every day in the Church, nevertheless they will be brought to fulfillment in the consummation of the world and at the second coming of our Savior.

Isaiah 61

1 The spirit of the Lord is upon me,
   because he has anointed me;
 he has sent me to bring good news to the poor,
   to heal the brokenhearted,
 to proclaim release to the captives,
   and recovery of sight to the blind;
2 to summon the acceptable year of the Lord,
   and the day of retribution;
 to comfort all who mourn;
3 so that to those who mourn for Sion
   be given glory instead of ashes,
 oil of joy to those who mourn,
   a garment of glory instead of a spirit of weariness.
 They will be called generations of righteousness,
   a plant of the Lord for glory.
4 They shall build the desolate places of old,
   they shall raise up the former devastated places;
 they shall renew the desolate cities,
   places devastated for generations.

5 Strangers shall come, feeding your sheep,
   and foreigners as plowmen and vinedressers;
6 but you shall be called priests of the Lord,
   ministers of God;
 you shall devour the strength of nations,
   and with their wealth you shall be admired.
7 Thus they shall inherit the land a second time,
   and everlasting joy shall be above their head.

8 For I am the Lord, who loves righteousness

and hates spoils obtained by injustice;
   I will give them their hard work righteously,
      and I will make an everlasting covenant with them.
9 And their offspring and their descendants
      shall be known among the nations;
   everyone who sees them shall acknowledge them,
      because these are an offspring blessed by God,
10   and they will rejoice with rejoicing in the Lord.
   Let my soul be glad in the Lord,
      for he has clothed me with a garment of salvation,
      and with a robe of joy;
   he has put on me a garland as on a bridegroom,
      and adorned me with ornaments like a bride.
11 And as the earth making its flowers grow,
      and as a garden its seeds,
   so the Lord will cause righteousness and gladness
      to spring up before all the nations.

According to the Gospel of Luke (4:18-19), on the Sabbath Jesus read from chapter 61 of Isaiah in the synagogue at Nazareth and said: "Today this scripture has been fulfilled in your hearing" (Luke 4:21). Following Luke the church fathers take the opening verses of Isaiah 61 to refer to the "marvelous things accomplished during the sojourn of the only Son on earth" (Cyril). The first verse, **The spirit of the Lord God is upon me**, *was seen as a reference to Christ's Baptism. The text, however, was not without difficulties. If Christ is God and one of the three persons of the Holy Trinity, how can he receive the Holy Spirit as though he was not always one with the Spirit? In a passage from one of his treatises against the Arians, Athanasius argues that the text does not mean, as the Arians thought, that Christ needed to be sanctified by the Holy Spirit. When Isaiah speaks of the Spirit descending on Christ, he means that Christ received the Spirit as man "that we might be sanctified and receive his anointing." Origen says that if one wishes to exercise the "priesthood of the soul" because* **You will all be priests of the Lord** *(61:6), one must never let the fire go out on one's altar. For Augustine the verse,* **he has put on me a garland as on a bridegroom, and adorned me with ornaments like a bride** *(61:10), was a key passage for his understanding of the "totus Christus" in the interpretation of the Psalms. In the Psalms Christ speaks at times as God according to his divine nature, at times as God become man, and at times as the head and the body of the church. The prophet "calls one and the same person bridegroom with reference to the head, bride with reference to the body."*

(1) The Gospel according to Luke

And he came to Nazareth, where he had been brought up; and he went to the synagogue, as his custom was, on the Sabbath day. And he stood up to read; and there was given to him the book of the prophet Isaiah. He opened the book and found the place where it was written, **The Spirit of the Lord is upon me, because he has anointed me to preach good**

news to the poor. He has sent me to proclaim release to the captives and recovering of sight to the blind, to set at liberty those who are oppressed, to proclaim the acceptable year of the Lord (61:1-2). And he closed the book, and gave it back to the attendant, and sat down; and the eyes of all in the synagogue were fixed on him. And he began to say to them, "Today this scripture has been fulfilled in your hearing."

(2) Cyril of Alexandria

In the previous chapter the Lord said this to those who were to be called to faith: *I the Lord will gather them in due time* (60:22). Now he speaks as though the promised time for gathering them has already come. It is as though he has already become man and *emptied himself, taking on human likeness* (Phil 2:7-8). For he maintains, **The Spirit of the Lord is upon me** (61:1). He is God by nature, the only Son, the holy of holies who sanctifies all creation. He has his being from the holy Father and sends the Spirit, who proceeds from him, into the heavenly powers and also on those who saw him when he appeared on earth. How then can he be sanctified? He exists as God and as man; as God he gives his Spirit to creation, and as man he receives the same Spirit from his God and Father. This we call his anointing.

The passage also explains the reason for the Incarnation. After saying what he has received from the Father, he adds: **because he has sent me to bring good news to the poor, to heal the brokenhearted, to proclaim release to the captives, and recovery of sight to the blind, to proclaim the day of retribution** (60:1-2). These are some of the marvelous things accomplished during the sojourn of the only Son on earth. In order to reclaim the region under heaven and return those who dwelled all over the world to God the Father, to transform everything into something better, and, as it were, *to renew the face of the earth* (Ps 104:30), he *took the form of a servant* (Phil 2:7), though he was Lord of all. The **poor** are to be understood as those who have been deprived of every good thing, as it is written, *having no hope and without God in the world* (Eph 2:12). They are the Gentiles who have become rich by faith in him and possess the divine and heavenly treasure, the gospel of salvation. Through it they have become partakers of the kingdom of heaven, and they will share the life of the saints and become heirs of things beyond reason and understanding. For Scripture says, *What no eye has seen, nor ear heard, nor the heart of man conceived, what God has prepared for those who love him* (1 Cor 2:9).

But the text might also be referring to the cornucopia of gifts that Christ gives to the *poor in spirit* (Matt 5:3). For the text mentions the **brokenhearted**, that is, those whose spirit is fragile and easily crushed, who are unable to resist the attacks of unruly passions. Indeed, they are so dominated by their passions that they seem like **captives**. To these he promises healing and **release** and **recovery of sight to the blind** (61:1). Are not those blind who worship creation and *say to a tree, "You are my father," and to a stone, "You gave me birth"* (Jer 2:27)? For they did not know the one true God. Are not their hearts devoid of the divine and spiritual light? These the Father has filled with the light of the true knowledge of God. They have been called through faith and they know God; rather, they are known by him (cf. Gal 4:9). Those who were children of night and of darkness have become children of light. On them the day has spread its light, the *Sun of Righteousness* (Mal 4:2) has risen, and the bright *morning star* has appeared (2 Pet 1:19)....

Those who are in Christ are called *a chosen race, a holy nation, God's own people* (1 Pet 2:9) on account of the beauty of the **righteousness** (61:3) that dwells in them. The prophet is not talking about **righteousness** according to the law, but that **righteousness** gained through the Savior's holy words. For what comes from Christ is incomparably better than what is in the law. That is why Christ warned his holy apostles, *For I tell you, unless your righteousness exceeds that of the scribes and Pharisees, you will never enter the kingdom of heaven* (Matt 5:20).

The text says that **they shall be called generations of righteousness**, and also **the plant of the Lord** (61:3). We are indeed God's field, and the inspired David says about us, *They are planted in the house of the Lord, they flourish in the courts of our God* (Ps 92:13). Hence the most-wise Paul says that those who have been called through faith in Christ are *God's field* (1 Cor 3:9). Moreover, he asserted, *I planted, Apollos watered, but God gave the growth* (1 Cor 3:6). The Savior tills the field through the holy sacraments. It is very likely that the apostles call themselves *fellow workmen for God* for the same reason (1 Cor 3:9). The most-wise David sings, *The righteous will flourish like the palm tree, and grow like a cedar in Lebanon* (Ps 92:12). We are then **the planting of the Lord, that he may be glorified** (61:3).

The text continues: **They shall build up the ancient cities, they shall restore the ruined cities** (61:4). By this it seems that he wishes to show that the number of those to be called will be so great that they will seek other cities besides those that already exist and they will renew those that were once deserted. Or perhaps it means the following. Although the churches were once empty and deserted, now they cannot accommodate the crowds of people. Hence the text indicates that they will act like people who want to rebuild deserted cities and are eager to lift up what has fallen to the ground. This is why the Church is exhorted, *Enlarge the place of your tent, and let the curtains of your habitations be stretched out; hold not back, lengthen your cords and strengthen your stakes* (54:2). Whether this is true only future events will certainly show....

The Lord has generously stretched out his hand to them and crowned them with many bountiful gifts, as the prophet affirms: **Everyone who sees them shall acknowledge them, because they are an offspring blessed by God** (61:9), to which he adds: **They will greatly rejoice in the Lord** (61:10), for he gives them joy at once. It is appropriate that these words personify the Church, for out of great joy she cries out: **Let my soul be glad in the Lord, for he has clothed me with the garment of salvation, and the robe of joy** (61:10).

Our Lord Jesus Christ is called the **robe of joy**. That is why the most-wise Paul writes to those who believe in Christ, *Put on the Lord Jesus Christ, and make no provision for the flesh, to gratify its desires* (Rom 13:14). Besides possessing salvation those who wear Christ as a **robe** will enjoy happiness and their days will be filled with joy. The Savior himself says, *The thief comes only to steal and kill and destroy; I came that they may have life, and have it abundantly* (John 10:10). For Christ not only saves, he also gladdens his followers with immeasurable **joy**. The word *abundance* here refers to life as it is known by the saints. Christ then is the garment from heaven above, the **robe** of immortality. If anyone receives this garment, he will wear a crown of many jewels. The passage is of course to be understood spiritually to refer to the honor one receives from doing good works. The text also indicates that such a person will be like a **bridegroom** decked with a **garland**, and like a **bride** adorned with every kind of **ornament** (61:10).

Those who are in Christ are strong and mighty and armed with spiritual fortitude, and they are rich and decorated with every form of virtue. They are also like **brides** who are fertile and whose offspring are many splendid virtues. One of the holy prophets showed that those who live a pure life are fruitful when he said: *Because of our fear of you, O Lord, we were with child, we writhed, we have as it were brought forth the Spirit of salvation, which we have wrought on the earth* (26:17-18). Therefore, the saints are comparable to a bride and a groom who are vigorous and fertile. Indeed, everything beautiful can be found in them. When the saints bring forth the gorgeous fruits of courage and bravely withstand the onslaught of the passions, they are beautiful.

This passage also shows that Christ made **righteousness** and **gladness** (61:11) dawn for the nations. They will blossom like a flowering plant that covers the earth, as the prophet expresses it: **For as the earth brings forth its flowers, and as a garden its seed, so the Lord God will cause righteousness and gladness to spring up before all the nations** (61:11). It seems likely that in this passage germination or shooting up as a seed and flowering **before the nations** refers to our Lord Jesus Christ himself. For he said in the Song of Songs, *I am a rose of Sharon, a lily of the valleys* (Song 2:1). Of course the passage could refer to the gospel of salvation and the righteousness that surpasses the righteousness of the law. Joy always accompanies this righteousness, and this leads to **gladness** (61:11). God will fill with boundless joy those who have accomplished the works of **righteousness**. They will hear Christ, the Savior of all, saying, *Well done, good and faithful servant; you have been faithful over a little, I will set you over much; enter into the joy of your master* (Matt 25:21). In another sense, **gladness** can refer to the proclamation of salvation. For the law could be harsh and admonitory. For example, *a man who has violated the law of Moses dies without mercy at the testimony of two or three witnesses* (Deut 17:6; Heb 10:28), but the word of the gospel bestows life and promises gifts and a genuine hope for good things beyond our understanding.

61:1
The Spirit of the Lord God is upon me.

(3) Athanasius of Alexandria

When the Spirit descended on him in the Jordan, the Spirit descended on us because he bore our body. The Spirit did not descend that the Word of God might be improved, but that we might be sanctified and receive his anointing. For then it could be asked of us: *Do you not know that you are God's temple and that God's Spirit dwells in you?* (1 Cor 3:16). For when the Lord was washed in the Jordan, we were washed in him and by him. And when he received the Spirit, we were made worthy to receive the Spirit by him. For this reason his anointing was unlike the anointing of Aaron or David or others, for he was anointed in another way, *with the oil of gladness beyond all his fellows* (Ps 45:7; Heb 1:9). He understands this anointing to be the anointing of the Spirit when he declares through the Prophet: **The Spirit of the Lord is upon me, because he has anointed me** (61:1), as the apostle also said: *How God anointed him with the Holy Spirit* (Acts 10:38). These things were said of him when he became flesh and was baptized in the Jordan, and the Spirit descended on him. Indeed, the Lord said: *The Spirit will take what is mine* (John 16:14) and *I will send him* (John 16:7), and to his disciples, *Receive the Holy Spirit* (John 20:22). Even though he who as the Word and *reflection* (Heb 1:3) of the Father gives to others, he is now said to be sanctified, because he has become man and the body that is sanctified is his. From him, then, we have begun to receive the anointing and the seal, as John says: *You have been anointed by the Holy One* (1 John 2:20), or the apostle puts it: *You were sealed with the promised Holy Spirit* (Eph 1:13).

(4) Jerome

The one who had said previously, *I the* LORD *in time shall gather them together* (or according to the Hebrew, *I am the* LORD; *in its time I will hasten it* [60:22]), now says: **The Spirit of the Lord God**[1] **is upon me** (61:1). He does not mean that the Lord God receives another **Lord God** or that he venerates another "Lord God," but that insofar as he has taken on flesh he speaks of those things which are lowly. About him the psalmist had written: *You love righteousness and hate wickedness. Therefore God, your God, has anointed you with the oil of gladness above your fellows* (Ps 45:7). The term *fellows* is used because Christ was in the flesh. As God he has no peers. Further, the *anointing* mentioned here is spiritual anointing, not of the human body, as was the case for the priests of the Jews. Therefore he is said to have been anointed above his fellows, that is, above those who are saints. His anointing took place when he was baptized in the Jordan and the Holy Spirit descended on him in the form of a dove and remained on him (John 1:32). This same prophet also spoke about this when he wrote: *There shall come forth a shoot from the stump of Jesse, and a branch shall grow out of his roots. And the Spirit of the* LORD *shall rest upon him, the spirit of wisdom and understanding, the spirit of counsel and might, the spirit of knowledge and the fear of the* LORD (11:1-2).

After being baptized in the Jordan, our Savior *came to Nazareth; and he went to the synagogue, as his custom was, on the sabbath day. And he stood up to read; and there was given to him the book of the prophet Isaiah. He opened the book and found the place where it was written: "The Spirit of the Lord is upon me, because he has anointed me to preach good news to the poor. He has sent me to proclaim release to the captives and recovering of sight to the blind, to set at liberty those who are oppressed, to proclaim the acceptable year of the Lord." And he closed the book, and gave it back to the attendant, and sat down; and the eyes of all in the synagogue were fixed on him. And he began to say to them, "Today this scripture has been fulfilled in your hearing." And all spoke well of him, and wondered at the gracious words which proceeded out of his mouth* (Luke 4:16-22). We understand this

---

1. Jerome follows the Hebrew version, which reads **Spirit of the Lord God**. The LXX reads, **Spirit of the Lord**.

prophecy to be fulfilled during Jesus' lifetime. Some interpreters, however, think that it is referring to the end times. Perhaps it was fulfilled in part when Jesus came to the synagogue in Nazareth, and will be fulfilled more fully when all the people of God become righteous. *For our knowledge is imperfect and our prophecy is imperfect; but when the perfect comes, the imperfect will pass away* (1 Cor 13:9-10).

He was **anointed** by the Holy **Spirit to bring good tidings to the poor** (61:1) or to the **meek**, as he put it in the Gospel: *Blessed are the poor in spirit, for theirs is the kingdom of heaven* (Matt 5:3), and *Blessed are the meek, for they shall inherit the earth* (Matt 5:5). And he was sent to **bind up the brokenhearted** (61:1), as it is written: *a broken and contrite heart, O God, thou wilt not despise* (Ps 51:17). However, according to the translation of Symmachus and Theodotion: the Spirit of the Lord was upon him **to bind up the wounds of sinners, to proclaim liberty to the captives, and the opening of the eyes to the blind that they might see**, or **the opening of prison to those that are bound**. Symmachus translated this latter phrase as **the breaking of the chains of those that are bound** (61:1). Earlier in the book of Isaiah it is said about him, indeed said to him: *I have given you as a light to the nations, to open the eyes of the blind, to bring out the prisoners from the dungeon, and from the prison house those who sit in darkness* (42:6-7).

(5) Ambrose of Milan

In the previous book[2] I have shown by the clear testimonies of the Scriptures that the apostles and prophets were appointed, the latter to prophesy and the former to proclaim good tidings. They were appointed by the Holy Spirit as well as by the Father and the Son. Now I say, and this is something that will astonish everyone, though it could hardly be doubted, that the Spirit was upon Christ; and that as He sent the Spirit, so the Spirit sent the Son of God, for the Son of God announces, **The Spirit of the Lord is upon me, because the Lord has anointed me to bring good tidings to the poor, to proclaim liberty to the captives and sight to the blind** (61:1). In the Gospel, after Christ had read from the book of Isaiah, he said: *Today this Scripture is fulfilled in your hearing* (Luke 4:21), indicating that the passage was speaking about himself.

One should not be surprised then that the Spirit sent both the prophets and apostles, for Christ declared: **The Spirit of the Lord is upon me** (61:1). Rightly did he say **upon me** because he was speaking of the Son of man. For he was anointed as the Son of man and sent to preach good tidings.

But if one does not believe the Son, let them hear the Father, who also asserts that the Spirit of the Lord is upon Christ. For he says to John: *He upon whom you see the Spirit descend and remain, this is he who baptizes with the Holy Spirit* (John 1:33). God the Father said this to John, and John heard and saw and believed. He heard from God, he saw in the Lord, he believed that the Spirit was the one who descended from heaven. It was not a dove that descended, but the Spirit descended like a dove. For it is written: *And I saw the Spirit descending from heaven like a dove* (Mark 1:10).

2. Of his treatise *On the Holy Spirit*.

Isaiah 61

(6) Irenaeus of Lyons

The apostles recorded that the Spirit of the Lord descended on Christ in the form of a dove. This is the Spirit mentioned by Isaiah when he wrote: *And the Spirit of the* LORD *shall rest upon him* (11:2). And again: **The Spirit of the Lord is upon me, because he has anointed me** (61:1). About this Spirit the Lord said: *For it is not you who speak, but the Spirit of your Father who speaks in you* (Matt 10:20). And again when he gave the power of rebirth into God, he commanded them: *Go therefore and make disciples of all nations, baptizing them in the name of the Father and of the Son and of the Holy Spirit* (Matt 28:19). For through the prophets God promised that in the *last times* (2:1) he would pour out this Spirit on his servants and handmaidens that they might prophesy. That is why he also descended on the Son of God who had become man. By dwelling in him the Spirit became accustomed to dwelling in the human race, to finding a resting place among men, and to dwelling in God's handiwork. In this way the will of God could be at work among them and transform their old ways into the newness of Christ.

David asked that this Spirit be sent to the human race: *Establish me with your governing Spirit* (Ps 50:14 LXX). Luke says that the Spirit also descended on the disciples after the Lord's ascension on the Day of Pentecost with the power to introduce all nations to life and to open the New Covenant to them (Acts 2). So, animated by the same Spirit, they sang a hymn to God, the Spirit bringing together into one the separate peoples and offering the first fruits of the nations to the Father. That is why the Lord promised to send the Paraclete (John 16:7), who would make us fit to live in God's presence.

For as one cannot make a ball of dough or a loaf of bread out of dry flour without adding liquid, so we could not, being many, be made one in Christ Jesus without the water that comes from heaven. As the dry earth does not bring forth fruit unless it is watered, in the same way we who were at first a dry tree could not have brought forth a life of fruit without the generous rain from above. For our bodies were joined to incorruption by that washing with water (cf. Eph 5:26), but our souls by the Spirit. Both are necessary, because both contribute to the life in God. So our Lord showed compassion to that unfaithful Samaritan woman who did not remain with one husband but committed fornication by being married many times. He pointed that out to her but also promised her living water so that she would no longer be thirsty and no longer have to labor to acquire refreshing water. For she had in herself a drink that gushes forth to eternal life. For the Lord had received this as a gift from the Father, and he gives it in turn to those who are partakers of himself by sending the Holy Spirit to all the earth.

(7) Faustus Luciferanus

Though they received only one anointing, those who were anointed with the oil of kingship or of priesthood were called messiahs [christs, anointed ones].[3] Our Savior, however, who is the Christ [the Anointed One], was anointed by the Holy Spirit in fulfillment

---

3. Christ, however, was anointed as king and priest.

of the passage in Scripture: *God, your God, has anointed you with the oil of gladness above your fellows* (Ps 45:7). The difference between the one Christ and the many christs [anointed ones] is in the anointing, since he was anointed with the oil of gladness, which signifies the Holy Spirit.

This we know to be true from the Savior himself. When he took the book of Isaiah, he opened it and read: **The Spirit of the Lord is upon me, because he has anointed me** (61:1). He then said that the prophecy was fulfilled in the hearing of those listening (cf. Luke 4:21).

Peter, the prince of the apostles, also taught that the chrism which made the Savior a Christ was the Holy Spirit, that is to say, the power of God. In the Acts of the Apostles when Peter spoke to that faithful and merciful man, the centurion, he said among other things: *After the baptism which John preached, Jesus of Nazareth, whom God anointed with the Holy Spirit and with power, began from Galilee and went about performing powerful miracles and freeing all who were oppressed by the devil* (Acts 10:37-38).

So you see that Peter, too, taught that Jesus in his humanity was anointed with the Holy Spirit and with power. So Jesus in his humanity did in truth become the Christ. By the anointing of the Holy Spirit, he was made both king and priest forever.

(8) John Chrysostom

When the letters from heaven are being read [in the Liturgy], people are chattering rather than paying attention, although the one who sent the letters is much greater than our emperor and the spectacle one sees here much more awesome. For there are present here not only men but angels. And the triumphs that are recounted here are much more fearful than earthly accomplishments. For that reason not only men, but angels and archangels, and the whole company of heaven, and all those on earth, are commanded to give praise. For the Scripture says: *Bless the* LORD, *all his works* (Ps 103:22). For the things God has done are not small, for they transcend all speech and human understanding.

These things the prophets proclaim every day, each in a different way announcing his glorious triumph. For one says: *Thou didst ascend on high, leading captives in thy train, and receiving gifts among men* (Ps 68:18) and *the* LORD, *strong and mighty in battle* (Ps 24:8). And another adds: *he will divide the spoil with the strong* (Isa 53:12). For he came for this purpose, **to proclaim release to the captives, and the opening of the eyes of the blind** (61:1).

And shouting a cry of victory over death, he asked: *Where, O Death, is your victory? Where, O Sheol, is your sting?* (Hos 13:14; 1 Cor 15:55). And another, proclaiming the goodness of the most profound peace, said: *They shall beat their swords into plowshares, and their spears into pruning hooks* (Isa 2:4). And another calls on Jerusalem: *Rejoice greatly, O daughter of Zion! For behold your king comes to you, humble and riding on an ass, and on a young colt* (Zech 9:9). Another proclaims his second coming: *The* LORD *whom you seek will suddenly come, and who can endure the day of his coming?* (Mal 3:1-2). *Leap like calves set free from their bonds* (Mal 4:2). And another, astounded at such things, shouted: *This is our God; no other can be compared to him* (Bar 3:36).

However, when these and many other things are being spoken, and we ought to tremble as though we were not on earth, we behave as though we are in the middle of the forum. We are noisy and restless and spend the whole time of our worship chattering about trivial things.

(9) Ephrem the Syrian

The Good one in his love
   wished to discipline us for doing wrong,
and so we had to leave Paradise
   with its bridal chamber of glory;
He made us live with the wild beasts,
   which caused us sorrow,
so that we might see how little
   our honor had become,
and so would supplicate him and beg to return
   to our inheritance.
Praise be to him who released
   these **prisoners** (61:1) who have no wish to be free.

61:2
To summon the acceptable year of the Lord

(10) Origen of Alexandria

If I consider that the true *high priest* (Heb 9:7), my Lord Jesus Christ, found in flesh, was with the people for the entire year,[4] that year about which it was said, **he sent me to bring good news to the poor, and to summon the acceptable year of the Lord and the day of forgiveness** (61:2), note that *once* in this *year* on the Day of Atonement he does enter into *the Holy of Holies* (Exod 30:10). When his mission is accomplished, he *penetrates the heavens* (Heb 4:14) and comes before the Father that he might make atonement for the human race and pray for all who believe in him. About this atonement by which he propitiates the Father for human beings, John the apostle said: *My little children, I am writing this to you so that you may not sin; but if any one does sin, we have an advocate with the Father, Jesus Christ the righteous* (1 John 2:1). And Paul also mentions this atonement, using similar language: *This is the one God put forward as an expiation by his blood, to be received by faith* (Rom 3:25). Therefore the Day of Atonement continues for us until the sun sets (cf. Lev 11:25), that is, until the world comes to an end.

---

4. Not "once in the year" on the Day of Atonement, as in ancient Israel (Exod 30:10).

61:6
You shall be called priests of the Lord.

(11) Origen of Alexandria

There ought always to be *fire on the altar* (Lev 6:12), if you want to be a priest of God, as it is written, **You will all be priests of the Lord** (61:6). For it is said that you are *a chosen race, a royal priesthood, God's own people* (1 Pet 2:9). If, therefore, you want to exercise the priesthood of your soul, never let the fire go out on your altar. This is what the Lord also taught in the gospels, that *your loins be girded and your lamps burning* (Luke 12:35). Thus let the *fire* of your faith and the *lamp* of your knowledge always be lit for you.

61:10
He has clothed me with a garment of salvation.

(12) John Chrysostom

Our responsibility is never to put off the *righteousness* (Eph 4:24) which the prophet calls **the garment of salvation** (61:10), so that we may be become like God. For he has put on righteousness. Let us then clothe ourselves in this garment.

(13) Augustine of Hippo

According to the Scriptures, Christ can be understood and named in three ways.... The first way is as God and according to the divine nature which is coequal and coeternal with the Father before he assumed flesh. The next way is when, after assuming flesh, he is now understood... to be God who is at the same time man, and man who is at the same time God....

The third way is how the whole Christ is predicated with reference to the Church, that is, as head and body. For indeed head and body form one Christ. Not that he isn't complete without the body, but that he was prepared to be complete and entire together with us too, though even without us he is always complete and entire, not only insofar as he is the Word, the only-begotten Son equal to the Father, but also in the very man whom he took on, and with whom he is both God and man together. All the same, brothers and sisters, how are we his body, and he one Christ with us? Where do we find this, that head and body form one Christ, that is, the body together with its head? In Isaiah the bride is speaking with the bridegroom as if in the singular; certainly it is the same person speaking; and see what is said: **He has decked me with a garland as for a bridegroom, and adorned me with jewels as for a bride** (61:10). As a bridegroom and bride; he calls the same person bridegroom with reference to the head, bride with reference to the body.

Otherwise, how are we the members of Christ, with the apostle saying as clearly as can be, *You are the body of Christ and its members* (1 Cor 12:27)? All of us together are the members of Christ and his body, not only those of us who are in this place, but throughout the world; and not only those of us who are alive at this time, but what shall I say? From Abel the Just right up to the end of the world, as long as people beget and are begotten, any of the just who make the passage through this life, all that now — that is, not in this place but in this life — all that are going to be born after us, all constitute the one body of Christ; while they are each individually members of Christ. So if all constitute the body, and are each individual members, there is of course a head, of which this is the body. *And he himself,* it says, *is the head of the body, the Church, the firstborn, himself holding the first place* (Col 1:18).

(14) Augustine of Hippo

We have seen and are witnesses (1 John 1:2). Where did they see? When it was made clear. What does it mean to make clear? In the sun, by its light. The Maker of the sun could be seen only by the light of the sun, because he *set his tent in the sun, going forth himself as a bridegroom out of his chamber, rejoicing as a giant running his course* (Ps 19:4-5). He who existed before the sun made the sun before the day star and all stars, before all angels. He is the true Creator (*because all things were made by him, and without him was nothing made* [John 1:3]). That he might be seen by the eyes of flesh which see the sun, he *set his own tent in the sun* (Ps 19:4). He showed his flesh clearly by this light: the Bridegroom's chamber was the Virgin's womb, because there Bridegroom and Bride, Word and flesh, were joined together. It is written: *And the two shall be one flesh* (Gen 2:24), or, as the Lord says in the Gospel, *therefore they are no longer two, but one flesh* (Matt 19:6). Isaiah says it best — that the two are one person — when he speaks of the person of Christ: **He put a band upon my head as on a bridegroom, and adorned me as a bride with her ornaments** (61:10). Here one speaker presents himself both as Bridegroom and as Bride; for they are *not two, but one flesh* since *the Word was made flesh and dwelt among us* (John 1:14). When the Church is joined to that flesh, there one finds the whole Christ, Head and Body.

Isaiah 62

1 Because of Sion I will not be silent,
    and because of Ierousalem I will not slacken,
  until my righteousness goes forth like a light,
    and my salvation shall burn like a torch.
2 And nations shall see your righteousness,
    and kings your glory;
  and he shall call you by your new name,
    which the Lord will name.
3 And you shall be a crown of beauty in the hand of the Lord,
    and a royal diadem in the hand of your God.
4 And you shall no more be called Forsaken,
    and your land shall not be called Desolate;
  for you shall be called My Will,
    and your land, Inhabited.
5 And as a young man lives together in marriage with a virgin,
    so shall your sons dwell with you,
  and it shall be that as a bridegroom shall rejoice over a bride,
    so shall the Lord rejoice over you.
6 And upon your walls, O Ierousalem,
    I have posted sentinels
  all day and all night,
    who shall never be silent,
    making mention of the Lord.
7 For you have none like him,
    if he should restore Ierousalem
    and make it a boast on the earth.
8 The Lord has sworn by his right hand
    and by his mighty arm:
  I will not again give your grain
    and your food to your enemies,

and not again shall alien sons drink your wine
   for which you have labored;
9 but those who gather shall eat them
   and praise the Lord,
and those who gather shall drink them
   in my holy courts.

10 Go through my gates,
   and make a way for my people;
and cast the stones out of the way,
   lift up a signal for the nations.
11 For see, the Lord has made it to be heard
   to the end of the earth:
Say to daughter Sion,
   "See, your Savior comes to you,
having his own reward
   and his work before him."
12 And he shall call it a holy people,
   redeemed by the Lord;
and you shall be called
   "A City Sought After" and "Not Forsaken."

Here, as in other places in the commentaries on Isaiah, **Zion** *is understood to refer to the Church, the "city of God" spoken about in Psalm 87. She will be adorned with a* **crown of beauty** *(62:3) whose precious jewels are the victories of the martyrs and the valorous deeds of the saints. Cyril takes the phrase* **I will not be silent** *(62:1) to mean that God will not rest and what he promised to Zion he will surely bring to fulfillment. Following the Gospel according to Matthew, the verse,* **Say to daughter Zion, "Your Savior comes to you"** *(62:11), was taken as a prophecy of the coming of Christ. The* **new name which the mouth of the Lord will give** *(62:2), says Jerome, is the name "Christian," for the Church is consecrated to the Lord.*

Although this chapter receives a full exposition in the commentaries, it is seldom cited in sermons or theological writings, perhaps because its themes were fully developed in exegesis of other chapters of Isaiah.

(1) The Gospel according to Matthew

And when they drew near to Jerusalem and came to Bethphage, to the Mount of Olives, then Jesus sent two disciples, saying to them, "Go into the village opposite you, and immediately you will find an ass tied, and a colt with her; untie them and bring them to me. If any one says anything to you, you shall say, 'The Lord has need of them,' and he will send them immediately." This took place to fulfill what was spoken by the prophet, saying, **Tell the daughter of Zion, Behold, your king is coming to you** (62:11), humble and mounted on an ass, and on a colt, the foal of an ass.

(2) Cyril of Alexandria

Zion (62:1) is here identified with the Church that gave birth to the inspired disciples, her firstborn children, and those who were called to the knowledge of Christ through them, including Israelites according to the flesh who came before others. A remnant was saved, and a great number came to faith through the apostles. Therefore, the text says, **I will not rest** (62:1), that is, I will not cease from my promise to bring to fulfillment what I promised to Zion. God the Father promised salvation through Christ to both Jews and Greeks. As Paul declares in his all-encompassing wisdom: *God is one; and he will justify the circumcised on the ground of their faith and the uncircumcised because of their faith. God is not only God of the Jews, but also of the Gentiles* (Rom 3:30, 29). That is why the text says, **I will not rest, until my righteousness goes forth like a light, and my salvation shall burn like a torch** (62:1).

Christ appeared to those on earth as **righteousness** and as **salvation** (62:1). He makes righteous and he saves, being himself the true **light**, a **torch** in the darkness as it were (62:1). He himself said, *As long as I am in the world, I am the light of the world* (John 9:5). Everything had remained in mist and darkness. The devil had darkened the hearts of all, and there was *no one who does good* (Rom 3:12) or knows **righteousness**, that is, the way to salvation. No one possessed the light from above that enlightens the mind, nor was anyone able to perceive with the eyes of understanding the true nature of God, who is Creator and Lord of all. However, after the Savior rose like a **light** and a **torch**, the world was illuminated and through him we have seen the way of salvation.

Then the prophet speaks to the Church that was gathered from the company of the Jews. The multitude of the Gentiles had not yet been drawn in. **Nations shall see your righteousness, and kings your glory** (62:2). The **righteousness** mentioned in this verse, as well as the **glory**, is nothing else than our Lord Jesus the Christ. We have been justified in him, and we have been enriched by his glory. We have become his, and we are called his chosen ones. We have been placed under his yoke and scepter and delivered from the cruel tyranny of the one who ruled us (cf. Matt 11:29-30).

Because Zion no longer worships God according to the law and has embraced the new life according to the gospel, she casts off her old name and has been given a new name that befits the God of all, as is indicated in the words: **He shall call you by your name, which the Lord will name** (62:2). No longer will she be called synagogue but Church of the living God, his *city* and his *house* (cf. Rev 3:12; 1 Tim 3:15). The inspired David was thinking of her when he said, *Glorious things are spoken of you, O city of God* (Ps 87:3).

Isaiah teaches that the Church will shine with splendor and be crowned with incomparable beauty. **You shall be a crown of beauty in the hand of the Lord, and a royal diadem in the hand of your God** (62:3). Every soul will be holy, together with the whole Church, and the ranks of the saints will be like a crown woven from many flowers or a royal tiara shining with stones from India and sparkling with splendor. For the deeds of the saints are valorous and many; like different ornaments they are not all alike but varied. Thus, the inspired David describes the Church of Christ clothed *in a many-colored garment* (Ps 45:14). The prophet also adds that the crown of beauty is **in the hand of the**

Lord (62:3), that is, *I will hide you in the shadow of my hand* (51:16). Christ himself also states about his own lambs, the flock of those who believe in him: *no one is able to snatch them out of the Father's hand* (John 10:29)....

Upon your walls, O Jerusalem, I have posted sentinels (62:6). The prophet speaks as if he were addressing a magnificent and heavily populated city. The most illustrious cities always have a great many vigilant watchmen guarding them, so that they are not vulnerable to an unexpected attack from their enemies. So also the Savior and Lord of the whole universe girded the Church with his invincible power and his angelic troupe. He appointed for her wise guards and watchmen, who attentively care for her. Clearly this has reference to the holy mystagogues[1] (cf. 1 Cor 4:1), who constantly proclaim in every possible way his glory and awe-inspiring works. Indeed, it is our custom always to proclaim the glories of the Savior to the people under our charge and to tell of God's abundant grace, that their faith in him may be certain and immovable....

The words **See, your Savior comes to you** (62:11; cf. Matt 21:5) foretell the coming of the Savior and everything we have gained through him, the great riches that will be given to those who believe in him. He calls **Zion** (62:11) a daughter. Now one can understand the text to refer to the **Zion** of old as already having obtained mercy and having been justified by faith. But if it is taken to refer to the new **Zion**, that is, the Church, then one could say that she is the daughter of **Zion**. The first to believe were Israelites by blood, hence the Church of the Gentiles can be called a daughter of the first church formed from them.

Whom does God command to tell good news to Zion? Is it not the holy mystagogues who have been appointed to lead the Churches and who in particular have been commanded to open the gates and clear the stones away? What is it, then, that is being announced? **See, your Savior comes to you, having his own reward and his work before him** (62:11). He names two notable and divine characteristics by which the glory of the Savior would be manifest. The inspired prophets called the people to live virtuous lives and to observe a law-abiding and honorable way of life. They also reminded them of the gifts they would receive from God in due time. However, it was not the prophets themselves who gave the spiritual gifts. They announced, as it is said, the promises of God. But the Savior of the universe, because he is very God, has the ability to give rewards and also to know what each has done and what is appropriate to each person. Only God can do this. *For a man's ways are before the eyes of the* LORD, *and he watches all his paths* (Prov 5:21).

He will come, the text says, having **his own reward with him** (62:11). For he himself will give the precious gifts to those who deserve them. Hence after Peter confessed the true faith, he said: *I will give you the keys of the kingdom of heaven, and whatever you bind on earth shall be bound in heaven, and whatever you loose on earth shall be loosed in heaven* (Matt 16:19). And he generously gave to the holy apostles as a body power over unclean spirits (cf. Mark 3:15) and the ability to *heal every disease and every infirmity among the people* (Matt 4:23). Indeed, he even made clear to the thief who joined him on the cross that his faith would have its reward: *Truly, I say to you, today you will be with me in Paradise* (Luke 23:43).

---

1. Spiritual leaders, in particular bishops and teachers in the Church.

When Christ comes, the text says, those who believe in Christ **shall be called a holy people, redeemed by the Lord** (62:12). For it was neither a messenger nor an angel, but the Lord himself who saved us. You, **Zion** (62:12), that is, the Church, **shall be called "Sought After," and "Not Forsaken"** (62:12). The text reads, **Sought After**, not simply worthy of being remembered. Yet what is sought is of course what has been remembered. She was not abandoned as the first Zion was, that is, those who did not believe. It was said by Christ through the mouth of Jeremiah: *I have forsaken my house, I have abandoned my heritage* (Jer 12:7). And through his own mouth, Christ the Savior of us all, said: *Behold, your house is forsaken and desolate* (Matt 23:38).

(3) Jerome

The words, *The Spirit of the Lord GOD is upon me, because he has anointed me* (Isa 61:1), up to, *all who see them shall acknowledge them, that they are a people whom the LORD has blessed* (61:9), are spoken by our Lord and Savior. After this promise, the Church responds: *I will greatly rejoice in the LORD* (61:10), which she joyfully sang in the third song of ascents in the person of a penitent people, *I was glad when they said to me, "Let us go to the house of the LORD"* (Ps 122:1). Now the person of the prophet is introduced with the words: **For Zion's sake I will not keep silent, and for Jerusalem's sake I will not rest** (62:1). Day and night, he says, I shall not close my mouth, and my voice will not be silent, but I shall shout and heap prayers upon prayers until he who was promised will come and illuminate the whole world with his glory. These words set forth more plainly who is the one she seeks and whose coming she yearns for: **until his just one goes forth as splendor, and her savior as a torch** (62:1). In the Gospel Christ spoke of these things when he said: *I am the light of the world* (John 8:12). After the Church has been kindled in Zion and Jerusalem, she will shine not only in Judea, but elsewhere, for to her was said: "The light that was kindled in you, and which came from the Father, began to glow on your boundaries, and it will illuminate the nations."

And all the kings shall see your glory (62:2), O Jerusalem and Zion; he who was born from your stock and was lifted up by a cross among you has drawn all men to himself, so that the nations might see his righteousness by which the Creator of all has shown mercy toward the nations. **Kings will see the glory** through which he was glorified on the cross, and all their kingdoms will be subject to his authority. Further, she will no longer be called Jerusalem and Zion but will receive a new name which the Lord gave when he spoke to the apostle Peter: *You are Peter, and on this rock I will build my church, and the powers of death shall not prevail against it* (Matt 16:18). This name, Christian, is derived from the Lord's name, for the Church is consecrated to the Lord. Therefore his people are not called by the old name Israel, but by a new one, Christian.

And she will be as it were **a crown of beauty in the hand of the Lord, and a royal diadem in the hand of your God** (62:3). This will take place when a host of believers crowns the Church, and an imperial diadem, which the martyrs adorned with their many precious jewels, will be in the hand of God so that he may crown his own Son with their victories. Hence the apostle Paul used to address the saints as *my joy and my crown* (Phil 4:1). . . .

The apostle commands: *Husbands, love your wives as Christ loved the church* (Eph 5:25). In another place he gives an example: *For this reason a man shall leave his father and mother and be joined to his wife, and the two shall become one flesh* (Eph 5:31). Then he adds: *This mystery is a profound one, and I am saying that it refers to Christ and the church* (Eph 5:32). If then because of the shortness of the time that remains *those who have wives should live as though they had none* (1 Cor 7:29), how much more will there be a sacred union between the bride and bridegroom. For this is the bridegroom sung about in Psalm 19: *He comes forth like a bridegroom leaving his chamber* (Ps 19:5). And the bride is the one mentioned often in the Song of Songs, who has neither wrinkle nor *flaw* (Song 4:7). Paul wishes to offer this chaste virgin to one husband, that she may be holy in body and in spirit. Psalm 45 sings about this one under the name of the beloved: *The queen stands at your right hand clothed in a gown of gold and many colors* (Ps 45:13-14). In the way that a bridegroom rejoices in his bride, and a young man with a virgin (examples in which the union is seen as holy), so too will the Lord rejoice in her, whose names shall never again be changed.[2]

62:11
See, the Lord . . . and his work before him

(4) Clement of Alexandria

We ought to have works that cry out *as becoming those who walk in the day* (Rom 13:13). *Let your works shine* (Matt 5:16). Look, a person's works go before him. **Look, God and his works** (62:11). The Gnostic[3] must imitate God with all his power. Even the poets call the elect among them godlike and gods and equal to the gods and a rival of Zeus in wisdom. For "their thoughts are like gods,"[4] and they seem godlike, nibbling as it were at the words *in the image and likeness* (Gen 1:26).

---

2. Once the bride is given a "new name" by the Lord (62:2), her name will never again be changed.
3. For Clement the term "Gnostic" refers to a spiritually mature Christian.
4. *Odyssey* 13.89.

Isaiah 63

1 "Who is this that comes from Edom,
   a redness of garments from Bosor,
so beautiful in apparel,
   in might, with strength?"
"I discourse about righteousness
   and judgment of salvation."

2 "Why are your garments red,
   and your clothes as if from a trodden winepress?"

3 "I am full of a trampled winepress,
   and of the nations no man is with me,
and I trampled them in wrath
   and crushed them like earth,
   and brought down their blood to the earth.
4 For a day of retribution has come upon them,
   and a year of ransom is here.
5 And I looked, but no one was a helper,
   and I observed, but no one was assisting;
so my own arm delivered them,
   and my wrath was present.
6 And I trampled them down in my anger,
   and I brought down their blood to the earth."

7 I called to mind the mercy of the Lord,
   the excellences of the Lord
   in all the things with which the Lord rewards us;
the Lord is a good judge to the house of Israel,
   he provides for us according to his mercy,
   according to the abundance of his righteousness.

8 And he said, "Are they not my people —
    children who will not deal falsely?"
   And he became to them salvation
9   out of all affliction.
   It was no ambassador or angel
     but the Lord himself that saved them,
   because he loved them and spared them;
     he himself ransomed them and took them up
     and lifted them up all the days of old.

10 But they disobeyed
     and provoked his holy spirit;
   therefore he turned to them in enmity,
     and he himself warred against them.
11 Then the one who brought up from the land
     the shepherd of the sheep
     remembered the days of old:
   Where is the one who put within them
     his holy spirit,
12 who led Moyses with his right hand?
     Where is his glorious arm?
   He overcame the water from before him
     to make for himself an everlasting name.
13 He led them through the deep
     like a horse through a desert,
     and they did not become weary,
14   and like cattle through a plain.
   A spirit came down from the Lord and guided them.
   Thus you led your people,
     to make for yourself a glorious name.
15 Turn from heaven and see
     from your holy house and glory.
   Where are your zeal
     and your strength?
   Where is the abundance of your mercy
     and of your compassions,
     that you have held back from us?
16 For you are our father,
     because Abraam did not know us
     and Israel did not recognize us;
   but you, O Lord, are our father;
     deliver us: from the beginning your name is upon us.
17 Why, O Lord, did you make us stray from your way
     and harden our hearts, so that we would not fear you?

> Turn back on account of your slaves,
>> on account of the tribes of your inheritance,
> 18 so that we may inherit a little of your holy mountain;
>> our adversaries have trampled down your sanctuary.
> 19 We have become as at the beginning,
>> when you did not rule us,
>> nor was your name called upon us.

In the early Church the opening verses of chapter 63 were understood to refer to the passion of Christ and his ascension into heaven. **Edom** *signified "from the earth," and the words* **Who is this that comes from Edom?** *(63:1) were taken as a question addressed to Christ by the heavenly powers on his return to glory after his passion and resurrection.* **Scarlet garments** *(63:1) was thought to signify Christ's bloodstained clothing. So widespread was this interpretation in the early Church that it could be considered the "sensus communis." The passage also prompted discussion of the nature of Christ's risen body, and as the excerpt from Didymus indicates, some writers struggled trying to explain what St. Paul meant by a "spiritual body" (1 Cor 15:44). Tertullian and Cyprian also suggest a Eucharistic interpretation of the words* **scarlet garments** *and* **wine** *(63:2). In the Catholic liturgy prior to the reforms of Vatican II the opening verses of this chapter were read on Wednesday of Holy Week. They are also echoed in the first verse of the "Battle Hymn of the Republic": "He is trampling out the vintage where the grapes of wrath are stored."*

(1) The Revelation to John

He is clad in a robe dipped in blood, and the name by which he is called is The Word of God. And the armies of heaven, arrayed in fine linen, white and pure, followed him on white horses.

(2) Cyril of Alexandria

This prophetic oracle wisely and artfully gives a true-to-life portrayal of Christ, the Savior of all, as he makes his return to heaven. In order to accomplish fully the work of the divine plan in the flesh, he ascended to God the Father in heaven. He was seen by the powers above[1] in the form which he had among us, that is, as a man, and also displayed to them the signs of his passion. This passage teaches not only that the perforations from the nails and the other marks remained in his holy flesh after he rose from the dead, but that he showed the nail wounds in his side to Thomas, who had doubted the holy apostles when they said that they had seen the Lord risen from the dead. In ascending Christ also showed the signs of his passion to the heavenly powers *that through the church the manifold wisdom of God might now be made known to the principalities and powers in the heavenly places* (Eph 3:10).

---

1. See 1 Tim 3:16: "He was manifested in the flesh, vindicated in the Spirit, seen by angels...."

His appearance was altogether strange and foreign to the powers above. They were astonished at seeing him come up and asked: **Who is this that comes from Edom?** (63:1). **Edom** can be translated either "of wheat" or "of earth," **Bozrah** (63:1) as either "of flesh" or "fleshly." So they are asking, "Who is this one from the earth, this earthling?" The **scarlet garments from Bozrah** (63:1) means that his clothes were reddened from flesh, or, rather, from blood. **He is beautiful in his apparel** (63:1). The heavenly powers, strong, and wise, and filled with heavenly glory, were looking upon Christ, even in the flesh, as a mighty one, thoroughly invincible, that is to say, he manifested his divinity as well as his humanity to them.

While the angels were asking him or perhaps questioning each other, **Who is this?**, he answers, **It is I, announcing justice [or righteousness] and judgment of salvation** (63:1). By **justice** he means the proclamation of the holy gospel, for the Word of God is just. And by **judgment of salvation** he is referring to his intervention on our behalf. For Christ brought judgment on the region under heaven, a judgment against Satan who had brought injustice into the world, and he delivered those who were oppressed by Satan's insufferable insolence. He cast him out as a rebel who resisted his rule among men. For that reason he once said: *Judgment is of this world; now shall the ruler of this world be cast out; and I, when I am lifted up from the earth, will draw all men to myself* (John 12:31-32).

After Christ speaks, they ask another question: **Why are your garments red, and your clothes as if from treading on the winepress?** (63:2). This brings to mind what the patriarch Jacob said, *He washes his garments in wine and his vesture in the blood of grapes* (Gen 49:11). His clothes were clearly reddened with blood, as if they had been drenched red by wine.

(3) Jerome

Beginning at Isaiah 60, where according to the Septuagint it is said: *Shine, Shine, O Jerusalem, for your light has come, and the glory of the Lord has arisen upon you* (60:1), and up to the present chapter, where it is said, **Who is that one who comes from Edom, in dyed garments from Bozrah** (63:1), the subject, according to many interpreters, is the end of the world. At that time these things are to be fulfilled either physically or spiritually. However, opinion on this matter diverges considerably. We are, however, convinced that these things should be applied to the first advent of our Savior because we also read above in the same section, *The Spirit of the Lord GOD is upon me,* and, *because he has anointed me, has sent me to bring news to the poor* (61:1). When the book of Isaiah had been read in the synagogue of the Jews, our Lord and Savior pointed out that this passage was fulfilled in himself, saying, *Today this scripture has been fulfilled in your hearing* (Luke 4:21). And now Isaiah asserts that after his passion he ascended bloodstained to the Father. For it is not reasonable, as some interpreters think, that events that are linked together should have their fulfillment at different times. We do not deny that it is very difficult to relate all these things to one another and to explain how they are fulfilled in a spiritual sense, yet we do hold that they have all come to pass in Christ according to the flesh as well as according to the Spirit.

Therefore, because the Savior of the *daughter of Zion* (1:8) has come *whose reward is with him, and whose recompense is before him* (40:10), the just one has gone forth in splendor, the Savior has shone like a lamp, and he rejoiced as a bridegroom over his betrothed, the Church. Indeed, God, who is both Bridegroom and Lord, exulted over her. Hence because he took on human flesh and suffered on the cross, it was said of him: *that you may stain your feet in blood* (Ps 68:23). And using the name Judah, it is prophesied in Genesis: *Judah, your brothers will praise you; your hands shall be on the necks of your enemies; your father's sons shall bow down before you. Judah is a lion's whelp; from the prey, my son, you have gone up. He stooped down, he crouched as a lion and as a lioness; who dares rouse him?* (Gen 49:8-9). And again it is written: *Binding his foal to the vineyard and to the vine, he will wash his garment in wine, and his cloak in the blood of the grape* (Gen 49:11). This is the One whom the angelic powers saw ascend bloodstained to the Father, and those who accompanied him called out to the others: *Lift up your gates, O princes! and be lifted up, O ancient doors! and the King of glory will come in. Who is this King of glory? The* Lord, *strong and mighty, the* Lord, *mighty in battle!* (Ps 24:7-8). And again: *The* Lord *of hosts, he is the King of glory!* (Ps 24:10). . . .

The words **Who is this that comes from Edom?** were spoken by the angels. In our language **Edom** means both "from the earth" and "bloody." Hence the angels inquire who this is, because they are astonished at the strangeness of what they have seen. For the mystery of Christ's passion and resurrection, according to the apostle Paul, was unknown to previous generations (cf. 1 Cor 2:6-7). . . .

The Lord answers the inquiring angels, "Do you ask who I am that ascends bloodstained to the Father, who though splattered with blood is not ugly but **beautiful?** (63:1). I am the one to whom the Father hands over all judgment (cf. John 5:22), about whom the psalmist exclaimed: *Give the king thy justice, O God, and your righteousness to the royal son!* (Ps 72:1). I am the one who speaks justice that I may repay evil for evil, good for good. I am he who has come to fight against evil powers, to proclaim freedom to the captives and liberate from prison those in chains (cf. Isa 61:1). I have come to punish my adversaries and free the captives."

Why are your garments red, and your clothes as if from a trodden winepress? (63:2). In Hebrew the term **red** (63:2) is **Edom**. Hence in verse 1 **Edom** is not the name of a place but a term for blood. The angels again ask and say, "We have learned who you are, you who speak justice and in whose justice all have been saved. Now we want to know why your vestments are dyed as if with new wine. What is your tunic, one that was woven from above and cannot be rent, you who from your birth of a virgin had a whiteness that no launderer on earth can produce, why are you stained with blood? For mercy is more fitting for you than cruelty, and whiteness more than gore." The Lord answers them not with a single sentence as at first, but with many words he tells them everything so that they don't have to ask him again.

63:1
Who is this that comes from Edom, with scarlet garments from Bozrah, so beautiful in apparel, in might, with strength?

(4) Tertullian

When Christ established the covenant sealed with his own blood by referring to the cup (Matt 26:27-28), he affirmed the reality of his body. For there can be no blood except from a body which is flesh. For even if it is objected that there can be a body that is not flesh, surely it cannot have blood if it is not of flesh. So proof that there is a body is firmly established by the evidence of flesh, just as proof that there is flesh stands by evidence of the blood. Isaiah helps us see in wine an ancient figure for blood, when he asks: **Who is this that comes from Edom with his garments scarlet from Bozrah? He is beautiful in apparel, which is violent with strength. Why are your garments red, and your clothes as from the outlet of a winepress, fully trodden down?** (63:1-2). The prophetic spirit, contemplating the Lord coming to his passion, clothed of course in the flesh in which he would suffer, indicates by that redness of apparel the bloodstained garment of his flesh that was trodden on and pressed down by the violence of the passion, as in the outlet of a winepress. Men come down from a winepress as though stained with blood from the redness of the wine. This is even clearer in the book of Genesis at the blessing of Judah, from whose tribe Christ took his flesh. There Christ is depicted as Judah: *He shall wash his garment in wine and his vesture in the blood of the grapes* (Gen 49:11). By *garment* and *vesture* the text signifies his flesh, and by *wine* his blood. So now he consecrated his blood in wine, which of old he had used as a figure for blood.

(5) Cyprian of Carthage

The figure of Christ is portrayed in the blessing of Judah (Gen 49:10), because Judah was to be praised and worshiped by his brethren. Christ was destined to press down upon the necks of his enemies as they turned and fled — using those very hands by which he bore the cross and conquered death. For he is himself the lion of the tribe of Judah (Gen 49:9; Rev 5:5). He lies down to sleep during his passion, but then he arises to become the hope of the nations. To which the Holy Scriptures add these words: *He will wash his garments in wine and his robe in the blood of the grape* (Gen 49:11). When it speaks of the blood of the grape, what else is this than the wine of the cup, the blood of the Lord?

In Isaiah the Holy Spirit bears witness to this same thing when he speaks of the Lord's passion in the words: **Why are your garments red, and your clothes as if from treading a full and well-trodden wine vat?** (63:2). Can water make clothing red? In the **wine vat** is it water which is trodden by the feet and squeezed out by the press? Clearly **wine** is referred to here, so that by **wine** we may understand the blood of the Lord. What was made known later in the cup of the Lord was foretold by the proclamation of the prophets. It also mentions **treading** and pressing down, because one cannot prepare wine for drinking without the bunch of grapes first being trodden and pressed. In the same way we could not drink the blood of Christ if Christ had not first been trodden upon and pressed down and first drunk the cup that he would pass on for his believers to drink.

(6) Origen of Alexandria

After he had destroyed his enemies by his passion, *the LORD, mighty in battle and strong* (Ps 24:8) needed purification[2] for his great deeds of valor that only the Father could give. So he forbids Mary to hold him[3] and says: *Do not hold me, for I have not yet ascended to the Father. But go to my brethren and say to them, I am going to my Father and your Father, to my God and your God* (John 20:17).

When he goes to the Father, victorious and bearing trophies, with the body that had been raised from the dead (for how else are we to understand, *I have not yet ascended to my Father*, and *but I am going to my Father?*), some of the powers say: **Who is this that comes from Edom in scarlet garments from Bozrah, so beautiful?** (63:1). And those escorting him cry to those stationed at the gates of heaven: *Lift up your gates, you princes! and be lifted up, everlasting doors! and the King of glory will come in* (Ps 24:7).

When they see his right hand dripping with blood — if one must speak this way — and his person covered with blood because of his valorous deeds, they inquire further: **Why is your apparel scarlet, and your garments as if fresh from a full winepress that has been trampled down?** (63:2). To which he answers: **I trampled them** (63:3). Indeed, this is why he had to *wash his robe in wine and his garments in the blood of grapes* (Gen 49:11). For after he *bore our infirmities* and *carried our sicknesses* (Isa 53:4), and after he *took away the sin of the whole world* (John 1:29) and had done so much good to so many, then he received the Baptism that is greater than any imagined by men, to which he alluded when he said: *I have a baptism to be baptized with; and how I am constrained until it is accomplished!* (Luke 12:50). . . .

After he had performed these valorous deeds against his adversaries, as we have mentioned, he needed to wash *his robe in wine and his garment in the blood of grapes* (Gen 49:11). So he went up to the vinedresser of the true vine, the Father (cf. John 15:1), that being washed there after *he ascended on high leading captivity captive* (Eph 4:8), he might descend bearing all sorts of gifts, for example, tongues of fire distributed among the apostles and the assistance and protection of the holy angels in all their undertakings.

(7) Didymus the Blind

And the King of glory will come in (Ps 24:7). The angels who advance before the Savior during his ascent say these words to the powers above, to those who lift up the heavenly gates. Then the powers inquire, *Who is this King of glory?* (Ps 24:8), whose arrival you an-

---

2. Christ needed purification because in contending against sin and death in his passion he had been contaminated with evil. See selection #8 below, from Gregory of Nyssa.

3. Origen is commenting on John 20:17.

nounce, for whom one must lift up the gates and raise up the *eternal gates* (Ps 23:7 LXX) — not the temporal ones, but the immortal ones? In Isaiah something similar is said when they ask: **Who is this who comes from Edom, with scarlet garments from Bozrah? Why are your garments red?** (63:1). Although this is the body that belonged to the Savior when he was risen from the dead and certainly before that, it does not have the marks of the flesh since it has been transformed into a *spiritual body* (1 Cor 15:44). However, by the grace of the one who ascends, certain marks were preserved so that it was possible to recognize where he had come from. Therefore the text reads **scarlet garment from Bozrah** (63:1).

When he rose from the dead he appeared to the disciples, for he wished to confirm for them that he possessed a risen body. He showed them the impressions of the nails, and the wounds, not that that body has wounds — for it is a property of a hard and resistant body to bear wounds — but so that he might give assurance that he was the Risen One. Then, to keep them from thinking wrongly about the resurrection (because he had shown them a sign as evidence of the resurrection), namely, that the risen body will again bear the distinctive properties of the corruptible body, he entered through closed doors (John 20:19). In the same way, here in Isaiah, when he was being taken up, immediately upon the ascension he showed the marks of the flesh, not however, to suggest that they would remain. Neither does he still possess those things he had shown the disciples, for example, eating or the impressions of the nails and the other things. He did not eat after the resurrection, as though to indicate that we might later eat, but so that they might see that he was the one he had said he was, the Risen One. Indeed, Luke mentions this, *He also presented himself alive after the passion with many proofs, appearing to them and having fellowship with them* (Acts 1:3).

(8) Gregory of Nyssa

The remainder of this psalm [Psalm 24] may be even more profound than the teaching of the gospel itself. For the gospel recounted the Lord's way of life while on earth. But this sublime prophet David experiences ecstatic release to the point that he is no longer limited by his body and mingles with the heavenly powers. He transmits their voices to us as they accompany the Lord on his return to heaven and command the angels to whom he had been entrusted during his sojourn among men to fling open the doors, *Lift up your gates, O rulers! and be lifted up, O everlasting doors! that the King of glory may come in* (Ps 24:7). Wherever he is, the One who embraces all things in himself adapts to the one who receives him. He not only became a man among men, but also among angels he condescended to their nature. For this reason the gatekeepers ask the one who presents him, *Who is this King of glory?* (Ps 24:8). And they announce that he is the one *strong and mighty in battle* (Ps 24:8), who contended against the one who had taken human nature captive. His mission was to put down the one who holds the power of death so that when the last enemy is destroyed (1 Cor 15:26), human nature may be called back to freedom and peace.

Moreover, the prophet says something quite similar elsewhere (for already the mystery of death has reached its end and the enemy has been vanquished and the cross lifted high as a trophy against its foes): *He ascended on high who takes captivity captive* (Ps 68:18) and gives life and the kingdom as good gifts to all. So it was fitting that the heavenly gates should be thrown open for him. Our guardians meet the triumphal procession and command that the heavenly gates be opened for him so that they may see his glory. But they do not recognize him clothed in filthy human apparel, **his clothes stained red from the wine vat** (63:2) from contact with human evil. Hence the question to those who are approaching: *Who is this King of glory?* But the reply is no longer, *the one who is strong and mighty in battle* but *The Lord of hosts* (24:10), on whose power all things depend, who *sums up all things in himself* (Eph 1:10), who *is preeminent in everything* (Col 1:18), who restores all things to their original creation, he is the *King of glory* (Ps 24:10).

(9) Ambrose of Milan

The angels were in doubt when Christ rose from the dead, and the powers of heaven were in doubt when they saw his flesh coming up to heaven. So they asked: *Who is this King of glory?* (Ps 24:8). And others said: *Lift up your gates, O princes! and be lifted up, eternal gates! and the King of glory will come in* (Ps 24:7). Others were in doubt and inquired: *Who is this King of glory?* (Ps 24:10). In Isaiah you learn that the powers of heaven also were in doubt and asked: **Who is this that comes from Edom with scarlet garments from Bozrah, beautiful in a white stole?** (63:1).

(10) Augustine of Hippo

In the virgin's womb Christ received human flesh as a kind of pledge; on the cross he shed his blood as a priceless dowry; in his resurrection and ascension he confirmed the contract of this eternal marriage. *For he ascended on high, he led captivity captive, he gave gifts to men* (Eph 4:8). What gifts? The Holy Spirit, through whom love has been poured out upon human minds (cf. Rom 5:5) and the Church has been attached inseparably to Christ as her husband.

So he came forth today[4] like a bridegroom from his sacred chamber, and as the psalm continues, *he exulted as a giant to run the course* (Ps 19:5). He came forth as a bridegroom, he exulted as a giant. Beautiful and strong; beautiful as a bridegroom, strong as a giant. Beautiful so as to be loved, strong so as to be feared; beautiful to give pleasure, strong to win victories. Where in the Sacred Scriptures is the beauty of this bridegroom to be found? *Handsome in form above the sons of men; grace is poured upon your lips* (Ps 45:2). Where is the giant's strength to be found? *The Lord, strong and mighty, the Lord, mighty in battle* (Ps 24:8). Each quality, though, that is, both beauty and strength, had been seen and understood by Isaiah when he asked: **Who is this that comes from Edom, in scarlet garments from Bozrah, so handsome in the robe of his garment and**

---

4. This passage is taken from a sermon preached on Christmas Day.

strength? (63:1). So this prophet, who called him both handsome and strong, knew him as bridegroom and *giant*.

(11) Gregory the Great

Long ago Isaiah looked upon the garment of Christ, which was stained with the blood of the passion on the cross, and inquired, **Why are your garments red, and your clothes as if from a trodden winepress?** (63:2). To which he answered, **I alone have trodden the winepress, and of the nations no man is with me** (63:3). He alone trod the winepress in which he was trodden, he who by his own power conquered the passion which he endured. For he who suffered *unto death on a cross* (Phil 2:8) rose from the dead in glory. And rightly is it said, **And of the nations no man is with me**, since those on whose behalf he came to suffer ought to have shared in his passion. But, inasmuch as at that time the nations had not yet come to believe, in his passion he laments those whose life he sought in that passion.

63:5
I looked, but no one was a helper.

(12) Eusebius of Caesarea

Then he says, **I looked, but no one was a helper; I observed, but no one was assisting; so my own arm delivered them** (63:5). We can understand that the Word is being referred to here if we consider that he alone *emptied himself, taking the form of a servant . . . and he humbled himself and became obedient unto death, even death on a cross* (Phil 2:7-8). The things which no man or angel or supernatural power ever attempted, he alone undertook for our salvation. Therefore, the Father *bestowed on him alone the name which is above every name* (Phil 2:9) and entrusted him with the universal judgment. He who received power from the Father rescued those who were worthy of salvation and turned back his hostile enemies. That is why the text says, **my wrath was present. I trampled them down in my anger, and I brought down their blood to the earth** (63:5-6). Instead of **their blood** other translators have rendered the phrase **their victory**. It seems that there had been some who were obstinate and would concede victory to no one; perhaps he indicates their defeat and humiliation by declaring, **he has poured out their victory on the ground**.

63:9
It was no ambassador or angel, but the Lord himself that saved them.

(13) Irenaeus of Lyons

The *Lord himself,* who is *Emmanuel* from the *Virgin,* is the *sign* (7:14) of our salvation. For it was the Lord himself who saved them because they were not able to save themselves.

For this Paul spoke about human weakness when he said: *I know that nothing good dwells within my flesh* (Rom 7:18). By this he meant that the good that is our salvation is not from us but from God. And again: *Wretched man that I am! Who will deliver me from this body of death?* (Rom 7:24). Then he presents the deliverer: *Thanks be to God through Jesus Christ our Lord!* (Rom 7:25). And Isaiah also says this: *Be strong, you weak hands and feeble knees. Take courage, faint of heart, be comforted, fear not. Behold, our God is repaying judgment with recompense. He himself will come and save us* (35:4). So we see that we will be saved not by ourselves but only with God's help. That it was not a mere man who would save us nor a being without flesh (for the angels are without flesh), Isaiah proclaimed: **It was no ambassador or angel but the Lord himself that saved them, because he loved them and spared them; he himself ransomed them** (63:9). And to show that he would be fully human and visible when he comes as the Word bringing salvation, Isaiah adds: *Behold, city of Zion; your eyes shall see our salvation* (33:20).

63:10
They disobeyed and provoked his holy spirit.

(14) Basil of Caesarea

Scripture says that *the Spirit himself intercedes for us* (Rom 8:26). It would seem that as the intercessor must always be inferior to a benefactor, so the Spirit must be inferior to God. But have you never heard what is said about the Only-Begotten? *He is at the right hand of God and intercedes for us* (Rom 8:34). Do not, because the Spirit is in you — if indeed he is truly in you — shy away from confessing the pious and holy teaching concerning him. He is the one who teaches us who were blind and guides us to choose what is good. It would be a grievous affront to repay the loving-kindness of our benefactor with ingratitude. *Do not grieve the Holy Spirit* (Eph 4:30). Listen to what Stephen, the first martyr, said when he reproached the people for their rebellion and disobedience: *You always resist the Holy Spirit* (Acts 7:51). And Isaiah says: **They grieved the Holy Spirit; therefore he became their enemy** (63:10). And elsewhere: *The house of Israel provoked the Spirit of the Lord* (cf. Ps 106:33). Are not these passages evidence of his sovereign might? I leave it to the judgment of my readers to decide how these passages are to be interpreted. Are we to regard the Spirit as an instrument, a subject, of equal rank with creatures, a servant like us? Or should we say that even the merest hint of such blasphemy is intolerable to the ears of the pious? Do you say that the Spirit is a servant? How can that be when it is written: *The servant does not know what his master is doing* (John 15:15). But the *Spirit knows the things of God as the spirit of man knows the things of man* (1 Cor 2:10-11).

Isaiah 64

1 If you should open heaven,
   trembling from you would seize the mountains,
   and they would melt
2(1)[1]as wax melts from the fire.
   And fire shall burn up your adversaries,
      and the name of the Lord shall be manifest among your adversaries;
      nations shall be confused at your presence!
3(2)When you do your glorious deeds,
   trembling from you will seize the mountains.
4(3)From ages past we have not heard,
      nor have our eyes seen any God besides you,
      and your works, which you will do to those who wait for mercy.
5(4)For he will meet those who do what is right,
      and they will remember your ways.
   Look, you were angry, and we sinned;
      therefore we went astray.
6(5)And we have all become like unclean people,
      all our righteousness is like the rag
      of a woman who sits apart.
   And we have fallen off like leaves because of our transgressions,
      thus the wind will take us away.
7(6)And there is no one who calls on your name,
      or remembers to take hold of you;
   because you have turned your face away from us,
      and have delivered us over because of our sins.
8(7)And now, O Lord, you are our Father,
      and we are clay;
      we are all the work of your hands.

---

1. Editions of the LXX begin numbering the verses of chapter 64 with the second verse.

9(8)**Do not be exceedingly angry,**
>   **and do not remember our sins in season.**
>   **And now look upon us, because we are all your people.**
10(9)**Your holy city has become a wilderness,**
>   **Sion has become like a wilderness,**
>   **Ierousalem a curse.**
11(10)**The house, our holy place,**
>   **even the glory that our ancestors blessed,**
> **has been burned by fire,**
>   **and all our glorious places have fallen in ruins.**
12(11)**And for all this**
>   **you have restrained yourself, O Lord,**
>   **and have kept silent, and have humbled us severely.**

The opening words of chapter 64, **If you would open the heavens** *(64:1), were understood to refer to the Incarnation, as Jerome indicates in the passage from his commentary. Verse 4,* **From ages past we have not heard, nor have our eyes seen any god besides you,** *was cited in 1 Cor 2:9, "What no eye has seen, nor ear heard, nor the heart of man conceived," and it is in the version of 1 Corinthians that the text was most often cited in sermons and others writings. It was sometimes related to the beatitude, "Blessed are the pure in heart, for they shall see God" (Matt 5:8), as in the selection from Leo the Great. The verse,* **Look, you were angry, and we sinned** *(64:5), posed difficulties for interpreters. The order of the verse seemed reversed. The sentence should, it seems, read,* **Because we sinned, you were angry.** *Cyril tries to make sense of the original version, but others simply interpret it to mean that God was angry because of our sin.* **All our righteousness is like a menstrual rag** *(64:6) was interpreted in light of St. Paul's contrast between our righteousness and the righteousness of Christ (Phil 3:8-9).*

(1) 1 Corinthians

We impart a secret and hidden wisdom of God, which God decreed before the ages for our glorification. None of the rulers of this age understood this; for if they had, they would not have crucified the Lord of glory. But as it is written, **What no eye has seen, nor ear heard, nor the heart of man conceived, what God has prepared for those who love him** (64:4), God has revealed to us through the Spirit. For the Spirit searches everything, even the depths of God.

(2) Jerome

These things were said at the time before the Savior had come and before he had assumed from a virginal womb of our nature and substance that humanity which he was going to save — so that we, who have borne the image of what is earthly, may in turn bear the image of the heavenly (1 Corinthians 15). If you would come down, they say, and the **heav-**

Isaiah 64

ens were opened, at your coming in majesty the **mountains would overflow** and the **mountains would quake** (64:1) and be consumed as **wax** is when touched by **fire**.

The heavens opened for Ezekiel, and he saw a great vision (Ezekiel 1). Moses, too, prays in the "blessings" in Deuteronomy: *The LORD will open to you his good treasury the heavens, in order to give you a blessing* (Deut 28:12). And in the Gospel John the Baptist is said to have seen the heavens opened and the Holy Spirit descending upon the Lord in the form of a dove (Matt 3:16). Moreover, it is written, *The LORD is a consuming fire* (Deut 4:24). Hence, when the text says that at the coming of the Lord the mountains will be consumed and melted like wax, this signifies the powers which stood against him and all who raise themselves up against the knowledge of God. Psalm 97 also speaks about these things: *He looked and the land was shaken. The mountains melted like wax before the LORD, before the Lord of all the earth* (Ps 97:4-5).

In the version of Symmachus the text reads: **If you come down and fulfill your promises, the waters of the sea would waste away and fire would consume the entire salty expanse of those waters** (64:1). Another psalm speaks about these things: *As smoke fails, let them fail; as wax melts before fire, let the wicked perish before God!* (Ps 68:2). And, it should be noted, when the waters of the sea will have been consumed by divine fire, then the name of the Lord and Savior will be made known to his enemies. Concerning these things it is spoken in Psalm 68: *the tongues of your dogs may have their portion from the foe* (68:23), in order that through their own captivity and the overthrow of their city they may learn of him whom they did not perceive through his kindnesses.

And the nations will tremble at thy presence (64:2) means that they will be stirred (as it is expressed more clearly in the Hebrew), so that what formerly did not move may come to salvation. When he does **glorious deeds** (64:3), as in the gospel, and works signs which he once displayed in Egypt and in the wilderness, they would confess that they are unable to bear the glory of his coming, that is, **trembling will seize the mountains** (64:3). The passage is beautiful in the Hebrew, for it makes clear that the words they prayed, **O that you would rend the heavens and come down, and the mountains would flow down at your presence** (64:1), had been clearly heard. For they go on to say: **You did come down** (64:3). That is, *The Word was made flesh and dwelt among us* (John 1:14). Indeed, he is *Emmanuel, which means, God with us* (Matt 1:23). For this reason all the mountains flowed down at your presence, as we have discussed above. . . .

In the sentence, **Behold, you were angry, and we sinned** (64:5), the order is inverted. We have sinned not because you are angry; but you are angry because we have sinned. It is because we have sinned that you are angry at us, O Lord. We have wandered and abandoned the straight path. Or, according to the Hebrew, **we have been a long time in our sins and have brought uncleanness upon ourselves, and are saved only by your mercy** (64:5). Whatever righteousness we seem to have is comparable either to the **rags of a beggar** (according to the Hebrew) or to a **menstrual rag** (64:6). . . . This text means that in comparison to the purity of the gospel the righteousness of the law is called uncleanness. *Indeed, what once had splendor has come to have no splendor at all because of the splendor that surpasses it* (2 Cor 3:11). Hence the apostle Paul, who had fulfilled everything according to the righteousness of the law, says that he had considered all these things as worthless *in order that he might gain Christ* (Phil 3:8). Because of the surpassing knowledge of our Lord Jesus Christ, he considers everything to be dung and desires only to gain Christ and to be found in him, not having a righteousness of his own which is from the law, but the righteousness which comes from God through faith in Christ (Phil 3:7-9).

A righteous man will die in his own righteousness if, after knowing the truth of the gospel, he desires to follow the shadows of the law and pursue that which is righteous in an unrighteous manner. Hence, according to the very wise Solomon, every man appears righteous to himself when he lives by the law. To these the Lord speaks in the Gospel: *You are those who justify yourselves before men* (Luke 16:15). But Paul will have nothing to do with this: *I am not aware of anything against myself, but I am not thereby acquitted* (1 Cor 4:4). Concerning the righteousness of God that has nothing to do with sin, Solomon enjoins: *Understand true righteousness* (Prov 1:3 LXX). There is then another righteousness that is not the true righteousness, but true righteousness is that about which it is said in the Gospel: *Blessed are those who hunger and thirst for righteousness* (Matt 5:6).

64:1
If you should open heaven, trembling would seize the mountains, and they would melt.

(3) Cyril of Jerusalem

It is impossible to behold God with the eyes of the flesh. For what is without a body cannot be perceived by eyes of flesh. The only Son of God himself bore witness, saying: *No one has seen God at any time* (John 1:18). If, however, one should think that Ezekiel saw God because of what is written in the book of Ezekiel, let him read what the Scripture actually says. He saw the *likeness of the glory of the* LORD (Ezek 1:28). He did not see the Lord himself, but the *likeness of his glory*, not the glory itself as it truly is. But even when he saw only the *likeness of his glory* and not the glory itself, he fell to the earth in fear. Now if the sight of the *likeness of God's glory* filled the prophets with fear and apprehension, then someone who attempted to behold God would surely die, as it is written: *No one shall see my face and live* (Exod 33:20).

For this reason, out of his great love God spread out the heavens as a veil to shield us from his godhead, that we might not perish. It is not I but the prophet who said: **If you should open heaven, trembling would seize the mountains, and they would melt** (64:1). Why then do you wonder that Ezekiel fell on his face when he saw the *likeness of God's glory* (Ezek 1:28)? Even Daniel, when he saw Gabriel who was only a servant of God, immediately fell on his face, and even though he was himself a prophet, he dared not answer him until the angel transformed himself into human form.[2] If the sight of Gabriel made the prophets tremble in fear, would not all have perished if they had seen God himself? It is impossible, then, to behold the divine nature with the eyes of the flesh. We are, however, able to gain some sense of God's power from his works, as Solomon said: *From the greatness and beauty of created things comes a corresponding perception of their Creator* (Wis 13:5).

---

2. See the account in Daniel 10. The figure who appears to Daniel was understood to be the angel Gabriel.

64:4
From ages past we have not heard,
nor have our eyes seen any God besides you.

(4) Augustine of Hippo

For the faithful seeking their homeland, this world is as the desert was for the people of Israel. The Israelites were still wandering about and seeking their homeland, but with God as their leader they could not go astray. God's command was the way for them. For where they wandered about for forty years, the journey itself had but a few stopping places, as is well known. They made their way slowly because they were being trained, not because God had abandoned them. What God promises us therefore is unspeakable sweetness and a good, as Scripture says, and you have often heard me speak of it, namely, **no eye has seen, nor ear has heard**, *nor the heart of man conceived* (64:4; 1 Cor 2:9). But we are disciplined by our labors in this world and are trained by the temptation in this life. But if you do not wish to die of thirst in this desert, drink love. It is the spring that the Lord wished to put here in order that we may not faint on the way. And we shall drink of it more abundantly when we come to the homeland.

(5) Augustine of Hippo

What does, *go into your room and shut the door and pray to your Father in secret* (Matt 6:6), mean? That you should ask God for what God alone knows how to give. What is it you wish to obtain when you shut your door and offer your petition? It is **what eye has not seen, nor ear heard, nor has it entered into the heart of man** (64:4; 1 Cor 2:9). And it may not even have entered into that bed of yours, that is, your heart. However, God knows what he intends to give you. But when will that be? When the Lord is revealed, when the judge appears. For what can be clearer than his greeting to those who are to be at his right hand? *Come, O blessed of my Father, inherit the kingdom prepared for you from the foundation of the world* (Matt 25:34).

(6) Cyril of Alexandria

God is by nature invisible. As it is written, *No one has ever seen God* (John 1:18). God is perceived by the eyes of the mind through the things he does in marvelous and surprising ways. *Ever since the creation of the world his invisible nature, namely, his eternal power and deity, has been clearly perceived in the things that have been made* (Rom 1:20). But he is most often known through his merciful actions and gives proof of his compassion by unexpectedly rescuing those who have lost all hope. For he extends his consoling hand to those who are fallen down and as it were lying on the ground. Such is the conviction of those who offer the prayer found in this passage.

From the beginning of the world, they say, we have **not heard nor seen a God be-**

sides you (64:4), and you alone. To those who wait on you, meaning those who place their hopes in you, you lavish your grace. It follows that those who are **workers of righteousness** (64:5) are fit to receive your grace and **remember your ways** (64:5), that is, to remember what your acts of will have accomplished. The ways of the Lord are his commandments. Therefore wise David sang in the psalm: *I live in your way,* and again, *I have run the way of your commandments since you have widened my heart for them* (Ps 119:11-15).³

(7) Leo the Great

Blessed are the pure in heart, for they shall see God (Matt 5:8). Great is the happiness, beloved, of the one for whom so great a reward is made ready. What, then, is it to have a pure heart but to strive to achieve those virtues mentioned in the other beatitudes? What mind can conceive and what tongue can declare how great is the blessedness of seeing God? Yet this will take place when human nature is transformed and it will no longer look *in a mirror nor in a riddle but face to face* (1 Cor 13:12) and will see what *no man can see* (1 Tim 6:16), God *as he is* (1 John 3:2). Through the unspeakable joy of the eternal vision one will obtain that **which eye has not seen, nor ear heard, nor entered into the heart of man** (64:4; 1 Cor 2:9). This happiness is rightly promised to the *pure in heart.* For the brightness of the true light cannot be seen by those whose vision is clouded. What brings happiness to the minds that are bright and clean will be punishment to those that are stained. So shun the dark clouds of earth's vanities and purge your inner eyes from all filth of wickedness, so that your sight may be fed on the magnificent vision of God.

64:5
But you were angry, and we sinned; therefore we went astray.

(8) Gregory the Theologian

We have sinned, we have transgressed, we have done wrong (Bar 2:12), because we have forgotten your commandments and followed our own evil thought. We have behaved unworthily of the calling and gospel of your Christ, and of his holy sufferings and emptying for us (Phil 2:7); we have become a reproach to your beloved. Priest and people together, we have erred, we have all gone wrong and become worthless. *There is no one who judges rightly or acts justly, not one* (Ps 14:3)! We have cut short your mercies and kindness, and we have turned away from the compassion of our God by our wickedness and our perverse behavior.

You are good, but we have done wrong; you are long-suffering, but we deserve punishment. Though we acknowledge your goodness, we lack understanding. Yet, though our sins are great, we have been scourged but little. *You are terrible! Who can stand before you?* (Ps 76:7). The mountains will **tremble before you** (64:1), and who will strive against the might of your arm? If you shut the **heaven**, who will **open** (64:1) it? And if you let

---

3. Cyril's citation of the psalm is very free.

loose the torrents, who will restrain them? In your eyes it is a small thing to make poor and to make rich, to bring to life and to kill, to strike and to heal. Your will and your act are in perfect harmony. **You were angry, and we have sinned** (64:5), says one of old, making confession. But now it is the time for me to say the reverse: "We have sinned, and you are angry." For that reason we have become a reproach to our neighbors. You turned your face from us, and we were filled with dishonor. But stay your hand, Lord; cease, Lord; Lord, forgive. Lord, do not abandon us forever because of our iniquities, and let us not be the ones whose punishment instructs others. Rather, let us learn wisdom from the trials of others. From whom? From the nations that do not know you, and kingdoms that have not been subject to your rule. For *we are your people* (Ps 79:13), O Lord, *the rod of your inheritance* (Ps 73:2 LXX). So correct us, but in goodness, not in your anger, lest you belittle us and we are mocked by all who dwell on earth (cf. Ps 79:1, 4, 12).

(9) Cyril of Alexandria

Some interpreters think it is necessary to transpose the meaning of this verse, **But you were angry, and we sinned** (64:5). By reversing the order of the phrases, or at least giving them a different sense, it would be possible to read it in the following way: **We sinned, and you were angry** (64:5). Such interpreters wish to rule out the possibility that divine wrath was a factor contributing to sin. However, I think one must insist that it is no indictment of God's wrath if those overtaken by it find themselves incapable of escaping the onslaught of sin.

As long as the one who saves takes pleasure in us, we are able to overcome sin, and when we are emboldened to put aside our inclinations toward vice, we are crowned with spiritual strength. If, however, we offend the one who gives us strength, the captain who bestows courage, we are overcome by impotence and our mind is enfeebled. For God is the LORD *of hosts* (Ps 24:10). And Christ said, *Apart from me you can do nothing* (John 15:5). With respect to the saints the inspired David somewhere said to God: *For thou art the glory of their strength* (Ps 89:17). Moreover, in another place, he sings that the ability to accomplish a good deed comes not from himself but from God's power. He declares, *For not in my bow do I trust, nor can my sword save me. But thou hast saved us from our foes* (Ps 44:6-7). In this way the gentle grace that comes from above gives us strength and steels us to oppose the assault of evil. In the same way when we fall under divine anger, of necessity we become slaves to pleasures that debase us further.

64:6a
All our righteousness is like a menstrual rag.

(10) Origen of Alexandria

The boasting of the Jews is excluded (Rom 3:27), not through the law of works but through the law of faith in Christ Jesus, in whose cross the apostle gloried (Gal 6:14). Who can have any reason for boasting about his chastity when he reads what is written: *if someone looks at a woman lustfully, he has already committed adultery with her in his heart* (Matt 5:28)? So also the prophet asks: *How can anyone boast that he has a pure heart?* (Prov 20:9). Or who can boast about his wisdom, when he sees that it is written: *since the world did not know God through wisdom, it pleased God through the folly of what we preach to save those who believe* (1 Cor 1:21)? And again: *God has chosen what is foolish in the world to shame the wise* (1 Cor 1:27). Moreover, who can boast about his righteousness when he hears what God said through the prophet: **all your righteousness is like a menstrual rag** (64:6)? The only proper boasting is in faith in the cross of Christ that excludes all boasting derived from doing the works of the law.

(11) Martyrius Sahdona

At his *voice the earth quakes* (Ps 46:6), and who can endure the sight of his face? Nothing that has breath is able to speak in his presence. Our entire inner being is *overwhelmed* (Dan 10:8), and at the sight of him, out of awe our mouths are stopped in silence. And even if we regain just a little strength to speak before him, our consciences rebuke us, seeing that *we have sinned and done wrong* (Ps 106:6) in his presence. If we should imagine that we have been put in a state of righteousness, then all our righteousness is **like a menstrual rag** (64:6), for the victory belongs to him, whereas *ours is the shamefacedness* (Bar 1:15).

64:6b
We all have fallen off like leaves, and our transgressions have carried us away like the wind.

(12) Gregory the Great

Will you show your power against a leaf driven by the wind and pursue dry stubble (Job 13:25 Vg.)? What is man but a leaf who fell from the tree in paradise? What is he but a leaf driven by the wind of temptation and lifted up by the gusts of his desires? Indeed, the human mind is tossed around by gusts as it suffers so many temptations. Anger often perturbs it, and when the anger dissipates, empty pleasure follows. It is beset by the stings of luxury, and the fever of avarice causes it to stretch far and wide in seeking earthly things. Sometimes pride lifts it up, and at other times inordinate fear pulls it down to the depths. Therefore, since man is lifted up and led by so many gusts of temptation, he is rightly compared to a leaf. Thus it is well said through Isaiah: **We all have fallen off like leaves, and our transgressions have carried us away like the wind** (64:6). Our transgression has carried us away like the wind because, since we are not steadied by any weight of virtue, it has lifted us up to a state of vain pride.

Isaiah 64

64:8
O Lord, you are our Father.

(13) Cyril of Jerusalem

If anyone wishes to learn why we call God Father, let him listen to Moses the most excellent teacher: *Is not he your father, who made you and created you?* (Deut 32:6). And also Isaiah the prophet: **O Lord, thou art our Father; we are the clay, the work of thy hands** (64:8). The prophetic grace has made clear that we call God Father not by nature but by God's grace and by adoption.

64:9
Do not be exceedingly angry.

(14) Didymus the Blind

The Lord renders to each person according to his deeds. Toward those who commit many large and grave sins **he is exceedingly angry** (64:9). But his anger is mild to those who fall in little things and only occasionally. He also said about chastisements that are the instruments of his wrath: *While I was angry with them but a little, they added to their evils* (Zech 1:15). And those who accuse themselves by their transgressions cry out to the compassionate and merciful Lord: **Be not exceedingly angry, O Lord** (64:9). Since God is a *righteous judge, firm and patient, and he does not require vengeance every day* (Ps 7:12 LXX), he tempers his wrath toward those he judges, and does not count all their evil deeds against them.

Isaiah 65

1 I became visible to those who were not seeking me,
   I was found by those who were not inquiring about me.
I said, "Here I am,"
   to the nation that did not call my name.
2 I stretched out my hands all day long
   to a disobedient and contrary people,
who did not walk in a true way
   but after their own sins.
3 These are the people who provoke me
   to my face continually;
they sacrifice in the gardens
   and burn incense on bricks
   to the demons, which do not exist;
4 and they fall asleep in the tombs
   and in the caves for the sake of dreams —
those who eat swine's flesh
   and broth of sacrifices
   (all their vessels are defiled);
5 who say, "Stay far away from me,
   do not come near me, for I am clean."
This is the smoke of my wrath,
   a fire burns in it all the days.
6 See, it is written before me:
   I will not keep silent
until I repay into their bosom
7   their sins and those of their ancestors — says the Lord —
who burned incense on the mountains
   and reviled me on the hills;
   I will repay their works into their bosom.
8 Thus says the Lord:

Isaiah 65

As the grape will be found in the cluster,
  and they will say, "Do not destroy it,
  because the blessing of the Lord is in it,"
so I will do for the sake of the one who serves me:
  for the sake of this one I will not destroy them all.
9 And I will bring forth the offspring
  that comes from Iakob and from Ioudas,
  and it will inherit my holy mountain;
  and my chosen ones and my slaves
  shall inherit it and dwell there.
10 And there shall be in the forest folds of flocks,
  and the Valley of Achor shall become a resting place of herds
  for my people who have sought me.
11 But as for you who forsake me,
  and forget my holy mountain,
  and prepare a table for the demon
  and fill a mixed drink for Fortune:
12 I will deliver you over to the sword,
  all of you shall fall by slaughter;
  because I called you and you did not answer,
  I spoke and you misheard,
  and you did what was evil before me,
  and chose the things I did not desire.
13 Therefore this is what the Lord says:
  See, those who serve me shall eat,
    but you shall be hungry;
  see, those who serve me shall drink,
    but you shall be thirsty;
  see, those who serve me shall rejoice,
    but you shall be put to shame;
14 see, those who serve me shall be glad with joy,
    but you shall cry out because of the pain of your heart,
    and shall wail for crushing of spirit.
15 For you shall leave your name for fullness to my chosen ones,
    but the Lord will do away with you.
  But to those who serve him a new name shall be called,
16   which shall be blessed on the earth;
  for they shall bless the true God,
    and those who swear on the earth
    shall swear by the true God;
  for they shall forget their first affliction,
    and it shall not come up into their heart.

17 For heaven will be new,

>   and the earth will be new,
>   and they shall not remember the former things,
>   nor shall they come upon their heart,
> 18 but they shall find joy and gladness in it;
>   because look, I am making Ierousalem as gladness,
>   and my people as a joy.
> 19 And I will be glad over Ierousalem,
>   and rejoice over my people;
>   and no more shall a voice of weeping be heard in it,
>   nor a voice of crying.
> 20 And there shall not be there
>   one who dies untimely,
>   or an old person who will not fulfill his time;
>   for the young person will be a hundred years old,
>   but the one who dies a sinner will be a hundred years old and accursed.
> 21 And they shall build houses and themselves shall inhabit them,
>   and they shall plant vineyards and themselves shall eat their fruit;
> 22 and they shall not build and others inhabit;
>   they shall not plant and others eat;
>   for according to the days of the tree of life
>   shall the days of my people be;
>   they shall make old the works of their labors.
> 23 And my chosen ones shall not labor in vain,
>   nor bear children for a curse;
>   because they are an offspring blessed by God.
> 24 And it shall be that before they have cried out I will listen to them,
>   while they are yet speaking I will say, What is it?
> 25 Then wolves and lambs shall feed together,
>   and a lion shall eat straw like an ox;
>   but a serpent shall eat earth as bread!
>   They shall not do wrong or destroy
>   on my holy mountain,
>   says the Lord.

*This chapter was read on two levels. The early verses were understood to refer to God's judgment on the ancient Israelites who practiced idolatry (**sacrificing in gardens, burning incense on bricks** [65:3]) and his **blessing** (65:8) on those who remained faithful. But the latter part of the chapter, **heaven will be new, and the earth will be new** (65:17) and **no more shall there be heard weeping** (65:19), was thought to refer to the final resurrection and the new Jerusalem, on the basis of the climactic prophecy at the end of the book of Revelation (cf. the allusions to 65:17 in Rev 21:1 and to 65:19 in Rev 21:4). The phrase **new heaven and new earth** also occurs in 66:22, and other selections dealing with the new heaven and the new earth can be found in chapter 66. One textual variant is significant: at 65:22, for **days of a tree**, the Septuagint and Latin versions have **tree of life**. This reading allowed early Christian interpreters to see this passage as referring*

Isaiah 65

back to the original paradise as well as to the "sublime happiness" of the future age. Some took the words of the first verse, **I was ready to be found by those who did not seek me** *(65:1), to mean that God's grace precedes our actions. Clement of Alexandria offers a beautiful meditation on the verse,* **a new name will be given to those who serve him** *(65:15). One of the names, he says, is "little child," which means one who is gentle, tender, mild, guileless, and truthful. He also observes that the Spirit, prophesying through Isaiah, called the Lord a "child": "Behold, a child is born to us" (9:6).*

(1) Epistle to the Romans

Then Isaiah is so bold as to say, **I have been found by those who did not seek me; I have shown myself to those who did not ask for me** (65:1).

(2) Second Letter of Peter

But the day of the Lord will come like a thief, and then the heavens will pass away with a loud noise, and the elements will be dissolved with fire, and the earth and the works that are upon it will be burned up. Since all these things are thus to be dissolved, what sort of persons ought you to be in lives of holiness and godliness, waiting for and hastening the coming of the day of God, because of which the heavens will be kindled and dissolved, and the elements will melt with fire! But according to his promise we wait for **new heavens and a new earth** (65:17; 66:22) in which righteousness dwells. Therefore, beloved, since you wait for these, be zealous to be found by him without spot or blemish, and at peace.

(3) The Revelation to John

Then I saw a **new heaven and a new earth** (65:17; 66:22); for the first heaven and the first earth had passed away, and the sea was no more. And I saw the holy city, new Jerusalem, coming down out of heaven from God, prepared as a bride adorned for her husband; and I heard a loud voice from the throne saying, "Behold, the dwelling of God is with men. He will dwell with them, and they shall be his people, and God himself will be with them; he will *wipe away every tear from their eyes* (25:8), and death shall be no more, neither shall there be mourning nor crying nor pain any more, for the former things have passed away."

(4) Eusebius of Caesarea

In the previous section, the prophet, speaking in the name of the people, had presented them as suppliants confessing their wrongdoings. Yet their words make it sound as though God is responsible: *O LORD, why have you have made us stray from your way and hardened our hearts so that we do not fear you?* (63:17). To which this answer is given through the prophetic spirit: *How could it be that I, who do not want the death of the sinner, but desire his repentance* (Ezek 18:23, 32; 33:11), would ignore those who beseech me and confess their sin in this way (cf. Isa 64:7)? How could it be that I, who desire to turn all people from error to truth and to encourage the fallen to rise (Jer 8:4), *make you stray from my way or harden your heart that you do not fear me* (Isa 63:17)? If someone genuinely loves the truth and desires to see how much I love mankind, he will discover that even on those who **did not seek** (65:1) by grace I bestowed a share in it and anticipated their entreaties for further things. Even before they uttered a prayer, even before they made petition, I said, **Behold, here am I** (65:1).

If I was good and gracious to strangers who did not know me, how could I be fierce and cruel and unjust to you?[1] For my grace had its beginning with you, and I first **stretched out my hands** (65:2) to you, beseeching you and longing to take you in my arms as my own dear children. But you were unwilling and went your own way even though I beckoned and encouraged you to embrace the salvation I had prepared for you.

You turned to your own way and multiplied troubles for yourself. Do you not **provoke me continually** (65:3), you who have not raised your children to worship me? Have you not given yourselves over to idolatry and been deceived into worshiping many gods? You are **sacrificing in gardens and burning incense** to unclean spirits, and evil demons on altars you have built from **bricks** (65:3), and you even spend the night in **tombs** and in **caves** (65:4). You consider such things sacred and use them as auguries. What else remains but to make yourselves altogether strangers to my laws since you now take your fill of **swine's flesh** and do not hesitate to defile your household **vessels** with abominable **sacrifices** (65:4)? . . .

What is said here is directed against the irreligious among the people. If, however, someone would be found among their number longing for salvation, such a person would be exempted from what has been said. For *the vineyard of the LORD of hosts is the house of Israel* (5:7). Yet, instead of edible grapes *it yielded wild grapes* (5:2), instead of justice lawlessness, and instead of *righteousness a cry* (5:7b). If among those who are condemned there should be found someone like a plump **grape** in a dry **cluster** (65:8), this one will escape my judgment and will not be destroyed with the others, since he has a share of **blessing** (65:8). This rare **grape** will be honored by me and will be the model for dealing with every nation. For if someone among them is found worthy of salvation, **I will not destroy them all** (65:8). I will lead out **my servant** from among them, setting him apart from those being destroyed. An **offspring will come forth from Jacob** (65:9) who is fecund and life-giving and able to bear fruit for others.

Earlier in his book Isaiah had said: *If the LORD of hosts had not left us a seed* (1:9). This good and rare seed clearly refers to the chorus of apostles set apart from the mass of those being destroyed. For they will **inherit my holy mountain** (65:9), about which one of the apostles wrote: *But we have come to Mount Zion and to the city of the living God, the heavenly Jerusalem* (Heb 12:22). He promises that **my chosen and my servants** (65:9) will

---

1. The Israelites.

Isaiah 65

receive this heavenly **inheritance** and **shall dwell there**. His **chosen** and his **servants** are the apostles, those **grapes** that he chose for himself. These he chose to watch over others, and he calls them a *holy seed* (6:13) and elect....

And **I**, God, **will rejoice** (65:19) to see **Jerusalem**, the godly commonwealth of those who are going to serve me. In my sight she has greater esteem than the earthly Jerusalem. Therefore, **I will rejoice** over her, **and be glad in my people** (65:19). That future godly commonwealth of my servants will be the kind of place in which there will no longer be heard **weeping and the voice of crying, nor shall there be a child that dies untimely, or an old person who does not fulfill his time** (65:19-20) For when the time has come for the promises to be fulfilled and everyone is raised with me, they will have attained *mature manhood, the measure of the stature of the fullness of Christ* (Eph 4:13). Everyone will be in the prime of life, there will be no immature child, no life cut down early, and there will be no one old and feeble among them. All will be the same age, remade at the same time through the resurrection and sharing the same rebirth. A youngster who has lived to be **a hundred years old** (65:20) will be in perfect health and in the prime of life, and the sinner who is perishing will be the same age. Though they will all come to life at the same time in the one resurrection, some will be destined for eternal life but others will be subjected to punishment and retribution and handed over to the *second death* (Rev 2:11). It is quite astonishing that in mentioning the youngster preserved for **one hundred years** and the sinner who is also a hundred years, the text asserts that the same amount of time from the resurrection of the dead has passed for them both. Then the sinner himself will be **one hundred years old** and still accursed. In the prime of life he will be mature in his wickedness and will continue to die in his sin. On the other hand, the new man will be **one hundred** and will be continually renewed and perfected in every way for salvation.

And **they** themselves **shall build houses and they shall inhabit them** (65:21). By their works and by their own deeds they procure for themselves *rooms in the Father's house* (John 14:2), and they *shall eat the fruit of the labor of their hands* (Ps 128:2). What they have planted they will gather, and when they have ceased their work they will be fed from their own labors, and others will be unable to seize the fruits of their labors. Hence the text says: **They shall not build and another inhabit; they shall not plant and another eat**, that is, they shall live forever in immortal blessedness. It continues, **For the days of my people shall be like the days of the tree of life** (65:22).[2] This signifies the tree planted by God in paradise, for the promises are not fulfilled outside the paradise of God. The prophet clearly announces the hope of eternal life without end when he writes: **For the days of my people shall be like the days of the tree of life** (65:22). Solomon taught elsewhere that the tree of life is the wisdom of God; *She is a tree of life to those who lay hold of her, security belongs to those who rely on her as on the Lord* (Prov 3:18 LXX). Since the wisdom of God is eternal and a *spring of water welling up to eternal life* (John 4:14), the word of the prophet promises that such **shall be the days of my people**. What else does he foretell than the most sublime happiness for them? He adds: I will do these things for my people, and **I will be glad in my people** (65:19), for **like the days of a tree shall be**

---

2. The Hebrew text reads "the days of a tree," but the LXX reads **the days of the tree of life.**

the days of my people (65:22). Through all this we see clearly that he gathers to himself another people along with the people of the Jews. Though he says that **the works of their labors will grow old** (65:22), they themselves will not grow old, nor will they hand on the fruits of their labors to others, but they will enjoy the products of their own labors and delight in the fruits they have cultivated.

65:1
I was ready to be found by those who did not seek me.

(5) Irenaeus of Lyons

Matthew says that the Magi, coming from the East, exclaimed, *For we have seen his star in the East and have come to worship him* (Matt 2:2)! After they had been led by a star into the house of Jacob (cf. Num 24:17) and to Emmanuel, they showed, by the gifts they offered, who it was that they were worshiping: myrrh to signify that he would die and be buried for our mortal human race; gold because he was a king *whose kingdom will have no end* (Luke 1:33); and frankincense because he was God who was *made known in Judea* (Ps 76:1), and was revealed **to those who did not seek him** (65:1).

(6) Leo the Great

Isaiah says: **I have been found by those not seeking me, and have appeared openly to those who were not looking for me** (65:1). How this was fulfilled the apostle John demonstrates when he asserts, *We know that the Son of God came and has given us discernment so that we might recognize the true God and be in his true Son* (1 John 5:20). On another occasion he urges, *Let us love, therefore, since God first loved us* (1 John 4:19). It is by loving that God refashions us in his image. That he might find in us the image of his goodness, he gives us the very means by which we can perform the works that we do — by lighting the lamps of our minds and inflaming us with the fire of his love, so that we might love not only him but also whatever he loves.

65:2
I stretched out my hands.

(7) Cyril of Jerusalem

Christ **stretched out his hands** (65:2) on the cross that he might embrace the ends of the world. For Golgotha is the very center of the earth. It is not my word but that of the prophet who said: *You have worked out salvation in the midst of the earth* (Ps 74:12). He who had established the heavens with his spiritual hands **stretched** forth human **hands**. They were fastened with nails so that his humanity, by being nailed to the tree and suffer-

Isaiah 65

ing death, might bear the sins of men. For in his death sin also died that we might rise again to righteousness. *Since sin came into the world through one man, so also through one man came life* (Rom 5:12, 17); this one man was the Savior, who died out of his free choice. Recall what he said: *I have power to lay down my life, and I have power to take it up again* (John 10:18).

65:13
Those who serve me shall eat, but you shall be hungry.

(8) Origen of Alexandria

The multitude that is being taught receives its food from the disciples of Jesus, who are commanded to distribute food to the crowds (Luke 9:16), and Jesus' disciples receive their food from Jesus himself, though occasionally from the holy angels (cf. 1 Kgs 19:5-8). The Son of God, however, receives his food from the Father alone without the intervention of any other human being....

One should also read the parables in the gospels that deal with meals. For example, the parable of the great supper deals with being called and chosen. *A man once gave a great supper, and invited many; and at the time of the supper he sent someone to call those who had been invited* (Luke 14:16-17). One needs then to collect the parables about suppers recorded in the gospels.

But Isaiah also mentions promises of eating and drinking: **Behold, my servants shall eat, but you shall be hungry; behold, my servants shall drink, but you shall be thirsty** (65:13).

Further, in the book of Genesis God places man in the garden of luxuries and gives laws about eating some things and not eating others. Indeed, man would have remained immortal if he had eaten from every tree in the garden given for his nourishment and had not eaten from the tree of the knowledge of good and evil (Gen 2:16-17).

Consider also what Psalm 22 says about those who worshiped because they had eaten: *All the fat ones of the earth have eaten and worshiped*[3] (Ps 21:30 LXX). Therefore, *the LORD will not afflict a just soul with famine* (Prov 10:3 LXX), but whenever we become unjust, he will send forth *a famine on the land, not a famine of bread nor a thirst for water, but a famine of hearing the word of the LORD* (Amos 8:11).

The more we progress, then, the more we shall eat better food until we reach the point that we eat the same food that nourishes the Son of God, a nourishment that the disciples did not know when Jesus said to them: *I have food to eat of which you do not know* (John 4:32).

---

3. For the Hebrew "to him shall all the proud of the earth bow down," the LXX reads: *all the fat ones of the earth have eaten and worshiped, all that go down to the earth shall fall down before him* (Ps 21:30 LXX).

65:15-16
But my servants will be called by a new name.[4]

(9) Clement of Alexandria

Tutoring *(paidagogia)*, as is evident from the name, has to do with the training of children.[5] So we must consider whom the Scripture has in mind when it speaks symbolically of children who are to be entrusted to the tutor *(paidagogos)*.

We are the children! Scripture celebrates us often and introduces variety into the simple language of faith by frequently using symbolic language to refer to us by different names.... At times God calls us *children* (Ps 112:2; Isa 8:18), at other times *chicks* (Matt 23:37), sometimes *little ones* (Matt 10:42), here and there *sons* (Rom 8:23; Gal 4:5-6), often *offspring* (Acts 17:29), and "a new people" and "a young people."[6] **A new name**, he says, **shall be given my servants** (65:15). By **new name** he means one that is fresh and everlasting, pure and simple, childlike and true. **That name shall be blessed on the earth** (65:16)....

He also calls us **lambs**, as the Spirit bears witness in the words of Isaiah: *He shall feed his flock like a shepherd; he shall gather together the lambs with his arm* (40:11). Because lambs lack experience, they are a figure for simplicity....

So the name "little child" is not used in the sense of lacking intelligence. The word for that is "childish," meaning someone who is silly. "Little child" means someone who has recently become gentle and meek. St. Paul points this out clearly when he writes: *Although as the apostle of Christ we could have claimed a position of honor among you, still while in your midst we were children, as if a nurse were cherishing her own children* (1 Thess 2:6-7). A little child is therefore gentle, tender, mild, simple, guileless and incapable of hypocrisy, straightforward and lacking duplicity. To be childlike is the basis for simplicity and truthfulness. *For upon whom shall I look,* Scripture says, *if not the meek and the peaceful* (66:2)? The speech of a young child is gentle and unaffected. This is why we also speak of a virgin as a tender maid and of a child as tenderhearted. We are tender, too, in the sense that we are open to persuasion, ready to be formed in the virtuous life, free of anger, without malice or deviousness....

Indeed, if those who look down on spiritual childishness call us simpleminded, you can see that they are really speaking blasphemy against the Lord. For they think that those who seek refuge in God lack intelligence. But even if they understand the term "little one" to mean "simple ones" — as indeed it does — we glory in that name. For little ones are the new spirits who have been born according to the New Covenant and recently become wise when one considers their former folly, since it was not long ago that God became known in the coming of Christ. *For no one has known God but the Son, and he to whom the Son has revealed him* (Matt 11:27).

---

4. The LXX reads **new** for the Hebrew "different."

5. The title of the work from which this excerpt is taken is *Tutor (paidagogos)*. The Greek term for tutoring or education, *paidagogia*, is derived from the Greek words for "child" *(paidion)* and "leading" or "guiding" *(agogia)*.

6. It is not evident which biblical texts, if any, Clement has in mind.

The new people, by contrast to the older people, are called young because they have heard the new good tidings. We have the exuberance of youth that knows nothing of old age. We are always at the height of our powers, quick to learn, always youthful, always meek, always fresh. Those who have partaken of the new Word must themselves be new. For whatever partakes of eternity becomes habituated to incorruptibility. The term "childhood" signifies a lifelong springtime, for the truth that does not age abides in us, and our life overflows with that truth. Wisdom always blooms, remains the same, is constant and unchanging.

Their children, according to Scripture, *shall be carried on their shoulders, and comforted on their knees; as a mother will comfort someone, so also I will comfort you* (Isa 66:12-13). A mother gathers her children near her; we seek our mother, the Church. Whatever is weak and young, and because of its weakness needs help, is viewed kindly and is pleasing and lovable. God does not withhold his help from such a person. As fathers and mothers look tenderly on their young — whether it be horses on their colts, cows their calves, lions their cubs, deer their fawns, or human beings their children — so too does the Father of all draw near to those who seek his aid to give them a new birth by the Spirit and adopt them as children. He knows they are gentle, he loves them alone, and he comes to their aid and defends them. That is why he calls them children. . . .

The Spirit prophesying through Isaiah also called the Lord himself a child: *Behold, a child is born to us, and a son is given us, and the government is upon his shoulders: and his name shall be called Angel of great counsel* (9:6). Who is this child, this little one, in whose image we also are little ones? Through the same prophet the Spirit goes on to describe Christ's greatness: *Wonderful Counselor, mighty God, everlasting Father, Prince of peace, that he might increase his training;[7] of his peace there shall be no end* (9:6-7). O the great God; O the perfect child! The Son is in the Father, and the Father is in the Son. How can the tutoring of this child not be perfect since it extends to all of us his children and tutors us as his little ones. The **hands he stretches out** (65:2) are certainly to be trusted.

(10) Cyril of Alexandria

All things have been made new in Christ, worship and life and the making of laws. For we do not adhere to shadows and ineffective types. We offer adoration, and *worship in spirit and in truth* (John 4:23). Unlike Israelites in the flesh we do not take our name from one of the original ancestors or fathers, such as Ephraim or Manasseh or some other tribe; nor do we traverse the path of the scribes and Pharisees who value the antiquity of the letter above everything else. We have instead embraced the new life in Christ by the gospel, and have been given his **name** (65:15) to wear like a crown. For we are called Christians. This celebrated and blessed **name** has spread throughout the world. Since we have been blessed by Christ, we in turn strive to gladden him with endless praise and adora-

---

7. Clement adds the phrase "that he might increase his training" (reflecting the theme of his treatise, *The Tutor*) to the passage from Isaiah.

tion. Of old, before we believed, in him we composed songs for gods that do not exist. For this we were rightly derided. But once we have come to know the true God, we sing hymns to him and offer him the fruit of our lips and tongues, remembering him in our praises. And if there should be need to confirm assurances we give with oaths, we swear by the true God. For it is the custom of those who worship idols to swear oaths by heaven or by one of the heavenly powers. But those who have embraced the Christian faith abandoned this sinful practice even as youths. They swear oaths only by the God of all, since they know that he is truly Lord by nature and there is no other god besides him. This was also decreed by the law of Moses: *You shall worship the* LORD *your God; you shall serve him alone, and swear by his name* (Deut 6:13).

(11) Theodoret of Cyrus

The prophet has already mentioned that there will be a **new name** (65:15).[8] It is **new**, not old. After the appearance of our Lord Christ, Christian believers received the name "Christians" (Acts 11:26). No name is worthy of greater praise. For when one wishes to praise someone, it is customary to say, "He is truly a Christian." Indeed, so worthy of praise and honor is the name that it is also customary to say: "Behave like a Christian," or "Do what a Christian would do."

65:17
For heaven will be new, and the earth will be new.

(12) Irenaeus of Lyons

John says: *Then I saw a new heaven and a new earth; for the first heaven and earth had passed away; and the sea was no more. And I saw the holy city, the new Jerusalem, coming down out of heaven from God, prepared as a bride adorned for her husband; and I heard a loud voice from the throne saying, "Behold, the dwelling of God is with men, and he will dwell with them, and they shall be his people, and God himself will be with them as their God. And he will wipe away every tear from their eyes, and death shall be no more, neither shall there be mourning nor crying nor pain any more, for the former things have passed away"* (Rev 21:1-4). Isaiah declares the same things: **There shall be a new heaven and a new earth; and the former will not be remembered, neither shall they come to mind. But they will be glad and rejoice** (65:17-18). Now this is what has been spoken of by the apostle: *For the form of this world is passing away* (1 Cor 7:31). In the same way the Lord also said: *Heaven and earth shall pass away* (Matt 24:35). When these things pass away, John, the Lord's disciple, says that the new Jerusalem will descend to a new earth as a bride adorned for her husband. This is the tabernacle in which God will dwell with men. The Jerusalem that existed on the former earth is an image of the Jerusalem above. In the

---

8. See 62:2.

earthly Jerusalem the righteous learned to practice immortal life and to prepare themselves for salvation.... As it is truly God who truly raises man up, so it is man who truly rises from the dead, not spiritually, as I have abundantly shown.

(13) Ephrem the Syrian

In the world there is struggle,
in Eden, a crown of glory.
At our resurrection
both **earth and heaven will God renew** (65:17),
liberating all creatures,
granting them paschal joy, along with us.
Upon our mother Earth, along with us,
did he lay disgrace
when he placed on her, with the sinner, the curse;
so, together with the just, will he bless her too;
this nursing mother, along with her children,
shall he who is good renew.

(14) Gregory of Nyssa

All the statements in the Song of Songs about the Bridegroom's beauty[9] point not to the invisible and incomprehensible realities of the Godhead, but to the things revealed in the Incarnation, when God, having put on human nature, was revealed on earth and held converse with human beings. By that it means, as the apostle says, *the invisible things of him . . . have been clearly apprehended in his works* (Rom 1:20), revealed through the founding of the cosmos of the Church. For the founding of the Church is the creation of a cosmos[10] in which, according to the word of the prophet, **a new heaven is created**, which is *the firmament of faith in Christ* (Col 2:5), as Paul says, and **a new earth** (65:17) is established. The earth drinks the *rain that falls upon it* (Heb 6:7),[11] and another man is formed according to the *image of his Creator* (Col 3:10) through his birth from above (cf. John 3:3), and there comes into existence another nature that is shining with light, as it is written, *You are the light of the world* (Matt 5:14) and *among whom you shine as lights in the world* (Phil 2:15). And so many stars arise *in the firmament of faith* (Col 2:5).

---

9. "His head is the finest gold, his locks are wavy . . . his cheeks are like beds of spices yielding fragrance" (Song of Songs 5:11-12)
10. Gregory is thinking of Eph 3:9-10.
11. An allusion to Baptism.

65:18
They shall find joy and gladness in her.

(15) Cyril of Alexandria

Instead of their former affliction, the prophet affirms, **they shall find joy and gladness in her** (65:18). To what does **in her** refer? There can be no doubt that it refers to the Church of Christ. It should be noted that some commentators refer this passage not to the time of our earthly life but to what will come after this present age. For the prophet says that the just will find **joy and gladness** and will enjoy endless delight, that is, spiritual delight, when this creation has been transformed and renewed. For one of the holy apostles said: *The day of the Lord will come like a thief, and then the heavens will pass away with a loud voice, and the elements will be dissolved with fire, and the earth and the works that are upon it will be burned up. But according to his promise we wait for new heavens and a new earth* (2 Pet 3:10, 13). Choose, therefore, whichever of these interpretations appeals to you, the former or the latter. For one should not reject what offers some benefit to the reader.

65:22
They shall not build and others inhabit; they shall not plant and others eat.

(16) Theodoret of Cyrus

The prophet is using figurative language. By **houses** (65:21) and **vineyards** he signifies virtues. In the same way the apostle wrote: *Whatever a man sows, that he will also reap. For he who sows to his own flesh will from the flesh reap corruption; but he who sows to the Spirit will from the Spirit reap eternal life* (Gal 6:7-8). And again: *He who sows sparingly will also reap sparingly, and he who sows bountifully will reap bountifully* (2 Cor 9:6). And yet in another place: *Each shall receive his wages according to his labor* (1 Cor 3:8).

65:22
According to the days of a tree of life shall the days of my people be.

(17) Augustine of Hippo

After he has given promise of a *new heaven and a new earth* (65:17), Isaiah goes on to give descriptions of the bliss of the saints in allegorical and figurative language. However, since I do not want to go on too long, I will refrain from a full explanation of them all. Yet one statement calls for comment: **As the days of the tree of life will be the days of my people** (65:22). Anyone with a minimal knowledge of the Holy Scriptures knows where God planted the **tree of life** (65:22), and that human beings were forbidden to eat this fruit. And when they were driven from paradise by their wickedness, a terrible flaming guard was set around that tree. Now one could say that the **days of the tree of life**, mentioned by the prophet Isaiah, stand for the present days of the Church of Christ, and that Christ himself is prophetically called **the tree of life** because he is himself the Wisdom of God, of which Solomon writes: *Wisdom is a tree of life to those who embrace her* (Prov 3:18).

(18) Theodoret of Cyrus

How does what is said here apply to mortal human beings? Well, the word of the prophet promises eternal life, because about that **tree of life** (65:22) God warned: *Lest Adam put forth his hand, and eat of the tree of life, and live forever* (Gen 3:22). For us, however, it is the cross of salvation that has become the **tree of life**. For its fruit was the life-giving body, and those who put forth their hands to takes its fruit will have eternal life.

Isaiah 66

1 Thus says the Lord:
  Heaven is my throne
     and the earth is the footstool of my feet;
  what kind of house will you build for me,
     or of what kind will be the place of my rest?
2 For all these things my hand has made,
     and all these things are mine, says the Lord.
  And to whom will I look,
     but to the one who is humble and quiet
     and trembles at my words?

3 But the transgressor who sacrifices to me a calf
     is like one who kills a dog;
  and he who offers fine flour,
     like one who offers swine's blood;
  he who has given frankincense for a memorial,
     like a blasphemer.
  And these have chosen their own ways
     and their abominations, which their soul wanted;
4 so I will choose mockeries for them
     and repay them their sins;
  because I called them and they did not answer me,
     I spoke and they did not hear;
  but they did what was evil in my sight,
     and chose the things I did not desire.
5 Hear the word of the Lord,
     you who tremble at his word;
  speak, our brothers,
     to those who hate and abominate us,
  so that the name of the Lord may be glorified

and seen in their joy;
   but those ones shall be put to shame.

6 A voice of crying from the city!
   A voice from the temple!
  The voice of the Lord,
   rendering retribution to his adversaries!

7 Before she who was in labor
   gave birth,
  before the pain of her pangs came,
   she escaped and gave birth to a male.
8 Who has heard of such a thing?
   And who has seen thus?
  Did the earth give birth in one day?
   Was also a nation born all at once?
  Because Sion was in labor,
   and she gave birth to her children.
9 But I am the one who gave you this expectation,
   and you did not remember me,
   said the Lord;
  see, was it not I who made the woman who gives birth
   and the one who is barren?
   said God.

10 Rejoice, O Ierousalem,
   and celebrate a festival in her, all you who love her;
  rejoice with joy,
   all you who mourn over her —
11 that you may nurse and be satisfied
   from her consoling breast;
  that by much nursing you may take delight
   from the entrance to her glory.

12 Because this is what the Lord says:
   See, I myself turn to them like a river of peace,
    and like a torrent overflowing the glory of nations;
   their children shall be carried on shoulders,
    and comforted on knees.
13 As a mother will comfort someone,
    so also I will comfort you,
    and you shall be comforted in Ierousalem.
14 You shall see, and your heart shall rejoice,
    and your bones shall grow like grass;

and the hand of the Lord shall be known to those who worship him,
and he shall threaten those who disobey him.
15 For see, the Lord will come like fire,
and his chariots like a tempest,
to render vengeance with wrath,
and repudiation with a flame of fire.
16 For by the fire of the Lord shall all the earth be judged,
and all flesh by his sword;
many shall be wounded by the Lord.

17 Those who sanctify and purify themselves for the gardens, and who in the porches eat swine's flesh, the abominations, and the mouse, shall be consumed together, said the Lord.

18 And I understand their works and their reasonings; I am coming to gather all the nations and tongues, and they shall come and shall see my glory. 19And I will leave signs upon them, and from them I will send forth those who are saved to the nations, to Tharsis and Phoud and Loud and Mosoch and Thobel, and to Greece and to the islands far away — those who have not heard my name or seen my glory; and they shall declare my glory among the nations. 20They shall bring your kindred from all the nations as a gift to the Lord, with horses and chariots, in mule-drawn litters with sunshades, into the holy city Ierousalem, said the Lord, so that the sons of Israel may bring to me their sacrifices with psalms into the house of the Lord. 21And I will take for myself some of them as priests and as Leuites, said the Lord.

22 For as the new heaven and the new earth,
which I am making, remain before me, says the Lord;
so shall your offspring and your name stand.
23 And it shall be that month after month,
and sabbath after sabbath,
all flesh shall come before me to worship in Ierousalem,
said the Lord.

24And they shall go forth and see the limbs of the people who have transgressed against me; for their worm shall not die and their fire shall not be quenched, and they shall become a spectacle to all flesh.

In their expositions of the final chapter of the prophet Isaiah, the church fathers focus on eschatological themes, the heavenly Jerusalem, the new heavens and new earth, eternal bliss and eternal punishment (66:24). The phrase **new heaven and new earth** *also occurs at 65:17, and the relevant New Testament texts, 2 Pet 3:13 and Rev 21:1, are cited there, as well as other excerpts that comment on the expression. Other topics that appear in this final chapter of the prophet are God's majesty and transcendence (***Heaven is my throne** *[66:1]), that all things subsist in God* *and were made by his Word (interpreting* **hand** *in 66:2 as Christ the Word of God), humility as a mark of the Christian life (66:2), divine mercy (66:12-13), and the calling of the nations (66:18). Augustine's commentary on the final verse of Isaiah (in* The City of God*) considers at some length whether the words* **the worm that shall not die** *and* **the fire that shall not be quenched** *(66:24) are to be referred to the body or to the soul.*

(1) The Gospel according to Matthew

Again you have heard that it was said to the men of old, *You shall not swear falsely, but shall perform to the Lord what you have sworn* (cf. Lev 19:12; Num 30:2). But I say to you, **Do not swear at all, either by heaven, for it is the throne of God, or by earth, for it is his footstool** (66:1), or by Jerusalem, for it is the city of the great King.

(2) Acts of the Apostles

But it was Solomon who built a house for him. Yet the Most High does not dwell in houses made with hands; as the prophet says, **Heaven is my throne, and earth my footstool. What house will you build for me, says the Lord, or what is the place of my rest? Did not my hand make all these things?** (66:1-2).

(3) Cyril of Alexandria

God speaks through the prophets to those who do not know the splendor and magnificence of his glory, saying: **Heaven is my throne and the earth is my footstool; what is the house which you would build for me, and what is the place of my rest?** (66:1). Does not God fill all things? Does not his majesty fill heaven and earth? Yet when using human language we can say: **heaven is his throne and the earth his footstool.** What space can enclose him? Or what house has room for him? **All these things my hand has made, and so all these things are mine, says the Lord** (66:2). What are these things? Clearly, things that can be seen and things that cannot be seen. For all creation is his, and by his command what did not exist came to be. What can we give him that is not already his? As God puts it, using the words of the psalmist: *If I were hungry, I would not tell you; for every beast of the forest is mine, the herds and cattle on the mountains. I know all the beasts of the field and all the birds of the air, and the produce of the field is mine* (Ps 50:10-12).

To whom will I look? (66:2), he asks. Is it not to one who is truly **humble and contrite** (66:2), who is meek and obedient, who eagerly does God's will and trembles at his words? Here he is referring to the life-giving message of the gospel. God has regard for the humble and cares for the meek, but turns away from the swaggering blowhard who lifts himself up against the divine commandments. . . .

He enjoins the new and spiritual Zion to **rejoice** (66:10). He is speaking of Jerusa-

lem, the Church of the living God, the city that he presented to himself pure and blameless. From the tribes of the Jews and the multitude of the nations he joined the two peoples into one new person, bringing *peace* and *reconciling both with the Father in his one body* (Eph 2:15-16). How right to rejoice with her! For her hopes transcend words and thoughts. *What no eye has seen, nor ear heard, nor the heart of man conceived, what God has prepared for those who love him* (1 Cor 2:9). He commands those who live in Jerusalem and love her to rejoice. He has in mind those who support her, hold fast to her true teachings, defend her, and lift her up. He even mentions those **who mourn over her** (66:10), as the Savior himself said, *Blessed are those who mourn, for they shall be comforted* (Matt 5:4).

Mourning signifies that they have begun to change their lives. They struggle to live holy lives not to win some earthly reward but to receive God's gifts, and they endure all tribulations that their hearts may be filled with gladness. This is the meaning of the words **that you may suckle and be filled from her consoling breast** (66:11). Using the figure of a woman, he compares the consolation of the Holy Spirit to breasts and milk. The Song of Songs uses similar language: *Your breasts are better than wine* (Song 1:2 LXX).

When someone first comes to faith in our God, Jesus Christ, he eats food fit for infants, that is, he learns the simple fundamentals of the faith. Thus, Paul writes somewhere, *I fed you with milk, not solid food; for you were not ready for it; and even yet you are not ready* (1 Cor 3:2). But those who drink what is offered to the catechumens will not remain infants. The prophet teaches that they must grow "to mature manhood, to the measure of the stature of the fullness of Christ" (Eph 4:13). Then they will understand the fine points of Christian doctrine. Hence he adds: **having suckled deeply, you may fare sumptuously from the visitation of her glory** (66:11). The phrase **having suckled deeply** means that a baby has been removed from the breasts and nipples, that is, weaned, and is no longer an infant, but a youth on the way to maturity or an adult longing for solid food. Hence he says: **You fare sumptuously from the visitation of her glory** (66:11). Like the psalmist he calls Christ **glory**: *may glory dwell in our land* (Ps 85:9). He calls the mystery of his earthly sojourn a **visitation**, for though he was God by nature, through the Incarnation he came into the world as a human being.

Those who know the deeper mysteries of Christ **fare sumptuously** (66:11). They know that **glory** (66:11), meaning Christ, has entered the world. For this reason, the divine prophet immediately mentions his visible manifestation in the flesh. Speaking in the person of the Lord, he says: **Behold, I am turning to them like a river of peace, and like torrents I am flooding the glory of the nations** (66:12). The **river of peace** and the **flood** of delights is Christ. So also the divinely inspired David called him a river: *How precious is thy steadfast love, O God! The children of men take refuge in the shadow of thy wings. They feast on the abundance of thy house, and thou givest them drink from the river of thy delights* (Ps 36:7-8). And again: *There is a river whose streams make glad the city of God* (Ps 46:4)....

Beginning with the words **I am coming to gather all nations and tongues** (66:18ff.), Christ sums up the central message of the Scriptures. In a few succinct words he sets forth what has happened from the beginning to the end of time and points to the significance of Christ's coming in the flesh. He also mentions the calling of the nations and shows that through the proclamation of the gospel by the apostles Christ would be worshiped throughout the world.

Isaiah 66

The ancient law had gathered together only one people and one tongue, the people of Israel. But by his coming in the flesh our Lord Jesus Christ gave power not only to the people of Israel but to all peoples and languages. For the psalmist sang: *Hear this, all peoples. Give ear, all inhabitants of the world* (Ps 49:1). And Isaiah promises: **I will gather them all, and they shall come and shall see my glory** (66:18). Those who were far off were called through faith and have come near and beheld his glory. Through the proclamation of the gospel they learned that in deed and in authority he is equal to God the Father. When he raises the dead from their graves and gives light to the blind, he astounds us and we also marvel at all the other things he did. Put another way, that the nations have **seen his glory** means that they have come to know the mystery of the divine Word made flesh.

66:1
Heaven is my throne and earth my footstool.

(4) Origen of Alexandria

The universe is held together by the power and reason of God as by a single soul. This truth, I believe, is set forth in the Holy Scripture in words spoken by the prophet: *"Do I not fill heaven and earth?" says the* LORD (Jer 23:24); also in another prophet: **Heaven is my throne and the earth is my footstool** (66:1); and when the Savior prohibits swearing *neither by heaven, for it is the throne of God, neither by the earth, for it is the footstool of his feet* (Matt 5:34-35); and in St. Paul's speech to the Athenians: *in him we live and move and have our being* (Acts 17:28). For how do we *live and move and have our being in God* except that God holds together and contains the universe by his power? And how is heaven the *throne of God* and earth *the footstool of his feet,* as the Savior himself declares, except that in heaven and on earth God's power fills all things, as he declares, *"Do I not fill heaven and earth?" says the* LORD (Jer 23:24). On the basis of these passages I do not think it difficult to acknowledge that God, the source of all things, fills and contains the whole universe in the fullness of his power.

(5) Cyril of Jerusalem

God is not confined to any space. He is the creator of all space, existing in all things but circumscribed by none. **Heaven is his throne**, but he that sits on the throne surpasses even heaven, **and earth is his footstool** (66:1), but his power extends to all things under the earth. God is the one who is everywhere present, seeing all things, perceiving all things, creating all things through Christ. *For all things were made by him, and without him was not anything made that was made* (John 1:3). God is an abundant and unfailing fountain from which flow all good things, a river of blessings, an eternal light of unceasing splendor, an invincible power who sympathizes with our infirmities, whose name we speak with awe. *Can you find the traces of the Lord,* asks Job, *or have you come to the limit of the things the Almighty has made?* (Job 11:7 LXX). If the extent of his works is beyond our grasp, can we comprehend the one who made them all? *Eye has not seen, nor ear heard, nor the heart of man conceived what God has prepared for those who love him* (1 Cor 2:9). If the things God has prepared are incomprehensible to our thoughts, how can we comprehend with our mind the one who prepared them? *O the depth of the riches and wisdom and knowledge of God! How unsearchable are his judgments, and how inscrutable his ways!* says the apostle (Rom 11:33). If his judgments and his ways are incomprehensible, how can God himself be comprehended?

(6) Jerome

Before Stephen was martyred he proclaimed: *Solomon built a house for him* (Acts 7:47). By *him* he meant God. *Yet the Most High does not dwell in houses made by human hands, as the prophet says:* **Heaven is my throne, and earth my footstool** (Acts 7:48-49, citing 66:1). And Paul in the same book of Acts says: *The God who made the world and everything in it, being Lord of heaven and earth, does not live in shrines made by man* (Acts 17:24). If God is likened to someone whose throne is the heavens and whose footstool is the earth, how can he who fills all things, and in whom all things exist, be enclosed in a tiny place?

This is why Moses said: *Do not say in your heart, he is far away. For God is in the heaven above you and on the earth beneath. And there is no other besides God* (Deut 4:39). And the psalmist: *Whither shall I go from thy Spirit? Or whither shall I flee from thy presence? If I ascend to heaven, thou art there! If I make my bed in Sheol, thou art there!* (Ps 139:7-8). To which Jeremiah adds: *I am a God at hand and not a God afar off. Can a man hide himself in secret places so that I cannot see him?* (Jer 23:23-24). *In him we have our being and are moved* (Acts 17:28). The prophet says these things to correct the error of Jews who thought that the invisible and immaterial and incomprehensible God could be enclosed within the temple in Jerusalem. Solomon, the builder of the temple, expressed the same thoughts in his lengthy prayer to the Lord (cf. 1 Kgs 8:27ff.). Lest we think that the greatness of God can be measured by heavenly and earthly standards, in another place we read: *He holds the heaven in his palm, and the earth in his fist* (Isa 40:12). These passages show that God is at once transcendent and immanent, in all things and embracing all things. He does not sit on a throne that can hold him, yet he holds all things in the palm of his hand. He is not only the creator of the heavens and the earth, but he also made the invisible angels and archangels, dominions, powers, and all men, as the apostle said (Col 1:16). Or in the words of Isaiah: **My hand made all these things** (66:2). Job and the psalmist also spoke about this: *Your hand made me and fashioned me* (Job 10:8 and Ps 119:73). And John says: *All things were made through him, and without him was not anything made that was made* (John 1:3). And also: *He was in the world, and the world was made through him* (John 1:10). *For he spoke, and they came to be; he commanded, and things were created* (Ps 33:9). This is what the book of Genesis expresses mystically in the words: *God said* and *God made* (Gen 1:3). Also: *By the word of the* LORD *the heavens were established, and all their host by the breath of his mouth* (Ps 33:6). It is understandable, then, that the Lord can find no resting place except on what the prophet speaks about in the next verse, the **humble and contrite in spirit** (66:2).

(7) John of Damascus

Now God, who is immaterial and uncircumscribed, is not "in" a **place** (66:1). He is himself his own **place**, at once filling the universe, transcending the universe, and containing the universe. But we also speak of God being "in" a **place**, by which we mean the **place** of God where his activity is made manifest. For he himself extends throughout the universe without being enmeshed by it, and imparts to each thing a share in his activity, in proportion to its distinctive character and receptivity, by which I mean both its innate and its acquired purity. For what is immaterial is purer than what is made from matter, and what is virtuous is purer than what is yoked with evil. We therefore say that the **place** of God is that which has a larger share of his activity and his grace, hence **Heaven is** his **throne** (66:1). That is where the angels who do his will exist and glorify him always. For this is his **rest**. **And the earth is** his **footstool** refers to the place where in his flesh he sojourned with human beings, God's **foot** standing for his sacred flesh. We also call the Church the **place** of God because we have set it apart for glorifying him, like a temple in which we hold converse with him. Similarly those other places in which his activity is made manifest to us, whether it occurs in the flesh or without it, are called the "places" of God.[1]

(8) Gregory the Great

What does it mean that Satan is said to *go forth from the presence of the* LORD (Job 1:12)? For how does one *go forth* from him who is everywhere present? For this reason God asks: *Do not I fill heaven and earth?* (Jer 23:24). Likewise his Wisdom says, *I alone made the circuit of the vault of heaven* (Sir 24:5), and concerning his Spirit it is written, *For the Spirit of the Lord fills the world* (Wis 1:7). The Lord says again, **Heaven is my throne and the earth is the footstool of my feet** (66:1), and it is also written of him, *He measures heaven with his palm, and holds all the earth in his fist* (40:12). He remains both within and without the **throne** from which he governs. Because he *measures the heavens with his palm* and *holds the earth in his fist,* it is evident that he contains everything he has created. For that which is within is surrounded by what is without and is enclosed by it. Therefore, the **throne** from which he governs means that God is within and above, and the **fist** with which **he holds** means that he is outside and beneath, because he himself is within all things, outside all things, above all things, and beneath all things. He is above by virtue of his power and beneath by virtue of his forbearance; without by his greatness, and within by his intangibility. He rules from on high, holds together from below, encompasses from all around, and penetrates from within. He is not above in one part, below in another, outside of one, inside of another. Rather, he remains the same, wholly everywhere, sustaining in ruling, ruling in sustaining, penetrating in encompassing, encompassing in penetrating. Hence he rules from above, sustains from below, enfolds from without, and fills up from within. He rules from above without restlessness, sustains from below without labor, penetrates from inside without being diminished, and encompasses without being overextended. So,

---

1. For example, the sacred sites in the Holy Land.

he is both beneath and above, yet not in any place; he is greater without being extended, and more intangible without being lessened.

66:2
All these things my hand has made.

(9) Athanasius of Alexandria

All things that came to be were made by the **hand** (66:2) and the *Wisdom* (Wis 9:1-2) of God, who himself declares: **All these things my hand has made** (66:2). And David says in the psalm: *In the beginning thou didst lay the foundation of the earth, and the heavens are the work of thy hands* (Ps 102:25). David also says, *I remember the days of old, I meditate on all that thou hast done; I muse on what thy hands have wrought* (Ps 143:5). If then these works are done by the hand of God, and it is written that *all things were made through the Word*, and *without him was not anything made* (John 1:2-3), and again, *one Lord Jesus Christ, through whom are all things* (1 Cor 8:6) and *in him all things hold together* (Col 1:17), it is evident that the Son cannot be one of God's works. He is the **hand** of God and the *Wisdom* of God.

(10) Gregory of Nyssa

If anyone thinks it unreasonable that the creature is clearly distinguished from God, let him take note of what the prophets and apostles say. For the prophet, speaking in the person of the Father, asserts: **My hand made all these things** (66:2). **Hand** in his enigmatic language signifies the power of the Only-Begotten. And the apostle says that all things are *from* the Father and *through* the Son (1 Cor 8:6). The prophetic spirit surely agrees with the apostolic teaching which was also given by the Spirit. For when the prophet says that all things are the work of the **hand** of him who is over all, he defines the nature of those things which have come into being in relation to the One who made them. The One who made them is the God of all, who has the **hand** and makes all things through it.

66:2
Humble and contrite in spirit

(11) Clement of Rome

Be then humble, free of pretentiousness and arrogance and thoughtlessness and anger. Act as Scripture urges us, for the Holy Spirit says: *Let not the wise man boast of his wisdom, nor the strong man of his might, nor the rich man of his wealth. But let him that boasts boast of the* L<small>ORD</small>, *and seek for him, and act justly and uprightly* (Jer 9:23-24). Remember especially the words of the Lord Jesus spoken to teach us gentleness and patience. Here is what he said: *Show mercy, that you may be shown mercy. Forgive, that you may be forgiven. Do to others as you would have them do to you. Give as you expect to receive. Judge as you would be judged. Be kind as you expect to receive kindness. The measure you give will be the measure you get* (Matt 5:7; 6:14-15; 7:1-2). Let us hold firmly to this commandment and these injunctions so that in what we do we obey his holy words and live humbly. For Holy Scriptures asks: **To whom will I look, but to the one who is humble and gentle and trembles at my words?** (66:2).

(12) Augustine of Hippo

When sins are forgiven in the sacraments, the house is cleaned out, but it needs an occupant, the Holy Spirit, and the Holy Spirit lives only in the humble of heart. God, you see, inquires, **Upon whom shall my Spirit rest?**[2] And he answers the question: **Upon the humble and the quiet and the one who trembles at my words** (66:2). So when the Holy Spirit becomes the occupant, he fills and guides and leads the person, restrains from evil and spurs on to good, and makes justice delightful, so that the person does good out of love for what is right, not out of fear of punishment. No one is capable on their own of doing what I have said. But if you have the Holy Spirit as the occupant of your house, you will find him also assisting you in everything good.

There are some proud people, however, who, once their sins have been forgiven, rely solely on the free choices of the human will for living a good life, and by that very pride shut their doors in the Holy Spirit's face, and the house remains apparently cleaned up from the mess of sins, but vacant, with nothing positively good in it. Your sins have been forgiven, you have been cleansed of evils, but it is only the Holy Spirit who will fill you with good things. And he is repelled by pride. If you are relying on yourself, he leaves you to yourself; if you trust in yourself, you are handed over to yourself. But once that greed which made you bad has been driven out of a person, that is to say, from your consciousness when your sins were forgiven, it wanders through desert places looking for rest, and not finding any rest, that greed comes back to the house, finds it cleaned up, brings with it seven other spirits more wicked than itself, and the last state of that person will be worse than the first (cf. Matt 12:43-45).

66:12ff.
See, I myself turn to them like a river of peace, and like a torrent overflowing the glory of nations. . . .

(13) Ambrose of Milan

The Holy Spirit is the **river** (66:12), indeed an abundant **river** which, according to the Hebrews,[3] flowed from within Jesus, as we have learned from the prophet Isaiah (66:12). This is the great **river** that always flows and never fails. It is not only a **river** but a great

---

2. For the Hebrew, **This is the man to whom I will look, he that is humble and contrite in spirit**, Augustine's Latin text read: **Upon whom shall my Spirit rest?**
3. Ambrose seems to have in mind the apocryphal *Gospel of the Hebrews*.

torrent overflowing with abundance, as David said: *There is a river whose streams make glad the city of God* (Ps 46:4).

(14) Augustine of Hippo

With respect to God's promise of good things we should certainly understand the **river of peace** (66:12)[4] to mean the overflowing abundance of that peace of which there can be nothing greater. In the end we will be refreshed with this peace as with water.... He will direct this **river** toward those to whom he promises such felicity that we may understand that in this land of felicity located in the heavens this **river** will satisfy us with all things. But because the peace of incorruption and immortality will flow also to earthly bodies, he says that he will direct this **river** so that it may flow, as it were, from the realms above even to the lower regions and put men on the same footing as the angels.

By **Jerusalem** (66:13) we should understand not the Jerusalem who is in slavery with her children but our free mother, which, according to the apostle, is eternal in the heavens (Gal 4:26). There, after the tribulations and cares of this life, we will be **comforted like children carried on their mother's shoulders or held on her knees** (66:12). For though we are untrained and immature, that unaccustomed felicity will lift us up and support us with the most gentle caresses. There **we shall see, and our heart shall rejoice** (66:14). The prophet did not indicate what we shall see, but what can it be but God? For thus will be fulfilled in us the promise of the Gospel: *Blessed are the pure in heart, for they will see God* (Matt 5:8). And we will see all those things that we do not see now. Yet even now, because we believe, we are able to conceive them insofar as our human minds are capable. Our idea of them is, however, infinitely less, indeed incomparable, to what they are. **And you will see**, says the prophet, **and your heart will rejoice** (66:14). Here you believe; there you will see.

However, for fear that we should suppose, because he says **Your heart will rejoice**, that the good things of that Jerusalem belong only to the spirit, he adds: **Your bones shall grow like grass** (66:14), thereby touching on the resurrection of the body, as though to clarify what had not been expressed. For this will happen not after we have seen; we shall see after it has taken place. For he had already spoken about the new heaven and the new earth when talking more than once and in different ways about those things promised to the saints at the end of time. *There will be new heavens and a new earth, and the former things shall not be remembered; but they will be glad and rejoice in the new creation. See, I will make Jerusalem a rejoicing, and her people a joy; and no more shall be heard in it the sound of weeping* (65:17-19) and the other promises that some try to refer to the establishment of an earthly kingdom of a thousand years.[5] It is customary for the prophets to intermingle figurative and literal manners of speech. It is both useful and salutary that we give careful attention to the text and apply ourselves diligently so that we might arrive at its spiritual meaning. Our natural human indolence and unwillingness to be instructed

---

4. Augustine's Latin text read **river of peace** for **extend prosperity like a river** (66:12).
5. Augustine is referring to a common early Christian belief, based on Rev 20:1-5, that Christ would return to earth to reign for a thousand years before the final consummation of all things.

and directed, however, makes us content with the superficial literal meaning and leads us to think that there is no deeper meaning to be discovered.

66:13-14
As a mother will comfort someone, so I will comfort you.

(15) Jerome

We learn the mercy of the Creator toward his creatures by the example of mothers who tenderly nurse their children at their loving bosom. Thus, when God wants to show how he loves those he created, he asks: *Can a woman forget her suckling child, that she should have no compassion on the son of her womb? Even these may forget, yet I will not forget you* (Isa 49:15). Is not that what the Gospel means when the Lord laments over Jerusalem: *How often would I have gathered your children together as a hen gathers her brood under her wings, and you would not!* (Matt 23:37)? And Deuteronomy sounds much the same note: *Like an eagle that protects its nest, that flutters over its young, spreading out its wings, catching them, bearing them on its pinions* (Deut 32:11).

Naturalists say that all wild animals and cattle and sheep and birds have an intense affection for their offspring. Yet the eagle's love is the greatest, since they make their nests in the highest and most inaccessible places to prevent snakes from harming their young. They are even found to place among their young the so-called "eagle stone" that repulses anything harmful. If this is so, the love of God for his creatures is rightly compared with the affection of eagles, who diligently watch over their young, lest the dragon and the ancient serpent (the devil and Satan) steal upon the newborn children. God stands guard so that all the deceits of the enemy may be dashed against the rock that has become the foundation of Zion (cf. 28:16). This is the Jerusalem where the sons are **comforted** (66:13) by a mother, and **dandled on her knees** (66:12). This is the city about which the apostle writes: *But the Jerusalem above is free, and she is our mother* (Gal 4:26). Being filled with the comfort that comes from her breasts, the apostle comforts others who crave his preaching, saying, *Blessed be God, the Father of mercies and God of all comfort, who comforts us in all our affliction, so that we may be able to comfort those who are in any affliction, with the comfort with which we ourselves are comforted by God* (2 Cor 1:3-4).

After they are comforted, they will hear, **You shall see, and your heart shall rejoice; your bones shall flourish like the grass** (66:14). That is, they will rise, or, according to Symmachus, they will blossom. Indeed, they will see God himself, who is our true joy. As the Lord promises: *Blessed are the pure in heart, for they shall see God* (Matt 5:8). The vision of God is perfect bliss that delights those who are mature in faith.

66:22
New heaven and a new earth

(16) Irenaeus of Lyons

Neither the substance nor the essence of the created order will be destroyed, because the one who established it is faithful and trustworthy. But *the form of this world is passing away* (1 Cor 7:31), that is, those things that were the occasion for sin, for man has grown old in them. That is why the *form of this world* has been created temporal.... But when the *form of this world* passes away, man has been renewed and flourishes in an incorruptible state and does not grow old, then there will be a **new heaven** and a **new earth** (66:22) in which the new man shall persevere, always engaged in fresh conversation with God. And since these things shall continue without end, Isaiah declares, **For as the new heavens and the new earth, which I will make, shall remain before me, says the Lord, so shall your descendants and your name remain** (66:22). And as the teachers of the Church say, those who are deemed worthy of a dwelling place in heaven shall go there, some enjoying the delights of paradise, and others possessing the splendor of the city. For everywhere God will be seen insofar as each is able to behold him.

(17) Ambrose of Milan

If the **earth** and **heaven** are made new, why should we doubt that man, on account of whom heaven and earth were made, can also be made new? If the transgressor is to be punished, why should the just not be glorified? If the **worm** (66:24) of sin does not die, shall the flesh of the just perish? For the resurrection, as the very form of the word shows, is this: that what has fallen should rise again, that what has died should come to life again.

66:24
For their worm shall not die, their fire shall not be quenched.

(18) Gregory of Nyssa

The blessings promised to those who have lived a good life defy description. For how can one describe *what the eye has not seen, nor the ear heard, nor the heart of man conceived* (1 Cor 2:9)? Further, the grief from physical pain in this life is in no way to be compared to the torment inflicted on sinners in the future life. Even if we can name some of those torments with terms that are familiar to us from this life, still there is no comparison between the one and the other. When you hear the word **fire** (66:24), you have been taught to think of something quite different from the **fire** spoken of here, since it has a quality not found in fire as we know it. For that **fire is not quenched** (66:24; cf. Mark 9:44), while there are many ways to quench the fire we know. The difference between fire which can be quenched and fire which cannot be quenched is very great indeed. This **fire**, then, is a quite different kind and unlike anything we know.

In the same way when one hears the word **worm** (66:24), the similarity of expression must not lead one to envision the familiar earthly creature. Here, too, the addition of the phrase **that does not die** (66:24; cf. Mark 9:48) indicates that it is a quite different creature from the one we know.

These, then, are the things we are to expect in the life to come, depending on the choice each person has made. By God's just judgment each will be judged in accord with the life one has led. Let the wise then set their eyes on the life to come, not this present life, laying the foundations in this brief and fleeting existence for unspeakable happiness. If they choose to live virtuous lives and shun evil, in this life as well as in the life to come they will receive an eternal reward.

(19) Augustine of Hippo

What God said through the mouth of his prophet about eternal punishment of the damned will come true; it will most certainly come true that **their worm will never die and their fire shall not be quenched** (66:24). Our Lord Jesus himself took care to emphasize this with even greater vehemence when he spoke of the bodily parts which cause a man to go wrong, making them stand for the people whom a man loves as he loves his own right hand. He bids him cut them off: *It is better for you to go into life maimed*, he says, *than to keep both hands and go to hell, into the inextinguishable fire, where their worm never dies, and their fire does not go out* (Mark 9:43-44). Similarly, he says of the foot: *It is better for you to go lame into eternal life than to keep both feet and be consigned to hell, to the inextinguishable fire, where their worm never dies, and their fire does not go out* (Mark 9:45). He says the same about the eye: *It is better for you to enter the kingdom of God with one eye than to keep both eyes and be consigned to the hell of fire, where their worm never dies, and their fire is not quenched* (Mark 9:47-48). He did not find it irksome to repeat the same form of words three times in the same passage. Who could fail to be appalled at this repetition, this vehement emphasis on that punishment, uttered from his divine lips?

Now as for this **fire** and this **worm**, there are some who want to make both of them refer to the pains of the soul, not of the body. They contend that those whose penitence is too late, and therefore ineffectual, those who have thus been separated from God, are burnt in the fire of the soul's sorrow and pain; and therefore, they maintain, **fire** (66:24) is quite appropriately used as a symbol for that burning pain. That is why the apostle says, *If anyone is led astray, do I not burn with indignation?* (2 Cor 11:29). They suppose that the **worm** (66:24) is to be taken in the same way; for, they hold, the Scriptures say, *Like the moth in a garment, or the worm in timber, so does sorrow enter the heart of a man* (Prov 25:20 Vg.).

Those, on the other hand, who feel sure that in that punishment there will be pain of both soul and body declare that the body is burnt by the **fire** while the soul is, in a sense, gnawed by the **worm** of sorrow. This is a more plausible suggestion, inasmuch as it is obviously absurd to suppose that in that state either soul or body will be exempt from pain.

And yet for my part I should be more ready to ascribe both of them to the body than neither of them, and to assume that the scriptural statement is silent about the pain of the soul for this reason, that, although it is not stated, it is taken as implied that when the body is thus in pain, the soul also will be tortured with unavailing remorse. For in the Old Testament we have this saying, *The punishment of the flesh of the wicked is the fire and the worm* (Sir 7:17); which could be put more briefly as *the punishment of the wicked.* The reason for the addition of *the flesh* can surely be only that both the fire and the worm will be punishments of the body. Or it may be that the writer chose to say *the punishments of the flesh* because what will be punished in a man is his wickedness in having lived a life of fleshly sensuality; for that is why he will come to the second death, which is what the apostle means when he says, *If you live on the level of fleshly sensuality, you will die* (Rom 8:13).

Well, then, each one of us must choose as he thinks fit between those interpretations. He may ascribe the **fire** to the body, and the **worm** to the mind, the former literally and the latter metaphorically; or he may attribute both, in the literal sense, to the body. For in any case I have sufficiently argued that it is possible for living creatures to remain alive in the fire, being burnt without being consumed, feeling pain without incurring death, and this by means of a miracle of the omnipotent Creator. Anyone who says that this is impossible for the Creator does not realize who is responsible for whatever marvels he finds in the whole of the world of nature. It is, in fact, God himself who has created all that is wonderful in this world, the great miracles and the minor marvels . . . and he has included them all in that unique wonder, that miracle of miracles, the world itself.

Then let each one choose the alternative he prefers; he may think either that the **worm**, along with the **fire**, refers, in the literal sense, to the bodily punishment, or that it refers to the punishments of the soul, the word being used by a transferal of sense from the material to the immaterial. Which of these is the true explanation will be all too swiftly revealed by the actual event, when the knowledge of the saints will be such as to need no experience to teach them the truth about those pains; that wisdom, which will then be full and perfect, will then suffice by itself for them to know this also — for *now our knowledge is partial* (1 Cor 13:9), until perfection comes. The important thing is that we should never believe that those bodies are to be such as to feel no anguish in the fire.

APPENDIX 1

Authors of Works Excerpted

Aelred of Rievaulx (1109-67), Cistercian monk and spiritual writer. He is the author of *The Mirror of Charity*, a series of meditations on love addressed to his fellow monks, and a beautiful treatise, *Spiritual Friendship*. He also wrote a spiritual commentary on the oracles of the nations in Isaiah 13–23 entitled the "Burdens" of Isaiah, the title coming from the Latin word for "oracle."

Ambrose (ca. 339-97), bishop of Milan, the capital of the western Roman Empire in the late fourth century, one of the four Latin "doctors" (teachers) of the Church (along with Augustine, Jerome, and Gregory the Great). He is the author of many works, including *Commentary on the Gospel according to Luke*, a treatise on Christian ethics, exegetical homilies, theological treatises, several writings on virginity, two series of homilies on Baptism and the Eucharist for the newly baptized, and hymns.

Ambrosiaster (probably fourth century) is a name given to an unknown early Christian writer who wrote commentaries in Latin on the thirteen letters of Paul, perhaps in Rome at the time of Pope Damasus (366-84). His commentaries were attributed to Ambrose (hence the name "Ambrosiaster"), but this attribution has been rejected by scholars since the Renaissance. Ambrosiaster is also assumed to be the author of a work called *Questions on the Old and New Testaments*.

Anaphora of the East Syrian Liturgy. *Anaphora* is the Greek term for the Eucharistic prayer, the great prayer over the gifts of bread and wine, and East Syrian refers to the rite of the Nestorians or Chaldaeans, the eastern rite-Catholics.

Anselm of Canterbury (1033-1109), theologian, philosopher, bishop, and spiritual writer. He is most famous for his argument for the existence of God solely by an appeal to reason. Following Augustine, however, he interpreted Isa 7:9, "if you do not believe you shall not understand," to mean that the knowledge of God begins with faith. From that he derived the maxim *fides quaerens intellectum*, faith seeking understanding. The passage is quoted in the first chapter of his *Proslogion,* and his interpretation gained wide currency within medieval thought and in later Christian thinking.

Aphrahat (fourth century), Syriac Christian writer, sometimes called the "Persian Sage." He lived in the Sassanid Empire (in present-day Iran) and is the author of twenty-three "Demonstrations," that is, orations, on doctrinal and ascetical topics.

Apostolic Constitutions, a collection of liturgical and legal sources dating from the late fourth century, probably from Syria. It includes such works as the *Didache* and the *Apostolic Tradition.*

Athanasius (ca. 296-373), bishop of Alexandria, was a strong supporter of the creed adopted at Nicea (325). In his writings against Arius he defended the full divinity of the Son. His works include a treatise, *On the Incarnation,* and a life of the desert monk Antony.

Augustine (354-430), bishop of Hippo, was the preeminent Latin theologian of the patristic period. Trained as a teacher of rhetoric, he spent many years as a Manichean before being baptized by Ambrose in Milan in 387. The immense corpus of his writings includes the autobiographical *Confessions,* the *Trinity,* his most important dogmatic work, and *The City of God,* in which he answers pagan critics of Christianity through a synthesis of philosophical, theological, and political ideas that was to become a foundational text for Western civilization. Augustine wrote commentaries on Genesis (the *Literal Commentary on Genesis*), the Psalms, the Gospel of John, and Galatians, but none on Isaiah. His writings, including his sermons, are a rich source of commentary on many key passages in the prophet.

Basil of Caesarea (ca. 330-79), was bishop of Caesarea in Cappadocia (modern Turkey) and founder of a monastery and charitable institutions. One of the three Cappadocian fathers, he was the brother of Gregory of Nyssa and the friend of Gregory of Nazianzus. His rules for monks, published in several different forms, are still influential in Eastern churches. A commentary on chapters 1–16 of Isaiah bears his name, but today it is not considered the work of Basil.

Bede (673-735), the "Venerable," monk at Jarrow in England, Anglo-Saxon historian, biblical commentator, chronographer, and educator. He is the author of the *Ecclesiastical History of the English People,* works on Latin grammar, a work on the date of Easter, biblical commentaries, and other writings.

Bernard of Clairvaux (1090-1153), was the founder of the famous Cistercian abbey at Clairvaux. In the course of his career he became, through his connections with the papacy, a leader in the wider Church. Author of many writings dealing with the spiritual life, among which are a series of homilies on the Song of Songs, a treatise, *On Loving God,* and homilies, *In Praise of the Virgin Mother.*

Authors of Works Excerpted

Cassiodorus (485/90–ca. 580) was a Roman statesman who served the Ostrogothic rulers in Ravenna and founded a monastic community near Naples. A bibliophile, he founded a library and collected many theological writing, including biblical commentaries. His works include the *Institutes of Divine and Secular Literature,* a church history, and a commentary on the Psalms.

Clement of Alexandria (ca. 150–ca. 215), Christian apologist, was the first Christian to attempt a thoroughgoing synthesis of the Bible and Greek philosophy. He is known primarily for a trilogy that consists of the *Exhortation,* an invitation to the Christian faith directed at educated Greeks, the *Pedagogue,* a moral treatise that focuses on the elementary stages of the Christian life, and the *Stromateis* or *Miscellanies,* an enigmatic, diffuse work in seven books that discusses various theological and moral topics.

Clement of Rome, bishop of Rome at the turn of the first century, author of a letter to the church at Corinth.

Council of Chalcedon (451), fourth ecumenical council, whose bishops issued a formal confession of faith that identified Christ as "one person in two natures (divine and human) united unconfusedly, unchangeably, indivisibly, inseparably."

Cyprian of Carthage (d. 258). A rhetorician by profession, he converted to Christianity in his forties and was elected bishop of Carthage shortly afterward. He guided the church of Carthage during the dark days of the Decian persecution and proved a decisive leader in the churches of North Africa at a time of disagreements and schisms occasioned by differences over the treatment of the many Christians who had fallen away during the persecution. He is the author of theological, moral, and devotional works and a large number of letters.

Cyril of Alexandria (d. 444) was the patriarch of Alexandria and an influential theologian who played an important role in the formulation of the classic doctrine of the person of Christ. He led opposition to the teaching of the Antiochene Nestorius, bishop of Constantinople. His writings include theological treatises, letters, and many commentaries, including a complete commentary on the prophet Isaiah.

Cyril of Jerusalem (315-87), bishop of Jerusalem, was the author of a series of catechetical homilies addressed to candidates for Baptism and five "mystagogic catecheses" delivered in Easter week after Baptism.

Didymus the Blind (ca. 313-98), head of the Catechetical School in Alexandria, was much influenced by Origen. His writings include a treatise on the Holy Spirit and many commentaries on Scripture, most of which are lost.

Dionysius the Pseudo-Areopagite (ca. 500) wrote a series of works dealing with the union of the whole created world with God. The *Divine Names* deals with the attributes of God, and *Mystical Theology* with the ascent of the soul to God. He also wrote on the orders of angels that mediate between God and humankind and on the sacraments.

Ephrem (306-373), Syriac writer and poet, native of Nisibis in southeastern Turkey. He is the author of many hymns and verse homilies dealing with biblical persons and events, ascetical topics, and theological themes, as well as biblical commentaries. Only Syriac writer recognized by the Catholic Church as "Doctor of the Universal Church" celebrated in the Eastern Church as "The Lyre of the Holy Spirit."

Eusebius of Caesarea (260-339), bishop of Caesarea in Palestine, prolific and learned Christian scholar and father of church history. He wrote the first history of the church and other historical works, a Life of Constantine, theological and apologetic writings, and various works on the Bible, including a complete commentary on Isaiah.

Faustus Luciferanus (fourth century), a relatively unknown Christian writer who lived in the early part of the fourth century. He was the author of a treatise on the Trinity.

Fulgentius (468-533?), bishop of Ruspe in North Africa during the years of the rule of the Vandals, who were Arians. Augustinian in theology, he is the author of treatises against Arianism and Pelagianism as well as letters and sermons.

Gregory the Great (540-604), bishop of Rome; an energetic, practical, and thoughtful administrator of the papacy at a difficult time, author of many letters, a collection of exegetical sermons on the gospels and on the prophet Ezekiel, and a popular spiritual commentary on the book of Job, the *Moralia*.

Gregory the Theologian (329-389), Gregory of Nazianzus, was bishop of Sasima and a prominent preacher in Constantinople. Along with the other two Cappadocian fathers (Basil of Caesarea and Gregory of Nyssa), he defended the orthodox teaching formulated in 325 at Nicea. Well educated in Greek culture and rhetoric, he was known for his eloquence, evident, for example, in his *Five Theological Orations*.

Gregory of Nyssa (ca. 330–ca. 395), bishop of Nyssa, a leading theologian and mystical writer, was the brother of Basil of Caesarea and one of the three Cappadocian fathers. He championed the creed of Nicea (325) against Arians who denied the full divinity of Christ, as is evident in the extracts included in this volume from his homily on 1 Cor 15:28 and from his polemical work *Against Eunomius*. Among his many works are his *Great Catechesis*, an introduction to the Christian faith and sacraments, *On Virginity*, which recommends the ascetic life, his *Life of Moses*, and homilies on the Beatitudes, the Lord's Prayer, and the Song of Songs, which he understands as an allegory of the love between God and the soul. His exegesis, which emphasizes the mystical sense of Scripture, was influenced by Origen.

Hesychius of Jerusalem (fifth century), monk and preacher in Jerusalem in the early fifth century. He is the author of a commentary on Leviticus, a series of homilies on the book of Job, and commentaries on the prophets.

Hilary of Poitiers (317-367), Latin theologian, biblical commentator, and hymn writer. His most important work, *The Trinity*, is a defense of the teaching of the Council of Nicea. He is also the author of a commentary on the Gospel of Matthew as well as on the Psalms.

Hippolytus (170-236), Greek Christian writer, most important theologian of the Roman Church in the third century, author of polemical and theological works, commentaries on Daniel and the Song of Songs, and an early church order, *The Apostolic Tradition*.

Irenaeus (ca. 130–ca. 200), bishop of Lyons in southern Gaul (modern France), wrote *Against the Heresies* to oppose Gnostic teachers such as Valentinus and Ptolemy. He defends Christian use of the Old Testament and argues that it forms a unity with the New Testament, which he is one of the first to cite as Scripture. His theology emphasizes God's action in the world and encapsulates the main themes of the biblical narratives: creation, redemption, and eschatological fulfillment.

Isidore of Seville (560-636), bishop of Seville in Spain, doctor of the Church, prolific author. His most important work, the *Etymologies*, is an encyclopedia of information drawn from earlier writers on the liberal arts, medicine, geography, the books of the Bible, liturgy, and theology. He also compiled a little book of collected citations from Isaiah that narrates the principal events in the life of Christ and their significance.

Jerome (ca. 345-420), biblical scholar and ascetic, was educated in Rome and then devoted himself to the ascetic life, spending several years as a hermit in the Syrian desert and then serving as head of a monastery in Bethlehem. He is best known for the Vulgate, his translation of the Bible from Hebrew and Greek into Latin, and for his many biblical commentaries, including commentaries on Ezekiel, the Minor Prophets, and Isaiah.

John Cassian (360-430?), monk and influential spiritual writer who founded monasteries in southern France. He wrote several works on the monastic life, including the *Conferences*, a series of conversations with outstanding leaders of Eastern monasticism.

John Chrysostom (ca. 347-407) studied rhetoric under the pagan orator Libanius and theology under Diodore of Tarsus, head of the Christian school of Antioch. As a priest at Antioch and later bishop in Constantinople he was known especially for his high moral tone, his courage in difficult political circumstances, and his eloquence. His honorific title "Chrysostom" means "golden tongued," and it reflects his great reputation as a preacher. He preached extended series of sermons on many biblical books, including homilies on Isaiah 6, a collection of homilies on chapters 1-8, and a complete commentary on Isaiah preserved in Armenian.

APPENDIX 1

John of Damascus (ca. 655–ca. 750), an important Greek theologian who lived under the Muslims and defended the use of images during the Iconoclastic Controversy (726-73). His major work, *The Fount of Wisdom,* gives a comprehensive synthesis of the teaching of the Greek fathers on the central points of Christian doctrine.

Justin Martyr (d. 165), author of two apologies in defense of Christianity, the first to Emperor Antoninus Pius and the second to the Roman Senate. He is also the author of the *Dialogue with Trypho,* a debate with a Jewish teacher on the meaning of passages from the Old Testament. He was martyred (beheaded) with a group of his disciples for refusing to sacrifice to the Roman gods.

Lactantius (250-325), Latin Christian apologist, sometimes called the Christian Cicero. His *Divine Institutes* is the first attempt by a Latin author to present a systematic account of Christian teachings to a learned audience.

Leo the Great (d. 461) was pope from 440 and greatly enhanced the authority of the see of Rome over all the western provinces during an unstable time. He wrote many letters and sermons.

The Liturgy of Saint James is an early Christian order for the Eucharist associated with the church in Jerusalem, and used in Syria, Egypt, Ethiopia, Armenia, and Georgia. It dates at least to the early fifth century.

Martyrdom and Ascension of Isaiah, an apocryphal work, in origin Jewish but transmitted in Christian versions. It depicts the circumstances that led to Isaiah's martyrdom and the revelations he received when he ascended to the heavens. The date of the original is uncertain.

Martyrius (Sahdona), a Syriac monk who lived in the vicinity of Kirkuk in modern Iraq. He is the author of several letters to fellow monks, a set of spiritual maxims, and the *Book of Perfection,* a work on the monastic life that includes a section on prayer.

Maximus the Confessor (580-662), Eastern theologian who wrote on theological, cosmological, and ascetic topics. He is most noted for his critique of monotheletism, the teaching that Christ had only a divine will, and his brilliant interpretation of the double will of Christ. He was imprisoned, his tongue was cut out and his right hand cut off, and he died in exile. For his faithfulness he was honored with the name "confessor."

Maximus of Turin (d. 408/423), author of more than a hundred sermons, some of which were widely read in the Middle Ages.

Origen of Alexandria (ca. 185–ca. 254), the true godfather of Christian biblical scholarship and interpretation. Despite posthumous condemnations occasioned by some of his bolder theological speculations, Origen exerted an unrivaled influence on early Christian biblical interpretation not only in the eastern Christian tradition but in the West as well, through the medium of Latin translations. He wrote many commentaries and series of homilies on Old and New Testament books (e.g., on Genesis, Exodus, Leviticus, Jeremiah, Luke, and John), and apparently commented on all the Pauline epistles. Known especially for his allegorical or symbolic exegesis, Origen also concerns himself with historical and philological questions. His philological training is evident in his careful attention to the definitions of words, to shades of meaning expressed by similar phrases, and to textual variants. He is the author of nine homilies on Isaiah dealing with the first ten chapters, particularly chapter 6.

Pacian of Barcelona (fourth century), bishop of Barcelona, admired for his learning and holiness. Author of treatises on Baptism and on penance.

Proclus (d. 446), patriarch of Constantinople, outstanding preacher and author of a series of highly rhetorical sermons, the most famous of which is on Mary as the *Theotokos*.

Prudentius (348-410), Latin Christian poet and hymn writer. He wrote a collection of poems for the hours of the day, a series of poems on early Christian martyrs, and an allegorical epic entitled *Psychomachia* on the spiritual struggle of the soul against the vices.

Romanos the Melodist (fl. 540), Greek Christian poet, author of metrical hymns to be sung in the liturgy. The best known are *The Nativity, The Presentation in the Temple,* and *The Resurrection.*

Symeon the New Theologian (949-1022), Byzantine monk and spiritual writer. He is the author of several collections of essays, the *Theological and Ethical Discourses* for learned readers, a series of *Catechetical Discourses,* delivered to his fellow monks, and a body of hymns. He is noted for his mysticism and his ability to depict his experience of the vision of God. He is called the "new" theologian to distinguish him from Gregory of Nazianzus, who was called "the Theologian."

Syro-Malabar Rite. The Syriac Liturgy of Christians living in the Kerala area in southwest India who are sometimes known as the Thomas Christians.

Tertullian (ca. 160–ca. 225), from Carthage in North Africa, was the first to write theological treatises in Latin. He also wrote apologetic, antiheretical, and moral works, all of which display great skill in rhetoric. In his *On the Resurrection of the Dead,* which is directed against Gnostics, he argues vigorously for the physical reality of the resurrection body. For a time Tertullian was a Montanist, attracted in part by the rigorous moralism of this movement.

Theodore of Mopsuestia (ca. 350-428), bishop of Mopsuestia in Cilicia in southeastern Asia Minor, theologian and biblical commentator. He is also the author of a series of catechetical homilies dealing with the Nicene Creed, the Lord's Prayer, the liturgy of Baptism and the Eucharist, and a commentary on the Minor Prophets.

Theodoret (ca. 393–ca. 460), bishop of Cyrus in Syria (near Antioch), was educated in Antioch and defended Nestorius and Antiochene Christology against the criticisms of Cyril of Alexandria. His works include an apology that compares Christian and pagan teaching, a church history, biographies of monks, a refutation of heresies, and commentaries on many Old Testament books, including a complete commentary on Isaiah.

Thomas Aquinas (1225-74), outstanding Dominican theologian and philosopher in the high Middle Ages. His most famous work, the *Summa Theologiae*, is a systematic treatment of questions concerning God, creation, the human person, the moral law, Christ, sacraments, and the like. He also wrote biblical commentaries, for example, on Job, Isaiah, the Gospel of John, and he prepared a commentary on the gospels based on patristic texts (not unlike The Church's Bible).

Venantius Fortunatus (530-610), a Latin poet and hymn writer, was the author of two hymns sung during Holy Week, "Pange lingua gloriosi" (Sing, My Tongue) and "Vexilla regis prodeunt" (The Royal Banners Forward Go).

APPENDIX 2

Sources of Texts Translated

1. Abbreviations of Source Titles

ACW   Ancient Christian Writers. New York: Newman Press, 1946–.
CCCM   Corpus Christianorum: Continuatio mediaevalis. Turnhout (Belgium): Brepols, 1971ff.
CCSL   Corpus Christianorum: Series latina. Turnhout (Belgium): Brepols, 1953ff.
CSCO   Corpus scriptorum Christianorum orientalium. Paris, 1903–.
CSEL   Corpus scriptorum ecclesiasticorum latinorum. Vienna, 1866ff.
FOC   Fathers of the Church. Washington, DC: Catholic University of America Press, 1948–.
GCS   Die griechischen christlichen Schriftsteller der ersten drei Jahrhunderte. Berlin: Akademie Verlag, 1901ff.
GNO   Werner Jaeger et al., ed., Gregorii Nysseni opera. Leiden: Brill, 1960-72.
PG   J.-P. Migne, ed., Patrologiae cursus completus: Series graeca. 161 vols. Paris, 1857-66.
PL   J.-P. Migne, ed., Patrologiae cursus completus: Series latina. 221 vols. Paris, 1844-64.
PLS   A. Hamann, ed., Patrologiae latinae supplementum. Paris, 1957ff.
SC   Sources chrétiennes. Paris: Éditions du Cerf, 1948ff.
WSA   Works of Saint Augustine. Brooklyn, N.Y.: New City Press, 1990ff.

2. Sources of Individual Excerpts

Preface

(1) Hebrews 11:32-39.
(2) Luke 4:16-21.
(3) John 12:36-41.
(4) Acts 8:26-38.

545

APPENDIX 2

(5) *Martyrdom and Ascension of Isaiah* 3:8-12; 5:1-8, *The Old Testament Pseudepigrapha,* trans. M. A. Knibb, ed. James H. Charlesworth (New York, 1958), 2:160, 163, slightly revised.
(6) Origen of Alexandria, *Homilies on Joshua* 9.8, SC 71:260.
(7) Eusebius of Caesarea, *Commentary on Isaiah, Eusebius Werke,* vol. 9, ed. J. Ziegler (GCS; Berlin, 1975), 3.
(8) John Chrysostom, *Commentary on Isaiah,* ed. J. Dumortier, SC 304:36-40.
(9) Jerome, *Commentary on Isaiah,* ed. M. Adriaen, CCSL 73:1-2.
(10) Augustine of Hippo, *Confessions* 9.5.1, PL 32:769; trans. H. Chadwick, 163.
(11) Augustine of Hippo, *City of God* 18.29, CCSL 48:617 and PL 41:585-86.
(12) Augustine of Hippo, *Revisions* 1.5.2, PL 32:591.
(13) Cyril of Alexandria, *Commentary on Isaiah,* PG 70:9A-13B.
(14) Isidore of Seville, *Isaiah's Testimony concerning Christ the Lord,* PLS 4:1822-37.

Chapter 1

(1) John Chrysostom, *Commentary on Isaiah,* SC 304:42-52.
(2) Cyril of Alexandria, *Commentary on Isaiah* 1:2, PG 70:16D-17A, 17C-20A.
(3) Origen of Alexandria, *Homily* 11.3 *on Genesis,* SC 7:286-90.
(4) Didymus the Blind, *Commentary on Zechariah* 4:8, SC 83:360.
(5) Augustine of Hippo, *Sermon on the Birthday of the Lord* 4, *Miscellanea Agostiniana* (Rome, 1930), 1:211.
(6) Gregory the Theologian, *Oration* 38.17, SC 358:142-44.
(7) Tertullian, *On Prayer* 28-29, CCSL 1:273-74.
(8) Augustine of Hippo, *Sermon* 42.1, PL 38:252; trans. Edmund Hill, WSA III/2:234, revised.
(9) Clement of Rome, *Letter to the Corinthians* 8.1–9.1, SC 167:112-14.
(10) Origen of Alexandria, *Homily* 6.2 *on Leviticus,* SC 286:272.
(11) Aphrahat, *Demonstrations* 4.18; Syriac text: I. Parisot, ed., *Aphraatis Demonstrationes,* Patrologia Syriaca (Paris, 1894), 1:180.
(12) Cyril of Jerusalem, *Catechetical Lectures* 1.1, PG 33:369-72.
(13) Gregory of Nyssa, *On the Baptism of Christ,* PG 46:592-93.
(14) Didymus the Blind, *Commentary on Psalm* 33:18, *Psalmenkommentar,* vol. 3, ed. Michael Gronewald (Bonn: Habelt, 1969), 201:12-15.
(15) Didymus the Blind, *Commentary on Zechariah* 7:11-12, SC 84:508.
(16) Augustine of Hippo, *Sermon* 341.13, PL 39:1500-1501; trans. Edmund Hill, in WSA III/10:27-28, revised.
(17) Martyrius, *Book of Perfection,* second part, 8:3-4, Martyrius (Sahdona), *Oeuvres spirituelles,* 3: *Le livre de la perfection, 2me partie (chs. 8-14),* ed. André de Halleux (CSCO 252; Scriptores Syri 110), 1-2; trans. S. Brock, *The Syriac Fathers on Prayer and the Spiritual Life* (Kalamazoo: Cistercian Publications, 1987), 203.
(18) Basil of Caesarea, *Epistle* 46, PG 32:380C.
(19) Augustine of Hippo, *Sermon* 78.2, PL 38:490-91; trans. Edmund Hill, WSA III/3:341, slightly revised.

Sources of Texts Translated

(20) Augustine of Hippo, *Perfection in Righteousness* 40, 42, PL 44:313-14, 315.

Chapter 2

(1) Hebrews 1:1-2.
(2) Cyril of Alexandria, *Commentary on Isaiah* 2:1-3, PG 70:65D-68A, 68C-D.
(3) Eusebius of Caesarea, *Commentary on Isaiah* 2:1-4, *Eusebius Werke*, vol. 9, ed. J. Ziegler (GCS; Berlin, 1975), 14-16.
(4) John Chrysostom, *Commentary on Isaiah* 2:2, SC 304:98, 104-6.
(5) Theodoret of Cyrus, *Commentary on Isaiah* 2:1-2, ed. J. Guïnot, SC 276:188-90.
(6) Origen of Alexandria, *Commentary on John* 2:2-7, SC 120:208-12.
(7) Theodore of Mopsuestia, *Theodori Mopsuesteni Commentarius in XII Prophetas*, ed. Hans Norbert Sprenger (Göttinger Orientsforschungen V.1; Wiesbaden, 1977), 206-8.
(8) Augustine of Hippo, *Sermon* 62A, PLS 2:673; trans. Edmund Hill, revised, WSA III/3:171.
(9) Augustine of Hippo, *Sermon* 223H, PLS 2:739; trans. Edmund Hill, WSA III/6:234.
(10) *Acta Conciliorum Oecumenicorum*, ed. E. Schwartz (1933); 2.1, 325.23-326.3, trans. Edward Rochie, *Christology of the Later Fathers* (Philadelphia: Westminster, 1954), 373.
(11) Gregory the Great, *Commentary on the First Book of Kings* 1:1, SC 351:174-78. This commentary may come from a later writer.
(12) Justin Martyr, *Apology* 1.39, *Iustini Martyris: Apologiae pro Christianis*, ed. M. Marcovich (Berlin, 1994), 87.
(13) Irenaeus of Lyons, *Against Heresies* 4.34.4, SC 100:856-58.
(14) Cassiodorus, *Explanation of Psalm* 49 (50), CCSL 97:441-42; trans. P. G. Walsh, (New York: Paulist, 1990), 1:481.
(15) Tertullian, *Against Marcion* 3.21, SC 399:182-84.
(16) Athanasius of Alexandria, *On the Incarnation* 52, SC 199:452.
(17) Cyril of Alexandria, *Commentary on Isaiah* 2:8-9, PG 70:81D-84A.
(18) Didymus the Blind, *Commentary on Zechariah* 11:1-2, SC 85:812.

Chapter 4

(1) John Chrysostom, *Commentary on Isaiah* 4:1-5, SC 304:202-8.
(2) Cyril of Alexandria, *Commentary on Isaiah* 4:5-6, PG 70:133B-D.
(3) Origen of Alexandria, *Homilies on Isaiah* 3.1, *Origenes Werke*, vol. 8, ed. W. A. Bährens (GCS; Leipzig, 1925), 253.
(4) Eusebius of Caesarea, *Commentary on Isaiah* 4:1, *Eusebius Werke*, vol. 9, ed. J. Ziegler (GCS; Berlin, 1975), 25-26.
(5) Irenaeus, *Against Heresies* 4.22.1, SC 100:684-86.
(6) Origen of Alexandria, *Homilies on Jeremiah* 2.2-3, SC 232:242-46.
(7) Didymus the Blind, *Commentary on Job* 9:30-33, *Job Toura* 3:261.21–62.8.
(8) Gregory of Nyssa, *That There Are Not Three Gods to Ablabius*, GNO 3.1:49-52.

APPENDIX 2

Chapter 5

(1) Matthew 3:16-17 and parallels: Mark 1:10-11 and Luke 3:21-22; Matthew 17:5 and parallels: Mark 9:7 and Luke 9:35; Matthew 21:33-46 and parallels: Mark 12:1-12 and Luke 20:9-19.
(2) John Chrysostom, *Commentary on Isaiah* 5:1-7, 21, SC 304:210-14, 216-18, 220-26, 244.
(3) Eusebius of Caesarea, *Commentary on Isaiah* 5:1, *Eusebius Werke*, vol. 9, ed. J. Ziegler (GCS; Berlin, 1975), 28-29.
(4) Theodoret of Cyrus, *Commentary on Isaiah* 5:1-4, SC 276:228-32.
(5) Pseudo-Athanasius, *Oration against the Arians* 4.24, PG 26:504C.
(6) Augustine of Hippo, *Sermon* 376A, PL 39:1670-71; trans. Edmund Hill, WSA III/10:349.
(7) Augustine of Hippo, *Tractates on the Gospel of John* 10.5.2, CCSL 36:103; trans. John Rettig, FOC 78:215-16.
(8) Gregory the Great, *Homilies on the Gospels* 7.4, CCSL 141:51.
(9) Symeon the New Theologian, *Discourse, On Partaking of the Holy Spirit, #9: Obtaining the True Knowledge of God*, SC 113:264-66; trans. C. J. deCatanzaro (New York: Paulist, 1980), 345.

Chapter 6

(1) Matthew 13:10-17.
(2) John 12:36-40.
(3) Acts 28:23-29.
(4) Revelation 4:6-11.
(5) Origen of Alexandria, *Homilies on Isaiah* 1.1-2, 1.4-5, 5.2, *Origenes Werke*, vol. 8, ed. W. A. Bährens (GCS; Leipzig, 1925), 242-47, 264-65.
(6) Eusebius of Caesarea, *Commentary on Isaiah* 6:1-4, *Eusebius Werke*, vol. 9, ed. J. Ziegler (GCS; Berlin, 1975), 36-39.
(7) Jerome, *Commentary on Isaiah* 6:1-3, CCSL 73:84-87; *Epistle* 18a 4.1, CSEL 54:78; *Commentary on Isaiah* 6:4-8, CCSL 73:87-90.
(8) John Chrysostom, *Commentary on Isaiah* 6:1-3, SC 304:256-66.
(9) Gregory the Theologian, *Oration* 28.17-19, SC 250:134-40.
(10) Gregory of Nyssa, *Homily 12 on the Song of Songs*, GNO 6:368,7–369,12.
(11) Didymus the Blind, *Commentary on Genesis*, SC 244:156-58.
(12) Augustine of Hippo, *Letter* 147.12-22, PL 33:601-6; trans. Roland Teske, S.J., WSA II/2:324-30, slightly revised.
(13) *La Liturgie de Saint Jacques* ed. Dom B.-Ch. Mercier (Patrologia orientalis 26.2, no. 126; Brepols, 1997), 198-200.
(14) Ambrose of Milan, *On Faith* 2.107, CSEL 78:96-97.
(15) Basil of Caesarea, *On the Holy Spirit* 38, *Über den Heiligen Geist,* ed. Hermann Josef Sieben (Fontes Christiani 12; New York: Herder, 1993), 190-91.

Sources of Texts Translated

(16) Prudentius, *Cathemerinon* 4, CCSL 126:19, trans. David Slavitt, *Hymns of Prudentius* (Baltimore: Johns Hopkins University Press, 1996), 14-15.
(17) Cyril of Alexandria, *Commentary on Isaiah*, PG 70:176A-B.
(18) Gregory the Great, *Moralia on Job* 29.70, CCSL 143B:1482-83.
(19) Pseudo-Dionysius the Areopagite, *Celestial Hierarchy* 7.4, *Corpus Dionysiacum*, ed. Heil and Ritter, 2:31-32; trans. Colm Luibheid, *Pseudo-Dionysius: The Complete Works* (New York, 1987), 165-66.
(20) Martyrius, *Book of Perfection* 8.8, Martyrius (Sahdona), *Oeuvres spirituelles*, 3: *Le livre de la perfection, 2e partie (chs. 8–14)*, ed. André de Halleux (CSCO 252; Scriptores Syri 110), 3; trans. S. Brock, *The Syriac Fathers on Prayer and the Spiritual Life* (Kalamazoo: Cistercian Publications, 1987), 204-6.
(21) Maximus the Confessor, *Chapters on Charity* 1.12, PG 90:964B.
(22) John Cassian, *Conference* 23.17.1-3, SC 64:162-63.
(23) *Anaphora* of the East Syrian Liturgy, *Taksa* of the Priests of the Church of the East (Mosul: Press of the Assyrian Church of the East, 1928), 27-29.
(24) Theodore of Mopsuestia, *Commentary on the Eucharist and Liturgy*, ed. A. Mingana (Woodbrooke Studies; Cambridge: Heffer, 1933), 6:118-19; Syriac text on p. 260.
(25) Cyril of Alexandria, *Commentary on Isaiah* 6:6-7, PG 70:181A-84A.
(26) Divine Liturgy of the Syro-Malabar Rite, *The Book of Anaphoras* (Pampakuda, India: Mar Julius, 1976), 77-78.
(27) Ephrem the Syrian, *Hymns on the Nativity* 6.13-14, CSCO 186:53; *Hymn on Faith* 10.10, CSCO 154:50; trans. Sebastian Brock, *The Luminous Eye* (Kalamazoo: Cistercian Publications, 1992), 103-4.
(28) Jerome, *Commentary on Isaiah* 6:9-10, CCSL 73:91-94.
(29) John Chrysostom, *Homily on Matthew* 13:10-11, PG 58:472-73.
(30) Augustine of Hippo, *Tractate* 53.4-6 *on John* 12:37-40, CCSL 36:453-55 and PL 35:1775-77.
(31) Theodoret of Cyrus, *Commentary on Isaiah* 6:9-10, SC 276:268-70.

Chapter 7

(1) Matthew 1:18-25.
(2) John Chrysostom, *Commentary on Isaiah* 7:1, 10-16, SC 304:290, 294-96, 308-24.
(3) Augustine of Hippo, *Sermon* 126.1, PL 38:698; trans. Edmund Hill, WSA III/4:270.
(4) Augustine of Hippo, *Against Faustus* 12.46, CSEL 25:374-75.
(5) Augustine of Hippo, *Letter* 120.1.2-6, PL 33:453-54; trans. Roland Teske, WSA II/2:130-31.
(6) Augustine of Hippo, *On the Trinity* 15.2, CCSL 50A:460-62 and PL 42:1057-58.
(7) Cyril of Alexandria, *Commentary on Isaiah* 52:13-15, PG 70:1168A.
(8) Anselm of Canterbury, *Proslogion* 1, ed. Franciscus Salesius Schmitt, O.S.B. (Florilegium Patristicum Fasciculus XXIX; Bonn, 1931), 11.
(9) Tertullian, *On the Flesh of Christ* 17.1-5, CCSL 2:903-5.

APPENDIX 2

(10) Origen of Alexandria, *Against Celsus* 1.34-35, SC 132:168-172; trans. Henry Chadwick (Cambridge: Cambridge University Press, 1953), 33-35, slightly revised.
(11) Ambrose of Milan, *Commentary on Luke* 2:15, SC 45:79.
(12) Pseudo-Basil of Caesarea, *On the Holy Birth of Christ* 3, PG 31:1464A-D.
(13) Gregory of Nyssa, *On the Birth of Christ*, GNO 10/2:246-47.
(14) Jerome, *Against Jovinian* 1.32, PL 23:254D-55A.
(15) Pacian of Barcelona, *On Baptism* 3.1, SC 410:152.
(16) Augustine of Hippo, *Sermon* 370.3, "On the Lord's Nativity," PL 39:1658; trans. Edmund Hill, WSA III/10:309, slightly revised.
(17) Cyril of Alexandria, *Commentary on Isaiah* 7:14-16, PG 70:204B-5D.
(18) Theodoret of Cyrus, *Commentary on Isaiah* 7:14, SC 276:286-88.
(19) Ephrem the Syrian, *Hymns on the Nativity* 19.7-9, CSCO 186:100; trans. Kathleen McVey (New York: Paulist, 1989), 168.
(20) Leo the Great, *Sermon* 23.1, "On the Nativity of the Lord," CCSL 138:102-3.
(21) Venantius Fortunatus, "In Praise of Saint Mary," *Venanti Fortunati opera poetica*, ed. Friedrich Leo (Monumenta Germaniae historica: Auctores antiquissimi, vol. 4, pt. 1; Berlin: Weidmann, 1881), 371.1–72.26.
(22) Cassiodorus, *Explanation of Psalm 119(118).130*, CCSL 98:1116-17.
(23) Bernard of Clairvaux, *Homilies in Praise of the Virgin Mother* 2.11, *Sancti Bernardi opera* 4:28-29.

Chapter 8

(1) Romans 9:32-33.
(2) Hebrews 2:11-14.
(3) 1 Peter 2:4-8.
(4) Jerome, *Homilies on Isaiah* 3.8.1-4, CCSL 73:110-12.
(5) Eusebius of Caesarea, *The Proof of the Gospel* 7.1.96-113, *Eusebius Werke*, vol. 6, ed. I. A. Heikel (GCS; Leipzig, 1913), 316-20; see also PG 22:517B-24B (as 7.1).
(6) Eusebius of Caesarea, *The Proof of the Gospel* 7.1.115-19, *Eusebius Werke*, vol. 6, ed. I. A. Heikel (GCS; Leipzig, 1913), 320-21.
(7) Origen of Alexandria, *Commentary on Romans* 7.19.7-9, *Römerbriefkommentar*, ed. Theresia Heither (Fontes Christiani 2; Freiburg: Herder, 1990), 4:183-89.
(8) Augustine of Hippo, *Sermon* 352.5, PL 39:1554-55; trans. Edmund Hill, WSA III/10:143.
(9) Jerome, *Homilies on Isaiah* 3.8.18, CCSL 73:118-19.
(10) Origen of Alexandria, *Homilies on Isaiah* 7.3, *Origenes Werke*, vol. 8, ed. W. A. Bährens (GCS; Leipzig: J. C. Hinrichsche, 1925), 283.
(11) John Cassian, *Conference* 8.23.1, "On the Principalities," SC 54:31-32; trans. Boniface Ramsey, *John Cassian: The Conferences*, ACW 57:308, slightly revised.

Chapter 9

(1) Matthew 4:12-17.
(2) Cyril of Alexandria, *Commentary on Isaiah* 9:1-3, PG 70:245B-48D and 253D-57A.

Sources of Texts Translated

(3) Eusebius of Caesarea, *Commentary on Isaiah* 9:6, *Eusebius Werke*, vol. 9, ed. J. Ziegler (GCS; Berlin, 1975), 65.
(4) Gregory the Theologian, *Oration* 38.1-4, SC 358:104-10.
(5) Augustine, *Sermon* 362.24, PL 39.1627-28.
(6) Proclus of Constantinople, *Homily* 4.3 *on the Nativity of the Lord*, PG 65:713B-16A.
(7) Leo the Great, *Sermon* 29.3, SC 22 bis: 182-84.
(8) John of Damascus, *Exposition of the Orthodox Faith* 3.29, *Die Schriften des Johannes von Damaskos*, vol. 2, ed. P. Kotter (Patristische Texte und Studien 12; New York, 1973), 172.
(9) Symeon the New Theologian, *Discourses* 34.12, SC 113:298-300.
(10) Irenaeus of Lyons, *Against Heresies* 3.19.1-2, CCSL 1:533.
(11) Tertullian, *Against Marcion* 3.19.1-3, SC 399:164-66.
(12) Pseudo-Ephrem the Syrian, *Hymns on Mary* 11.4-7, ed. T. J. Lamy, *Sancti Ephraem Syri Hymni et Sermones*, vol. 2 (Mechliniæ: H. Dessain, Summi Pontificis, et al., 1886), 567-69; trans. S. Brock, *Bride of Light* (Kerala, India: St. Ephrem Ecumenical Research Institute, 1994), 57ff.
(13) Ambrose of Milan, *Epistle* 41.5-6, CSEL 82.3, pars 10:148.
(14) Jerome, *Commentary on Isaiah* 9:6-7, CCSL 73:126-27.
(15) Maximus of Turin, *Sermon* 54.2, CCSL 23:219; trans. Boniface Ramsey in ACW 50:132, slightly revised.
(16) Fulgentius of Ruspe, *Epistle* 14.16, CCSL 91:403; trans. Robert B. Eno, FOC 95:518, slightly revised.
(17) Eusebius of Caesarea, *Commentary on Isaiah* 9:7, *Eusebius Werke*, vol. 9, ed. J. Ziegler (GCS; Berlin, 1975), 67-68.

Chapter 11

(1) Romans 15:9-12.
(2) Revelation 5:5; 22:16.
(3) Cyril of Alexandria, *Commentary on Isaiah* 11:1-3, PG 70:309D-16B.
(4) Jerome, *Commentary on Isaiah* 11:1-3, CCSL 73:147-49.
(5) Justin Martyr, *1 Apology* 32, ed. M. Marcovich, *Iustini Martyris: Apologiae pro Christianis* (Berlin, 1994), 79.
(6) Tertullian, *Against Marcion* 5.8.4, SC 483:182-88; trans. Ernest Evans, *Tertullian: Adversus Marcionem* (Oxford, 1972), 557-61.
(7) Hippolytus, *On Christ and Antichrist* 8, *Hippolytus Werke*, vol. 1.2: *Hippolytus Kleinere: Exegetische und homiletische Schriften*, ed. H. Achelis (GCS; Leipzig, 1897), 9-10; see also PG 10:736A-B.
(8) Didymus the Blind, *Commentary on Zechariah* 1.253-57, SC 83:324-26.
(9) John Chrysostom, *Against Jews and Gentiles That Christ Is God* 2, PG 48:815.
(10) Leo the Great, *Sermon* 24.1, "On the Nativity of the Lord," CCSL 138:109-10.
(11) Romanos the Melodist, *Kontakion* 1, "On the Nativity," Preface, 1-2, *Sancti Romani melodi cantica: Cantica genuina*, ed. P. Maas and C. A. Trypanis (Oxford, 1963), 1-2; trans. Ephrem Lash, *On the Life of Christ: Kontakia of St. Romanos the Melodist*

APPENDIX 2

(New York, 1995), 3-4; *Kontakion* 37, "On the Mother of God," Preface, 1, 4, *Sancti Romani melodi cantica: Cantica genuina*, 289-91; trans. E. Lash, 17-18 (slightly revised).

(12) Maximus the Confessor, *Questions to Thalassius* 29, CCSL 7:211-13.
(13) Bernard of Clairvaux, *Homilies in Praise of the Virgin Mother* 2.5, *Sancti Bernardi opera* 4:24.
(14) Irenaeus of Lyons, *Against Heresies* 3.17.1-3, SC 211:328-38.
(15) Origen of Alexandria, *Homilies on Isaiah* 3.1-2, *Origenes Werke*, vol. 8, ed. W. A. Bährens (GCS; Leipzig, 1925), 253-55.
(16) Origen of Alexandria, *Homilies on Numbers* 6.3, SC 415:148-50.
(17) Aphrahat, Demonstration 1.9 on Faith, in I. Parisot, ed., *Aphraatis Demonstrationes* (Patrologia Syriaca 1; Paris, 1894), 20, 24-21, 9, trans. K. Valavanolicki (Changanassery: HIRS Publications, 1999), pp. 25-26, slightly revised.
(18) Gregory the Theologian, *Oration* 41.9, SC 358:334-36.
(19) Ambrose of Milan, *On the Mysteries* 7.42, SC 25 bis: 178.
(20) Augustine of Hippo, *The Lord's Sermon on the Mount* 1.4.11, CCSL 35:9-11 and PL 34:1234-35.
(21) Augustine of Hippo, *Sermon* 72A.2, on Matthew 12:41-45, *Miscellanea Agostiniana*, vol. 2: *Sancti Augustini: Sermones post Maurinos reperti*, ed. D. G. Morin (Rome: Typis Polyglottis Vaticanis, 1930), 156-57; and PL 46:933-34; trans. Edmund Hill, WSA III/3:282-83.
(22) Augustine of Hippo, *Grace and Free Choice* 18.39, PL 44:904-5; trans. Roland Teske, WSA I/26:97-98.
(23) Gregory the Great, *Moralia on Job* 29.74, CCSL 143B:1486-87.
(24) Irenaeus of Lyons, *Against Heresies* 5.33.4, SC 153:418-20.
(25) Cyril of Alexandria, *Commentary on Isaiah* 11:6-9, PG 70:320D-28D.

Chapter 12

(1) Jerome, *Commentary on Isaiah* 12:1-5, CCSL 73:157-58.
(2) Theodoret of Cyrus, *Commentary on Isaiah* 12:1-5, SC 295:60-62.
(3) Irenaeus of Lyons, *Against Heresies* 3.10.3, SC 211:122-24.
(4) Gregory of Nyssa, *On the Making of Man* 19, PG 44:196C-D.

Chapter 13

(1) Mark 13:3-6, 21-27.
(2) Jerome, *Commentary on Isaiah* 13:1-22, CCSL 73:160-62, 164-65; CCSL 73:223-25.
(3) Cyril of Alexandria, *Commentary on Isaiah* 13:1, PG 70:345B-48B.
(4) Pseudo-Basil of Caesarea, *Commentary on the Prophet Isaiah* 13:1, PG 30:565C-68B.
(5) Aelred of Rievaulx, *The Burdens of Isaiah*, Homily 2, "On the Burden of Babylon," PL 195:365A-67D.

Sources of Texts Translated

Chapter 14

(1) Cyril of Alexandria, *Commentary on Isaiah* 14:1-3, PG 70:365B-68C.
(2) Theodoret of Cyrus, *Commentary on Isaiah* 14:4-30, SC 295:84-100.
(3) Origen of Alexandria, *On First Principles* 1.5.5, SC 252:190-92.
(4) Augustine of Hippo, *Literal Commentary on Genesis* 11.24.31, PL 34:441-42.
(5) John Cassian, *Institutes* 12.4-6, CSEL 17:208-10; trans. B. Ramsey, ACW 58:256-57.
(6) Cyprian of Carthage, *Letter* 59.3, CSEL 3.2:669.
(7) Augustine of Hippo, *Sermon* 198.27, *Vingt-six sermons au peuple d'Afrique*, ed. François Dolbeau (Paris: Institut d'Etudes Augustiniennes, 1996), 386; trans. E. Hill, WSA III/11:200.
(8) John Cassian, *Conferences* 5.7.2, SC 42:195-96.
(9) John Chrysostom, *Homily 25 on Matthew* 7:28, PG 57:332-33.
(10) Thomas Aquinas, *Literal Exposition on Isaiah* 14:9-20, Opera Omnia 28: *Expositio super Isaiam ad litteram* (Rome, 1974), 90.69–91.187.

Chapters 15 and 16

(1) Eusebius of Caesarea, *Commentary on Isaiah* 15:1–16:5, *Eusebius Werke*, vol. 9, ed. J. Ziegler (GCS; Berlin, 1975), 107-10.
(2) Cyril of Alexandria, *Commentary on Isaiah* 15:1, PG 70:396D-400A.
(3) Aelred of Rievaulx, *The Burdens of Isaiah*, Homily 28, "On the Burden of Moab," PL 195:477D-80D.

Chapter 19

(1) Cyril of Alexandria, *Commentary on Isaiah* 19:1, 16-20, PG 70:449D-53A, 468A-B, 469D-72A, D.
(2) Theodoret of Cyrus, *Commentary on Isaiah* 19, SC 295:128, 138-40, 142.
(3) Gregory of Nyssa, *On the Inscriptions of the Psalms* 2.9, GNO 5:106.
(4) John Chrysostom, *Homily 56.3 on Matthew* 16:28, PG 58:553.
(5) The Venerable Bede, *Homily 2.15 on the Gospels*, CCSL 122:286.

Chapter 20

(1) Cyril of Alexandria, *Commentary on Isaiah* 20:2-3, PG 70:480B-81A, 481D-84A.
(2) Clement of Alexandria, *The Teacher*, SC 108:212.
(3) Origen of Alexandria, *Against Celsus* 7.7, SC 150:30-32.
(4) Gregory the Great, *Moralia on Job* 10.9, CCSL 143:541-42.

Chapter 24

(1) Eusebius of Caesarea, *Commentary on Isaiah* 24:1-2, *Eusebius Werke*, vol. 9, ed. J. Ziegler (GCS; Berlin, 1975), 153-54.

APPENDIX 2

(2) Cyril of Alexandria, *Commentary on Isaiah* 24:14-15, 23, PG 70:545A-48C, 553C-56A.
(3) Origen of Alexandria, *Homily 4.1 on Ezekiel*, SC 352:162.
(4) Ambrose of Milan, *On Isaac* 4.32-33, CSEL 32.1:661-62.

Chapter 25

(1) 1 Corinthians 15:54-55.
(2) Revelation 7:13-17.
(3) Cyril of Alexandria, *Commentary on Isaiah* 25:1-9, PG 70:556B-60C, 561A-65C.
(4) Theodoret of Cyrus, *Commentary on Isaiah* 25:1-6, SC 295:196, 200-202.
(5) Cyril of Jerusalem, *Mystagogical Catecheses* 3.7, PG 33.1093B-C.
(6) Irenaeus of Lyons, *Against Heresies* 5.12.1-2, SC 153:140-48.
(7) Tertullian, *Against Marcion* 5.10.14-16, CCSL 1:695.
(8) Augustine of Hippo, *Sermon* 128.10, PL 38:718.
(9) Aelred of Rievaulx, *The Mirror of Charity* 1.29.85, CCSL: Continuatio mediaevalis 1:49-50.
(10) Irenaeus of Lyons, *Against Heresies* 4.9.2, SC 100:482-84.

Chapter 26

(1) Matthew 6:6.
(2) Cyril of Alexandria, *Commentary on Isaiah* 26:1-8, 19, PG 70:568C-72A, 572D-73A, 588A-89A.
(3) Jerome, *Commentary on Isaiah* 26:1, CCSL 73:329.
(4) Didymus the Blind, *Commentary on Zechariah* 1.127, SC 83:260.
(5) Gregory the Great, *Homilies on Ezekiel* 2.2.5, CCSL 142:228.
(6) Athanasius of Alexandria, *Epistle* 20.1, PG 26:1431B-32A.
(7) Ambrose of Milan, *Exposition of Psalm 118*, 19.30, CSEL 62:437-38.
(8) Gregory the Great, *Homily 25.2 on the Gospels*, CCSL 141:207.
(9) Irenaeus of Lyons, *Against Heresies* 5.35.1, SC 153:436-38.
(10) Gregory of Nyssa, *Homily 6 on the Beatitudes*, GNO 7.2:138.
(11) Augustine of Hippo, *Sermon* 65.8 PL 38:430.
(12) Augustine of Hippo, *Sermon* 127.12-13 PL 38:711-12.
(13) John Chrysostom, *Homily 12.3 on John 1:14*, PG 59:85-86.
(14) Augustine of Hippo, *Sermon* 77A.2, Miscellanea Agostiniana 1:578; trans. E. Hill, WSA III/3:328.
(15) Augustine of Hippo, *Confessions* 13.35.50-52, PL 32:867; trans. H. Chadwick, 304.
(16) Augustine of Hippo, *Sermon* 169.15, PL 38:924; trans. E. Hill, WSA III/5:232.
(17) Augustine of Hippo, *Expositions of the Psalms, Sermon 2.18 on Ps 32:18*, CCSL 38:267 and PL 36.295; trans. M. Boulding, WSA III/15:418, revised.
(18) Augustine of Hippo, *Exposition of Psalm 131:3*, CSEL 95.3:293-94 and PL 37:1717; trans. M. Boulding, WSA III/20:157.
(19) Gregory the Great, *Moralia on Job* 17.21.30, CCSL 143A:868.

Sources of Texts Translated

(20) Augustine of Hippo, *Sermon* 210.7, PL 38:1051.
(21) Tertullian, *On the Resurrection of the Flesh* 31, CCSL 2:960-61.
(22) Gregory of Nyssa, *Against Eunomius* 2.224-25, GNO 2:406-7.
(23) Ambrose of Milan, *On His Brother, Satyrus* 2.67-68, CSEL 73:286-87.
(24) Didymus the Blind, *Commentary on Zechariah* 2.341-43, SC 84:596.
(25) Augustine of Hippo, *City of God* 20.21, CCSL 48:736 and PL 41:690.
(26) Gregory the Great, *Moralia on Job* 4.26.47, CCSL 143:192.

Chapter 28

(1) Romans 9:32-33; 10:11-11.
(2) 1 Peter 2:6-8.
(3) Irenaeus of Lyons, *Against Heresies* 3.21.7, SC 211:420.
(4) Origen of Alexandria, *Commentary on Romans* 8.2.8, *Römerbriefkommentar*, ed. T. Heither (Fontes Christiani 2; New York: Herder, 1995), 4:206-8.
(5) Ambrose of Milan, *On Duties* 1.142, CCSL 15:51.
(6) Ambrosiaster, *Commentary on Romans* 10:10-11, CSEL 81:348.
(7) Jerome, *Commentary on Isaiah* 28:16-20, CCSL 73:363.
(8) Gregory of Nyssa, *On the Baptism of Christ*, PG 46:588B-89B.
(9) Augustine of Hippo, *Sermon* 279.9, PL 38:1280.
(10) Augustine of Hippo, *Tractate* 7.23 on John 1:34-51, PL 35:1449.
(11) Cyril of Alexandria, *Commentary on Isaiah* 28:16, PG 70:632D-33B.
(12) Theodoret of Cyrus, *Commentary on Isaiah* 28:16, SC 295:240-42.

Chapter 29

(1) Matthew 15:8-9; cf. Mark 7:6-7.
(2) Romans 9:19-21.
(3) 1 Corinthians 1:18-19.
(4) Eusebius of Caesarea, *Commentary on Isaiah* 29:1, *Eusebius Werke*, vol. 9, ed. J. Ziegler (GCS; Berlin, 1975), 187-88.
(5) Jerome, *Commentary on Isaiah* 29:1, CCSL 73:370.
(6) John Cassian, *Conferences* 9.5.1, SC 54:44-45; trans. Boniface Ramsey, *John Cassian: The Conferences*, ACW 57:332-33.
(7) Origen of Alexandria, *Commentary on John* 5.7, SC 120:386.
(8) Origen of Alexandria, *Homily* 12.4 on Exodus, SC 321:364.
(9) Jerome, *Letter* 53.5, CSEL 54:451-52.
(10) Theodoret of Cyrus, *Commentary on Isaiah* 29:11, 295:254-56.
(11) Symeon the New Theologian, *Discourse* 24.4, SC 113:42-46.
(12) Irenaeus of Lyons, *Against Heresies* 4.12.4, SC 100:516-18.
(13) Origen of Alexandria, *Commentary on Matthew* 15:1-20, SC 162:320-24.
(14) Origen of Alexandria, *Exhortation to Martyrdom* 5, *Origenes Werke*, vol. 1, ed. Paul Koetschau (GCS; Leipzig, 1899), 6-7.
(15) Gregory of Nyssa, *Against Eunomius* 1.541-42, GNO 1:182-83.

(16) Augustine of Hippo, *Exposition on Psalm* 4:6, CCSL 38:16 and PL 36:80.
(17) Augustine of Hippo, *Exposition on Psalm* 94:2, CCSL 39:1331-32 and PL 37:1217.
(18) Gregory the Great, *Moralia on Job* 33.6.12, CCSL 143B:1681-82.
(19) Augustine of Hippo, *Letter* 186.18, CSEL 57:59-60.

Chapter 35

(1) Matthew 11:5-6.
(2) Eusebius of Caesarea, *Commentary on Isaiah* 35, *Eusebius Werke*, vol. 9, ed. J. Ziegler (GCS; Berlin, 1975), 227-30.
(3) Theodoret of Cyrus, *Commentary on Isaiah* 35:1-2, SC 295:336-38.
(4) Gregory of Nyssa, *On the Baptism of Christ*, PG 46:593B-C.
(5) Irenaeus of Lyons, *Against Heresies* 3.20.3, SC 211:392-94.
(6) Augustine of Hippo, *Sermon* 293.5, PL 38:1330; trans. E. Hill, WSA III/8:152.
(7) Leo the Great, *Sermon* 54.4, CCSL 138A:319-20.
(8) Origen of Alexandria, *Homily 11.18 on Matthew*, SC 162:374-76.
(9) Cyril of Jerusalem, *Catechetical Lecture* 17.21, "On the Holy Spirit," PG 33:994.
(10) Cyril of Alexandria, *Commentary on Isaiah* 35:8-10, PG 70:753D-56B.
(11) Tertullian, *On the Resurrection of the Dead* 58.1-5, CCSL 2:1006.
(12) John Chrysostom, *Homily 55.6 on Matthew*, PG 58:540.
(13) Augustine of Hippo, *On the Trinity* 1.21, CCSL 50:57-58; trans. E. Hill, WSA I/5:80, slightly revised.
(14) Augustine of Hippo, *Sermon* 158.8, PL 38:866.

Chapter 40

(1) Luke 3:1-6.
(2) Romans 11:33-36.
(3) 1 Peter 1:22-25.
(4) Cyril of Alexandria, *Commentary on Isaiah* 40:1-4, PG 70:797B-812A.
(5) Origen of Alexandria, *Commentary on John* 6.94-96, 98-102, SC 157:200-206.
(6) Gregory the Great, *Homily on the Gospels* 17.2, CCSL 141:117.
(7) Ambrose of Milan, *On Faith* 5.99, PL 16:695-96.
(8) Origen of Alexandria, *Homily 1.2 on Psalm 36:1-2*, SC 411:62-66.
(9) Gregory of Nyssa, *Homily 5 on the Song of Songs*, GNO 6:168-170.
(10) Augustine of Hippo, *Sermon* 33A.3, *Miscellanea Agostiniana* 1:138; trans. E. Hill, WSA III/2:162.
(11) Augustine of Hippo, *Newly Discovered Sermon* 293a.12 (Dolbeau 3) "On the Birth of John the Baptist," *Vingt-six sermons au peuple d'Afrique*, ed. François Dolbeau (Paris: Institut d'Etudes Augustiniennes, 1996), p. 491; trans. E. Hill, WSA III/11:259, slightly revised.
(12) Hilary of Poitiers, *On the Trinity* 1.5-6, SC 443:212-16.
(13) Gregory of Nyssa, *Homily 7 on the Beatitudes*, GNO 7.2:149-50.
(14) Gregory of Nyssa, *On Holy Easter* 665, GNO 9:256.

Sources of Texts Translated

(15) Basil of Caesarea, *On the Holy Spirit* 5.7 SC 17 bis: 272-76.
(16) John Chrysostom, *On the Incomprehensibility of God* 5.230-50, SC 28 bis: 290-92.
(17) Ambrose of Milan, *Exposition of Psalm* 12:1.49-50, CSEL 64:41-43.
(18) Origen of Alexandria, *Commentary on John* 13.274-78, SC 222:178-80.

Chapter 41

(1) Eusebius of Caesarea, *Commentary on Isaiah* 41, *Eusebius Werke*, vol. 9, ed. J. Ziegler (GCS; Leipzig, 1975), 258-59, 261-64, 266-67.
(2) Origen of Alexandria, *Homily 5.1 on Isaiah*, PG 13:234C-35A.
(3) Cyril of Alexandria, *Commentary on Isaiah* 41:4, PG 70:832C-33A, 833C-36B.
(4) Origen of Alexandria, *On First Principles* 4.3.14, SC 268:392-96.

Chapter 42

(1) Matthew 12:15-21.
(2) Eusebius of Caesarea, *Commentary on Isaiah* 42:1-4, *Eusebius Werke*, vol. 9, ed. J. Ziegler (GCS; Leipzig, 1975), 268-69.
(3) Cyril of Alexandria, *Commentary on Isaiah* 42:1-3, PG 70:849B-52B.
(4) Augustine of Hippo, *City of God* 20.30, CCSL 48:756-57.
(5) Irenaeus of Lyons, *Against Heresies* 5.12.1-2, SC 153:140-48.
(6) Ambrose of Milan, *On the Holy Spirit* 3.2.10, CSEL 79:154.
(7) Origen of Alexandria, *Commentary on Lamentations* 1, *Origenes Werke*, vol. 3, ed. Erich Klostermann (GCS; Berlin, 1983), 235-36.
(8) Gregory of Nyssa, *Refutation of the Confession of Eunomius* 2.116-18, GNO 2:361-62.
(9) Gregory of Nyssa, *Homilies on the Beatitudes* 4.5, GNO 7.2:117-18.
(10) Cyril of Alexandria, *Commentary on Isaiah* 42:10, PG 70:860B-61C.
(11) Jerome, *Commentary on Isaiah* 42:10-17, CCSL 73A:483-85.

Chapter 43

(1) 1 Peter 2:9-10.
(2) Cyril of Alexandria, *Commentary on Isaiah* 43, PG 70:884B-85B, 888D, 889B-92C, 897A-C, 901C-4A, 904D-8B; 909B-D, 912C-13B.
(3) Origen of Alexandria, *Homilies on Samuel* 5.9, SC 328:204-6.
(4) Irenaeus of Lyons, *Against Heresies* 4.5.1, SC 100:424-26.
(5) Origen of Alexandria, *Commentary on Romans* 1.10.1, *Römerbriefkommentar*, ed. T. Heither (Fontes Christiani 2; New York: Herder, 1990), 1:114.
(6) Augustine of Hippo, *Newly Discovered Sermon* 374.16-20, "On Epiphany," *Vingt-Six sermons au peuple D'Afrique*, ed. François Dolbeau (Paris, 1996), 607-12; trans. E. Hill, WSA III/11:401-5, revised.
(7) Ambrose of Milan, *Commentary on Psalm* 118, 3.10, 5.44, 7.3, CSEL 62:46, 106-7, 127-29.

APPENDIX 2

Chapter 44

(1) Cyril of Alexandria, *Commentary on Isaiah* 44:2-7, PG 70:917B-25B.
(2) Tertullian, *Against Praxeas* 18.3–19.6, CCSL 2:1183-85.
(3) Basil of Caesarea, *On the Holy Spirit* 44-45, *Über den Heiligen Geist*, ed. Hermann Josef Sieben (Fontes Christiani 12; Freiburg: Herder, 1993), 208.
(4) Gregory of Nyssa, *Against Eunomius* 3.3.8-11, GNO 2:109-11; *Against Eunomius* 3.6.3-4, 7-8, in GNO 2:186-87, 188.
(5) Origen of Alexandria, *Commentary on Romans* 7.10, *Römerbriefkommentar*, ed. T. Heither (Fontes Christiani 2; New York: Herder, 1990), 4:108-10.
(6) Eusebius of Caesarea, *Commentary on Isaiah* 44:24-26, *Eusebius Werke*, vol. 9, ed. J. Ziegler (GCS; Berlin, 1975), 287-88.
(7) Athanasius of Alexandria, *Orations against the Arians* 3.9, *Athanasius Werke*, vol. 1.1, ed. Karin Metzler and Kyriakos Savvidis (Berlin, 2000), 315-16.
(8) Ambrosiaster, *Book of Questions from the Old and New Testaments* 23.1-2, CSEL 50:49-50.
(9) Didymus the Blind, *Commentary on Zechariah* 8:9, SC 84:578.

Chapter 45

(1) Romans 9:20-21; 14:10-11.
(2) Philippians 2:9-11.
(3) Cyril of Alexandria, *Commentary on Isaiah* 45:1-7, PG 70:949D-53B.
(4) Irenaeus of Lyons, *Demonstration of the Apostolic Preaching* 49, SC 406:154-56.
(5) Lactantius, *Divine Institutes* 4.12.17-21, SC 377:108-10.
(6) Eusebius of Caesarea, *Commentary on Isaiah* 45:1-3, *Eusebius Werke*, vol. 9, ed. J. Ziegler (GCS; Leipzig, 1975), 288-89.
(7) Jerome, *Commentary on Isaiah* 45:1-4, CCSL 73A:504-5.
(8) Theodoret of Cyrus, *Commentary on Isaiah* 45:1-4, SC 315:18-20.
(9) Hesychius of Jerusalem, *Interpretatio Isaiae Prophetae* 45.1, ed. Michael Faulhaber (Freiburg: Herder, 1900), 139.
(10) Venerable Bede, *On Ezra and Nehemiah* 1.148-70, 178-79, CCSL 119A:244-45.
(11) John Cassian, *Institutes* 5.2, CSEL 17:82-83; trans. B. Ramsey, 117-18, revised slightly.
(12) Irenaeus of Lyons, *Against Heresies* 4.40.1, SC 100:974.1-14.
(13) Origen of Alexandria, *Against Celsus* 6.54-55, SC 147:314-18.
(14) Augustine of Hippo, *Against an Enemy of the Law and the Prophets* 1.23.48, CCSL 49:79-81; trans. R. Teske, WSA I/18:390-91, slightly revised.
(15) Gregory the Great, *Moralia on Job* 3.15-16, CCSL 143:124.
(16) Jerome, *Commentary on Isaiah* 45:8, CCSL 73A:507.
(17) Leo the Great, *Sermon* 24.3, "On the Birth of the Lord," CCSL 138:111-13.
(18) "Rorate coeli," traditional Advent hymn; taken with slight changes from *A Manual of Prayer for the Use of the Catholic Laity* (Third Plenary Council of Baltimore; Baltimore: John Murphy, 1889), 603-4.
(19) Augustine of Hippo, *Letter* 186.18, PL 33:822-23; trans. R. Teske, WSA II/3:218.

Sources of Texts Translated

(20) Eusebius of Caesarea, *Commentary on Isaiah* 45:13, *Eusebius Werke*, vol. 9, ed. J. Ziegler (GCS; Leipzig, 1975), 292-93.
(21) Gregory of Nyssa, *Against Eunomius* 3.15-16, GNO 2:269-70.
(22) Origen of Alexandria, *On Prayer* 31.3, in *Origenes Werke*, vol. 2, ed. Paul Koetschau (GCS; Leipzig, 1897), 396-97.

Chapter 46

(1) Theodoret of Cyrus, *Commentary on Isaiah* 46:1-7, SC 315:42-46.
(2) Jerome, *Commentary on Isaiah* 46:3-11, CCSL 73A:517-19.
(3) Augustine of Hippo, *Confessions* 4.16.31, PL 32:706; trans. H. Chadwick, 71.
(4) Augustine of Hippo, *Newly Discovered Sermon* 90A.10, *Vingt-Six sermons au peuple d'Afrique*, ed. François Dolbeau (Paris, 1996), 64; trans. E. Hill, WSA III/11:82.
(5) Augustine of Hippo, *Sermon* 102.2, PL 38:611; trans. E. Hill, WSA III/4:73-74.
(6) Augustine of Hippo, *Exposition of Psalm* 57.3, CCSL 39:711 and PL 36:676; trans. Maria Boulding, WSA III/17:124-25, revised.
(7) Augustine of Hippo, *Confessions* 4.12.19, PL 32:701; trans. H. Chadwick, 64.
(8) Gregory the Great, *Moralia on Job* 26.61, CCSL 143B:1313.
(9) Origen of Alexandria, *On First Principles* 2.4.1, SC 252:276-80.
(10) John Cassian, *Conferences* 9.20.1-2, "On Prayer," SC 54:57-58; trans. B. Ramsey, 342-43, slightly revised.
(11) Cyril of Alexandria, *Commentary on Isaiah* 46:10, PG 70:996D-97B.
(12) Origen of Alexandria, *Dialogue with Heraclides* 22, SC 67:98-100.

Chapter 48

(1) Cyril of Alexandria, *Commentary on Isaiah* 48:12-13, PG 70:1021B-24C.
(2) Ambrose of Milan, *Homily* 13.3 on *Psalm 118*, CSEL 62:282-83.
(3) Origen of Alexandria, *Commentary on Matthew* 13.18, PG 13:1144.
(4) Origen of Alexandria, *Against Celsus* 1.46, SC 132:196-98.
(5) Augustine of Hippo, *On the Trinity* 2.5.8, CCSL 50:89-90 and PL 42:849-50.
(6) Theodoret of Cyrus, *Commentary on Isaiah* 48:16, SC 315:66-68.
(7) Augustine of Hippo, *Exposition on Psalm* 96.19, CCSL 39:1370 and PL 37:1251-52.

Chapter 49

(1) Acts 13:44-49.
(2) 2 Corinthians 6:1-2.
(3) Revelation 7:13-17.
(4) Cyril of Alexandria, *Commentary on Isaiah* 49:1-3, PG 70:1033D-41A.
(5) Origen of Alexandria, *Commentary on John* 1.133-36, SC 120:128-30.
(6) Origen of Alexandria, *Commentary on the Song of Songs* 3.8.3-15, SC 376:574-76.
(7) Gregory of Nyssa, *Homily 4 on the Song of Songs*, GNO 6:127-28.
(8) Gregory of Nyssa, *On the Inscriptions of the Psalms*, 2.11, GNO 5:119-20.

APPENDIX 2

(9) Ambrose of Milan, *Homilies on Psalm 118*, 5.16-17, CSEL 62:90-91.
(10) Gregory of Nyssa, *On Faith to Simplicius*, GNO 3.1:62-63.
(11) Origen of Alexandria, *Commentary on John* 1.158-9, SC 120:138.
(12) Augustine of Hippo, *Sermon* 199.1, PL 38:1026.
(13) Theodoret of Cyrus, *Commentary on Isaiah* 49:6, SC 315:80-82.
(14) Origen of Alexandria, *Exhortation to Martyrdom* 42, *Origines Werke* (GCS) 1:39-40.
(15) Augustine of Hippo, *Letter* 186 3.7, PL 33:818; trans. R. Teske, WSA II/3.
(16) Eusebius of Caesarea, *Commentary on Isaiah* 49:9, *Eusebius Werke*, vol. 9, ed. J. Ziegler (GCS; Leipzig, 1975), 312.
(17) Cyril of Alexandria, *Festal Letter* 5.1, SC 372:284.
(18) Jerome, *Commentary on Isaiah* 49:14-21, CCSL 73A:542-44.
(19) John Chrysostom, *Homily* 22.5-6 on Matthew 6:22, PG 57:306-7.
(20) Ambrose of Milan, *Hexameron* 6.7.42-43, CSEL 32.1:233-34.
(21) Ambrose of Milan, *Homilies on Psalm 118*, 14.43, CSEL 62:327-28.
(22) Gregory of Nyssa, *On the Baptism of Christ*, PG 46:577.

Chapter 50

(1) Matthew 26:67-68.
(2) Jerome, *Commentary on Isaiah* 50:2-4, CCSL 73A:553.
(3) Origen of Alexandria, *Homilies on Exodus* 6.9 SC: 321:192-94.
(4) Eusebius of Caesarea, *Commentary on Isaiah* 50:4, *Eusebius Werke*, vol. 9, ed. J. Ziegler (GCS; Leipzig, 1975), 318-19.
(5) Cyril of Jerusalem, *Mystagogical Catechesis* 3.4, PG 33:1091 and *Mystagogische Katechesen*, ed. Georg Rowekamp (Fontes Christiani 7; New York: Herder, 1992), 126-28.
(6) Ambrose of Milan, *On Duties* 1.2.5, CCSL 15:2-3.
(7) Cyril of Alexandria, *Commentary on Isaiah* 50:4-5, PG 70:1089-92.
(8) Cyril of Alexandria, *Festal Letters* 5.7, SC 372:318.
(9) Bernard of Clairvaux, *Sermons on the Song of Songs* 28.6, SC 431:356-58.
(10) Origen of Alexandria, *Series of Commentaries on Matthew* 113, *Origenes Werke*, vol. 11, ed. Erich Klostermann (GCS; Berlin, 1976), 234-35.
(11) Athanasius of Alexandria, *The Festal Letters of Athanasius: Discovered in an Ancient Syriac Version*, ed. William Cureton (London: Society for the Publication of Oriental Texts, 1848), 49.
(12) Cyril of Jerusalem, *Catechetical Lectures* 13.13, PG 33:789-92.
(13) Ambrose of Milan, *Exposition of Psalm 118*, 5.26, CSEL 62:95-96.
(14) Cyril of Alexandria, *Commentary on Isaiah* 50:6-7, PG 70:1093.
(15) Origen of Alexandria, *On First Principles* 2.10.4, SC 252:382.

Chapter 51

(1) Cyril of Alexandria, *Commentary on Isaiah* 51:1-5, PG 70:1108B-9A, 1112C-16A.
(2) Theodoret of Cyrus, *Commentary on Isaiah* 51:1-2, SC 315:112-16.

(3) Eusebius of Caesarea, *Commentary on Isaiah* 51:1, *Eusebius Werke*, vol. 9, ed. J. Ziegler (GCS; Leipzig, 1975), 321.
(4) Gregory of Nyssa, *Life of Moses* 1.10-12, GNO 7.1:5.
(5) Theodoret of Cyrus, *Commentary on Isaiah* 51:5, SC 315:118.
(6) Gregory the Theologian, *Oration* 6.14, SC 405:158.
(7) Origen of Alexandria, *Exhortation to Martyrdom* 4, *Origenes Werke*, vol. 1, ed. Paul Koetschau (GCS; Leipzig, 1899), 5-6.
(8) Augustine of Hippo, *Sermon* 340a.8, *Miscellanea Agostiniana*, vol. 1: *Sancti Augustini Sermones post Maurinos reperti*, ed. D. G. Morin (Rome, 1930), 569-70; trans. WSA III/9:301, slightly revised.
(9) Theodoret of Cyrus, *Commentary on Isaiah* 51:7-8, SC 315:120.
(10) Gregory the Great, *Homily 31.7 on the Gospels*, CCSL 141:275.

Chapter 52:1-12

(1) Romans 10:14-17.
(2) Cyril of Alexandria, *Commentary on Isaiah* 52:1-8, PG 70:1144A-49A, 1152C-57D.
(3) Eusebius of Caesarea, *Commentary on Isaiah* 52:1-12, *Eusebius Werke*, vol. 9, ed. J. Ziegler (GCS; Leipzig, 1975), 328, 330-32.
(4) Theodoret of Cyrus, *Commentary on Isaiah* 52:7-11, SC 315:136-38, 140-42.
(5) John Chrysostom, *Homily 32.6 on Matthew* 9:27-30, PG 57:384.
(6) Origen of Alexandria, *Commentary on John* 32.77-82, SC 385:220-22.
(7) Leo the Great, *Sermon* 36.1, "On the Feast of the Epiphany," CCSL 138:195-96.
(8) Origen of Alexandria, *Homily 11.1.5 on Leviticus*, SC 287:146.
(9) Augustine of Hippo, *Sermon* 88.23, 25, PL 38:551-53.

Chapter 52:13–53:12

(1) Matthew 8:14-17.
(2) Luke 22:35-37.
(3) John 12:36-38.
(4) Acts 8:26-38.
(5) Romans 10:14-17.
(6) Romans 15:18-21.
(7) 1 Peter 2:18-25.
(8) Cyril of Alexandria, *Commentary on Isaiah* 52:13–53:6 and 53:10-11, PG 70:1164D-89C.
(9) Eusebius of Caesarea, *Commentary on Isaiah* 52:13–53:8, *Eusebius Werke*, vol. 9, ed. J. Ziegler (GCS; Leipzig, 1975), 332-33.
(10) Augustine of Hippo, *Exposition of Ps 85[86]:11*, CCSL 39:1188; trans. M. Boulding, WSA III/18:235.
(11) Augustine of Hippo, *Sermon* 44.1-2, PL 38:258-59; trans. E. Hill, WSA III/2:244-45.
(12) Augustine of Hippo, *Sermon* 27.6, PL 38:181.
(13) *The Apostolic Constitutions* 2.25.7, 9-12, SC 320:230-32.

(14) Theodoret of Cyrus, *Commentary on Isaiah* 53:5, SC 315:152.
(15) Irenaeus of Lyons, *Against Heresies* 4.23.2, SC 100:694-98.
(16) Augustine of Hippo, *Sermon* 17.1, PL 38:124; trans. E. Hill, WSA III/1:366, slightly revised.
(17) Origen of Alexandria, *Commentary on John* 1.233-34, SC 120:174-76.
(18) Origen of Alexandria, *Commentary on John* 6.273-81, SC 157:336-42.
(19) Augustine of Hippo, *Sermon* 375A.1-2, PL 46:828-29; trans. E. Hill, WSA III/10:330-31, slightly revised.
(20) Gregory the Great, *Moralia on Job* 29.69, CCSL 143B:1482.
(21) Basil of Caesarea, *Against Eunomius* 1.12, SC 299:212-14.
(22) Augustine of Hippo, *Sermon* 184.2-3 on Christmas Day, *PL* 38:996-97; trans. E. Hill, WSA III/6:18-19, slightly revised.
(23) Gregory of Nyssa, *On "When All Things Will be Subject to Him"* (1 Cor 15:28), GNO III/2:13-14.
(24) John of Damascus, *Exposition of the Orthodox Faith* 3.27, *Die Schriften des Johannes von Damaskos*, ed. P. Bonifatius Kotter (Patristische Texte und Studien 12; Berlin: Walter de Gruyter, 1973), 170; and PG 94:1096-97.

Chapter 54

(1) Galatians 4:25-27.
(2) John 6:45.
(3) Jerome, *Commentary on Isaiah* 54:1, CCSL 73A:599-600.
(4) Cyril of Alexandria, *Commentary on Isaiah* 54:1-3, PG 70:1192D-96D.
(5) Irenaeus of Lyons, *Against Heresies* 1.10.3, SC 264:162-64.
(6) Origen of Alexandria, *Commentary on Romans* 6.7, *Commentarii in Epistulam ad Romanos*, vol. 3, ed. T. Heither (Fontes Christiani; New York, 1991), 240-42.
(7) Augustine of Hippo, *Exposition 1 of Psalm 58.11*, CCSL 39:738-39 and PL 36:700; trans. M. Boulding, WSA III/17:158-59.
(8) Augustine of Hippo, *City of God* 18.29, CCSL 48:619-21 and PL 41:585-86.
(9) Gregory the Great, *Homilies on Ezekiel* 2.6.3-4, SC 360:276-78.
(10) Augustine of Hippo, *Grace of Christ and Original Sin* 1.13.14, PG 44:367-68; trans. R. Teske, WSA I/23:410-11.

Chapter 55

(1) Acts 13:33-34.
(2) Cyril of Alexandria, *Commentary on Isaiah* 55:1-2, PG 70:1217C-20C.
(3) Clement of Alexandria, *Exhortation to the Greeks* 10.93.1–94.2, SC 2:161-62.
(4) Ambrose of Milan, *On Joseph* 7.42, CSEL 32.2:101-2.
(5) Theodoret of Cyrus, *Commentary on Isaiah* 55:1, SC 315:176-78.
(6) Gregory the Great, *Moralia on Job* 1.29, CCSL 143:40.
(7) Gregory the Theologian, *Oration* 40.27, SC 358:258-60.
(8) Tertullian, *Against Marcion* 3.20.1-8, 10, CCSL 1:534-37.

Sources of Texts Translated

(9) Leo the Great, *Sermon* 33.5, "On Epiphany," CCSL 138:175-76.
(10) Jerome, *Commentary on Isaiah* 55:6-7, CCSL 73A:623-24.
(11) Gregory of Nyssa, *Homily 7 on Ecclesiastes*, GNO 5:400-401.
(12) Augustine of Hippo, *The Trinity* 15.2.2, CCSL 50A:460-62 and PL 42:1057-58.
(13) Origen of Alexandria, *Exhortation to Martyrdom* 18, *Origines Werke*, vol. 1, ed. P. Koetschau (GCS; Leipzig, 1899), 16-17.

Chapter 56

(1) Matthew 19:10-12.
(2) Mark 11:15-17, parallels in Matthew 21:12-13 and Luke 19:45-46.
(3) Jerome, *Commentary on Isaiah* 56:1-6, CCSL 73A:629-34.
(4) Clement of Alexandria, *Stromateis* 3.91, 98, *Clemens Alexandrinus*, vol. 2, ed. O. Stählen (GCS; Berlin, 1960), 238, 241.
(5) Augustine of Hippo, *Holy Virginity* 24-25, PL 40:408-10.

Chapter 60

(1) Revelation 21:22-26.
(2) Cyril of Alexandria, *Commentary on Isaiah* 60:1-4, PG 70:1321B-28C.
(3) Jerome, *Commentary on Isaiah* 60:4, CCSL 73A:695.
(4) Tertullian, *Against Marcion* 3.24.11-12, CCSL 1:543-44.
(5) Clement of Rome, *Letter to the Corinthians* 42.5, SC 167.
(6) Irenaeus of Lyons, *Against Heresies* 4.26.5, SC 100:726-28.
(7) Origen of Alexandria, *Homily 3.9 on Psalm 36:18*, SC 411:158.
(8) Ambrose of Milan, *Commentary on Psalm 118*, 12.26, CSEL 62:266.
(9) Jerome, *Commentary on Isaiah* 60:20, CCSL 73A:704-5.
(10) Cyril of Alexandria, *Commentary on Isaiah* 60:19-20, PG 70:1345C-48A.
(11) Jerome, *Commentary on Isaiah* 60:21-22, CCSL 73A:705-6.

Chapter 61

(1) Luke 4:16-21.
(2) Cyril of Alexandria, *Commentary on Isaiah* 61:1-4, 9-11, PG 70:1349D-52C, 1357C-60B, 1365B-68C.
(3) Athanasius of Alexandria, *Orations against the Arians* 1.47, *Athanasius Werke*, vol. 1.1, ed. K. Metzler and K. Savvidis (Berlin: Walter de Gruyter, 1998), 156-57.
(4) Jerome, *Commentary on Isaiah* 61:1, CCSL 73A:706-7.
(5) Ambrose of Milan, *On the Holy Spirit* 3.1-3, CSEL 79:149-50.
(6) Irenaeus of Lyons, *Against Heresies* 3.17.1-2, SC 211:328-34.
(7) Faustus Luciferanus, *On the Trinity* 39-40, CCSL 69:341.
(8) John Chrysostom, *Homily 19.9 on Matthew 6:1*, PG 57:285-86.
(9) Ephrem the Syrian, *Hymns on Paradise* 13.10, CSCO 174:44; trans. S. Brock, *Hymns on Paradise* (Crestwood, New York: St. Vladimir's Seminary Press, 1990), 172.

APPENDIX 2

(10) Origen of Alexandria, *Homilies on Leviticus* 9.5, SC 287:92-94.
(11) Origen of Alexandria, *Homilies on Leviticus* 4.6, SC 286:180.
(12) John Chrysostom, *Homilies on Ephesians* 13.3, PG 62:97A.
(13) Augustine of Hippo, *Sermon* 341.1, 11, PL 39:1493, 1499; trans. E. Hill, WSA III/10:19, 26, revised.
(14) Augustine of Hippo, *Tractates* 1.2 on 1 John 1.1–2:11, PL 35:1979.

Chapter 62

(1) Matthew 21:1-5.
(2) Cyril of Alexandria, *Commentary on Isaiah* 62:1-3, 6, 11-12, PG 70:1368D-69D, 1373C-D, 1380A-81A.
(3) Jerome, *Commentary on Isaiah* 62:1-3, CCSL 73A:713-14, 715-16.
(4) Clement of Alexandria, *Stromateis* 4.171, SC 463:342.

Chapter 63

(1) Revelation 19:13-14.
(2) Cyril of Alexandria, *Commentary on Isaiah* 63:1-2, PG 70:1381B-84B.
(3) Jerome, *Commentary on Isaiah* 63:1-2, CCSL 73A:720-22.
(4) Tertullian, *Against Marcion* 4.40.4-6, CCSL 1:657.
(5) Cyprian of Carthage, *Epistle* 63.6-7, CCSL 3C:395-97.
(6) Origen of Alexandria, *Commentary on John* 6.287-92, SC 157:348-52.
(7) Didymus the Blind, *Commentary on Psalm* 23:7-8, in *Psalmenkommentar*, vol. 2, ed. M. Gronewald (Bonn: Rudolf Habelt, 1968), 62-64.
(8) Gregory of Nyssa, *Sermon on the Ascension of Christ*, GNO 9:325-27.
(9) Ambrose of Milan, *On the Mysteries* 36, SC 25 bis: 174-76.
(10) Augustine of Hippo, *Sermon* 372.2, PL 39.1662; trans. E. Hill, WSA III/10:317, slightly revised.
(11) Gregory the Great, *Homilies on Ezekiel* II.1.9, SC 360:68-70.
(12) Eusebius of Caesarea, *Commentary on Isaiah* 63:5-6, *Eusebius Werke*, vol. 9, ed. J. Ziegler (GCS; Leipzig, 1975), 388.
(13) Irenaeus of Lyons, *Against Heresies* 3.20.3, SC 211:392-94.
(14) Basil of Caesarea, *On the Holy Spirit* 19.50, SC 17 bis: 422-24.

Chapter 64

(1) 1 Corinthians 2:7-10.
(2) Jerome, *Commentary on Isaiah* 64:1-6, CCSL 73A:733-34, 736-37.
(3) Cyril of Jerusalem, *Catechetical Lecture* 9.1-2, PG 33:637A-40B.
(4) Augustine of Hippo, *Tractates on 1 John* 4:4-12, PL 35:2029.
(5) Augustine of Hippo, *Sermon on Psalm* 35.5, CCSL 38:324 and PL 36:343-44.
(6) Cyril of Alexandria, *Commentary on Isaiah* 64:4-5, PG 70:1397D-1400A.
(7) Leo the Great, *Sermon* 95.8, CCSL 138A:588-89.

(8) Gregory the Theologian, *Oration* 16.12, PG 35:949B-51A.
(9) Cyril of Alexandria, *Commentary on Isaiah* 64:5, PG 70:1400B-D.
(10) Origen of Alexandria, *Commentary on Romans* 3.9.7, *Römerkommentar*, ed. T. Heither (Fontes Christiani 2; New York: Herder, 1990), 2:138-40.
(11) Martyrius Sahdona, *Book of Perfection* II.8.10, CCSO 252:3-4; trans. S. Brock, *The Syriac Fathers on Prayer and the Spiritual Life*, 206.
(12) Gregory the Great, *Moralia on Job* 11.60, CCSL 143A:619-20.
(13) Cyril of Jerusalem, *Catechetical Lecture* 7.8, PG 33:613B.
(14) Didymus the Blind, *Commentary on Zechariah* 2.192, SC 84:514-16.

Chapter 65

(1) Romans 10:20.
(2) 2 Peter 3:10-14.
(3) Revelation 21:1-4.
(4) Eusebius of Caesarea, *Commentary on Isaiah* 65:1-4, 8-9, 19-22, *Eusebius Werke*, vol. 9, ed. J. Ziegler (GCS; Berlin, 1975), 392-94, 397-98.
(5) Irenaeus of Lyons, *Against Heresies* 3.9.2, SC 211:106.
(6) Leo the Great, *Sermon* 12.1, CCSL 138:48-49.
(7) Cyril of Jerusalem, *Catechetical Lectures* 13.28, PG 33:805B.
(8) Origen of Alexandria, *Commentary on John* 13.220-25, SC 222:150-52.
(9) Clement of Alexandria, *The Tutor* 1.5.12-24, SC 70:132, 136, 144-48, 152-54.
(10) Cyril of Alexandria, *Commentary on Isaiah* 65:16-18, PG 70:1417B-D.
(11) Theodoret of Cyrus, *Commentary on Isaiah* 65:15-16, SC 315:320-22.
(12) Irenaeus of Lyons, *Against Heresies* 5.35.2, SC 153:446-50.
(13) Ephrem the Syrian, *Hymns on Paradise* 9.1, CSCO 174:35-36; trans. S. Brock (St. Vladimir's Seminary Press, 1990), 136.
(14) Gregory of Nyssa, *Homily 13 on the Song of Songs*, GNO 6:384-85.
(15) Cyril of Alexandria, *Commentary on Isaiah* 65:16-18, PG 70:1420B.
(16) Theodoret of Cyrus, *Commentary on Isaiah* 65:21-22, SC 315:326.
(17) Augustine of Hippo, *City of God* 20:26.1-2, CCSL 48:749-50 and PL 41:701.
(18) Theodoret of Cyrus, *Commentary on Isaiah* 65:22, SC 315:326-28.

Chapter 66

(1) Matthew 5:33-35.
(2) Acts 7:48-50.
(3) Cyril of Alexandria, *Commentary on Isaiah* 66:1-2, 10-12, 18, PG 70:1429B-C, 1437C-40C, 1445A-B.
(4) Origen of Alexandria, *On First Principles* 2.1.3, SC 252:238-40.
(5) Cyril of Jerusalem, *Catechetical Lectures* 6.8-9, PG 33:552B-53B.
(6) Jerome, *Commentary on Isaiah* 66:1-2, CCSL 73A:769-70.
(7) John of Damascus, *On the Orthodox Faith* 13, *Die Schriften des Johannes von*

Damaskos, vol. 2, ed. P. B. Kotter (see Patristische Texte und Studien 12; New York: Walter de Gruyter, 1973), 38; also PG 94:852A-C.

(8) Gregory the Great, *Moralia on Job* 2.20, CCSL 143:72-73.
(9) Athanasius of Alexandria, *Orations against the Arians* 2.71, *Athanasius Werke*, vol. 1.1, eds. M. Tetz and K. Savvidis (Berlin: Walter de Gruyter, 1998), 248.
(10) Gregory of Nyssa, *Against Eunomius* 3.5.30, GNO 2:170-71.
(11) Clement of Rome, *Letter to the Corinthians* 13, SC 167:120-22.
(12) Augustine, *Sermon* 72a.2, in *Miscellanea Agostiniana*, vol. 1, ed. D. G. Morin (Rome, 1930), 156-57.
(13) Ambrose, *On the Holy Spirit* 1.16.157, CSEL 79:81.
(14) Augustine, *City of God* 20.21.1-2, CCSL 48:737-38 and PL 41:690-91.
(15) Jerome, *Commentary on Isaiah* 66:13-14, CCSL 73A:780-81.
(16) Irenaeus of Lyon, *Against Heresies* 5.36.1, SC 153:452-56.
(17) Ambrose of Milan, *On the Death of His Brother Satyrus* 2.87, CSEL 73:297.
(18) Gregory of Nyssa, *Great Catechism* 40, GNO 3.4:105-6.
(19) Augustine, *City of God* 21.9, CCSL 48:774-75 and PL 41:723-24; trans. H. Bettenson, St. Augustine, *Concerning the City of God against the Pagans* (Harmondsworth: Penguin Books: 1972), 983-85, slightly revised.

Index of Names

Aelred of Rievaulx, xxv, 160, 165-67, 184, 187-91, 215-16, 537
Ambrose, xv, xxv, 6, 77, 92, 100, 129, 147-48, 189, 204, 207, 223, 229-30, 236, 273, 279-80, 298, 314-15, 358-60, 372, 378, 381, 384, 388-89, 443, 461, 467, 476, 496, 531, 534, 537
Ambrosiaster, 236, 318, 327, 537
Anselm of Canterbury, 98, 537
Aphrahat, 25, 147, 538
Athanasius, 32, 41, 222, 318, 327, 388, 471, 474, 530, 538
Augustine, xiv-xv, xx, xxv, 1, 6-7, 17, 21-22, 24, 27-29, 32, 37-38, 53, 59, 62, 75, 87-89, 91, 95-97, 102-3, 114-15, 125, 134, 148-49, 171, 175-78, 189, 215, 219, 224-28, 230-31, 238, 243, 250-51, 258, 261-62, 275, 296, 305, 313, 332, 340, 344, 348, 350-52, 358, 360-62, 366, 373-75, 393, 398, 401, 410, 413-14, 422-25, 427, 429, 437-39, 441, 448, 451-52, 457-58, 471, 480-81, 496-97, 502-3, 520, 525, 531-32, 535, 538

Basil of Caesarea, xxv, 28, 77-78, 266, 278-79, 323, 414, 428-29, 498, 538
Bede, 194, 197-98, 338, 538
Bernard of Clairvaux, xi, xvii, xxx, 107, 143-44, 381, 386, 538

Cassiodorus, 41, 106, 539
Clement of Alexandria, 200, 443, 451, 456-57, 487, 511, 516-17, 539
Clement of Rome, 24-25, 461, 466, 530-31, 539
Cyprian of Carthage, 177, 189, 490, 493, 539
Cyril of Alexandria, xi, xiv, xvi, xxi, xxiii, xxv, 1, 7-8, 19-20, 33-34, 42-45, 78-79, 82-83, 98, 103-4, 121-23, 134-36, 151, 160, 163-64, 171-73, 186-87, 194-96, 199, 204-6, 209-12, 219-21, 239, 260, 266-71, 288-89, 295-96, 300-301, 305-11, 318-21, 333-34, 348, 349n.1, 354, 358-59, 367-69, 376, 381, 384-86, 389, 393-95, 402-6, 413, 416-21, 434-36, 442, 462-64, 468, 472-74, 484-86, 490-91, 503-4, 505, 517-18, 520, 525-27, 539
Cyril of Jerusalem, 25-26, 213-14, 260, 381, 384, 388, 502, 507, 514-15, 527, 539

Didymus the Blind, 21, 26-27, 42-43, 48, 75, 140, 222, 230, 328, 490, 494-95, 507, 539
Dionysius the Pseudo-Areopagite, 79-80, 539

Ephrem, xxv, 40, 83-84, 104-5, 479, 519, 540
Eusebius of Caesarea, xxi, xxiii, xxv, 1, 4, 32, 34, 43, 45, 53, 57, 68, 109, 111-13, 123-24, 130-31, 184-86, 204-5, 244-45, 254-57, 266, 284-87, 294-95, 318, 326-27, 332, 335-36, 345, 349n.1, 375, 383-84, 395-96, 406-7, 421-22, 497, 511-14, 540

Faustus Luciferanus, 477-78, 540
Fulgentius, 130, 540

Gregory the Great, xxv, 32, 39-40, 60, 79, 150, 201, 222-23, 227-28, 231, 251, 273, 332, 341-42, 352, 399, 428, 433, 438-39, 444, 497, 506, 529, 540
Gregory the Theologian, xxv, 17, 22, 74, 124-25, 134, 147, 393, 397, 444-45, 504-5, 540
Gregory of Nyssa, xi, xvii, xxv, xxvii, 26, 43, 48-49, 74-75, 101, 155, 157, 197, 219, 224, 229, 234, 237-38, 243, 250, 257-58, 274, 277-78, 284, 294, 299-300, 318, 324-25, 345-46, 366, 371-73, 379, 393, 396, 414, 429-30, 441, 447-48, 494n.2, 495-96, 519, 530, 534-35, 540

Hesychius of Jerusalem, 338, 540

INDEX OF NAMES

Hilary of Poitiers, 266, 276-77, 541
Hippolytus, 139, 140, 541
Homer, xv

Irenaeus, x, xxv, 40-41, 46, 127-28, 134, 144-45, 150-51, 157, 214, 216, 224, 235, 248, 258, 297-98, 312, 332, 334-35, 339, 424-25, 436, 461, 466, 477, 497-98, 514, 518-19, 534, 541
Isidore of Seville, 1, 8-13, 541

Jerome, xiii, xviii, xxiv-xxvii, 1, 6, 62, 69-71, 84-86, 101-2, 109-11, 115, 120, 129, 133, 137-38, 141n.9, 154, 155-56, 160-63, 188n.3, 189, 221, 237, 245, 247, 301-2, 332, 336-37, 342, 348-50, 366, 376-77, 382-83, 433-34, 447, 451-56, 461, 464-65, 467, 475-76, 483, 486-87, 491-92, 500-502, 528, 533, 537
John Cassian, 81, 109, 116-17, 171, 176-78, 245, 338-39, 348, 354, 451, 456, 541
John Chrysostom, xxv, 1, 4-5, 17-19, 34-35, 43, 44, 53-57, 62, 71-73, 86-87, 92-95, 133, 140-41, 178, 197, 225, 261, 266, 279, 377, 408-9, 478-80, 541
John of Damascus, 120, 126-27, 430, 529, 542
Josephus, xxiii, 336
Justin Martyr, 40, 128n.3, 138, 542

Lactantius, 332, 335, 542
Leo the Great, 105, 120, 126, 141, 259, 343, 401, 409-10, 446-47, 500, 504, 514, 542

Martyrius (Sahdona), 27, 80, 506, 542
Maximus the Confessor, 80-81, 143, 542
Maximus of Turin, 129-30, 542
Melito of Sardis, xvi

Origen of Alexandria, x, xiv, xvii, xxii, xxv, 1, 3-4, 17, 20-21, 25, 32, 35-36, 43, 45-47, 62-67, 70n.5, 99-100, 109, 113-14, 116, 145-47, 175, 201, 204, 206-7, 234-36, 243-44, 246, 248-50, 259, 271-74, 280, 284, 287-90, 298-99, 311-13, 318, 325, 332, 337n.4, 339-40, 346, 348, 353, 355, 358, 360, 370-71, 373-75, 382-83, 387-89, 393, 397-98, 401, 409-10, 414, 425-26, 436-37, 449, 456n.3, 466-67, 471, 479-80, 494, 505-6, 515, 527, 540

Pacian of Barcelona, 102, 543
Proclus, 125-26, 543
Prudentius, 78, 543
Pseudo-Athanasius, 53, 58
Pseudo-Basil, xxiv, 101, 164
Pseudo-Ephrem, 128-29

Romanos the Melodist, 134, 142-43, 543

Silva, Moisés, xii, xxvi
Symeon the New Theologian, xxv, 60, 127, 247-48, 543

Tertullian, xxv, 17, 23-24, 32, 41, 98-99, 128, 139, 215, 219, 228-29, 260-61, 318, 322-23, 441, 445-46, 465, 490, 493, 543
Theodore of Mopsuestia, 32, 36-37, 82, 235, 239n.3, 543
Theodoret, xxv, 32, 35, 53, 57-58, 89, 104, 154, 156-57, 173-74, 196-97, 213, 234, 239-40, 247, 257, 332, 337, 348-49, 361, 374, 395-97, 398, 408, 424, 444, 518, 520-21, 544
Thomas Aquinas, 160, 171, 179-81, 544

Xenophon, xxiii, 336

Venantius Fortunatus, 106, 544

Index of Subjects

Aaron, 25; rod of, 107, 142-43, 474
Abel, xvi, 201, 428, 481
Abraham, xv, 5, 27, 68-69, 74, 178, 211, 393, 395-96, 454; offspring of, 151, 176, 285, 288, 294; promise to, 141, 279, 463. *See also* Hagar, Sarah
Adam, 98-99, 125, 142, 176, 190n.8, 212, 236, 378
Age, 134, 150n.15, 184, 269, 335, 511, 520; end of, 210, 461-62, 468; present, 33, 65, 286, 466
Ahaz, 7-8, 17, 91, 93, 103-5, 110-12, 170, 174
Allegory. *See* Scriptural exegesis
'*Almah*, 92, 99, 102
Angel (Messenger) of great counsel, 120, 122-24, 127, 129
Angels, xvi, 76-82, 215, 280, 287, 350, 449, 485, 489-92, 494-98. *See also* Cherubim, Gabriel, Seraphim
Anna, 83, 126
Anointed One, 335, 337; Christ as, 2, 296, 332, 474-78
Apostles, 18, 163, 294, 319-20, 406-9, 466, 512-13; calling of, 121-22; mission of, 11-12, 40-41, 301, 381, 401
Arians, xxv, 53, 318, 327, 471, 540
Ascension of Christ, xvi, 10-11, 421, 490-92, 494-96
Asceticism, 199, 201, 451, 538, 540-42
Assyrians, 36, 91, 109-10, 133, 170, 173-74, 184-85, 194, 199, 267, 326, 400, 435

Babylonians, 36, 160, 167, 171-74, 184-87, 267, 327, 333-34, 337
Baptism, xiv, xxvii, 12, 17, 26, 195, 209, 211, 255-57, 260, 338, 444, 477; of Christ, 53, 144, 234, 254, 293, 471
Beloved, Christ as, 53, 57-58, 293-94, 327

Bible. *See* Scriptures
Bishops, x, 184, 186, 393, 424, 461, 466, 485n.1
Blood of Christ, xvi, xxii, 10, 134, 138, 152, 209, 226, 256, 313, 383, 403, 418, 426, 428, 430, 443, 464, 493. *See also* Cross of Christ, Death of Christ
Blossom: Christ as, 133, 135, 137-42; Mary as, 143-44
Body of Christ, 37, 67, 171, 480-81
Bozrah, xvi, 10, 491, 493-96
Branch: Christ as, 47, 145-46, 150, 475; Mary as, 9, 39, 106n. 8, 137-38, 141
Bride, Church as, 27, 377, 435, 474, 480-81, 487, 492
Bridegroom, Christ as, 471, 480-81, 487, 496
Burning Coal, Christ as, xxii, 62, 82-83

Canticles, xxi, 155, 209
Cherubim, 69-70, 72, 77, 80-81, 311-12
Choice, free, 27, 103, 149, 252, 344, 515, 531. *See also* Free will
Chosen arrow, xxii, 363, 366, 369-72
Christ: humanity of, 94, 98, 102-5, 110, 194, 196-98, 366, 496; divinity of, 42, 104-5, 130, 299, 318, 322-24; nature of, 39, 68, 373, 417-21, 471-72, 480, 490. *See also* Anointed One, Ascension, Baptism, Beloved, Blood of Christ, Blossom, Body of Christ, Branch, Bridegroom, Burning Coal, Chosen arrow, Cloud, Cornerstone, Cross of Christ, Death of Christ, Emmanuel, Incarnation, Israel, Jacob, Judah, Lamb, Life, Light, Mountain, Names of Christ, Passion of Christ, Peace, Righteousness, Second coming, Son of God, Wisdom, Word
Church, xx, 28, 104, 124, 130, 196, 204-6, 219-22, 237, 255, 286, 318, 414, 437-39, 463-64, 467,

INDEX OF SUBJECTS

473, 519-21; gathered from nations, 32, 432-37, 461, 526-27; mission of, 32, 40, 266, 293. *See also* Bride, Gentiles, Islands, Jerusalem, Mountain, Temple, Tent of David, Zion

Christology. *See* Christ, Incarnation, Son of God, Word

Cloud, Christ as, 43, 45, 160, 194-98

Cornerstone, Christ as, xxi, 9, 110, 113, 233, 235, 237-39, 328, 374

Covenant, 445-46, 451, 455-56

Creation, 109, 117, 226; new, 254, 278, 300, 305, 307, 519-20, 532. *See also* Creator

Creator, 42, 79, 105, 141, 150, 215, 259, 306, 319, 343, 372, 527-28

Creeds, xviii, xxvi, 78, 212n.1; Apostles', 209; Chalcedon, 38-39, 539; Nicea, 219, 318, 538, 540, 544. *See also* Faith, confession of

Cross of Christ, 10-11, 27, 122, 128, 157, 196, 244, 270, 372, 424, 486, 514-15, 521. *See also* Blood of Christ, Death of Christ

Cyrus, 172, 267, 318, 326, 329, 332-38, 342, 345, 350

Darkness, xxii, 120-22, 124-27, 298-99, 305-6, 462-63

David, xvii, 5, 22, 39, 186, 227, 244, 315, 339n.5, 441-42, 445-46; Christ from line of David, 9, 81, 100, 104, 131, 133-35, 139-41, 145, 171

Day star, 160, 171, 173, 175-77, 179. *See also* Devil

Death, 110, 212, 220, 224; shadow of, 120-22, 124-26, 446; victory over, 128, 209, 214-16, 221, 376, 430, 478, 511. *See also* Death of Christ

Death of Christ, 10-11, 95, 152, 190n.8, 270, 352, 387-89, 413, 416-18, 422, 426. *See also* Blood of Christ, Cross of Christ

Descent into Hades, 120, 126, 420

Devil, 109-10, 177, 179-80, 190, 227, 325, 394, 402-3. *See also* Lucifer

Easter, 32, 38n.3, 171, 278n.4, 384n.2

Economy, Divine, xxvii, 309, 416, 421, 428. *See also* Incarnation; Plan, Divine

Edom, xvi, 10, 488, 490-96

Edomites, 163

Egypt, 20, 124, 160, 165, 196-97, 305

Egyptians, 160, 163, 186, 194-96, 199, 300, 349

Emmanuel, xiii, xx, 6, 9, 92-94, 98-107, 111-12, 122-23, 129, 141, 155, 368, 501

Epiphany, xxii, 366, 373n.4, 409, 446n.5, 461

Eternal life, 85, 225, 257, 260-61, 366, 420, 513, 521

Eucharist, xxii-xxiii, 10, 58, 62, 67n.3, 81-84, 121, 155, 204, 209, 211, 441-42, 490, 493

Eunuchs, 450-58; Ethiopian, xiii, xx, 2-3, 247, 415, 424-25, 454

Eve, 99, 176, 190n.8

Evil, origin of, 176-77, 332, 339-42

Exegesis. *See* Scriptural exegesis

Exile, 5, 37, 156, 173, 265, 305, 318, 401

Faith, 91, 220-22, 234, 236, 251, 371, 375, 415, 423, 441-43; confession of, xxiv, 83, 212, 244, 442, 539; seeking understanding, 92, 95-98, 448

Fall: of Adam, 151, 184, 378; of Satan, 160, 169, 171, 173, 175-77

Fellowship: with angels, 94, 224; with Christ, 144, 495; with God, 339, 342, 358

Fire, 47-48, 83-84, 222, 229, 306, 311-12, 382, 389, 480, 501, 525, 534-36

Fleshly, xviii, 491. *See also* Bozrah

Forgiveness, xxii-xxiii, 83, 102, 142, 211, 226, 266, 305-6, 314-15, 318, 325, 375, 444, 479

Free will, 62, 176-77, 231, 360. *See also* Choice, free

Gabriel, 73, 92, 99, 103, 107, 111, 126, 155, 368, 502

Garments: red, xvi, xxii, 10, 488, 490-97; white, 28

Gentiles, 279-80, 374, 437, 441, 446; calling of, 6, 35, 123, 134, 186, 294, 305, 308, 407, 433, 463, 525, 526-27; conversion of, 12-13, 286-87; light to the nations, 85, 373, 476. *See also* Church, Islands

Gifts of the Spirit, xxi, xxvi, 133-36, 138-41, 143-50

Gnostics, x, xxv, 353n.5, 451, 541, 543

God: transcendence, 266, 277, 284, 358, 524, 527-30; oneness of, 288-89, 318, 321-26, 348, 353

Grace, 29, 45, 102, 269, 311, 375, 392-94, 441-42, 511-12; of Baptism, 12, 26, 205, 257; of the Spirit, 139, 223. *See also* Mercy

Hades. *See* Hell

Hagar, xv, 237, 433

Heaven, 9, 69, 161, 207, 273, 276-80, 312, 322-23, 326-27, 342-44, 397, 461, 465, 500-501, 502, 511, 524, 527-29; new heaven, 229, 468, 510-11, 518-20, 524, 532, 534. *See also* Ascension

Hell (Hades), 51, 149, 168-69, 171, 173, 179-80, 233, 237, 535; Christ's descent into, xiii, 6, 94, 120, 126, 153, 376, 416, 420

Heretics, xxv, 116, 125, 189-90, 226, 322-23, 353, 404

Index of Subjects

Hezekiah, 7-9, 17, 103, 111, 174, 235, 239, 266-67
Holy, holy, holy, xxii, 61, 64-65, 68-69, 73, 77-81, 289
Holy Spirit, xviii, 43-49, 57, 62, 214, 226, 247-48, 260, 286, 293-98, 358, 360-61, 498, 531; as dew, 219, 221; given to believers, 11, 298, 320; Spirit of the Lord, 9, 247, 471-72, 474-78, 486; Spirit of Salvation, 228, 230. *See also* Gifts of the Spirit, Trinity
Homilies, x, xvi, xix, xxv, 32, 43, 53, 109, 160, 305, 366, 381, 414, 537-43
Hope, 134, 138, 152-53, 205-6, 212, 228-29, 262, 294-95, 315, 393-96, 420
Humility, 60, 427, 525

Idolatry, xxiv, 35, 42, 163, 194-97, 284, 299, 322, 348-50, 366, 510
Immortality, 78, 127, 209, 215-16, 231, 436, 473, 532
Incarnation, xxiii, xxvii, 10, 43, 92, 133, 135-41, 204, 209-10, 288, 296, 305, 343, 366, 369, 382, 404, 421, 472, 500, 519, 526
Incorporeality: of God, 37, 73, 97, 419; of soul, 328
Incorruptibility, 127, 416, 477, 517, 534
Interpretation of Scripture. *See* Scriptural exegesis
Isaac, xvi, xxvii, 20, 336, 353, 433
Isaiah: as apostle, xiii, 6; as evangelist, xiii, xxii, 1, 6, 8-9, 413, 438; martyrdom of, 1-3, 8-9, 66, 542; nakedness of, 160, 199-201; vision of God, xxii, 62, 64-82
Islands, 12, 301-2, 366-67, 394; church as, 205, 284, 301-2, 366-67, 394
Israel, 32-33, 53-56, 109, 163, 171-72, 319, 462-64; Christ as, 293-94, 296-97, 309, 369

Jacob, xxvi, 138, 171, 234, 238, 284, 286, 288, 310, 319-21, 358, 512; Christ as, 293-94, 296-97, 309
Jerusalem, 12, 32-34, 40-41, 109, 257, 318; above, xv, xx, 376, 432-33, 518, 533; church as, 33, 172, 206, 287, 376, 401-2, 432, 485-86, 525-26; heavenly, xxi, 77, 256, 376, 512, 524; new, 209, 432-33, 510-11, 518. *See also* Zion
Jesse, root of: 9, 39, 47, 106, 134, 139-46, 150, 152, 163
Jews, xxiv-xxvi, 84-85, 156, 167, 377, 454, 484
John the Baptizer, xx, 138, 146, 199-200, 266, 268, 271-72, 454, 501
Joseph (patriarch), xvi, xvii, 4, 142, 196
Joseph (father of Jesus), 92, 101, 107, 122, 235
Joshua, 26, 146, 311, 409

Judah, 7-10, 32, 56, 110, 161, 172, 187, 194-96, 327, 492; Christ as 220-21, 493
Judaism, Christian critique of, xxiv-xxv, 53, 58, 62-64, 85-89, 109, 243, 248-49
Judgment, 43-44, 72, 88-89, 284, 289, 314, 333, 340, 491, 507, 510; by Christ, 48, 125, 135, 166, 185-86, 239, 294-97, 425, 492; final, 180, 184, 204-5, 230, 236, 239, 534-36
Justice, 9, 28, 37, 88, 151, 156, 231, 236, 287-88, 294, 299-300, 332, 335, 342-44, 351-52, 372, 397, 444, 452-53, 491. *See also* Righteousness
Justification, 195, 236, 375

Kingdom of God, 54, 63, 95, 123, 130, 210, 215, 254, 256, 261, 426, 465-66, 535
Knowledge, 60, 211, 267, 278, 289, 301, 320, 338, 536; of Christ, 20, 95, 121, 321, 370, 409; of God, xxi, 17, 20-21, 34-36, 79-81, 83, 96-97, 122, 135, 210, 279, 284-86, 302, 307, 312, 420, 428, 462. *See also* Gifts of the Spirit

Lamb (sheep), Christ as, xiii, xx, 3, 11, 95, 184, 187-90, 209, 344, 367, 370, 372, 414-15, 418, 422, 424-28, 434, 462
Last days, xix, 32-40, 46, 139, 201, 214, 404, 463, 477
Law, 29, 37, 40-41, 113, 116-17, 201, 239, 246, 359, 436-37, 501-2, 505-6, 515; of Moses, xxiii, 3-4, 63, 220, 248, 255, 353, 393, 416, 474, 518; natural, 109, 116-17; new, 12, 34; and the prophets, xxii, 1, 7, 28, 83, 122, 246, 312, 417, 434, 462; as tutor (pedagogue), 20, 117, 151, 210, 385, 402
Lebanon, 42, 56, 255, 257, 473
Life: Christ as, 367; eternal, 85, 219, 221, 225-26, 257, 261, 366, 419-20, 438, 513, 520-21; life to come, 458, 534-36; new, 133, 254, 420, 484, 517; present, 45, 74, 116, 204, 229, 300, 309, 367, 458
Light: Christ as, xxi, 124-26, 223, 268, 366, 461-63, 467, 484, 486; light to the nations, 85, 373, 476
Liturgy, x, xxii, 62, 77, 81-83, 478, 490
Living water, xvii, 21, 155, 209, 237, 286, 320, 367, 442, 445, 477, 513
Logos. *See* Word
Lord's Supper. *See* Eucharist
Love, 5, 22, 54-58, 80, 97, 129, 148, 201, 222, 226, 247-48, 266, 293-94, 342, 375, 388, 397, 411, 443, 503, 514; for Christ, 153, 216, 225, 423, 456, 466; Christ's, xxii, 41, 95, 273, 420; for God, 60, 64, 98, 143, 187, 206, 219, 244, 251, 269-70, 319, 336, 358-60; God's, 20, 166, 237, 261, 268, 288, 299, 310, 315, 377, 395, 419, 426,

479, 498, 517, 533; wounded with, 366, 369, 370-72
Lucifer, 160, 171, 175-76, 179. *See also* Devil

Manicheans, 372, 538
Marcionites, 215n.3, 340n.7
Marriage, xv, 101, 196, 352, 451-52, 454, 458, 496
Martyrdom, of Isaiah, 1-3, 8-9, 66, 542
Mary, 143, 235, 360-61, 446; Mother of God (Theotokos) 126, 129, 134, 142-43, 543; as mountain, 32, 39-40; virginity of, 9, 32, 39-40, 92, 98-107, 111, 137, 141, 366, 368. *See also* Branch
Medes, 161-62, 172-74, 185, 350. *See also* Persians
Mercy, 27, 29, 85-86, 134, 172, 184-85, 191, 239, 306, 310-11, 376-77, 392-95, 406, 423, 452-54, 525, 533. *See also* Grace
Messenger of great counsel, 120, 122-24, 127, 129
Messiah, 238, 332, 477-78. *See also* Anointed One
Miracles, 107, 144, 157; performed by Christ, xx, 10, 89, 106, 206, 254, 269, 417, 478, 536. *See also* Signs
Moabites, 160, 163, 184-89
Money, 205, 336, 441-43
Monasticism, 60, 160, 245n.1
Moses, 18, 25, 28, 62, 66, 68-71, 75-76, 101, 114, 155, 163, 272, 409, 447. *See also* Law of Moses
Mountain: Christ as, 34, 38, 41; Church as, 34-35, 152, 212, 214; Mary as, 32, 39-40

Names of Christ, 113, 129, 135, 138, 155, 220, 284, 297, 309, 367-68, 370, 372, 473, 521, 526
Nations. *See* Gentiles
Nature: of God, 19, 42, 72-76, 82, 103, 266, 277-78, 306-9, 321, 324, 358-59, 502-4; human, 89, 133, 221, 277, 295, 298, 305, 307, 328, 403, 504; of the Trinity, 65, 69, 77-79, 130, 323. *See also* Christ, nature of

Natural law, 116-17
Nebuchadnezzar, 161-62, 171, 173-74, 179-80, 267, 337
New Covenant, 5, 12, 19, 40, 126, 144, 267, 421, 446, 477, 516
New heavens and new earth, 229, 468, 510-11, 518-20, 524, 532-34
Nicea, 219, 293, 318

Old Testament, xxiv, xxvi, 150, 215n.3, 286, 301, 337n.4; interpretation of, xiii-xix, xxii, 1, 243, 461. *See also* Septuagint

Paradise, 22, 26, 94, 142, 312, 479, 485, 506, 511, 513, 520
Passion of Christ, xvi, xxii, 10, 67, 114, 122, 153, 196, 335, 381-83, 387-89, 413, 418-19, 424-28, 490-97. *See also* Blood of Christ, Cross of Christ, Death of Christ
Peace, 32, 34, 41, 113, 122-24, 134, 174, 219-20, 225-26, 339-42, 401, 404-11, 526, 531-32; Prince of, 10, 120, 129-31
Persians, 326, 332, 335-36, 338, 345, 350. *See also* Medes
Pharaoh, 18, 63, 69, 71, 85, 272, 309
Philip, xiii, xx, 2-3, 121-22, 247, 414-15, 424-25
Plan, Divine, xxvii, 116, 135, 490; formed of old, xxiii, 209-11, 213. *See also* Economy, Divine
Prayer, 17, 21, 23-25, 66-67, 78n.8, 80-82, 155, 197, 209, 219, 222-23, 227, 243, 345, 348, 353-54, 452, 486, 503
Promise, 134, 211, 226, 433, 462, 483-86, 501, 511; of Christ's coming, 41, 110, 123, 138-44, 150, 188, 196, 255, 270, 334-35, 267; to David, 39, 131, 315, 441, 445-46
Providence, 48, 141, 201, 309, 313, 371
Punishment, 48, 179-80, 204, 268, 297; eternal, 167, 224, 524, 535-36
Purification (washing), 24-27, 46-48, 67, 74-75, 82, 260, 494
Purity, 46-48, 78, 81, 102, 176, 257, 274, 343, 501, 529

Reason, 22, 38, 56-57, 96-97, 148, 274, 278, 472, 527
Redemption, xxiii, xxvii, 10, 114, 189, 260, 284, 287, 305-6, 309-10, 326, 402-3, 444. *See also* Salvation
Repentance, xxiv, 24-25, 28, 86-87, 121, 157, 266, 305-6, 311, 314, 318, 325, 341, 346, 351, 354, 377
Resurrection, 120, 125-27, 204, 209, 212, 219, 221, 228-31, 260-61, 278n.4, 420, 513, 534; of believers, 151, 215, 224; of the body, 125, 215, 219, 225, 495, 532; of Christ, 11, 67, 123, 198, 295, 335, 421, 427, 490, 495; final, 510, 518-19
Reward, 270, 315, 397-98, 448, 455-57, 485, 535
Righteousness, 131, 185-86, 257, 284-85, 332, 345, 393-96, 398, 444, 466, 473-74, 480, 491, 500-502, 504, 505-6; Christ as, 140, 236, 268, 284, 287-88, 342-43, 385, 467, 484; through faith, 113, 439; girded with, 368. *See also* Justice

Sabbath, xxiv, 2, 226, 366, 451, 453, 455-57, 471
Sacraments, 148, 163, 410n.3, 464, 473, 531. *See also* Baptism, Eucharist

Index of Subjects

Sacrifice, 4, 17, 24, 222, 255, 269, 305-6, 310, 313, 405, 512; of Christ, xxvii, 414, 426-28, 430; Eucharist as, 58, 211; spiritual, 23, 82, 110, 235, 301. *See also* Blood of Christ, Cross of Christ, Death of Christ

Saints, 4-5, 39, 88, 96, 178, 181, 190, 222, 312, 421, 463, 469, 474-75, 483, 484, 486, 520

Salvation, 28, 112, 126, 154, 205, 211-14, 219-20, 343, 354, 366, 373-75, 405-9, 498, 443, 452; through Christ, 258, 269, 393-94, 484; garment of, 402, 473, 480; of Gentiles, 64, 85; spirit of, 228-30; wells of, 155-57, 286. *See also* Plan, Divine; Redemption

Samaritan woman, xvii, 37, 442, 445, 477

Sanctification, 26, 82, 110, 113-14, 284, 287, 307, 471-72

Sanctus. *See* Holy, holy, holy

Sarah, xv, 237, 393, 395-96, 433

Satan. *See* Devil

Savior, 6, 9, 12, 154-55, 157, 196, 219, 221, 269, 338, 342, 483, 485-86

Scriptural exegesis, allegorical, xv, xvii, 4, 17, 43, 53, 56, 91, 109, 116, 150, 160, 171, 184-85, 188-89, 237, 433, 520; attention to textual variants xviii-xix, 34, 57, 104, 137, 244-45, 255, 284-85, 294-95, 422, 476, 501, Christological, 43, 53, 109, 184, 239n.3, 332, 461; foreshadowing, xvii, 74, 220, 237, 257, 305, 401; historical, xvii, xxiii, 7, 17, 91-92, 109, 160-63, 171, 184, 200, 265-66, 318, 402; by Jews, xv, xxiv, 66, 92, 137, 243, 345n.9, 350, 376, 382, 385; literal, 34, 43, 46, 91, 115, 156, 171, 332, 532; multiple senses, xvii, 4, 7, 109, 536; philological, 133; plain meaning, xiv, 172; spiritual meaning, xv, xvii, 7, 33, 91, 152, 180, 189, 402, 404, 410, 466-67, 491, 532; typological, xxvii, 32, 37, 58, 102, 195, 200, 237-38, 305, 332, 435

Scriptures, inspiration of, xxiii, 256, 277, 375

Second coming, of Christ, 255, 335, 351, 387, 532

Septuagint (LXX), xviii, xxvi, 104

Seraphim, xxii, 62, 65-74, 77-79, 81-82, 84, 195, 289

Sermons. *See* Homilies

Servant Songs, xxi, 293, 381, 413

Signs, 9, 34, 93-94, 98-100, 103-4, 151, 161. *See also* Miracles

Siloam, 112

Simeon, 86, 102, 166, 209, 211-12

Sin, 28, 43, 47, 53, 59, 62, 268, 305, 311, 314-15, 325, 372, 401-5, 410, 414, 416, 418-21, 426, 429-30, 500, 504-6; of Adam, 190

Son of God, 10, 57, 62, 98, 105, 128, 130, 204, 334-35. *See also* Christ, Christology, Incarnation, Word

Stone of stumbling, Christ as, 109-10, 113-14

Spirit of the Lord, xx, 2, 9-11, 136-39, 144, 471-72, 474-78. *See also* Holy Spirit

Temple, 55, 65, 69-70, 173, 244-45, 451; Christ as, 41; church as, 37, 196, 227, 328, 433, 435; rebuilding of, 267, 318, 326, 328, 337, 345

Tent of David, Church as, xxii, 186, 191, 433, 435, 473

Theotokos (Mother of God), 39, 134, 368. *See also* Mary

Thirst, 12, 155, 157, 211, 222-23, 257-58, 367, 422-23, 442-45, 515

Transfiguration, 53, 155, 194

Trinity, 43, 48-49, 62, 65-66, 69, 77-79, 81, 96, 293, 323-24, 358, 471. *See also* Christ, God, Holy Spirit, Son of God, Word

Trisagion. *See* Holy, holy, holy

Uzziah, 7-8, 17, 19, 62, 64, 69, 71, 92

Vineyard, song of, xxiv, 53-59

Virgin birth (of Christ), xiii, xxi, 9, 92-94, 98-107, 137-44, 366, 368

Virginity, 101-2, 137n.5, 451-52, 455

Virtue, 10, 55, 60, 138, 150, 178, 299-300, 335, 339, 378, 453, 520

Vision of God, by Isaiah, xxii, 62, 64-82

Vulgate, xviii, xxvi, 171, 332, 541

Widows, 25, 44, 45, 435, 437

Wine, 209, 211-13, 245, 249, 441-45, 490-94, 496-97; feast of, xxii-xxiii. *See also* Eucharist, Vineyard, song of

Wisdom, 36, 209, 244, 381, 384, 504; Christ as, 284, 287, 322-23, 367, 388, 521, 530; of God, 371; spirit of, xxvi, 45, 133-36, 138-41, 143-50

Word: Christ as, 36, 48, 269, 275, 323, 414; of God, 92, 269, 275. *See also* Christ, Christology, Incarnation, Son of God

Works, good, 214, 221, 236, 375, 402, 474

Zechariah (father of John), 100, 209, 211-12, 268

Zerubbabel, 172, 345

Zion, 37, 40-41, 115, 189, 257, 366, 376, 401-3, 405-7; church as, 34, 45, 156, 206, 236, 239, 287, 295, 393, 483-86, 525. *See also* Jerusalem

Index of Scripture References

OLD TESTAMENT

Genesis

Ref	Pages
1:3	528
1:3-4	124
1:6	42
1:26	19, 378, 487
1:26-27	42, 406
1:28	42
1:31	226
2:2-3	226
2:7	42, 206, 214, 298
2:16-17	515
2:24	xv, 481
3:5	176
3:8	236
3:19	378
3:22	521
3:24	311-12
4:1-8	xvi
4:4	428
6:1-3	146
8:21	311
9:5 LXX	355
9:25-27	201
11	162
11:7	273
12:1	288
12:3	280
12:7	68, 75
17:1	68, 69
17:16	336n.2
18:1	68, 69
18:1-8	74
18:11	395
18:21	65
18:22-33	5
18:27	27, 178, 277
19:24	336
19:30	188
19:37	188n.4
21:10	433
21:19	237
22:1-9	xvi
22:18	141
24:42-44	102
25:11	20
26:23-24	68
27:27-29	201
28:10-22	238
28:17	20
29:1-12	234, 238
31:13 LXX	68
32:22-32	74
32:24-30	69
32:28	68
32:30	68-69, 76
35:6-7	68
35:9	68
37:5-8	4
37:6-7	4
37:9-10	4
37:28	xvi
41:1-36	4
49:1	201
49:8	220
49:8-9	492
49:9 LXX	139-40
49:9	113, 427, 493
49:10 LXX	112
49:10	493
49:11	10, 491-94
49:18	157

Exodus

Ref	Pages
2:3	xvi
2:11-15	18n.1
2:23	69
3:1-6	82
3:2	72, 101, 107
3:2-4	142
3:3	101
3:5	409
3:10	71
3:11–4:17	18
3:14	266, 276, 300, 321, 324, 358-59
3:15	300
4:11	164
4:13	71
7:1	272
7:17ff.	155
7:21	382
9:16	85, 309
10:21-23	124
10:22-23	382
13:21	45
14:15	272
14:19-20	45
15:1	54, 155
15:16	359
20:3	250
21:22-23	328
22:27	300
23:13	250
23:26	455
25:29	410
27	435

Index of Scripture References

30:10	479	31:30	57	**1 Kings**	
32:13	395	31:30–32:44	54	10:1	445
32:32	5	32:2	230		
33:11	76	32:6	507	**2 Chronicles**	
33:13 LXX	75-76	32:8-9	358, 434	26:16ff.	7
33:20	3, 62, 66, 68-69, 71, 76, 502	32:9	321, 449	29:1-2	111
33:23	66, 72	32:11	533	**Job**	
34:6	237	32:16	54	1:4	444
		32:21	302	1:12	529
Leviticus		32:32	245	2:10	332, 340-41
6:12	480	32:33 LXX	245	3:3	225
6:15	255	32:39	174	3:19	205
8:1	25	32:43 Vg.	454	9:30-31	48
11:25	479	32:43	134, 405	10:8	528
15:2	237n.1	32:46	54	11:7 LXX	527
16	xiv	32:49-50	114	13:25 Vg.	506
17:8 Vg.	453			14:4-5 LXX	146
20:7	410	**Joshua**		15:15	27
		1:8	246	19:26 LXX	229
Numbers		3:16	311	21:13 Vg.	180
2:17	350n.2	5:15	409	35:7	266
12:7	456	7:1	67	38:31	150
14:20-21	70	20:7	40	40:20	175
14:21	205				
17:8	107, 142-43	**Judges**		**Psalms**	
18:17	410n.2	5:1ff.	54	1:1	20, 453
21:9	157	5:20	181	1:2	410
22:1-3	186	6:36-38	142	2:3	403
22:6	186	6:37-40	107	2:6 LXX	345
23:7–24:19	186			2:6	64
24:17	138, 350, 514	**Ruth**		2:7	xiv, 58, 441
25:1-3	187	1:4	189n.5	2:7-8	126, 334, 434, 445
				2:8	280, 338
Deuteronomy		**1 Samuel**		2:9	135
1:17	452	2:5	434	2:11	124
4:10-12	82	3:10	386	3:5	140
4:24	501	15:17	60	4:4	250
4:39	528	23–26	xvi	6:2	229
6:4	289, 386	24:6	336	7:12 LXX	507
6:5	359			9:1 LXX	58
6:13	518			9:4	72
7:6	358	**2 Samuel**		9:24 LXX	114
7:14	455	6:14	22	9:38 Vg.	386
10:14	358	7:8-9	315	11:4	69
16:20 Vg.	453	7:11	315	12:6	444
17:6	474	7:14	xiv	14:2	448
22:15	104	7:18-19	315	14:3	81, 136, 151, 310, 404, 504
22:23-26	99	7:28-29	315		
23:1	451, 457	18:14	371	14:12	97
28:12	501	24:17	5	15:2 Vg.	313
30:15	29n.13			15:2	453

575

16:1	442	37:19 LXX	311	57:8	402
17:8	73	39:7-9 LXX	418	58:6 Vg.	437
18:6	352	40:1	395	61:2 LXX	66
18:10	73	40:2	403	61:4	350
18:11	163	40:8	350	62:12	166
18:49	134	41:7	398	63:1-2	222
19:1-4	397	42:2	219, 223, 257	65:8	223
19:3-4	12, 427	42:5	397	65:9	286
19:4	310, 481	44:1 LXX	58	66:12	339
19:4-5	481	44:6-7	505	67:5-6	39
19:5	487, 496	45:1	17, 467	67:6-7	79
19:6	301	45:2	41, 296, 427, 496	67:7	79
19:8	273	45:2 Vg.	423	68:2	501
19:12	81	45:6	xiv, 135	68:4	273
19:14	222	45:7	333, 475, 478	68:9	144
21:1 LXX	xix	45:12	377	68:18	111, 478, 496
21:29 LXX	352	45:13-14	487	68:23	492, 501
21:30 LXX	515	45:14	484	68:23-24 LXX	85
22:1	xix	46:2	38	68:26	156, 286
22:2	110	46:4	221, 286, 442, 526, 532	68:27	122
22:6	178, 286	46:6	506	71:6 LXX	142
22:16-17	396	47:1	124	72:1	492
23:1-2	375	47:3-4	436	72:7	124, 131
23:4	135	47:7-8	405	72:8	188
23:7 LXX	495	47:8	403	72:11	280
24	495	48:10	301	72:19	70
24:1	65, 204, 319	48:12 LXX	42	72:20 LXX	378
24:3	278	49:1	405, 527	73:2 LXX	505
24:7	494-96	49:23 LXX	156	73:5	166
24:7-8	492	50:2	41	73:23-24	333
24:8	478, 494-96	50:2-3	406	73:27	447
24:10	492, 496, 505	50:3	425	73:28	447, 453
25:15	222, 448	50:10-12	525	74:12	514
27:1	371	50:12 LXX	144	76:1	34, 151, 514
27:13	468	50:14 LXX	477	76:4	38
31:10	215	50:14	156	76:7	504
32:1	26, 447	50:16	71	77:1	272
32:9 LXX	326	50:20	41	78:24-25	20
33:6 LXX	111	51:3	311	78:36	251
33:6	323, 528	51:7	22n.6	79:1	505
33:9	528	51:10	147	79:4	505
34:5	26	51:12	147	79:12	505
34:7	402	51:17	476	80:1	70, 72
34:8	314	51:18	156	80:8	58
34:10-14	339	52:4	176	80:13 Vg.	166
34:12	278	52:5	177	82:1	452
36:6	38, 89	52:6-7	177	85:1-2	394
36:7-8	526	53:3	81	85:8	386
36:7-9	442	57 LXX	352	85:9 LXX	270
37:2	273-74, 277	57:2 LXX	352	85:9	526
37:17	135	57:3	453	85:11	342-43
37:18	466-67	57:4 LXX	434	86:9	79

86:11	422	106:3	453	3:18 LXX	513
87	483	106:4 LXX	229	3:18	521
87:1-2	376	106:6	506	3:19	138
87:3	221, 484	106:7 LXX	229	3:34	42
87:5	106	106:33	498	5:17	56
88:11 LXX	394	109:3 LXX	58, 171, 349	5:19	56
88:11 Vg.	179	110:1	288, 334-36	5:21	485
89:13	359	111:10	148, 285	5:22	26, 375
89:17	402, 505	112:1	410	8:22	366, 372-73, 388, 389
89:19	21	112:2	516	8:25	58
89:22-24	369	113:9	434	8:27	322, 326
89:32-33	166	117:1	134	9:5	157
92:3 LXX	310	118:8	239	10:3 LXX	515
92:12	473	118:22	110, 235, 237, 374	12:5	452
92:13	469, 473	118:22-23	54	17:25	206
94:7-8 LXX	306	118:24	467	18:13	xvii
94:10	21	119:11	267	18:17 LXX	311
94:16	278	119:11-15	504	18:17	80
95:4	72	119:17	314	20:9	81, 506
95:6	28	119:20	222	21:6	228
96:1	124, 221	119:43-44	222	22:1	404
96:10	128	119:73	528	25:20 Vg.	535
96:11	124	119:97	359	25:25	223
97:1	367, 405	119:103	165	26:12	57
97:2	197	119:105	394	27:6	372
97:4-5	501	121:6	467	29:12	180
97:12	358, 361	122:1	486	30:19	256
98:2	157	126:1	229	31:10	107
98:8	449	128:2	513		
99:7	197	128:5	224	**Ecclesiastes**	
99:8	197	130:3-4	311	1:2	277
100:1 Vg.	191	132:11	39, 141, 446	3:6	447
102:18	308	137:4	37, 221	3:7	302
102:25	530	137:8-9	162	7:20	146
103:8	268	139:6	428	7:23-24	289
103:10	268	139:7-8	447, 528	10:14	65
103:22	478	139:7-10	276		
103:24 LXX	301	143:2	81	**Song of Songs**	
103:25 LXX	301	143:5	530	1:2 LXX	526
104:2	327	143:6	257	1:2	xix
104:3	194, 197	143:10	147	2:1 LXX	135, 137
104:3-4 LXX	97	145:8	237	2:1	474
104:4	xiv, 70, 73, 350	145:13	28	2:3	372
104:24	138, 416	145:15	279	2:5	xxii, 366, 369-72
104:25	205	145:16	279	2:8	207
104:27	279	146:3	239, 275	2:9	188, 207
104:29-30	221	146:4 Vg.	181	2:10-12	404
104:30	472	147:3	416	2:12	254
105:3	447			2:16-17	274
105:3-4	448	**Proverbs**		2:17	314
105:4	223, 441, 447	1:3 LXX	502	4:6	314
105:15	336-37	3:12	166	4:7	487

INDEX OF SCRIPTURE REFERENCES

4:15	xvii
4:16	404
5:7	74
5:11-12	519n.9
7:13	254

Isaiah

1–16	xxv
1–8	xxv
1	14-17
1:1	17-21, 32-33, 204
1:2	xxi, 17, 19-21, 54, 465
1:3	21-22, 54
1:4	xxiv, 209
1:6-7	47
1:8	58, 492
1:9	512
1:10	382
1:11	4, 17, 23-24
1:11-12	24
1:15	25, 67
1:16	17, 24-27
1:16-17	25-26
1:16-20	25
1:18	25, 27-28, 325
1:18-19	67
1:19-20	29
1:21	140, 245
1:26	94
2	30-32
2:1	32-36, 477
2:1ff.	432
2:1-4	34
2:2	xix, 32, 34-40, 214, 456
2:2-3	12, 463
2:2-4	36
2:3	37, 41, 464
2:3-4	12, 40-41
2:4	xxi, 32, 41-42, 478
2:8-9	42
2:12	42
2:12-13	42
2:13	42
2:20	349
2:21	468
3:25	46
3:25-26	46
4	43
4:1	43, 45-46, 145
4:2	39, 43-44
4:3	44
4:4	43-44, 46-49
4:5	43-45
4:6	43-45
4:15	xvii
5	xxiv-xxv, 50-53
5:1	4, 53-55, 57-58
5:1-2	53-54, 58
5:2	53, 55, 59, 469, 512
5:4	58
5:6	55, 342
5:7	53, 56, 512
5:18	53, 59
5:20	60
5:21	56, 60
5:22	43
6	xxii, xxv, 61-62
6:1	1, 3, 63-65, 69, 71-72, 74-76, 78, 194-95, 201, 428
6:1-3	195
6:2	65, 72, 74, 78-80
6:2-3	69, 73, 289
6:3	xxii, 64-66, 68, 70, 77-81
6:4	74
6:5	66-68, 70-71, 80-82
6:6	xxii, 62, 74, 82-84
6:7	74
6:8	6, 71, 382
6:9	85
6:9-10	xxiv, 53, 62-64, 69, 84-89
6:10	2, 63, 85, 88-89
6:12	224
6:13	513
7	x, 90-91, 109, 111, 120
7:1-2	92
7:2	104
7:3-11	110
7:4	112
7:8	111
7:9	91, 95-98, 165, 417, 448
7:10-14	9, 93, 99
7:11	100, 103-4
7:12	110
7:14	xx-xxi, 92-93, 98-107, 111, 137, 141, 155, 324, 368, 497
7:14-15	102, 123
7:15	103
7:15-16	94
7:16	95, 103-4, 111
8	xxv, 108-9, 120
8:1	110, 155
8:1-4	111
8:2	110-11
8:3	110-11
8:3-4	123
8:4	111
8:5	112
8:5-6	155
8:5-7	112-13
8:7	56
8:9	196
8:14	109-10, 113-15, 235
8:14-15	109
8:16	115
8:17-18	110
8:18	109, 115, 121, 516
8:19	116
8:20	109, 116-17
9	x, 118-20
9:1	121
9:1-2	120-22, 126
9:2	124-27, 211, 446
9:5	142
9:6	xxi, 11, 101, 120, 122-24, 127-30, 511, 517
9:6-7	10, 517
9:7	120, 123-24, 130-31
10:5	47n.2
10:34	42
11	132-34
11:1	xxi, 39, 45, 47, 134-35, 137-44, 145n.11, 163, 294-95
11:1-2	141, 146-47, 475
11:1-3	139-40, 150
11:2 LXX	xxi, xxvi
11:2	xxvi, 135-37, 144, 295, 477
11:2-3	45, 46, 144-50
11:3	134, 136
11:3-5	9
11:4	368
11:5	368
11:6	151
11:6-8	143
11:6-9	134, 150-53
11:9	152
11:10	134, 152, 163
11:15	155
12	154
12:1	155-56

Index of Scripture References

12:1-6	xxi	15–16	182-84	25:4	210
12:2	155, 157	15:1	165, 185-86	25:6	xxii-xxiii, 204, 209, 211, 213-14, 432
12:3	155-57, 286	15:2	185		
12:3-4	12	15:5	189	25:6-7	213-14
12:4	156	15:7	185	25:7	211, 213-14
12:4-5	156	16	160	25:7-8	28
12:5	156	16:1 Vg.	344	25:8	209-11, 214-16, 297, 511
13–23	xxi, 160	16:1	184	25:8-9	229
13	137n.3, 158-60	16:1-2	188	25:9	212, 216
13:1	160-66	16:1-5	187-91	25:10	212
13:1-22	185	16:2 Vg.	189	26	217-18
13:2	163	16:4	189-90	26:1	219-22
13:3	161-62	16:5 Vg.	191	26:2	220
13:5	162	16:5	184-85	26:3	220
13:9	163, 224	17:1	165	26:7	220
13:10	160-61	19	160, 192-94	26:9 Vg.	453
13:11	163	19:1	160, 165, 194-98	26:9	219, 222-23
13:14	162	19:16	195	26:10	219, 224-25
13:16	162	19:17	194-96	26:12	219, 225-26
13:17	161, 185	19:19	194-96	26:13	219, 226-27
13:21	162	19:20	194, 196	26:14	227-28
14	160, 164-71	20	160, 199	26:17-18 LXX	474
14:1	171-72	20:2	160, 200	26:18	220, 228
14:2	160, 172	20:2-3	200-201	26:18-20	228-31
14:3	172	20:3	201	26:19 LXX	229
14:3-21	171	20:7	381	26:19	204, 219-21, 229-30
14:4	173	21:1	165	26:20	219, 231
14:9	171, 173, 179	21:13	165	27:1	368
14:9-20	179	22:1	165	27:5	123
14:10	179	22:4	5	28	xxv, 232-35
14:11	175, 179	22:13	xxin.1	28:1-3	245
14:12	171, 173, 175-76, 179	22:22	246	28:14	237, 239
14:12-15	175	23:1	165	28:15	237
14:12-21	175-77	23:33 LXX	447	28:16	xxi, 9, 109-10, 113-14, 234-40, 533
14:12-22	175	24–27	204		
14:13	173, 176, 178, 180	24	202-4	28:17	239
14:13-14	162, 177-81	24:1	204	28:18	237
14:14	176, 179-80	24:2	205	29	xx, 241-43
14:15	173, 179-80	24:5	204, 206-7, 211	29:1	244
14:15-16	177	24:6	205	29:9	245
14:16	179-81	24:10	496	29:9-15	249
14:17	173, 180	24:14	204-5, 207	29:10	85
14:18	173	24:14-15	205	29:11	246-48
14:19	180	24:15	204-5	29:11-12	246
14:20	180	24:16	205	29:12	246
14:21	173	24:18	204, 207	29:13	163, 243-44, 248-51
14:22	174	24:22	206	29:13ff.	249
14:25	174	24:23	206, 210	29:14	188, 244
14:27	174	25	xxiii, 208-9	29:16	244, 251-52
14:28	165, 174	25:1	xxiii, 209-11, 213	30–39	xxi
14:29	174	25:2	210	30:6 Vg.	165
14:30	174	25:3	211	30:28	11

579

… INDEX OF SCRIPTURE REFERENCES

Ref	Pages
31:7	359
32:15	11
33:10	11
33:20	498
34:4	xxin.2
34:6	72
34:8-9	256-57
35	xx, 253-54
35:1	254-55, 257
35:1-2	257-58
35:2 LXX	254
35:2	255-56
35:3	255
35:3-4	258
35:4	254-55, 258, 498
35:5	254
35:5-6	xxin.2, 10, 255, 259
35:6	256, 259-60
35:8	256, 260
35:9	256, 260
35:10	254, 256-57, 260-62
39	267
40–66	266
40–55	265
40	263-65
40:1	xxi, 267, 269, 344
40:1-3	268
40:2	267-68
40:3	xx-xxi, 266, 268, 271-73
40:3-5	266, 268, 272
40:4	268
40:5	269
40:6	266, 269, 272-75, 277
40:6-7	273-75
40:6-8	266-67, 275
40:7	274, 302
40:8	269, 274-75
40:9	302, 406
40:9-10	270
40:9-11	269
40:10	270, 492
40:11	270, 274, 516
40:12 Vg.	528-29
40:12	266, 276-79
40:12-13	278
40:12-14	271
40:13	266, 271, 278-79, 322
40:14	271
40:15	279-280
40:26	280
40:27	284n.1
40:31	284
41	281-84
41:1	284-85
41:2	284-85, 287-88
41:4	284-85, 288-89, 312, 323, 348
41:4-5	285
41:5	285, 288
41:5-6	285
41:6	288
41:8	285-86, 288, 294
41:9	285, 288-89
41:10	285, 289
41:11-12	286
41:13-14	286
41:15	286-87
41:17-18	286
41:18	286
41:20	287
41:21	284
41:21-23	289-90
41:22-23	65, 289
41:24-26	287
41:25	287
41:27	12, 287, 295
41:29	294
42	xx, 291-93
42:1 LXX	293
42:1	53, 293-97
42:1-4	137, 293-94, 297
42:2	296-97
42:2-3	295
42:3	295, 299
42:4	294-95, 324
42:5	214, 297-98
42:6-7	298-99, 445, 476
42:7	299
42:8	293, 299-300
42:9	301
42:10	293, 300-302
42:11	302
42:14	302
42:15	301
42:18	259
43	xxiii, 303-5
43:1	xxiii, 306
43:2	306-7, 311-12
43:5	307
43:5-6	305
43:6	307
43:7	307-8
43:10	308, 312, 361
43:10-11	312
43:12	308, 312-13
43:13	308
43:15	308-9
43:16	309
43:17	309
43:18	309, 313
43:18-19	306, 314
43:19	310, 313-14
43:20	306, 314
43:21	306
43:22	310
43:23	310
43:24	310
43:25	305, 311, 394
43:25-26	314-15
43:26	311
43:27-28	319
44	316-18
44:1	319
44:1-2	319, 327
44:2	319-20
44:3	320
44:3-4	11
44:4	320
44:5	320
44:6	284, 318, 321-25, 348
44:7	321
44:21-22	394
44:22	325
44:23	326
44:24	318, 322-23, 326-28
44:25	327
44:25-26	323
44:28	328, 332
45	329-32
45:1	332-38, 345
45:1-2	333
45:1-3	335
45:2	336-39
45:2-3	333, 338
45:3	336-37
45:4	334, 336-38
45:5	322
45:6	334, 345
45:7	332, 334, 339-42
45:8 Vg.	342-44
45:8	9, 332
45:9	252, 332, 344
45:13	332, 345
45:14	345-46, 361
45:20	349

Index of Scripture References

Reference	Pages	Reference	Pages	Reference	Pages
45:23	333, 346	50:7	389	53:10	420-21
45:23-24	332	50:7-8	389	53:10-12	433
46	347-48	50:11	381, 389	53:11	416, 420-21
46:1	348-49	51	390-92	53:12	414, 424, 478
46:1-2	349	51:1	395-96	54	xx, 1, 431-33
46:3	349	51:1-2	393	54:1	xxi, 433-34, 436-38
46:3-4	349	51:2	393, 395, 396	54:1-5	6, 438
46:4	350	51:3	393	54:2	xxii, 433, 435, 473
46:5	277, 349	51:5	138, 393-94, 396-97	54:2-3	437
46:7	349	51:6	393, 397	54:3	433-37
46:8	348, 350-52	51:7	393, 397-98	54:3-4	437
46:9	284, 348, 350, 353	51:7-8	398	54:4-5	437
46:10	348, 350, 354	51:16	485	54:12	433
46:11	335, 350	51:23	399	54:12-13	438-39
46:12	355	52-53	413	54:13	433, 439
48	356-58	52:1	401-3, 406	54:17	443
48:12	358-59, 361	52:1-12	400-401	54:17–55:1	443
48:13	359	52:2	403	55	440-41
48:14 LXX	324	52:3	403	55:1	12, 272, 366, 441-45
48:14	358-60	52:5	403	55:3	442, 445-46
48:16	358, 360-61	52:6	404	55:3-4	441
48:22 LXX	362	52:6-7	404	55:4	446
48:22	358, 361-62	52:7	6, 67, 401, 404-9, 415	55:4-5	445-46
49	363-66	52:8	405-7	55:5	126, 446-47
49:1	366-68, 370	52:10	106, 401, 407, 409-10, 417	55:6	97, 441, 447
49:1-3	370	52:11	401, 408, 410-11	55:6-7	447-48
49:2	xxii, 366, 368-72	52:12	407	55:8-9	271
49:3	369-70	52:13	11, 416, 421-22	55:12	449
49:5	366, 372-73	52:13–53:12	xxi, 6, 412-13, 438	55:13	452, 454
49:5-6	370	52:14	416-17	56	450-51
49:6	85, 366, 370, 373-74	52:15	409, 415, 417	56:1	452
49:8	366, 374-75	53	1, 433	56:2	453
49:9	375-76	53:1	2, 63, 87, 122, 388, 401, 414-15, 422	56:3	451, 453, 455-57
49:10	367	53:1-2	417	56:3-5	457
49:14	366, 376-77	53:2	414, 417, 422-23	56:4	451, 457
49:15	377	53:2-3	422-24	56:4-5	455
49:16	377-78	53:3	417, 422-23, 427	56:5	451, 457-58
49:17	377	53:3-4	418, 422	56:6-7	456
49:18	377, 465	53:4	414, 424, 494	56:7	451
49:20	379	53:4-6	418	57:16	214, 298
50	380-81	53:5	403, 416, 418-19, 424	58:9	223
50:1	382	53:5-7	xxi	58:13	453
50:2	382	53:6	11, 419	59:2	1, 6
50:2-3	382	53:7 Vg.	188	59:19-20	11
50:2-7	387	53:7	xx, 414, 416, 424-28	60	xxi, 459-61
50:3	387	53:7-8	xiii, 3, 11, 415, 422, 425	60:1	xxi, 462, 491
50:4	17, 381-85, 387	53:8	105, 127, 414, 419, 427-29	60:1ff.	432
50:4-5	384-85	53:9	94, 102, 414, 416, 429-30	60:1-3	xxii
50:4-7	381			60:2	462
50:4-11	382			60:3	463
50:5	381, 385-86			60:4	461, 463-65
50:6	381-82, 387-89, 418			60:4-7	463

INDEX OF SCRIPTURE REFERENCES

60:8	197, 379, 465	65:1	4, 12-13, 511-12, 514	2:27	472
60:17 LXX	466	65:2	512, 514-15, 517	2:27-28	308
60:19	462, 467	65:3	510, 512	2:31	393
60:19-20	466-69	65:4	512	4:4	33
60:20	467	65:8	510, 512	4:5	210
60:21-22	468-69	65:9	512	5:1	81
60:22 LXX	472	65:13	515	5:3	166
60:22	469, 475	65:15	511, 516-18	5:17	210
61	xx, 470-72	65:15-16	516-18	6:16	220
61:1	10, 144, 298, 416, 472, 474-79, 486, 491-92	65:16	516	6:30	444
		65:17	510-11, 518-20, 524	8:4	512
61:1-2	2, 472	65:17-18	518	8:14	210
61:2	479	65:17-19	532	9:23-24	530
61:3	473	65:18	520	11:15 LXX	163
61:4	473	65:19	510, 513	11:19	188, 370, 414, 426
61:6	471, 480	65:19-20	513	12:7	486
61:9	473, 486	65:20	513	13:1	200
61:10	402, 471, 473-74, 480-81, 486	65:21	224, 513, 520	14:21	36
		65:22	510, 513-14, 520-21	15:9	434
61:11	474	66	xxvii, 522-24	15:20	210
62	482-83	66:1	276, 353, 524-25, 527-29	17:5	200, 239
62:1	381, 383, 483-84, 486			17:7	200
62:2	483-84, 486, 487n.2, 518n.8	66:1-2	525	17:9	127
		66:2	xxvii, 149, 516, 525, 528, 530-31	17:16 LXX	362
62:3	483-86			22:17 LXX	421
62:6	485	66:10	526	22:19	180
62:11	483, 485, 487	66:11	526	23:18	74n.7
62:12	486	66:12	442, 526, 531-33	23:23 LXX	447
63	xvi, 488-90	66:12ff.	531-32	23:23-24	528
63:1	xvi, 72, 490-97	66:12-13	517, 525	23:24	273, 527, 529
63:1ff.	xxii	66:13	532-33	25:9	161n.3
63:1-2	493	66:13-14	533	27:6	161n.3
63:1-3	xvi, 10, 59	66:14	229, 532-33	31:21	403
63:2	490-94, 496-97	66:18	525, 527	31:22	107
63:3	494, 497	66:18ff.	526	31:31-33	268
63:5	497	66:18-19 Vg.	12	33:14	106
63:5-6	497	66:20-21	13	43:10	161n.3
63:9	497-98	66:22	229, 510-11, 533-34	48:17	135
63:10	498	66:23	229	48:25-26	187
63:17	512	66:24	229, 524-25, 534-36	48:41-42	187
64	499-500			51:50	463
64:1	500-502, 504, 510	**Jeremiah**			
64:2	501	1:1-2	18	**Lamentations**	
64:3	501	1:4-5	326	4:4 Vg.	444
64:4	178, 206, 261, 500, 502-4	1:5	71, 106	4:20 LXX	157
		1:6	71		
64:5	500-501, 503-5	1:9	71	**Ezekiel**	
64:6	48, 500-501, 505-6	1:14	287	1	501
64:7	512	1:18	18, 210	1:4	72
64:8	506-7	2:13	xvii	1:4-28	74
64:9	507	2:21	58, 469	1:22-27	195
65	508-10	2:22	46-48	1:24	80

Index of Scripture References

1:28	502
2:6	18
2:10	246
3:8-9	382
3:12 LXX	80
8:2	69
10:12	80
12:13	161
17:12	257
17:3	257
17:3-6	56
18:23	87, 512
18:31	25
18:32	512
24:24	115
28:2	180
32:25	180
33:6	355
33:11	24, 512
33:11-20	24
34:14	152
36:25-27	26
37	219, 228n.3
43:13	244
43:15-16	244
47–48	376
47:1ff.	531

Daniel

1:11-16	201
2:34	37, 235, 238
2:34-35	237
2:38-39	179
2:45	238
3	93
3:15	173
5:25	174
5:28	174
6	93
6:22	23
7:9	64, 72
7:9-13	195
7:10	27, 70, 78, 181
7:13	128, 197, 465
7:14	335
9:21	73
10:2-3	5
10:8	506
12:3	181

Hosea

1:1	36
2:6	114
2:23	436
4:13	7
5:14	166
6:3	223
9:10	55
12:10	72, 164
13:14	478
14:9	426

Joel

2:28	35, 139, 214, 298
2:28-29	144
3:12	65
3:18	442

Amos

7:14	18
8:11	157, 515
9:6	465
9:11	131
9:11-12	186

Micah

1:3	65
1:12-13	340
3:8	18
4:1	456
4:1-3	36n.2
6:1-2 LXX	19
7:14	135

Nahum

1:1	18, 20

Habakkuk

2:3	394
3:2	135, 416
3:3 Vg.	188

Zephaniah

1:5	8
3:14	465

Haggai

2:3	435
2:9	435

Zechariah

1:15	507
2:5	104
2:10-11	465
3:4	66
3:8 LXX	140
3:8	115
3:9 LXX	138
3:9	140, 147, 150
4:2	150
4:9	345
4:10	147
6:12 LXX	140
9:9	xiv, 478
12:1	328
14:8	xvii

Malachi

1:6	319
2:7	111
3:1	272
3:1-2	478
4:2	126, 140, 223, 268, 340, 385, 467, 473, 478
4:2-3	229, 403

NEW TESTAMENT

Matthew

1:5	189n.5
1:18	361
1:18-25	92
1:21	155, 368
1:22-23	105
1:23	xx, 92, 99, 102, 345, 501
2:1-12	409
2:2	514
2:23	137
3:1-3	xx
3:3	8, 124
3:6	255
3:9	454
3:10	372
3:12	437
3:16	297, 500
3:17	58, 261, 293, 296, 323
4:9	162
4:12-17	120-21
4:13-16	121
4:16	211
4:18-22	121
4:19-20	121
4:23	485
5:2-12	280

583

INDEX OF SCRIPTURE REFERENCES

5:3	148, 472, 476	11:29	151, 295	21:43	xxiv
5:4	374, 467, 526	11:29-30	484	22:1-14	437
5:5	148, 300, 476	12:15-21	xx, 294	22:11-13	261
5:6	148, 299, 467, 502	12:17-18	137	22:29	312
5:7	148, 531	12:18	293, 295	22:30	215
5:8	68-69, 75, 148, 216, 224, 500, 504, 532, 533	12:18-21	293	22:31-32	353
		12:20	295	22:37	420
5:9	148	12:24	86	23:2-4	248
5:10	397	12:25-32	210	23:8	436
5:11	398	12:28	48	23:8-10	18n.3
5:11-12	398	12:29	394	23:10	18
5:12	xvi, 398	12:37	384	23:13	114
5:14	175, 519	12:42	445	23:37	86, 114, 376, 516, 533
5:16	36, 487	12:43-45	531	23:37-38	58
5:20	473	12:45	149	23:38	486
5:28	67, 506	13:10-17	53, 63	24:16-17	408
5:34-35	353, 527	13:13	86	24:27	175
6:4	26	13:14	87	24:29	xxi, 160, 468
6:6	219, 503	13:16	87	24:31	469
6:9	353	13:17	103	24:35	518
6:9-10	66	13:19	425	24:45-46	466
6:10	29, 354	13:23	190	25:1-3	261
6:13	29	13:28	175	25:21	474
6:14-15	531	13:31-32	423	25:34	213, 503
6:19-20	443	15	243	25:41	339
6:24	236	15:1-3	243	26:18	417
7:1-2	531	15:8-9	244	26:27-28	493
7:7	29	15:13	468	26:37	417
7:21	251	15:24	267	26:38	420
7:24	274	15:31	259	26:39	381, 386
7:24-25	45, 307	16:16-17	367	26:53	382
7:25	34	16:18	197, 219, 237, 345, 486	26:64	387
8:11	454	16:19	485	26:67-68	382, 387
8:12	339	16:24	130, 420	26:68	417
8:14-17	414	17:1-8	28	27:26	388
10:20	144, 477	17:5	53, 194	27:59-60	395
10:22	386	17:20	38	28:18	66
10:26	398	17:27	126	28:18-19	421
10:28	149, 378, 398	18:3	115, 129	28:19	144, 156, 213, 407, 477
10:29-30	279	18:10	76-77	28:19-20	464
10:32	308, 313	19:6	481	28:20	285, 407
10:37	420	19:10-12	452		
10:42	516	19:12	451, 454, 457	**Mark**	
11:2-5	255	19:25	454	1:3	268
11:2-6	xx	19:27	127	1:6	200
11:5-6	xxin.2, 254	20:28	421	1:10	476
11:10	272	21:1-5	483	1:11	57
11:15	89, 381, 384	21:5	xiv, 485	3:15	485
11:19	416	21:9	77, 81	3:27	403
11:27	279, 516	21:33	58	4:12	xxiv
11:28	26, 28, 212	21:33-46	53	5:25-34	28
11:28-29	405	21:40	58	7:8	377

Index of Scripture References

9:7	57
9:43-44	535
9:44	534
9:45	535
9:47-48	535
9:48	535
11:15-17	452
12:30	359
13:3-6	161
13:21-27	161
13:24	160
14:3-4	417, 420
14:34	420
14:61	383
14:65	418
15:5	427

Luke

1:18	100
1:26-27	107
1:28	126
1:30-31	368
1:33	514
1:34	100
1:34-35	361
1:35	39, 103, 111, 419
1:41	22
1:42	39
1:51	403
1:68-79	211
1:69	212
1:76	268
2:1	22
2:1ff.	32
2:10-11	368
2:14	70, 126, 374
2:19	360
2:29-32	211
2:30-31	212
2:34	86, 166
2:40	422
3:1-6	266
3:4-6	272
3:6	269
3:8	454
3:16	47
4:16-21	2, 471-72
4:16-22	475
4:18-19	471
4:18-21	247
4:21	xx, 476, 478, 491
5:31-32	28

6:21	467
6:22	397
6:37-38	24
6:46	251
7:14	83
7:18-23	255
7:35	36
7:50	129
8:1	34
8:43-48	28
9:16	515
9:35	323
9:44	267
10:1	273
10:18	171, 175
10:19	190
10:30	145
10:33-34	145
10:35	145
11:28	386
12:4	149
12:5	149
12:32	395
12:35	480
12:50	67, 494
13:11	280
13:16	256
13:19	423
14:16-17	515
15:7	25, 314
15:12	351
15:17	351
15:20	447
15:23	156
16:15	502
16:22-23	454
16:23	280, 312
18:11-12	311
18:13	311
18:26	5
19:17	469
19:17-18	435
19:19	469
20:36	215
21:20	376, 408
21:34	245
21:14	267
22:35-37	414
23:11	417
23:34	130
23:42-43	94
23:43	485

24:27	xiii, xxiiii, 1, 4
24:32	xxiii, 4, 246
24:46-47	189

John

1	32
1:1	35-36, 124, 127, 271, 323-25, 367, 421, 423, 427
1:1-2	456
1:2-3	530
1:3	49, 138, 258, 323, 326-27, 427, 481, 527-28
1:4	325
1:4-5	373
1:5	127, 467
1:6-7	272
1:7	272
1:9	28, 373, 436
1:10	352, 528
1:11	66
1:13	115, 127
1:14	83, 105, 157, 197, 325, 343, 427, 481, 501
1:15	272
1:18	62, 68, 69, 71, 75, 325, 502
1:23	272, 275n.3
1:29	95, 157, 188-89, 372, 414, 418, 426-28, 430, 494
1:32	136, 141, 475
1:32-33	138
1:33	146, 476
1:33-34	146
1:43-45	122
1:47-49	122
2:14	353
2:16	353, 410
2:19	37, 123
2:19-21	376
3:3	519
3:5	130
3:6	274
3:13	288
3:14	157
3:16	58, 419
3:17	393-94
3:30	275
3:33-34	122
4:7-15	xvii
4:10	xvii

4:10-11	21	10:30	105, 323	19:34	396
4:13-14	155, 258, 442	10:33	404	20:17	494
4:14	21, 445, 513	12:15	xiv	20:19	223, 495
4:21	37	12:24	270	20:22	475
4:22	373	12:25	388	20:28	345
4:23	517	12:27	417	21:15	360
4:23-24	23	12:31	175	21:22	389
4:24	32, 37, 220, 247, 393	12:31-32	206, 296, 491		
4:32	515	12:32	270	**Acts**	
4:35	4, 280, 377, 464	12:35	467	1:3	495
5:20	278	12:36-38	414	1:8	313
5:22	43, 48, 166, 297, 492	12:36-40	63	1:9	197
5:22-23	239	12:36-41	2	2	464, 477
5:35	268	12:38	8, 87	2:1-11	144
5:39	188	12:39	88	2:17	32, 35, 214, 298
5:39-40	385	12:39-40	62, 88	2:17-18	144
6:27	453	12:40	xxiv, 5n.12, 88	2:24	345
6:32-33	372	12:41	62, 69	2:41	406
6:33	274	13:1-17	407	3:1	260
6:38-39	389	13:5	46	3:6	443
6:44	123	13:8	67	3:15	345
6:45	433	13:23	455	4:11	372
6:46	71, 279	13:31	153	4:29	270
6:63	393	13:33	457	5:41	397
6:70	176	14:2	261, 455, 513	7:47	528
7:37	157, 258, 272, 444	14:6	45, 113, 256, 310, 312, 372, 409, 422	7:48-49	528
7:37-38	272, 442			7:48-50	525
7:37-39	155	14:9	76, 369	7:51	498
7:38	223	14:16	298	8:26-38	2-3, 414-15
7:38-39	xvii, 320	14:17	147	8:26-40	xx
8:12	373, 467-68, 486	14:21	225, 423	8:27-38	454
8:28	157	14:23	153, 371	8:30-31	247
8:34	453	14:27	122, 129, 408	8:32-33	xiii
8:39-59	454	14:28	105	8:34-35	xiii
8:46	94	14:30	94, 325	9:15	408, 433
8:51	269	15:1	227, 494	10:37	478
8:53	404	15:3	386	10:38	475
8:56	447	15:5	227, 505	11:26	518
9:5	373, 468, 484	15:14-15	122	13:2	147
9:6	83	15:15	498	13:4	147
9:31	67	15:19	453	13:33-34	441-42
9:39	86, 89, 164, 166	16:7	475, 477	13:44-49	366
10:7	113, 372	16:14	475	13:46	285
10:9	312	16:21	228	13:46-47	85
10:10	473	16:25	261	15:13-18	186
10:11	135, 349, 403	16:26-28	261	15:28-29	464
10:14	274	16:33	307	16:28	406
10:16	469	17:1	152, 462	16:33	406
10:18	426, 515	17:3	225	17:24	528
10:27-28	219	17:4	205, 308	17:28	527-28
10:27-29	308	17:9-10	123	17:29	516
10:29	485	19:11	386	28:23-29	63-64

28:24-27	69	8:28	375, 439	15:10	405
28:25-27	84	8:29	213	15:12	134
28:26-27	62	8:29-30	421	15:18-21	415
28:28	84	8:32	326, 418	16:20	394
		8:33-34	325		
Romans		8:34	261, 498	**1 Corinthians**	
1:1	18, 456	9	109	1:1	18n.2
1:3	100, 131, 185-86	9:5	346	1:3	407
1:3-4	145	9:14	88	1:8	250
1:7	407	9:16	29	1:10	230
1:9	312	9:19	251	1:18	188
1:20	42, 75, 259, 503, 519	9:19-21	244	1:18-19	244
1:22	57	9:20-21	252, 332, 344	1:19	188
1:25	79, 151, 359, 369, 434, 463	9:31	113	1:20	256
		9:32	113	1:21	96, 506
2:11	205	9:32-33	109, 234-35	1:23	372
2:28-29	33	10:3-4	113, 248	1:24	48, 130, 138, 322
3:6	48	10:4	7, 250	1:27	96, 115, 506
3:10	81	10:8-10	83	1:30	113-14, 284, 287, 453
3:12	136, 151	10:9	235	1:31	165
3:20-21	28	10:10	238, 250	2:2	163
3:25	479	10:10-11	235, 238	2:6-7	492
3:26	402	10:14-17	401, 415	2:7	213
3:27	505	10:15	401, 406	2:8	299, 425
4:18	395, 447	10:20	4, 8, 511	2:9	148, 178, 206, 225, 261, 467, 472, 500, 503-4, 526, 528, 534
4:19-21	395	11	211		
4:25	236	11:7	88		
5:1	220, 405, 407	11:8	85	2:10	77
5:4-5	394	11:9-10	85	2:10-11	498
5:5	226	11:11	86	2:11	279, 322
5:6	428	11:15	86	2:12	3
5:9	403	11:16	430	2:12-13	xxiii
5:12	430, 515	11:20	148	2:14	385
5:12-14	128	11:22	340	2:16	397
5:17	515	11:25-26	86	3:1-2	385
5:20	29, 125, 402	11:27	418	3:2	464, 526
6:1	194	11:28-32	86	3:6	469, 473
6:4	236	11:32	85	3:7	59, 87
6:9	352	11:33	36, 62, 85, 89, 252, 284, 369, 429, 436, 528	3:8	520
6:9-10	95			3:9	473
6:12	64	11:33-34	271	3:9-15	236
7:18	258, 498	11:33-36	266	3:10	237
7:24	258, 277, 498	11:34	279	3:11	237, 240
7:25	258, 498	11:36	79, 278-79	3:12	389
8:3	436	12:2	307	3:16	147, 474
8:13	536	12:16	57, 60	3:16-17	147
8:15	126, 147, 216	13:12	124	3:18	57, 369
8:15-16	307	13:13	487	4:1	485
8:17	126	13:14	25, 401-2	4:4	502
8:22-23	373	14:10	204-5	4:5	338
8:23	228, 261-62, 516	14:10-11	333	4:7	136
8:26	250, 261, 498	15:9-12	134	4:9	449

4:15	320, 457	15:47	124	3:13	372, 383
4:21	145n.11, 146	15:50	215	3:16	176, 447
5:7	427	15:53-55	215	3:19	29
6:11	147	15:54	209, 215-16, 436	3:24	20, 117, 385
6:15-16	67	15:54-55	209	3:27	402, 454
6:19-20	443	15:55	212, 478	3:28	456
7	455n.2			3:29	176

2 Corinthians

7:5-6	455	1:3-4	229, 533	4	432
7:6	455	1:5	374	4:4	35, 46, 135, 139, 361, 388, 436
7:7	320	1:7	374, 393	4:5	127
7:23	383	2:14-16	135	4:5-6	427, 516
7:29	139, 454, 487	2:15	372, 384	4:6	20, 216, 307
7:31	518, 534	2:15-16	341	4:9	248, 472
7:36	29	3:2	268	4:19	115, 421, 457, 465
8:6	xxvii, 322, 530	3:3	268, 301	4:21-31	237
9:16	165	3:6	124	4:22-24	xv
10	xv	3:9	421	4:25-27	433
10:1	194-95	3:11	501	4:26	376, 432, 532-33
10:1-5	43	3:12-16	247	4:27	xx, 436
10:4	xiv, 189, 302, 307, 372, 396	3:14-15	385	4:28-31	433
10:11	xiv, 200	3:15	246	5:1	453
11:1	469	3:17	137, 147, 246, 295	5:22-23	59
12:4	143	3:18	21, 384, 421	6:7-8	520
12:8	320	4:4	385	6:14	196, 424, 505
12:8ff.	143	4:18	458		

Ephesians

12:8-10	139	5:8	397	1:4	34, 141, 209-10, 369
12:8-11	150	5:10	239	1:5	420
12:11	49, 136, 147	5:14-15	420	1:9	210, 420
12:12	176	5:15	418	1:9-10	xxiii, 209
12:27	480	5:16	454	1:10	xxiii, 35, 123, 211, 305-6, 496
12:28	466	5:17	124, 300, 305, 307	1:13	475
12:31	189	5:19	259	1:19-20	120
13:9	536	5:21	372	1:19-21	124, 131
13:9-10	309, 476	6:1-2	366	1:21	269
13:11	453	6:2	375	1:22	211
13:12	97, 216, 230, 504	6:16	273	2:3	375
14:40	181	9:6	520	2:7	312
15	500	9:7	386	2:11-13	134, 152
15:8	178	10:17	165	2:12	394, 434, 465, 472
15:8-9	28	11:14	175	2:12-13	464
15:9	163, 178	11:25	372	2:13	465
15:20	221, 376, 430	11:29	535	2:14	113, 207, 239, 374, 404, 407, 419
15:22	125	12:4	428	2:14-15	129, 405
15:24	254, 261	13:3	428	2:14-16	419
15:26	371, 495				

Galatians

15:28	426, 429	1:1	140	2:15	374, 421
15:32	xxi, 160	1:4	340	2:15-16	463, 526
15:41	181	2:15-16	310	2:16	419
15:44	490, 495	2:16	205	2:17	374, 407, 463
15:45	98-99, 393	2:19-21	420		
15:45-46	214, 298				

Index of Scripture References

2:20-21	239
2:20-22	328
3:6	436
3:8	178, 469
3:9	213
3:9-10	519
3:10	490
3:14-15	346
4:8	111, 191, 494, 496
4:10	100
4:13	385, 453-54, 464, 513, 526
4:22	403
4:24	188, 403, 480
4:30	402, 498
5:8	375, 385, 421, 443
5:14	125, 223
5:16	467
5:25	487
5:26	477
5:27	27, 34, 405
5:31	xv, 487
5:31-32	xv
5:32	487
6:11	384
6:12	368
6:14	188, 384
6:17	368

Philippians

1:23-24	5
2	413
2:5	397
2:6	140
2:6-8	416
2:7	44, 135-36, 212, 273, 297, 309, 389, 416, 419, 421-22, 472, 504
2:7-8	367, 386, 472, 497
2:8	38, 383, 387, 418, 421, 497
2:8-9	421
2:9	191, 497
2:9-11	270, 332-33
2:10	127, 346
2:10-11	79, 369
2:11	152
2:13	375
2:15	519
3:7-9	502
3:8	501
3:8-9	500
3:9	439
3:13	290, 453
3:13-14	27
3:14	368
3:15-16	96
3:19	116n.4
3:20	181, 206
3:21	393
4:1	59, 406, 486
4:7	36, 226, 397
4:13	384

Colossians

1:12-13	385, 446
1:15-16	427
1:16	65, 258, 280, 289, 404, 528
1:17	530
1:18	481, 496
1:19	83, 136, 237
1:26	213
2:5	519
2:9	136-37, 295
2:14	184, 190, 314
2:14-15	191
2:15	211, 269, 375
3:1	125
3:9-10	308
3:10	115, 188, 519
3:11	454, 456

1 Thessalonians

2:6-7	516
2:7	465
2:8	465
3:16	219
4:8	298
4:13	212
4:17	465
5:5	275, 463
5:17-18	222

2 Thessalonians

3:16	226

1 Timothy

1:15	352
2:4	354, 404
2:6	206
3:15	196n.1, 197, 328, 484
3:16	346, 490n.1
4:8	458
6:15-16	27
6:16	504

2 Timothy

1:7	149
2:21	408
3:4-5	64
3:12	306
4:7-8	315
4:8	257

Titus

1:16	251
2:13	302, 346
3:5	27, 205

Hebrews

1:1	35, 46, 141, 406
1:1-2	33, 404
1:2	32
1:3	475
1:4	123
1:5-14	xiv
1:9	475
1:14	70
2	109
2:9	221
2:11-12	115, 427
2:11-14	110
2:13-14	115
2:14	416
2:16-17	151
3:5	456
4:12	47, 371
4:14	479
4:15	212
5:7	140
5:12	359
5:14	452
6:7	519
7:19	402
8:1	426
9:7	479
10:4	310, 418
10:5-7	418
10:11	416
10:28	474
11:32-39	2
11:37	1, 9
11:37-38	201
12:2	270, 418
12:6	166

12:13	115	2:4	251	22:10	417
12:22	115, 256, 376, 512	2:14	206	22:16	134, 171
12:23	427	2:16	410		
12:29	47	2:20	475		

APOCRYPHA

13:8	125	2:20-27	211		
13:12	418	2:20-28	213	**Judith**	
13:16	393	3:2	75-76, 181, 225, 228, 423, 504	16:21 Vg.	179
James		4:8	370-71, 375	**Wisdom**	
2:1	402	4:19	375, 514	1:1-2	447
2:20	251	5:16-17	47	1:2	75
4:7	447	5:19	175	1:7	147, 529
4:8	447	5:20	514	2:23	341
				3:13-14	455
1 Peter		**Revelation**		6:6	180
1:3	393-94	1:3	417	7:23	147
1:3-4	438	1:17	124	9:1-2	530
1:8	216	2:11	513	13:5	502
1:18-19	256	2:12	223		
1:20	141	2:16	223	**Sirach**	
1:22-25	266-67	2:28	171	1:16	148
2:2	270, 465	3:7	246, 247	4:26	311
2:4-8	110	3:12	484	7:17	536
2:5	345, 438	3:14	223	15:9	71
2:6-8	234-35	3:19-20	223	16:21	290
2:9	195, 249, 473, 480	4:6-11	64	20:7	381, 384
2:9-10	305-7	4:8	xxii	24:5	529
2:18-25	415-16	5:1	246	24:29	97, 441, 448
2:22	102, 325	5:5	113, 134, 246, 427, 493	43:9	181
2:22-24	xxi	5:6	414, 426	50:6	181
2:23	130, 388	7:13-17	209-10, 367		
2:24	424	7:17	254, 260	**Baruch**	
3:15	96	8:10	171	1:15	506
3:19	126, 376	9:1	171	2:12	504
5:4	152	10:10	246	3:3	72
5:8-9	447	12:1	181	3:36	478
		14:2	80		
2 Peter		14:4	427	**Song of the Three Young Men**	
1:17	299	19:13-14	490	27	23
1:19	95, 171, 473	19:16	335		
3:10	520	20:1-10	467n.3	**Susanna**	
3:10-14	511	20:10	261	35	384
3:13	520, 524	21:1	510, 524		
		21:1-4	511, 518	**2 Maccabees**	
1 John		21:1-5	532	11:23	180
1:2	481	21:4	261, 510		
1:5	47	21:10-22:5	376		
1:9	83	21:22-26	462		
2:1	145, 479	21:27	378		

www.ingramcontent.com/pod-product-compliance
Lightning Source LLC
Chambersburg PA
CBHW080528300426
44111CB00017B/2645